# Shakespeare
and the Mediterranean

# The International Shakespeare Association

# Previous volumes of proceedings

*Shakespeare: Pattern of Excelling Nature*, Shakespeare Criticism in Honor of America's Bicentennial from the International Shakespeare Association Congress, Washington, D.C., April 1976, ed. David Bevington and Jay L. Halio (Newark: University of Delaware Press; London: Associated University Presses, 1978).

*Shakespeare, Man of the Theater*, Proceedings of the Second Congress of the International Shakespeare Association, 1981, ed. Kenneth Muir, Jay L. Halio, and D. J. Palmer (Newark: University of Delaware Press; London and Toronto: Associated University Presses, 1983).

*Images of Shakespeare*, Proceedings of the Third Congress of the International Shakespeare Association, 1986, ed. Werner Habicht, D. J. Palmer, and Roger Pringle (Newark: University of Delaware Press; London and Toronto: Associated University Presses, 1988).

*Shakespeare and Cultural Traditions*, The Selected Proceedings of the International Shakespeare Association World Congress, Tokyo, 1991, ed. Tetsuo Kishi, Roger Pringle, and Stanley Wells (Newark: University of Delaware Press; London and Toronto: Associated University Presses, 1994).

*Shakespeare and the Twentieth Century*, The Selected Proceedings of the International Shakespeare Association World Congress, Los Angeles, 1996, ed. Jonathan Bate, Jill L. Levenson, and Dieter Mehl (Newark: University of Delaware Press; London: Associated University Presses, 1998).

# Shakespeare and the Mediterranean

The Selected Proceedings of the
International Shakespeare Association
World Congress
Valencia, 2001

*Edited by*
Tom Clayton
Susan Brock    Vicente Forés

DELAWARE

Newark: University of Delaware Press

Associated University Presses
2010 Eastpark Boulevard
Cranbury, NJ 08512

The paper used in this publication meets the requirements of the American National Standard for Permanence of Paper for Printed Library Materials Z39.48-1984.

Library of Congress Cataloging-in-Publication Data

International Shakespeare Association. World Congress (7th : 2001 : Valencia, Spain)
    Shakespeare and the Mediterranean : the selected proceedings of the International Shakespeare Association World Congress, Valencia, 2001 / edited by Tom Clayton, Susan Brock, Vicente Forés.
        p.   cm.
    Includes bibliographical references and index.
    ISBN 0-87413-816-7 (alk. paper)
    1. Shakespeare, William, 1564–1616—Knowledge—Mediterranean Region—Congresses.   2. Shakespeare, William, 1564–1616—Stage history—Mediterranean Region—Congresses.   3. Shakespeare, William, 1564–1616—Appreciation—Mediterranean Region—Congresses.   4. Mediterranean Region—Literatures—English influences—Congresses.   5. Mediterranean Region—Intellectual life—Congresses.   6. Mediterranean Region—In literature—Congresses.   I. Clayton, Thomas, 1932–   II. Brock, Susan, 1948–   III. Forés, Vicente.   IV. Title.
    PR3069.M44I58    2004
    822.3'3—dc22                                                          2003058163

PRINTED IN THE UNITED STATES OF AMERICA

*In memory of Sam Schoenbaum (1927–1996),*
*Sir John Gielgud (1904–2000),*
*Maynard Mack (1911–2001),*
*and Yasunari Takahashi (1932–2002),*
*Shakespeareans*

# Contents

# Foreword

IN AN ESSAY PUBLISHED FOR THE OCCASION IN APRIL 2001, GIORGIO MELCHI-
ori asks, "Why choose Valencia as the venue of a World Shakespeare Conference?" The question proves rhetorical because "the reply is obvious: in
the first place Valencia is a most hospitable city, an ideal setting for *any*
conference on any subject in the world, because of its location, its climate,
the mere beauty of the place" ("The Valencian Connection," 1). A perfect
match for the theme of the seventh World Shakespeare Congress, "Shakespeare and the Mediterranean," Valencia hosted over 500 delegates from
more than thirty countries.

The social and cultural program for the Congress took full advantage of
its site. Ranging through the arts, it included Spanish versions and adaptations of Shakespearean plays (*Much Ado About Nothing*, *The Merchant of
Venice*, and *King Lear*); an exhibition titled "Thirty Years of Shakespeare
Translations in Spain"; *honoria in cyberspazio*, an opera based on a text
by Madelyn Starbuck and presented by Carles Padrissa and Vicente Forés;
and a performance scripted from the work of Valencian poet Ausiàs
March. The Congress was timed to conclude on 23 April, a date coinciding
not only with Shakespeare's birthday but also with the feast of San Vicente, patron saint of Valencia. As a result, visitors had an opportunity to
see the city mount a religious celebration, the streets filled with colorful
processions and various spaces offering miracle plays enacted by citizens
of all ages. There were optional tours through Valencia and its environs,
providing additional access to such places as the city's museums and cathedral, the monastery of Puig, the castle and theater of Sagunto.

While making the most of its venue, the social and cultural program
extended beyond it with performances illustrating conventions of Italian
theater and music, and with screenings of several American and British
films. It complemented the rich and diversified academic program of forty-
three papers and thirty-two seminars. Appearing in this volume, the five
plenary papers by Jonathan Bate, Michael Coveney, Robert Ellrodt, Stephen Orgel, and Marina Warner explore topics from Shakespeare's islands
and magic to the ambivalence of Shylock to correspondences between
Shakespeare and Montaigne. Comparable to their subjects, the backgrounds of these speakers—distinguished scholarship, theater criticism,

13

creative writing—informed their presentations with wonderful variations in both content and style. Thirty-eight short papers and the seminars also investigated many aspects of the Congress theme, among them performance history, Shakespeare in music and film, translation, travel writing, and pedagogy.

When it organized the academic program, the Congress Committee of the International Shakespeare Association (ISA) made a special effort to involve participants from countries outside Great Britain and North America. Their project was successful: contributions came from six continents, representing nations from Brazil to Malaysia and from Croatia to South Africa. Funding to support travel grants for delegates and fees/expenses for speakers was made available by the Shakespeare Birthplace Trust and, in some measure, by the Generalitat Valenciana. The ISA Congress Committee is most appreciative of the funding received.

The success of the academic program owes an immeasurable debt to Stanley Wells, chair of the ISA Congress Committee, and Susan Brock, Executive Secretary and Treasurer of the ISA. Working with the Shakespeare Foundation of Spain, in particular Vicente Forés, they are responsible for arranging a conference of such uniformly high quality. The editors who assembled this collection of twenty-eight essays—Tom Clayton, Susan Brock, and Vicente Forés—had the difficult job of selecting a fraction of the submissions from short-paper sessions and seminars. If resources had permitted, they could have filled another volume with material that stimulated much valuable discussion at the conference. The ISA Congress Committee is grateful to them for the expertise and time they have given to the demanding tasks of preparing this volume for the press.

The published book serves as one important reminder of a conference that allowed delegates to address Shakespearean (and non-Shakespearean) issues at formal sessions in suitable buildings and at large throughout the city of Valencia. Like Sycorax in Marina Warner's *Indigo*, however, the volume looks both "back into the past and forward into the future" (93). It charts the latest stop in a journey that has taken the World Shakespeare Congress from its first meeting in Vancouver to Washington, D.C., Stratford-upon-Avon, Berlin, Tokyo, and Los Angeles. Echoing tributes delivered at the Congress, it marks in this Foreword the retirement of Stanley Wells and Susan Brock from their positions on the ISA Executive with gratitude for the skills and dedication they have brought so generously to their work. At the same time it looks forward with great anticipation to the next Congress, which will take place in Brisbane, hosted by the University of Queensland, in the year 2006.

—Jill L. Levenson, Chair
International Shakespeare Association Executive Committee

# Acknowledgments

SHAKESPEARE USES *MEDITERRANEAN*, A RELATIVELY NEW WORD, ONLY once, but that did not prevent him from creating many a virtual world in its environs. We feel sure he would have enjoyed some birthday revelry in this city by the sea at festival time, and we like to think he would have shared the instruction and delight so many of the contributions brought to this seventh Congress held in Valencia and hosted by the Fundación Shakespeare España. The occasion afforded participants the opportunity to hear plenary lectures of impressive range and diverse expertise, along with a great variety of stimulating shorter papers. The seminars and workshops in turn generated lively discussion of papers read in advance on their specialized topics. We would gladly have selected twice or three times the number of papers space allowed, but having to stop with the present representative selection, we look forward to seeing published in books and journals elsewhere many we regretfully could not include. We are grateful to the contributors to this volume, to the International Shakespeare Association for providing assistance toward the costs of Publication, to the University of Minnesota for funding editorial assistance, and to the University of Delaware Press for their help and cooperation.

All quotations from Shakespeare's plays and poems are taken from *The Riverside Shakespeare*, ed. G. Blakemore Evans, 2nd ed. (Boston: Houghton Mifflin Company, 1997), except as otherwise noted (editors have used their own editions).

# Shakespeare
# and the Mediterranean

# Part One
## Theaters and Performance

# John Gielgud: Tradition, Magic, and Continuity in the Modern Shakespearean Theater

## Michael Coveney

First, I would like to say what a pleasure it is to speak in this tremendous city on this delightful subject. It is exactly eleven months since John Gielgud died, aged ninety-six. On Shakespeare's birth and death day, it is therefore especially appropriate that this actor should be celebrated. And I'd like to suggest why Valencia is a good place to do so.

John Gielgud was not a Hispanophile of note, though he much enjoyed working on location near Madrid with Orson Welles when he made *Chimes at Midnight* in the early 1960s.

Kenneth Tynan, however, one of Gielgud's leading witnesses and the greatest British theater critic since Shaw (he died in 1980), was a devotee of Spain and of this city in particular. Valencia was Tynan's favorite place on the whole Mediterranean seaboard. He loved the food, the fireworks—and the bullfights.

And he loved the fact that Valencia had an especial appeal to those anti-tourists who required sun on their holidays, and the company of fellow human beings who are not fellow tourists: "Above all," he said, "we seek to escape the company of our compatriots, apart from any we may happen to be traveling with."

This sentence may serve to define the unusual mixture of glamor and remoteness that always attended Gielgud as an actor. No other English actor of the last century was better bred to the tradition he sought to continue—that of the great Ellen Terry dynasty, to whom he was connected on his mother's side; while his air of aloofness, almost sanctity, placed him above the rabble both onstage and off.

Yet no actor was more loved in his lifetime by his traveling companions in the theater. He exerted an exemplary influence on British theater and acting from the moment he decided to take his new-won West End stardom to the Old Vic in 1929 and to learn how to play Shakespeare.

Tynan's devotion to Valencia was understandable in one whose temper-

21

ament drew him violently towards the meteoric career and volcanic stage personality of Laurence Olivier. And yet he could force even Gielgud into a metaphor of the bullring: "In the serenity of his pride," he said, "in his sure-footed assumption of poise and authority, Gielgud is something of a matador himself, particularly in his attitude towards his audience. He avoids moving them too drastically, as might happen if he surrendered himself, and permitted his intestines to be gouged out in their sight. He gazes at them instead, with a prudent coolness, controlling them by skill rather than strength."[1]

Where Olivier pounced like a lion, Gielgud, Tynan said, not quite accurately, picked at his parts in kid gloves and left no fingerprints. The two titans rarely appeared together, but they did so in 1935, when Gielgud more or less rescued his rival's then-floundering career by casting him as both Romeo and Mercutio, and sharing the roles with him.

In both roles Gielgud reckoned Olivier his superior, marvelously Italianate and dashing. Gielgud himself had already played Romeo twice, once aged nineteen in 1923. A silent film shows him in this production spreading his arms imploringly at the balcony like a beseeching, rather well-mannered pauper at the gates; the actor always relished the humorous cruelty of James Agate in the *Sunday Times,* who declared of this performance that "Mr. Gielgud from the waist downwards means absolutely nothing. He has the most meaningless legs imaginable."[2]

Olivier wanted to make the poetry of Romeo real and modern. He refused point-blank to follow Gielgud's example of modulated intonations and a more refined expression. Tynan therefore, as part of his campaign to play Boswell to Olivier's Dr. Johnson, set about discrediting, or at least ridiculing, Gielgud's physical appearance. He was running after the ball set rolling by Gielgud's first drama teacher, Lady Benson, who told him that he walked exactly like a cat with rickets.

When Gielgud played Prospero at Stratford-upon-Avon in 1957, Tynan said that he was "perhaps the finest actor, from the neck up, in the world today." To which Gielgud replied, "[He] said I had only two gestures, the left hand up, the right hand up. What did he want me to do, bring out my prick?"[3]

I might interject here that, while Gielgud was an acquaintance of some critics, he had an admirable dislike of back-slapping and hob-nobbing. Unlike Olivier, who was memorialized with full pomp and splendor in Westminster Abbey, Gielgud, who had cancelled a big dinner at the Garrick Club to mark his ninetieth birthday, insisted on no memorial and no speeches.

Those who went to bury Gielgud did so silently. He hated listening to his own recordings. And he had a horror of other actors, and critics, using his death to wallow in their own self-advertising egoism. So I'll try to be discreet in this lecture, for fear of prompting that shuddering wince of disapproval beyond the grave.

Fanfares and self-importance were not his thing at all. "Critics, like clergymen, always seem out of place behind the scenes," he said. He once rang the critic, and his official biographer, Sheridan Morley, in a blind panic. "You'll never believe this," he said; "in America they are actually about to name a theater after a drama critic. . . . Oh my God, you are one. Goodbye." And on the habit of reading the cavalier, coruscating Tynan, he said, "It's wonderful when it isn't you."

Even Tynan could not have predicted that Gielgud would at the very end of his career play Prospero in the nude on film for Peter Greenaway, one of the most visually eccentric and original movie directors of our day. Still, the idea took hold early on that heart and passion were Olivier's trademark, while cerebral, intellectual interpretations were Gielgud's forte. There is something, but not everything, in this.

Tynan elaborated the difference by noting Olivier's shattering effects of passion as opposed to Gielgud's smaller, more exquisite effects of temper: "It is rather like the contrast between what was known as 'beautiful' and what was known as 'sublime.' As Gielgud says, when you quiz him on the point," says Tynan, "It's obvious, isn't it? I'm Macready, and Larry's Edmund Kean."[4]

And yet the more you look at, and listen to, Gielgud, the less the idea of him as a remote exquisite holds true. How exactly his place in the British theater was won, and maintained, was illustrated for me one cold Saturday night at the Old Vic just over twenty-five years ago.

The National Theatre was saying goodbye to the Vic as a prelude to moving into the new concrete fortress on the South Bank. Actors came and went, doing their party turns. Sybil Thorndike was making what proved to be her last appearance in public, rising on sticks to acknowledge the cheers in the stalls.

Then Gielgud was announced. He entered upstage left in immaculate evening dress and made for center stage with those characteristic, quick, foreshortened steps, beaming pinkly the while as the light bounced ecstatically around his noble, bald, and glistening dome. He absorbed an ovation that tumbled, like crashing waves, at his feet. He simply stood to attention and shed a few tears.

Eventually, silence and stillness. Then he launched, at top speed and with stunningly perfect articulation, into Hamlet's "Oh, what a rogue and peasant slave" soliloquy. It was amazing, electrifying. Just remembering it sends shivers down my spine. If, there and then, the Old Vic had announced a Hamlet revival with Gielgud in the part he had played over five hundred times, but not since 1944, the queue would have formed on the pavement overnight.

Olivier may well have been the definitive Romeo and Macbeth of his time—Gielgud, with characteristic generosity certainly thought that he was—but Hamlet is the role with which Gielgud is more permanently fixed in the public memory.

He never filmed his performance, unlike Olivier, who prefaced his black-and-white 1948 version with the deadly voice-over simplification, "This is the tragedy of a man who could not make up his mind." In that same year, Gielgud recorded Hamlet for the BBC on radio, and it feels as though the sum of his experience is in the role.

"Oh, what a rogue and peasant slave" is much slower than I heard it in 1976, starting as a whisper, hardening into steel on "what's Hecuba to him, or he to Hecuba, that he should weep for her," accelerating with sudden purpose at "I have heard that guilty creatures sitting at a play" and throughout spoken with a sparingly deployed, rapid, controlled vibrato.

The most striking thing about it is how absolutely natural it sounds; Gielgud's voice is perfectly attuned to the shape and tenor of the rhetoric. "To be or not to be" is not sung, nor is it apologized for in the modern manner. That intelligent actor Michael Pennington, a Royal Shakespeare Company Hamlet himself in 1980, concluded that the speech hovers over the play like a great wing, "its greatness lying in its very detachment."[5]

There is no old-laddie-style quaver at all in the voice—for that one will have to re-imagine Beerbohm Tree and Irving—and throughout one marvels at how meaning is carved among arcs of verse: "what dreams must come . . . when we have shuffled off this mortal coil . . . must give us pause" is perfectly pitched for clarity; Gielgud can do this over much longer paragraphs when the meaning is only revealed after several parenthetical, or subsidiary, statements. He does it almost habitually in any passage of Shakespeare.

Then, the speech to the Players is indeed spoken trippingly on the tongue, very fast, consonants hit like clashing cymbals, and all the while Hamlet is hurrying the actors along to the evening's revels. In a most extraordinary way, the listener can almost feel and smell the scene going on. In the closet scene, he is grave and possessed in the frenzy of disgust, allowing the drift of his speech to rise above a sea of rushing words.

Did anyone ever speak as brilliantly as this, one wonders, and how on earth did Gielgud? And what is his peculiar individuality of sound? A tenor voice, certainly, it has been variously compared to a violin and a cello, while to the writer and actor Emlyn Williams it was "an unbridled oboe." Alec Guinness, who was a protégé of Gielgud's, coined the famous phrase, "like a silver trumpet muffled in silk." Musical, this voice certainly was, but musicianly, too, in the sense that, at his best, Gielgud never sang for effect. Rarely, in fact. It is as if he beat and bent the verse to his vocal armory in order best to reveal its meaning; this was a two-way process forged between his own, idiosyncratic vocal quality and the raw material which, in a way, demanded that treatment.

Color, intonation, variety of pace, an undulating landscape of emotion: these are not fashionable virtues in speaking Shakespeare today, though Sir Peter Hall, founding director of the Royal Shakespeare Company, believes that there is only one way to speak him. Hall says he learned this from Edith Evans, who had in turn learned it from William Poel, who directed Evans as Cressida in 1912.

The technique of giving shape to the rhetorical structure of verse, the taking of breaths and the emphasis of syllables, says Hall, can be traced back to Kean and Garrick.[6] And yet the big debate in contemporary criticism of Shakespeare production always rests on the extent to which the plays are enhanced or diminished by production styles as well as by speaking habits.

The first Hamlet I saw, at Stratford-upon-Avon in 1965, was David Warner's, directed as it happens, by Peter Hall. This was the student prince of the new rock and pop era, not yet fully politicized but resentful and, we thought, anarchic, swathed in a red scarf, gangly and sullen, flat of speech and desultory of thought. At the time, it was the most powerful theater experience of my life.

In the same year, I saw Gielgud on stage for the first time, in Chekhov's Ivanov, at the Phoenix Theatre, and my impatience with that performance was reflected in an angry, adolescent poem I wrote to myself the moment I got home: "Ivanov, Ivanov, we've all had enough of your whimpering, simpering whine. Your tiresome self-pity is not even witty . . ." and here, thank God, my memory gives up!

This only demonstrates how taste changes with our age and moods. Theater is an ephemeral art, and no one embodied the ephemeral better, or understood it more, than Gielgud. As he once said, Hamlet "must be rediscovered, re-created, every ten or fifteen years. The changes in the world must affect the directors and actors who seek to create him, as well as the reactions of the audience."[7] David Warner was "my" Hamlet just as, I dare say, the luminously sensitive and highly musical Simon Russell Beale has just been the perfect prince for another generation at the National Theatre in London.

A clue to Gielgud's success in the role has surely something to do with his own character. This was brilliantly defined by Peter Brook, the director with whom Gielgud, as Angelo in *Measure for Measure* in 1950, enjoyed one of his many milestone moments. "In John," said Brook, "tongue and mind work so closely together that it is sufficient for him to think of something for it to be said.

"Everything in him is moving all the time, at lightning speed—a stream of consciousness flows from him without pause; his flickering, darting

tongue reflects everything around and inside him: his wit, his joy, his anxiety, his sadness, his appreciation of the tiniest detail of life and work. . . .
John is a mass of contradictions which happily have never been resolved
and which are the motors of his art. . . . He seems to have no method,
which is in itself a method that has always worked wonders. His inconsistency is the truest of consistencies."[8]

You could hardly invent a better definition of Hamlet himself. No wonder, then, that Gielgud, as in no other part, found it difficult to know
whether he became Hamlet or Hamlet, he.

As an actor, his restless quest for truth and new meaning defined, for
Brook, his modern quality. And his sense of tradition, his passionate sense
of quality, came from the past. In linking two ages, said Brook, he was
unique. With Gielgud, that suspension between past and present gave him
his identity and defined his talent, especially as he got older.

Destiny, of course, came into it, too. Through his aunt, Ellen Terry,
Henry Irving's leading lady, he inherited the style and poise of a true star,
as well as the Terry tears, the ability to cry at the drop of a hat. Gielgud's
mother always told him that this ability was due to weak lachrymal glands.

His second cousin was Gordon Craig, the innovative stage designer and
theoretician. And he knew of the legendary actor-managers through his
great uncle, Fred Terry, to whom he was devoted.

Gielgud's stockbroker father was of aristocratic Polish émigré extrac-
tion and his paternal great grandmother had been a Shakespearean actress
of some reputation.

So, on the Terry side he inherited a commitment to the theatrical life,
while his Slav ancestry no doubt explains his enduring enthusiasm for
Russian music and ballet and his affinity with the works of Chekhov,
whom he championed in London in the 1930s.

At the same time, while he was addicted to the grand, expansive manner
of the Victorian and Edwardian touring theater, he was exposed from an
early age to all manner of entertainment. He enjoyed musical comedies
and revues as much as he enjoyed Shakespeare or J.M. Barrie; and he always insisted, perhaps over-insisted, that he wanted color and beauty and
drama and magic in the theater. He once told a magazine interviewer that
he couldn't read *Troilus and Cressida* or *Coriolanus* with any great pleasure; he much preferred to bolt down a cheap thriller.

The young Gielgud attended first nights, with friends or his family, as a
matter of course. In the early 1920s, as a teenager, he saw the London
premieres of Shaw's *Heartbreak House* and *Saint Joan*, Eugene O'Neill's
*Anna Christie*, and Karel Capek's *The Insect Play*. Whether seated in the
stalls or perched in the upper circle, he scribbled opinionated and perceptive notes on his programs in the neat and tidy scrawl known to all his
correspondents down the years.

Many of the actors he watched at this stage of his life, such as Edith Evans, Gladys Cooper, and Frank Vosper, he would later act with and direct, although at first he had to persuade his father to allow him to try his luck in the theater. His parents were hoping he might follow his brother to Oxford and become an architect.

Edith Evans he revered as a comedienne and miraculous technician, Gladys Cooper as a talented and beautiful actress of both tragedy and comedy, and Frank Vosper for his warmth, charm, and generosity.

Frank Vosper, now forgotten, died tragically in 1937. When he played Claudius to Gielgud's 1934 Hamlet, he was visited in one of the intervals by an important Army major, who much impressed Vosper and the rest of the cast with his enthusiasm for the production. In the final scene when Claudius says, "Cousin Hamlet, you know the wager," Vosper, according to Gielgud, still thinking of his visitor and unaware of his mistake, demanded sonorously, "Cousin Hamlet, you know the major!"[9]

One difference between Gielgud and a Victorian sacred monster like Henry Irving was Gielgud's sense of self-mockery and fun. This went hand in hand with an instinctive, thoroughly modern preference for an overall standard of ensemble acting. He understood how certain crudely fashioned situations could be improved by an actor's effects.

But he disapproved of this in Shakespeare and followed Shaw, who wrote to Ellen Terry with the firm instruction to play on the lines, within the lines, and never in between the lines. Shaw's big complaint about Irving in Shakespeare was that the actor somehow inserted his performance between the lines and was therefore regardless of them.

This side of Gielgud's interpretative rigor was no doubt due to the Slav strain, influenced by the intellectual integrity and practical brilliance of Harley Granville-Barker and the Russian director Komisarjevsky. Both men exerted huge influence upon him. As a result, Gielgud was inevitably drawn to directing plays, and always tried to gather the best possible actors around him. Generosity of spirit came naturally, more naturally than it may have done to Olivier.

Throughout the 1930s, with his New Theatre Hamlet at the center of the decade in 1934, he produced, directed, and acted in a way that surely laid the foundations of the two great British companies, the Royal Shakespeare and the National, that were created, at last, in the early 1960s. In his first Old Vic season, he played Romeo, Richard II, Oberon, Macbeth, and Hamlet. In the second season of 1930–31, he played Antony, Prospero, Lear, Hotspur, and Benedick.

The Old Vic was the mission of the remarkable Lilian Baylis, who believed that the working classes should be improved by going to see Shakespeare at reasonable prices. Her chief lieutenant, and the main director, was a man called Harcourt Williams, whom Gordon Craig denigrated but

Gielgud thus celebrated: "Trained by Benson and coached by Ellen Terry, he combined the ideals of Poel, Craig and Granville-Barker with the best traditions of the theatre that preceded them—the theatre of Irving, Tree and Alexander—and so linked in his work the most valuable lessons of both generations."[10]

Gielgud then directed a Romeo and Juliet at Oxford with a cast that included Edith Evans and Peggy Ashcroft—"Two leading ladies," he declared at the first night curtain calls, dropping one of his famous bricks, "the like of whom I hope I shall never meet again."

The cast also included George Devine as Mercutio. Devine later founded the English Stage Company at the Royal Court and transformed the English theater by putting on *Look Back in Anger* in 1956. Gielgud worked with the new design team collectively known as Motley, who would also become a transforming influence on the British stage, embracing Gielgud's enthusiasm for simplicity and swiftness.

Gielgud professed an aversion to the hackneyed Gothic style of decoration for Hamlet "in which the King and Queen look like playing-cards, and Hamlet like an overgrown Peter Pan."[11] The Motleys came up with costumes inspired by Lucas Cranach, the contemporary of Dürer, and a setting of a large, revolving rostrum with a cyclorama for the exterior scenes.

"All the dresses," recalled Gielgud of his 1934 triumph, "were made of canvas, but trimmed with silk and velvet, and with rich autumnal colors patterned on to them with a paint spray. The cost of these clothes was amazingly little, and the results looked magnificent. . . . [W]e wore great chains round our necks, which appeared imposing and massive from the front. Actually, they were made of rubber, painted with silver and gold, and were as light as a feather."[12]

In 1937 he presented a nine-month commercial season at the Queen's Theatre—unthinkable today—of *Richard II, The School For Scandal, The Merchant of Venice,* and *Three Sisters*—this, the first Chekhov ever seen in the West End, with Gielgud as Vershinin, Michael Redgrave as Tusenbach, and Peggy Ashcroft as Irina.

The nature of the creative network of theater in Britain has never been better exemplified than in Gielgud's career during this revolutionary decade of the 1930s. Traditions were meshed, collaborations forged, old lessons incorporated, and new directions considered.

The British theater is in many ways a story of continuous evolution; Peter Hall has often said that the theatrical community is really a large village with about four hundred people working continuously within it. The Shakespearean legacy was central to this process, as it remains today, largely thanks to the careers of Olivier, Ashcroft, Ralph Richardson, and, especially, John Gielgud.

He had conquered New York in 1936 with that same Hamlet, seeing off competition from Leslie Howard in the same role at another theater. This was a victory he savored with a typical mixture of embarrassment and gratification. His Ophelia was Lillian Gish—"she wore a stocking on her arm in the mad scene," he delightedly told a television interviewer in 1988.

After the war years, he cemented his reputation in comedy, notably as John Worthing in *The Importance of Being Earnest*, opposite the hilariously intimidating Lady Bracknell of his adored Edith Evans. The mock-funeral scene was widely enjoyed as a send-up of his own Hamlet. He was never above lampooning himself; indeed, he started to use this healthy tendency very early in his career.

Then a new start in a different style as Angelo at Stratford-upon-Avon in 1950. *Measure for Measure* was established in the modern repertoire by this production; surely today we think of it, alongside *Troilus and Cressida*, as the most contemporary in tone and subject matter of all the plays. Gielgud's Angelo was nerve-wracked, vinegary, petulant, and spinsterish; under Brook's careful tutelage, he learned to play against his self-acknowledged weakness for wanting always to be liked on stage.

He had seen Charles Laughton play the part, directed by Tyrone Guthrie, and obviously felt there was room for a less sweaty, overtly evil reading. Again, a BBC recording of 1950 invokes a new Gielgud, one suddenly wracked by desire, almost taken off guard by it, in his meetings with Isabella. By the time he gives his sensual race the rein, this buried, other-Angelo has outstripped the political façade of the official Angelo.

One of Gielgud's obituarists last May argued that "many of Gielgud's greatest performances were often marked by such piercing moments of self-discovery."[13]

Murkiness invades his private thoughts like a stain, and it must have given his audiences quite a shock to see him not only desiring a nun despite himself, but also coating his lust in a thick veneer of smarminess; a smarminess unaccustomed even in one who had made such a career-enhancing success of the duplicitous Joseph Surface in Sheridan's great comedy *The School For Scandal*.

A striking and particular note of cruelty is sounded when he weighs Claudio's life against his sister's chastity: "But thy unkindness shall his death draw out to ling'ring sufferance," those last two words hit with chilling severity on a rising, metallic pitch, a good example of the old-fashioned effect absorbed into a non-extravagant flow of argument.

Just how determined he was to go for broke is clear in Peter Brook's anecdote of Gielgud's wig. Initially, the actor had responded to the name of Angelo by spending secret hours with the wigmaker and preparing an angelic wig of shoulder-length blond locks.

"At the dress rehearsal," Brook recalls, "no one was allowed to see him until he came onto the stage, delighted by his new disguise. To his surprise, we all howled our disapproval. 'Ah!' he sighed, 'Goodbye my youth!' There were no regrets and the next day he made a triumph, appearing for the first time [in his career] with a bald head."[14]

Years later, in 1968, Brook was encouraging Gielgud in some preparatory exercises while rehearsing a violent and experimental production of Seneca's *Oedipus* at the Old Vic during the National Theatre regime of Olivier. Brook asked all the actors to come, one by one, to the front of the stage and reveal the most terrifying thought that occurred to them. Gielgud lingered at the back until his turn came. He stepped forward and simply said, "We open on Tuesday."

Paradoxically, he harbored both a horror of the avant-garde and a belief that he should know something about it. Brook reports that Gielgud joined in all these exercises, some of them physically demanding, with a good grace, even though he found doing so extremely difficult; he bridged the generation gap and was held in true admiration and respect by the younger actors.

In the same Stratford-upon-Avon season in which he played Angelo, Gielgud also played Cassius, Benedick, and Lear. Cassius is interesting because it is the only performance we can see on film, albeit with a different group of actors, soon after his first stab at it, as it were, on stage.

He always trusted first stabs, feeling that, especially when younger, he had more success with a role when he flew at it instinctively, without the baggage of too much study.

He never much enjoyed playing in *Julius Caesar* because of the lack of variety in the verse, the difficulty of projecting a performance among a seething mass of citizenry and soldiers, and, he said, the small amount of feminine interest to provide domestic warmth and relaxation. Classical costumes, too, were hazardous. Togas do not suit actors of irregular shapes and sizes. "There is always a danger," he said, "of the effect of a lot of gentlemen sitting on marble benches in a Turkish bath."[15]

But the film, directed by Joseph Mankiewicz in black and white in 1953, is something of a landmark in Shakespeare on celluloid. It is faithful to the text, with a certain amount of cutting but nothing more drastic than the second scene of Brutus and Portia, the lynching of Cinna the Poet, and some of the huff-and-puff at the end. Marlon Brando is a magnificently brooding Antony, though Gielgud felt he was aping Olivier too much with his shouting over Caesar's corpse, and James Mason a splendidly decent and distracted Brutus.

Today, the best Shakespearean films seem effortlessly engaged with our own fragmenting culture—Baz Luhrmann's *Romeo and Juliet* among the youth gangs of Little Italy, or the recent Hamlet starring Ethan Hawke in

the urban desolation of high-rise, corporate Manhattan, the Ghost material-
izing by the Coca Cola machine—but this Caesar is a straight period
drama with no fancy references.

The camera gets around the characters, shoots them from dramatic
angles, closes in on disputes, and captures all the narrative developments
with Spartan clarity. The storms, too, are terrific. Gielgud is tense, quick,
and manipulative as Cassius, ironically and accurately described as one
who reads and thinks too much, loves no plays and hears no music.

No one further from the real Gielgud could be imagined, yet he con-
vinces at every step of the action—except, perhaps, when he sits uncomfortably on a horse at Philippi. If I remember it correctly—I have not seen
*Chimes at Midnight* for twenty years—this is the one dodgy aspect of his
magisterial, melancholic, and authoritative Bolingbroke in the Welles
movie: mounted on a horse at the Battle of Shrewsbury, he looks desperate
either to fall off or be whisked away to his caravan. Gielgud could no more
be a supreme horseman than he could a swaggering deadly swordsman.
The Errol Flynn aspects of Hamlet, for instance, were happily left to
Olivier.

But in *Julius Caesar*, the tent scene with Mason at Sardis is thrilling in
its ebb and flow of accusation, and in the mocking, sardonic, controlled
delivery of "Come Antony, and young Octavius, come, revenge your-
selves alone on Cassius, for Cassius is aweary of the world." This is one
of the most supple of all his speeches in the canon, though not, significantly, one of the most bejeweled.

Much of Gielgud's verse-speaking, surprisingly perhaps, is about under-
cutting luxuriance—as in Oberon's "I know a bank where the wild thyme
blows" in his *Ages of Man* recording. This Gielgud version has more eagerness than magic in it, as though the urgency of the actor comes solely
from wanting to describe the experience of seeing, not from painting the
picture itself. In contrast, he enlivens the more prosaic meaning of a difficult speech, such as this of Cassius, with real immediate force and a technique so breathtaking it becomes transparent.

Gielgud believed in throwing one's self into the verse like a swimmer,
but a swimmer who remembers the contours of the pool or the currents in
the ocean because he has been there and done it so many times. The metaphor reminds us of his cameo as the Duke of Clarence in Olivier's 1955
film of *Richard III*, and the premonition of his death by drowning in a butt
of malmsey.

It is not a well shot scene, and Gielgud has to wander around his cell
competing with some dreary background music. But the journey he makes
in the speech of just sixty or so lines is astonishing. He starts in a whisper,
then grows to both describing and conveying the tempest to his soul; then,
a creeping sense of anxiety and of his own impending fate, followed by a

devout prayer for his wife and children; then a naked upsurge of pure fear
and then a troubled lassitude, "I fain would sleep." By the end, the viewer
knows the man completely, and he haunts the rest of the film, for all Olivier's crowd-pleasing pyrotechnics.

Which reminds me: all great actors, even Gielgud, have a vulgarian
streak. They cannot survive without it. Gielgud won his first and only
Oscar as Dudley Moore's valet in *Arthur*, one of many films he made in
the last thirty years of his life, partly for fun, mostly for money.

In the case of *Arthur*, I imagine it was mostly for money. Leaning solici-
tously over the bath, Gielgud adopted a non-Shakespearean tone in addressing his nakedly repellent master thus: "I suppose I am now expected
to wash your dick, you little shit."

This was another new, scatological Gielgud, one who was more than
happy to take a dig at his own dignity while assured of his impregnable
status. This later period began on stage in 1968, when, on leaving Olivier's
National—where he had not prospered as either Orgon in *Tartuffe* directed
by Tyrone Guthrie, or in *Oedipus* directed by Brook—he appeared as a
befuddled, regretful headmaster of Albion House—symbolic name!—in
Alan Bennett's *Forty Years On*. "The crowd had found the door into the
secret garden," was the final sentence in a speech of sudden, poignant perception. The world was rushing by, and Gielgud found a way of exploiting
his own ageing process.

Then, renewing his partnership with Ralph Richardson, he scored two
of his greatest ever successes in *Home* by David Storey and *No Man's
Land* by Harold Pinter. In the first, he was a tear-stained amnesiac resident
of a lunatic asylum; in the second, a pot-bellied, garrulous, and ingratiat-
ing, failed old poet, blinking through spectacles, mincing around the stage
in cheap sandals and gray socks. This portrait, he acknowledged, was
modeled on the shambolic, bitchy figure of the poet W. H. Auden.

The whole point of these performances was that they confirmed his classical past, worked on the memory of an audience. We knew that this was
not a new Gielgud, on holiday from Hamlet and disavowing his past, but
a fantastically pliable, inventive artist elaborating on familiar themes of
loss, grief, and resignation in painfully unfamiliar modern settings.

Not even Olivier as Archie Rice in John Osborne's *The Entertainer*, a
character forging new tragic vitality in the loss of Empire and death of the
music hall, made a more decisive or creative break from his own repertoire
to more telling, or more poetic, effect. Prospero beckoned once more, and
more conclusively.

Gielgud further revealed a willingness to exploit his evolving status in
the title role of an otherwise lackluster revival by John Schlesinger of *Julius Caesar* at the National Theatre. This, in 1977, was his last appearance
in Shakespeare on the stage. One or two critics even suggested that the

assassination of Gielgud's Caesar was the result of a plot to kill off the best verse-speaker in the English language.

But even after death, this Caesar, through a series of production tricks and ornaments, continued to dominate the play in a remarkable way. The stage was bedecked with images of Gielgud's countenance, disapproval crinkling imperiously around his noble nose, as if what the new democracy got up to had nothing to do with him and pretty despicable even if it had.

In between Storey and Pinter, in 1974, Gielgud appeared at the Royal Court as William Shakespeare himself in the mischievously titled *Bingo* by Edward Bond. Bond's bard was a writer living his final days off the fat of the land, the land he has cynically consigned to the socially evil consequences of the enclosures. Gielgud never endorsed this view of Shakespeare, nor was he all that happy playing the role. But his performance was a perfect example of how his own personality and standing as an actor had become inextricable from the work itself.

Having just played Prospero for the fourth time at the National Theatre, he gave an even more telling valedictory. Shakespeare found himself, drunk and in despair, exiled in a landscape of harsh white snow. Gielgud rose heroically to the challenge of Bond's unfond farewell: "I didn't want to die. I could lie in this snow a whole life. I can think now, the thoughts come so easily over the snow and under my shroud. New worlds. Keys turning new locks—pushing iron open like lion's teeth. Wolves will drag me through the snow. I'll sit in their lair and smile and be rich. In the morning or when I die the sun will rise and melt it all away. The dream. The wolves. The iron teeth. The snow. The wind. My voice. A dream that leads to sleep."[16]

Is it just me, or do I hear writing there written specifically for one actor alone? No great actors are written for today by contemporary playwrights, more's the pity. Think of Shakespeare with no Burbage to write for. Gielgud, along with Olivier, Maggie Smith, and Paul Scofield, perhaps Michael Gambon, was about the last. And I also hear echoes of the end of *A Midsummer Night's Dream*, as in "the iron tongue of midnight hath told twelve" and "now the hungry lion roars and the wolf behowls the moon."

Gielgud the Shakespearean, playing Shakespeare at death's door, had come across a text that both energized his gift for nostalgia and provided a blanket as protection against the icy winds of change. The blanket, however, was electric. It clung to him like Prospero's cloak and confirmed his final persona as the unchallenged spirit of Shakespearean farewell.

Towards the end of his life Olivier made a television recording of *King Lear*. Gielgud was determined to film *The Tempest*, and spent fifteen years in the attempt. The result, *Prospero's Books*, in 1993, was as unexpected as it was extraordinary, and put the seal on his later role in life, that of him as his own living memorial, heedless—and indeed needless—of the contribution of others in a church service.

Anti-intellectual to the last, Gielgud had no defining concept of what kind of Prospero he might inhabit, but on Greenaway's invented Renaissance Island, Shakespeare, Prospero, and Gielgud himself all merged. He spoke all the lines of all the characters—until the final scenes of reunion. Those of Caliban, who was danced entirely in the writhing nude by Michael Clark, were strained through a curious Gielgud gargle.

The film is far from perfect and Gielgud tartly remarked that he felt Greenaway didn't know what he was doing and didn't understand the relationship between Prospero and Ariel at all.

On the other hand, he was also quite proud of it, as he told me at the time. "Haroun al-Rashid I was trying to be! I've never done the part quite like that. It's a conglomeration of all my performances and I think the film is so clever and so beautiful. I've fought against Prospero being a bore each time I've played it, and audiences seem to like the play better when I do it."[17]

In all, he played the role five times, testing it for different aspects of the character in the context of different visions of the director. This, I believe, betrays more than anything else Gielgud's interest in theatrical ideas, though he is adamant on one point: "In all the times I acted Prospero, I never once looked at Ariel. He was always behind me or above me, and I saw him only in my mind's eye."[18]

His first Old Vic Prospero, in 1930, marked his first collaboration with Ralph Richardson, as Caliban. He thought Richardson perfectly combined that character's elements of comedy and pathos, and placed him in a longer tradition: "I once saw an old actor called Louis Calvert play Caliban," he said. "He was dressed in a kind of animal skin and walked on all fours like a pantomime bear: quite ridiculous. Sir Frank Benson used to hang from a tree with a fish in his mouth, and Beerbohm Tree had a tableau at the end of the play in which Caliban was left lonely and forlorn on the island, crouching on a cliff with the ship sailing away in the distance."[19]

His 1957 Prospero, directed by Peter Brook, was a sort of El Greco hermit, naked to the waist, bare legs, an exile and watchful outcast, and even, according to the *Guardian*'s critic Philip Hope Wallace, first cousin of Timon of Athens.

J. C. Trewin confirmed this impression of Gielgud—absolutely not playing a fuzzy recluse—when the production transferred to the Theater Royal, Drury Lane, later that year: "[Here] is a man who has fought hard for his knowledge, the power of giving fire to the dread rattling thunder, and rifting Jove's stout oak with his own bolt. . . . He speaks with a noble austerity, and he bids farewell to his art as a man who has challenged and overcome."[20]

The special resonances Gielgud brought to Prospero, the reasons why it became his signature role in later life just as Hamlet had been in his early career, stemmed from two things: first, his sense of the past and uneasy truce with the future; and, second, the way an audience both esteemed and cherished him as their favorite Shakespearean.

All of this was brought into play in a 1974 National Theatre production by Peter Hall that was, at the time, rather underrated. Gielgud played the magician as an explorer of the possibilities and limits of art, and Hall made a fascinating statement about that moment in theatrical history when artificial moons, storms, and masques became a practical proposition for producers and playwrights.

Gielgud was made up to look like Dr. Dee, the Elizabethan alchemist, swaddled in voluminous robes, with beard, ruff, and spectacles. He knew that Hall was mad on the masque, but he felt that neither he nor Peter Brook made it work properly.

They also, he said, "had completely different ideas about the end of the play. Brook felt that Prospero in the last act goes back to his kingdom as a kind of god; Hall was convinced, because of the Epilogue and Prospero's attitude in the last act, that Shakespeare means him to be disillusioned, very reluctant to take his dukedom back, and finally returning to it in despair, knowing that everything is beyond redemption except for the young people, who are a kind of forlorn hope."[21]

Gielgud was not convinced by this. But the conclusion is scarcely resolved in *Prospero's Books*, where Gielgud abandons his character in the reunion scenes, throws his books into the swimming pool—these are the thirty-five plays of Shakespeare and the thirty-sixth, *The Tempest*—and asks us to draw near to him for the epilogue as, well, who? As Gielgud, or at least as the unguarded Prospero, who could surely now be no one but this actor.

The cue for the film is the line that, for Prospero, his library was dukedom large enough. So, we are then treated to an indulgently, entertainingly animated library of books related to the story at convenient moments.

These books of anatomy, bestiary, utopias, travelers' tales, mythologies, and so on, are ingeniously linked to the main narrative, which is enormously helped by such episodes as the long expositionary scene with Miranda done in flashback—a long cherished notion of Gielgud's—and such visual bonuses as the sight of Ariel excruciatingly trapped in his cloven pine.

The magic volumes and their applications were unleashed in a film language that Greenaway likened to the Gutenberg revolution: a digital, electronic Graphic Paintbox associated with the newest Japanese Hi-Vision television technology.

This was a far cry indeed from the creased hose and shaky rostra of the

Old Vic in the 1930s. Gielgud had made an amazing journey, and there he was, still pink and mischievous, his carriage impeccable, his dignity intact, his magnificent nose still wrinkled beneath his dancing blue eyes and his vertically furrowed brow.

His revels now were ended, but his place in our memories is unalterably secure, not just as Hamlet, but now as Prospero. His ability to laugh at himself, not take himself too seriously, was the secret of his greatness and the guarantee of our affection.

Gielgud was always embarrassed by his propensity for making terrible, sometimes hurtful gaffes, but these merely reinforced the idea that a great figure had feet of clay, an essential requirement in Shakespearean heroism. They became known as Gielgoodies. He himself once said he had dropped enough bricks to build a new Great Wall in China.

For instance, one old character actor, Clive Morton, was so terrified of Gielgud when touring with him in a play that he hardly dared speak to him. Eventually, he summoned up courage to knock on his dressing room door. "Thank God it's you," said Gielgud as Morton put his head nervously around the door. "For one dreadful moment I thought it was going to be that ghastly old bore Clive Morton."

The actor became a legend in his own lifetime, a summary of his roles and an embodiment of his own past. At last, in 1994, the West End theater renamed one of its most illustrious houses after one of its most illustrious sons.

The Globe became the Gielgud. At the informal ceremony in the theater circle-bar, on a magical sunlit morning, Gielgud recalled not the great figures he had known, not the great Shakespearean triumphs he had enjoyed, but his very first, unlucky appearance on the new Gielgud Theatre's stage. In 1928 he had acted, badly, in a play called *Holding out the Apple*, and he quoted a favorite silly line, "You've a way of holding out the apple that positively gives me the pip."

He giggled so much he nearly had to sit down.

More plaintively, he then revealed that when he walked down Shaftesbury Avenue these days, he never knew any of the names on the marquees. At least now, at the Gielgud, he said, there would be one that he recognized.

And one that we would, too. What a marvelous, magical man. Not *an* actor, said Kenneth Tynan, despite all those early strictures, but *the* actor. We shall not, as they say, look upon his like again.

## Notes

1. Tynan, *Profiles* (London: Nick Hern Books, 1989), 47.
2. John Gielgud, *Early Stages* (1939; London: Sceptre, 1990), 51.

3. John Mortimer in *The Ages of Gielgud: An Actor at Eighty*, ed. Ronald Harwood (London: Hodder and Stoughton, 1984), 68.

4. Tynan, *Profiles*, 47.

5. Michael Pennington, *"Hamlet": A User's Guide* (London: Nick Hern Books, 1996), 21.

6. Peter Hall interview, *New York Times*, 1 April 2001.

7. John Gielgud, *Stage Directions* (London: Heinemann, 1963), 59.

8. Peter Brook, *Ages*, 101.

9. Gielgud, *Early Stages*, 151.

10. Ibid., 181.

11. Ibid., 149.

12. Ibid., 150.

13. Obituary, *The Independent*, 23 May 2000.

14. Brook, *Ages*, 103.

15. Gielgud, *Stage Directions*, 48.

16. Edward Bond, *Bingo* (London: Methuen, 1974), 43.

17. Interview with the author, *The Observer*, 4 August 1991.

18. Ibid.

19. Ibid.

20. J. C. Trewin, *Illustrated London News*, 5 December 1957.

21. Interview with the author, *The Observer*, 4 August 1991.

# Shylock's Tribe

STEPHEN ORGEL

SHYLOCK IS CONVENTIONALLY IDENTIFIED AS AN OUTSIDER IN VENETIAN society, though generally as a prelude to observing how he also embodies all the essential Venetian qualities. I don't intend to question what seems to me a critical truism, but I do want to think about what kind of outsider he is, and what it means to be either an insider or an outsider in the world the play presents. If Venice was an exotic locale to Shakespeare, it is for us a familiar enough place, easily fitting a number of modern models—of early capitalism, of evolving notions of finance, of the beginnings of modern racial stereotyping—as well as some less familiar ones, such as those of the largely fictitious ideal Renaissance republican society, and of English law at a moment of accelerating change in concepts of both equity and citizenship. It is also a truism that the Venice of the Rialto and the dogana is really Shakespeare's London, but here surely the distinctions are more important than the similarities. The Italian setting is everything Elizabethan middle-class mercantile London is not for Shakespeare: a world of romance, glamour, poetry, and danger.

If Shylock is an outsider, what kind of outsider is he? In English and American productions since the late nineteenth century, he has been for the most part a member of a recognizable underclass, often speaking, even in productions with Italian Renaissance settings, with London East End or New York Lower East Side Jewish intonations—that is, not an outsider at all, just the insider we prefer not to know. Before that, from the beginning of the eighteenth century (which is as far back as our records go), he was first, as played by Thomas Dogget, a comic character: this was in George Granville's adaptation, called, significantly, *The Jew of Venice*, the only form in which the play survived the Restoration. As the title attested, the comic villain here was the center of the play. Charles Macklin, starting in the 1740s, and returning more or less to Shakespeare's text, was the first performer to conceive Shylock as a tragic figure, in this case a terrifying villain with no redeeming features, eaten up with malice and vindictiveness, a counterpart to Iago, the villain of the other Venetian play. Macklin's "badge of all our tribe" was a red beard, conventional for stage

Jews; the "Jewish gabardine," the rough wool robe that sets him off from the high fashion of his Venetian clients, was a cloak covering unfashionably wide black trousers, and he wore a red skullcap. Pope, who saw the performance on its third night, was puzzled by the skullcap and questioned Macklin about it. The actor claimed it as a gesture toward historical accuracy: he explained that he had read that sixteenth-century Venetian Jews did in fact wear red skullcaps, and Pope, suitably impressed, is said to have composed a distich on the subject: "This is the Jew / That Shakespeare drew." In fact, in various parts of sixteenth-century Italy, Jews were required to wear *yellow* hats—Macklin was misinformed on two counts. I'll return to the source of Macklin's information and its implications.

The transformation to the sympathetic Shylock, psychologically human and essentially a martyr to Christian intolerance, was the work of Edmund Kean. Kean's Shylock was far less localized than Macklin's had been, a victim but not recognizably an outsider. It was not until Henry Irving's Shylock at the end of the century, with Ellen Terry as Portia, that the Jew was rationalized historically, in this case as oriental; though Irving believed Shylock probably came from Frankfurt, he said he had based his interpretation on Jews he had seen in Morocco, "magnificent" Jews.[1] London Jews for once were off the hook: the Jew was at last an authentic outsider. Subsequently, however, he was generally played closer to home, whether as an East End Jew or, starting in the thirties, an East European refugee, instantly identifiable by his accent and costumed essentially as a used-clothing peddler—the Jewish gabardine itself was often distinctly seedy. Shylock the banker, for all his ready money, remained the thoroughly déclassé Jew, the Jew one had necessary dealings with but didn't recognize socially—this throughout almost two centuries of Rothschilds, Salomons, Montefiores, Warburgs, and Sassoons, in the London financial world, to say nothing of Rachel, Beerbohm Tree, Pinero, Sarah Bernhardt, Ada Reeve, and Leslie Howard on the London stage. For modern Shylocks, the great watershed production was Jonathan Miller's in 1970, in which Olivier's Shylock was a high Victorian banker—a stroke of genius that made sense out of Portia's question, "Which is the merchant here, and which the Jew?" by presenting a Shylock basically indistinguishable from Antonio, a thoroughly British financier, his gabardine as fine as Antonio's worsted, recognizable as a Jew only when he removed his top hat to reveal his (quite inauthentic and anachronistic) skullcap. Even in this production, even with a thoroughly assimilated, incontestably successful Jewish director, it was necessary to invoke the secret Chasid beneath the English gentleman.

The issue of how to play Shylock is significant because in the history of production the Merchant who is the play's titular subject tends to get lost—George Granville's adaptation was in this respect acutely perceptive.

The play is, even in the Revels accounts, called *The Jew of Venice;* and though the most famous actor of the era where our records begin, Betterton (at the age of sixty-six!), played the romantic lead Bassanio, the starring roles—definitively so since Macklin—have always been Shylock and Portia. As for the Merchant, he isn't even the second lead; Venice, for the stage, belongs to Shylock, not Antonio. What, then, is an outsider?

Let us return now to Macklin's red skullcap. He almost certainly found it in Coryate, where the Venetian Jews are said to be "distinguished and discerned from the Christians by their habits on their heads; for some of them doe weare hats and those redde, onely those Jewes that are borne in the westerne parts of the world, as in Italy, &c. but the easterne Jewes being otherwise called the Levantine Jewes, which are borne in Hierusalem, Alexandria, Constantinople, &c. weare Turbents upon their heads as the Turkes do."[2] Note that these are *hats*, not caps. The caps only appear later, when Coryate attends a service at the synagogue and observes that the rabbi is "discerned from the lay people onely by wearing of a redde cap, whereas the others doe weare redde hats."[3] Note too that these Jews are *not* outsiders, they are the Italian Jews; the outsiders, the Levantine Jews, wear turbans.

Shylock is clearly not a rabbi at prayer. Why then did Macklin wear a skullcap, rather than the hat stipulated by his source? Because by the 1740s, the skullcap was a marker of Jews in England. The routine wearing of the skullcap by Jews was in fact an innovation; it dates from the eighteenth century, and was practiced only among orthodox Ashkenazim, Jews from the German tradition. Its point was to devise a dress code specifically differentiating Jews from gentiles, for whom uncovering the head was a sign of respect; it was based on the Christian practice, and designed as a distinguishing alternative. By the mid-eighteenth century it would have been noticeable among Dutch and German Jews trading in London. Macklin's skullcap was in fact not history but sociology, and his performing style too was considered authentically Jewish. According to a report in *The Connoisseur* in 1754, "he made daily visits to the centre of business, the 'change and the adjacent coffee houses, that by a frequent intercourse and conversation with the 'unforeskinned race' he might habituate himself to their air and deportment."[4] Despite Macklin's claim to Pope, then, his audience recognized him as neither historically correct nor Venetian, but as an authentic contemporary Jew.

Pope's question, then, must have been not about the skullcap but about its color. Why is the skullcap *red*? The decor of Shylock's orthodoxy was thus brought into keeping with his Jewish red hair; but the cap would have had a deeper, if unacknowledged, significance. The production as a whole was costumed in modern dress—Pope might well have wondered why Shylock should have been the only historically correct Venetian—and for

Macklin's audience the red skullcap was the badge not of Jews, but of cardinals of the Roman Catholic church. Paradoxical as this juxtaposition sounds, it is probably the only point at which Macklin's conception of the play had a real historical validity, and I shall return to it.

Shylock's Jewishness is insisted on throughout the play; it serves, indeed, as a principle of explanation for his character, and of justification for his treatment at Portia's hands. The play's anti-Semitism is regularly accounted for by invoking the notorious case of Roderigo Lopez, a physician of Portuguese Jewish descent, who was executed in 1594 on charges of spying and plotting to poison the queen. The relevance of the case to the play was first discussed by Sir Sidney Lee in 1880 and has since appeared almost axiomatic. Since its relevance seems to me, on the contrary, both dubious and far-fetched, I shall give a brief account of this complex and confusing affair. Lopez was a respected and successful doctor. He may have been born in England—there were physicians named Lopez in England from the time of Henry VIII—but in any case he was there by 1559, and by 1569 was a member of the College of Physicians. In the 1570s he was attending first Walsingham, the head of the Elizabethan secret service, and then the earl of Leicester, Elizabeth's chief minister. In 1586 he became the queen's chief physician. He was not a Jew, except in the sense defined by the Nuremberg laws; he was either descended from converts or a convert himself, and was a regular communicant in the Anglican Church. (Gabriel Harvey, who disliked him, described him as "descended of Jewes: but himself A Christian."[5]) Before his trial he was occasionally referred to as a Jew, but this may well have been considered an asset, establishing his expertise in one of the few professions open to Jews and in which they were acknowledged to excel. Even when the charge is hostile, it is also admiring, as in a passage in the scurrilous pamphlet *Leicester's Commonwealth*, published in 1584, which lists Leicester's agents "for divers affairs": "two Galenists for agents in the university: Dee and Allen (two atheists) for figuring and conjuring: Julio the Italian & Lopez the Jew, for poisoning, and for the art of destroying children in women's bellies."[6] Jews are among the experts.

As a Portuguese speaker with connections in high places, however, his usefulness was not limited to his medical skills. He was a logical person to install as adviser and interpreter to Don Antonio, the chief claimant to the Portuguese crown, who was for a few years a key figure in Walsingham's and Essex's anti-Spanish machinations. Philip II of Spain had annexed Portugal in 1581, on the death of the Portuguese king, and Don Antonio spent a fruitless decade in Paris and London seeking support for his claim. Essex talked of leading a Spanish invasion to place Antonio on the Portuguese throne, but it eventually became clear that the project had less to do with Portugal than with Essex's plans for his own advancement;

and Antonio, blaming Lopez for misleading him, dismissed his adviser. Essex had also employed Lopez to deal with Spanish agents, hoping thereby to lure the Spanish king into some action that would justify open warfare against Spain, with himself as the heroic general. The Spanish duly proposed a payment to Lopez of fifty thousand ducats—eighteen thousand pounds, a gigantic sum in the period—if he would poison the queen. Lopez agreed, but demanded payment in advance; the matter went no further. In all this, of course, Lopez was acting on Essex's orders.

The whole scheme fell apart when Lopez revealed some part of it to the queen, who had no interest in a war with Spain, and had a showdown with Essex over the business. Essex was understandably furious, and in any case had no further use for Lopez. Two underlings were got to confess that Lopez had discussed the poisoning plot with them, and had had more correspondence with Spain than he had revealed to his employers; and although a search of Lopez's house produced nothing incriminating, he was threatened with torture and confessed to plotting against the queen's life. Tried for high treason by a court headed by Essex, he was found guilty and sentenced to death. The queen for many months refused to sign the death warrant and, after the execution was finally carried out, returned his fortune to his widow. Camden, who was not an eyewitness, later claimed that Lopez cried from the scaffold that he loved the queen more than he loved Jesus Christ, to which the crowd replied "He is a Jew, he is a Jew." This is exceedingly improbable, and Camden is the only source for the story, but even as it stands there is nothing disingenuous in Lopez's assertion: he was in fact a practicing Anglican. It is more likely, however, that he became a Jew only to justify his execution.

To represent him as a Jew, in fact, was not a significant part of the prosecutorial rhetoric, if indeed it was present at all. Robert Cecil reported that at his trial Lopez was condemned as a "murdering traitor and Jewish doctor . . . worse than Judas himself," and that the judge referred to him as "that vile Jew."[7] But this too seems to be a later addition to the story, recorded in none of the records of the trial; and in the longest and most widely circulated account of the affair, a pamphlet called *A True Report of Sundry Horrible Conspiracies* published in November 1594, which gives a very detailed if confused narrative of the case, the fact that he is a Jew is nowhere mentioned. The tract is all about Lopez's dealings with Spanish agents and his part in the international Jesuit conspiracy. The case is most interesting, in fact, in its ambivalences: Lopez is of course assumed to be Machiavellian and untrustworthy; but he is being *used* by the English throughout. And though Essex was surely justified in feeling that Lopez had betrayed his confidence, it was to the queen that Lopez had betrayed it, and he did so because his loyalty to the queen was greater than his loyalty to Essex—the queen herself perceived this, and protected Lopez until the weight of judicial pressure and public opinion made it impossible to do so any longer. The charge of villainy and betrayal obviously contains a lot of psychological projection in it: the Machiavel here really is Essex, and the unforgivable crime is that he has been exposed.

What has all this to do with Shylock? Not much: Readers of *Sundry Horrible Conspiracies* wouldn't even have been aware that Lopez was a Jew. Being a Jew here is tantamount to being an agent of the papacy and a tool of the Jesuits—this is the sense in which Macklin's red skullcap has a real historical validity. The case does, however, seem to have a tangential relevance to Marlowe's Jew, who claims to go around poisoning people. *The Jew of Malta* was probably written in 1589 or 1590, and the first re-corded performance was in 1592, long before Lopez was an available model; but the play was performed twice within ten days of the execution, in June 1594, and this is unlikely to have been coincidental. That *The Merchant of Venice*, written in 1596 or 1597, has something to do with Marlowe's play is not a matter for dispute. Jay Halio points out that *The Jew of Malta* was performed by the Lord Admiral's Men, the rivals of Shakespeare's company, eight times in 1596, and *The Merchant* was doubtless designed to capitalize on its continuing popularity.[8] In short, Shylock is a Jew not because Lopez was, but because Barabas was.

But what kind of Jew is Shylock? Barabas is identifiable as a reprehensible Jew simply from his name, that of the biblical thief released instead of Jesus. Shakespeare's other Jews, too, have immediately recognizable biblical names: Leah, Tubal, Chus (or Cush in the Authorized Version); but Shylock and Jessica come from another onomastic world entirely. Commentators since the eighteenth century have been baffled by Shylock's name, and have attempted to rationalize it by deriving it from *Shiloh*, a word for the Messiah; or from a genealogy in Genesis where the name "Shelah" is found; or from a pamphlet entitled *Caleb Shillocke his prophecy, or the Jew's Prediction*, which, since it was published in 1607, is more likely to derive from Shakespeare's Shylock than Shylock from it. The point of all this critical energy is to avoid the awkward fact that Shylock is, quite simply, an English name; this was first pointed out in 1849 by M. A. Lower, who found a power of attorney granted to a Sir Richard Shylok of Hoo, Sussex, in 1435. Subsequent commentators looking for keys to Shakespeare dismissed Sir Richard Shylok because he had no evident connection with either Shakespeare or usury, as if he were the only person in England who ever bore that surname. But Sir Richard Shylok had ancestors, and siblings, and relatives, and descendants; and over several hundred years there were other Shylock families who were not related to him. The surname "Shylock" appears in the Hundreds Rolls, and the name had been since Saxon times a native one. It means "white-haired" and is the same name as its more common English equivalents "Whitlock" and "Whitehead." The original name is still in use: there is a Christopher Shylock currently living in London, and the Shylock Beauty Salon may be found in Sydney. Shylock is not some form of a biblical name; in Shakespeare's time it was clearly and unambiguously English.

As for Jessica, it too is not a biblical name, though unlike Shylock it is also not English. It might be like Sidney's Pamela, an invented name that has passed into the culture. Pamela, however, reveals its sources easily: all honey, or sweetness, or melody. Jessica is less easy to locate. It might conceivably be intended as a female diminutive of the name of David's father Jesse, which would be appropriate because *Jesse* means "wealth"; but there is no reason whatever to believe that Shakespeare knew any Hebrew or was being advised by someone who did. Attempts to extract Jessica more directly from the Old Testament are even more far-fetched. They depend on a brief genealogy of Abraham's family in Genesis 11.29, in which a daughter is mentioned whose name is given in the Geneva Bible as "Iscah" and in the Bishops' Bible as "Jisca," and who is never referred to again. But surely in the world of Leah, Tubal, and Cush, this is clutching at straws: "Jessica" is in fact a common enough name in Scotland, a diminutive of the woman's name "Jessie." If Shakespeare knew any Jessicas, they were Scottish.

What does this mean? To begin with, it may reveal more about us than about Shakespeare. There are many parallels. The Navarre of *Love's Labor's Lost* includes Nathaniel and Costard (the most English of apples); all the Athenian workmen in *A Midsummer Night's Dream* have English names—Snout, Bottom, Snug, Quince, Flute, Starveling; the Mediterranean duchy of Illyria is home to the relentlessly English Sir Toby Belch and Sir Andrew Aguecheek; the servants in the Verona of *Romeo and Juliet* are Sampson, Gregory, Peter, and Abraham (and no critic to my knowledge has ever claimed that Sampson and Abraham were Jews); the villain in *Much Ado About Nothing*—a world of Pedros, Leonatos, Claudios, Borachios—is Don John. Shakespeare often wanted his clowns and grotesques to be recognizably English—why is only Shylock's name a problem?

Where do we go from there? If I were hunting for the real Shylock of Shakespeare's imagination, I'd look not in Old Testament genealogies but in the continuing Elizabethan debates on banking and interest—for example, in Thomas Wilson's *Discourse Upon Usury* (1572) and more particularly in R. H. Tawney's masterful long introduction to the 1925 edition of it. The Shylocks of Shakespeare's world were ubiquitous, but by the end of the sixteenth century they began to be localized in a few groups: goldsmiths, mercers, and, most visibly of all, scriveners, who combined the functions of accountant and legal adviser. None of these had anything to do with Jews—the association of Jews with usury in England was entirely conventional. Wilson, on the contrary, is convinced that the rise of usury was precisely a function of Protestantism, of Reformation morality and the abandonment of canon law. As Tawney says, "Calvin approached [economic life] as a man of affairs, who assumed, as the starting point of his social theory, capital, credit, large-scale enterprise,"[9] and therefore sanctioned the taking of interest on loans.

So one way to play Shylock "authentically" would be as one of the Puritan moneylenders of Shakespeare's London, for whom the Old Testament rhetoric would be entirely in character, and the Jewishness a moral comment on the profession. I am not, however, looking for a "real" Shylock, I'm simply following out the implications of his English name. What about the fact that he is a Jew? What would an authentic Jew be like for Shakespeare's stage? To begin with, not a lower-class Londoner or an East European refugee with a yarmulke, but Spanish or Portuguese: such figures carried with them, as in the Lopez case, the villainous subtext of Jesuit subversion. James Shapiro cites a wonderfully paranoid passage from William Prynne that makes the point: "If extraordinary care be not taken . . . under pretext of Jews, we shall have many hundreds of Jesuits, Popish priests, and friars come over freely into England from Portugal, Spain, Rome, Italy, and other places, under the title, habit, and disguise of Jews."[10] The Jew is the mask of the papist—we return to Macklin's red skullcap.

To play Shylock as a Renaissance Spaniard would not, of course, have much resonance for a modern audience. To play him as a modern Latino, however, would make a striking kind of sense for American audiences: Shylock, after all, isn't an outsider, any more than Latinos are in American society. He's as Venetian as the Christians are, but he's part of an underclass, marginalized within the society. Latinos aren't associated with money in our culture, but a production might make real capital out of that. After all, if, as Antonio says, there are Christian moneylenders who don't charge interest, then why are Bassanio and Antonio involved with Shylock at all? But the point is surely that Bassanio has already gone to all the classy mainline banks, and none of them will give him the time of day— Antonio's obviously a bad risk, and he's an even worse one. So he ends up with Shylock—that means, let's say, in our American production, that he ends up at a barrio bank. The Latino banker also sees perfectly well that Antonio and Bassanio are a bad investment, but he never gets any business from the Anglo community, and he thinks that if he does a favor for Antonio perhaps that will get him some clout in the mainstream financial world—at least Antonio will be in his debt, owe him some favors. So he makes the loan, with a jokey stipulation substituting a body part for his usual interest—a joke, that is, that precludes his charging interest. And then he gets completely screwed by the Anglo world he's trying to become a part of, losing not just his money but also his daughter to the Anglos, and he goes crazy and gets very vindictive. That actually would be, for us, a quite comprehensible psychological scenario.

But as I've already suggested, there is another side to Shylock, and to the Jew figure, for the Elizabethans, and that is his Old Testament component. Jews have a special status theologically: they are neither heathens nor heretics, categorically different from pagans and Moslems because they were God's chosen people, and in them Renaissance Christianity saw its own past. The conversion of the Jews was a holy mission, because it would mark the historical completion of Christ's work—the Turks were to be destroyed, but the Jews had to be converted. Coryate expresses the cultural ambivalence very clearly, observing from his Venetian experience that "our English proverbe: To looke like a Jewe (whereby is meant sometimes a weather beaten warp-faced fellow, sometimes a phreneticke and lunaticke person, sometimes one discontented) is not true. For indeed I noted some of them to be most elegant and sweet featured persons, which gave me occasion the more to lament their religion."[11] And for Christians who saw the church as corrupt, or as having fallen away from its proper function and its original purity, the Jews represented a tradition to be embraced and returned to, a way of starting afresh. Various radical Protestant sects used the Jews as a model, both for the ordering of society and for their rhetoric; and there's a lot in Shylock's language that recalls Puritan ways of speaking and arguing. Such sects quite explicitly emulated Judaism, calling their priests rabbis and using Hebrew—Jonson satirizes the practice with Rabbi Zeal-of-the-Land Busy in *Bartholomew Fair*. In 1655 Cromwell convened the Whitehall Conference to discuss formally readmitting the Jews to England—they had been formally expelled in 1290. There were even negotiations to sell the decaying St. Paul's Cathedral to the Jewish community as a great central synagogue, and while the Whitehall Conference ended inconclusively, the government granted various privileges to resident Jews, though it stopped short of allowing them to be naturalized. They were technically "denizens," legally resident in the society but not finally integrated into it.

Shylock can be seen as a kind of Puritan. Shakespeare is not at all sympathetic to the Puritan cause, but his distaste for it isn't a distaste for foreigners. Shylock is very deeply part of Venetian society: he expresses a good deal of its deepest nature; the success of both Antonio's love for Bassanio and Bassanio's love for Portia depends not only on Shylock's capital, but on his willingness to see it used merely to enable a Venetian romance. This helps to explain the strange ambivalence Shakespeare exhibits about this villain; and it also helps to explain why he's unwilling to destroy or expel him after the trial scene, but wants to incorporate him into the Christian world, to force him to convert. He *is* an essential part of

Venice, which is to say, of England. Hence the most striking point about him, his English name: Shakespeare's ambivalence epitomized. Just what kind of subversion does this figure represent? All those pleasure-loving types in the play are Italians, but for an Elizabethan audience, Shylock is one of us.

The other side of this, of course, is the continuing, corrosive, paranoid anti-Semitism so thoroughly chronicled and analyzed by James Shapiro. The most dangerous aspect of Jews was precisely how much like "us" they were, the fear that they were in fact indistinguishable, that anyone might be a secret Jew. The telltale sign of circumcision was, after all, to any but the most intimate of observers, invisible, and for women there was no sign whatever. Shapiro cites a fascinating fantasy of a minister named Josselin in Essex in 1655, who had dreamt that "one came to me and told me that Thurloe [Oliver Cromwell's Secretary of State] was turned Jew; I answered perhaps it was a mistake, he might declare he was a Jew born, the Jews having lived here, and he pretend by old writings his pedigree from them, to ingratiate with the Jews, or some compliance with them." Shapiro asks, "What are we to make of Josselin's response in his dream that news of John Thurloe's conversion was 'a mistake'? Not that this report was false, but that Thurloe was not really 'turned Jew'; rather, he was simply pretending to be 'a Jew born' for politic reasons. It is not entirely clear (Shapiro continues) what it means here to 'turn' Jew. Is this something one chooses to do, or is it somehow beyond one's control? Have religious or national identity become so unstable as to be vulnerable to such an unlikely transformation? Perhaps the most interesting feature of the dream is Josselin's notion that Thurloe would defend this claim by reinventing his 'pedigree' through antiquarian records, 'old writings' connecting his lineage back to the Jews who, centuries earlier, had lived in England. Here was the repressed returning with a vengeance."[12]

The baffling question here of why one would choose to be a Jew, or to represent oneself as one, however, conceals a deeper and more disturbing question: how can one ever know who is a Jew and who is not? Indeed, if one traced one's own impeccably British ancestors far enough back, one might find Jews among them, "the Jews having lived here," as Josselin says. In this fantasy, the very wellspring of British history is contaminated with the alien presence. One might, then, "really" be a Jew oneself and not know it: the question of what it means "really" to be a Jew remained unanswerable. Is it a matter of lineage, of belief, of practice? Is someone who does not perform Jewish rituals, pray as a Jew, profess the faith— someone like Dr. Lopez, for example—"really" a Jew? Is an uncircumcised Jew (like Daniel Deronda) "really" a Jew? In orthodox Jewish law, Jewish identity passes through the mother; the child of a Jewish father and a gentile mother is not a Jew. This of course makes the racial identification even more problematic, since the woman bears no sign of her religion—Jessica says her husband has made her a Christian, but is this the case? *Can* a Jewish woman become Christian? What will be the status of her children then—are they Jewish or gentile? If "Jewish blood" is involved, does a change in belief affect the bloodline? In fact, a child may be either Jewish or gentile depending on whether one applies the Mosaic or the patriarchal law. Those who are Jews to the English may not be Jews to the Jews.

For Shakespeare's England, the fantasy of secret contamination is not at all limited to the Jews; but the Jews provide an essential model. In *Titus Andronicus*, when Tamora gives birth to Aaron's black child, the villainous Moor, never at a loss for a stratagem, determines to substitute another:

> Not far, one Muliteus, my countryman,
> His wife but yesternight was brought to bed.
> His child is like to her, fair as you are.

> (4.2.153–55)

This is the same fantasy even more racially charged, a testimony to the impossibility of determining not only whether one's child is one's own, but even whether it is "really" white or black: blackness in this case is not at all a function of skin color. It is surely not coincidental that Aaron is the name of the brother of Moses.

How does all the ambivalence about Shylock, the tragic energy, the dangerous and subversive potential, get accommodated to comedy? Why is it an element in comedy at all? The idea that comedy and tragedy are not opposites but complements is not a new one: at the end of the *Symposium* Socrates tells Agathon and Aristophanes, tragic and comic playwrights, that their crafts are the same, and every Shakespeare comedy, from *The Comedy of Errors* to *The Tempest*, has its tragic elements. What distinguishes comedy from tragedy is not the problems they act out, but what they accept as solutions. Many commentators have remarked the similarities between Shylock and that stock figure of the Italian comedy the Pantaloon. Pantalone is the heavy father, morbidly protective of his daughter Columbine. Sixteenth- and seventeenth-century depictions of him might be depictions of the original Shylock: he is elderly, has a hooked nose, and carries a large, wickedly curved knife in his belt. Irascible and vindictive, he is driven wild by Columbine's flirtations with Harlequin and other young men. Making off with his daughter and his ducats is no more than a condign punishment, an entirely predictable comic conclusion. What is missing from this as a model for Shylock is, obviously, a complex psychology, an explanatory history, a credible motivation—in short, Shake-

speare—but it is difficult to imagine Shylock without Pantalone
somewhere in the background.

But comic or tragic, does Shylock in fact sum up the play's threatening
potential? After the trial scene, after the tragic plot has been resolved, the
play nevertheless still includes an insistent sense of danger, ominous overtones that derive not from Shylock but precisely from the conventions of
comedy itself, the complexities of courtship, and the promise—and, in
Shakespeare, the very ominous implications—of marriage. Shylock both
is and is not part of that structure, and banishing him or converting him
does not remove him. In one way, as I've said, he is essential to it: his
money is required for the success of Bassanio's love for Portia and of Antonio's love for Bassanio, because that is an essential relationship in the
play too. But what is essential, it turns out, is also subversive: the translation of love into money, money into love, isn't a simple matter. It remains
benign only so long as money can be thought of merely as *riches*—as in
the case of Portia, the lady richly left: she *has* her money, who doesn't
*make* it. As soon as money is conceived to be *finance*, however, the essence of commerce, venture capital, capital in the Marxist sense, it becomes threatening both to love and to that sense of self that love depends
on—it controls us, instead of our controlling it. Hence the dangers of
choosing the gold or silver caskets. What Venice requires also undermines
it.

Most critical treatments of the play until very recently have said that it
ends with heavenly harmony, and the happy marriages of Portia and Bassanio, Nerissa and Gratiano, Lorenzo and Jessica. But in fact, most of the
fifth act is taken up with the consequences of Portia's ring trick. This is
commonly either dismissed as a joke, if a rather malicious one, or defended as a way of insisting on the primacy of marriage over all other
relationships. But it has implications that have little to do with harmony,
least of all the harmony of marriage. To begin with, the women have made
their husbands' love equivalent to the rings they have given them. This
is the same translation Othello does with Desdemona's handkerchief and
Posthumus does with Imogen's bracelet, and if Othello and Posthumus are
at fault, so are Portia and Nerissa: the material basis of love is as powerful
at the play's conclusion as at its beginning, and as powerful in this comedy
as it is in Shakespearean tragedy. The model of marriage here, moreover,
is Shylock's: he had a ring from Leah when he was a bachelor, he would
not have given it up for a wilderness of monkeys. The test of the men's
faith is both a trap and exceedingly revealing about the nature of marriage
in the play. Portia and Nerissa know perfectly well that Bassanio and Gratiano have not given the rings as love tokens to other women, but as a
compelled recompense for an overwhelming debt of gratitude to two
young men: the whole reason the women disguise themselves as men,

rather than come to the court in their own persons or disguised as other women, is precisely that this is the only way to get the rings away from their husbands. Other women have nothing to do with the matter, and they know it. All the ruse does, all it is designed to do, is give the wives a grudge to hold over their husbands forever: this is what the primacy of marriage depends on, this is the reason that husbands should be faithful. On the other hand, if their husbands' interest in young men is really a significant menace, if this is really the danger the grudge is a prophylactic against, then keeping any number of rings safe will hardly ensure the sanctity of the marriage vow.

The blatant materialism of the play's conclusion is surely part of its point: Portia's money has rescued Bassanio, just as Shylock's has done, and however clever, charming, or beautiful Portia is, both Bassanio and the play itself make it quite clear from the outset that she is nothing to him without money—"In Belmont is a lady richly left . . . / And many Jasons come in quest of her" (1.1.161–72). This Jason does indeed obtain the golden fleece; does he also marry Medea? The insistent sense of threat and danger no doubt accounts for the fact that, for all its high romance, the play has been, as far back as our records take us, a play about Shylock; many productions over the years have simply ended the play with the trial scene. Ask people who the merchant of Venice is, and nine out of ten will reply that it is Shylock. But the play, nominally at least, is about Antonio, and the threat posed by Shylock to his lavish altruism, which is the path to love. As a summary of the play, however, this doesn't quite do it, because if Antonio is necessary to the successful outcome of love in the play, so is Shylock—Antonio's money is Shylock's money, there is no Antonio without Shylock. Credit, bonds, trust, above all cash—these are central to the worlds of both Venice and Belmont: the loan isn't incidental, and you can't have love without money.

Venice, then, contains its own dangers: not only Shylock presents us with tragic possibilities, they exist even without him. If we look at the play symbolically, we might say that Shylock sums up the destructive tendencies of both Venice and Belmont—the overwhelming concern with money, the literalizing of bonds, whether Shylock's bond or Portia's ring, the emphasis on the flesh, not on the spirit. Why does Shylock ask for a pound of flesh nearest the heart? Obviously not for any reason having to do with character, but precisely because the flesh *is* what is closest to the heart.

Even in overcoming its dangers and signaling its romantic triumphs, the play has a kind of overkill. In the love scene between Lorenzo and Jessica at the opening of act 5, the lovers are finally free, and together, and rich; and they have the support of the most powerful people in their world. How do they celebrate their victory? They entertain each other with mythological stories of tragic love affairs: the faithless Cressida, suicidal Thisbe, betrayed Dido, murderous Medea—and then themselves: the extravagant, untrustworthy Lorenzo, the rash and slanderous Jessica. The disasters of passion, the dangers of the flesh, are the substance of poetry and the resolution of comedy—you can't have comedy without tragedy.

Let us turn finally to the triumph over Shylock, the trial scene, with its eulogy on unconstrained mercy. Portia's—or Shakespeare's—behavior toward Antonio is in fact as cruel as anything Shylock does. The scene is drawn out excruciatingly, and its theatrical power has much less to do with the quality of mercy than with the pleasures of sadism on the one hand and revenge on the other. Gratiano, who simply wants to see Shylock drawn and quartered, obviously expresses a good deal of what Shakespeare's audience would have felt—this is a particularly clear case where Shylock and the Venetians are mirror images of each other. Gratiano doesn't get his way, but he gets more of his way than Portia's speech about mercy would lead us to expect; in particular, he gets the deep satisfaction of Portia's invocation of the forgotten law about plots against the lives of Venetian citizens. Shylock has already lost his case on technical grounds: why bring another case against him?

Consider the trial as a whole, and particularly where we stand during it. Suppose Portia had stopped the proceedings at the point where Shylock has lost his case on technicalities: how would the play be changed if, after her close reading of the bond, Shylock were sent home unsatisfied, with Antonio's life intact, and only the return of his principle, or not even that, for comfort? But no, we'd say, that wouldn't do it. He has been too much of a threat; not only the action of the play but his own vindictiveness demand more retribution than that. Gratiano no doubt overstates the case when he's outraged that any mercy at all is being shown to the Jew, but he expresses something that we *do* feel—that Shylock has to be exorcised, requires a degree of retribution that isn't provided for in the mere forfeiture of the pound of flesh. The old law that Portia suddenly invokes allows for this—allows, that is, for *us* to have *our* revenge. It also allows for a degree of mercy to be shown to Shylock far greater than any he was willing to extend to Antonio. The law calls for the forfeiture of all his goods and his life; in fact, he keeps half his goods and his life.

But does *this* really satisfy us, even as Renaissance Christians? Because there's something deeply problematic about the old law: it is trumped up. No one has ever heard of it before; only Portia knows about it, and she springs it on Shylock, and on all of us, at the last possible moment. After Shylock has lost his case, she reveals that he never had a case at all. The threat against Antonio was never anything but a threat against himself, potential suicide. Anybody can see through the bond; but the old law is a secret, in effect an *ex post facto* law, which applies only to Shylock, and has been invoked—indeed invented—solely to put him at the mercy of the court. This is a striking example of the play's tendency toward overkill, because the forgotten law is Shakespeare's invention, appearing in none of the sources, and quite unnecessary to the plot.

Viewed in this way, the court's mercy looks rather different. Shylock is deprived of half his property and forced to abandon his faith. Does this really constitute mercy? The answer is, it does and it doesn't; it is an utterly ambiguous resolution that satisfies both our charity and our vindictiveness in the same dramatic moment. It also contributes significantly to the oddly schizoid response that Shylock, in the trial scene in particular, seems to demand of us. Shylock is, unquestionably, the villain of the play; but there's something in the character that we are asked to sympathize with and are unwilling to reject.

In one sense he is antithetical to the altruism of Venice and the generosity of Christianity, but in another he confronts the Venetians with the truth about themselves: that they are versions of him, not only in their essential humanity—"hath not a Jew eyes . . ."—but in their inhumanity as well:

> You have among you many a purchased slave
> Which, like your asses and your dogs and mules,
> You use in abject and in slavish parts,
> Because you bought them. Shall I say to you,
> "Let them be free, marry them to your heirs"?
> . . . You will answer
> "The slaves are ours." So do I answer you.
>
> (4.1.90–98)

This might in fact have touched some nerves—England was heavily involved in the slave trade by the 1590s (Venice was not), and it is not at all clear where an Elizabethan audience's sympathies would have been at this point. Shylock also confronts his audience with their hatred, for Antonio has set the terms of the bond as much as Shylock. Shylock is presented as the heavy, the disapproving father interfering with our fun and against whom we naturally rebel. But surely we also feel that he just might be right—and Shakespeare's moralizing culture would have felt it far more strongly. *Is* Bassanio's extravagance a virtue? Isn't it true that Lorenzo and Jessica are spendthrifts—do we want to see our children (to say nothing of our elders) act that way? After all the parties, *won't* there be a day of reckoning? When we start thinking in this way, the whole moral structure of the play starts to look different. "Antonio is a good man": *is* Antonio a good man—good in either sense? Would *we* lend him money? In fact, Shylock agrees to the loan knowing that Antonio is a bad risk; he says he's trying to be friendly. Is Antonio trying to be friendly—is he even willing to try? To which one of the two is it a cold business arrangement? And however romantic we find the fine careless rapture with which Antonio and Bassanio treat their money, do we really believe, in our own lives, that extravagance is a virtue and thrift isn't? And so forth: Shylock touches on profoundly ambivalent attitudes in all of us, and this effect would have been far more powerful to Elizabethan audiences, many of whom were strongly sympathetic to Puritan attitudes.

I conclude my history of Shylock as an inescapable presence both for the play and for England with a bit of originary bibliography. The title page of the first quarto reads, "The Excellent History of the *Merchant of Venice*. With the extreme cruelty of Shylock the Jew towards the said Merchant, in cutting a just pound of his flesh, and the obtaining of Portia by the choice of three caskets. 1600." This seems to promise a quite different trial scene, in which Shylock is awarded his just pound of flesh, and takes it. The final clause implies that he obtains Portia too. By 1600, the play had already become Shylock's.

# Notes

Note: for information and advice I am indebted to Peter Holland and John Stokes. I am especially grateful to Charles Edelman, who called several errors to my attention and shared his unpublished work on the Lopez trial with me.

1. Joseph Hatton, *Henry Irving's Impressions of America* (Boston: Osgood, 1884), 231.

2. Coryate, *Crudities* (1611), 231.

3. Ibid.

4. Cited by Toby Lelyveld, *Shylock on the Stage* (Cleveland: Case Western Reserve University Press, 1960), 26.

5. From a marginalium transcribed by Frank Marcham, *Lopez the Jew* (Harrow Weald, Middlesex: n.p., 1927).

6. *Copie of a Leter Wryten by a Master of Arte at Cambridge to his friend in London* (1584; reprinted 1641 and thereafter invariably referred to as *Leicesters Commonwealth*), 80.

7. The remarks are cited in Hermann Sinsheimer, *Shylock, the History of a Character or The Myth of the Jew* (London: Victor Gollancz, 1947), 66. I am indebted to Charles Edelman, whose study of the case is forthcoming, for the information that the claims are unfounded.

8. Jay L. Halio, ed., *The Merchant of Venice* (Oxford: Oxford University Press, 1993), 28.

9. Thomas Wilson, *A Discourse Upon Usury* (London: Bell, 1925), 111.

10. James Shapiro, *Shakespeare and the Jews* (New York: Columbia University Press, 1996), 27.

11. Coryate, *Crudities*, 231.

12. Ibid., 55–56.

# Staging Shakespeare and Calderón: Comparison and Contrast

JOHN J. ALLEN

W HEN THE FIRST PERMANENT PLAYHOUSE IN MADRID OPENED ITS DOORS in 1579, Lope de Vega was seventeen years old. Miguel de Cervantes returned from captivity in Algiers a year later, ending his career in the marines, and began to seek his fortune by writing twenty or thirty plays for this playhouse, the Corral de la Cruz, and for another, the Corral del Príncipe, that shared with it the monopoly on theatrical productions in Madrid for the following 150 years.

Commercial theater in Renaissance Spain had begun with performances in city squares by people like Lope de Rueda, whom Cervantes in 1615 recalled having seen as a boy, in the 1550s or '60s:

> In the time of that celebrated Spaniard, all the equipment of the manager of a company of actors fit into a single basket, and it consisted of a few fancy shepherds' cloaks, a few beards and wigs, and four shepherds' crooks, more or less. The plays were eclogue-like colloquies between two or three shepherds and a shepherdess. There was no machinery in those days, no figures who arose or seemed to arise from the bowels of the earth through a trapdoor in the stage, which was made up of four benches in a square with a few planks on top of them, which raised it about three feet off the ground. Nor were there clouds bearing angels or blessed souls to be let down. The stage decoration was an old blanket drawn by two ropes from one side to the other, which created what they call a *vestuario*—a tiring or "attiring" room, and behind it the musicians, singing some old ballad without even a guitar.[1]

Before the construction of the permanent theaters, then, these were the basic elements of theatrical production in Spain: a rectangular platform surrounded on three sides by spectators, with a curtained-off area at the rear for entrance and exit, which also served as dressing room and discovery space. This is the same sort of outdoor platform stage that appears in drawings and engravings from all over Western Europe at the time.

These performances in public squares soon moved to enclosed open-air Spaces of great variety—innyards and hospital patios, etc.—providing the key to commercial success: no longer obliged to pass a hat for voluntary contributions, theatrical entrepreneurs henceforth controlled admission to the spectacle. By the turn of the century, *corral* playhouses were being built all over the peninsula, with major theatrical activity in Madrid, Seville, and here in Valencia. At the same time—from the 1560s and 70s on—two other important theatrical innovations took place: first, the arrival in Spain of *commedia dell'arte* troupes from Italy, most notably the company of Alberto Naseli, called "Ganassa"; and secondly, the presentation of one-act religious plays celebrating the sacrament of communion, called *autos sacramentales*, staged on carts as part of the processions at Corpus Christi and employing staging arrangements that soon appear in the commercial *corrales de comedias*.

The tiring-room arrangements on these carts necessitate the construction of buildings, mountains, or some sort of elevation at each side to conceal them. The actors must have a place offstage to dress and to enter from and retire to, and there is no space behind or under the carts for this purpose, which must thus be served by the space available within these lateral elevations, which became fundamental elements in the subsequent development of staging.

Later on, platforms analogous to the two carts drawn up at either end of a third were provided in the Madrid *corrales* at each side of the main stage, used for bench seating for spectators at urban, simply staged, "cape and sword" performances; but also, alternatively, to facilitate the more elaborate staging needed for the common "mountain" or two-mountain scene, making a virtue out of what had originally been a necessity: room offstage for the actors. This is one of the distinctive elements that characterize the Madrid playhouses as compared to their contemporary counterparts in London, and this unique stage design was so successful that as far as we can tell it persisted with little fundamental modification for a century and a half.

The distinctive Spanish *corral* stage, then, seems to have arisen from this confluence of three public theatrical traditions early in the second half of the sixteenth century: (1) indigenous secular street theater, involving people like Lope de Rueda; (2) the evolution of processional tableaux into increasingly elaborate sacramental plays performed on carts at Corpus Christi; and (3) the arrival in Spain of Italian *commedia dell'arte* troupes. What the combination of these three traditions produced was a stage and scenic arrangements remarkably similar to those of Shakespeare and his contemporaries, but that could also be expanded, using the lateral platforms, for much more elaborate sets that seem to have no counterpart in the English open-air playhouses.

\*     \*     \*

The database called *Teatro Español del Siglo de Oro* (hereafter *TESO*) was created by a group of scholars directed by María del Carmen Simón Palmer and produced on CD-Rom by Chadwyck-Healey.[2] It allows us to search sixteenth- and seventeenth-century editions of nearly nine hundred *comedias* and *autos*, including some 145 works by Calderón. This new resource together with the *Dictionary of Stage Directions in English Drama, 1580–1642,* by Alan Dessen and Leslie Thomson,[3] facilitates the kind of comparative research of Elizabethan and Golden Age staging practice that has previously been quite difficult to carry out. In what follows I have also depended heavily upon Dessen's *Recovering Shakespeare's Theatrical Vocabulary.*[4]

My remarks today will be restricted to the staging terms and practices in the works of Calderón for *commercial* theater, with such allusions to his contemporaries and to his sacramental plays as clarify or otherwise bear upon examples of his *corral* staging. Before discussing staging practices, I will briefly address the theater itself, the *corral de comedias*.

Theatrical spaces varied greatly then as they do now. A play written for a *corral* stage might have been performed almost anywhere, from a room in a palace to some specially built festival stage. The size, shape, and decoration of the more than two dozen *corrales* scattered throughout Spain that we know about are surprisingly varied, but within these playhouses the dimensions and shape of the stage itself remain fairly constant in venues as different as the *corral* in Toro, a relatively small square hospital yard, and the Corral de la Montería, elliptical in shape and the largest public theater in Seville. In each case the stage is a rectangle about twelve feet deep by twenty-four feet wide. An appropriate point of comparison with the stages in the London playhouses would be the two stages, from 1587 and 1592, respectively, of the Rose, as revealed in the excavation a little over a decade ago. In the case of the Madrid playhouses and others that featured the lateral platforms described above, those platforms added a variable amount of staging space at each side of the main stage.

With these fundamental circumstances in mind, we can begin to illustrate the staging features that characterize Calderón's *corral* plays with the texts provided by the *TESO* data base, drawing comparisons where appropriate with what we know of Shakespeare's staging. Although we cannot ignore the chronological disparity between the two playwrights— Calderón was only sixteen when Shakespeare died, and he wrote plays for the *corrales* until the middle of the century—all of the staging features I will discuss in what follows are established as available to the Spanish dramatists who were Shakespeare's strict contemporaries, unless I specify to the contrary. I will, however, use citations from Calderón wherever possible and unless otherwise indicated.[5]

We can begin by examining staging for the *comedia de capa y espada*, the "cape and sword" plays and other genres written for stages quite similar to the two Rose stages in dimensions and proportions, although more strictly rectangular. The tiring-room or *vestuario* at the back of the *corral* stage had three openings, for entry, exit, and discovery: *El conde Lucanor* mentions entries "on one side," then "on the other," and finally through "the middle door" (10:408), as is the case in *The English Traveller* and in *Eastward, Ho* (*Dictionary*, s.v. "door"). The outer two of the three doors or openings are the usual entry and exit points for the actors coming onstage. The central door (or opening) is the default discovery space, although discoveries are frequently staged at other points: a curtain is drawn to reveal Doña Mencía bled to death in her bed in *El médico de su honra* (5:118), just as in the quarto *2 Henry VI*, "the Curtains being drawn, Duke Humphrey is discovered in his bed" (*Dictionary*, s.v. "curtain"). These doors may be covered or disguised: "[a door with] a hanging" in *Casa con dos puertas* (2:30v), "a door that is painted as a wall" in *El encanto sin encanto* (10:165). In *Roaring Girl*, "three shops open in a rank" (*Dictionary*, s.v. "open"), apparently corresponding to three openings to the stage from the tiring house in the *corrales*. These stage-level spaces, with or without doors and other coverings, constitute the first level of the façade of the *vestuario*, the vertical structure at the back of the stage, at least the width of the central stage and perhaps extending along the back of the lateral platforms in playhouses like the Príncipe and the Cruz in Madrid. The whole *vestuario* façade can be exposed or differently covered, as for example in *Orígen, pérdida y restauración de la Virgen del Sagrario*, where the stage directions for opening act 2 specify the decor as follows: "cover the tiring-house with sections of wall" (5:126v), and those for opening act 3: "cover the whole façade with curtains" (5:134r). Simultaneous use of virtually the entire space can be seen in *El postrer duelo de España*: "draw the curtain from the whole tiring house and let Charles be seen on the throne, and below the 'condestable' on another throne, with a table in front . . . and two tents, that will be placed at each side" (11:23v). The façade of the *vestuario* must thus be thought of as a three-story blank space structurally divided into nine niches, three at each level. Lope once referred to it as a kind of "chest of drawers," but the similarity to a typical Baroque altar-piece is obvious, and offers us another point of contact with contemporary religious art and decor.

The first level above the stage, then, is another curtaincd tripartite gallery, once again at least the width of the central stage: "Discover in a gallery Beatriz, Leonor, and Isabel with pillows, embroidering" (*La desdicha de la voz*, 16:433); it can easily convert to windows, bars, etc.: "Clori and Nise appear at a window, and at another Lísida y Celia," in *La banda y la flor* (17:318). Dessen and Thomson record "the King, and Butts, at a Window above" from *Henry VIII* (*Dictionary*, s.v. "window"). This level is curtained as well in the Elizabethan works, as in "the curtains drawn above," from *Emperor of the East* (*Dictionary,* s.v. "curtain"). The second level above is "the top" (*lo alto*), also divisible into three segments; and it may represent, for example, the top of a castle or wall, or a mountain peak: "Singing at the top on one side . . . on the top on the other side" (*Darlo todo y no dar nada*, 12:183r/v). In London, the "top," as Dessen and Thomson indicate, may serve "for a location where one figure appears above the main platform and possibly above the upper playing level, as when having breached the walls of Rouen, Pucell enters "on the top" (*1 Henry VI*) and "in yonder turret," then appears "on the walls," which perhaps differentiates the two locations; in *The Tempest*, Prospero watches "on the top (invisible)" (*Dictionary*, s.v. "top"). The below-stage area, excavated in the principal *corrales* to allow easy standing movement and activity, certain types of staging machinery, and sometimes wardrobe and dressing-room space, provided access to the stage through a number of *escotillones*, or trapdoors. In London, in *Antony and Cleopatra*, the "music of the Hoboys is under the stage" (*Dictionary*, s.v. "hoboy").

Calderón's characters usually come on (*salen*) and go off the stage (*entran*) through the two rear lateral doors or openings in the tiring-house or, rarely, through the center door, sometimes referred to as a pair of doors. They may also appear above, *en lo alto*, at a window or balcony, atop a wall or mountain; or they may emerge from a cave, pit, or dungeon, or rise up out of hell.

The usual method for characters to travel from one place to another is exemplified in *El escondido y la tapada* (15:535): "they go in one door and come out the other." I have observed this convention in at least ten of the Calderón plays in the *TESO* collection. This corresponds to Elizabethan practice, in which, as Dessen says, a character "'goes in at one door and comes out another' to go 'from one room to another'" (*Recovering*, 165). Calderón sometimes combines the procedure with the use of discovery curtains in the change of scene, as when, in *Los tres afectos de amor* (10:287), "the temple of Venus is discovered . . . and having gone in one door, they come out another." It is possible, however, to change locale without clearing the stage, much as in the Elizabethan practice where, as Dessen says, "scenes regularly move from street to interior or vice versa without a clearing of the stage" (*Recovering*, 167). A standard convention in both *comedia* and Elizabethan practice appears to be that a character may bring with him or her a change from outside to inside contiguous space, or the reverse, as seems to happen in act 1, scene 2, of Calderón's *El alcalde de Zalamea* (16:488). Dessen says that "in at least some scenes the actors were not suddenly revealed 'in' this place . . . but rather brought 'the shop' with them onto the main stage" (*Recovering*, 156).

Designation of relative stage position in the stage directions is rare, except for characters' appearing "at the curtain," or expressions such as "looking within." Two other terms used by Calderón are *la punta* (the edge, or perhaps the right or left front corner), and *la esquina* (the corner, probably one of the corners where the stage meets the tiring-house): "the kings," armed, go to "*la punta*" of the stage, from *El postrer duelo* (10:48) and "the two *puntas* of the stage," used in *La exaltación de la Cruz* (16:167). The latter case, where the discovery of "two peaks" is to be executed at "*las dos puntas del tablado*," seems clearly to designate the forward edge of the lateral extremities of the stage and/or the lateral platforms, as the case may be. *Esquina* (corner) is used contrastively: "*a la esquina del tablado* [at the corner of the stage] there is to be a table," in *El Gran Príncipe de Fez* (11:129v); "both retire to the corner of the stage," in *Para vencer a Amor* (15:569), followed by "she is to be *ala punta*, as he was" (573).

The precise meaning of a number of theatrical terms in use in Calderón's day is still not entirely clear to me, and in some cases was not firmly fixed even for him and his contemporaries. The word *t[h]eatro* can mean "la parte del tablado que se adorna con paños o bastidores para la representación,"[6] that is, the tiring-house, or its façade; or it can refer to the stage itself—the *tablado*—as it does in many of the theater-repair documents. It can refer as well, of course, to the entire *corral* or playhouse. The word *apariencia*, which was often used by earlier dramatists to signal a discovery, covers a multitude of special effects in Calderón's plays, from "la apariencia del incendio y de la nieve" (the simulation of fire and snow), in *La aurora en Copacabana* (10:384), to "sube la apariencia hasta lo alto" (the machine or device rises up to the top), in *El purgatorio de San Patricio* (2:59v). For Shakespeare's Spanish contemporaries, including Calderón, a scene revealed by drawing a curtain is conventionally signalled by "descúbrese" (is discovered), or "córrese una cortina" (a curtain is drawn). In Calderón's plays, curtains are drawn on the different stage levels and niches to reveal a boat, a throne, a raised dais, or a bed, among many other things.

The supernumerary required for delivery and removal of bodies and other objects in thrust-stage performance was called a *metemuertos y sacasillas* (body-snatcher and chair-bringer; *Diccionario de Autoridades*, s.vv. "metemuertos"; "sacapelotas"). Machines and standard props in use in the Elizabethan playhouses all have counterparts in the *corrales*: the tree and the hell-mouth found in Henslowe's inventory, the onstage "tombs," the chair or throne lowered from "the top," the scaling ladders, the "hoboys" (*chirimías* in Spain) used frequently for supernatural events and to announce or accompany the entry of nobility or royalty, and the lanterns and torches to indicate night in these open-air daytime productions.

In short, I have found a very broad correspondence between the two traditions, and no notable differences between the playing space and the staging practices of Calderón and his predecessors in Spain, in their standard *capa y espada* productions, on the one hand, and Shakespeare and his contemporaries in London, in a playhouse like the Rose, on the other.

*     *     *

It remains to be said what sorts of thing are done with the expanded stage provided by the lateral platforms analogous to the staging carts used at Corpus Christi. First of all, it must be recognized that when the spectators are cleared from both sides of the stage, the situation immediately approximates a much more modern, single-perspective theatrical experience, even without the crucial device of a front curtain to mask scene changes. It also provides for the importation, with appropriate modification, of some of the more elaborate staging practices of court drama, which coexisted with the *corrales* in Madrid for over a century after the inauguration of Philip IV's Coliseo del Buen Retiro in 1640. The number and kind of machines used in these more elaborate productions greatly exceeds anything in the stage directions of Shakespeare and his contemporaries: the *canal* was a track mounted on one or more of the upright posts that framed the tiring-house discovery space that was used for raising saints and lowering angels, as was the cloud or similar devices such as the *gloria* or the *araceli*. Rapid lateral motion was effected using the *bofetón*, which operated like a door or gate; flying machines could be quite elaborate, even permitting flights out over the standing audience to the "stewpan" or women's *cazuela* facing the stage at the other end of the yard. A revolving platform mounted in the tiring-house wall permitted the rapid disappearance or the illusion of shape-changing.

The *palenque* was a ramp from the yard to the stage for processions, entry on horseback from behind the audience, and the like. A sizeable number of plays utilize the elevations accommodated on the lateral platforms. I will provide two examples, both graphically documented. The first is an example of the two-mountain or mountain-tower sets that appear with some frequency in plays from Cervantes through Lope to Calderón, and which I believe developed out of their origin in the *auto* staging, with the elevations at each side of the main acting stage that I described earlier. *El Cardenal de Belén* (1610) is an elaborately staged "saint's play" by Lope de Vega, a work in that particularly popular genre of the early seventeenth-century *comedia* characterized by elaborate staging. This play, which is preserved in an autograph manuscript, includes a representation of the Nativity scene, in which the following stage direction appears: "They raise [the saint] up to the top, and a curtain is drawn to reveal Mary and Joseph and the child, and down one mountainside come shepherds and down another three kings." Just below the stage direction Lope has drawn in the narrow margin a rough sketch indicating how he wants this sequence staged, with mirror-image inclined planes descending from each side, shepherds coming down one slope and kings down the other, to converge at the discovery space at center stage.[7]

The second example is another "saint's play" by Blas de Mesa—undated and unpublished until quite recently, and called *La fundadora de la Santa Concepción*, probably from about the middle of the seventeenth century—that calls for staging a scene "as it is customarily painted." This sort of reference is common enough in the plays of the time, but in this manuscript from the Biblioteca Nacional in Madrid the playwright has actually included both a copy of the picture to which he is referring and extensive description of how the machines involved in staging it work:

> At the second level, in the middle and extending out over the stage, there is to be a *"gloria,"* and in the upper part of it is to be placed the girl who . . . played the Virgin Mary in Part I, standing above a crescent moon, and with the same dress, and on her left the actors who played Saint Francis and Saint Anthony of Padua in Act II, Saint Francis with a crucifix in his left hand, leaning against his shoulder, and his right hand and arm extended downward toward the ground, with his wounds showing. At his left is to be the actor who plays Saint Anthony of Padua, holding in his left hand and arm a child . . . on a book, and in his right a bouquet of lilies.
>
> An actor playing the first angel is to be in the *"gloria"* with the Bulls in his right hand, and the left hand and arm raised; and Doña Beatriz de Silva is to be separate, standing in the way she was when Saint John of Toulouse appeared to her, holding the Bulls in her hand, together with the angel.
>
> Shafts of light should be emanating from the area where the girl who plays the Virgin is. This whole discovery can be covered with screens so it will be more hidden and can be revealed and covered easily.
>
> At the same time that this scene is discovered, the actor who plays the second angel comes out from under the roof over the stage on a machine at the place where Doña Beatriz de Silva is, playing on a harp the song that is to be sung; the machine must be placed so as not to block the view of any of the stage decor, and as it comes down even with Doña Beatriz de Silva it stops, and when the action requires, it goes back up again.
>
> The discovery of the angel should be brought out as far above the stage as the roof allows, if it doesn't block the view.[8]

This kind of spectacle is infrequent; in fact, this description is the only one of its kind to have surfaced, and it is worlds away from the simple *capa y espada* staging so strikingly similar to that of the London productions of Shakespeare's day. It clearly must be thought of as the exception in an age when all indications are that theatergoers in the late sixteenth and early seventeenth centuries customarily went to the playhouses with virtually the same expectations in Madrid as they did in London.

## Notes

1. *Obras completas de Miguel de Cervantes Saavedra. Comedias y entremeses*, (Madrid: Bernardo Rodríguez, 1915), 1, 6. The translation and subsequent translations are mine.

2. *Teatro español del Siglo de Oro*, Sixteenth- and Seventeenth-Century Spanish Drama Full Text Database, http://teso.chadwyck.com, CD-ROM (Bell and Howell Information and Learning Co., 1997–2000).

3. Alan C. Dessen and Leslie Thomson, *A Dictionary of Stage Directions in English Drama, 1580–1642* (Cambridge: Cambridge University Press, 1999). Subsequent citations to this dictionary are parenthesized in text.

4. Alan C. Dessen, *Recovering Shakespeare's Theatrical Vocabulary* (Cambridge: Cambridge University Press, 1995).

5. D. W. Cruickshank and J. E. Varey, comps., *Comedias, a Facsimile Edition*, 19 vols. (Farnborough, England: Gregg International, 1973). All citations are taken from this edition; they are identified in parentheses in the text by volume and page or folio number, e.g., "(10:408)."

6. *Diccionario de la Real Academia de la Lengua* (Madrid: Gredos, 1969). Facsimile reproduction of the first Academy dictionary (1726–37) is known as (and hereafter referred to as) the *Diccionario de Autoridades*. s.v. "theatro."

7. Lope de Vega Carpio, *El cardenal de Belén*, ed. T. Earle Hamilton (Lubbock: Texas Tech Press, 1948), plate 2, f. 10v, act 3. My attention was drawn to this forgotten volume by Patricia Kenworthy of Vassar College.

8. Blas Fernández de Mesa, *La fundadora de la Santa Concepción. Comedia en dos partes*, Ibérica 15, ed. Nancy K. Mayberry (New York: Peter Lang, 1996), 153.

# Elizabethanism in Verona: Giorgio Strehler's *Henry IV, Part 1*

### John H. Astington

If we set aside Verdi's *Falstaff* of 1893, which contains a sung version of Sir John's catechism on honor, the first production of either of the *Henry IV* plays in Italy took place in 1951, performed by the company of the Piccolo Teatro of Milan under the direction of Giorgio Strehler. *Henry IV, Part 1*, translated by Cesare Vico Lodovici, was presented in a large-scale outdoor production, first in the Roman theater at Verona, in July, and then at the Villa Floridiana in Naples, in August.[1] With only nine performances in Verona and five in Naples, this production was hardly seen by the large numbers of people who saw one version or another of Strehler's later renowned productions of the adapted *Henry VI* plays, *King Lear*, and *The Tempest;* but it came at a crucial cultural moment and further defined the director's approach to staging Shakespeare. These issues form my chief subject in this paper.

Since *1 Henry IV* continues the story of Henry Bolingbroke's career and initiates that of his unthrifty son, one would expect Strehler to have taken some interest in it, since he had begun his Shakespearean directing with *Richard II*—also the first Italian production and also translated by Lodovici—in the second season of the Piccolo Teatro, in 1948. Following this, in 1950 Strehler directed *Richard III*; after 1951 it would be another fourteen years before he returned to the English Histories, in the adaptation to which he gave the title *The Power Game*, or more strictly, *The Game of the Powerful* (*Il gioco dei potenti*). Games of power perhaps governed other Shakespeare plays that Strehler chose to produce between 1948 and 1965, *The Tempest*, *The Taming of the Shrew*, *Macbeth*, *Julius Caesar*, and *Coriolanus* among them.[2] But the immediate relevance of the drama of political and military struggle to the cultural life of northern Italy in the years directly following 1945 is easy to grasp—in fact, the stories of internal civil discord, contested authority, division, recrimination, and bitterness would have been far more sympathetically read there than in the countries of the English-speaking allies, for whose population the paradigmatic wartime Shakespeare was the Olivier film of *Henry V* (1944), in which a heroic nation gains a great victory on foreign soil.

Yet in their outward aspects—setting, costuming, and staging—Strehler's early Shakespeare productions made no reference to contemporary conditions or recent history, unlike, say, earlier productions such as Orson Welles's fascist *Julius Caesar*, or subsequent ones such as Ian McKellen's *Richard III*. His general model, rather, was an adapted Elizabethanism, which he saw as importantly connected to the rhythms and shapes of the plays.[3] In the outdoor production of *1 Henry IV* this principle was given particularly extravagant expression in stage design, whereby an entire Globe theater in cutaway form faced the audience seated in the old Roman *cavea*. This stylistic mixture was a quite deliberate choice, but the grand scale of the Verona staging had grown out of Strehler's governing idea of an "Elizabethan" façade as best suiting the Shakespeare plays produced on the relatively small proscenium stage of the Piccolo Teatro. For *Richard II*, designed by Gianni Ratto, a fixed, polygonal façade faced the audience, with three entries through it at stage level and three matching entries above, giving on to balconies with slim balusters. The anonymous commentator on the production for *Shakespeare Survey* characterized the setting as "an Elizabethan-type stage inspired by the film of *Henry V.*"[4] Photographs of the production show that the balconies were used ceremonially (in addition to their internally required use in the Flint Castle scene, for example), to add height and symmetry to the visual effect of the stage composition.[5] The balconies projected, and in the central upstage position a raised platform directly in front of the stage-level entry gave the effect of what in the 1940s would have been called an "inner stage." But if the framework was inspired by the Elizabethan stage façade, its decorative treatment, with painted relief and cutout details, was designers' Gothic, to suggest the medieval period of the play; costumes were similarly medievalized.

The general plan of a permanent two-level stage façade was repeated in the production of *Richard III* in 1950 ("con concetti molto vicini a quelli che ci avevano guidati nel rappresentare *Riccardo II*" [with very similar conceptual guidelines to those followed in the production of *Richard II*]);[6] the setting had a more squared-off effect, with the vertical surfaces covered with hangings and valances—a more neutral and "interior" atmosphere than that of *Richard II*: the designer was Giulio Coltellacci. Coltellacci had designed the setting for *Julius Caesar* in the second year of the Verona theater festival, 1949;[7] this was not a Strehler production, but the work of this designer represents the first intersection between Strehler's productions in Milan and the very different conditions at Verona. For *Richard III* three symmetrically arranged entry points—stage left and right, with double doors at the center—gave access to the stage. The center doors were raised by two steps with a small platform directly in front of them, covered by a canopy supported on slender columns; as in

*Richard II* this was the site of the royal throne. The "Elizabethan" structure survived until the Piccolo Teatro productions of *Macbeth* in 1952, and
*Julius Caesar* in 1953, both the work of a third designer, Piero Zuffi. The
*Macbeth* design in particular still used three openings at each level of a
two-story façade, although its architectural frame was disguised by skewed
angles, hanging curtains, and rugged surface relief.

For his first six years as a director of Shakespeare, then, Giorgio Strehler
took as one of his guiding principles the permanent architectural set on an
Elizabethan model, with upstage entry doors and a balcony level, a neutral
or unchanging space to which life is given by the movement and grouping
of actors within its limits. From this work he undoubtedly learned more
about the precise placement of actors in space, which marks his subsequent work so strongly, and is so apparent in photographs and video of his
famous final Shakespearean production of *The Tempest* in 1978. He perhaps also learned that to the modern eye the Elizabethan façade is not neutral, but antiquarian—often fussily or clumsily so. The neutral background
in the modern indoor playhouse is the variously lit—or unlit—cyclorama,
to which he turned in his production of *Coriolanus* in 1957, designed by
Luciano Damiani, Strehler's chief collaborating designer from that date
onward. Strehler's initial interest in Elizabethan principles was perhaps informed by his reading about the Elizabethanism of Poel and his followers
in England and America, and is likely to have had something to do with his
professed admiration for Jacques Copeau, who had combined an interest in
Elizabethan drama with a desire to simplify the stage space, and to make
it an unchanging sculptural medium for the movement and gesture of the
performers. Copeau's *Twelfth Night* of 1914, influenced by Granville
Barker's Savoy production of 1912, remains a landmark in the performance history of that play.

The Elizabethan theater itself had famously appeared in Laurence Olivier's film of *Henry V* in 1944; the film was well known in Italy,[8] and the
Roger Furse version of the Globe where the opening of the film is set undoubtedly influenced the designer Pino Casarini when he came to create
the very large outdoor setting for *1 Henry IV* at Verona in 1951. To be quite
clear about the venue of this production, the Roman theater at Verona, to
the north of the town and across the Adige river, is quite distinct from the
more famous, and nearer intact, amphitheater, or arena, in the center of the
town plan, where the summer opera festival takes place. Casarini's prior
experience in outdoor design, in fact, had included opera settings for the
arena, and he continued to work on large-scale outdoor projects, including
a *Hamlet* at the Castello di Malcesine on Lake Garda, in 1953, as well
as other Shakespeare productions at the Roman theater in Verona.[9] The
production of *1 Henry IV* was mounted for the fourth theater festival at the
Roman theater, and the resulting scenic solution might be said to combine

four governing elements: first, Strehler's own stipulations concerning his
current directorial model, the Elizabethan façade; second, a relatively recent cultural reference that any audience might recognize, Olivier's filmed
Globe; third, the perhaps rather light-hearted air of a summer gathering
outdoors; and, fourth, the considerable logistical problem of filling the site
of the ruined Roman *scena*, over three hundred feet wide (figure 1).

It may be observed that the result echoes the semicircular plan of the
Roman auditorium as it simultaneously invokes the polygonal shape of an
Elizabethan outdoor playhouse. De Witt's famous comparison of the
wooden Swan to a Roman theater is given particular local point; his well-
known drawing is fairly evidently the basis for the central structure of

**1. Pino Casarini's setting for *1 Henry IV* at Verona in 1951, "a Globe within a
Roman theater within an Italian theater festival."**

stage roof, huts, and playhouse flag (which also feature at the start of the Olivier film). At the center of Casarini's plan sits a level stage platform in the form of a twelve-sided regular polygon; the downstage five segments project into the Roman *orchestra*, forming a five-sided forestage. From the upstage side projects a slightly raised, squarish platform, like an Elizabethan stage platform placed within a yard, descanting further on the theme of theater set within theater. Large caryatid figures on this platform hold up a sloping stage roof, and a curtain was used to conceal the space beyond them from view: this evidently was a larger and more elaborate version of the central upstage platform used in the preceding productions of the Histories. As in *Richard II* and *Richard III* the throne was placed there, and, as far as one can judge from photographs, the tavern scenes were focused there also: a thematically appropriate staging, even if it may have made Falstaff's relationship with the audience harder to sustain. Columns looking rather more like de Witt's stage pillars mark six of the angles of the central polygonal platform: they hold up a lower roof that runs penthouse fashion over an area of stage stretching around and behind seven of the angles of the twelve-sided space, and they thus define six entry points from beyond its limits. The level stage also extends in Roman fashion in a corridor-like strip to the limits of the *scena* on either side; steps at the front of these runways lead down to the level of the orchestra. The structure behind this complex area of level stage might be described as a combination of Elizabethan tiring-house and Roman *parascenia*: symmetrically arranged roofed structures facing the audience at either limit of the entire scene.

Those parts of the façade visible in photographs are treated in painterly style as the walls of timbered buildings—Eastcheap, Rochester, or where you will, but suggestive of urban townscape of no great pretension. Or, indeed, of certain versions of the reimagined Globe: the huts structure of the Globe in Olivier's film has a particularly marked "half-timbered" character. The roofline of Casarini's setting partly continued the urban theme, with little dormer windows, while the timbering motif reappears on the hut structure, which also featured a large central clock that appears to have worked. If on the one hand these touches seem rather too bourgeois for the play, on the other, the "time of day," the "time for frighted peace to pant," and "time, that takes survey of all the world" truly did survey the entire audience from a high central point. But the roof motifs were mixed: above the clock appears a decorative window in more palatial taste; turrets with heraldic vanes and pennants capped the rising line of the pillars, and the military note was heavily sounded by a prominent, curving, battlemented structure that ran above the line of the lower roof like a defensive town wall. This mixture of styles and motifs was designed partly to match the effect of the towers, roofs, and buildings of the town of Verona on view beyond the limits of the stage wall, in every style from

Roman to modern, and particularly visible to those seated in the upper levels of the hillside *cavea*. This historical play, the audience was reminded visually, has a presence and immediacy that Verona itself expresses in physical space.

So if in some ways the Verona theater appears to resemble the Festival Theatre at Ashland, Oregon, built eight years later, it was in fact considerably larger and more complex. The vast town-like structure surrounding the stage seems to resemble a film set rather than a theatrical space, and the actors used to the modest confines of the Piccolo Teatro must have found it rather intimidating. The problems of focus were no doubt helped by lighting—the performances were in the evening, beginning at nine and running approximately four hours, and hence performed mostly in darkness; several reviews mention the play of light beams in the battle scene, for example. Yet the physical stage remained enormous, and, in order to make something of the decidedly non-Elizabethan flanking platforms, Strehler, for example, elaborated the carters' scene, 2.1, with practical wagons, which were trundled on down the stage-right runway. The extended platform and the steps came into their own after act 3. In scenes of marching, assembly, and battle, Strehler used banner-waving extras, "sbandieratori," experienced Palio marchers from Siena who created colorful movement and varying speed and rhythm across the whole extent of the space. In doing so he was applying lessons taught by Max Reinhardt in his productions set within large spaces, indoor and outdoor. Strehler's first independent Shakespeare production outdoors had been *The Tempest* in June 1948. This was set in the Boboli Gardens in Florence, in an elaborate dispersed setting that was deliberately reminiscent of Renaissance Medici entertainments; it also had the air of some of Reinhardt's more extravagant productions.[10] Reinhardt himself had staged *A Midsummer Night's Dream* in the Gardens in 1933; Strehler, aged twelve at the time and living in Milan, is unlikely to have seen it, but he had undoubtedly heard and read about it as an adult. Strehler, then, was not unacquainted with the spectacular and the grand, nor averse to handling their practical problems. The legacy of such experiments, perhaps, may be seen in the effects of the 1978 *Tempest*. He was also, from early in his career, a director of opera, at La Scala in Milan and elsewhere—although never, it appears, at the arena in Verona.[11]

The Roman theater in Verona made necessary the enlargement and extension of Strehler's Elizabethanized model for the production of Shakespeare's histories. It produced another kind of hybrid Elizabethanism. The experiment was never repeated, and one may take it to be a particularly fascinating blind alley. What it achieved, however, was to set before the audience a far more thoroughgoing evocation of Shakespeare's own theater than the allusive façades, doorways, and balconies, set within a proscenium frame, of the preceding indoor productions. At least this is true if one had been prepared to have concentrated one's gaze on the central area, with its dominating stage roof and turret. The Verona audience was set outside the ring of the wooden O rather than within it, of course, but this would have increased the effect of contemplation of theater itself.

For all its unusual qualities, the stage did give certain "Elizabethan" opportunities to the actors. The polygonal thrust would have allowed performers to advance to a position where spectators and listeners surrounded them on three sides, hardly the kind of encirclement the Shakespearean actor experienced but the evident place to play intimate moments—"I know you all," or the "honor" speech. Hence movement up and down-stage, the Elizabethan dynamic that Strehler endeavored to retain through his settings, was perfectly possible on the Verona stage. But what the entire structure invited—or rather required—in terms of movement and grouping was something far larger and more extended than what was possible on even the largest Elizabethan stages, let alone those at the Rose or the Blackfriars. The long lateral extensions to the central polygon, with their steps leading down to a polgonal corridor on the *orchestra* itself, between the raised stage and the first row of seats, called for complex processional movement and dispersed visual composition. These means of staging Shakespeare were being explored by other directors at almost exactly the same time—a matter I will turn to shortly. But physical extension inevitably slows the pace of spoken dialogue, and it is not surprising that Strehler had recourse to both orchestral music and a choir, since the visual language of such a theater is nearer to that of the cinema, or of opera. If one principle of Elizabethanism is economy, synecdoche, the Verona festival stage worked against it. The production ran for four hours, and more than one reviewer complained about the late hour at which the entertainment ended.[12]

There is every reason, however, for regarding this production as integral to Strehler's work and consonant with his later Shakespeare productions, visually so very different. Throughout his career, Strehler, like his mentor, Brecht, remained fascinated with the aesthetics of illusion and pretense, and frequently drew the audience's attention to the boundaries between the real and the fictional, to the end of emphasizing the continuity of the one with the other. So his trademark production of *The Servant of Two Masters* evolved into a "framed" staging, whereby the actors of the Piccolo Teatro played a touring troupe who put on a performance of the Goldoni play on a platform stage set on the proscenium stage.[13] When not "onstage" as Goldoni characters they sat casually "offstage" in the characters of the individual eighteenth-century actors they had each developed through improvisation. Such Chinese-box effects, or effects of *mise en abîme*, as we know, are common in Shakespeare's plays, and in both Shakespeare and

Strehler's Goldoni they are there to question the line drawn between the stage and the auditorium, between theater itself and the theater of human life, and between the imaginative projections of the actors and their reception in the imaginations of the observers. In *1 Henry IV* the extempore playmaking that goes on in act 2 reminds us of the connection between performance and perception, and of the larger play's exposure of mythology, opinion, and seeming. Playing is intimately connected with history making, and history writing.

When Strehler returned to *The Tempest* as his final Shakespearean production, he conducted his most remarkable contemplation of theatricality, if I may call it that. Prospero's theater in 1978 was not that of Shakespeare but that of the Italian Renaissance and its durable successor, the proscenium stage. The magic that the central character controlled was that of Sabbattini, Torelli, Bérain, and Inigo Jones, backed up by the inventions of the nineteenth and twentieth centuries, steel technology and subtly variable artificial lighting. It was such a technological theater, not the great Globe itself, which collapsed when Prospero broke his staff, and magically reassembled itself during the epilogue, restored by applause. Once again, however, the actors played their play within a setting that evoked the entire history of the theater, and hence the history of invention and imagination. Prospero stood within a vast empty space, a bare island that grew or shrank as the light defined it. The breaking ship was a shadow play, the great blue sea a cloth with stagehands beneath it, Ariel an acrobat on a circus wire. The effect was both amazing and disillusioning, in that it made its means of pretense quite plain. Such a demonstration of means and invocation of layers, I have been suggesting, also governed Strehler's early productions of Shakespeare, and thus constitute a consistent principle of his approach to the plays. In the Verona production the stretch of time and the interpenetration of imaginative realms were largely borne by the vehicle of the physical setting—a Globe within a Roman theater within an Italian theater festival. And within Verona, real place and place of the Shakespearean imagination. Physicality of the Elizabethan village variety brought with it too much that was awkward, robust, and unchanging, and in the case of *1 Henry IV*, arguably, allowed too little room for the melancholy of the play. The magical effects Strehler achieved with light and the bare space in his 1978 *Tempest* successfully suggested the dangers of darkness and emptiness ready to eclipse the creative act. A more neutral stage, in short, allowed the original sense of the play to breathe. As Elizabethan costume may bring an actor no nearer to a living incarnation of a given part, Elizabethanism worn externally may yield little vitality on the stage.

Whatever its place in Strehler's own development, the 1951 production holds a significant position internationally within the theater of its time, that of the ten years following World War II. The postwar period saw unusual activity in the creation of summer theater festivals, and perhaps of festivals generally—1951 was the year of the Festival of Britain. Created in the spirit of reconstruction, optimism, a new attempt at internationalism, and no doubt primed with a certain amount of U.S. funding, theater festivals attracted international attention and a good deal of press coverage.[14] The particular economics of outdoor productions in Italy during this period were commented on in an article by Paolo Grassi, Strehler's collaborator, and cofounder of the Piccolo Teatro. Shows such as those at Verona, he writes, cost at least 30 percent more to mount than those in the normal season, and at best recoup only half the expenses in box office receipts. Hence they are underwritten by various government agencies, national and local, and by subventions from commercial bodies, led by the banks. The terms for the government support of *Henry IV* were that it be shown at a second venue, hence the productions in Naples.[15]

The theater festivals at Avignon and Edinburgh both began in 1947; the more modest festival at Verona followed a year later. Outdoor performance suited southern Europe only, but the fashion for staging plays within non-theatrical spaces was widespread; in Verona the model was partly that of the long tradition of using classical auditoria for modern events.[16] In Avignon the medieval windows and walls of the Papal Palace loomed behind a plain platform stage picked out with light: *un tréteau nu*, in Copeau's phrase.[17] Jean Vilar's renowned production of *Richard II* appeared there in the year before Strehler's mounting of the play.

At Edinburgh in 1948, Tyrone Guthrie staged his experimental production of Lindsay's *Satire of the Three Estates*, planting a platform stage in the center of the Assembly Hall of the Church of Scotland so that it was surrounded by audience, through which actors moved in procession to and from the stage. This model, standard accounts of Guthrie's work tell us, was the genesis of his Shakespearean stages and staging in the years that followed: at Stratford, Ontario, and at Minneapolis—the theater plan was copied at Chichester and Sheffield in England.[18] My general question here, it may be gathered, is whether the Edinburgh stage was the *only* inspiration for what was built at Stratford, first in 1953, and then in the permanent theater that followed in 1957.

The original Canadian proposal for a summer Shakespeare festival was for an outdoor stage. Ontario summer evenings can be pleasant, if their mosquitoes are not; violent thunderstorms, which tested the temporary theater during its first season, are also not unknown. Guthrie insisted on cover, and the great circus tent above the theater was the result. The effect of the original proposal, however, might be imagined in a photograph taken while the tent was in the process of raising (figure 2): a round sweep of seats, in the fashion of the classical *cavea*, surrounds a polygonal thrust stage backed by a two-story wooden façade; beyond the limits of the

2. The circus tent goes up over Guthrie's first festival theater at Stratford, Ontario, in 1953. Photograph by Peter Smith, courtesy of the Stratford Festival Archives.

scene, the theater is in dialogue with a rural or suburban landscape rather than the Verona townscape. The overall visual effect is less grand and extended than that of the Verona stage, but the elements are generally similar: a polygon formed by the angles of the scene wall and the limits of stage, steps, and surrounding runway is set within a larger half-circle (or approximately so) of banked seating. Classical ideas about theater space seem at least as important in the Stratford model as do Elizabethan or Elizabethanized conceptions, and it seems particularly significant that the plan came into being just two years after Giorgio Strehler and Pino Casarini had married the Globe to the theater of Vitruvius.

If Guthrie and Tanya Mosiewitsch, his designer, may have been influenced by what they had seen at or read about European theater festivals, it is a commonplace to point out that the Stratford façade and stage have very little of the Elizabethan about them. Mosiewitsch's design is all angles, levels, and lines, and it is finished in an austere dark wood tone. Strehler's own schema was followed (in the original version of the stage) so far as providing three entries at each of the two levels of the façade, aligned on a prominent central entry: a covered dais was placed directly in front of this central door.[19] But the non-Elizabethan character of the stage can be appreciated by considering that from no point offstage is it possible to enter the central platform area without stepping either up or down. Mosiewitsch's principles are different from those of Strehler's early designers. She came to Stratford, Ontario, from designing a permanent wooden setting for the tetralogy of *Richard II*, the two parts of *Henry IV*, and *Henry V* at Stratford-upon-Avon in England, in 1951. This was an arrangement of platforms, galleries, posts, and steps that receded within the proscenium frame, and could be decorated with hanging curtains.[20] At the time, reviewers called it an Elizabethan setting, though this seems to be stretching the term to absurd lengths. Mosiewitsch is a Modernist, as was revealed when at Stratford, Ontario, she turned her earlier setting around, as it were, making it project rather than retreat, as well as regularizing its symmetry. The ancestry of all the steps at Stratford lies in the designs and theories of Adolphe Appia, who made stages for movement, light, and music, and not principally for speech. The operatic and choreographic style imposed on Strehler by the sheer scale of the Verona theater is rather an implicit principle of the Stratford Festival stage: it is what Appia would have called a rhythmic space.

The temporary conditions of postwar festival theater were made permanent at Stratford; the particular style of its construction, altered somewhat over the past half century—although in the direction of further complexity of steps and levels rather than that of Elizabethan simplicity—imposes a corresponding structural style on all the Shakespeare produced there. Although Giorgio Strehler demanded of his earlier designers certain elements of the Elizabethan stage, he was not wedded, I have suggested, to any particular physical model; and the considerable limitations of the unwieldy design for *Henry IV* might have pushed him toward abandoning his Elizabethanism, such as it was. The point of a historical theatrical reference, allusive in the Milan designs and explicit in the Verona Globe, was to theatricalize the theater, to include the art of theater itself within the audience's contemplation of the entertainment. If one of Strehler's chief influences in this direction was the theater practice and playwriting of Brecht, it seems as if another early inspiration was Shakespeare's *Henry V*, seen through the medium of Olivier's film, with its placing of the performance and its reception within the frame of an older performance. Theatricalization would remain a central element of Strehler's aesthetics, but the special associations of the Verona production of *1 Henry*, with one ancient theater enclosed within another yet more ancient, were particular, remarkable, and never repeated.

## Notes

1. David L. Hirst, *Giorgio Strehler* (Cambridge: Cambridge University Press, 1993), 65–66; Arturo Lazzari, *Piccolo Teatro, 1947–58* (Milan: N. Moneta, 1958), 119–21.

2. Hirst, *Giorgio Strehler*, 125–28.

3. Lazzari, *Piccolo Teatro*, 55.

4. "International News," *Shakespeare Survey* 2 (1949): 129.

5. See Lazzari, *Piccolo Teatro*, 53–56.

6. Lazzari, *Piccolo Teatro*, 90.

7. A photograph of this setting appears in Guido Frette, *Stage Design* (Milan: G. G. Görlich, [1955]): 69. The director was Guido Salvini. A brief English-language notice of the production by Mario Praz appears in "International Notes," *Shakespeare Survey* 4 (1951): 128.

8. Hirst, *Giorgio Strehler*, 64–65.

9. See Frette, *Stage Design*, 52–58. Casarini's short essay, "Scenic Art Applied to the Amphitheatre," appears as part of the introduction to the book, xvii–xix.

10. The designer was Gianni Ratto, who had designed the Milan *R2* in the preceding year, but on entirely different principles. In this instance there seems little connection between the Elizabethanism of Strehler and his designers and the experiment in outdoor production.

11. Hirst, *Giorgio Strehler*, 117–30.

12. Two reviewers also mention the set with disapproval, finding it too massive and operatic: Roberto Rebora, "Successo di *Enrico IV*," *La fiera letteraria* (Rome), 15 July 1951; and Antonio Valenti, *"Enrico IV* a Verona," *Teatro Scenario* (Rome), 31 July 1951, 9–11. I am grateful to Gian Giacomo Colli for his assistance in research and translation of material in the archives of the Piccolo Teatro di Milano.

13. Hirst, *Giorgio Strehler*, 40–51.

14. The article on the Verona *1 Henry IV* in *Il Gazzetino* (Venice) for 8 July 1951 ("E' cominciata l'Estate teatrale") notes congratulatory telegrams from the Italian government ministers Guido Gonnella and Giulio Andreotti, and from the British and American ambassadors.

15. Paolo Grassi, "A solo di *Enrico IV* con commento dell' Adige," *Epoca*, July 1951, 58–60.

16. Other venues for outdoor productions of Shakespeare in Italy during this period, apart from those mentioned in the course of this essay, include the castle at San Giusto in Trieste (*A Midsummer Night's Dream*) and the Greek theater at Taormina (*Othello*).

17. For a photograph see Denis Bablet, *Revolutions in Stage Design in the Twentieth Century* (Paris: Leon Amiel, 1977), 299.

18. See, for example, J. L. Styan, *The Shakespeare Revolution* (Cambridge: Cambridge University Press, 1977), 180–205; Dennis Kennedy, *Looking at Shakespeare* (Cambridge: Cambridge University Press, 1993), 154–64.

19. See Richard and Helen Leacroft, *Theatre and Playhouse* (London: Methuen, 1984), 176–77.

20. See John Dover Wilson and Thomas C. Worsley, *Shakespeare's Histories at Stratford, 1951* (1952; New York: Theatre Arts Books, 1970), frontispiece; Kennedy, *Looking at Shakespeare*, 157.

# Off the Book: Extra-Textual Effects in Trevor Nunn's *Twelfth Night*

## ANN JENNALIE COOK

THOUGH NOT SO DARING IN CASTING AS FRANCO ZEFFIRELLI NOR SO gifted in camera work as Orson Welles, Trevor Nunn's *Twelfth Night* is solid, sensual, and subtle. Freed from the limitations of his televised versions of prior staging, as in *Macbeth* and *Othello*, the film takes full advantage of this director's strengths.[1] The actors, the locations in Cornwall, the period costuming and set designs, above all the sure grasp of visual realizations of the text create a clear rationale for the production. While deeply immersed in Shakespeare's language, Nunn does not hesitate to move off the book to further his particular reading of its cinematic possibilities.

Nunn chooses experienced British performers, just as he does in the theater. And for a thoroughly Victorian English Illyria, those selections are commendable.[2] Imogen Stubbs plays Viola/Cesario as if made for the role.[3] Vulnerable whether bereft of her brother or swaggering in the strange freedom of trousers or nearly surrendering to secret desire, she also captures the inherent appeal that leads both Olivia (Helena Bonham Carter) and Orsino (Toby Stephens) to love her so passionately—and so quickly. Entering the dim, candlelit parlor, Stubbs whispers seductively to the black-veiled object of her mission. Once outdoors with the captivated countess, this Cesario crescendoes the description of his/her imaginary wooing into a cry of "Olivia!" that echoes back inside to startle the household, especially Malvolio (Nigel Hawthorne). Intimacy with Orsino increasingly eroticizes the attraction between master and servant. Stubbs shows her discomfort at physical touch, flinching when the fencing master adjusts the position of her bound chest and her buttocks, resisting Stephens's fingers on her lips and his grasp of her jacket front by leaning back, defensively putting up her hands, and finally making a playful shove that topples her companion onto his injured shoulder. Such preludes logically build to the bath scene, when Stubbs agonizingly averts her gaze from Stephens's naked body and then, behind him, melts into the pleasure of sponging his bare back. The climax comes during the stable serenade by Feste (Ben Kingsley), when an arm around a "boy"'s shoulder brings

75

two heads slowly, sensuously, wordlessly closer into an almost-kiss. Under Nunn's direction, Stubbs indicates the difficulties of impersonating a male in countless non-textual details—the handkerchief stuffed in a pocket to swell the crotch of trousers, the gasp when a broad red band constricts her breasts and the sigh of release when she removes it, the terror in her eyes as she gallops across treacherous terrain, and the legs sore from straddling a horse.

Against Viola, anchoring any successful *Twelfth Night*, stand the roles of Sebastian, Orsino, and Olivia. With the camera's brutal eye, twins must be either virtually identical or else played by the same actor.[4] Seeking a match for Stubbs, Nunn has chosen Steven Mackintosh, who not only looks like her but also turns in a competent performance, especially in his dazzled reactions to Olivia and his moving reunion with Viola. As Orsino, Toby Stephens also looks right, his sensual, beautiful face and air of inherent ennui exuding self-indulgence. A couple of times he breaks through the narcissism into genuine feeling—while listening to the story of Cesario's "sister" and while experiencing the pain of supposed betrayal. The growing intimacy with the "boy" he enjoys without considering its ramifications, reacting to the near-kiss by striding out onto the cliffs to rival a stormy sea with his angry speeches. He cries out "What dost thou know?" as if to shout down an unacknowledged desire with his publicly proclaimed desire. Perhaps no actor can redeem Orsino from his innate selfishness, but at least audiences can like Stephens better as he abandons his sling and his audience for the lesser vices of hot baths, cigars, cards, billiards, and conversations with a trusted young friend.

The Olivia-Viola pairing often involves fine performers whose acting style or physical appearance undercuts the believability of their relationship. Here the director has tapped Helena Bonham Carter to play opposite Imogen Stubbs. Carter's petite figure is just a trifle shorter than Stubbs's slender one, her skin paler, her masses of dark auburn curls a contrast to the straight, chopped blond hair of the twins. Moreover, this Olivia is a fiery, reckless young heiress, mercurial of mood and relentless in pursuit of her passion. From the first sobs, Carter hints that her grief is not wholly sincere, though tears involuntarily spring to her eyes as she seeks comfort from Feste. In her household she has no other true companion, for Nunn opts to make Maria (Imelda Staunton) a housekeeper, subject to the authority of the steward, rather than a friend and confidante to her mistress. Class thus dictates that the wealthy but inexperienced countess be as isolated and vulnerable and freed from ordinary restraints as is Viola. The surprise of her embrace with Kingsley, then their sitting together on the sofa like equals, hints at indecorum yet to come. The pair's barely suppressed laughter when a drunken Sir Toby (Mel Smith) stumbles in and out of the room further evidences high spirits barely contained. Visually, this sequence signals that, even though she sets up a scene of inconsolable loss before Cesario is admitted, Carter will quickly switch to a more intriguing game with an irresistible young "gentleman." A brief shot where she holds up a black gown and then discards it in favor of a brilliant blue one confirms her altered status. Furthermore, the slower, more controlled pace of Carter's words and actions give way to increasingly frantic movement. She pins Cesario against the garden door with her own body. She races out of her room, hurls herself between drawn swords, lavishes fervent kisses upon her beloved, and rushes him to the altar. She can more sedately (and scornfully) face Orsino, but only the appearance of two Cesarios stops her altogether. Instead of pouts, frowns, smiles, sidelong glances, and nervous little gestures, Carter's huge expressive eyes now command the camera's focus, silently expressing the shocked disbelief of all the other beholders. She creates a genuinely likeable Olivia. There is wistfulness in her isolation and her attempts at dignity, kindness in her refusal to take offense at Malvolio's clutches and her pity for his abuse, appeal in her need for love and her swift embrace of both husband and sister.

For a *Twelfth Night* that emphasizes melancholy, Ben Kingsley is an unexpected but splendid Feste,[5] his raspy song opening and closing the movie. Enigmatic eyes, stillness of face and presence, mimicry of other voices, shaved head, anonymous greatcoat all set him apart. Nunn presents him as the quintessential outsider, welcomed and moving freely from one group to another but belonging to none. Kingsley first appears on the cliffs, observing the shipwrecked survivors below. The necklace Viola throws down upon the sand he mysteriously restores to her at the end of the action. An inveterate watcher, he lingers at doors or peers through windows or pops up, hooded, at night. Repeatedly, the camera rests on his face at critical moments, particularly during the reunion of Viola and Sebastian. Kingsley plays as if he has an omniscience, perhaps even an authority, higher than that of the other characters, as if he may control the wind and the rain, the merry and the sad, not merely sing about them.[6] Yet he does display powerful feelings, most notably against Malvolio. In their first encounter, Hawthorne's eyes lock on Kingsley's in a prolonged, hostile stare. Thus, when the fool, wearing the steward's wig, descends the long staircase lined with servants, his bitter tone extends all the way from "Why, 'some are born great'" to "And thus the whirligig of time brings in his revenges"—not ironic observation but deliberate retribution. Hence his concluding words, "And I'll strive to please you every day" (sung and then repeated), "Every day. Every day" (spoken but not sung), resonate with ambiguity.

Abetting the somber strain of Nunn's film, Mel Smith plays an unusually debauched Sir Toby Belch, Imelda Staunton an unhappy Maria, Rich-

ard E. Grant a pitiable Sir Andrew Aguecheek,[7] Peter Gunn a sturdy
Fabian, and Nicholas Farrell a restrained Antonio. This last role gets some
fleshing out with Farrell's presence on the ship bound for Messaline,
clearly captivated by the androgynous twins. He mutes his homosexuality
but not his hostility towards the duke. Though released from chains in a
silent gesture of magnanimity, the state's enemy does not attend his
friend's nuptial festivities. Fabian does not appear in the text until act 2,
scene 5, but the gardener gets a purely visual introduction when Gunn
fetches Maria to assist with Sir Toby, who lies outside, wine bottle in hand
and still in his dinner clothes, giving point to Staunton's line, "you must
come in earlier a'nights." The tacit alliance among the trio here explains
why he is invited to watch Malvolio take the bait for his comeuppance.
Gunn's brown work clothes distinguish him from the house servants and
the gentry as he stands in the entry hall confessing, regretfully and hon-
estly, what has been done to Malvolio. As for Sir Andrew, Grant under-
plays the role, offering innocence and a bit of pathos.[8] With Maria's
declaration that Olivia "abhors" the color yellow, there is a pause, the
other conspirators look at him, and he stops laughing, staring sadly down
at his yellow vest and the matching stockings. Grant's "I was ador'd once
too" sounds almost tragic. The comic business accompanying his attempted departure works particularly well, as bags, trunk, cricket guards,
fencing foils, golf clubs, tennis racquet, violin case, and birdcage get carried down the stairs, out to the waiting cart, and back inside when he is
persuaded to challenge Cesario.

Maria and Sir Toby, as played by Imelda Staunton and Mel Smith, are
both well past their prime, Sir Toby gray and paunchy, Maria vainly longing for a marriage less likely to materalize with each passing year. Nunn
involves Feste in her fate. At his first arrival, she spies him from the library
window, hurries down to him in the kitchen, feeds him, and reproves him
for his absence. At the line "if Sir Toby would leave drinking, thou wert
as witty a piece of Eve's flesh as any in Illyria," two maids stop working
and exchange knowing looks, while she says, "Peace, you rogue, no more
o' that." When Smith suddenly pulls her into his arms for a kiss and bids,
"Come by and by to my chamber," she looks to Kingsley, who silently
nods assent. With a smile of pleasure he observes the couple seek out the
priest. Yet aside from desperation and a wish to escape a tyrannical steward, it is hard to see why she finds Smith's Sir Toby attractive. He punctu-
ates lines with belches and seems too drunk to be very amusing. For Nunn,
the issues of class distinction may well be involved. He has pinpointed
"the all-important trigger for Toby's extreme vendetta" against Malvolio
as the fact that "a *servant* has reproached him" (Laroque, 95). Yet Maria
is a servant too, Staunton's speech marking her as lower in status than her
mistress or the mistress's titled cousin. Their marriage would be yet an-

other step down for Sir Toby. Ominously, the pair silently board a hired coach while within their former home others celebrate.

Predictably, Nigel Hawthorne makes a splendid Malvolio, his capacity for the telling gesture fully exploited. Between glimpses of the silent, black-clad figure in the graveyard who supports a weeping mistress with his arm and the man who kneels just a moment longer after she leaves her chapel pew, the audience sees a frowning Hawthorne sweep through an inspection of cowed, curtsying kitchen maids, Maria and two lesser minions following him. He turns over the hands of one girl and makes the peremptory hand signals that will inform his character, especially the raised forefinger. He claps and points and makes a rapid circular motion to insist a servant speed up the pace of her beating. His rigid posture, his carefully combed and frequently adjusted dyed wig,[9] his glares of disapproval, his silent hostility, his eyebrows arched with self-importance, the little alteration of a sun dial to accord with his watch all set him up for ridicule. Hawthorne's juxtaposition with a nude statue of Venus and his grimaced attempt at smiling offer fine comic touches. Yet the moment of ultimate disgrace wrenches. Filthy, bare-headed, baffled, he stumbles into the entry hall to be further humiliated before the tittering staff he has tyrannized over, as well as the mistress he has desired and all those gentlefolk whose ranks he will never join. As he listens to Carter's explanation, the hand lifts one last time in a caress that never quite touches her face. Making his way up the long staircase, he stumbles just toward the top, shrugging off help from the now-hushed servants and proceeding to his chamber. Nunn provides a final glimpse of a balding, white-haired man in a gray traveling suit with a single small suitcase and a rolled umbrella, the last exile from the estate.

Besides attending to the essential off-book task of casting and eliciting effective performances, a director aspires to integrate the plot line with intelligent scene sequences (Laroque, 89). This *Twelfth Night* works with a text tailored to fit Trevor Nunn's filmic vision. The opening action in particular relies upon his interpolations (marked with *), alterations (departures from the Riverside text follow the film's soundtrack), rearrangements, and cuts, always marrying verbal with visual information as its elements set up the motifs which unify the whole. Over the first credits comes Feste's raspy song,

> I'll tell thee a tale, now list to me,*
> With hey, ho, the wind and the rain,
> But merry or sad, which shall it be,*
> For the rain it raineth every day.

At the first "rain," streaks of rain cross the screen, followed by a pitching sea and then a masted ship emerging out of the night. A voiceover (not

Kingsley) begins lines of blank verse as the camera moves to the ship's interior.

> Once, upon Twelfth Night, or what you will,*
> Aboard a ship bound home to Messaline,*
> The festive company, dressed for masquerade,*
> Delight above the rest in two young twins.*

A faint snatch of "The First Noel" backs the first line, and then the sound dissolves into laughter from the dining salon, crowded with guests in evening attire or in costumes. The twins wear blue tunic blouses sashed over red harem pants, gold coin necklaces, gold bands circling long black hair, and white, gold-embroidered veils covering nose, mouth, and chin. One plays the piano, the other a concertina, as both sing, watched intently by a solitary male listener.[10]

> O mistress mine, where are you roaming?
> O, stay and hear, your true-love's coming,
> That can sing both high and low,
> That can sing both high and lo-o-o-ow.

A further burst of laughter comes as the twin at the piano apparently sends the pitch deeper and deeper, while the other apparently stops singing to stare at him/her, finally reaching down to rip off the veil and reveal a mustached face. That twin, in turn, stands up, rips off the other's veil, and reveals an identical mustached face. When the second person unmasked removes the mustache from his sister, she reaches across to remove his.

At that moment the ship lurches, sending furnishings flying and terrified guests screaming from the room. The voiceover continues,

> The storm has forced the vessel from its course,*
> And now they strike upon submerged rocks.*

The attentive listener checks the situation on deck through a porthole window, then looks back at the fearfully embracing twins. Outside a toppling mast breaks away a section of the railing, while crewmen in slickers struggle to control the ship. The twins, now in their cabin, hastily change clothes and put mementoes in a trunk, including a photograph of themselves as children gathered with their father around a piano. The narrative explains,

> Uncertain what to leave and what to save,*
> Brother and sister often since their father's death*
> Have but themselves in all the world.*

The next shots show fierce wind whipping the rain, lifeboats lowered, then the twins dragging their trunk across the deck, the sister now in dress and shawl. When she slips and falls overboard through the missing rail, her brother breaks from the grip of the mysterious stranger to plunge in after her. Underwater, the action proceeds in slower motion, deep romantic background music replacing the din of the storm above. The girl struggles, her long hair sweeping across her face like another veil; she and her brother clasp hands but then lose their grip. She swims upward to the surface, sees no sign of her twin, and goes back down for him. When his head surfaces, a man at the railing dives in toward the struggling swimmer. Briefly, a band encircles his head, but when the sister rises, to be seized by the captain, the brother has vanished. According to the narrator,

Deep currents and the sinking bark above them*
Divide what naught had ever kept apart.*
When a small, half-drowned band make it to a beach, the audience hears,
The poor survivors reach an alien shore,*
For Messaline with this country is at war.*

The couplet ends Nunn's interpolation, but he supplies new dialogue or altered speeches in the next few scenes. Thus the appearance of mounted soldiers at the far end of the beach sends the survivors scurrying into a cave under the cliffs while the troopers examine the wreckage, menacing silhouettes of horses and rifles and torsos and tall helmets with square mortarboard tops perceived by their prey within the cave.[11] According to the Captain,

The war between these merchants here and ours*
Too oft hast given us bloody argument.*
We must not be discovered in this place.*

A quieter interlude in the woods elicits the information from the Captain that Orsino rules here, that not only is he still a bachelor but "'Tis said no woman may approach his court,"* and that he woos Olivia. Passing mourners prompt the Captain to identify a grieving Olivia and to squelch Viola's wish to serve the lady, at which point she devises her plan to serve Orsino by disguising herself as a man. Credits run through a marvelous scene of hair cropped, trousers stuffed, breasts bound (with the sash from her harem costume), shirt and jacket buttoned, shoes exchanged. It ends with a practice run of masculine voice and walk, a stretch beside the sea, a look at the leather photograph case, now with both sides open to show Sebastian and Viola together, and an application of a small false mustache against her picture. As the newly-made young man strolls across the rocky causeway toward a castle on the promontory of an island, darkly outlined against the sky, "Twelfth Night or What You Will" flashes on the screen and then "By William Shakespeare." Music swells throughout.[12] Nine minutes have elapsed.

In matters large and small, Trevor Nunn has initiated the film's motifs. The initial music signals his homage to excess of it. Characters sing and play music, listen to music, caper to music, riot to music, defy Puritans to music, mourn to music, yearn to music, rejoice to music. The piano and the concertina on shipboard multiply into Orsino's piano and Olivia's several pianos, her harp, the chapel organ, Feste's concertina and guitar, and Sir Andrew's violin case. Songs recur at critical points, to reinforce the problems of adversity and love. Symmetrically, the conclusion repeats Feste's first song but with new verses. "A foolish thing was but a toy" shows Sir Andrew leaving in his open cart, alone save for a driver. "'Gainst knaves and thieves men shut their gate" accompanies Antonio's exit from the gates into the wind, rain, and mud. "But when I came, alas, to wive, . . . By swaggering could I never thrive" ushers Sir Toby and Maria into their coach. Finally, "With toss-pots still had drunken heads" sends Malvolio out into a bitter world. The merry wedding dance to an instrumental adaptation of the same melody proceeds after the departures, and a sun sets over a calm sea, but Feste's last lines presage future wind and rain. The film's opening also establishes other persistent patterns, such as uncertainty of identity, confusion of gender roles,[13] festive celebration, separation, reconciliation, storms (both literal and figurative), loss, grief, danger, excess, miracle. Even minor devices like veils, mirrors, windows, and photographs appear here. As a result, the reverberations among, between, and within scenes are rooted in Nunn's clear introduction of the elements which unify his *Twelfth Night*. Subsequently, the director uses the freedom of film to create off-book scenes or to intercut scenes where the events and the lines mutually comment on one another. Some long sequences remain undisturbed, their rhythm integral to their success. For example, act 1, scene 5, runs straight through, though the location shifts from the kitchen to the chapel to the grounds outside the chapel to the parlor and back outdoors again. The gulling of Malvolio and the final scene of reconciliation also play through with shifts only in location. Here the logic of the deception and the miracle of restoration would be ruined by interruption.

By contrast, some scenes or speeches in the text are rearranged as a sequence of jumps from one event to another so that they mutually comment on a shared subject, rather like a conversation. As a result, both the action and the language gain in power. Thus Nunn sets up a discussion of love between Viola/Cesario and Orsino simultaneously with the night revels of Sir Toby, Sir Andrew, Feste, and Maria, using music as a crucial link. The sequence begins with a long shot of the duke's island, moving to the castle interior, where Stephens leans across a table to light a slim cigar for Stubbs, who barely stifles her choked coughs. His "O, when mine eyes did see Olivia first" is lifted from act 1, scene 1, and at "pursue me" the camera shifts to Olivia's garden, where the revelers' noise and their pebbles against her window rouse Staunton, who joins them in the kitchen. With "Let's have a song," the setting returns to the castle, where Stubbs at the piano replaces Kingsley on the table with his concertina. Stephens strolls over, bottle and glasses in hand, to request "That old and antique song." His attendant's reference to "a fool that the Lady Olivia's father took much delight in" sends the viewer back to Kingsley's face and his question, "Will you have a love-song, or a song of good life?" Here Smith's Sir Toby presides over the party's bottle and glasses. At the lyric "your true-love's coming," Nunn inserts a shot of Carter upstairs in bed, waking to sounds of the now distant music, smiling at "That can sing both high and low." With the same song at the same point in the melody picked up by a background piano, Stephens and Stubbs play at cards, bottle and glasses now on their table. He asks, "How dost thou like this tune?" Two lines later "Thou dost speak masterly" segues into the kitchen party and the related "Every wise man's son doth know." The camera rests on a wistful Staunton at "'Tis not hereafter; / Present mirth hath present laughter," voicing her unspoken longings. The tune continues without words at the castle, linking, like an affirmation of the song's truth, with "My life upon't." Stubbs, whose Viola now describes but does not identify her love, is paired with Staunton, Cesario's line "To die, even when they to perfection grow" cutting to the song's "What's to come is yet unsure," while the camera focuses first upon the pensive housekeeper and then upon the drunken knight she loves. She joins Kingsley at "In delay there lies no plenty" and sings to the end of the piece, when she looks away. The complications for those in both households having been revealed so poignantly, a sad, prolonged silence falls on the kitchen, broken finally by an enigmatic little "Hm" from Kingsley, a silence repeated in quick shots of Stubbs, then Stephens, both reflective.

A radical shift of tone occurs as the revelers, singing raucously, parade out of the kitchen, down the hall, and into the gallery, where they dance to the fool's piano and his vocal accompaniment. There Hawthorne comes to confront them, the move from his chamber cued by the loud chorus of "O' th' twelf day of December. / My true love said to me."* He is defied by more song, a music hall routine by Kingsley and Smith at the piano. Then Staunton deliberately allies herself against Malvolio by bringing a bottle of wine and glasses from the cupboard. After the plot against him is hatched, another touching sequence occurs. Staunton's "For this night, to bed" heralds a long pause that is a tacit invitation to Smith, who stands with her on the staircase. She covers his silent refusal with "dream on the event"; but his line "'tis too late to go to bed now" as he goes off to drink with Sir Andrew moves the camera to her, closing the bedroom door—and her hopes—as her face collapses into tears. A jump to another disappointed woman shows Stubbs, also in her bedroom, unbinding her breasts and removing her mustache while she begins the relocated speech "Disguise, I see thou art a wickedness,"[14] a speech with far greater resonance at this point in the film than in its textual site. Looking into the mirror and at the photograph of herself and her brother further integrates the scene into Nunn's cinematic motifs. After "As I am woman," Stubbs's voice continues, "What thriftless sighs shall poor Olivia breathe" through a shot of Carter dreaming in bed. It has been a night of thriftless sighs for everyone.

While music and the melancholy of unrequited love link episodes in the night sequence, madness and deceit inform two parallel explorations of what is and is not real—the torment of Malvolio in dark confinement and the meeting between Olivia and Sebastian/Cesario. The action begins with a brief shot of Nigel Hawthorne through a coal shed's wide wooden bars that shut out most of the light. He wails, "They have wronged me. They have put me into darkness."* By contrast, Helena Bonham Carter, in her sunny bedchamber, sees Ben Kingsley and Stephen Mackintosh through her open window, and Kingsley's line, "No, I do not know you" runs through her hasty attention to her hair in the mirror and her dash out the door. He continues with "Nor I am not sent to you by my lady" as the camera moves to the argument outside. "Nothing that is so is so" sets up one side of the equation in this sequence, while "Are all the people mad?" sets up the other. The duplication of Viola's coin trick by the new "Cesario" confirms one reality for Kingsley, but the fight with apparent strangers and the intervention of a beautiful lady confirm another reality for Mackintosh. His line "I am mad, or else this is a dream" ties in to the next shot of Stubbs on the sea cliff, saying, "Prove true, imagination, O, prove true." The subsequent glimpse of Kingsley opens with "I would I were the first that ever dissembled in such a gown" as he garbs himself to play Sir Topas. The confusion as to what one can trust or not trust, who is mad or not mad, what is true or not true expresses itself here in Hawthorne's designation as "Malvolio the lunatic" and his denial, "do not think that I am mad." His dark imprisonment cuts to the brightness of Olivia's parlor, where Carter, in bright pink, lies atop Mackintosh on the sofa and rains passionate kisses upon him. When she exits, he continues the debate with "This is the air," proceeding to "I am ready to distrust mine eyes, / And wrangle with my reason that persuades me / To any other trust but that I am mad." The camera promptly returns to Hawthorne's insistence, "I am no more mad than you are." His plea for pen, ink, and paper to write a letter "to my lady" cues "Or else the lady's mad," which continues Sebastian's speech. The same kind of echo joins his vow "And having sworn truth, ever will be true" to Kingsley's "But tell me true, are you not mad indeed, or do you but counterfeit?" back at Malvolio's cell. The ping pong of terms and ideas strengthens the themes inherent in the text while increasing the film's comic effects.

Essential to Nunn's interpretation are the physical surroundings and the Victorian setting. Rigidities of the period in dress, decorum, and degree work brilliantly in a comedy like *Twelfth Night*, which flaunts all three. Viola's discarded corset, Sir Toby's disheveled hair and garments, Malvolio's descent from impeccable black to nightgown and robe to the ludicrous cross-gartered yellow stockings to the filth of his confinement all offer visual constructions of meaning, particularly within this social realm. Similarly, the clumsy capering of Sir Andrew, the duel where swords get stuck in apple baskets, the impetuous movements and frantic kisses of a besotted Olivia, and the soldiers' chase after Antonio all enact the chaos of the storm that has precipitated the disruption of correct behavior. It is not simply the aspirations of a Malvolio that violate class distinctions. Shot after shot shows a countess intimate with a fool, a gardener and two knights duping a steward, a wedding party where household servants join the gentry in dancing. Degree, Nunn suggests, has been permanently breached rather than temporarily threatened, even though the most serious offenders are sent packing. The Cornish locations provide near perfect visual metaphors for the action. The sea surges throughout the movie to unite it from opening to closing. In steep gray precipices that drop down to beach or breakers and in slippery rocks there lies a patent danger, as if the possibility of falling were ever close at hand. By selecting St. Michael's Mount for the site of Orsino's court,[15] Nunn not only has an authentic nineteenth-century village for town shots but a gloomy gray stone castle at its summit. In splendid isolation, the island can be reached at low tide only by a causeway, used in several scenes, or a boat to the harbor moles that appear in other scenes. At the height of rank and power as well as self-absorption, the duke lives cut off from the wider, greener, sunnier world just across the way, where all the fun occurs. Olivia's mansion is surrounded by carefully tended orchards, gardens, and parks, with benches, a gazebo, a nude Venus in a scallop-shell grotto, a chapel, a formal gatehouse, stables, and outbuildings.[16] If the exterior testifies to vitality, the interior testifies to wealth. Persistent references to money—the coin necklaces and coin tricks of Viola and Sebastian, the purses of Olivia and Antonio, the ducats of Sir Andrew, the rich jewel of Malvolio's imagination, the ring sent to Cesario, the pearl given to Sebastian, the fees paid to Feste—culminate in Olivia's plea, "Fear not, Cesario, take thy fortunes up." Like his sister, Sebastian's fortunes will go up, and not just figuratively. His new home is crammed with evidence of solid Victorian money. The retinue of servants, the enormous kitchen with its array of expensive foods, the lace on bed sheets, the stained glass windows—thousands of visual details attest to Olivia's wealth and, in part, silently explain why Sebastian readily accepts her proposal of marriage.

The preceding analysis by no means exhausts the extra-textual techniques employed by Trevor Nunn in *Twelfth Night*. Obviously some could work equally well on the stage, but the director has a good eye for the unique possibilities of film. He enhances the credibility of an improbable plot, first by placing it in an appropriate historical setting and then by drenching it in a realism that includes a prequel with a slightly altered plot.[17] The shipwreck is absolutely believable, so swift and confusing that no viewer can tell whether Sebastian drowns or not. The locations and the set decoration and the costuming further enhance the air of authenticity. With an exceptionally fine cast, both in looks and skills, Nunn has the basis for a production that persuasively yet perceptively addresses the text. Sometimes re-siting lines or speeches, sometimes running an uninterrupted scene, sometimes cutting back and forth between or among scenes, often relying on wordless shots, he creates resonant connections that theater cannot provide. Throughout, the comic vision has an autumnal melancholy,[18] rooted especially in music and Feste but tied to love denied, to hopes disappointed, to dear ones lost for a while or forever.

# Notes

1. According to Nunn, "This time I recognized that I was doing Shakespeare on *film*, and even though the budget was really quite small it seemed to me it was very important that I made a movie rather [than] a filmed play, so I did much more adaptation of the text than I ever would have done if I'd been doing 'the play' for television." François Laroque, "Interview given by Trevor Nunn," *Cahiers Elisabéthains* 52 (October 1997): 92.

2. Geoffrey O'Brien feels that "Despite the clothes and the furniture," the film did not have a particular nineteenth-century feel; it's more a question of meeting the seventeenth-century half way, . . . inventing a historical era which—like the period in which a cowboy movie takes place—never quite happened." "The Ghost at the Feast," *New York Review of Books*, 6 February 1997, 15.

3. Stanley Kaufmann thinks Stubbs "has all the warmth and color of a popsicle" ("Blanking Verse," *New Republic*, 2 December 1996, 40), and Richard Alleva says that she "entirely lacks the androgynous glamour Viola must possess" ("Romance Old & New," *Commonweal*, 20 December 1996, 14).

4. Nunn rejected the idea of doubling Stubbs "for two reasons. The first one is not terribly important, I suppose, but I think an audience always knows when technology is involved, always withholds a little bit of their belief and their investment in the characters. . . . But the second reason is the much more important one. Shakespeare's theme is gender" (Laroque, 92). Furthermore, "the audience is not

the object of the joke, it must be in on the joke." *Twelfth Night* website, www.flf.com/twelfth/about.htm.

5. Geoffrey O'Brien disagrees: "Feste, conceived rather scarily as a prophetic beggar lurking in the background and seeing all, a figure whose intimations of latent violence and mad wisdom suggest that Lear's fool has been grafted onto Olivia's" (14). David Ansen says, "Kingsley (overworking his Rasputin stare) becomes the surprisingly severe truth-teller of the play [*sic*], to the point where this clown can seem almost as morally smug as party pooper Malvolio." "It's the '90s, So the Bard is Back," *Newsweek*, 4 November 1996, 74.

6. Brian H. Johnson notes his "sphinxlike gravity" ("Souping up the Bard," *Maclean's*, 11 November 1996, 75), and Alleva adds, "One feels the inner strength of this shamanistic clown resides in his regarding himself as beyond all hope" (14). Kingsley himself says, "I think there is something Shamanistic about Feste, even I don't know what it is. But he seems to have been given by the author more than his fair share of knowledge about what's going on (Stan Schwarz, "Ben and the Bards Clown," Internet interview, http://desires.com/2.5/Performance/Kingsley/kingsley.html). Nunn too conceives of Feste as the supreme truth teller (Laroque, 91).

7. For John Mullan, Sir Toby and Sir Andrew are "sad oldies trying desperately to have fun" ("Mourning glory," *Times Literary Supplement*, 1 November 1996, 20), and Ansen finds the two "more pathetic than hilarious" (74). Nunn admits, "I wanted it to be clear that Toby is not socially graceful, he's an embarrassment to Olivia. And I think that there is something garrulous and physically dangerous about Toby that you can detect in his text" (Laroque, 95). Sir Toby, Sir Andrew, and Maria "are in one way or another trying to parade to the world as young, but each of them is aware that the parade is passing them by" (*Twelfth Night* website).

8. "Grant refused to read the whole play. 'Because I'm playing somebody so confused, I thought it would be a great help to keep myself in a state of confusion'" (*Twelfth Night* website).

9. The wig was nicknamed "Colin" during the shooting (*Twelfth Night* website).

10. Antonio's seeing the twins on the ship creates a logical problem for the plot's resolution, since he knows that Sebastian has a double. Nunn apparently just lets the matter slide, hoping audiences will, too.

11. Mullan sees "a militarized state of the 1890s, continually patrolled by men in uniform" (20), while Alleva declares that "Illyria is a vaguely Near-Eastern country, part nineteenth-century Greece, part Turkey, or even a touch Serbian. Its army is uniformed like a Central European force in service to the Austro-Hungarian Empire" (14). Even Nunn thinks of Orsino as presiding over "an all male military court, such as many middle European principalities once boasted" (*Twelfth Night* website). Apparently no one has looked at the bizarre range of uniforms worn by British troops at the end of the nineteenth century.

12. Mullan objects: "Only the often unnecessary accompanying music occasionally loses faith in the interpretation" (20).

13. H. R. Coursen has a first-rate discussion of the function of gender in the film. "The Recent Shakespeare Films," *Shakespeare Bulletin* 17, no. 1 (1999): 38–41.

14. Angela Maguin mistakenly follows the text, not the film, when she places this speech and the removal of the moustache to Viola's reception of the ring from Olivia. Review, *Cahiers Elisabéthains* 51 (April 1997): 84.

15. John St. Aubyn provides further information. *St. Michael's Mount: Illustrated History and Guide* (St. Ives: Beric Tempest and Company, 1978).

16. Llanhydrock and Prideaux Place supplied the major locations, along with Cothele, Trerice, Mount Edgecombe, and Bedruthan Steps. The grotto was created by set designer Sophie Becher (*Twelfth Night* website).

17. Nunn "felt the urge to make the content of the play seem real and not pantomime or stylized, so that the contrary extremes of sexual behavior in the central characters are seen in a believable social context" (*Twelfth Night*). Alleva objects that "Shooting on location, no matter how stylish the production values, entails a certain inalienable naturalism which is at odds with the fairy-tale doings of *Twelfth Night*" (14).

18. The film was shot in November and early December with surprisingly good weather (Laroque, 94). "Director of photography Clive Tickner shot the film through a tobacco filter to 'age' it while keeping the autumn skies luminous." Though Nunn declares, "*Twelfth Night* is the most autumnal of Shakespeare's comedies because it touches on mortality, the end of youth, and how fleeting our lives are" (*Twelfth Night* website), that season would not arrive three months after a Twelfth Night shipwreck. Some critics see no darkness at all, referring to "Nunn's sunny, athletic adaptation" (Ansen, 75) and a "pre-Raphaelite glow" (Donald Lyons, "Lights, Camera, Shakespeare," *Commentary* 103, no. 2 [1997]: 59).

# The Corral de Comedias at Almagro and London's Reconstructed Globe

FRANKLIN J. HILDY

SINCE 1984 I HAVE BEEN INVOLVED WITH THE PROJECT TO RECONSTRUCT the first Globe playhouse near its original site in London. This reconstruction opened as Shakespeare's Globe in 1997, but it remains a work in progress (figure 3). The limited historical information we have available offers us a number of options when it come to issues like the design of the stage, its decoration, the arrangement of doors, and the relationship the audience has with the actors and with itself. Scholars who have been writing about such issues for the last hundred years have argued for their preferences and list the alternatives, but when an actual working theater is being constructed, only one alternative can be shown at a time. It makes sense, then, to let the work of the actors inform our thinking about the alternatives we choose, and that is what has been done at the Globe. As the actors discover a problem, as they did with the shape of the column bases or the poor sightlines to the stage balconies, for example, we return to the historical evidence to see if other options suggest themselves.[1] It will be up to the next generation of scholars to speculate about the degree to which we may, or may not, have gotten this reconstruction right; there is, after all, no way to know for sure. But if the consensus is that we have not, there is a lot of room in the exhibition hall underneath the Shakespeare's Globe for them to explain our errors to the general public.[2]

The Globe project, however, is only a small part of my wider interest in historic theater architecture. The Globe had to be reconstructed because not a single one of the playhouses that inspired the dramaturgy of Shakespeare and his contemporaries survived the seventeenth century. But examples of other important forms of theater architecture have survived, and one of the most important is the Spanish Golden Age playhouse at Almagro. This "corral" theater is the only remaining example of an architectural form that had some remarkable and intriguing similarities to the playhouses of Shakespeare's London, and there are certainly lessons to be learned from it (figure 4).

In *The Human Stage: English Theatre Design, 1567–1640*,[3] John Orrell

**3. Shakespeare's Globe (1999), London, view towards the stage. © F. J. Hildy**

argues that there could have been little relationship between the theaters of Golden Age Spain and the those of Shakespeare's London, because the Spanish theaters were "ad hoc structures, developed piecemeal over the years to satisfy the demands for revenue and changing audience conditions," while the theaters of London were "more clearly of a piece" (12–14). This is a compelling argument, but one that is worth some scrutiny. Orrell himself admits that his assertion does not really apply to London's Boar's Head playhouse of 1597, which was as ad-hoc a structure as any playhouse in Spain (12). But his statement implies that we know a lot more about the design of the Red Lion, the Theatre, Newington Butts, and the Curtain than we actually do. He says of the Theatre, for example, that "once built . . . its main frame could hardly be adapted so all of a piece was its conception and design." And he confidently concludes this first chapter by saying that, "no one ever added a new story of boxes, or expanded the ground plan, or radically changed the relation of the stage to the auditorium" in the Elizabethan playhouses, as, presumably, was commonly done in Spain, because, he says, "such alterations, however desirable for commercial or even theatrical reasons, were entirely precluded by the highly integrated design of the original structure" (29). Ironically, just

**4. The Corral de Comedias at Almagro (1628), view towards the stage. © F. J. Hildy**

as this book came out, the excavations of the Rose Playhouse were under-way. By the time they were finished we knew that someone had "expanded the ground plan" of one of these theaters and had "changed the relation-ship of the stage to the auditorium."[4] So the design of these structures was perhaps not as highly integrated as Orrell believed. The Rose discoveries gave us the evidence that the Elizabethans could and did alter their play-house designs when it seemed desirable. We do not know if the Theatre was equally transformed at any point in its history or what kind of alter-ations may have been undertaken at Newington Butts or the Curtain. But we do know that prior to 1988 the scholarly consensus was that the alter-ations undertaken at the Rose in 1592 were little more than a redecorating project. The archaeology has shown us that they were much more than that, so we really cannot assume, as Orrell does, that when the Theatre was dismantled, moved across town, and reassembled as the Globe, its ground plan remained the same. There could easily have been as much difference between the Theatre of 1576 and the Globe of 1599 as there was between the Rose of 1587 and Rose II of 1592.

If the Elizabethan playhouses were not as "of a piece" as Orrell pro-posed, it is also true that the corral theaters of Spain were not as "ad hoc" as he had been led to believe. Research into Renaissance theater structures has tended to focus on capital cities, so theater historians are quite familiar with Madrid's Corral de la Cruz of 1579 and the Corral del Principe built just a few blocks away in 1583. These theaters were owned by charities and were indeed the kind of "ad hoc" structures Orrell had in mind. In fact the Corral del Principe was the example he used to stand for all when he talked of Spanish playhouses. But Spain, unlike England, had theaters in cities all over the country, and the Madrid Corrales represented only one of at least three possible models of construction and ownership. There were, for example, many corral theaters that were like the Bel Savage Inn in London or the Red Lion Inn at Norwich; that is, existing spaces with their own functions that were set up occasionally for the performance of plays. Other structures were purpose-built. The Corral de las Atarazanas at Seville, for example, was built in 1574, two years before the Theatre in London, by the Italian architect, Juan Marin Modeñin Bellini, who had been the chief architect for the cathedral there. His theater was built of wood and had to be dismantled and reassembled on another site (in 1585) just as the Theatre was.[5] A number of other Spanish theaters were not only purpose-built from the ground up but—like the Red Lion, the Rose, the Swan, and the Fortune playhouses in London—were also entrepreneurial investments owned by a single individual, not by a charity. This is certainly true of the Corral de Comedias at Almagro, perhaps the last of the great corral theaters to be built and the only one to have survived.[6]

The Corral de Comedias at Almagro was discovered during renovation work being carried out on the city's unusual Plaza Mayor in 1953. It was restored by M. Gonzalez Valcarcel and reopened as a National Monument on 29 May 1954, when it was declared to be a sixteenth- or seventeenth-century theater. At that time, the theater could not be dated with certainty. Its construction followed the building codes established in Spain in 1584, and a lawsuit from 2 August 1715 confirmed that the theater was well established by 1680, but no more precise information was available.[7] Documents recently discovered by Concepción García de León Álvarez and published in *La Construcción del Corral de Comedias de Almagro* in 2000, however, have filled in some of the key missing details.[8]

We now know that the Corral de Comedias at Almagro was built in 1628 for Don Leonardo de Oviedo, a priest of the order of the Calatrava. It was purpose-built within the courtyard of his inn, the Bull, located on the south side of the Plaza Mayor in the heart of the city. There is no evidence of its being connected to charity as the Madrid playhouses were, though Don Leonardo did make charitable donations from the profits. When Don Leonardo died in 1640, his sister Dõna Beatriz inherited the property. She left it to her daughter, Dõna Maria de Bivero y Prado, who then passed it on to her son, Bernardino de Villarreal y Oviedo, who owned it in 1715. Its

last recorded use was in 1802, and by 1857 all signs of its having been a
theater had been covered over while the patio had reverted to use as a
courtyard (Rodrigo 53 and 87).

Almagro, located 120 miles south of Madrid and eighteen miles south-
east of Ciudad Real, seems a small town of little importance today. But
from the twelfth century to 1499 it was an important holding of the Military Order of the priests of the Calatrava, who defended the southern
boundaries of La Mancha from the Moors of Granada. Lope de Vega's
most famous play, *Fuenteovejuna* (1614), is set in Almagro during this
period. In the early sixteenth century, Almagro became an important administrative center for the mining monopoly that Charles V had granted to
Europe's richest family, the Fuggers, making it one of the most cosmopolitan cities in the country. A Franciscan college was built there in 1597,
and a Jesuit college was added in 1638. By the seventeenth century, then,
Almagro was a city of major importance. We have no records of Italian
and French troupes visiting there as they did in Valencia (Falconieri 31),
but we do know that important acting companies from Madrid were con-
tracted to play in Almagro as soon as the theater was built. A company
under the *autor*, Juan Martinez, played there in 1629, while the companies
of Francisco Lopez and Alonzo Olmedo Tofino performed there in the
1631 season (Álvarez 9). But still, by 1628 corral theaters, just like the
open-air playhouses of London, were on the wane. The second Fortune of
1626 was the last of the open-air theaters to be built in London, and Almagro's Corral de Comedias of 1628 is the last known open-air theater to
have been built in Spain.[9]

Corral theaters had their own geography, which was in many ways similar to the theaters of Shakespeare's London. The Fortune playhouse of
1600 would have made quite a fine corral. The central area of a corral, the
equivalent of the yard in English theaters, was called the *patio*. At the Almagro today this patio averages twenty-eight feet east to west and forty-
one feet, six inches north to south (figure 5).[10] Many corrales had a system
of canvas awnings that, like the classical Roman *vela*, were stretched
across the opening to protect the audience from the sun. The awnings at
Almagro have recently been restored and are remarkably effective not only
in shading the space but in creating a translucent ceiling.[11] With the awnings in place, the corral undergoes a remarkable transformation that suddenly makes the presentation of a play like Calderon's *Life is a Dream*
visually extraordinary. The experience of discomfort caused by the sun at
Shakespeare's Globe in London suggests that the theaters of Shakespeare's day could certainly have benefited from such an arrangement. But
to date, only John Corbin has suggested that "heavens," when used in the
context of Elizabethan playhouses, meant "a cloud of canvas thrown out
from the loft above the stage towards the top of the amphitheater," and

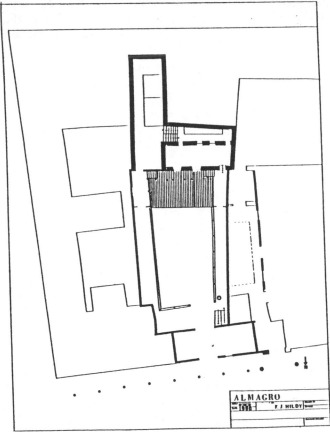

5. **Ground plan of the Corral de Comedias at Almagro.** © F. J. Hildy

that was back in 1911. If he got this idea from the canvas awning of the Spanish playhouses, he does not say so.[12] The patio was occupied primarily by *mosqueteros*, men of the lower classes, who stood to watch the plays. The yard of the English theaters was also predominantly a male domain. The *mosqueteros* were quite active, making trips to the well (in the northwest corner at Almagro) and to the bar (*alojero*) at the back of the theater throughout the performances. There were no wells inside the English playhouses, and at the Rose and the Globe, at least, the refreshment house was outside in a separate structure, making it less distracting.[13] A few benches (*taburetes* or *bancos*) were sometimes placed near the stage in the patio, a feature we don't find in the English playhouses. In most corrales, bleacher style seats (*gradas*) were set laterally along the side walls under the galleries, making them the equivalent of the lower gallery of the London playhouses. The *gradas* have not been restored at the Almagro, and that distorts the feel of this theater.

On three sides of the patio in corral theaters there were combinations of galleries (called *corredores* or sometimes *barandillas*) and boxes (usually called *aposentos*, but also known as *camarillas, rejas, ventanes, vistas*, and, when at the top-most level, *desvanas*). The galleries could be at two levels, as they are in this theater; or three, as they were in the larger theaters of Madrid and Seville. The contract for London's Fortune Playhouse calls for gallery floors at about two feet above yard level, thirteen feet above, and twenty-four feet above.[14] At Almagro the missing *gradas* would have to stand for the first gallery; but the second-gallery floor is only nine feet, two inches above the yard, while the third level is only at fifteen feet, eight inches, which is more than eight feet lower than the third level at the Fortune.[15] Boxes (*aposentos*) began as rooms in the houses that surround the theater patio, where the plays could be watched from windows. Gradually they developed into standard theater boxes, since the windows were enlarged to allow more people to see from them. They were probably not unlike the Lord's Rooms or gentlemen's rooms at a theater like the Globe, but the *aposento* openings were covered with grills or lattice work to protect privacy and prevent unauthorized access, and this is something for which there is no historical evidence in the English playhouses. In some theaters there were no galleries on walls where the *aposentos* existed. In other theaters, galleries were mounted in front of and slightly below the *aposentos*. A third arrangement was simply to divide the galleries closest to the stage into boxes, and this is the solution used at the Almagro. There are two *aposentos* on the stage end of each of the galleries. Documents indicate that there was also a city *aposento*, reserved for public officials, which was probably located in the normal position on the second-gallery level at the north end of the patio opposite the stage.

The gallery directly below the city box was reserved for women and is commonly called the *cozuela* but was also known as the *jaula* or the *corre-dor de las mujeres*. It was the usual practice for this area to be partitioned off from the rest of the theater and to have its own stairway entrance. Nothing remains of any such partitions in this theater today, but the women's stairway may well be sealed within the walls that take up the northeast corner of this corral. The side galleries on both levels would have been occupied mostly by men sitting in chairs, though women could also be found there and in the *aposentos*, providing they were accompanied by a male blood-relative. It is interesting to note that in Spain, where women acted on stage from the mid-sixteenth century, women were carefully segregated from the men in the auditorium. In England, where women were not allowed on the public stage until 1660, the women in the audience had almost no restrictions put on them.

On the corral's south side is a raised platform stage (*encenario*). It is at a height of four feet, nine inches today, but the level of the doors at the back of the stage suggest that it was originally at a height of five feet, six inches, just slightly higher than the five feet we think was average for stages in England (see figure 4). The stage is twenty-eight feet, nine inches wide at the rear but tapers to twenty-seven feet, two inches at the front (figure 6). It is twelve feet, six inches from the front of the stage to the row of posts that support the overhanging balcony, and three feet, two inches from there to the back wall. Allowing for the size of the posts, this leaves

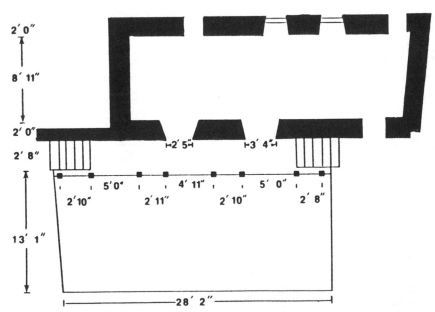

6. **Drawing of stage area of Corral de Comedias at Almagro.** © F. J. Hildy

a corridor about thirty-two inches wide between the posts and the façade. At the rear of the stage is a stage house (*vestuario*), which, like the tiring-houses in England, served as both back stage and dressing room. Because there were both men and women on stage in corral theaters, there had to be additional dressing rooms. In this theater there are dressing rooms below stage level for the men and dressing rooms at balcony level for the women. A stage balcony projects out from the stage house over the rear three feet of the platform stage in this corral. A row of eight posts supports this balcony and forms a series of openings in the symmetrical width pattern of roughly three feet, five feet, three feet, five feet, three feet, five feet, and three feet. Curtains or scenic pieces would probably have been mounted between these posts, providing for a wide variety of entrances and for up to three five feet wide (but only three feet deep) discovery spaces.[16] Small stairways in the corners of the stage near the stage house allow the performers who are behind the curtains easy access to the patio level under the first gallery and from there down to the cellar below the stage, where there is also access to men's dressing rooms. At stage level, two asymmetrically placed doors lead into a large waiting room within the *vestuario*. From this room a small stairway leads up to the balcony on the west side (this would be on the audience's right). In the rear wall of this room two doors lead out to an open walkway that provides access to rooms on the east side of the theater. From those rooms it is possible to go up to the east side of the stage balcony, and to the dressing rooms on that level, or to go down to the dressing-rooms in the cellar.

As it exists today, the Almagro corral is a wonderfully eccentric theater and an effective performance facility. With few exceptions, it fits all of the expectations we have of the corrales based on the available documents (Shergold, 206–8). The most unusual feature about this building is that both the entrance to the patio and the *vestuario* building itself are located well west of center (again, west is on the audience's right-hand side). This may have been part of the original design, which could have been dictated by land ownership and existing structures, or it may have been caused by the insertion of the present west wall at some time after the original construction of the building. It is difficult to determine the original size of the corral, or courtyard, of Don Leonardo's Bull Inn. It looks to have been something on the order of eighty-four feet square, but the east side (on the left-hand side of the audience) is now very irregular and not accessible for measurements, so it is impossible to know what has been added or taken away since 1628. The west side appears to have been defined by a dividing wall separating this courtyard from that of the next one, the courtyard of the Eagle Inn, perhaps; but that courtyard is now a house, so again it is hard to know the original layout. To create his theater, it seems that Don Leonardo had a dividing wall built along the east side of his courtyard, roughly parallel to the dividing wall on the west side. He had the tiring-house (*vestuario*) built on the south end centered in the resulting space, and this left him with a corral that was uniformly fifty-four feet east-to-west and not quite so uniformly sixty-six feet north-to-south. (While this compares favorably with the fifty-five-feet-square yard of the Fortune theater, it is to be remembered that the Fortune was fifty-five-feet square when measured along the front of its galleries; while the Almagro is fifty-five feet by sixty-six feet when measured along the back walls that supported its galleries.) But here is where things get difficult. In the theater as it exists today, another dividing wall appears to have been inserted along the west side of the corral. It is, on average, just about fourteen feet, nine inches inside the west wall that I believe originally separated the Bull Inn from the Eagle Inn. This new wall is not parallel to that old wall, nor is it parallel to the theater's east-side wall. This slanting wall makes the *vestuario* and the entrance to the corral itself off-centered so that they both seem too far west; that is, too far to the audience's right as they face the stage to be appropriate for the space. For this reason, I have argued elsewhere that the existing west wall is a late addition put in some time after 1715 to make room for the prominent Casa de Molina, which we see there today, at a time when the theater was no longer attracting large crowds.[17]

If we were to remove the existing west wall, expanding the theater by fourteen feet, nine inches up to where the exterior wall of the Casa de Molina now stands with one level of balconies still on it, the Corral de Comedias at Almagro suddenly becomes a symmetrical building (figure 7). With the stage also raised to the level of the doors, it would have a look that would be not inappropriate for London's Fortune Theatre of 1600. Certainly any play by Shakespeare could have been done here and with the awnings in place: *Macbeth* or *The Tempest* would be in a magical world indeed (figure 8). And such an adjustment in the width of the building and the height of the stage gives this venerable corral a more satisfying appearance. Fortunately, along with her recently published document on the Almagro, Álvarez cites an ordinance survey of Spain taken in the eighteenth century that indicates that the Bull Inn at Almagro occupied 266 square meters more then than it does now. This would seem to confirm my hypothesis, but this is more than twice as much space as would have been lost by the insertion of the slanted west wall I would like to see removed. Worse, the survey seems to indicate that the Bull Inn property measured forty feet east-to-west, about what the theater measures today, but was over 148 feet north-to-south, much larger than it is now. This suggests that the entire Bull Inn was located behind the tiring-house of the theater. The slanted west wall, then, may have been an original feature put in to allow guests of the Inn to gain access to it without going through the Corral de Comedias. Of course, the survey may have been misinterpreted, and it is

**7. Ground plan of proposed reconstruction of the original Corral de Comedias at Almagro.** © F. J. Hildy

8. Comparison of current Corral de Comedias at Almagro with proposed reconstruction. © F. J. Hildy

part of my continued project to obtain a copy and view it for myself. The issue requires a lot more investigation.

But whether this theater was intentionally built asymmetrically to fit an awkward space, in the way the Rose playhouse was built in London in 1587, or whether it was modified at a later date as the Rose was in 1592, the Corral de Comedias at Almagro remains the only existing theatrical space in Europe with any resemblance to the open-air playhouses of Shakespeare's day. As such, it has much to tell us about the workable size of such a space; about the advantage of shallow stages; about the value of an overhanging balcony; and about the use of curtains, working doors, working windows, temporary stage stairways, and all the other effects employed on the Spanish stages. It also has much to tell us about the effectiveness of theater buildings that are "of a piece," as Orrell would have it, but yet eccentrically and perhaps asymmetrically laid out, as the builders of the Rose did have it.

# Notes

1. Such findings are written up in *Shakespeare's Globe Research Bulletin* at the end of each season. These are available on the web at http://www.reading .ac.uk/globe/.

2. In "'If you build it they will come': The Reconstruction of Shakespeare's Globe Gets Underway on Bankside in London," *Shakespeare Bulletin* 10 (Summer 1992), 9; I noted that building this theater has been much like the story of the Brontosaurus. We know now that the discoverer of the first Brontosaurus put the wrong head on a perfectly good Apatosaurus body. The Brontosaurus never existed, so the New York Museum of Natural History now explains the error to its visitors. Yet generations have been inspired to study dinosaurs because of their encounter with the fictitious Brontosaurus. If our Globe makes a fraction as many people take up the study of theater history, we will have done well.

3. Cambridge: Cambridge University Press, 1988.

4. For details of the Rose excavation, see Julian M. C. Bowsher and Simon Blatherwick, "The Structure of the Rose," in *New Issues in the Reconstruction of Shakespeare's Theatre,* ed. Franklin J. Hildy (New York: Peter Lang, 1990), 56–78; and Julian Bowsher, *The Rose Theatre: An Archaeological Discovery* (London: Museum of London, 1998). While it may be argued that the changes seen at the Rose were not radical, they were certainly more significant than Orrell's argument would allow for.

5. John J. Allen, "The Spanish *Corrales de Comedias* and the London Playhouses and Stages," in *New Issues,* 212.

6. The Teatro Cervantes at Alcala de Henares of 1601 has been restored, but this theater was modified several times, most notably in 1769, 1831, and 1927, when it was converted to a cinema. Archaeologists chose to preserve it in its first three forms. An international competition was held, and the winning architect presented a plan that would allow people to see the theater in something of its 1601 configuration, its 1769 configuration, and its 1831 configuration. Unfortunately, the theater has been closed since the restoration was completed. When I received

a special tour of the theater in April 2001, it was in its nineteenth-century configuration, and one had to go to the basement and peer under the false floor to see the seventeenth-century patio. See Miguel Angel Coso Marin, Mercedes Higuera Sánchez-Pardo, and Juan Sanz Ballesteros, *El Teatro Cervantes de Alcala de Henares: 1602–1866, Estudio y Documentos* (London: Tamesis Books, 1989).

7. See John V. Falconieri, "The Old Corrals of Spain," *Theatre Survey* 4 (1963): 35; and Antonina Rodrigo, *Almagro y su Corral de Comedias* (Ciudad Real: Instituto de Estudios Manchegos, Consejo Superior de Investigaciones Cientificas, 1971), 40, 46–50.

8. Concepción García de León Álvarez, *La Construcción del Corral de Comedias de Almagro, 1628* (Almagro: Ciudad del Teatro, Patimonio de la Humanidad, 2000).

9. The theater at Huesca was built by José Garro in 1624, and the oval-shaped Corral de Montería was built in 1626, but there are no later ones that I am aware of. See Falconieri, "The Old Corrals," 33 and 34.

10. There are few straight lines in this building and fewer consistent measurements. The building was also laid out in Castilian feet, each one being eleven English inches. The measurements provided here were taken on site during multiple visits to Almagro.

11. This awning was first used by the Italian *autor*, Ganassa (Alberto Nazeri or Naseli), in 1574 in a temporary corral in Madrid. It became a common feature of the Spanish Golden Age playhouses. See Hugo Albert Rennert, *The Spanish Stage in the Time of Lope de Vega* (New York: Hispanic Society of America, 1909), 29; and Melveena McKendrick, *Theatre in Spain 1490–1700* (Cambridge: Cambridge University Press, 1989), 48.

12. John Corbin, "Shakespeare His Own Stage Manager," *Century Magazine* (December 1911): 260–70. Corbin proposes that such a canvas was used for special effects like night scenes in Elizabethan theaters. In Spain, however, it was to shade the audience; but if its effectiveness at Almagro is any indication, it could be of the greatest help for such effects. These awnings were not designed to keep off rain.

13. Gabriel Egan, "John Heminge's Tap-House at the Globe," *Theatre Notebook* 55, no. 2 (2001): 72–77.

14. The contract calls for a one-foot foundation with a twelve-foot gallery on top of it. That would put the floor of the first gallery at about two feet above ground, and the floor of the second at about thirteen feet. The contract says the second gallery is to be eleven feet high, making the third level twenty-four feet above the yard. The third gallery is only nine feet high, so the eaves would be thirty-three feet from the yard.

15. The lower gallery levels give a better angle of view to the stage in this theater where the yard is so narrow. Reconstructions for the only slightly larger Rose playhouse will also have to lower the gallery heights specified in the Fortune contract.

16. N. D. Shergold, *A History of the Spanish Stage* (Oxford: Clarendon Press, 1967), 233–34.

17. Franklin J. Hildy, "'Think when we talk of horses, that you see them': Comparative Techniques of Production in the Elizabethan and Spanish Golden Age Playhouses," *Text & Presentation* 11 (1991): 61–68.

# The Tempest's Masque and Opera

## DAVID LINDLEY

THIS PAPER APPROACHES BOTH THE SUBJECT OF THE CONFERENCE AND THE topic of its original seminar in a somewhat sidelong fashion.[1] Its focus is neither directly on the setting of *The Tempest* in a Mediterranean island nor upon the history of operatic *Tempests*—a history characterized by Gary Schmidgall as "a long, melancholy one, punctuated by bursts of unintended hilarity."[2] Instead, it takes the betrothal masque in act 4 as a starting point for reflection on the ways in which Shakespeare's employment in the play of the most European of Renaissance dramatic genres has generated problems in subsequent theatrical history, problems that have on occasion been solved by converting the masque into that other most Italian of genres (one that some have seen as a direct descendant of the masque), a through-composed mini-opera. I conclude with specific consideration of Stephen Oliver's pastiche operatic setting of it for the Royal Shakespeare Company (RSC) performance at Stratford in 1982, which usefully raises both general questions about what "opera" might signify in this kind of theatrical context, and particular issues that derive from Oliver's deliberate choice of a historically and culturally "marked" musical style.

*The Tempest* is perhaps the most spectacular, and certainly the most musical, of all of Shakespeare's plays. The climactic combination of these elements comes in the betrothal masque in act 4, introduced modestly by Prospero as "some vanity of mine art" (4.1.41). It is, says Prospero, "such another trick" (4.1.37) as the disappearing banquet and apparition of Ariel as a Harpy in the previous scene, but here the spectacle is presented in a fashion that emphasizes its generic distinctness from the play surrounding it. Its verse is of rhyming couplets, and it presumably featured rich, symbolic costumes for its three goddesses of the kind employed in the court masque itself. It concludes with a dance, as did the court masque—though, since Prospero's is a court peopled only by spirits, it is the "country footing" of spirits dressed as nymphs and reapers, rather than an elegant aristocratic dance that is offered to our eyes. No contemporary music for this part of the play survives,[3] and one can only conjecture whether, stylistically, its song, "Honor, riches, marriage blessing," might have gestured

103

towards the declamatory air, imported in self-conscious imitation of Italian style, and just beginning to make its mark on contemporary court performances. It is perhaps unlikely that the boy actors of the King's Men who took the parts of the goddesses would have aspired to any great vocal complexity, and thereby have differentiated this song from the more straightforward settings Robert Johnson provided for the songs "Full fathom five," and "Where the bee sucks,"[4] but I would argue, nonetheless, that it is the *distinctness* of theatrical vocabulary in the masque as a whole that is an important part of its meaning in the play.

To an audience at Blackfriars, the Globe, or at the court, the primary signification of the genre was of aristocratic courtliness, but one equally as appropriate to a Duke of Milan as to the court of King James. Much recent critical attention devoted to the court masque has so concentrated on its function within the English court that its international character has tended to be obscured. Yet Shakespeare's contemporary masque writers and designers pillaged continental sources for their inspiration; his fellow dramatists inserted masques in plays set in Rhodes (Beaumont and Fletcher, *The Maid's Tragedy*, 1611), Cyprus (Chapman, *The Widow's Tears*, c. 1605), and Italy (Middleton, *The Revenger's Tragedy*, 1607) to name but three. The masque is therefore coded both as an elite and an exotic genre. But it is also the self-evident artfulness of the masque that permits Prospero to interrogate the limits of art's capability to transcend the realities of ambition, insurrection, and the ravages of time in his meditation on mortality that follows the masque's sudden ending. "Our revels now are ended" blurs the boundaries between the real and the theatrical, and complicates the court masque's conventional preoccupation with its own transience by pointing to the fact that Prospero's actors are not the flesh-and-blood aristocrats who strutted at court, but airy, insubstantial spirits.[5]

Though set off from the play surrounding it, the masque offers a representation of the blessings of chaste marriage and a celebration of fertility that is integrated with *The Tempest's* wider preoccupation with the rewards for the proper regulation of appetite. Furthermore, Ferdinand's response to its vision—that "so rare a wondered father, and a wife, / Makes this place paradise"[6]—links the masque to other golden-age visions within the play, Gonzalo's ideal commonwealth in 2.1.141–63 and Caliban's dream of a musical heaven in 3.2.131–41. Like them, it is doomed to fade, and its dramatic dissolution thereby recapitulates the pattern of frustrated expectation and disappointment that is pervasive in the play's narrative. Far from being a late and inessential addition as some have argued, then, the masque in *The Tempest* sits at the heart of the play's theatrical meaning.

Yet in Dryden and Davenant's Restoration adaptation of Shakespeare's play, *The Enchanted Island* (1669), and its 1674 recension by Shadwell, although more songs were introduced, the complication of the plot by the introduction of a second pair of young lovers rendered the original masque inappropriate, and it was replaced by a concluding masque of Neptune and Amphitrite much less integrated into the play's action and theme. Irena Cholij, in her authoritative survey of the successive adaptations of the play during the eighteenth century, notes that it was not until the 1745–46 season that Shakespeare's text was (partially) restored.[7] For that performance, although the concluding masque of Neptune and Amphitrite was retained, Thomas Arne also composed music for the restored "Grand Masque" of act 4. The British Library manuscript, in which part of this setting survives, indicates that he through-composed the whole masque, with a sequence of recitatives and arias leading up to the song for Ceres and Juno indicated by Shakespeare's text. This is an interesting precedent for the modern settings I will later be considering, but seems not to have been much followed in the next 150 years. Boyce's music for Garrick's 1757 performance, according to Cholij, sets only fifteen lines of Shakespeare's masque, while Linley's music for Sheridan's popular adaptation, though it opens the play with a marvelous storm-chorus, has no setting at all of the act 4 masque.

During the nineteenth century, although Shakespeare's text was gradually more and more fully restored, Kean's 1857 performance, for example, abbreviated the speeches of Iris and Ceres before Juno descended, accompanied by non-Shakespearean "Graces, Seasons, and other spirits," to sing "Honour, riches." The poster for a performance at Leeds Amphitheatre in 1865 advertised a "Grand Masque and dance of Reapers and Nymphs" as one of its highlights, and states that the music was Arne's setting of "Honour, riches." It is interesting to speculate where the company obtained the music, since, as far as I am aware, it was not published.[8] Sadly, if there were a score in Leeds, it almost certainly perished in the fire that destroyed the theater later in the century. It is not, therefore, clear whether the performance incorporated the whole of Arne's operatic setting, or only its final number. A few weeks before the show opened, the local newspaper had advertised for sixty children to take part in the dances, which would suggest some considerable elaboration of the dance of nymphs and reapers rather than of the music. More spectacularly, Beerbohm Tree's 1904 rendition of the play, which significantly rearranged Shakespeare's text to give greater prominence to the actor-manager's own performance as Caliban, abbreviated the first part of the masque, and followed it with a massive balletic expansion of the dance, turned into a miniature drama of its own.[9] It would seem that to expand the dance was the common practice in the later nineteenth and early twentieth centuries, rather than to follow the operatic treatment of Arne in the eighteenth.

But, of course, Arne's setting was part of a more general "operatic" treatment of the play during the eighteenth century—"operatic" at least in the sense of "English dramatic opera—essentially spoken drama in which music, dancing, and spectacle . . . played critical parts." Cholij observes that, "In contrast to continental opera, however, in these works the principal characters did not usually sing" (Cholij, 79). Michael Dobson, indeed, has argued that the descendant of the "operatic" versions of the Dryden/ Davenant *Enchanted Island* was not full-blown opera, but "Panto as the London stage still knows it."[10] In this context, the genre of the whole play has been transformed, and to set the masque operatically is not to mark it as generically different from the play surrounding it, but merely to present it as one of the more highly elaborated moments in the patchwork of music and speech the play had become.

In the twentieth century, the problems of dealing with the masque at all were considerable. Material was substituted for, or added to, the text; it was radically pruned, or entirely cut. When staged, it has not infrequently been a theatrical flop.[11] Directors have, however, attempted to find some modern generic equivalent for the masque's introduction into the play of a distinct theatrical vocabulary. So, for example, Mendes (RSC, 1993) flew in a kind of pop-up theater, and his goddesses imitated puppets, whereas a New York production by George C. Wolfe transformed the masque into "a blissful celebration of the rites of marriage . . . presented as a jubilant Brazilian carnival" (Dymkowski, 289).

In the 1980s, two major productions of the play—Ron Daniels's RSC production of 1982, and Peter Hall's 1988 production for the National Theatre—both chose to "frame" the masque by setting it as a through-composed mini-opera, the first with music by Stephen Oliver, the latter set by Harrison Birtwistle. Both were enthusiastically received by the majority of critics. Stephen Oliver's score made the masque "the showpiece of this magical production," and gave real celebratory weight to its idealized vision of fertile marriage;[12] while Hall's production had "a masque of beauty and charm, much of which is provided by Harrison Birtwistle's music."[13] In what follows I consider only the first; Birtwistle's music survives in the National Theatre (NT) archives, but only as individual instrumental parts: as is sadly not at all unusual, it would seem that someone made off with the full score.

Oliver's score is preserved in the RSC archives at the Shakespeare Centre in Stratford, and I have set out the text as adapted by him below. He omits and reorders some of the Shakespearean material in a way that reveals his musical priorities. Perhaps the most noticeable feature of the setting is that a good deal of it is in aria or arioso form rather than, as one might have expected, employing recitative (as Birtwistle does much more freely) for the first part of the masque. It is not surprising, then, that Iris's opening aria cuts the text, and, ingeniously, adds the words "the goddess of all the earth,"[14] so that the "rich leas," "turfy mountains," and the rest become instances of that which she commands rather than, as in the

Shakespeare text, an enormous sequence of subordinate clauses suspended before the arrival of the main clause at "the queen o'th'sky . . . bids thee leave these." Instead, Oliver makes a clear distinction between the pastoral 6/8 rhythm that characterizes Ceres, and the instruction Iris bestows upon her, in a recitative that incorporates some word-painting on the word "fly" (examples 1 and 2). The other major rearrangement is of the final section of the masque, where the song of blessing is designed to build towards an emphatic musical climax, and is appropriately fashioned as a triumphant trio, over a rushing semi-quaver accompaniment, with Juno rising to high Cs to dominate its ending, as befits her queenly status (example 3). If, all too often, Ferdinand's characterization of the masque as a "most majestic vision and / Harmonious charmingly" rings hollowly in the theater, here it seemed an entirely appropriate response to the ecstatic musical celebration, as the three goddesses ended, arms raised, giving it all they had. (In this production the celebratory atmosphere continued as Ferdinand and Miranda joined in the dance of nymphs and reapers.)[15]

Shakespeare's text, then, is rearranged in a fashion dictated by musical logic and, in the first part, by a recognition of the need to simplify syntax in a way that makes it possible for an audience at some level to follow the words they hear. In the adaptation of the text, inevitably, some things are lost—perhaps most importantly the symbolic significance of the banishment of Venus from this masque of chaste betrothal. Although Oliver con-

Example 1

Example 2

veys some sense of threat with rushing upward scales accompanying Iris's account of the goddess's retreat, the recapitulation of the quaver-semiquaver rhythm in the accompaniment that had featured in Iris's earlier recitative suggests primarily the musical distinctiveness of the section, rather than the thematic significance of Venus herself—and Iris's recitative is then folded back into the musical structure as she placates Ceres by returning to the 6/8 rhythm of her opening aria (example 4). But what is gained is, I think, the way in which the masque achieves, through its operatic setting, what Auden characterizes as the quality of music's language to embrace "only the present indicative tense, and no negative."[16]

It is essential to the success of this setting of the masque in the dramatic context precisely that it is "operatic"; this is a score for singers rather than actors, and conspicuously more vocally demanding than the songs for Ariel, and it therefore establishes a generic distinction between the masque and the play that surrounds it. Freed by its music from ambivalence and ambiguity, it simply is a celebration of an abstract plenteousness. The use of aria, arioso, and recitative marks this out self-consciously as operatic, formally contained. In British culture, opera functions in a fashion not entirely dissimilar from the masque in the seventeenth century. It is perceived as an elite art form, and as European rather than native.[17] For many, if not most, of the audience at Stratford, opera is a distinct—and somewhat alien—genre. The reviewer who complained that "the songs, which veer from the light fantastic to the heavy operatic, are inclined to take our minds off the magic of the writing" witnesses, in his choice of adjective, to precisely that attitude.[18] Yet it is that alien distinctiveness that is vital to its formal and emotional effect.

The musical language Oliver uses is pastiche. Different reviewers placed it rather differently: Michael Billington called it "pastiche Monteverdi,"[19] Michael Coveney described it as including "pastiche elements of Purcell and Handel."[20] Elsewhere in Oliver's score, the setting of "Full fathom five" over a ground-bass is unambiguously Purcellian, and, for those with ears to hear, its recollection of the great Purcell laments added significantly to its effect. But in the masque, the general vocabulary is a rather lush version of the Baroque, though no eighteenth-century composer would have essayed the modulation from C major to B-flat major that triumphantly emphasizes "Spring come to you." For some, no doubt, this imitative style immediately disqualifies it as a composition meriting serious attention. Pastiche can be permitted for comedy—as in Britten's hilarious play of Pyramus and Thisbe in *A Midsummer Night's Dream*. But unless it is Stravinsky's neoclassicism, which signals its creative modernity in revisiting and reappropriating past musical forms and languages with an overt self-consciousness, pastiche is regarded as intrinsically second-rate, the sort of thing that any competent music student should be able to turn out. Such a verdict might be just if Oliver's music were being proffered in a concert environment (though I am not sure even of that), but in its theatrical setting something rather more complex is happening. Any production of a Shakespeare play is inevitably engaged in negotiating the historical distance of the text, and in this production, although Ariel was costumed as a distinctly space-age figure, for the most part the setting was

Jacobethan. It is generally true that theater audiences are much less sensitive to the historicity of musical vocabulary than they are to that of costume or setting—indeed the stage history of the music in *The Tempest* is proof enough of that proposition, since from the eighteenth century until comparatively recently the settings of "Purcell,"[21] Linley, Arne, and Sullivan have not infrequently happily coexisted within the same production. (Amusingly enough, the Leeds production proudly advertises that it is using the "original" music—though actually employing settings by Purcell, Linley, Arne, and J. C. Smith.) Nonetheless, any musical setting does carry with it, as part of its coding, a historical element, and composers might choose very different strategies and vocabularies. They might choose to preserve a twentieth-century integrity (as in Tippett's fine score for what was, apparently, a disastrous Old Vic production in 1962, or as Birtwistle did in his NT score);[22] they might imitate the musical style of the period in which the production is set; more often, sadly enough, perhaps, modern performances have gone for a bland, middle-of-the-road banality.[23] Oliver's well-crafted score seems to me to be playing a very intelligent game. His singers were unambiguously costumed in early seventeenth-century style, yet they sing in a musical vocabulary that, however one anatomizes its various elements, is clearly later than their dress. This establishes a productive gap between how his goddesses look and what they perform. The pastiche then becomes highly self-conscious—not a Poel-ish attempt at "authenticity" but a translation. Because the language is familiar, it enables an audience to respond directly and immediately to it; because it is archaic it establishes the necessary distinctiveness, the sense of alienness that I have argued is essential to, and appropriate for, the masque in this play. Neither quite "then" nor "now," this framed musical event, this explicitly time-bound quasi-opera, forms an entirely appropriate object for Prospero's instruction of Ferdinand in the evanescence of all art. Our sense of its irrevocable pastness coupled with the pleasure we have taken in its performance reinforces his melancholy message of inevitable dissolution.

The operatic solution of the problem of *The Tempest*'s masque is not, of course, the only one. That Oliver's score seems to me a particularly successful theatrical response to the difficulty of representing the betrothal masque before a modern audience is, ultimately, less important than the reflections it provokes on the often-neglected function of music in the performance and theatrical history of Shakespeare's plays. In particular, in the context of this congress, and of a seminar on Shakespeare and Opera, it suggests ways in which the cultural signification of "opera" as a genre is as significant to its theatrical effect as its musical creation of what Auden calls a "secondary world" is appropriate to the masque's generation within the play of a brief moment of paradisal stasis.

## Appendix: Shakespeare's text as adapted by Stephen Oliver

IRIS. Ceres, most bounteous lady, thy rich leas
Of wheat, rye, barley, vetches, oats and peas;
Thy turfy mountains, where live nibbling sheep,
And flat meads thatched with stover, them to keep;
Thy banks with pionèd, and twillèd brims
Which spongy April at thy hest betrims
To make cold nymphs chaste crowns; and thy broom-
groves,
Whose shadow the dismissèd bachelor loves,
Being lass-lorn; thy pole-clippèd vineyard,
And thy sea-marge, sterile and rocky-hard,
Where thou thy self dost air: the queen o'th'sky,
Whose wat'ry arch and messenger am I,
Bids thee leave these, and with her sovereign grace,
Here on this grass-plot, in this very place
To come and sport. Her peacocks fly amain.
Approach, rich Ceres, her to entertain.
                        *Enter* CERES
CERES.         Hail, many-coloured messenger, that ne'er
Dost disobey the wife of Jupiter;
Who, with thy saffron wings, upon my flowers
Diffusest honey drops, refreshing showers,
And with each end of thy blue bow dost crown
My bosky acres, and my unshrubbed down,
Rich scarf to my proud earth. Why hath thy queen
Summoned me hither, to this short-grazed green?
IRIS. A contract of true love to celebrate,
And some donation freely to estate
On the blest lovers.
CERES.         Tell me, heavenly bow,
If Venus or her son, as thou dost know,
Do now attend the queen? Since they did plot
The means that dusky Dis my daughter got,
Her and her blind boy's sandaled company
I have forsworn.
IRIS.         Of her society
Be not afraid. I met her deity
Cutting the clouds towards Paphos, and her son
Dove-drawn with her. Here thought they to have done
Some wanton charm upon this man and maid,
Whose vows are, that no bed-right shall be paid
Till Hymen's torch be lighted—but in vain.
Mars's hot minion is returned again;
Her waspish-headed son has broke his arrows,
Swears he will shoot no more, but play with sparrows,
And be a boy right out.
                        [*Juno descends*]
CERES.         Highest Queen of state,
Great Juno comes, I know her by her gait.
JUNO. How does my bounteous sister? Go with me
To bless this twain, that they may prosperous be,
And honoured in their issue.
[*singing*] Honour, riches, marriage-blessing,
Long continuance, and increasing,
Hourly joys be still upon you,
Juno sings her blessings on you.

IRIS. (Aria) Ceres, most bounteous lady,
the goddess of all this earth, thy rich leas,
thy turfy mountains,

thy banks
which April betrims
to make cold nymphs chaste crowns,
thy groves
whose shadow the dismissed bachelor loves,—

(recit) the queen of the sky
whose wat'ry arch and messenger am I
bids thee leave these, and with her sovereign grace

to come and sport. Her peacocks fly amain.
Approach, rich Ceres, her to entertain.

CERES. (Arioso) Hail, many-coloured messenger,
that ne'er dost disobey the wife of Jupiter,
who with thy saffron wings upon my flowers
diffusest honeydrops, refreshing showers,

rich scarf to my proud earth. Why hath thy queen
summoned me hither?
IRIS. (recit) A contract of true love to celebrate,
And some donation freely to estate
on the blest lovers.
CERES. (recit) Tell me,
if Venus or her son
do now attend the queen? Since they did plot
against my daughter,
her and her blind boy's scandalled company
I have forsworn.

IRIS. (Aria) Be not afraid of her. I met her deity
cutting the clouds toward Paphos, and her son
dove-drawn with her. Here they thought to have done
some wanton charm upon this man and maid,

but in vain.
Mar's hot minion is return'd again.

CERES & IRIS. Great Juno comes, highest queen of
state.
JUNO. (arioso) How does my beauteous sister? Go with
me to bless this twain, that they be
honoured in their issue.
(Aria) Honour, riches, marriage blessing,
Long continuance, and increasing.
Hourly joys be still upon you.
Juno sings her blessing on you.

[CERES.] [*singing*] Earth's increase, and foison plenty,
Barns and garners never empty,
Vines, with clust'ring bunches growing,
Plants, with goodly burden bowing;
Spring come to you at the farthest,
In the very end of harvest.
Scarcity and want shall shun you,
Ceres' blessing so is on you.

CERES. Earth's increase and foison plenty

Barns and garners never empty

Scarcity and want shall shun you
Ceres' blessing so is on you.
(with Juno—"Juno sings her blessing on you")
Trio: IRIS JUNO CERES. Spring come at the farthest
In the very end of harvest
Hourly joys be still upon you
Juno's blessing so is on you
Juno sings her blessing on you

FERDINAND. This is a most majestic vision, and
Harmonious charmingly. May I be bold
To think these spirits?
PROSPERO. Spirits, which by mine art
I have from their confines called to enact
My present fancies.
FERDINAND. Let me live here ever,
So rare a wondered father, and a wife,
Makes this place paradise.
*Juno and Ceres whisper, and send Iris on employment*
PROSPERO.          Sweet now, silence.
Juno and Ceres whisper seriously,
There's something else to do. Hush, and be mute,
Or else our spell is marred.
IRIS. You nymphs called naiads of the windring
brooks,
With your sedged crowns, and ever-harmless looks,
Leave your crisp channels, and on this green land
Answer your summons, Juno does command.
Come, temperate nymphs, and help to celebrate
A contract of true love. Be not too late.
          *Enter certain nymphs*
You sun-burned sicklemen of August weary,
Come hither from the furrow, and be merry,
Make holiday; your rye-straw hats put on,
And these fresh nymphs encounter every one
In country footing.

*Enter certain reapers, properly habited. They join with
the nymphs in a graceful dance, towards the end
whereof Prospero starts suddenly and speaks*

JUNO. (recit) You nymphs, call'd Naiades, of the windring
brooks,

leave your crisp channels.
Answer your summons: Juno does command.
IRIS. (recit) Come temperate nymphs, and help to
celebrate a contract of true love.

CERES. (recit) You sunburnt sicklemen of August
weary,
come hither from the furrow and be merry
IRIS. Make holiday: your ryestraw hats put on
and these fresh nymphs encounter ev'ry one
in country footing. (CERES and JUNO join the last
phrase).

DANCE

Example 3

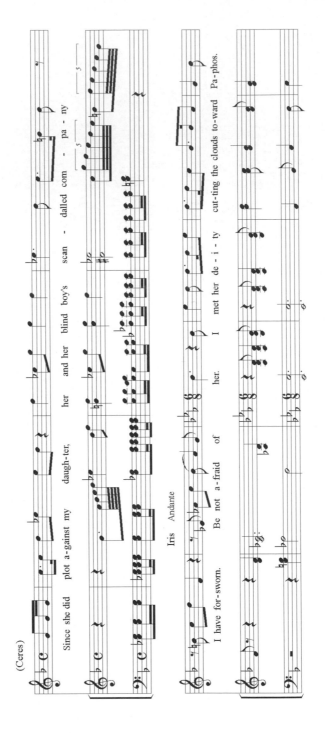

Example 4

# Notes

1. I am grateful to Stephen Oliver's family for kind permission to reproduce the musical quotations from the manuscript held at the Shakespeare Centre, Stratford-upon-Avon.

2. Gary Schmidgall, *Shakespeare and Opera* (New York: Oxford University Press, 1990), 280.

3. The conjecture that a dance called "The Tempest" in BL MS Add. 10,444 belongs to the play has generally been discounted by recent writers.

4. These songs are likely to have been used at early performances of the play, even if we do not know for certain that they were employed at its first performances in 1610/11.

5. For discussion of the relationship of Prospero's entertainment to the court masque, see Stephen Orgel, *The Illusion of Power* (Berkeley and Los Angeles: University of California Press, 1975); David Lindley, "Music, Masque, and Meaning in *The Tempest*," in *The Court Masque*, ed. Lindley (Manchester, England.: Manchester University Press, 1985); and introduction to *The Tempest* the New Cambridge Shakespeare edition of (Cambridge: Cambridge University Press, 2002), 13–18. I argue that Shakespeare intervenes in the debate between Jonson and Samuel Daniel about the possibility of the masque's exceeding its present moment.

6. Despite the fact that the First Folio (F) unambiguously prints "wise," I am convinced that the Second Folio (F2) emendation to "wife" is correct.

7. Irena Cholij, "'A Thousand Twangling Instruments'. Music and *The Tempest* on the Eighteenth-Century London Stage," *Shakespeare Survey* 51 (1998): 79–94.

8. *A Shakespeare Music Catalogue*, 5 vols., ed. Bryan N. S. Cooch and David Thatcher (Oxford: Clarendon Press, 1991) gives Percy M. Young's 1964 edition as the first of any part of Arne's Grand Masque.

9. Beerbohm Tree, *Shakespeare's Comedy, "The Tempest"* (London: J. Miles, 1904), 51–52. The text of this adaptation is available at http://www.leeds.ac.uk/english/staff/projects/treestempest.

10. Michael Dobson, "'Remember First to Possess His Books': The Appropriation of *The Tempest*, 1700–1800," *Shakespeare Survey* 43 (1991): 101.

11. For information on various forms the masque has taken, see Christine Dymkowski, ed., *"The Tempest": Shakespeare in Production* (Cambridge: Cambridge University Press, 2000), 298–99. Flops include Hytner's 1988 RSC production, where "Prospero conjures up busy little figures bearing black plastic hampers, and allows a soft-focus harvest to be projected onto the back of the stage. The rich and strange is briefly overtaken by the rich and kitsch" (Kate Kellaway, *Observer*, 30 July 1988); and Hall's 1974 NT production, which drew on the theatrical vocabulary of the Jacobean masque but was dominated by a "Juno whose [false] breasts are so enormous that whilst they are on the stage they absorb the attention to the exclusion of all else in fascinated horror" (Harold Hobson, *Sunday Times*, 10 March 1974).

12. *New Statesman*, 20 August 1982.

13. Charles Osborne, *Daily Telegraph*, 21 May 1988. It is curious, but revealing of the general temper of much stage history, that Warren's valuable detailed discussion of this production in *Staging Shakespeare's Late Plays* (Oxford: Clarendon Press, 1989) makes no mention of the music.

14. From the manuscript this seems to have been a second thought.

15. This is a not-infrequent device—interestingly varied in the current RSC touring production, where, to music of a rather different but no less impressive kind, there were no nymphs and reapers at all, but only Miranda and Ferdinand dancing.

16. W. H. Auden, *Secondary Worlds* (London: Faber and Faber, 1968), 91.

17. In her paper for this seminar, Marga Munkelt discussed critical responses to Samuel Barber's English-language operatic *Antony and Cleopatra*, noting that a number of reviewers wished it had been translated into Italian.

18. Eric Shorter in the *Daily Telegraph* (12 August 1982) complained.

19. *Guardian*, 12 August 1982.

20. *Financial Times*, 13 August 1982.

21. The music attributed to "Purcell" is now generally thought to be by Weldon.

22. In a brief conversation with me, however, Birtwistle indicated that he had had Dowland in mind.

23. I have tried to discuss some of these questions in my "Tempestuous Transformations," in *Translating Life: Studies in Transpositional Aesthetics*, ed. Shirley Chew and Alistair Stead (Liverpool: Liverpool University Press, 1999), 99–121.

# Northern Hamlet and Southern Othello?
# Irving, Salvini, and the Whirlwind of Passion

## Adrian Poole

IF YOU HAD BEEN WANDERING ROUND CENTRAL LONDON IN NOVEMBER 1874, your eye would have been caught by a poster for Bateman's Lyceum advertising the evening's fare: "A Fish out of Water. . . . Mr Irving in the Part of Hamlet." *Punch* thought the theater manager would do well to change the name of the farce that preceded Shakespeare on the bill.[1] (Its star, Mr. Compton, would later appear as the Gravedigger.) In the role of Hamlet, Henry Irving had never been less of a fish out of water. There were dissenting voices as always, and some of the praise was distinctly grudging: the *Saturday Review* thought him "much less disagreeable in Hamlet than he has ever been before."[2] But there was also widespread agreement that Irving was at last, at the age of thirty-six, in his element. Joseph Knight called his Hamlet "revolutionary";[3] a German witness hailed it as "the new Hamlet, the Hamlet of the future";[4] writing in the *Liverpool Town Crier,* the young Hall Caine spoke for many when he concluded that Irving will be "the leader of a school of actors now eagerly enlisting themselves under his name. His object will be—the triumph of *mental* over *physical* histrionic art."[5]

Tommaso Salvini *was* wandering round London the following spring, and he saw the posters advertising the seventy-second night of the Englishman's *Hamlet.* The Italian star was about to perform there for the first time the Shakespearean role he had made famously his own, on the Continent and more recently in the Americas, the Othello he had been playing for nearly twenty years. (Born in 1829, he was Irving's senior by nearly a decade.) He was also due to play Hamlet and "The Gladiator" (an Italian version of a popular French drama by Soumet). Salvini sneaked along to see Irving incognito, arriving too late for his scene with the ghost. By the end of the second act he had decided he would not play Hamlet in London. How could he compete with Irving's subtlety, with all his fine shades? But by the end of the next act he had changed his mind, for there was something missing in Irving "when the passion assumes a deeper hue."[6] Salvini could do the deeper hue, he thought, above all in *Othello*. There was little dissent from the overwhelmed London critics and audiences. "What a voice, what a style, what gentleness, what strength, what an astounding creation!" swooned Clement Scott.[7] The Drury Lane performances were greeted with an enthusiasm described by the *Times* as "one of the most extraordinary phenomena in the record of the modern London stage."[8] After seeing Salvini for a second time, G. H. Lewes noted that "Polly came home in a fever of excitement." George Eliot was not the only great novelist to acclaim him as a "genuinely great actor";[9] of the Othello he saw in Boston in 1883 and again in London the following year, Henry James averred that "No more complete picture of passion can have been given to the stage in our day."[10]

Irving's Hamlet and Salvini's Othello: comparison between them was unavoidable.[11] There was a consensus that together they were marking a significant historical juncture, and my concern is with the terms in which this consensus was framed. The *Times* believed that the interest in Salvini was closely connected with the revival of a taste for Shakespeare that Irving's Hamlet had fired after the comparative doldrums of the 1860s. The year 1875 also saw a couple of landmark publications: the *Reminiscences* of the leading English Shakespearean actor of the previous generation, W. C. Macready (who had died in 1873); and the collected essays *On Actors and the Art of Acting* by the finest English drama critic between Hazlitt and Shaw, George Henry Lewes, including a timely postscript on his "First Impressions of Salvini."[12]

The comparison between Irving and Salvini was sharpened by the fact that in 1875 Salvini overcame his momentary qualms to play Hamlet, while the following year Irving went on to play Othello. By March 1876 the Strand Theatre could put on a burlesque, *The Rival Othellos*, updating an earlier rivalry between Gustavus Brooke and Charles Fechter. And as if all this doubling were not enough, there arrived the same spring *another* Italian star prepared to play not only Hamlet but also King Lear and Romeo: Ernesto Rossi. He had not planned on giving London another Italian Othello, though he had been playing the role for as long as Salvini, but when his compatriot fell sick Rossi obligingly stepped in for him. But the Strand Theatre should really have gone one better with *The Rival Hamlets*, for this was the role on which the three actors most obviously converged. Frank A. Marshall prefaced his 1875 *Study of "Hamlet"* with a brief comparison. Rossi had not yet appeared in London, but Marshall had seen him in Paris, and he reported that the two great Italians were quite different in style and interpretation. His summary judgment was that "Salvini's interpretation was the most tender, Rossi's the most passionate, and Irving's the most intellectual."[13]

Foreign actors had played in London before, though they had not always been greeted with perfect courtesy. In 1848 a French company visiting

Drury Lane found themselves drowned by a pre-concerted tumult that drew the appalled Macready into controversy with his fellow professionals.[14] But twenty-five years or so later foreigners seemed to the English less of a menace, and the idea had even been broached that they might play our Shakespeare—to us. In 1856 Adelaide Ristori's Lady Macbeth had excited London audiences on the first of her seven visits to Britain, and in the 1860s Charles Fechter's Anglo-French and famously flaxen-haired Hamlet had been acclaimed.[15] So the moment, in the mid-1870s, must have seemed ripe enough for this Italian invasion. To a London audience it was flattering that our Shakespeare had mastered the imagination of these foreigners, and it was curious to see what they could—and could not—make of him. It was by turns exciting, disturbing, repellent, absurd. But this could all be true of our very own Irving.

*Punch* promptly hailed Salvini's Othello as the greatest of its time and "the highest expression of ideal tragic acting."[16] But within a little month (or two) his Hamlet had marked an impassable frontier: "All doubtless that an Italian can *conceive*, SALVINI can *be*; but to be SHAKESPEARE'S *Hamlet* is not, can never be, in his power. *Hamlet* is of the north, northern." *Punch* recalled Hazlitt's brave boast—"It is *we* who are *Hamlet*"—only to curtail it. Salvini had proved that this "we" did not include "men of the Latin race."[17] And so it was reiterated, endlessly: "The light that breaks over Hamlet can, indeed, scarcely be expected to come from the south"; Salvini had "not a jot of the Teuton in him."[18] As for poor Rossi, his main role in this discourse was to confirm the hardening consensus: "So essentially Northern in conception is 'Hamlet', it may be doubted whether a true notion of it can win its way into Spanish or Italian brains."[19] Thus Joseph Knight, throwing in the "Spanish" to toughen the visa restrictions. Rossi was moved to protest in a letter to the *Times* against these "ethnical" stereotypes. Surely Hamlet's temperament is "not more a product of Scandinavia than of Italy." Are there not, he pleaded, "vivacious Northerns and heavy apathetic Southerns?"[20]

Not everyone signed up to this racializing, protectionist position. G. H. Lewes freely admired Salvini's Hamlet, as did Robert Browning and the young William Poel. Salvini was himself understandably bullish about "the intention of Shakspere [*sic*] to render himself cosmopolitan."[21] The Italians encountered much less resistance to their alleged ethnical trespassing from American witnesses than from English, and the same was true for the Polish-born Helena Modjeska, of whom more anon. But then there are important questions about how such responses are first concerted and subsequently measured. In the middle decades of the century the astonishing Ira Aldridge enjoyed enormous success with his Othello touring round Britain and Ireland and across the Continent, from Hull to the imperial court at St. Petersburg and back again, but for most of his career he was effectively barred from London's West End (and never returned to his native America).[22] As regards Salvini's Hamlet, there were considerable differences between English and American reactions. On the first of his five tours to the latter in 1873–74, his passionate Hamlet initially received some severe reviews, especially in New York City, but it went on to command more widespread admiration than in England. By the time of his second tour in 1880–81 it could even elicit a favorable comparison with the dominant indigenous Hamlet of Edwin Booth: "Signor Salvini's Hamlet recalls the fire, spirit, and self-contained impersonation of Edwin Booth. . . . But the comparison ends there, for the American's art is cold in contrast with the warm, sun-land genius of the Italian."[23]

By the time of the third tour two years later (on which he did not play Hamlet), the ethnical issue posed by Salvini's impersonations had become familiar. There was the "racialist" position that saw some or all of Shakespeare's leading roles as impossible for players of non-English, Anglo-Saxon, or Teutonic origins. And there was the "internationalist" or "universalist" position, as expressed for example by the Jewish American poet, translator, and essayist Emma Lazarus, who wrote thus of Salvini's King Lear: "After every new Shaksperean [sic] interpretation offered by Salvini, a chorus of critics promptly exclaim against its non-Shaksperean inspiration, its essentially *Italian* quality. . . . It has always seemed to us a curious fact that any who speak the tongue of Shakspere should wish to rob him of his chief claim to immortality. There are those who insist upon his being insular and local, rather than comprehensive and universal; who resent as an impertinence the very suggestion that his genius may speak as clearly and as intimately to an Italian or a Frenchman as to an Anglo-Saxon."[24] Two years earlier her praise for his Macbeth included the emphasis that "Nothing of the Italian is visible in this tawny-bearded, tawny-haired, gigantic Thane." For this witness at least his ethnicity was not an unsurpassable issue; he could play Macbeth one night, "an embodiment of Saxon royalty," and the Gladiator the next, "a coarse Italian slave."[25]

But in the England of the last quarter of the nineteenth century such an enlightened position would have found few adherents. Americans had a different understanding of the opposition between the "North" and the "South"; their recent history had made it more than a figure of speech and they had good reasons for trying to put its bloody consequences behind them. English imaginations however were still being fueled by ideas of the cold Protestant North and warm Catholic South given such impetus earlier in the century by Goethe, Mme de Staël, and Byron. By the 1870s they had been affected by two particular developments that gave a deeper hue to this idea of difference. The first was the vigorous new interest in the "northern" origins of England's racial mix, in Anglo-Saxon, Teutonic, and Norse myth, language and history, and a corresponding enthusiasm for

what Charles Kean called the "homestead" of English history in the Middle Ages.[26] The second was the real history of the Italian Risorgimento
and the challenge to conventional English perceptions of contemporary
Italy as helpless, sensuous, feminized victim. As James Buzard sharply
puts it: "after the Risorgimento, the entire nation could be seen to undergo
what was for its visiting admirers a painful sex-change."[27] There is clearly
a sense in which for English audiences the magnificently masculine Salvini—who had fought with Garibaldi at the siege of Rome in 1848—
embodied the new Italy.[28]

So it is possible to discern the treacherously hospitable context into
which these London performances by Irving, Salvini, and Rossi would
have been received in the mid-1870s. The English refusal to admit the con-
ceivability of an Italian Hamlet must have been all the more galling for the
widely bruited commonplace that Hamlet was an easy part. Rossi insisted
on Hamlet's "universality," and the English could cheerfully agree, in
principle. In 1899 Clement Scott was roused to the usual thought that
"Shakespeare wrote for all men, all times, all ages, all nations. He is the
poet of humanity."[29] He might have added "all genders," given that it was
Sarah Bernhardt exciting him to this banality. Why, mused Scott, he had
seen German, French, Italian, English, American Hamlets, all "temperaments." On the spur of the moment the divine Sarah even made him express a supreme preference for "the French temperament." It was
generous of him to remember the Italian Hamlets in support of Shakespeare's theoretical universality, but as regards the real acclaim of English-
speaking audiences, they are the odd ones out from this list.

Othello was a different matter. There was general agreement that this
was a role as difficult as Hamlet was easy. Or rather, as this seemed rather
sharply to mean in the wake of Salvini's signal success, a role particularly
difficult for English or Anglo-Saxon or "Northern" actors. Lewes mentions Shylock alongside Othello as he makes this point, coupling together
the two great racial aliens in whom the Victorians took such an absorbing
interest.[30] But Shylock gave Irving one of his greatest triumphs, whereas
Othello was profoundly uncongenial to him. In this respect he was following the example of the actor who had most recently triumphed as Hamlet
on the English stage and failed as Othello, Charles Fechter. The *Athenaeum* noted that "Othello had not been a favourite with English exponents, happier always in presenting the sombre rage of Northern blood
than the fierce and burning passion of the South"; in the *Gentleman's
Magazine* "a Parisian Critic" asserted that "Signor Salvini's southern
blood serves him particularly well in the impersonation of the Moor."[31]
Many years later the myth of "southern blood" could help the actor
George R. Fosse explain why the role was so difficult for English actors,
and conclude that "the best Othellos have come to us from the south. Sal-

vini, Rossi, Grasso, Paul Robeson."[32] A remarkably elastic domain, it would seem.

So we can see a horde of binary oppositions queuing up to exploit the contrast between the two great fictional characters performed with such salience by Irving and Salvini. There is the North versus the South; the Teuton or Anglo-Saxon versus the Latin; there is the intellect, mind, spirit, restraint, gentility, refinement, inwardness, introversion, intensity, versus the senses, instincts, body, extravagance, animality, violence; there is conception (the writer's, the reader's, the witness's) versus execution (the actor's). These terms all recur in the service of making distinctions that confirm for English-speaking audiences that our Hamlet is as out of bounds for those Italians as that Othello is for us.[33] It would be easy to pile on the agony, exposing the structure of these dismally convenient dissociations. Reflecting on the way "genius" tends to concentrate itself in a single form of expression, W. B. Yeats recalls that Irving "never moved me but in the expression of intellectual pride," while Salvini, though he saw him only once, excelled in "a kind of animal nobility."[34] The contrast between Irving and Salvini assumes iconic force from the contrast between the characters they most memorably personate, and this helps to "prove" some comforting distances between northerners and southerners, the gentleman and the animal, and so on.

But the comfort of these conceptions depends on the discomfort of performance, its excitement and challenge and exposure, and it is this latter on which I want now to focus. Convenient as it was to insist on Irving's intellect and Salvini's physique, performance required an Irving who was more than all northern head just as it required a Salvini and Rossi more than all southern flesh and muscle. Again, we should observe a broad distinction between English and American responses. You would have been hard put to find an English counterpart to the enthusiasm with which Emma Lazarus applauded the "logical, scholarly, intellectual" interpretation she believed that Salvini brought to each part that he played, or to her claim that "The part of *Hamlet* reveals the purely intellectual and poetic side of Salvini's genius, and is therefore, to my mind, among all his creations, the noblest and loftiest."[35] Salvini himself saw the difficulty of the role in terms of a division between body and mind, and he was not above invoking ethnic differences to explain why Hamlet was still a student at such an advanced age: "In northern climates mental development does not always correspond with that of the body, and is often more slow." But he did not suppose that northern actors therefore had an advantage in seeking to portray Hamlet's particular balancing act: "it is equally necessary to have an audience of quick comprehension, and critics possessed of insight and appreciation."[36] We might lean on the word that Salvini himself uses to emphasize the point that performance entails several kinds of *correspondence*.

The Victorians were enthusiastic readers of "physique." Irving and Salvini were very different types. Both were tall (as Rossi was not), but Irving was angular, ascetic, slightly cadaverous. He had famously skinny legs, and the source of his power over audiences was focused in his face and hands. He had all sorts of mannerisms of gait and vocal delivery that provided detractors and mimics with an endless store of fun. "He sprawls in his walk and drawls in his talk," jeered Archer.[37] So how did he do it? Witnesses reach for the metaphors of mesmerism, magnetism, hypnotism, black magic, and Archer speaks of his "glittering eye," with conscious reference to the Ancient Mariner.[38] Irving encouraged his identification with a distinctively northern kind of (black) magic, through such roles as Vanderdecken, the Flying Dutchman, and Mephistopheles. As regards Hamlet himself, Irving's manager Bram Stoker takes up the hint from the source in Belleforest about the north being Satan's domain and the prince being skilled in necromancy, and suggests that the ghost at its second appearance was actively summoned by Irving's Hamlet.[39] But we have to remember that the impressionable Stoker also turned Irving into Dracula.

Where the sources of Irving's power in performance were mysterious, Salvini's were patent, even blatant. He was a fine figure of a man and he had a magnificent voice. Stanislavsky recalls his advice to a Russian actor who asked what a tragedian required. Three things, said Salvini: "voice, voice, and more voice!"[40] Lazarus was enraptured by it: "So extraordinary, indeed, is this organ, that some critics have ascribed to it alone the magnetic spell which he casts over his audience."[41] G. H. Lewes and many others testify to the beautiful force of Salvini's utterance. This was just as well, given that he always spoke in Italian, even when (later) surrounded by an English-speaking cast. In this respect he exactly complements Aldridge's practice across Europe when he played Othello and other Shakespearean roles in bilingual productions. For another kind of inverse instance that may throw some light back on Salvini, consider the hit made during the historic season played by the English actors in Paris in 1827, including "la belle Smidson" (a.k.a. Harriet Smithson, the object of Berlioz's passion). Alan Downer unkindly describes her as "an Irish actress with a thick brogue who had counted for little in London, but she captivated those whose ears were not very finely tuned to English speech and who may, in fact, have heard more music in her distortions than in the fine clarity of [Charles] Kemble's reading."[42]

Conversely, the English resistance to "foreign" Shakespeare should not go unnoticed. It was bluntly expressed by Dutton Cook when he opined that "To the foreign player, the Shakspearian [*sic*] drama is, in almost every instance, a sealed book." The actor prompting this rebuff was the

Polish-American Helena Modjeska (before Anglicization, "Modrzejew-ska"). Her Juliet had been much cried up in advance but it was not a great success with London audiences in 1881, and Cook for one thought that she murdered Shakespeare's English, reducing it "to a mere pulp, so to speak, of wrong emphasis, false accent, and mispronunciation."[43] At least Salvini did not make *that* mistake, to try playing in English. But the further terms of Cook's scorn are instructive. Modjeska was too much the modern woman for a Shakespeare heroine, "a clever woman of the world . . . who pertains much more to the Boulevards than to the bard of Avon." Cook berates her for her "skipping, ambling, skittish gait," and concludes that "she cannot reconcile the apparent inconsistency of Juliet's intensity of passion and innateness of purity."[44] There is a smack of Hamlet's censoriousness in this ("You jig and amble"), but there is also a memory of King Henry IV's fearful disdain when he invites his son to contemplate the example of the monarch they have displaced: "The skipping King, he ambled up and down."[45] What is calamitous about Modjeska's Juliet is its artfulness, its excessive self-consciousness: "Of the wild transport of sudden love, the intoxication of a first passion, no suggestions are forthcoming."[46] Doing "passion" was what these foreigners were supposed to be good at, but they needed to convince one that it was the real thing, "sudden" and "first," and when they failed, they were doubly culpable. As we shall see, this is the nub of the issue around which responses both to Salvini and to Irving congregate, the relations between art and passion.

Shakespeare might speak a "universal language" through the figure of Hamlet, but Salvini evidently drew on the universal language normally associated with nonverbal kinds of physical performance—musical, athletic, gymnastic, balletic. Edward Gordon Craig makes a daring attempt to recover for his beloved Irving the physical, musical grace denied him by his detractors and universally admired in Salvini. It was not that Irving lacked rhythm, Craig says, but that his critics could not perceive it. Irving did not speak badly—he *sang*; it was not that his gait was eccentric—he was *dancing*.[47] And if, like Archer and Shaw, you could not hear the melody and see the rhythm, it must be you who had no music in your self.

Craig is pointing to an important truth, not so much about Irving himself (about whose performance there can be no "truths") as about the terms on which any performance masters its witnesses (or fails to) before they know what they think of it, or think they think of it. I say "master" because the word indicates a problem about which writers on Irving and Salvini revealingly agree. One could never be entirely sure that Irving was in control of himself, of his legs and his voice: this was troubling, unnerving, exciting. One could always be sure that Salvini was in control of himself, of his immense physical and vocal force: this was exciting, unnerving, troubling. This sense of the actor's mastery is closely associated with an idea of manliness that encompasses both the force of self-control and the force that needs to *be* controlled, both the (northern) gentleman and the (southern) animal. This is why Irving made such unforgettable viewing. If he seemed obviously deficient in physical presence (those legs), he was also deficient in self-control, so that this double under-endowment created a perpetual sense of risk and unpredictability. Who knew what was pent up inside him, what was going to explode, to escape from him next? Salvini made unforgettable viewing for the comparably opposite reasons. Where Irving was all diffidence, both of physical presence and the hidden powers that lurk behind it, then Salvini was all justified confidence. It is tempting to transfer to Salvini the fine thing Keats says of the last English actor to make a great Othello before the role became so allegedly "difficult." At the moment when Edmund Kean utters the words, "Put up your bright swords or the dew will rust them [*sic*]," Keats wrote, "we feel that his throat had commanded where swords were as thick as reeds. From eternal risk he speaks as though his body were unassailable."[48] What Irving and Salvini converge on—from opposite points of the compass—is the question of "mastery." Irving approaches it from a state of deficiency, Salvini from one of excess.

The later Victorians took keen interest in Diderot's "paradox" about the role of the actor's intellect in the expression of the emotions.[49] They also had frequent recourse to the scene where Hamlet issues advice to the players, and writers often turn to this when they praise Salvini. Here is *Punch* hailing Salvini as "a great artist, in the ideal sense of the word—one whose art 'in the very storm and whirlwind of his passion, can beget a temperance that gives it smoothness.'"[50] Modern English actors found it hard to manage the whirlwind of passion. Dutton Cook thought they had become accustomed to a style of playing that was "easy, colloquial, and familiar, even to the verge of vulgarity." This made Iago an easy role but it put the great tragic roles beyond their reach, and this was more true of Othello than of any other. Reviewing the *Othello* of 1881 in which Booth and Irving alternated Iago and the title role, Cook lamented that "the stage of to-day knows little of the torrent, tempest, and whirlwind of tragic passion."[51] Cook discounted Salvini because of the language barrier, but he was in the minority. More representative was Joseph Knight, who like many others thought Salvini supremely impressive in the scene where he suddenly rounds on Iago, and then suddenly restrains himself. The key to it was the moment, Lewes said, when "the *gentleman* masters the *animal*."[52] Knight is describing the passage just after Othello has said farewell to his "occupation": "When the voice of Iago breaks the thread of his reflections, the animal nature springs to assert itself. Seizing fiercely Iago by the throat, he crushes the cowering miscreant to the ground, and in the whirlwind of his passion lifts his foot to stamp the heel upon his head, it might even be to stamp out his brains. Recalled, however, to reason, he turns away, and with averted head he stretches out his hand, and penitently, yet with a species of loathing, raises the prostrate wretch from the ground."[53] " Recalled to reason": it is telling that Knight should recall Hamlet's "whirlwind of passion" at just this moment, as if Othello were being recalled to the Hamlet in himself.

Or is it Salvini? The difficulty of distinguishing between Othello and Salvini gets witnesses excited and doubles their admiration for the mastery—both of character and of actor. By contrast Knight found himself complaining of Irving's Macbeth that it lacked exactly this masculine control: "His mourning and complaining are less than manly, and his mental struggles are those of a commonplace nature. . . . Macbeth's language in presence of the ghost of Banquo exhibits as much anger as fear. It is throughout that of a soldier ashamed of the tremors which he cannot command. In the very whirlwind of his fear he couples with words of defiance his protests against the unexpected species of torture to which he is exposed. To abandon this view is to lose sight of the character." In Irving's performance there was "not a point," he concluded, "at which the character is adequately masculine."[54] But what constitutes adequate masculinity for Hamlet, both the player and the character? That was something Irving *could* manage, it seems, a relation between manliness and whirlwinds very different from Macbeth's. Witnesses testify that one of the unforgettable moments in Irving's Hamlet was the end of the play scene. Bram Stoker recalls, "His whirlwind of passion at the close of the play scene which, night after night, stirred the whole audience to frenzied cheers."[55]

It is revealing then to find this same *Hamlet* allusion being used in support of a hostile response to what is perceived as the *excessive* mastery of the actor's art. Here is the *Saturday Review* accusing Salvini of cold-blooded artfulness, as if the actor were an Iago inside the character Othello: "Signor Salvini possesses great vigour, a fine presence, and a magnificent voice. His conception of Othello is at once improbable and revolting. Of true emotion he has little; and of unconsciousness of self, nothing. In the very torrent, tempest, and whirlwind of passion he ever seems to be thinking of what effect he will produce."[56] When Salvini played Hamlet two months later, the charge was repeated, specifically prompted by the scene with Ophelia, when "the appearance of cold-blooded self-command which disfigures the performance of Hamlet throughout is especially out of place."[57] So passionate, these foreigners, *and* so calculating. A few years later, on the legendary visit of the Comédie Française, Sarah Bernhardt's Phèdre provoked a similar response from Joseph Knight. It was something of a nineteenth-century commonplace to see Phèdre as the female equivalent to Othello. Thus Lewes, for instance, who describes Rachel's Phèdre as the French counterpart to Kean's

Othello.[58] In the famous third Act Phèdre is accusing herself of surrendering to passion and simultaneously seeking to seduce Hippolyte. Knight comments: "While . . . she exhausts herself in invective against herself for her crime, she is, in fact, in the very whirlwind of her passion studying, like a second Delilah, 'His virtue or weakness which way to assail.'"[59] We can see the allusion to Hamlet's "whirlwind of passion" recurring in anxieties about the duplicities entailed by performance—anxieties in which the distinction between actor and role become blurred. Too much self-command, too much art, or not enough? So hard to get it just right, all the time, every time, mastering every single witness.

These scenes in *Othello* (with Iago) and *Hamlet* (with Ophelia) are two of those to which the reviewers were most frequently drawn. We should add to them, in the case of Irving's *Hamlet*, the confrontation with the other woman in his life, his mother, and in the case of Salvini's *Othello* the final murder and suicide. All four are scenes of domestic violence, and they were clearly the moments in performance that touched the most intimate nerves.[60] Why these scenes in particular? All four of the "great" tragedies combine elements of the familiar and the strange: the domestic, home, family, "love," all that is "in here"; as against the barbaric, elemental, exotic, "passion," all that is—or we would like to think of as—"out there." Irving's *Hamlet* was firmly domesticating; his acting text excludes all reference to a world outside Denmark.[61] He aimed at the "lovability" that was a key element in the nineteenth century's conception of the character from Goethe onwards, and he passed this emphasis on to his heir in the role, the more aggressively cheerful and "English" Johnston Forbes-Robertson. Stoker recalls a typical Irving touch in the final scene involving a pretty cupbearer. Setting aside the poisoned goblet, Irving smiled at the child and "passed his hand caressingly over the golden hair."[62] But it was of course in the relationship with Ophelia—more emphatically after 1878, when Ellen Terry took over the Role—that the "love-interest" was concentrated, so much so that he was "accused of turning the play into a 'love poem.'"[63]

No one thought of calling the Italians "lovable." They were too thrillingly overt for that and the passion was disturbingly sustained. Irving could be scary out of what seemed like suppressed fear and guilt, but the Italians were far more simply extrovert, more fearsome than fearful. Of the four "great" tragic roles, it was only Hamlet in which Irving satisfied. He could turn it into a "character" part, as he could with Richard III, Shylock, and Iago, because he could find in them so much of the familiar and domestic. In Macbeth, Lear, and Othello, he could not. These required an "animal" force (it is the word on which Lewes insists) or a "whirlwind of passion" that put the familiar under much more pressure, or even overwhelmed it. Irving's passion came only in spasms, violent eruptions violently repressed. It was the uncertain control of his hidden resources that made him alarming. No wonder he favored such fitful stage lighting. With the Italians the violence was exposed to the broad light of day, and this was at once more satisfying and more disturbing. It explains why the moment when Salvini/Othello came close to Irving/Hamlet was so particularly admired. It was the moment when the whirlwind of Othello's passion was abruptly restrained by the Hamlet in him, the gentleman.

There is a further turn to this line of thought about domesticity and strangers. Irving's success was founded on the Lyceum, on the loyalty he won from its staff, company, and audiences. Salvini never enjoyed a theater of his own such as this, and no regular company for long. He was constantly on the move, a guest in other theaters, other lands, amid other languages, an extravagant and wheeling stranger. Irving toured too, of course, round Britain and North America, but he was never such an outsider, never outside his own language. For the long triumphant phase of his career, after the hesitant provincial beginnings and before the sad last years when he lost control of his Lyceum home, Irving was *chez soi*, head of the family, the lord and master who could afford to draw so daringly on his own insufficiencies.

There is then a real historical significance in the conjunction of these two star actors and their two great roles, their acting styles, and their kinds of theater. It is a key moment in the development of new kinds of international exchange. There is a limited sense in which Irving and Salvini met as equals in London in 1875, when both enjoyed wide public acclaim. Irving held a dinner in honor of the distinguished Italian guest. (He would also in due course have a signed photograph of Rossi on the wall of his living room.) But in most respects there was no real parity, for Irving had no need or incentive to perform in Italy. In the end it is not the fact that for his English audiences Salvini remained an exotic stranger that is cause for lament. Strangers should be welcomed, whether to stay and settle or to come and go. It is the force of Salvini's identification with a single, singular role that is dispiriting and even ominous. It is not the Italian Othello the English should have celebrated but the Italian Hamlet, the performances that rubbed against the grain of ethnical stereotypes and preconceptions. This is why poor Rossi's protest deserves to be remembered and honored.

Let me close with a glance at two other comparisons that bear on the one I have sketched. There is a diabolic Hamlet within *Othello* and his name is Iago. Irving was as brilliant an Iago as he was a hopeless Othello; so too was his American counterpart Edwin Booth, with whom he alternated the roles in 1881.[64] Virginia Mason Vaughan has written well on the "dissociation of intellect" promoted by the contrasting successes of Salvini's Othello and Irving's Iago.[65] My reading of this dissociation has followed her logic beyond the bounds of the single play. Another signal opposition is the one proposed by R. A. Foakes between *Hamlet* and *King Lear*—both characters and plays—when he meditates on the shifting identification of Shakespeare's "greatest" play.[66] Foakes is concerned with the altering paradigms that serve to distance if not to dissociate "us" from "them" across the last two centuries. It is a persuasive case. But if *King Lear* provides one kind of contrast to *Hamlet*, then I am suggesting that *Othello* provides another, that this complementarity came to particular prominence in the last quarter of the nineteenth century, and that its form and pressure were given to the very age and body of the time by Irving and Salvini.

# Notes

For their invitation to contribute this paper to the seminar on "Shakespeare's Nineteenth-Century Performers," I must thank Gail Marshall and Mariangela Tempera; and for the stimulus of their papers and subsequent discussion I must thank the other contributors: Nicholas Clary, Patricia Kennan, Krystyna Kujawinska-Courtney, Lisa Merrill, Robert Sawyer, and Isabelle Schwartz-Gastine.

1. *Punch*, 14 November 1874, 209.

2. *Saturday Review*, 7 November 1874, 604.

3. *Athenaeum*, 7 November 1874, 617; reprinted in Joseph Knight, *Theatrical Notes* (London: Lawrence & Bullen, 1893), 6.

4. *Times* (London), 18 January 1875.

5. Quoted by Bram Stoker, *Personal Reminiscences of Henry Irving*, 2 vols. (London: William Heinemann, 1906), 2:116.

6. Tommaso Salvini, *Leaves from the Autobiography of Tommaso Salvini* (London: T. Fisher Unwin, 1893), 166.

7. Clement Scott, *The Drama of Yesterday & To-Day*, 2 vols. (London: Macmillan & Co., 1899), 1:463.

8. *Times*, 4 June 1875.

9. *The George Eliot Letters*, ed. Gordon S. Haight, vol. 6 (New Haven: Yale University Press, 1954), 6:142, 147.

10. Henry James, *The Scenic Art: Notes on Acting and the Drama, 1872–1901*, ed. Allan Wade (London: Rupert Hart-Davies, 1949), 173. For a searching account of the impact of Salvini's Othello on the Anglo-American imagination, see Shaul Bassi, "Heroes of Two Worlds: Tommaso Salvini, Henry James, and Othello's Ethnicity," in *Shakespeare in Italy*, ed. Holger Klein and Michele Marrapodi, Shakespeare Yearbook, vol. 10 (Lewiston, N.Y.: Edwin Mellen Press, 1999), 38–69.

11. My argument and its supporting evidence draw primarily on the London performances of 1874–75. Irving continued to play Hamlet until 1885, notably in the revival with which he opened his own management of the Lyceum and began his long partnership with Ellen Terry at the end of 1878. Salvini played Othello for much longer: he began touring his signature role in 1856 in Paris, and it was the only Shakespearean role he played on his fifth and final North American tour of 1889–90. Marvin Carlson says of his London performances in 1884 that they never rekindled the enthusiasm of 1875 (*The Italian Shakespearians: Performances by*

*Ristori, Salvini, and Rossi in England and America* [Washington, D. C.: Folger Shakespeare Library, 1985], 56). For a convenient account of Salvini's Othello, see Marvin Rosenberg, *The Masks of "Othello"* (Berkeley and Los Angeles: University of California Press, 1961), 102–19.

12. William Charles Macready, *Reminiscences and Selections from his Diary and Letters*, ed. Sir Frederick Pollock, 2 vols. (London: Macmillan & Co., 1875); George Henry Lewes, *On Actors and the Art of Acting* (London: Smith, Elder, & Co., 1875). For the suggestion that George Eliot's *Daniel Deronda* (1876) may represent "a monumental expansion of Lewes's project in his essay on Salvini," see Joseph Litvak, *Caught in the Act: Theatricality in the Nineteenth-Century English Novel* (Berkeley and Los Angeles: University of California Press, 1992), 154–59.

13. Frank A. Marshall, *A Study of "Hamlet"* (London: Longmans, Green, & Co., 1875), x.

14. Alan S. Downer, *The Eminent Tragedian: William Charles Macready* (Cambridge: Harvard University Press, 1966), 278–79.

15. For Ristori, see Carlson, *Italian Shakespearians*, and Kenneth Richards, "Shakespeare and the Italian Players in Victorian London," in *Shakespeare and the Victorian Stage*, ed. Richard Foulkes (Cambridge: Cambridge University Press, 1986), 240–54. For Fechter, see John A. Mills, "The Modesty of Nature: Charles Fechter's *Hamlet*," *Theatre Survey* 15, no. 1 (May 1974): 59–78. Fechter's first language was French, though his father was German and his mother was English.

16. "A Salvo to Salvini," *Punch*, 24 April 1875, 181.

17. "Punch at the Play," *Punch*, 12 June 1875, 255.

18. *Athenaeum*, 5 June 1875, 762; *Academy*, 5 June 1875, 595.

19. *Athenaeum*, 29 April 1876, 609.

20. Ernesto Rossi, Letter to the Editor, *Times* (London), 9 May 1876.

21. Tommaso Salvini, "Impressions of Some Shaksperean Characters," *Century Magazine* (November 1881): 118.

22. Aldridge made his Covent Garden debut in 1833 (replacing the dying Edmund Kean), but he did not play in the West End again until 1865, shortly before his own death on tour in Poland in 1867. See Herbert Marshall and Mildred Stock, *Ira Aldridge: The Negro Tragedian* (London: Rockliff, 1958).

23. *New York Times*, 18 December 1880. I owe this particular reference and a general debt to Nicholas Clary's instructive paper for the seminar indicated at the head of these notes, "Tommaso Salvini and the Internationalization of *Hamlet*."

24. Emma Lazarus, "Salvini's 'King Lear,'" *Century Magazine*, (May 1883, 91. This significant writer is represented (and this review partly re-printed) in Ann Thompson and Sasha Roberts, eds., *Women Reading Shakespeare, 1660–1900: An Anthology of Criticism* (Manchester: Manchester University Press, 1997), 157–59.

25. Emma Lazarus, "Tommaso Salvini," *Century Magazine*, November 1881, 116. Compare the German reviewer in the *Prussische Zeitung* on Aldridge's Macbeth on his first Continental tour of 1852–55, quoted in Marshall and Stock, *Aldridge*, 182: "I was afraid that this hot-blooded son of the tropics could not cope with the galvanic, the metaphysical, fantastic and ghostlike in the first two acts of *Macbeth*, which was so Nordic; . . . but with every scene I felt growing in me, to my surprise, the conviction that this original genius is equal to everything."

26. See Richard W. Schoch, *Shakespeare's Victorian Stage: Performing History in the Theatre of Charles Kean* (Cambridge: Cambridge University Press, 1998), 113–39.

27. James Buzard, *The Beaten Track: European Tourism, Literature, and the Ways to Culture, 1800–1918* (Oxford: Clarendon Press, 1993), 133.

28. That England and Italy of course have their own "North" and "South"—recall the title of Elizabeth Gaskell's 1855 novel—is a matter of continuing political urgency.

29. Clement Scott, *Some Notable Hamlets of the Present Time* (London: Greening & Co., 1900), 43.

30. Lewes, *Actors and Acting*, ix.

31. *Athenaeum*, 10 April 1875, 497, reprinted in Knight, *Theatrical Notes*, 23; "Mr. Irving and Signor Salvini," *Gentleman's Magazine*, May 1875, 617.

32. George R. Fosse, *What the Author Meant* (London: Oxford University Press, 1932), 78, quoted in Virginia Mason Vaughan, *"Othello": A Contextual History* (Cambridge: Cambridge University Press, 1994), 179. Giovanni Grasso was a Sicilian actor who brought his sensational Othello to London in 1911. J. C. Trewin tells us that Grasso generated "a terrifying fury. He caught Iago by the throat and flung him to the floor; he collapsed in a convulsion of rage; he had a frantic outburst before the epilepsy; and he died with a hideous death-rattle"; *Shakespeare on the English Stage, 1900–1964* (London: Barrie and Rockliff, 1964), 44.

33. For continuing expectations about the predominance in Othello of physical over mental attributes, see these comments by Errol Hill on his own experience of playing the role professionally for the first time in Dartmouth in 1969. The reviewers caviled, he says, at "a tendency to make Othello too intellectual in the early scenes. This resulted from a conscious effort on my part to avoid the conventional image of the noble savage"; *Shakespeare in Sable: A History of Black Shakespearean Actors* (Amherst: University of Massachusetts Press, 1984), xxxv.

34. W. B. Yeats, *Autobiographies* (London: Macmillan, 1955), 125.

35. Lazarus, "Tommaso Salvini," 113, 115.

36. Salvini, "Impressions," 120–21.

37. William Archer, *Henry Irving: Actor and Manager: A Critical Study*, 2d ed. (London: Leadenhalle Presse, 1883), 70.

38. Archer, *Irving*, 46.

39. Stoker, *Reminiscences*, 1:76.

40. Constantin Stanislavsky, *My Life in Art*, trans. J. J. Robbins (1924; London: Methuen, 1980), 276.

41. Lazarus, "Tommaso Salvini," 111.

42. Downer, *Eminent Tragedian*, 113.

43. Dutton Cook, *Nights at the Play: A View of the English Stage*, 2 vols. (London: Chatto & Windus, 1883), 2:311, 313.

44. Cook, *Nights at the Play*, 312.

45. *Hamlet* 3.1.144, *1 Henry IV* 3.2.60.

46. Cook, *Nights at the Play*, 312. For a sustained retort on behalf of Modjeska, see the recent novel based on her career by Susan Sontag, *In America* (New York: Farrar, Straus, and Giroux, 2000). Of her temperate reception in England, Sontag has her leading actor conclude, "She was praised, but not embraced. Unlike Americans, the English didn't know what to do with questing foreigners (Allowing them to become English was not an option)" (341).

47. Edward Gordon Craig, *Henry Irving* (London: J. M. Dent and Sons, 1930), 76.

48. *Champion*, 21 December 1817, quoted in introduction to *"Othello": Shakespeare in Performance*, ed. Julie Hankey (Bristol: Bristol Classical Press, 1987), 59.

49. For Irving's own contributions, see his prefaces to Talma's *On the Actor's*

*Art* (1871) and Diderot's *The Paradox of Acting* (1883), in *Sir Henry Irving: Theatre, Culture and Society: Essays, Addresses and Lectures*, ed. Jeffrey Richards (Keele: Keele University Press, 1994), 29–30, 31–35.

50. "A Salvo to Salvini," *Punch*, 24 April 1875, 181.

51. Cook, *Nights at the Play*, 2:318.

52. Lewes, *Actors and Acting*, 269.

53. *Athenaeum*, 10 April 1875, 497; reprinted in Knight, *Theatrical Notes*, 23. This review can be conveniently consulted in Stanley Wells, ed., *Shakespeare in the Theatre: An Anthology of Criticism* (Oxford: Oxford University Press, 2000), 112–17.

54. *Athenaeum*, 18 September 1875, 740; reprinted in Knight, *Theatrical Notes*, 68.

55. Stoker, *Reminiscences*, 1:77.

56. *Saturday Review*, 39 (10 April 1875): 476.

57. *Saturday Review*, 39 (5 June 1875): 724.

58. Lewes, *Actors and Acting*, 27.

59. *Athenaeum*, 7 June 1879, 448–49; reprinted in Knight, *Theatrical Notes*, 258.

60. The last scene of Salvini's *Othello* was particularly controversial. The critics invariably expressed their repugnance, but the scene has a long history of arousing conflicting and ambivalent responses, as James Siemon has demonstrated; "'Nay, that's not next': *Othello* V.ii in Performance, 1760–1900," *Shakespeare Quarterly* 37, no. 1 (Spring 1986): 38–51.

61. See Alan Hughes, *Henry Irving, Shakespearean* (Cambridge: Cambridge University Press, 1981), 30.

62. Stoker, *Reminiscences*, 1:76.

63. Hughes, *Irving*, 55.

64. Salvini also played with Booth on his fourth American tour of 1885–86, but without alternation; he played Othello to Booth's Iago for nine performances, and the Ghost to Booth's Hamlet for three (Carlson, *Italian Shakespearians*, 57).

65. Virginia Mason Vaughan, "Salvini, Irving, and the Dissociation of Intellect," in *"Othello,"* 158–80.

66. R. A. Foakes, *Hamlet versus Lear: Cultural Politics and Shakespeare's Art* (Cambridge: Cambridge University Press, 1993).

# Part Two
## Textualities

# Self-Consistency in Montaigne and Shakespeare

### Robert Ellrodt

Revisiting "Shakespeare's reading," Robert Miola observes that readers in the new millennium, when alerted to influence, are likely to look "beyond the narrow range of texts indicated by the evidence of verbal echo," since "recent critical theory" has "shifted attention from the individual creative mind to the complex mix of factors—social, economic, political, and cultural—that go into the making of a text."[1] In my essay on "Self-consciousness in Montaigne and Shakespeare," I had already turned to a broader consideration of self-scrutiny as practiced by the French essayist and the English dramatist, and insisted on "the heightening of self-awareness as a process in which many minds were engaged by the end of the sixteenth century."[2] Yet I am not inclined to look on a text only as an "endless and bewitching array of intertexts."[3] Words and phrases, images and ideas, assembled in a literary work may be found elsewhere, but the "bewitching array" came into being through the operation of one mind. Since source-hunting is no longer the prime purpose, parallels may now be simply used either to demonstrate that "Montaigne and Shakespeare responded in similar ways to their reading," as Geoffrey Miles argues in *Shakespeare and the Constant Romans;*[4] or even to show that the essayist "is radically unlike the tragic Shakespeare," as Philip Davis concludes when studying the "Shaping of Shakespeare's Creative Thought."[5] Such parallels also enlighten our reading of the plays in books by Graham Bradshaw, Lars Engle, William Hamlin, and John Lee,[6] in several important articles,[7] and in papers prepared for the Shakespeare-Montaigne seminar.

The *Essays* are studded with peremptory statements harping on one theme: "*there is no constant existence, neither of our being, nor of the objects.*"[8] This rhapsody on all the forms of inconstancy, however, should not obscure Montaigne's genuine longing for a sober kind of constancy that would not exempt him "from perturbations of the mind, but moderate them" (1.12.48c; 1.59). Nor should it conceal his acknowledgment of a hidden order, his acceptance of customs, his recognition of values insusceptible of change, his observation of unvarying traits in himself, and the final emergence of his "essential form" out of the composition of his book.

"It is credible," Montaigne admitted, "that there be naturall lawes; as may be seene in other creatures, but in us they are lost," human reason "confounding and topsi-turving the visage of all things" (2.12.564–65b; 2.298). The contrast between man's "giddiness" and other creatures "tied to one sure state" was a commonplace, later echoed by George Herbert in "Giddinesse": "[Man] is twenty sev'rall men at least / Each sev'rall houre." Nature retains a permanence through its metamorphoses, but man "is by nature the being who has the power of disnaturing what he naturally is."[9] Nature is "an aenigmaticall poesie" (2.12.518c; 2.245), yet "*a gentle guide*" (3.13.1094b; 3.383), and Montaigne made his the ancient precept of the Stoics "That '*We cannot erre in following Nature*'" (3.12.1036–37b; 3.316).[10]

Despite the diversity of customs, some values proper to man are never questioned by Montaigne, whose "conscience was contented with it selfe; not of an Angels or a horses conscience, but as of a mans conscience" (3.2.784b; 3.25). He believed in loyalty,[11] truthfulness,[12] and benevolence.[13] Justice is said to be "in it selfe naturall and universall" (3.1.773b; 3.14), though the laws by which we are ruled are "a lively testimony of humane imbecility" (3.13.1047b; 3.328). Montaigne and Shakespeare had in common an abhorrence of cruelty[14]—whether man's inhumanity to man or the pangs suffered by the hunted deer or hare; nor could they admire "a martiall mind" in a child who takes pleasure in wring[ing] off a chickens necke" or mammocking a butterfly.[15] They both believed that "the rarer action is / In virtue than in vengeance."[16] They showed an acute awareness of injustice and a sympathy with suffering humanity. Barring recent political connotations, Montaigne might be said to display a "compassionate conservatism," extending compassion to those who suffer the death penalty (2.1.315a; 2.7; 3.4.811b; 3.54). He mainly found "rare vertue and exemplar goodnesse" among people of low birth,[17] and like the creator of Bottom he showed sympathy for the common man and "rude mechanicalls."[18]

Yet Shakespeare applied for a coat of arms in his father's name, and Montaigne, a magistrate, spoke of himself as belonging to the "old nobility"—"noblesse d'épée."[19] Apparently they both retained the reverence of their age for the heroic ideal while subjecting it to scrutiny. Montaigne praised the military profession (3.13.1075b; 3.361–62), yet declared military "valiancie" inferior to "another, true, perfect, and Philosophicall" vertue, Stoic constancy (362a; 2.63). Shakespeare usually exalted heroism, but could debunk it for comic purposes. The dramatist thought England had "long been mad and scarr'd herself" in the Wars of the Roses just as the "seigneur de Montaigne" denounced a "monstrous Warre" waged in France "inwardly and against her selfe."[20]

Montaigne and Shakespeare were only subversive inasmuch as they laid bare the artificial foundations of the social order. The essayist recognized that laws and customs are not universal but arbitrary and confined to a place or era,[21] but he thought it possible to have stable rules provided they were "the rarest, the simplest and most generall."[22] He was early praised by Samuel Daniel for having "made such bolde sallies upon / *Custome*, the mightie tyrant of the earth," but he only ascribed a "tyrannical countenance" to custom when it "force[d] the rules of Nature" (1.23.106a; 1.22.105). "Distasted with noveltie" (1.23.118b; 1.22.118–19), he later proclaimed that *"Onely change doth give forme to injustice, and scope to tyranny"* (3.9.935b; 3.198).[23] In the private sphere he had no objection to custom: "What is wanting to [my] custome, I hold it a defect" (3.10.987b; 3.261). Custom, as *"a second nature,"* can *"give our life what forme it pleaseth"* (3.13.1058; 3.340; cf. 3.13.1061b; 3.345). Hamlet, too, will remind Gertrude that "use almost can change the stamp of nature" (3.4.168). The minute account Montaigne gives of all the particulars of his way of life when growing old (3.3) discloses a general continuity. Custom, fortune, and nature become almost indistinguishable: *"By long custome, this forme is changed into substance, and Fortune into Nature"* (3.10.988b; 3.262).

Another element of stability was inborn. Montaigne, I admit, thought "the best of his corporall complexions" so "flexible" that he could momentarily leave his natural inclinations and "embrace the contrary" (3.13.1061b; 3.344), yet he found it difficult "to stray from them" (3.3.796b; 3.38), for "originall qualities are not grubd out" (3.2.788b; 3.29–30). He confessed his intellectual "volubilitie," but claimed that he had engendered "some constancy of opinions in [him] selfe" and "not so much altered [his] first and naturall ones" (2.12.533a; 2.284). "The most constant, and generall imaginations I have," he asserted, "are those, which . . . were borne with me" (2.17.641a; 2.385).[24] Thinking of his youth, he felt "in like circumstances, I should ever be the same" (3.33), found also his reason "to be the same" (3.35), and added, "I said so being young . . . and I say it againe" (3.37).

Montaigne often alluded to his complexion. He assumed that "a melancholy humor" "first put this humorous conceipt of writing into" his head (2.8.364a; 2.66), but it was bred by a special anxiety produced by the loss of a beloved friend. This melancholy was "a hatefull enemy to [his] naturall complexion" (ibid.), elsewhere defined as "betweene joviall and melancholy" (2.17.624b; 2.366). He often spoke in the plural of his "natural complexions":[25] their "commixture" gave its characteristic pliancy to his self. Besides, he thought a "stupid and insensible complexion" one of "the

better partes of [his] naturall condition" (2.37.738a; 2.492): "What I wish-
for, I commonly desire the same but mildely" (3.10.982b; 3.255). Owing
to this "priviledge of insensibility" he "engaged" himself with difficulty
(3.2.980b; 3.253), repeating the word: "I cannot so absolutely or so
deepely engage my selfe."[26] This inbred composure furthered the open-
mindedness, the abhorrence of all forms of intolerance—in religion, politics, and mores—displayed throughout the *Essays*.

Skepticism, and lately pragmatism, has provided a link between Montaigne's and Shakespeare's ways of thinking. Stanley Cavell's reading of
six plays in the light of Montaigne, [27] however, is challenged in the seminar paper of William Hamlin, who shows that the essayist, while promot-
ing "the avoidance of rash judgment," often abandons Pyrrhonian
"irresolution," not only in his "fideistic leap" but also in a reliance on
human reason as a criterion. Graham Bradshaw, in a more balanced view
of Shakespeare's skepticism, had defined it as an "interrogative perspec-
tivism," but acknowledged "the need to endow life with value and significance" as "an objective fact about human nature."[28] Lars Engle
discerns the same kind of "complex and socially specific explorations of
problems" in an essay by Montaigne or a play by Shakespeare, and calls
it pragmatism; that is, "a tendency to treat truth, knowledge, and certainty
as relatively stable goods," while rejecting any "fixed structure of fact,
truth, and knowledge."[29] The *Essays*, I agree, "allow thought experiments
to take their course," and frame "dual or multiple perspectives on characters and issues."[30] But this flexibility is reconcilable with the self-consistency, which is my present concern insofar as the various views or choices
adapted to different situations may be related to, if not dictated by, permanent inclinations. Montaigne's skepticism is extreme only when he echoes
theoretical assumptions on the impossibility of attaining any kind of
knowledge, but he rightly described himself as an "unpremeditated Philosopher and a casuall" (2.12.528c; 2.256). His own skepticism proved limited in its practical applications. Man has no knowledge of causes, but he
has a knowledge and use of things according to his needs and nature,
"without entering into their beginning and essence" (3.11.1003b; 3.278).

The three periods distinguished by Villey and retained by Miles—
conventional Neostoicism, a skeptical crisis, and finally a tolerant, Epicurean "philosophie de la nature"[31]—seem to overlap. The many additions
to the *Essays* at different periods were supposed to reveal an evolution, but
a close scrutiny shows that they either confirm earlier ideas or set them in
a slightly different light.[32] The author himself proclaimed, "I adde, but I
correct not. . . . My booke is alwaies one" (3.9.941c; 3.205). A statement
on the next page, "My selfe now, and my selfe anon, are indeede two," is
often quoted as a recognition of a plural self, but Montaigne here only
speaks of a change in the course of fifteen years, observing, "I doubt

whether I be encreased one inch in wisedome." Montaigne, of course, was aware that his opinions—as distinct from his fundamental inclinations— were changeable. But his relativism concerns man's apprehension of truth, rather than truth itself. He early acknowledged that "With our weaknes we corrupt and adulterate the very essence of truth (which is uniforme and constant)" (2.12.535a; 2.265). He recorded the opinions of the Academics who thought truth "in the deepest Abysses, where mans sight can no way enter"; and, with the Pyrrhonians, he even dismissed verisimilitude (2.12.544a; 2.275). Yet he constantly shows himself eager, if not "to establish truth," at least "to search for it," which might be a Pyrrhonian attitude, but he speaks as a Christian when asserting that "*wee are borne to quest and seeke after truth,*" though "*to possesse it belongs to a greater power*" (3.8.906b; 3.164), since "true and essentiall reason . . . lodgeth in Gods bosome" (2.12.523a; 2.251). Unlike the Stoics, he did not believe in universal consent (2.12.545a; 2.276); yet he thought himself endowed with a "capacitie of sifting out the truth."[33] He knew that he might find himself "convicted of a false opinion" (3.13.1051b; 3.333) and admitted his contradictions, yet claimed, "I may perhaps gaine-say my selfe, but truth (as *Demades* said), I never gaine-say" (3.2.782b; 3.23). This skeptic came to declare, "I cherish and I embrace truth, where and in whomsoever I find it" (3.8.902b; 3.160). Had he not believed in the possibility of attaining at least truth to himself, he could not have maintained that the *Essays* revealed his "essential form," a surprising statement.

In his essay "On the inconstancie of our actions," Montaigne, when observing contrarieties within his own nature, added, "All these I perceive in some measure or other to bee in mee, *according as I stirre or turne my selfe.*"[34] These contrasts had been observed by the Roman poets and moralists, but they were perceived only as a succession of moods and attitudes: here the various aspects of the self are embraced as if much depended on the observing gaze, "*selon que je me vire.*" Inconstancy is due to an ever-shifting point of view: "The blast of accidents doth not only remove me according to his inclination; for besides, I remove and trouble my selfe by the instability of my posture" (318–9b; 2.11). I have repeatedly called attention to this special kind of self-consciousness, first traced in Augustine and diversely displayed by Montaigne, John Donne, and several Metaphysical poets, as by Shakespeare's Hamlet.[35] This simultaneous apprehension of an experience and the experiencing self implied an "awareness of awareness" somehow akin to what Charles Taylor later called "radical reflexivity."[36] Its consequence was an elusiveness of identity, which anticipated modern forms of self-consciousness, from Hume to Amiel, from Amiel to Valéry or Sartre. But I have insisted on its different individual modes of operation in each author, a distinction blurred in a general notion of "reflexivity."

The first phase in Montaigne's exploration of the self did seem to lead to its dissolution: "We are all framed of flaps and patches and of so shapelesse and diverse a contexture, that every peece and every moment playeth its part" (2.1.321a; 2.14). That is why Antoine Compagnon assumed that like the Nominalists he looked upon the individual, Pierre or Guillaume, as "being but . . . an incomprehensible multiplicity of instantaneous subjects, a different 'I' each time there is a different *hic et nunc.*"[37] But this, I think, concerns the "self" rather than the "I," for, as in all later instances of self-analysis, this multiplicity and changeableness were observed by the constant gaze of a perceiving "I," and "inner eye," the ego.[38] This "I" is not the "I" of the enunciation, nor the Lacanian "I." It is both an awareness and a power, the power of directing one's attention, and choosing a point of view. It can deflect a tendency, alter an emotion. When held by a "violent imagination," Montaigne notes, "if I cannot substitute a contrary unto it, at least I present another unto it. . . . If I cannot buckle with it, I flie from it" (3.4.813b; 3.57; cf. 3.13.1092b; 3.381). This is a form of "self-managing" different from the full self-control he praised in Socrates and Cato but did not pretend to achieve (3.12.1014; 3.290). It seems to rest on a distinction Montaigne often makes between his soul and his own consciousness, a distinction Carol Clark, like Frame, found puzzling: "There are constant references in Montaigne to people doing things with or to their souls, just as they might be said to do things with or to their bodies."[39]

This view is consistent with the Freudian view of "the *Ich*, the conscious *I*, whose distinctive feature is the self-reflexivity that turns the very activity of the subject into an object, by position though not by nature." While retaining several levels—biological, psychological, and social—one may affirm "a certain unity of each individual psyche, at least as a common origin and binding coexistence of forces." Montaigne would have agreed that one should aim at "the unity which proceeds from a reflective representation of the self and from deliberate initiative."[40] His observing "eye-I" made the emergence of a constant-inconstant self possible. Geoffrey Miles has shown how the essayist associated "an ideal of consistent selfhood" with an acceptance of "diversity and mutability."[41] The contradictions noted by Montaigne are not in harmony with the Stoic ideal of "playing but one man," but they are reconcilable with a self-consistency understood as truth to the permanent impulses of one's own nature, however diverse they may be. Mere consistency belongs with the characters of classical comedy or Jonsonian humors.

When he says, "I write not my gests, but my selfe and my essence," Montaigne means that his interest is in the inner man, Hamlet's "that within" (2.6.359c; 2.60). But was he entitled to speak of a "Mistris forme" or "essentiall forme," which seems to imply a structured and unified personality? Rejecting uniformity, he delighted in the *"perpetuall variety of our natures shapes or formes"* (3.9.951b; 3.217) and in the union of "contraries" (3.3.1068b; 3.352). His self may be described as a "plural self," but only insofar as it implies a multiplicity of divergent impulses. His own awareness of this multiplicity is a characteristic feature of his self-consciousness, as it was of Augustine's, or even of Catullus's in his *odi et amo*.

The "form" Montaigne discerns in himself is never a transcendent Platonic form. It may be considered Aristotelian but often has a vaguer meaning.[42] It may define a condition, a way of behaving, a way of life (*"une forme de vie"*), or a way of speaking or writing (*"ma forme de parler,"* *"une forme d'escrire"*).[43] Yet it may prove stable: "My forme of life is ever alike, both in sicknesse and in health" (3.13.1057b; 3.340). In the opening address "to the Reader" (Florio 1.15), Montaigne pledges that his "naturall forme" will be discerned (*"ma forme naïfve,"* which meant native as well as natural). He may here echo the very words of Erasmus, reminding us that a painter can only convey *"vivam hominis speciem,"* whereas the inner man, *vera ac nativa hominis forma,*[44] is what matters most. In the essay "Of Repenting" he starts by acknowledging that he is *"bien mal formé"* (3.2.782b; 3.23), yet asserts that "There is no man that does not discover in himselfe a peculiar forme of his, a swaying forme, which wrestles against the institution, and against the tempest of passions, which are contrary unto him."[45] He is clearly implying that the "peculiar forme" of each individual resists the "reformation" that the "institution"—that is, education and society—seeks to impose on him. This "form" is closer to the Scotist haecceitas than to the Aristotelian entelechy, which he declares "as cold an invention as any other" (2.12.524a; 2.252).

The "peculiar forme" of Montaigne was apparently "flexible" like his complexion (3.13.1061b; 3.344), but he looked on "volubility and supplenesse" as a universal characteristic of the human mind (1.38.230a; 1.37.248). In his famous assertion, *"Every man beareth the whole stampe* ['la forme entiere'] *of humane condition"* (3.2.782b; 3.23–4), he does maintain that "humans possess an essence, however elusive of characterization";[46] but he may also suggest that he has imaginatively experienced whatever man can experience and succeeded in "totalizing in his own individual form all the forms of mankind."[47] When affirming his particularity, he stresses his singularity, not any strangeness.

The very flexibility of the inner form allows its control by the ego. Montaigne does not want to be "so addicted to his inclinations, as hee cannot stray from them, nor wrest them" (3.3.796b; 3.38). He found that he could "bend to the contrarie of [his] disposition" (3.10.991–2b; 3.265–66). There are many instances of his subtle self-mastery,[48] but he never claimed that his free will could thoroughly alter "the permanent content" of his self: he knew that "Naturall inclinations" do not change and are not easily overcome (3.2.788b; 3.29).[49] What this "self-managing" can achieve is a greater self-consistency. Starobinski has shown how Montaigne sought continuity and fixity through his identification with models in the history of mankind, yet found that the models contradicted each other.[50] Ultimately stability was attained through the writing of his *Essays*: "This publike declaration bindes me to keepe my selfe within my course" (3.9.958b; 3.225). This "register of my lives-Essayes" (3.13.1056b; 3.339) became "consubstantiall to his Author," though occasionally drawn "with purer and better colours" (2.18.648c; 2.392).

To reflect the life of his mind and his deeper self, the book had to be what Samuel Daniel long before modern critics described as "extracts of man; / Though in a troubled frame confus'dly set."[51] Yet a polyphonic orchestration holds the fragments together. Montaigne believed like Erasmus that "each mind has a peculiar face which his discourse must reflect as a mirror":[52] "All the world may know me by my booke, and my booke by me" (3.5.853b; 3.103); "my booke and my selfe march together, and keepe one pace" (3.2.783b; 3.24). Begun after the death of La Boétie with the sense of a dispossession of himself, this book, originally a surrogate friend, became a surrogate self.[53] The moral task of fixing his identity turned into an "artistic task,"[54] as in Shakespeare's *Sonnets*. And, as in the *Sonnets*, the engendering of the literary text became a substitute for engendering a whole lineage (2.8.383b; 2.87).

Turning from the essayist to Shakespeare, one may start from Montaigne's own "Apish and imitating condition" (3.5.853; 3.103). In his youth he had acted "the chiefest parts" in Latin tragedies (1.26.176; 1.25.189); he felt capable of entering a character different from his own, for he could "conceive a thousand manners of life" (1.37.225c; 1.36.243). This capacity, however, was largely confined to entering other people's thoughts with a tolerance of different opinions. He never was a dramatist,[55] though he showed an interest in drama unusual among magistrates, anticipating Prince Hamlet when he blamed those "that refuse good and honest Comedians . . . to enter our good townes" (1.26.177b–c; 1.25.190). When he notes that Comedians could be "so fare ingaged in a sorrowfull part, that they wept" (3.4.816c; 3.60), we think of Hamlet's remark on the tears in the eyes of the player acting Hecuba; but Montaigne was quoting an observation of Quintilian (*Institutio Oratoria* 6.1); Shakespeare may be indebted to Montaigne or Quintilian, or only speaking from experience.

I also refrain from ascribing Shakespeare's obsession with role playing to the influence of the essayist who had quoted the tag *"All the world doth practise stage-playing. Wee must play our parts duly"* (3.10.989b; 3.262).[56] For Montaigne it meant acting the part of "a borrowed personage"; he wanted to keep the "essential" self apart from the roles played in public life: "Of a visard and apparance, wee should not make a real essence. . . . The Maior of *Bourdeaux, and Michael* Lord of *Montaigne*, have ever been two, by an evident separation" (262–63). But when Antonio holds the world as "A stage, where every man must play a part, / And mine a sad one,"[57] there is no distinction between the social role and the inner life. The player-kings who "make [their] heaven to dream upon the crown" ( *3 Henry VI* 3.2.168) do not separate their inner selves from their kingship: they feel that losing their crown "they must nothing be" though they retain their griefs (*Richard II* 4.1.181–217). Does it mean that "acting" for Shakespeare could extend to the innermost longings of men as well as their actions? Perhaps. But it need not preclude some kind of sincerity and self-consistency. Roman actors consistently played the parts "fittest for themselves";[58] so did Elizabethan actors, and Shakespeare gave his *dramatis personae* "characters" appropriate to their roles in the play.

I can agree with Alan Sinfield when he claims that "characters" are only "textual arrangements which involve ideas about people,"[59] but the text when spoken and acted takes on a life of its own. Peter Brook, presenting his latest *Hamlet*, still assumes that "we have a keen desire to know this very special person."[60] The conventions of the Elizabethan stage were not an obstacle to this illusion. More damaging is the recent assumption that we hear several "voices" or "discourses" in a dramatic monologue.[61] The new critical interpretations, though subtle, take us back to the ancient apprehension of the passions as objective and warring forces within the individual.[62] The presentation of the inner debate in dialogue form, dominant in the Middle Ages, was gradually displaced in the Renaissance by a more subjective awareness, though there is no need to see Hamlet as "the decisive transitional moment" for its emergence.[63] To trace the ideology of a class, or social group, in the discourses of *dramatis personae* is legitimate, and I admit that these discourses at times do not build up a coherent personality. What I claim is that the play will only seem true to life when we hear a character speak with the same voice throughout, however rich and varied its inflexions may be. This is usually the case with Shakespeare, as with the author whose *Essays*, though interspersed with quotations and anecdotes, come to us through one voice, in one tone and temper, that of Michel de Montaigne.

Shakespeare could hardly doubt the unalterableness of fundamental dispositions acknowledged by the psychology of his age. He steered clear from a rigid application of it and probably believed like Montaigne that "Our being cannot subsist without this commixture" of contrary things (3.13.1068b; 3.353). Yet we are reminded that a man is what he is. "I should have been that I am, had the maidenl'est star in the firmament twinkled on my bastardizing," Edmund assures us (*King Lear* 1.2.131–33);

"Simply the thing I am / Shall make me live," assumes Parolles (*All's Well That Ends Well* 4.3.333–34), "I play the man I am," proclaims Coriolanus (3.2.15–16). In Sonnet 121 the poet himself states, "I am that I am" in self-justification. These assertions imply a sense of self-consistency. A distinction, however, must be drawn: some characters have only the kind of identity that "consists of the various functions a character acquires through participating in a number of social relationships."[64] For a parallel with Montaigne we must turn to those who, while fulfilling social roles, seem to act in an individual way. Since a full study would require a book, I chose Hamlet for obvious reasons.

As early as 1838 John Sterling saw the Prince of Denmark as "nearly a Montaigne" with "a somewhat more passionate structure of man."[65] This opinion has been echoed down to Harry Levin's *The Question of "Hamlet"* (1959).[66] An influence of Montaigne is possible, since Florio's translation was available to William Cornwallis when he wrote in 1600 (*Essays* 92): "I like nothing better in Montaigne than his desire of knowing Brutus' *private actions*," a desire obviously shared by Shakespeare. Catherine Belsey has described Hamlet as "the most discontinuous of Shakespeare's heroes,"[67] and Brian Vickers admits that there are "irreconcilable aspects" in his character.[68] Yet, in different ways, Harold Jenkins, Philip Edwards, and G. R. Hibbard in their editions of the play, John Lee in his exhaustive analysis, and psychoanalytical critics from Ernest Jones to Norman Holland, Arthur Kirsch, and Janet Adelman,[69] have offered complex but coherent interpretations.[70] In my present comment I shall stick to the text and refrain from any assumption about unmentioned experiences.

From the beginning of the play we hear that Hamlet is in a fit of melancholy, as Montaigne said he was when he started writing his essays (2.8.364a; 2.66). Hamlet's melancholy cannot be explained with reference *only* to Timothy Bright's treatise, but the many parallels traced by Harold Jenkins are incontrovertible.[71] With Hamlet as with Montaigne, this melancholy is not supposed to be a constant humor, since the Prince says, "I have *of late* . . . lost all my mirth, forgone all custom of exercises" (2.2.295–97). This mood had a definite cause: for Montaigne the death of a dear friend; for Hamlet his father's death and his mother's hasty remarriage. Burton found many references to the death of relatives as one of the chief causes of melancholy from antiquity.[72] Melancholy may at least partly account for the hero's recurrent death wish; death was also a constant preoccupation for Montaigne as the ultimate experience of identity.[73] Melancholy changes one's outlook upon the world:[74] Hamlet's dark view of the world, of society, of human nature, is the expression of a pessimism induced by special circumstances rather than an exposition of philosophical skepticism. When he says, "there is nothing either good or bad, but thinking makes it so" (2.2.249–50), he is explaining why Denmark now is to him a prison, not necessarily echoing the speculations of Montaigne in his essay, "That the taste of goods or evills doth greatly depend on the opinion we have of them."[75]

A melancholy man was expected to be given to "contemplations" and to be "not so apt for action."[76] Montaigne retired into his library; Hamlet intended to "go back to school in Wittenberg" (1.2.113). After the ghost's revelation, he feels bound to avenge his father, but he also feels unfitted for the role he has to play (1.5.188–89). To carry out his mission he adopts the common ruse of the avenger. His friends are warned of his decision to "put an antic disposition on" (1.5.172). It enables him to play many parts: the lunatic, the jester, the satirist. But these "actions that he [can] play" do not imply any change in "that within which passeth show" (1.2.85): the audience would know he was "essentially . . . not in madness / But mad in craft" (3.4.187–88).

This stratagem, I admit, cannot account for Hamlet's outrageous behavior toward Ophelia. But the son's love for his mother had suffered a sea-change when he imagined her "in the rank sweat of an enseamed bed" (3.4.92). Henceforth "Hamlet cannot talk to [Ophelia] in particular without thinking of women in general."[77] Even without resorting to an Oedipal interpretation, it is clear that sex, sullying the mother figure, now provokes the nausea also conspicuous in the ravings of Lear, the jealousy of Othello, or the loathing of lust in the Sonnet on "Th' expense of spirit in a waste of shame." Hamlet seeks to remake his mother "in the image of the Virgin Mother."[78] Despite Stanley Cavell's claims that Montaigne's "On Some Verses of Virgil's" influenced Shakespeare's views,[79] I fail to see any resemblance between a rabid revulsion from the physical aspects of sex and the calm, tolerant, yet temperate views of the French essayist for whom "*both male and female, are cast in one same mould*" (3.5.875b; 3.128) and unchastity is found excusable in either sex. Hamlet is obsessed by the sexual act seen as a breeding of "sinners" (3.1.121); Montaigne mentions original sin only once and looks on it as a sin of pride, unlinked to sensuality (2.12.467a–c; 2.186).

I have earlier stressed the immediacy of Hamlet's self-consciousness when, in a frenzied attempt to unpack his heart with words, he becomes ironically aware of his own ranting (2.2.582). He is self-conscious in the same way when parading his melancholy on his first appearance (1.2.76–86), or again parodying the emphatic expression of grief when he addresses Laertes over Ophelia's grave (5.1.254–58). Though more emotional than Montaigne, Hamlet is only capable of feeling by fits and outbursts (1.2.129; 1.5.92; 2.2.550; 3.2.390). He can be put "into a towering passion" (5.2.80), but he often has to whip himself into his emotions, as if he were conscious of acting.[80] This self-consciousness is responsible for his constant self-criticism. In their self-examination, both Montaigne and Hamlet find that "the best good [they have], hath some vicious taint."[81] They are both willing to "condemne and mislike [their] universall forme,"[82] but with a difference: Hamlet is incapable of Montaigne's serene acceptance of being "neither Angell nor *Cato*."[83] The secret of happiness according to Schopenhauer is not to wish oneself different.[84] Hamlet kept wishing himself different and, unlike the Shakespeare of Sonnet 29, could not find acquiescence in his own self through the love of another.

When the hero repeatedly charges himself with procrastination, we must remember that the melancholy man is "doubtful before, and long in deliberation."[85] Melancholy, however, is not the only cause for delay. Montaigne has confessed his "irresolution" in a striking way and declared it "a most incommodious defect in the negotiation of worldy affairs: I cannot resolve in matters admitting doubtfulnesse" (2.17.637a; 2.380). As a scholar "thinking . . . precisely on the event" (4.4.41) and distrusting his "imaginations" (3.2.83), Hamlet had to make sure that he was not abused by a "goblin damned" (1.4.41) or his own "melancholy" (2.2.602). The famous delays, or "deferrals," are accounted for by what is given in the text. When Hamlet's doubts are lifted, he seems ready to act, as he does when killing the overhearer behind the arras. But why did he put up his sword when he could have killed Claudius in prayer a moment before? Again he had been "thinking precisely": "That would be scanned" (3.3.75). In an age when many Christians thought that God wanted the reprobate to heap on himself damnation, the audience would not have been shocked by his wish to send the villain to hell. He is not seeking an excuse for a reluctance to kill a defenseless man at his prayers; he will have no such excuse for sending his former friends to death "not shriving-time allowed" (5.2.47). Hamlet himself had confessed he was "revengeful" (3.1.124). The Ghost had called for revenge, but he had mainly urged his son to put an end to usurpation and "damned incest" in the royal bed without tainting his own mind (1.5.81–85), which Hamlet does. The Prince had also declared himself "proud" (3.1.123), and he showed it when envenomed with envy of Laertes's fencing skill (4.7.103) and when he called upon Horatio to save his "wounded name" (5.2.344–49).

On his return to Denmark he is not "a second Hamlet," as some critics claim.[86] I admit that he is less anxious, but he shows the same inclination to discourse on death, the same obsession with the melting of "this too, too solid flesh," now imagined in "progress through the guts of a beggar."[87] He still declares himself "splenitive and rash" (5.1.261) and, in parodying the emphasis of Laertes's grief, he again ironically denounces the difference between the trappings of woe and "that within which passeth show" (cf. 5.1.254–58 and 1.2.76–86). He hardly mentions his father,[88] yet he alludes to his earlier "deep plots" (5.2.9) and tells Horatio that he is determined not "to let this canker of our nature [Claudius] come

In further evil," promising "It will be short" (5.2.63–70). Only his attitude has changed. The episode of the pirates has miraculously allowed him to be back at court; he therefore thinks he has just to wait for another opportunity offered him by providence: "There's a divinity that shapes our ends" (5.2.10–11). But this was the advice given by Montaigne to princes when they have to depart from their "ordinary duty": "When all is done . . . must wee often, as unto our last Anker and sole refuge, resigne the protection of our vessell unto the onely conduct of heaven" (3.1.779; 3.18). After killing Polonius, Hamlet already saw himself as "the scourge and minister" of Heaven (3.4.175). Horatio's call for flights of angels to sing the unshriven "sweet prince" to his rest (5.2.359–60) is morally questionable yet dramatically consistent, since Hamlet himself had thrice called upon "angels and ministers of grace" to defend him (1.4.39; 3.3.69; 3.4.103–4).

"At the centre of Hamlet," we are told, "there is, in short, nothing."[89] I could agree if it only meant that introspection may be self-defeated, that pure reflectivity cannot catch substance, only the "nothing" Amiel, Valéry, and Sartre diversely made evident.[90] Shakespeare's characters, however, were not meant to illustrate the workings of introspection, but to "hold, as 'twere, the mirror up to nature" (3.2.22). Notice the cautious phrasing in "as it were": mimesis is bound to be imperfect, but the aim is mimesis, which means that here the creation of a character whose "form" (Shakespeare here uses the word like Montaigne) must seem to be true. Questionable too is the "historical prematurity" of Hamlet's subjectivity.[91] John Lee argues that though "there is not in Hamlet, because there cannot be, direct evidence of the vocabulary of meaning of essentialist interiority," inward states existed and were expressed through metaphor.[92] The absence of a "vocabulary of interiority," however, should not be unduly stressed; from the early Renaissance states of mind were evoked and analyzed.[93]

Other similitudes between Hamlet and Montaigne might be traced. Both of them sought models: Montaigne in his friend La Boétie, then among the sages of antiquity; Hamlet in his friend Horatio, "more an antique Roman than a Dane" (5.2.341). Both needed to inscribe their experience in writing: Montaigne in his essays, Hamlet in his tables (1.5.107), then in his dying command to Horatio: "tell my story" (5.2.349). But a tragedy is not a self-portrait nor a psychological novel. *Hamlet* is a great tragedy because it offers action and language apt to stir emotion, enlarge the imagination, and tease our thoughts into wondering at the mystery of the human condition, the mystery of death and what may come after death, the mystery of fate or providence. Perhaps the mystery of self, but of this I am not so sure.

John Lee argues for a different Prince Hamlet in the Second Quarto and in the Folio.[94] The Quarto Prince insisted on personality as resulting from birth and on the part played by physiology. After the cuts, the Folio Prince's sense of "that within" and of his own "mystery" is said to be more dominant. The argument is persuasive, but too much is made, I think, of Hamlet's ironical remark about Guildenstern's attempt "to pluck out the heart of [his] mystery" (3.2.365–66); in context it may mean no more than pierce his real intentions. In none of his soliloquies is Hamlet intent on discovering his true self, his own "essence" or "form": he is concerned with "the uses of this world" and the ends of life, with the "ill . . . about [his] heart" and his doubts about what he should do, not what he is.

In a forthcoming edition of *King Lear* for the new Pléiade Shakespeare, I hope also to show that all the characters in the play are self-consistent despite their changes or impersonations. But I must now briefly turn to the *Sonnets*, since they alone can directly reveal the self-consistency of the speaker, who is generally assumed to be Shakespeare himself.[95]

In the *Sonnets*, as in the *Essays*, writing seems to become a way of preserving the identity of the friend and a close union with him. This was Montaigne's explicit aim concerning La Boétie.[96] In the *Sonnets*, the poet does not merely promise the young man a conventional immortality of fame: "thou in this shalt find thy monument" (Sonnet 107). The stress on the deictic, here as in other sonnets (18.14, 55.14, 74.14), calls attention to the perpetuation of the self of the beloved in the materiality of the sonnet sequence. Montaigne sought in his book more than the image of his friend: the image of himself he had lost when losing him.[97] Shakespeare, always in fear of losing his friend, and estranged from him at times, seems to look at his sonnets, "this" record of love and trust (present or lost), as enshrining a "presence"; the presence of the beloved and his own, and fusing their identities.

When he drops the "immortalizing" theme, Shakespeare often affects to devalue his writing;[98] so did Montaigne in speaking of his "galimafry" (3.13.1056b; 3.339). It is one more aspect of the self-criticism induced by self-consciousness, but this self-depreciation may have been for Montaigne a way of demonstrating his uniqueness;[99] for Shakespeare it was a means of asserting the sincerity of an unchanging love unchangingly expressed (Sonnet 76). In both cases it was, of course, partly ironical.

In their respective attitudes to time and transcendence, Montaigne and Shakespeare invite at once a parallel and a contrast. They had the same sense of ageing and being already near death in their thirties (1.20.82–83a; Florio 1.19.77), but the melancholy note of Sonnets 63 and 73 is not heard in the *Essays*. The author of the *Sonnets* is not merely "all in war with time for love" of the young man. His deep desolation at the waste of form is evoked by universal mortality, and his anger at Time's robbery of beauty is distinctive. Montaigne, quietly observing the universal flux, did not attempt to fight; he could even find enjoyment in the spectacle of change and the diversity it creates. In their intuition and representation of time Shakespeare and Montaigne also diverge. The essayist conceives of time as a *Before* and an *After*, leading from a past that no longer exists to a future as yet nonexistent (2.12.588a; 2.325). He will not "describe the essence but the passage," "not a passage from age to age," but "from minute to minute" (3.2.782b; 3.23). He refuses to be drawn "towards that which is to come" (1.3.18b–c; 1.25) and therefore seeks to take possession of the present instant, saying of his life, "I wil extend it in weight: I wil stay the readines of her flight, by the promptitude of my holdfast by it" (3.13.1092b; 3.380). In the first two books his emphasis is on constancy, for constancy allows the preservation of all the discrete moments of exis-tence. In the third book he insists on the experience of pleasure in each moment: time, when pleasant, must be arrested and "retasté" (3.13.1091b; 3.380). The form of the *Essays* is influenced by this intuition of time: no narrative progress, but a constant accretion of isolated moments of reflec-tion. These moments build "a reflective circle" according to Philip Davis,[100] but what I find dominant is rather a perpetual swaying movement, or an ebb and flow.[101] Having no sense of progress, Montaigne is not deeply interested in time, except as a constant anticipation of death. He apprehends it as beginning at birth (1.20.91a; 1.19.87) and as finality (82a, 1.20.82a, l. 76). He "enter[s] into confidence with dying" as a present ex-perience (3.9.949b; 3.215), which he wants to be *"voluptueuse, comme les commourants d'Antonius et de Cleopatra"*[102]—an allusion that may have attracted Shakespeare.

Montaigne was quietly obsessed with death, which, he thought, is "a great part of [life] and entermedleth, and ever where confounds it selfe with life."[103] Shakespeare was obsessed mainly with time: Time the De-stroyer in the *Sonnets* and the Tragedies, Time the Restorer in the Ro-mances. In the *Sonnets* time is not made up of isolated moments of experience; it is apprehended as a continuum. In all the works of Shake-speare, time is growth or decay "in sequent toil"—not a flitting from in-stant to instant as in Montaigne. In the plays and poems alike, succession, progress, and duration are conveyed by the movement of sentences related by "their being-in-time."[104] The high proportion of quatrains and even sonnets beginning or ending with "when" is significant. This is all the more remarkable, since the sonnet form by itself invites crystallization rather than continuity. Many Sonnets convey time's "thievish progress" (Sonnet 77), its duration or recurrent episodes; many others glide from past to present, from present to future or future to present, or encompass past, present, and future.[105]

Convinced that man has "no communication with being" (2.12.586a; 2.323) and seeing his life as only "a twinckling in the infinit course of an eternall night" (2.12.507; 2.232), ensconced in a present moment with no opening on infinity, Montaigne asserts the existence of a transcendent yet unknowable God.[106] Paradoxically it seems to allow him to ignore transcendence in his outlook on life and seek comfort in immediate enjoyment. Shakespeare, carried along on time's incessant current, cannot take shelter in a privileged moment and therefore needs a substitute for transcendence. A substitute, because "the world of the sonnets is enclosed in time."[107] The substitute for eternity is not merely the "longue durée" of Braudel,[108] but the whole of time. Whereas Montaigne's expectation for the survival of his essays was limited "to few men and to few years,"[109] the Sonnets claim that love "bears it out to the edge of doom" (Sonnet 116). But the poet's imagination never passes beyond, never evokes a paradise or an Elysium: only "So long as men can breathe or eyes can see, / So long" his love shall live (Sonnet 18). Indeed, Shakespeare's real substitute for transcendence may be love itself, his own love as enshrined in his poems. When he asserts that in the marriage of true minds "Love's not time's fool," the claim that love "alters not when it alteration finds" does not merely refer to the effects of time: it implies that one of the lovers may move away, prove untrue, as the young man actually did. But the love that is not love if "it bends with the remover to remove," ceasing to be reciprocal love, may be the love of the poet alone, unaltered by any change in the beloved and inscribed in the poem as "an ever-fixed mark." Just as the writing of his *Essays* shaped and fixed the elusive self of Montaigne, and determined his "essence," the writing of the Sonnets gave an essential permanence to the all-engrossing love of the poet. Not merely the assurance that the self-same voice will be heard in future days "by emperor and clown," like the song of Keats's nightingale, for this would only be a melancholy assurance; but a sense of triumphant permanence attained in the creation of form: "the essence sucked out of life and held rounded here— the sonnet."[110] Montaigne the essayist denied himself the shapeliness of form in his evasion of closure, but he also found a compensation for the lack of transcendence by projecting his own "essential form"—not the fixity of "being" but the fluctuation of "passage"—on to the variegated, repetitive, and incremental surface of his *Essays*.

# Notes

1. Robert Miola, *Shakespeare's Reading* (Oxford: Oxford University Press, 2000), 169.

2. Robert Ellrodt, "Self-consciousness in Montaigne and Shakespeare," *Shakespeare Survey* 28 (1975): 37–50.

3. Miola, *Shakespeare's Reading*, 169.

4. Geoffrey Miles, *Shakespeare and the Constant Romans* (Oxford: Clarendon Press, 1996), 84.

5. Philip Davis, *Sudden Shakespeare* (London: Athlone, 1996), 70.

6. Graham Bradshaw, *Shakespeare's Scepticism* (Brighton: Harvester Press, 1987); Lars Engle, *Shakespearean Pragmatism: Market of His Time* (Chicago: University of Chicago Press, 1993); William Hamlin, The Image of America in Montaigne, Spenser, and Shakespeare: Renaissance Ethnography and Literary Reflection (New York: St. Martin's Press, 1995); John Lee, *Shakespeare's "Hamlet" and the Controversies of Self* (Oxford: Oxford University Press, 2000).

7. Joan Lord Hall, "Role-playing in Montaigne and Jacobean Drama," *Comparative Literary Studies* 22 (1985): 73–86; Arthur Kirsch, "Virtue, Vice, and Compassion in Montaigne and *The Tempest*," *SEL: Studies in English Literature, 1500–1900* 37 (1997): 337–52; and "Sexuality and Marriage in Montaigne and *All's Well That Ends Well*," *Montaigne Studies* 9 (1997): 187–202; Jean-Marie Maguin, "*The Tempest* and Cultural Exchange," *Shakespeare Survey* 48 (1995): 147–54. Montaigne parallels in *The Tempest* attracted more comment in various articles.

8. 2.12.586a; 2.323; cf. 3.2.782b; 3.23, etc. All quotations in English are taken from *Montaigne's Essays*, trans. John Florio, Everyman's Library (London: Dent, 1965). References give first the numbers for book, essay, and page in *Oeuvres complètes*, ed. A. Thibaudet and M. Rat, Pléiade (Paris: Gallimard, 1962), in which the chronological layers of composition are indicated by a letter: a = 1580, b = 1588, c = 1595. This is followed by volume and page number of the Florio Everyman edition, with the essay number added only when different.

9. Jean Starobinski, *Montaigne en mouvement* (Paris: Gallimard, 1982), 321, 120.

10. In *The Politicall Philosophy of Montaigne* (Ithaca, N.Y.: Cornell University Press, 1990), D. L. Schaefer rightly claims that Montaigne "made his representation of nature the fruit of reason" (250), but he unduly restricts it to "an instinct toward self-preservation and the pursuit of pleasure" (141–42).

11. He stressed his respect for "the bond of [his] word": 2.17.630a; 3.9.944b; 2.373, 3.209.

12. 2.18.649a; 2.393: "The first part of customes corruption, is the banishment of truth."

13. "*debonnaireté et humanité*" (3.9.948c; 3.213).

14. See Kirsch, "Virtue, Vice, and Compassion," 344–46; to his references one may add 2.11, "Of Crueltie"; 2.12.502; 2.27.679–80; 3.6.889; 3.8.900 (Florio 2.227.426–28, 3.157). Cf. David Quint, *Montaigne and the Quality of Mercy* (Princeton: Princeton University Press, 1998), chap. 2.

15. Cf. 2.11. 412a–b (2.122) with *Venus and Adonis* 679–708 and *As You Like It* 2.1.21–43; and 1.23.107c (1.22.107) with *Coriolanus* 1.3.65.

16. First pointed out by Eleanor Prosser in "Shakespeare, Montaigne, and the 'Rarer Action,'" *Shakespeare Studies* 1 (1961): 221–26.

17. 2.25.724a; 2.476. See also 3.12.1017b, 1025b; 13.1079b (Florio 3.294, 304, 365–66).

18. He claimed that he had "seen a hundred Artificers, and as many labourers, more wise and more happie, than some Rectors in the Universitie, and whom [he] would rather resemble" (2.12.466b; 2.185). A similar inclination is suggested in Annabel Patterson's book, *Shakespeare and the Popular Voice* (Oxford: Blackwell, 1989).

19. Hugo Friedrich, *Montaigne* (Paris: Gallimard, 1949), 19.

20. *Richard III* 5.5.23; *Essays* 3.12.1018–20; 3.295 ff.
21. A recurrent theme; see particularly 1.23 and 3.13.
22. 3.13.1042b (3.323).
23. Admitting that "Innovation is of great lustre," he thought it unwise in his own time (3.10.1001; 3.276).
24. He later asserted: "in matters of generall opinions, even from my infancy, I ranged my selfe to the point I was to hold" (3.2.790b; 3.32).
25. See *Concordance des essais de Montaigne*, prepared by Roy E. Leake et al. (Geneva: Droz, 1981).
26. 3.10.989b; 3.263; adding, "When my will gives me to any party, it is not with so violent a bond, that my understanding is thereby infected."
27. Stanley Cavell, *Disowning Knowledge in Six Plays of Shakespeare* (Cambridge: Cambridge University Press, 1987).
28. Bradshaw, *Shakespeare's Scepticism*, 49, 251, 37.
29. Engle, *Shakespearean Pragmatism*, 8, 3.
30. Ibid., 59; Bradshaw, *Shakespeare's Scepticism*, 92.
31. Miles, *Shakespeare and the Constant Romans*, 85.
32. See F. Joukovsky, *Montaigne et le problème du temps* (Paris: Nizet, 1972), 215–25, 238.
33. 2.17.641a; 2.385; cf. 3.13.1052a; 3.333: "Judgement holds in me a presidentiall seate."
34. 2.1.319b–c; 2.12; emphasis added.
35. "Self-consciousness in Montaigne and Shakespeare"; *Genèse de la conscience moderne* (Paris: Publications de la Sorbonne, 1983); "The Search for Identity from Montaigne to Donne," in *John Donne and Modernity*, ed. A. Himy (Paris: University of Paris X, 1995), 7–23; *Seven Metaphysical Poets* (Oxford: Oxford University Press, 2000).
36. Charles Taylor, *Sources of the Self* (Cambridge: Cambridge University Press, 1994), 130–31.
37. Antoine Compagnon, *Nous, Michel de Montaigne* (Paris: Seuil, 1980), 162–63.
38. More space would be needed to show that this view is reconcilable, mutatis mutandis, with Frederick Rider's in *The Dialectic of Selfhood in Montaigne* (Stanford: Stanford University Press, 1973), Glynn Norton's in *Montaigne and the Introspective Mind* (The Hague: Mouton Publishers, 1975), and Donald Frame's in "Montaigne's Dialogue with his Faculties" in *French Forum* 1 (1976): 193–208.
39. Carol Clark, *Essays in Memory of Richard Sayce*, ed. I. D. McFarlane (Oxford: Clarendon Press, 1982), 71.
40. C. Castoriadis, *Topique* 38 (1986): 37; cf. Ellrodt, *Seven Metaphysical Poets*, 8.
41. Miles, *Shakespeare and the Constant Romans,* 97, 109.
42. See Michael Screech's *Montaigne & Melancholy* (London: Duckworth, 1983), 78–79, 107–8, 143.
43. Instances may be easily found under "form" in Leake's Concordance (see n. 25).
44. Erasmus, *Ciceronianus*, in *Opera Omnia*, ed. Jean LeClerc, 10 vols. (Leyden, 1703–6), 1:988 C–E.
45. 3.2.789b; 3.30; "swaying" here means dominant: "forme maistresse."
46. As Hamlin argues in *The Image of America*, 63.
47. Olivier Naudeau in *Journal of Mediaeval and Renaissance Studies* 6 (1976): 208.

48. Notably 2.31, end; 3.5, beginning; 3.12.1022b; 3.300–3.1 (quotation from Seneca).

49. Florio's "neither change nor exceed" is a mistranslation.

50. Starobinski, *Montaigne en monvement*, 29–31.

51. Florio, 1.14. Cf. Thomas Greene's "chaos" in *The Vulnerable Text* (New York: Columbia University Press, 1986), 123.

52. "*habet animus faciem quamdam suam in oratione velut in speculo relucentem*": *Ciceronianus Opera Omnia*, 1:1022 B.

53. 1.28.191a; Florio 1.27.207. T. Cave uses the phrase "surrogate self," yet assumes that "the presence of the text entails the absence of the author," a Derridean position; *The Cornucopian Text* (Oxford: Clarendon Press, 1979), 273–74.

54. Jean Starobinski in *Identität*, ed. Odo Marquard and Karlheinz Stierle (Munich: Wilhelm Fink, 1979).

55. Dialogue in the *Essays* (e.g., 3.9.949–79; 3.215 ff.) is only a rhetorical device.

56. As suggested by John Lord Hall, "Role-playing in Montaigne."

57. *The Merchant of Venice* 1.1.77–79.

58. Miles, *Shakespeare and the Constant Romans*, 34. Miles has noted Montaigne's "fundamental dichotomy between person and role" (100–10).

59. "*Macbeth*," New Casebooks (New York: St. Martin's Press, 1992), 6.

60. "cette personne exceptionnelle": *The Tragedy of Hamlet* (Paris: Bouffes du Nord, 2001).

61. Catherine Belsey, *The Subject of Tragedy* (London: Methuen, 1985), 45–46.

62. See Ellrodt *Seven Metaphysical Poets*, 300.

63. A view rightly criticized by David Aers in "*Hamlet*": *Culture and History, 1350–1600* (London: Harvester-Wheatsheaf, 1992), 177–78; cf. Robert Hilman's *Self-Speaking in Medieval and Early Modern English Drama* (London: Macmillan, 1997). I have traced the development of self-consciousness in several works (see n. 35).

64. Thomas Van Laan, *Role-playing in Shakespeare* (Toronto: University of Toronto Press, 1978), 25, 38.

65. In an essay in the *Westminster Review* quoted by Jacob Feis in *Shakespeare and Montaigne* (Geneva: Slatkine, 1984).

66. New York: Viking Press.

67. Belsey, *The Subject of Tragedy*, 41.

68. Brian Vickers, *Appropriating Shakespeare* (New Haven: Yale University Press, 1993), 338.

69. Holland offers a survey in *Psychoanalysis and Shakespeare* (New York: Octagon Books, 1979), 163–206. In "Hamlet's Grief" (*ELH* 48 [1981]: 17–37), Kirsch made sensible use of Freud's views in "Mourning and Melancholia." In *Suffocating Mothers: Fantasies of Maternal Origin in Shakespeare's Plays* (London: Routledge, 1992), chap. 2, Adelman's perceptive interpretation is based closely on the text. Most psychoanalysts after Freud "continue to find the idea of an organically unified psyche useful": see *Shakespeare's Personality*, ed. N. N. Holland et al. (Berkeley and Los Angeles: University of California Press, 1989), 3. For a different (Lacanian) view, see Philip Armstrong's essay in *Alternative Shakespeares*, ed. T. Hawkes, 2d ed. (London: Routledge, 1996), 216–37.

70. Another type of coherent interpretation is Alastair Fowler's British Academy lecture, "Shakespeare's Renaissance Realism," *Proceedings* 90 (1996): 29–64: "Recognising such dispersed aspects of character, far from disintegrating

Hamlet as an individual, helps to synthesize his Renaissance subjectivity" (48). Fowler's judgment of Hamlet's actions, however, seems to me at times unduly influenced by the moral sentiment of our own age.

71. *Hamlet*, 106–8. Hamlet himself believed in the influence of "some complexion" (1.4.27; Q2 only).

72. Robert Burton, *Anatomy of Melancholy*, pt. 1, sect. 2, mem. 4, subsect. 7 (London: J. M. Dent & Sons, 1932; reprint, New York: Vintage/Random House, 1977).

73. See Ellrodt, "The Search for Identity from Montaigne to Donne."

74. *Hamlet*, 2.2.295–301; cf. Timothy Bright, *A Treatise on Melancholy* (1586), quoted by Jenkins (ed. *Hamlet* 108).

75. Hibbard's edition of *Hamlet* (Oxford: Oxford University Press, 1987) calls attention to the proverb, "A man is weal or woe as he himself thinks so" (Tilley M 254).

76. Bright, *Treatise*, 200; quoted by Jenkins, 106.

77. Davis, *Sudden Shakespeare*, 86.

78. Adelman, *Suffocating Mothers*, 31–35. Hamlet's sexual disgust is essential in her interpretation (17–18). I had insisted on the widespread "sex nausea" at the turn of the century in my *Poètes métaphysiques anglais* (Paris: Corti, 1960), 3.52–70; it was not confined to Shakespeare.

79. In "Othello" in *The Claim of Reason: Wittgenstein, Skepticism, Morality, and Tragedy* (Oxford: Oxford University Press, 1979), 494, Cavell himself notes, however, that Shakespeare's heroes are incapable of taking their imperfections with the "'gay and sociable wisdom' of Montaigne" (see 3.13.1097b; 3.386). In "Virtue, Vice, and Compassion," Arthur Kirsch offers safer parallels with *All's Well That Ends Well*, but may overstate the influence of Montaigne.

80. As I pointed out in "Self-consciousness in Montaigne," 47.

81. *Essays*, 2.20.656b; 2.401; *Hamlet* 3.1.121–28; cf. 2.2.52, and *All's Well* 4.3.71–74.

82. *Essays*, 3.2.791b; 3.32; *Hamlet* 2.2.572–80; 3.1.129–36.

83. 3.2.791b; 3.32. Montaigne condemns the man "that maks himselfe a horror to himselfe" (3.5.857b; 3.108).

84. In *Die Kunst, glücklich zu sein*, trans. *L'art d'être heureux*, ed. F. Volpi (Paris: Seuil, 2001).

85. Bright, *Treatise*, 124; quoted by Jenkins, 106.

86. Notably Belsey, *The Subject of Tragedy*, 42. Other critics think that "Hamlet changes . . . from the undergraduate age to the near-maturity of thirty" (A. Fowler, "Shakespeare's Renaissance Realism," *Proceedings* 90, 34), but this would not create a "second self."

87. *Hamlet* 1.2.129, 4.3.31; cf. 5.1.199–212.

88. As Harold Bloom insists in *Ruin the Sacred Truths* (Cambridge: Harvard University Press, 1989), chap. 3.

89. Francis Barker, *The Tremulous Private Body* (London: Methuen, 1984), 36–37.

90. As I argued in *Genèse de la conscience moderne* 421–23.

91. Katharine Eisaman Maus also thinks it difficult to claim that Hamlet's boast of "that within" is anachronistic; *Inwardness and Theatre in the English Renaissance* (Chicago: University of Chicago Press, 1995), 3 ff.

92. *Shakespeare's "Hamlet" and the Controversies of Self*, 153–62, 162–65.

93. See Ellrodt, *Seven Metaphysical Poets*, chap. 16. Contrary to Lee's assertion (161), the term "individual" took on its modern meaning before 1646. Cf.

Donne's "the Ego, the particular, the individuall, I," *Sermons*, ed. Potter-Simpson, 5.70–71.

94. *Shakespeare's Hamlet*, chap. 8.

95. Which does not imply autobiographical accuracy.

96. 2.8.376a; 2.80: "For, as I know by certaine experience. . . ."

97. 3.9.961, n. 3 and p. 1652: "*luy seul jouyssait de ma vraye image et l'emporta*" (text of 1588 not in Florio).

98. See Sonnets 76, 78–80, 85, etc.

99. As Barbara Bowen shrewdly remarks in *The Age of Bluff* (Urbana: University of Illinois Press, 1972), 27.

100. Davis, *Sudden Shakespeare*, 95.

101. As argued by Marcel Conche in *Montaigne et la philosophie* (Paris: PUF, 1996), 47–50. "*Je ne fay qu'aller et venir*" is a characteristic statement (2.12.549b; 2.280).

102. 3.9.962b; mistranslated by Florio, 3.231.

103. 3.9.962b; 3.230; 3.13.1082b; 3.368.

104. As Philip Davis observes, "these long sentences lose their power of stationing and of finalizing; time has got into their very utterance" (*Sudden Shakespeare*, 78, 79).

105. See Ellrodt, "La perception du temps dans les Sonnets de Shakespeare," in *Le Char ailé du temps*, ed. Louis Roux (Sainte-Etienne: Publications de l'Université de Sainte-Etienne, 2003).

106. Mainly in 2.12, end. I need not engage in the debate on Montaigne's Christian faith.

107. As I pointed out in the 1986 edition of the *Cambridge Companion to Shakespeare*, ed. Stanley Wells (Cambridge: Cambridge University Press), 41.

108. Invoked by Lars Engle, *Shakespeare's Pragmatism*, 20–21.

109. 3.9.960b; 3.229 (cf.2.18.647a; 2.391). True philosophy in his eyes implied no desire of "further continuance, either of life or name" (1.39.242a; 1.38.263).

110. Virginia Woolf, *To the Lighthouse*, 1, sect. 19.

# Translating Arden: Shakespeare's Rhetorical Place in *As You Like It*

## SWAPAN CHAKRAVORTY

"SHAKESPEARE HAS HERE CONVERTED THE FOREST OF ARDEN INTO AN-other Arcadia," wrote William Hazlitt of *As You Like It*, "where they 'fleet the time carelessly, as they did in the golden world.'" Hazlitt names Arden, but it is not clear whether he is thinking of the forest or the play: "It is the most ideal of any of the author's plays. It is a pastoral drama in which the interest arises more out of the sentiments and characters than out of the actions or situations. It is not what is done, but what is said, that claims our attention. . . . Caprice and fancy reign and revel here, and stern necessity is banished to the court."[1] Such conflation of play and forest is not rare in later commentaries, especially in attempts to gloss the title. The Epilogue exhorts the women in the playhouse "to like as much of this play as please you" (13–14). Thomas Lodge had addressed not women, but gentleman readers in his preface to *Rosalynde*. But the sense of his invitation to them, which many feel to be the source of the play's title, "If you like it, so," was not much different.[2] But discussions of the title often drift away from this context of viewer esponse to that of the way the play's characters behave in Arden. For instance, an editor writes in 1975 that the title "is particularly suited to the do-as-you-please atmosphere of Arden, a place where a very mixed collection of people very happily go their own various ways."[3] More recently, Juliet Dusinberre, in the course of demonstrating the play's links with Rabelais's *Gargantua and Pantagruel*, has cited the single precept that governed life in the Abbey of Thelema, *fay çe que voudras*: do as you please. Dusinberre glosses the play's title in the light of the conceptual affinity between Rabelais's Abbey and Shakespeare's forest: "Do what thou wilt. As you like it. Arden, for all its pastoral echoes, is conceptually in harmony with the ideals of the Abbey of Thelema, in which those who enter are wealthy, free and chaste—not as celibates, but as people who will in due course marry and go back to a world they will transform through their new vision of concord between man and woman."[4] And, of course, as readers of Rabelais will recall, there was no clock in the abbey.[5]

One could explain this tendency to identify the play with the setting of only part of its action by exploring a deeper resemblance between their hermeneutic indeterminacy. After all, when the Senior Duke points to "This wide and universal theatre" (2.7.137), we are unsure whether he means the world, the forest, or the Globe playhouse. The setting and the action alike are varieties of heuristic fiction, challenging the interpretative skills of characters and playgoers. The title would then read like an invitation to this hermeneutic task, asking us to make of the play what we will, rather than telling characters to do what they wished, or playgoers to like as much of it as they pleased.

There was no preexistent forest for Shakespeare to "convert" to Arcadia or to anything else: one must interpret the representation in order to constitute a plausible object of the playwright's imitation. I am tempted to recall at this point Edmund Ludlow's comment about Isabel Archer in *The Portrait of a Lady*. When his wife objects that she does not see what he has against Isabel except that "she's so original," Edmund replies, " 'Well, I don't like originals; I like translations,' Mr Ludlow had more than once replied. 'Isabel's written in a foreign tongue. I can't make her out. She ought to marry an Armenian or a Portuguese.' "[6] That is indeed the trouble with originals. We cannot make them out or even perceive them to be originals unless we translate them. The process, I believe, engages some of the fundamental issues of the political and poetic functions of discourse, what in Shakespeare's time would have been understood as the major concerns of rhetoric. Arden, like the theater itself, speaks in many voices, and, like the Senior Duke, we must translate its speech to see what sense we can make of the scene wherein we all play. I propose to examine the implication of this idea of translation in the light of contemporary notions of rhetoric, with particular attention to the Senior Duke's exchange with his followers the first time we hear him in the play. The first words we hear in Arden are spoken by him:

> Are not these woods
> More free from peril than the envious court?
> Here feel we not the penalty of Adam,
> The seasons' difference, as the icy fang
> And churlish chiding of the winter's wind,
> Which when it bites and blows upon my body
> Even till I shrink with cold, I smile and say,
> "This is no flattery: these are counsellors
> That feelingly persuade me what I am."
>
> (2.1.3–11)

The speech draws on a set theme—the praise of the rural or sylvan retreat—for which Virgil's second *Georgics*, Horace's second and sixteenth

*Epodes*, and Seneca's *Hippolytus* (ll. 483–564) provided rhetorical models.[7] One is reminded of Valentine's praise in *The Two Gentlemen of Verona* (5.4.1–6), but the contrast with the treacherous court drawn by a deposed prince brings to my mind a closer parallel, Musidorus's eclogue in the *Old Arcadia*:

> O sweete woods the delight of solitarines!
> O how much I do like your solitarines!
> Here no treason is hidd, vailed in innocence,
> Nor envie's snaky ey, finds any harbor here,
> Nor flatterers' venomous insinuations,
> Nor conning humorists' puddled opinions,
> Nor courteous ruin of proffered usury,
> Nor time pratled away, cradle of ignorance,
> Nor causelesse duty, nor comber of arrogance,
> Nor trifling title of vanity dazleth us,
> Nor golden manacles, stand for a paradise,
> Here wrong's name is unheard: slander a monster is.[8]

Sidney's eclogue was cited by Abraham Fraunce as an instance of the *tetrametrum* or *Asclepiadicks* in *The Arcadian Rhetorike* (1588),[9] a book that, together with Fraunce's earlier unpublished work entitled *The Shepherd's Logic* (ca. 1585),[10] suggested links between the concerns of rhetoric and those of the pastoral.

A similar conjunction marks the Duke's speech, if not the play as a whole. Editors do not seem to have noticed that the Senior Duke, in this most rhetorically patterned of speeches, is also alluding to the discipline of rhetoric, especially in the phrase "feelingly persuade." Aristotle defined rhetoric as "the faculty of discovering the possible means of persuasion in reference to any subject whatsoever" (*Rhetoric* 1.2.1),[11] but he was not happy with an exclusive emphasis on the second of the three modes of persuasion he enumerated; namely, persuasion by awakening the emotions (pathos) of the hearers (1.2.5).[12] Aristotle preferred the convincing effected by the merits of the argument itself. But the notion of persuasion was still liable to be seen summarily in terms of pathos. Hence Quintilian warns against a definition of rhetoric as *vis persuadendi*. The trouble with the definition is that it privileges persuasion, but an ability to speak persuasively is morally neutral, "within the power of the bad man no less than a good."[13]

In spite of these reservations, the affective view of rhetoric as the art of persuasion that appealed to the emotions of the hearer was a commonplace inherited by Early Modern writers. It was the task of rhetoric to deck out the plain truth of logic through verbal amplitude and affective manipulation. In 1563, Richard Rainolde wrote in *A Booke called the Foundacion of Rhetorike* that rhetoric "dilateth and setteth out small thynges or woordes, in soche sort, with such aboundaunce and plentuousnes, bothe of woordes and wittie inuencion . . . that the most stonie and hard hartes, can not but bee incensed, inflamed, and moued thereto." [14]

The affective view of rhetoric can be detected behind some of the collocations in which the words "persuade" and "feeling," and their variants, appear in Shakespeare. In *Love's Labor's Lost*, Longaville says in a sonnet that also appeared in *The Passionate Pilgrim* (1599),

> Did not the heavenly rhetoric of thine eye,
> 'Gainst whom the world cannot hold argument,
> Persuade my heart to this false perjury?
>
> (4.3.58–60)

Persuasion is likewise linked to eloquence in Hotspur's curt direction to the soldiers in *Henry IV, Part 1*:

> . . . [F]ellows, soldiers, friends,
> Better consider what you have to do
> Than I, that have not well the gift of tongue,
> Can lift your blood up with persuasion.
>
> (5.2.75–78)

By "persuasion" Hotspur means stirring to action. The Porter in *Macbeth* uses the word in the allied sense of sexual arousal: "it [i.e., drink] persuades him, and disheartens him; makes him stand to, and not stand to" (2.3.33–34). This sense of "persuasion" is unwittingly evoked by Claudio in *Measure for Measure*, when he credits the persuasive skills of Isabella to her command of rhetoric:

> for in her youth
> There is a prone and speechless dialect,
> Such as move men; beside, she hath prosperous art
> When she will play with reason and discourse,
> And well she can persuade.
>
> (1.2.182–86)

The close link between persuasion and bodily stimulation may also be seen in Shakespeare's use of the word "feelingly." To speak "feelingly" was to speak precisely, to the purpose. The most recent editor of the play, Michael Hattaway, glosses the word as (1) "by experience," and (2) "intensely." [15] But it could also be construed as speaking persuasively, that is, in a way that affects the physical senses, as the following exchange in *Measure for Measure* clearly shows:

*1. Gentleman.* I had as lief be a list of an English kersey as be pil'd, as thou art pil'd, for a French velvet. Do I speak feelingly now?
*Lucio.* I think thou dost; and indeed with most painful feeling of thy speech.

(1.2.32–37)

The gentleman's joke is at the expense of Lucio's French pox, which has left him "pil'd" or bald. Hence, Lucio takes "feelingly" to mean "with feeling" or "in a way which provokes the feeling of pain," although the gentleman's primary sense was "to the purpose."[16] The word is used to mean "through the sense of touch" as well as "precisely" when the blinded Gloucester tells Lear that he sees the world "feelingly" (*King Lear* 4.6.149).

These examples suggest that the Senior Duke's phrase, "feelingly persuade," can be taken to mean "persuade to the purpose," "persuade with deep feeling," and "move in a manner involving physical sensation or response." As we have seen, to persuade or move or evoke sensations such as pain and pleasure through appropriate, copious, and emotionally appealing speech was the aim of rhetoric according to the affective view of the subject.

It seems, however, that a more direct connection between the phrase and the art of rhetoric is implied by the context. The Duke compares the persuasion of the winter wind to the counsel of the plain-speaking adviser, as opposed to the sugared speech of the flattering courtier. In the *Gorgias* Plato had grouped rhetoric with sophistry as the sham arts or flatteries. These were the false arts for the soul as cosmetics and cookery were for the body. The true arts for the soul were legislation and justice, and for the body, gymnastics and medicine.[17] In a well known passage in *Praise of Folly*, quoted below from Sir Thomas Chaloner's translation (1549), Erasmus borrows the Platonic parallel: "Lyke as *Phisike*, accordyng as many now a daies dooe wrest it, is naught els than a membre of *Adulacion*, as well as *Rhetorike*."[18]

The Duke, then, is saying that the winter wind is an honest counselor; and hence, unlike the flattering courtier who misuses the affective potencies of speech, it serves the true function of rhetoric, but does so, ironically, by moving the body more than the soul. It is the same contrast that is drawn in *King Lear*, a play whose connections with *As You Like It* and concern with the rhetorical production of feeling has been often noted:[19]

They flatter'd me like a dog, and told me I had the white hairs in my beard ere the black ones were there. To say "ay" and "no" to every thing that I said! "Ay," and "no" too, was no good divinity. When the rain came to wet me once, and the wind to make me chatter, when the thunder would not peace at my bidding, there I found 'em, there I smelt 'em out. (*King Lear* 4.6.96–103)

The courtiers who were disloyal to the Senior Duke presumably deceived him in the manner Joan proposes to entice the Duke of Burgundy in *Henry VI, Part 1*, "By fair persuasions, mix'd with sug'red words" (3.3.18). The interesting thing, however, is that in this speech the Senior Duke uses rhetorical embellishments more than plain logic. He is thus following the practice of the rhetorician who, wrote Leonard Cox in *The Art or Crafte of Rhethoryke* (first printed 1530), "seketh abought and boroweth where he can asmuche as he may for to make the symple and playne Logycall argumentes gay and delectable to the aere [*sic*]."[20]

One could justifiably say that the Duke, in trying to make exile bearable, is using rhetoric like cookery, making the unpalatable "sweet." He reads Arden as a text, translating trees into tongues, brooks into books, and stones into sermons. Arden as text is indeterminate and, as such, fit matter for rhetorical translation. The object of unqualified scientific knowledge, as Aristotle had said in the *Analytics*, is "something which cannot be other than it is."[21] On the other hand, the objects of the human sciences (*studia humanorum*), as Rudolf Agricola wrote in *De inventione dialectica libri tres* (1480; printed 1515), "are controversial and require the encounters of disputants for clarification."[22] The distinction had become almost axiomatic in Renaissance manuals of rhetoric and logic. Talking of human laws that were the proper concern of the orator, Sperone Speroni wrote in *Dialogo delle lingue* (1552), "It is rational that our states should not be governed by firm, demonstrable, and for all times secure, sciences; but by rhetorical, changing and variable opinions."[23]

But the rhetorical gloss, if it were to escape Platonic censure, could not be morally indifferent. Early Modern exponents sought to defend rhetoric from the charge of moral irresponsibility by combining the concept of rhetorical translation with the idea of nature as divine discourse. In order to read sermons in stones, one needed a cleansed will, as Erasmus has a character say in one of his *Colloquies*: "Socrates puts the Case . . . of a man's walking alone in the Fields; not as if any of the works of the Creation wanted a Tongue, for every part of it, speaks to the Instruction of any man, that has but a good will, and a Capacity to learn."[24]

One could connect Erasmus's point to that other mode of rhetorical efficacy mentioned by Aristotle, the one that depended upon the ethos or moral character of the speaker (*Rhetoric* 1.2.3). The rival claims of ethos and pathos were frequently debated in contemporary poetics, the question usually surfacing in discussions of catharsis. Giacopo Mazzoni, for instance, argued in *Della defesa della Comedia di Dante* (1587) that greater compassion is aroused by the character who bears "adverse fortune with a generous and firm mind" than by someone who screams and weeps.[25] Amiens compliments his master on possessing a similar fortitude:

Happy is your Grace,
That can translate the stubbornness of fortune
Into so quiet and so sweet a style.

*(As You Like It* 2.1.18–20)

Gonzalo will try translating Prospero's island in a similar vein in *The Tempest*, for which effort Antonio will call him "a spirit of persuasion" (2.1.235) in a passage that has baffled many, including Samuel Johnson.[26]

It is rarely noticed that, in addition to praising the ethos of the happy man, Amiens credits his master with a positive exercise of rhetorical skill. He uses the Latin word for metaphor, *translatio*,[27] that was the standard term in sixteenth-century treatises on rhetoric. Richard Sherry's *Treatise of Schemes and Tropes* (1550) defines the metaphor as "*Translatio*, translacion, that is a worde translated from the thynge that it properlye signifieth, vnto a nother whych may agre with it by similitude."[28] Metaphor was concerned with the substitution of a single word, but such substitution could be seen at work in the sentence and in the use of tropes in general. Henry Peacham's definition of the trope in *The Garden of Eloquence* (1577), for instance, is not far removed from Sherry's definition of the metaphor: "A *Trope*, is an alteration of a worde or sentence, from the proper and naturall signification, to an other not proper, yet nye and likely."[29]

The Duke translates Arden, and he translates it sweetly. The association of sweetness with eloquence was almost hackneyed, but the meaning of "sweetness" could be extended to include wholesome patience and wisdom. In *The Academie of Eloquence* (1654), Thomas Blount cites Proverbs 16:21, 24 to make the connection between ethos and eloquence: "For in the sacred Story we read, *the wise in Heart shall be called prudent and the sweetness of the lips increaseth understanding: Pleasant words are as an honeycomb; sweet to the soul and health to the bones*."[30] The Duke, while being suspicious of false rhetoric, might seem to exemplify in his own speech a decorative and affective ideal of rhetorical utterance. But he is also using speech in the service of social cohesion. His praise of Arden is not quite that of solitary life: he has his co-mates and brothers in exile to worry about. His translation is aimed at keeping this ad hoc community together: in fact, life in Arden is made to exemplify that freedom from intrigue and treason which ensures a cohesive polity.

This, again, is in keeping with the perceived goals of eloquence. The civic and republican ideals of rhetoric spelled out by Cicero in *De Inventione* (1.1–2),[31] were adapted by later writers to suit a princely state. In this revised interpretation, eloquence was the key means of ensuring social and political unity. As John of Salisbury wrote in *Metalogicon*, "Through harmony, it [rhetoric] holds human community together."[32] The idea recurs frequently in Tudor manuals of rhetoric. Richard Rainolde, for instance, in what is perhaps the first formulary rhetoric in English, writes that eloquence is that by which "kyngdomes vniversally are gouerned, the state of euery one priuatlie is maintained."[33]

Like Rosalind, Celia, Touchstone, Orlando, and Adam, the Duke is engaged in translating banishment into liberty, adversity into some settled, low content. His social station requires him to combine this ethical project of rhetoric with the political, and hence his praise of Arden can never quite be the praise of solitary life.

This attempt lends point to the scene's abrupt shift of attention to Jaques's moralizing on the deer. The Duke and Jaques both translate what they see around them. But Jaques's thousand similes turn sour as much because of his incapacity for contentment as because of his modish distaste for company. Stefano Guazzo, in explaining why conversation and fellowship are vital to human culture, describes the solitary man as one to whom "the hearbe Helleborum may be given . . . as to the foole."[34] When Jaques does seek out company, it is to flaunt his exclusive brand of melancholic seclusion, "compounded of many simples," the "sundry contemplation of my travels" (4.1.16–18). Such narcissistic indulgence in arcane discourse was singled out by Thomas Wilson in *The Arte of Rhetorique* (1553) as a perversion of the true social ends of eloquence: "Some farre iorneid gentleme[n] at their returne home, like as they loue to go in forrein apparell, so thei wil pouder their talke w[ith] ouersea language. . . . I knowe them that thynke Rhetorique, to stande wholy vpon darke woordes, and he that can catche an ynke horne terme by the taile, hym thei compt to bee a fine Englishe man, and a good Rhetorician."[35]

It is easy to see why the Duke rejects Jaques's defense of the socially corrective function of satire, a sensitive issue since the Bishops of London had banned satire in 1599, only months before the play was written. Jaques's unsociable hubris, as also his libertine past, fails to legitimate his social deployment of corrective rhetoric. His satiric persona is too heavily invested with claims of moral and intellectual superiority, and his libertine past hence becomes a matter different from, say, Touchstone's follies with Jane Smile. The genial and sociable jester sees folly all around him, the melancholy and withdrawn censor sees only evil.[36]

Arden, it has been said often enough, is a fabulous place. Lodge's Arden was in the southwest of France (not in the northeast, where the woods of the Ardenne are located), but Shakespeare's has shades of the Arden in his native Warwickshire, where Mary Arden's father had been a tenant farmer. James Joyce has Stephen say in *Ulysses* that Shakespeare's "mother's name lives in the forest of Arden," while Samuel Schoenbaum speculates on the possibility of the playwright's recalling in *As You Like It* his wife's cottage, which then stood almost at the edge of the Warwickshire forest.[37]

The Arden of the play, however, has both lionesses and olive trees, hedge-priest and Hymen. Even Charles the wrestler's mention of the "golden world" and "the old Robin Hood of England" (1.1.116–19) is not free from disturbing overtones. Richard Wilson has drawn attention to possible allusions to the anti-enclosure uprisings of 1596 by Midland foresters who were inspired by tales of Robin Hood and utopian notions of common un-enclosed woodland.[38] Even then, Arden is not a utopian alternative to re-pression. It feels the penalty of Adam, one has to kill deer for food, and the shepherd's life, in that it is not the life of the eclogue-spouting bucolics of pastorals, is naught. Corin has a hard time working under a churlish master, and Silvius, when he does not have Phoebe on his brain, considers investing in a farm. Orlando, who seeks to translate the trees of Arden into books that declare Rosalind's virtues (3.2.5–8), finds the forest a remote and savage desert, where good manners belong to those who are inland bred. Arden is a hermeneutic puzzle, to be pieced together, as Hazlitt cor-rectly guessed, by discourse and disputation.

I said earlier that there was no preexistent forest for Shakespeare to translate, the representation itself constitutes the putative object of the playwright's imitation. Speaking of Aristotle's idea of *mythos* and *mime-sis*, Paul Ricoeur draws our attention to the strangeness of the idea that the structure of the plot itself should constitute *mimesis*, that poetic imitation should compose and construct "the very thing it imitates." Ricoeur hence finds that in Aristotle's idea of poetic imitation "Reality remains a refer-ence, without ever becoming a restriction."[39]

It is tempting to draw a parallel here with the way Arden is discursively configured as an object of poetic imitation. More relevant perhaps is what Ricoeur has to say on metaphor or *translatio*. A fundamental rift in ancient and later theories of the metaphor, according to him, stems from the fact that poetry and oratory "mark out two distinct universes of discourse," although "Metaphor . . . has a foot in each domain" (12). In order to distin-guish between the poetic and rhetorical function of metaphorical transla-tion, one has to grasp the conjunction of fiction and redescription of reality. The rhetorical function "seeks to persuade men by adorning dis-course with pleasing ornaments," the poetic function "seeks to redescribe reality by the roundabout route of heuristic fiction" (247).

In spite of their differences, the Duke and Jaques both endorse a rhetori-cal function of *translatio* and a political ideal of rhetoric: they seek equally to prove and persuade for socially corrective ends. Rosalind's make-be-lieve game of love and her translation of Arden as the holiday world with-out a clock are an alternative, a piece of heuristic (that is, poetic) fiction. Ricoeur proposes a tensional model for such metaphorical truth, a tension that lies within the relational function of the copula of the verb *to be*: "The metaphorical 'is' at once signifies both 'is not' and 'is like.' If this is really so, we are allowed to speak of metaphorical truth, but in an equally 'tensive' sense of the word 'truth'" (7). This drama of "is" and "is not" concerns the tension of identity and difference, and is entirely different from the measured opposition of "is" and "is not/naught" in Touchstone's rhetorical dispute with Corin on the merits of country life. The truth that poetic fiction represents is not a verifiable truth: it is more akin to the truth of belief. It loses sight of its fictive nature and becomes, says Ricoeur, a species of true belief: "Can one create metaphors without believing them and without believing that, in a certain way, 'that is'?" (254).

Rosalind's metaphorical translation of Arden sets up this tensional model of metaphorical truth and belief: it is the natural perspective of theatrical fiction that is and is not. It is for this reason, I suggest, that Arden, where Rosalind becomes a busy actor in all sorts of plays, is very nearly a surrogate of Shakespeare's kind of theater. The Duke urges the playgoers to recognize the scene's location as not just Arden, but this wide and universal theater wherein the actors are playing, and Jaques follows it up with a clearer allusion to the Globe motto: "All the world's a stage" (2.7.139). The theater in its turn is seen as a creative and therapeutic analogue of the world where men and women have their exits and their entrances, but where roles can be played, even fashioned, with courage, good humor, and understanding. It is a place where "the creative dimension of language is consonant with the creative aspects of reality itself" (254).

The importance of rhetoric in *As You Like It* has been a subject of extensive comment.[40] More remarkable is the self-awareness with which its characters read, use, mimic, or mock language. Le Beau's account of the bereaved old man reminds Celia of the beginning of an old tale; Orlando's rhymes are read out and parodied; Touchstone raves at fortune in "good set terms" and mimics the language of chivalry, catechism, and scholastic dispute with equal skill; Jaques fears that Orlando and Rosalind will start talking in blank verse although his own speeches are bookish and rehearsed; he follows up one of Amiens's songs with a parodic *stanzo*; Rosalind makes fun of the cliches in Orlando's poems and in Phoebe's letter; Orlando finds Ganymede's accent too polished; Phoebe quotes Marlowe; and Touchstone compares his conversation with Audrey to Ovid's with the Goths.

Through such means the play distances us from stylized readings of experience, while keeping alive the sense of wonder that the romance narrative demands. It may be useful, I believe, to reconsider this discursive self-awareness and this preoccupation with rhetoricity in the light of the Duke's translation of what the wintry counselors in Arden "feelingly persuade."

# Notes

1. William Hazlitt, *Characters of Shakespeare's Plays* (London: Oxford University Press, 1916), 250.

2. Geoffrey Bullough, *Narrative and Dramatic Sources of Shakespeare*, 8 vols. (London: Routledge and Kegan Paul, 1957–75), 2:160.

3. *As You Like It*, ed. Agnes Latham, New Arden Shakespeare (London: Methuen, 1975), lxix.

4. Juliet Dusinberre, "As Who Liked It?" *Shakespeare Survey* 46 (1994): 12.

5. Francois Rabelais, *Gargantua and Pantagruel*, trans. J. M. Cohen (Harmondsworth: Penguin Books, 1955), 150.

6. Henry James, *The Portrait of a Lady*, ed. Leon Edel (Boston: Houghton Mifflin Co., 1956), 37.

7. The line reference to Seneca is to *Tragedies*, ed. and trans. Frank Justus Miller, 2 vols., Loeb Classical Library (Cambridge: Harvard University Press, 1917), 1:356–60.

8. Sir Philip Sidney, *The Poems,* ed. William A. Ringler, Jr. (Oxford: Clarendon Press, 1962), 69.

9. Abraham Fraunce, *The Arcadian Rhetorike: or the Praecepts of Rhetorike Made Plaine*, English Linguistics 1500–1800, no. 176 (facs. Menston: Scolar Press, 1969), sig. C2.

10. Abraham Fraunce, *The Shepherd's Logic*, BL MS Add. 34,361, English Linguistics 1500–1800, no. 185 (facs. Menston: Scolar Press, 1969); see dedicatory verse to Edward Dyer, fol. 2v.

11. Aristotle, *The "Art" of Rhetoric*, trans. John Henry Freese, Loeb Classical Library (Cambridge: Harvard University Press, 1926), 15.

12. Ibid., 17: "The orator persuades by means of his hearers, when they are roused to emotion by his speech; for the judgements we deliver are not the same when we are influenced by joy or sorrow, love or hate; and it is to this alone that . . . the present-day writers of treatises endeavour to devote their attention."

13. Quintilian, *Institutio Oratoria*, trans. H. E. Butler, 4 vols., Loeb Classical Library (Cambridge: Harvard University Press, 1920), 1:301.

14. Richard Rainolde, *A Booke called the Foundacion of Rhetorike*, English Linguistics 1500–1800, no. 347 (facs. Menston: Scolar Press, 1972), fols. 1r–v.

15. *As You Like It*, ed. Michael Hattaway, New Cambridge Shakespeare (Cambridge: Cambridge University Press, 2000).

16. See J. W. Lever's gloss in the New Arden *Measure for Measure* (London: Methuen, 1965), 11. The word means "to the purpose" or "with exactitude" also in Maria's speech in *Twelfth Night* 2.3.158–59: "he shall find himself most feelingly personated."

17. Plato, *Gorgias*, 463a–466a, in *Collected Dialogues Including the Letters*, ed. Edith Hamilton and Huntington Cairns (Princeton: Princeton University Press, 1963), 245–46.

18. [Erasmus], *The Praise of Folly*, trans. Thomas Chaloner, ed. Clarence H. Miller, Early English Text Society, no. 257 (London: Oxford University Press, 1965), 45.

19. See, for instances, Maynard Mack, *"King Lear" in Our Time* (Berkeley and Los Angeles: University of California Press, 1965), 64–65; Frank McCombie, "Medium and Message in *As You Like It* and *King Lear*," *Shakespeare Survey* 33 (1980): 67–80; and Lisa Jardine, Reading Shakespeare Historically (London: Routledge, 1996), 78–97.

20. Leonard Cox, *The Arte or Crafte of Rhethoryke*, ed. Frederic Ives Carpenter (Chicago: University of Chicago Press, 1899), 48.

21. Aristotle, *Posterior Analytics*, 1.2.15, in *The Basic Works*, ed. Richard McKeon (New York: Random House, 1949), 111.

22. Quoted in Marion Trousdale, *Shakespeare and the Rhetoricians* (London: Scolar Press, 1982), 34.

23. Quoted in Eugenio Garin, *Italian Humanism: Philosophy and Civic Life in the Renaissance*, trans. Peter Munz (Oxford: Basil Blackwell, 1965), 162.

24. Erasmus, *Twenty Select Colloquies*, trans. Roger L'Estrange (1680), ed. Charles Whibley, Abbey Classics 17 (London: Chapman and Dodd, n.d.), 69.

25. Quoted in Baxter Hathaway, *The Age of Criticism: The Late Renaissance in Italy* (Ithaca: Cornell University Press, 1962), 266.

26. See the editorial gloss on the passage in *The Tempest*, ed. Frank Kermode, New Arden Shakespeare, 6th ed. (London: Methuen, 1956), 55.

27. See Ernst Robert Curtius, *European Literature and the Latin Middle Ages*, trans. Willard R. Trask (New York: Pantheon Books, 1953), 128.

28. Quoted in Wilbur Samuel Howell, *Logic and Rhetoric in England, 1500–1700* (1956; New York: Russell and Russell, 1961), 130.

29. Henry Peacham, *The Garden of Eloquence Conteyning the Figures of Grammer and Rhetorick*, English Linguistics 1500–1800, no. 267 (facs. Menston: Scolar Press, 1971), sig. Bjv.

30. Thomas Blount, *The Academie of Eloquence Containing a Compleat English Rhetorique*, English Linguistics 1500–1800, no. 296 (facs. Menston: Scolar Press, 1971), sig. A3v.

31. See Cicero, *De Inventione, De Optimo Genere Oratorum, Topica*, trans. H. M. Hubbell, Loeb Classical Library (Cambridge: Harvard University Press, 1949), 3–9.

32. Quoted in J. B. Trapp, "Rhetoric and the Renaissance," in A. G. Dickens et al., *Background to the English Renaissance* (London: Gray-Mills Publishing, 1974), 92.

33. Rainolde, *Foundacion of Rhetorike*, fol. 1.

34. Stefano Guazzo, *The Civile Conversation*, trans. George Pettie and Bartholomew Young (1586), 2 vols. (London: Constable and Co., 1925), 1:46.

35. Thomas Wilson, *The Arte of Rhetorique, for the Vse of All Suche as are Studious of Eloquence* (facs. Gainesville, Fla.: Scholars' Facsimiles and Reprints, 1962), sig. Yii.

36. See Ruth Nevo, *Comic Transformations in Shakespeare* (London: Methuen, 1980), 185.

37. James Joyce, *Ulysses* (Harmondsworth: Penguin Books, 1969), 208; and Samuel Schoenbaum, *William Shakespeare: A Compact Documentary Life* (New York: Oxford University Press, 1977), 80.

38. Richard Wilson, "'Like the Old Robin Hood': *As You Like It* and the Enclosure Riots," *Shakespeare Quarterly* 43 (Spring 1992): 1–19.

39. Paul Ricoeur, *The Rule of Metaphor: Multi-disciplinary Studies of the Creation of Meaning in Language*, trans. Robert Czerny, Kathleen McLaughlin, and John Costello, S.J. (London: Routledge and Kegan Paul, 1978), 39, 42. Subsequent page references are given in parentheses after quotations.

40. See, for example, Karen Newman, *Shakespeare's Rhetoric of Comic Character* (New York: Methuen, 1985), 94–98; and Martha Ronk Lifson, "Learning by Talking: Conversation in *As You Like It*," *Shakespeare Survey* 40 (1987): 91–105.

# The Pronouns of Propriety and Passion: *you* and *thou* in Shakespeare's Italian Comedies

### Penelope Freedman

Petruchio opens his wooing of Katherine with

> Hearing *thy* mildness prais'd in every town,
> *Thy* virtues spoke of, and *thy* beauty sounded,
> Yet not so deeply as to *thee* belongs,
> Myself am mov'd to woo *thee* for my wife.
>
> (*The Taming of the Shrew* 2.1.191–94)

but concludes it with "And will *you*, nill *you*, I will marry *you*" (2.1.271). For a modern Anglophone audience the distinction between *you* and *thou* is virtually lost. We absorb both pronouns indiscriminately, and few would claim that they were aware of the choice of one pronoun or the other even at a subconscious level. Speakers of European languages that still employ a formal and an informal second-person-singular will, of course, be more attuned to the distinction; and it is significant that some of the most interesting studies that have been done on the *you/thou* distinction in Shakespeare in recent years have been by Clara Calvo in Spain on *As You Like It* and Manfred Draudt in Austria on *Love's Labor's Lost*.[1] But even those who are aware of the distinction between the two pronouns may be misled if they assume too close a parallel between them and the formal and informal pronouns in other languages.

Much of the discussion of *you/thou* use over the past forty years has been heavily influenced by a major paper first published in 1960 by Brown and Gilman, in which they attempted to trace and explain the changing use of second-person pronouns in European languages (in particular, French, German, Italian, and English) from the early medieval period to the present day.[2] They saw these changes as reflecting the changing values of European society and as relating particularly to issues of power relations, on the one hand, and group solidarity on the other. They attribute the use of the plural for singular address to the deferential plural addressed to the emperor in the late Roman Empire, which was extended to other people of

168

importance and found its way into the languages of Europe after the breakup of the Empire. Throughout the feudal period, they claim, the singular and plural pronouns were used non-reciprocally between those of unequal rank and reciprocally between those of equal rank, the plural being exchanged by the aristocracy and the singular by the lower orders. Only later, they suggest, did aspects of group solidarity become more important, with the result that the singular could be used to express solidarity between individuals in a wider range of social contexts, and came to carry, in addition, connotations of nearness or intimacy, in contrast to the distance implied by the plural form. The paper is hugely informative and wide-ranging, going beyond European languages to comparisons with Afrikaans, Gujarati, and Hindi; but I would suggest that, as far as English is concerned, it is quite misleading.

As Kathleen Wales demonstrates in her 1983 paper on Brown and Gilman's,[3] they make too simple a link between usage in English and in other European languages. She shows that *thou* always carried connotations not only of intimacy but of emotion, from the fourteenth century, when *you* first begins to appear in the courtly literature, and, more importantly, that it was always possible and easy to switch between *you and thou* to express temporary shifts of emotion or attitude, in contrast to the fixed relationships in other languages. In other words, *thou* always carried a powerful emotional charge and it is highly misleading to suggest that this emotional aspect was a late accretion or subordinate to the power and solidarity dyad. In spite of the work of Wales, Calvo, McIntosh,[4] and others, however, the Brown and Gilman view lingers on in the comments of editors of Shakespeare, and it is testimony to its power that the entire entry on the singular/plural distinction in David Crystal's 1997 *Cambridge Encyclopedia of Language* is taken from their paper.[5]

I would suggest that a major weakness of Brown and Gilman's argument is that they confine themselves almost exclusively to relationships and dialogue between men: their paradigms are officer and soldier, father and son, master and servant, older and younger brother; their historical examples Robespierre and George Fox; their literary examples, Valentine and Proteus, Toby Belch, Volpone and Mosca, Tamburlaine. Even the survey they conducted of European students studying in the United States was "limited": "Although we have data from a small number of female respondents," they say, "the present analysis is limited to males" (262). We seem to have elements of the self-fulfilling prophecy here: having settled on power and solidarity as the significant dyad, they have then confined their examples to an all-male world where these are bound to be significant elements. (Even the terms "power" and "solidarity" carry connotations of old-style British industrial relations, from which women were generally excluded.) When we look at dialogue between men and women, however, we see how inadequate the power and solidarity model is and what a delicate, subtle, and flexible indicator of attitude and feeling *you/ thou* switches can be. In particular, in dialogue between lovers and would-be lovers, we see how Shakespeare uses *you/thou* shifts to guide us through the emotional and psychological paths of a scene, issues of power or status for the most part secondary, and the power of emotion taking over.

*Thou* is the pronoun for wooing, and Romeo and Juliet as iconic lovers provide us with a benchmark in this respect: Romeo uses *thou* to Juliet from the moment of their first meeting, Juliet uses it from the balcony scene onwards, and they use it with absolute consistency. No other pair of lovers exchanges *thou* with anything like this consistency: for Romeo and Juliet, their love is a given, fixed and unalterable; it is threatened not from inside but from the world outside. The lovers in the comedies are assailed by the vagaries of their own emotions, by pride, anger, uncertainty, infidelity, misunderstanding, confusion, desperation, devotion; and these fluctuations of feeling are reflected in their pronoun choices. We can see that overall there are certain norms for *thou* use between mutual lovers: *thou* is not generally used at a first meeting; it is almost always initiated by the man and is, in general, used more freely by men; it is used in private rather than in public. In other words, it follows the same kind of conventions that have generally governed physical contact between lovers. Where the love is not mutual, or where one of the pair has become disaffected, then *thou* may be used to express anger, hurt, hate, or contempt. This is not as contradictory as it sounds: what links the expression of love with the expression of anger or hate is the power of the emotion, emotion so strong that it dispenses with the plurality of *you*—*you* which addresses a person's many faces, his or her social roles both private and public—and instead uses the old singular, which addresses the person intimately and directly, one human being to another, regardless of status or propriety.

Examination of lovers' dialogue in any of the plays will shed light on the significance of these shifts, but I have chosen three Italian comedies, *The Two Gentlemen of Verona*, *The Taming of the Shrew*, and *Much Ado About Nothing*, because they cover a time span of at least ten years and a spectrum of lovers' relationships, and because I like the idea of the *thou/ you* distinction's being returned to its origins, the Latin *tu* and *vos* absorbed and transformed almost beyond recognition and taken back to a fictional Italy different, in many respects, from Shakespeare's England.

In his only English comedy, *The Merry Wives of Windsor*, *thou* use is lower than in any of his other comedies. These buttoned-up English will not easily use such a dangerously emotional pronoun. The use of *thou* is, in fact, highly polarized between the characters: Falstaff, Pistol, the Host, and Fenton use it quite freely; Shallow and Slender, the Pages and the

Fords, the indigenous Windsor middle classes, use it very little, each use having a marked significance. We must assume that the paucity of their use of *thou* reflects the level of use, at least in that stratum of society, at that time. In a prose play set among the English middle class, contemporary in all but the anachronistic presence of Falstaff, Shakespeare must be using the discourse conventions of the time, and these are the conventions that he brings to the fictional Italy of his plays. In the more expansive atmosphere of the Mediterranean, his characters follow the conventions that his London audiences understand, but they are more ready to shift the emotional and social boundaries, to go to the limits of what is appropriate. His Italy is a place where hearts are worn on sleeves, and intimate, emotional *thou* is poised on the tips of tongues.

In *The Two Gentlemen of Verona* we find that Proteus is the major user of *thou* and half his *thou* uses are to Valentine; Valentine and Silvia both use *thou* extensively too, and in each case more than half their uses are to Proteus. Since *thou* between young people such as these can only be evoked by intimacy or emotional intensity, this use confirms our sense that Proteus stands not only at the apex of a love triangle but at the revolving emotional core of the play. The play opens with an emotional *thou* parting between devoted friends, Valentine and Proteus: "Wilt *thou* be gone? Sweet Valentine, adieu, / Think on *thy* Proteus" (1.1.11–12); but when it comes to the farewell between Proteus and his beloved, Julia, the picture is rather different. Julia gives Proteus a ring: "Keep this remembrance for *thy* Julia's sake" (2.2.5). It is unusual for the woman to use *thou* first, and Proteus's reply makes the situation even more unusual: "Why then we'll make exchange: here, take / *You* this" (2.2.6–7). He does move to *thou* after their farewell kiss, but the initiation of *thou* by Julia, combined with the asymmetry of Proteus's response, in a poignant leave-taking between devoted lovers, does suggest at least a subliminal awkwardness, if not a deliberate mismatch of emotional intensity, even at this stage in the play. The next time they meet, Julia is disguised as a boy, "Sebastian," and Proteus now uses *thou* freely to her, the affectionate address of a master to a favored servant. Since he is employing her to carry messages to Silvia, his new love, there are several levels of irony here, just as there are in Orsino's consistent use of *thou* to Viola as he sends her, as Cesario, to Olivia. As Sebastian, Julia must, of course, use *you* to her master, but when she drops her disguise in the final scene she moves immediately to *thou*:

> Behold her that gave aim to all *thy* oaths,
> And entertain'd 'em deeply in her heart.
> How oft hast *thou* with perjury cleft the root?
> O Proteus, let this habit make *thee* blush!

(5.4.101–4)

These are lines of strong emotion and lines that blur the distinction between the love and anger associations of *thou* use: the force of Julia's feeling expresses itself, and we do not need to ask whether love or anger predominates. Her switch to *thou* also marks her dropping of her assumed persona and return to her own identity.[6]

Between Silvia and Proteus, the pronouns are very different. With one significant exception, Proteus does not woo Silvia with *thou*. A clear finding, from looking at lovers' language across the plays, is that a man will use *thou* to woo a woman only where he believes his feelings to be reciprocated; rejected lovers do not use *thou*. Silvia, on the other hand, *thou*'s Proteus frequently, spitting contempt and anger at him. It is unusual for a woman to use *thou* to a man who is not her husband, lover, or son; but a woman may be moved by moral outrage to use *thou*. A striking example of this is Isabella's use to Angelo. She has treated him with scrupulous respect, even while arguing fiercely against him, but at the moment when she finally understands the corrupt bargain he is offering her she cries,

> I will proclaim *thee*, Angelo, look for't!
> Sign me a present pardon for my brother,
> Or with an outstretch'd throat I'll tell the world aloud
> What man *thou* art.
>
> (2.4.151–54)

*Thee*, like the bare "Angelo," strips away the trappings of authority from the Duke's Deputy and threatens to reveal the rotten individual, the man within. Not only gender but power relations are against Isabella, whereas Silvia has social status on her side as well as the high moral ground—she is the daughter of the Duke. It is not coincidental that another woman who consistently *thou*'s unwelcome wooers is Innogen, the daughter of a king. (Innogen, interestingly, spurns her wooers with *thou* but consistently uses respectful *you* to her lowborn husband.) In 4.2 and 5.5, Silvia submits Proteus to a barrage of contemptuous *thou*ing and in 5.4, under the pressure of this verbal assault, Proteus attempts to rape her:

> Nay, if the gentle spirit of moving words
> Can no way change *you* to a milder form,
> I'll woo *you* like a soldier, at arm's end,
> And love *you* 'gainst the nature of love—force *ye*.
>
> (5.4.55–58)

> I'll force *thee* yield to my desire.
>
> (5.4.59)

His shift to *thou* strips away chivalry and courtesy, and marks the change to a new identity—attacker rather than wooer.

When we look at Silvia's *thou* use in this scene, we can see how she has, albeit unconsciously, prepared the ground for Proteus's assault. Proteus is an arrogant, impatient man who has already endured scathing attacks at Silvia's hands. At the start of the scene, he feels that he has a strong advantage: chance has given him the opportunity to save Silvia from outlaws and he eagerly presses his claim to her favor. Instead of receiving thanks, he is submitted to a devastating attack on his faithlessness, couched in the most contemptuous terms. Proteus, at this point, exhibits the classic mixture of emotions that fuel the rapist—anger and low self-esteem. Proteus is angry not only with Silvia but with himself: the faithlessness she taunts him with affects his own self-image, for she attacks not his public *you* persona, but the *thou* that is the core of his self. Through her words he sees himself as irredeemably bad, and there is nothing to stop him from going to the limit; he has betrayed the two people he thought he loved, so why should he not betray another? For Proteus to be redeemed in his own eyes, he has to go to the limit before seeing himself as again lovable through the forgiveness of Valentine and Julia. It is important to see how Silvia's language drives him to that limit.

Petruchio uses *thou* quite cynically in his wooing of Katherine. He starts with the deliberately over-familiar greeting, "Good morrow, Kate" (2.1.182) and follows up the diminutive with a shift to *t* pronouns:

> Hearing *thy* mildness prais'd in every town,
> *Thy* virtue spoke of, and *thy* beauty sounded,
> Yet not so deeply as to *thee* belongs,
> Myself am mov'd to woo *thee* for my wife.
>
> (2.1.191–94)

This is conventional wooing language, but by launching into it without polite preliminaries and by starting with talk of her famous mildness, Petruchio ensures that she can take nothing about the proposal seriously. Knowing that there is a battle to come, he simply fires this as an opening salvo, and his use of *thou* heightens its irony. He continues with *thou*, in the wooing vein, until he makes a sudden switch to *you*: "Come, come, *you* wasp, i' faith *you* are too angry" (2.1.209). With the new pronoun he assumes a new identity: no longer her ironic wooer but her critic, as confirmed by his threat soon after: "I swear I'll cuff *you*, if *you* strike again" (2.1.220). *You* tells her, if she needs to be told, that this is a threat to be taken seriously, but three lines later he is back to lover's talk: "A herald, Kate? O, put me in *thy* books!" (224). And so he swings to and fro, soon producing another ironic paean of praise:

> *thou* art pleasant, gamesome, passing courteous,
> But slow in speech, yet sweet as spring-time flowers.
> *Thou* canst not frown, *thou* canst not look askaunce.
>
> (2.1.245–47)

His final speech in the scene, before the arrival of Baptista, again switches between *thou* and *you* as he moves from one identity to another. When she snubs him with "Yes, keep *you* warm" (2.1.266), he replies,

> Marry, so I mean, sweet Katherine, in *thy* bed;
> And therefore setting all this chat aside,
> Thus in plain terms: *your* father hath consented
> That *you* shall be my wife; *your* dowry 'greed on,
> And will *you*, nill *you*, I will marry *you*.
>
>                                        (2.1.267–71)

We see quite clearly here the two personae that Petruchio will continue to use for the rest of the play: the *thou* persona of the lover and later the attentive husband whose protestations always defy her to take them seriously, and the *you* persona in which he tells her how things really are. It is worth noting here what Katherine's experience of being *thou*'d has been: her father uses *thou* to her not affectionately, as he does to Bianca, but in anger: "For shame, *thou* hilding of a devilish spirit" (2.1.26). It is not surprising if Katherine is suspicious of *thou* address.

She herself uses *thou* in this scene: when Petruchio tells her father, "to conclude, we have 'greed so well together / That upon Sunday is the wedding-day" (297–98), she retorts, "I'll see *thee* hang'd on Sunday first" (2.1.299). There is, of course, extreme provocation for her outburst: she sees herself being dragooned into a marriage with this "half-lunatic," with no "tender fatherly regard" to save her. She is also herself reverting to another persona: with a single exception, she has maintained, throughout her exchanges with Petruchio, the *you* of a respectable woman; in the presence of her father she reverts to the *thou* she has used to bully Bianca, the *thou* that fits her identity in the family—that of the uncontrollable "hilding," "curst Katherine."

We can follow the progress of Petruchio's two personae in the subsequent scenes: the more he is bullying Katherine, the more likely he is to use *thou*. This is consistent with his plan to "kill a wife with kindness": the lover metamorphoses into the protective husband; cruelty is ironically dressed as affectionate concern. Thus after the wedding he snatches her away from her wedding feast, crying, "Fear not, sweet wench, they shall not touch *thee*, Kate! / I'll buckler *thee* against a million" (3.2.238–39). In the same spirit, he sends her meat away—"I tell *thee*, Kate, 'twas burnt and dried away" (4.1.170)—and snatches away her coveted silk cap:

> Why, *thou* say'st true, it is [a] paltry cap,
> A custard-coffin, a bauble, a silken pie,
> I love *thee* well in that *thou* lik'st it not.
>
>                                        (4.3.81–83)

But in his *you* persona he makes explicit the rules of the game: "The poorest service is repaid with thanks, / And so shall mine before *you* touch the meat" (4.3.45–46). And when Katherine asserts about the cap that "I'll have no bigger, this doth fit the time / And gentlewomen wear such caps as these" (4.3.69–70), he answers, "When *you* are gentle, *you* shall have one too, / And not till then" (4.3.71–72).

Although he is laying down the law, he accords her the respect of addressing her as an equal: she is neither child nor chattel. It is Katherine who recovers *thou* from the debased sense it has acquired in their relationship and restores it to its place as a signifier of genuine affection. When they arrive back in Padua, they find themselves onlookers to a scene of chaos and conflict; then, as the stage empties, they are left alone:

> *Katherine.* Husband, let's follow, to see the end of this ado.
> *Petruchio.* First kiss me, Kate, and we will.
> *Katherine.* What, in the midst of the street?
> *Petruchio.* What, art *thou* asham'd of me?
> *Katherine.* No, sir, God forbid, but asham'd to kiss.
> *Petruchio.* Why then let's home again. Come, sirrah, let's away.
> *Katherine.* Nay, I will give *thee* a kiss; now pray *thee*, love, stay.
> (5.1.142–48)

This is the first time that Katherine uses *thou* to Petruchio not in anger but with a wife's intimacy. If Petruchio's "art *'thou'* ashamed of me?" threatens a return to his ironic *thou* persona, Katherine subverts it, transforming the exchange from another test of obedience into a declaration of love.

In the shifting, ambivalent relationship of Beatrice and Benedick, too, their pronouns to each other mark the ebb and flow of their emotions. Their early sparring is entirely in *you* form; in contrast to the sparring of Katherine and Petruchio, there is no overt wooing going on, nor is there any real animus in their jibes. Though their exchanges suggest the familiarity of old opponents, they keep their distance by their *you* use, maintaining the fiction of their mutual unconcern. The first *thou* comes from Beatrice when, "overhearing" that Benedick loves her, she breaks out into verse for the only time in the play—into a formal quatrain, in fact, which moves to the ringing declaration, "And, Benedick, love on, I will requite *thee*, / Taming my wild heart to *thy* loving hand" (3.1.111–12).

*Thou* address is in fact standard for an absent addressee: one of the functions of *thou*, as the marked pronoun, is its rhetorical use, and so we find it in self-address, in address to inanimate objects, in address to the sleeping and the dead, and, indeed, in prayer. The change of pronoun for an internal monologue can have a striking effect. Banquo, for example, marks Macbeth's ascent to the throne with the revealingly direct

> *Thou* hast it now: King, Cawdor, Glamis, all,
> As the weird women promis'd, and I fear
> *Thou* play'dst most foully for't;

> (*Macbeth* 3.1.1–3)

and this contrasts strikingly with the lavish respect markers that he uses to Macbeth's face. Beatrice's use is, in its way, equally shocking, compounded as it is by the move into verse. Where Benedick's response to his gulling has been straightforwardly comic and robust ("I will be horribly in love with her"), Beatrice's hovers between comedy and pathos: the woman who has rejected an offer of marriage from the Prince, unless she "might have another for working days," who has fiercely protected the heart which Benedick once won off her "with false dice," and who looks forward with equanimity to leading her apes into Hell, suddenly capitulates. We see her stripped of her defenses and her cynicism, naively in love, set on "taming" her "wild heart." These feelings, glimpsed once, are never seen again. She never uses *thou* to Benedick in the flesh; the capitulation which has taken place in her heart is never revealed to him.

We do not see them together until they are left alone, suddenly quiet, after the clamor and distress of Claudio's and Hero's aborted wedding. Benedick moves tentatively, starting with the markedly respectful, "Lady Beatrice, have *you* wept all this while?" (4.1.255). Their talk is solemn, the topic Hero, but even when Benedick takes the plunge and declares his love, "I do love nothing in the world so well as *you*," he says, "is not that strange?" (4.1.267–68). I said earlier that a man will woo a woman with *thou* only if he has reason to believe that his love is reciprocated. Benedick has reason to believe it: he has the word of the Prince, Leonato, and Claudio; but Beatrice herself has given no indication that her attitude towards him has changed, and Benedick knows that it will be unwise to take anything for granted, especially in the fraught aftermath of Hero's disgrace. But Beatrice's half-reciprocating, evasive reply both exasperates and encourages Benedick enough to push him into a *thou* outburst: "By my sword, Beatrice, *thou* lovest me" (4.1.274). He retreats to *you* again as they start to exchange puns about eating swords and eating words; they are back to the raillery of their earlier scenes, but he wrenches himself out of this for another declaration in earnest: "I protest I love *thee*" (4.1.279–80). Beatrice's declaration is no less heartfelt: "I love *you* with so much of my heart that none is left to protest" (4.1.286), but she will not use *thou*. Her habit of self-protection remains with her, as it will to the bitter end, in spite of her earlier chagrin at being "condemned for pride and scorn so much." Benedick presses on with *thou*, to his euphoric challenge "Come, bid me do any thing for *thee*" (4.1.288) and beyond, in spite of Beatrice's fury, but in the end he reverts to *you* when he undertakes to challenge Claudio, another example of the pronoun switch marking a move to a new persona. Benedick has used *thou* in his persona as lover, but in undertaking to challenge Claudio, he adopts a new persona, a somber, grown-up Benedick, Beatrice's champion:

> Enough, I am engag'd, I will challenge him. I will kiss *your* hand, and so I leave you. By this hand, Claudio shall render me a dear account. As *you* hear of me, so think of me. Go comfort *your* cousin. I must say she is dead, and so farewell. (4.1.331–36)

At their next meeting, Benedick launches confidently into *thou* from the start: he has issued a challenge to Claudio, he knows that Beatrice loves him, and for the first time they indulge in conventional lovers' talk: "For which of my bad parts didst *thou* first fall in love with me?" (5.2.60–61). Though Beatrice never returns *thou*, Benedick maintains it until he makes a sudden switch from lovers' banter to serious enquiry:

> And now tell me, how doth *your* cousin?
> *Beatrice.* Very ill.
> *Benedick.* And how do *you*?
> *Beatrice.* Very ill too.
>
> (5.2.88–92)

In the context of his prevailing *thou* use, *you* here becomes the marked form, signaling real closeness. The effects of the two pronouns are almost reversed: *thou*, though familiar and affectionate, has been used for joking and posturing, while *you* marks the real intimacy of the genuine question which probes the pain that still overshadows their delight in each other. As the shadow lifts, with Ursula's news that all is resolved, Benedick celebrates with a return to *thou* and teasing: "I will live in *thy* heart, die in *thy* lap, and be buried in *thy* eyes; and moreover I will go with *thee* to *thy* uncle's" (5.2.102–4).

In the final scene, they revert to the mutual *you* of their public personae as a couple: neither is prepared to admit to love in public. Benedick adopts *thou* for his final, less than chivalrous proposal: "Come, I will have *thee*, but by this light, I take *thee* for pity" (5.4.92–93), but then goes back to *you* as he brings her protestations to a close: "Peace, I will stop *your* mouth" (5.4.97). Having moved to *thou*, why does he return to *you* for this confidently intimate line? In both the 1600 Quarto and the Folio, the line is actually Leonato's. Subsequent editors, following Theobald, have all taken this as an error and given the line to Benedick. One can see why: if we are deaf to the *thou/you* switch, then the line seems obviously Benedick's, a conclusion to the bickering, a reminder of Beatrice's own exhortation to Hero: "Speak, cousin, or (if *you* cannot) stop his mouth with a kiss, and let not him speak neither" (2.1.310–11). But the *you* should make us wonder whether the Folio attribution is right: *you* is Leonato's usual address to Beatrice and he has just intervened a few lines earlier to urge her to acquiesce: "Come, cousin, I am sure *you* love the gentleman" (5.4.84). Seeing that neither of these two lovers will be the first to give in, even after their love letters have been revealed, does Leonato step in to bring their bickering to an end by silencing Beatrice? Just as their friends had to bring them to acknowledge their feelings for each other initially, so Leonato has to step in to finish the job. The stage direction "*kissing her*" is part of Theobald's emendation giving the line to Benedick. If we take the Q1 text as it stands, we can imagine that Leonato steps in to stop Beatrice, possibly putting a hand to her mouth, that there is a pause as she stands in surprised silence and she and Benedick look at each other, and that the Prince then takes his turn, seizing the pause to clinch the match, allowing Benedick no way out: "How dost *thou* 'Benedick, the married man'?" (5.4.99). Audiences may expect the conventional closure of the kiss, but the alternative ending is more in keeping with all that has gone before. It is not an ending that we see played, but it is feasible and would be interesting.

The example of these three plays demonstrates, I hope, the subtle complexities of *you/thou* choice between lovers as Shakespeare uses it. In particular, the instances from *Shrew* and *Much Ado* suggest the limitations of *thou* as the conventional form of address for a wooer.[7] Although we are accustomed to it as the literary lover's mode, Shakespeare makes clear its weakness for use in a relationship with a woman who is not merely an idealized love object: *thou* addresses the woman only as the loved creature, the object of the man's affections. Used mutually, as in *Romeo and Juliet*, between lovers who are all in all to one another, it can suggest soul speaking to soul; but to a Katherine or a Beatrice, each an intelligent, spirited, difficult woman with her own place in her society, it can be used only sparingly. These women, like their men, have to engage with their social world, and in that world their public, you faces are significant and must be restored to them, their social roles acknowledged. For an example of the way *thou* can exclude a woman from the public world, we can bring the argument back to Britain: when Macbeth excludes Lady Macbeth from his plot on Banquo's life, he says, "Be innocent of the knowledge, dearest chuck, / Till thou applaud the deed" (3.2.45–46). The words are affectionate but they reveal only too clearly that she will never be what she was promised—his "dearest partner in greatness."

It is, of course, impossible to restore to modern audiences the linguistic sensibility of a sixteenth- or seventeenth-century English audience, but I would argue that it is still possible for actors and directors to be aware, to their advantage, of the conventions within which Shakespeare and his contemporaries were operating. If they are prepared to use pronoun choice as one of the markers to guide them in tracking the dynamics of scenes, identifying crisis moments, exploring relationships, and interpreting meaning, then they will find sometimes that patterns emerge with startling clarity, that confusions resolve themselves, and that uncertain relationships acquire substance. The next stage of my exploration is to discover how the actors' enhanced understanding of these dynamics can be translated into stage performance.

## Notes

1. Clara Calvo, "Pronouns of Address and Social Negotiation in *As You Like It*," *Language and Literature: Journal of the Poetics and Linguistics Association* 1 (1992): 5–27; and Manfred Draudt, *Shakespeare's Use of "You" and "Thou": The Subtext of "Love's Labor's Lost"* (Vienna: Braunmuller, 1984).

2. R. Brown and A. Gilman, "The Pronouns of Power and Solidarity," in *Style in Language*, ed. Thomas A. Sebeok (New York: MIT Press and John Wiley, 1960), 253–76.

3. K. Wales, "'Thou' and 'You' in Early Modern English: Brown and Gilman Reappraised," *Studia Linguistica* 37, no. 2 (1981): 107–25.

4. A. McIntosh, "*As You Like It*: A Grammatical Clue to Character," *Review of English Literature* 4, no. 2 (1983): 41–68.

5. David Crystal, *The Cambridge Encyclopedia of Language* (Cambridge: Cambridge University Press, 1997), 45.

6. This is an example of Calvo's finding (see n. 1 above) that one of the functions of *you/thou* shifts is to negotiate a new identity, to mark the adoption of a new role or persona.

7. Calvo writes convincingly on the effects of the ambiguity of *thou* as the pronoun both of wooing and of social patronage: "'Too wise to woo peaceably': The Meanings of *Thou* in Shakespeare's Wooing Scenes," *Actas del III Congreso del SEDERI* (Grenada, Spain, 1992), 49–59.

# "Action and accent did they teach him there": Shakespeare and the Construction of Soundscape

## Ros King

THE SOUND OF SHAKESPEARE IS A PECULIARLY NEGLECTED AREA OF study.[1] This is strange. We have more evidence for sound than we have for the visual aspects of the plays, since sound is an integral part of the words that are our main evidence. But we have, I think, become deaf to the subtlety of the construction of sound in Shakespeare for a number of historical reasons. Firstly, we know on an intellectual level that words change their pronunciation over time, although we have no real evidence in the period before recording machines for what those changes mean in practice. Consideration of the original sound of Shakespeare has therefore been left to the philologist on the (probably correct) assumption that Shakespeare done in "original" accents, even were it achievable, would be of merely antiquarian interest. Indeed until very recently, there has been an expectation that, even in North America or Australia, Shakespeare—except for the "low-life" characters—should be spoken in the current form of received (English) pronunciation. There is still lingering anxiety about this issue that surfaces regularly in discussions on Shaksper, the electronic discussion group; while the British theater company, Northern Broadsides, gets the bulk of its publicity from the fact that it does Shakespeare "irreverently" in Yorkshire accents. Secondly, taking accent in its other meaning as "stress," there is still, despite the work of George T. Wright,[2] a received understanding that Shakespeare wrote uniformly in iambic pentameters—except of course for the prose for those same low-lifers. This has maintained, even in editions at the forefront of the textual revolution of the1980s, some very traditional approaches to the regularization of Shakespearean meter.

There is a wide variety of accent (in the sense of regional or personal "intonation") to be found amongst English speakers. In English words of more than one syllable, however, the position of the accent (in the sense of "stress") is fairly stable, whatever the dialectical pronunciation of the speaker.[3] It is this consistency of stress in English that allows speakers, according to their individual preference at the time of speaking, not only to incorporate a range of emotional intonation into their speech, but also to underline sentence structure through the creation of one-off patterns in relative *degrees* of stress without affecting comprehensibility at the level of the word.[4] Indeed, this discretion can add to comprehensibility at the level of the sentence. When using our own words, expressing our own emotions, this comes naturally. But, as my title quotation from *Love's Labor's Lost* indicates (5.2.99), the correct placing of the accent when reciting works written by someone else is a matter in which most people need instruction. Indeed it is likely that the "learning" period of two or more weeks generally allotted to new plays in Elizabethan times would include such instruction for individual actors in both gesture and speaking, either from the playwright or from leading members of the company.[5] It is a practice that, in my experience working with actors, can still pay enormous dividends. This essay argues that the same techniques can also be used to offer a new approach to some old contentious issues in criticism, and explores the soundscapes created by the interplay of the two aspects of accent in a range of different plays.

If the exact intonation of English words can differ not only between speakers but at different times and according to different emotional states in the same speaker, then a dramatist with the technical facility and experience of a Shakespeare, both as a writer and as an actor, might be expected to try to write the accent of emotion into his poetry in order to create a sense of characterization. The only way for a writer to influence a speaker's accent is through the precise disposition of individual words and rhetorical patterns within the line and the sentence. Shakespeare's frequent departure from a strict tally of syllables for each line therefore needs to be considered as part of that patterning. When in *Love's Labor's Lost*, for example, Holofernes impatiently takes the paper containing Berowne's "canzonet" from Sir Nathaniel's hands on the grounds that he finds "not the apostraphas, and so miss[es] the accent" (4.2.119–20), the joke is on a rather higher level of poetic discourse than the simple mistaking of the commas in Quince's prologue to the play of Pyramus and Thisbe in *A Midsummer Night's Dream*.[6] Holofernes's objection carries two distinct senses. Firstly, the poem takes the form of an apostrophe to the poet's mistress. But as it limps along in twelve-syllable iambics (the limping is the result of its very regularity), it also notches up ten different grammatical subjects in as many lines (love, faith, thoughts, study, pleasures, art, knowledge, tongue, soul, I). In these circumstances the direction of the poet's address is difficult to determine and a reader may well be at a loss. Secondly, Nathaniel's delivery has, we may safely assume, sounded very wooden. Holofernes, by contrast, has just been seen in a reverie of delight, perhaps transported back to his schooldays through the recitation of the rhythmic hexameter that opens the First Eclogue of Mantuan, i.e., the poet Johannes Baptista Spagnolo (1448–1516).[7] He has followed this by an apostrophe to that poet, "Old Mantuan, old Mantuan! who understandeth thee not, loves thee not." This is adapted from the proverbial encomium to Venice, *Venetia, Venetia, chi non ti vede, non ti pretia* (Venice, Venice, who sees you not, values you not) and, of course, consciously plays on the conceit that the poet is the town (Mantua) from which his popular name is taken. He then breaks into a snatch of song, "Ut, re, sol, la, mi, fa." Sadly, these names for the degrees of the gamut only tell us the relative pitch of the notes, rather than their length. The tune (if indeed a recognizable tune was intended) is therefore not identifiable, but this snatch of melody is evidently a direct response to the poetry he has been quoting and an indication that he regards it as music to his ears.[8] In short, Holofernes seems to appreciate poetry in the manner described by Abraham Fraunce in *The Arcadian Rhetoric:* that proper pronunciation occurs with the "pleasant and delicate tuning of the voyce which resembleth the consent and harmony of some well ordred song."[9] His pleasure, both here and in the little puzzle poem that he extemporizes himself, evidently stems from a delight in the way in which words can be fitted into patterns—whether of semantics, rhetoric, or rhythm. Quite simply, he is enraptured by the quantitative quality of Latin prosody, which fits words into a rhythm according to metrical patterns. In English, as in Latin, however, the effect of easy, natural tunefulness is only achieved through art. In order to realize the writer's intended effect, the sensitive speaker is expected to recognize the need to use apostrophe in its other sense: the omission or elision of one or more letters in a word.

As I have written elsewhere, an analysis of the surviving contemporary musical settings for some eleven poems of *The Paradise of Dainty Devices* (1576) shows just how regularly this was done. If allowed the natural prose accent of the words, poems that appear to us, now, on the page as relentlessly regular runs of fourteeners or poulter's measure can be revealed as the charming lyrics that gained the book its huge reputation.[10] In English accentual poetry, poems come to life when the rhythms of sense and sentence are made to dance around the underlying pulse of the meter or the syllable count.

Holofernes thus initially assumes that Nathaniel just hasn't got the necessary skills in speaking. His disappointment in the poem, once he looks at it for himself, is palpable: "Here are only numbers ratified, but for the elegancy, facility, and golden cadence of poesy, *caret*." This poem has obeyed the meter—the "numbers"—of its chosen iambic, twelve-syllable verse, but no speaker, no matter his skill in elision, could release rhythm from it. Berowne's canzonet is technically inept because its rhythm and meter coincide so absolutely.

The core poems in *The Paradise* were originally collected (and some of them written) by the court poet and composer Richard Edwards. If the surviving contemporary music reveals the natural prose rhythms enclosed in the regular syllables in that poetry, Edwards's one known surviving play, *Damon and Pythias*, achieves a similar effect but with the reverse method. It is written in rhyming couplets in which the lines can consist of anything from four to twenty-one syllables. The principle of giving accent to syllables according to the prose meaning of the sentence, however, reveals that these apparently rambling lines actually consist of a regular four-stress meter. Here, the varying number of unstressed syllables between stresses (which is a reflection of colloquial English prose) again means that the true rhythm of the line is not enslaved to this underlying metrical organization, but works in counterpoint to it. The result is "a kind of orchestration for the spoken voice, utilizing a variety of techniques designed to simulate different linguistic registers, but which all play with the tension between poetic metre and natural word rhythms."[11]

So how then does Shakespeare write rhythm into his verse? The most cursory glance at a Shakespeare concordance shows that he limits his vocabulary in order to create a sense of definition for a particular play world. Our received wisdom that he wrote in blank verse of iambic pentameters (albeit pentameters that changed as he matured as a poet), has perhaps prevented us from appreciating the extent to which he also chose a distinctive sound system for each play. Not least, this is because of the tendency of editors to relineate the text in cases where, on mere syllable count, the line appears unmetrical, and to reproduce the original printed apostrophe marks (or lack thereof), while often adding stress marks to "ed" endings. These contradictory actions have one intention: to regularize the rhythm and subdue it to meter. If Holofernes is right, and that finding the apostrophe is, at this period, the responsibility of the speaker as much as of the writer, then we, as modern readers and editors, may need to pay greater attention to distinguishing between apostrophes inserted by printers according to their own taste, ability to read poetry, or pragmatic typography, and those, whether marked or not, that contribute to the living rhythm of the passage.

The purpose of this essay is to explore this problem from a dramaturgical point of view. I want to start by comparing the prosody of two plays, *Antony and Cleopatra* and *Julius Caesar*, which share a common source in North's translation of Plutarch's *Lives of the Ancient Grecians and Romans*. I have chosen these partly because North's prose style provides a constant against which to measure two evidently extreme examples, and partly because Plutarch himself, in the opening sections both of the life of

Marcus Antonius and of the life of Marcus Brutus, supplies us with an entry into their respective characters through an analysis of the language patterns that each favored.

Marcus Brutus was, in Plutarch's account, a serious-minded man, who would spend even the few hours before a battle studying and writing: "Furthermore, when others slept, or thought what woulde happen the morrowe after: he fell to his booke, and wrote all day long till night, wryting a breviarie of Polybius."[12] Plutarch has already remarked that he was "properly learned" in the Latin tongue, capable of writing "long discourse in it beside that he could also plead verie well in Latine," but that when it came to writing epistles in Greek, he "counterfeated that briefe compendious maner of speach of the Lacedaemonians." So intrigued is this Greek writer by the Spartan linguistic habits adopted by the Roman that he quotes several of Brutus's brutal but balanced epistles, notably one to the Samians: "Your counsels be long, your doinges be slowe, consider the ende," and another to the Patareians: "The Xanthians despising my good wil, have made their countrie a grave of dispaire: and the Patareians that put them selves into my protection, have lost no jot of their libertie. And therefore whilest you have libertie, either choose the judgement of the Patareians, or the fortune of the Xanthians."[13] The preparation for the conspiracy against Caesar is likewise a matter for the careful use of language. Brutus listens to debates on the relative dangers of suffering tyranny or embarking on civil war but keeps both his countenance and his own counsel. It is political action through measured and careful discourse, although its very secretiveness forces Portia, his wife, to take desperate measures, inflicting a wound on her thigh to prove herself worthy of his confidence. This intrinsic dichotomy between measured word and violent action well expresses the political conundrum of when and whether to take action against a tyrant that would have resonated so strongly with Shakespeare's audience.

Nothing, however, could be further from the habits in both life and language of Mark Antony. Plutarch tells us, significantly, that Antony bore a "cruell and mortall hate" towards Cicero, the very embodiment of the art of public speaking and of the governing right of the Senate, and that he fell in with Curio, a "dissolute man, given over to all lust and insolencie, who to have Antonius the better at his commaundement, trayned him on into great follies, and vaine expences upon women in rioting and banketing."[14] Antony, accordingly, made a study not of rhetoric but of eloquence. "He used a manner of phrase in his speeche, called Asiatik, which caried the best grace and estimation at that time, and was much like to his manners and life: for it was full of ostentation, foolishe braverie, and vaine ambition."[15] The style of oratory referred to in this label "Asiatic" is described by Cicero as "redundant and lacking in conciseness," and later as "swift," "ornate" but lacking in symmetry, suitable only for young men. Quintilian is even more scathing and blames a group of men who wanted to "class themselves as orators before they had acquired sufficient command of the language, and who consequently began to express by periphrases what could have been expressed directly, until finally this practice became an ingrained habit." He ends with the racist observation that "Asiatics, being naturally given to bombast and ostentation, were puffed up with a passion for a more vainglorious style of eloquence."[16]

Recent editors for both plays naturally draw attention to Plutarch's observations concerning the oratorical styles of the two protagonists. David Daniell takes the hint and goes so far as to enumerate the preferred word and even phoneme choices for a range of characters in *Julius Caesar*: Cassius employs recent coinages; Brutus more established ones; the two tribunes have a penchant for "o" sounds on stressed syllables; numerous characters refer to themselves repeatedly in the third person. Daniell also cites the impressions expressed by earlier critics such as Chambers and Bradley that the play's meter seems curiously, solidly "Roman," and comments that the spare, logical style of this play is "political": "seven great men of Rome, moderate of word and phrase, coolly and intellectually convinced of their rightness, act together to stab Caesar bloodily to death."[17]

Editors of *Antony and Cleopatra*, however, have not considered the implication that the flamboyance and bombast associated with the Asiatic style of rhetoric might apply to that play's notorious problems of lineation and the scansion of short lines, as well as to the choice of word and extravagant image. Indeed, one of Quintilian's references to Asiatic style comes in a chapter devoted to detailing different types of meter, the rhythmic effects of different types of foot in combination, and the use of elision and hiatus (whether the emphatic pause, or the necessary introduction of a break between syllables for the purposes of enunciation, i.e., the glottal stop).[18] In oratory, as in dramatic literature and performance, pauses are necessary to make the point. Quintilian in fact stresses that prose writing, like poetry, should always be rhythmic:

> My purpose in discussing this topic at length is not to lead the orator to enfeeble his style by pedantic measurement of feet and weighing of syllables: for oratory should possess a vigorous flow, and such solicitude is worthy only of a wretched pedant, absorbed in trivial detail. . . . Poetry was originally the outcome of a natural impulse and was created by the instinctive feeling of the ear for quantity and observation of time and rhythm, while the discovery of feet came later.[19]

The distinction that Quintilian is making here is precisely the distinction between meter and rhythm.

Quintilian also advises that the orator will only communicate effectively with his audience if he thinks himself into the emotional values behind the imagery of his rhetoric so as to sound convincingly natural. His tone of voice must be supplemented with appropriate gestures taken from the observation of real people. The suggestion is adopted by Thomas Wright, a Jesuit campaigner who nevertheless publicly sought to persuade his fellow Catholics to adopt the Oath of Allegiance. For Wright, the art of persuasion, and the art of finding the mind's construction in the face, were therefore professional and political necessities. His book, *The Passions of the Mind in General* (1601), is probably the first book, in English, of detailed observation of human behavior, or of nature working "in her kind":

> love, desire and joy require a plain, pleasant, soft, mild, gentle voice, and the like countenance. . . . Hatred and ire exact a vehement voice and much gesture, a pronunciation sharp, often falling with pathetical repetitions, iterated interrogations proving, confirming, and urging reason. The manner of this action we may best discover in witty women when they chide, because although their excess be vicious and not to be imitated, yet for that they let nature work in her kind, their furious fashion will serve for a good mean to perceive the external manage of this passion. Their voice is loud and sharp and consequently apt to cut, which is proper to ire and hatred, which wish ill and intend revenge; their gestures are frequent, their faces inflamed, their eyes glowing; their reasons hurry one in the neck of another; they with their fingers number the wrongs offered them, the harms, injuries, disgraces and what not, thought, said and done against them. If a prudent orator could in this case better their matter, circumcise the weakness of the reason, abate the excess of their fury, certainly he might win a pretty form for framing his action.[20]

The real art of Shakespeare's very careful and highly patterned language is similarly that it gives the impression of natural speech, differentiated by character. For the effect to work, however, the art and the naturalism need to be kept in balance. Unfortunately, modern actors are broadly divided between those who want to deliver Shakespeare in naturalistic prose without regard to the line and rhetorical pattern, and those who speak line by line (as indeed literally and metrically conducted by the British theater director, Sir Peter Hall[21]) with stops at the end, regardless of enjambment. Neither approach fully considers that there is a distinction to be drawn between meter and rhythm, and that the most powerful effects are created when one is played off against the other.

The normalizing of accent (i.e., stress patterns) by editors of Shakespeare through the relineation of lines that do not fit the perceived iambic pentameter norm is so well entrenched that it often goes unremarked. The rococo (to use a less racist term) rhythms of *Antony and Cleopatra* were first smoothed out in the edition by the eighteenth-century poet, Nicholas Rowe, according to his understanding of the rules and decorum of prosody.

He may also have been influenced in his approach to the soundscape of the play by hearing performances of Dryden's very different version of it: *All for Love*.

Since it is difficult to recognize something when it has become barely visible, there has been a tendency amongst editors to assume that the surviving passages of anomalous meter in Shakespeare are the result of interpolation. The witching octosyllabics in *Macbeth*, particularly those spoken by Hecate, are a case in point. This is an old suggestion, although it has recently gained widespread acceptance, reinforced by the fact that the song titles referred to in the stage directions of the scenes in which Hecate appears seem to relate to songs in Middleton's play, *The Witch*. By extension, then, Hecate herself has come to be regarded as an interpolation, added when the play was revised after Shakespeare's death. The Oxford edition of the *Complete Works* went further and expanded the scene by including passages that surround the songs in Middleton's play. The editors cited the unpublished work of R. V. Holdsworth for this decision without further elaboration or much examination. Their decision is in turn simply cited by later editors of both *The Witch* and *Macbeth*, again without much discussion even when it is somewhat at odds with their own theses.[22] It seems to be a case of something becoming true by virtue of endless repetition.

Only someone relentlessly counting syllables and completely deaf to rhythm could consider the soundscape of Hecate's speech in Folio *Macbeth* to be the same as that in the songs and their surrounding text from *The Witch*. Nothing else—whether in the tone of the language (*The Witch* is humorous, indeed blackly satirical), the vocabulary, the rhyme (*The Witch* has successive lines with internal rhymes), or the rhythm—bears any relation to these disputed passages in *Macbeth*. In both Middleton's *Witch* and Davenant's version of the *Macbeth* witch scenes, meter and rhythm tend to coincide. By contrast, pronunciation of the words in Hecate's lines in *Macbeth* as if they were normally accented prose frequently creates a three-stress rhythm out of the four-stress, octosyllabic, iambic meter. These three-stress lines are composed of the same number of syllables as the others, but the natural prose rhythm of the words creates a hiatus where one of the iambic stresses would be expected to be. The resulting stray, unstressed syllable forms an amphibrach ($\smile\prime\smile$), and the substitute unstressed syllable makes an anapest in the next foot ($\smile\smile\prime$). Thus, for example, in only one of the following six lines does rhythm coincide with meter:

> Tŏ tráde | ănd tráffic ‖ wĭth Măcbéth,
> Ĭn ríddlĕs ‖ ănd ăffaírs | ŏf deáth;
> Ănd Í, | thĕ místrĕss ‖ ŏf yoŭr chárms,

Thĕ clóse | cŏntrívĕr ‖ ŏf ăll hárms,
Wăs né | vĕr cáll'd | tŏ beár | mў párt,
Ŏr shów | thĕ glórў ‖ ŏf oŭr árt?

(*Macbeth* 3.5.4–9)

The amphibrach is likewise a feature of the rest of the play and is found particularly in Macbeth's speeches.[23]

*Macbeth*'s Hecate in fact has a plot function that has been almost universally ignored.[24] Before she appears, the weird sisters are merely fooling around, doing nothing very much out of the normal ambit of merely human agency: demanding chestnuts, cutting thumbs off drowned pilots, and making one "prediction" that the court (and even we in the audience) already know about and a second that is not beyond the bounds of probability in an elective monarchy like Scotland. True, they can summon up a storm, but, even so, they can only make human lives uncomfortable and cannot themselves cause death. It takes a human to do that—whether the Macbeths, at one end of the social scale, or the unmarried mother at the other, destroying the evidence in a ditch. It is only after Hecate has intervened and gone to fetch her "vap'rous drop" from the corner of the moon that their activity turns to the conjuring of apparitions deliberately to mislead Macbeth into a false sense of security, on the grounds that "security is mortals' chiefest enemy." Hecate's presence therefore marks an emotional and psychological turning point in the play. Anyone can want to be thane of Cawdor or to be king. That aspiration, and the criminal act that might accompany it, is well within human imagination and ability. But to be secure is another matter. The recurrent theme in Cicero's oratory is that tyrants cannot and should not feel secure because their violation of proper government and human values exposes them to assassination. This is the theme of Edwards's *Damon and Pythias* as it is of Shakespeare's *Julius Caesar*—two plays from opposite ends of the reign of Elizabeth. *Macbeth* is partly a return to that old theme, but recast according to James's particular predilections: act like a tyrant and you will not feel secure unless you resort to magic, and even that will be an illusion. Shakespeare, however, complicates the issue by suggesting that all members of the commonwealth have a part to play in allowing tyranny to take root. Those who know and do nothing like Banquo (who of course has aspirations of his own regarding the witches' "prophecies"), those who are prepared to overlook faults like Macduff in his interview with Malcolm, those like the old man and Lennox who stand by, wringing their hands at disasters in the air, and the Porter who quite enjoys being porter of Hell gate, are all part of the social system that allows tyranny to flourish. The witches only become an active force in this generally hellish social set-up after the appearance of Hecate.

The borrowing of extra bits of *The Witch* and of Davenant's reworking of Shakespeare's play for incorporation into modern editions of *Macbeth*, however, has ignored—even in the commentaries—the fact that the expansion of the witch scenes in the Davenant version goes hand in hand with a hugely increased role for Lady Macduff and a refocusing of the political agenda. Davenant is partly making her a foil to Lady Macbeth: for instance, they are given a scene together near the beginning of the play when they compare notes on how to cope with the husbands' absences. But whereas Lady Macbeth invokes witchcraft, Lady Macduff actually meets the witches herself, although without coming to believe in them. When her husband starts to listen to their veiled prophecies foretelling the deaths of their family and the death of Macbeth at his hands, she restrains him:

> He that believes ill news from such as these,
> Deserves to find it true. Their words are like
> Their shape; nothing but fiction.
>
> (2.5.88–90)[25]

Two scenes later she is berating him for wanting to take a stand against the tyrant. She tells him that "Heavens Justice" will work without the aid of his sword and expresses the fear that he has an ulterior purpose:

> I am afraid you have some other end,
> Than meerly Scotland's freedom to defend.
> You'd raise your self, whilst you wou'd him dethrone;
> And shake his Greatness, to confirm your own.
> That purpose will appear, when rightly scan'd
> But usurpation at the second hand.
>
> (3.2.17–22)

Another two scenes further on, Macduff prepares to fly to England and Lady Macduff, who has previously been stoical in his absence, is now fearful: "Can you leave me, your daughter and your son / To perish by that Tempest which you shun?" His response to this is the entirely unShakespearean reason that her weakness as a woman encumbered with children, which would endanger her on the road and slow his flight, would be a protection for her if she stays:

> He will not injure you, he cannot be
> Possest with such unmanly cruelty:
> You will your safety to your weakness owe
> As grass escapes the syth by being low.
>
> (3.6.11–14)

Finally in 4.2, talking to Lennox and Seyton, she blames her husband for abandoning her (as indeed she does with Ross in Shakespeare), but here the scene ends before the entrance of her murderers.

The effect of this expansion of her role is to replace the wider, political aspects of the story as found in Shakespeare with a much more domestic, politically conservative one that concentrates on personal honor. The social spectrum has narrowed. There is no old man and, of course, no porter, while the notion that the governed might get the governor they are prepared to put up with has completely disappeared. Along with this, there is systematic ironing out of the Shakespearean deliberate mismatches between rhythm and meter. The curious reversals of syntax found, for example, in the language of Shakespeare's Duncan, and which to my ear sound like an attempt to represent a Scottish idiom without transliterating a Scots accent, have been turned around and regularized. There is, on the other hand, and rather depressingly, a marked increase of servants doing and saying servant-like things. As indicated above, the expanded role of the witches loses the differentiation that I have argued is present in Shakespeare. Now the witches are in possession of knowledge belonging to the future of this particular story dressed up in the veiled language of threat rather than the veiled language of promise, but which, on moral grounds, because they know the witches to be evil, the Macduffs refuse to believe.

Usually, when Shakespeare writes or borrows an existing song, he incorporates it as part of the intrinsic dramaturgy of the scene. It is therefore found written in full. In the scenes as given in the Folio *Macbeth*, the songs have no bearing on the dramaturgy except as sound effects to cover an exit and a dance. If the entire Hecate scenes were interpolations added at a later stage, one would likewise expect to find the songs completely written out. The fact that the songs appear in vestigial form, just as titles, would suggest, on the contrary, that they, and they alone, have been added to the existing manuscript at a later date.[26] This later stage tradition then easily carried over into the scenes as they occur in Davenant's version.

Comparison with the use of song in other plays shows the difference. In *Othello, The Tempest, 1 Henry IV*—the list goes on and on—songs are incorporated seamlessly into the plotline and the dialogue. If the songs are cut, the dialogue has to be cut too—as in the case of Quarto *Othello*. The Oxford editors for *Macbeth* obviously appreciate this, which is why they have added the surrounding dialogue from *The Witch* to their edition. My point is that Hecate's speech from Folio *Macbeth* does not occur in *The Witch* and does not match the soundscape of that play.

I want to conclude with the song, "Hark, hark the lark" from *Cymbeline* (2.3.20–6), the dramaturgy of which had always puzzled me until, as Festival Dramaturg, I started to prepare for rehearsals for a production for Shakespeare Santa Cruz.[27] The charming lyrics, of course, are nothing to do with the awful Cloten. Even he realizes that his boasted (but repeatedly undemonstrated) ability to penetrate does not extend to song and has hired a musician to serenade Imogen for him. On the face of it, it looks like a simple pause for music—and a wholesale borrowing of accent—as if the play we have been watching until that point just stops for a few minutes. Fortunately, the setting of the song by Robert Johnson still survives. Johnson was the composer for the King's Men and had a keen sense of drama, and a tremendous ability to translate that into musical sound. His music for the song in *The Duchess of Malfi*, for example, makes extensive use of chromatic variation to suggest the howling of madmen and wolves—to haunting effect. His setting for the song in *Cymbeline* likewise tries to convey the sense of the words in musical sound. It is extremely attractive, but further consideration reveals something very weird about it. A florid run on the second "hark," three extra repetitions of that word, and then the setting of "lark" to a very long, high note are just too over-the-top even for music of this period. The same is true at the end, where the play-text's command "my lady sweet, arise: / Arise, arise!" culminates, in the musical setting, with a final triumphal run up the scale and an extra "my lady sweet, arise." For what? Nothing! *She doesn't appear*! Hilarious.

I have seen this song performed deliberately badly (on the grounds, presumably, that it is Cloten's song). But that was just embarrassing. It was also trying for the wrong kind of joke and so allowed the possibility that Imogen stays away because of the performance, whereas the joke as written is that she does not come because no one in her right senses— particularly one who thinks of herself as loyally married—would respond to that kind of hubris. Thus, although the music puts Cloten's characterization into a different medium and even a different, more cultivated register, it is written so that his essential arrogance and stupid boastfulness come bursting through. The song is both part of and reinforcement for the play's dramatic pattern. Clothes do not make the man—as the play will demonstrate in exactly those terms a few scenes later.

We must, therefore, in all our dealings with the text of Shakespeare, start to consider the particular soundscape for each play, including, as in this last instance, the sound created by an artistic collaborator in performance, whose choices interpret and enhance the purely linguistic material. This is a subject area that has huge implications for research, for textual bibliography, for performance, and for teaching, and it is capable of giving a much-needed fillip to the old, and now slightly tired, page versus stage debate.

## Notes

1. I would like to thank Andrew Gurr and Charles Edelman for the invitation to participate in their seminar, " 'I other accents borrow that can my speech diffuse' ": Accents, Pronunciation, and Dialects on the Elizabethan Stage."

2. George T. Wright, *Shakespeare's Metrical Art* (Berkeley and Los Angeles: University of California Press, 1988). See also Philip Hobsbaum, *Meter, Rhythm, and Verse Form* (London: Routledge, 1996).

3. For example, variant spellings for the name Henslowe (Hinchley, Hensley) and Shakespeare (Shaksper, Shagsberd) seem to be shortening the length of the second vowel in each case, and perhaps also the "a" in *Shaksper/d,* but the accent remains unchanged. Charles Butler, *The English Grammar* (London, 1634), chap. 4, sets out systematic rules for observing the accent according to the number of syllables in any given word.

4. By contrast, in many other languages (e.g., Chinese) the identification of individual words depends on precise intonation.

5. Tiffany Stern, *Rehearsal from Shakespeare to Sheridan* (Oxford: Clarendon Press, 2000). Cf. B. L. Joseph, *Elizabethan Acting,* 2d ed. (Oxford: Oxford University Press, 1964).

6. The same joke is also found in the earlier play *Ralph Roister Doister,* ed. John M. Manly, *Specimens of the Pre-Shakespearean Drama,* 2 vols. (New York: Dover, 1967), 2:3.4.36 ff. and 3.5.49 ff.

7. Both F and Q *Love's Labor's Lost* 4.2.85–107 assign Holofernes's lines to Nathaniel and vice versa, but the clear difference in register between the two characters, and the fact that Costard addresses the speaker of the joke on person/parson as "schoolmaster" (4.2.85), make the emendation certain.

8. It is much easier to recognize a tune from its rhythm than from the relative pitches of notes without rhythm. Commentators, convinced of the stupidity of Holofernes, have suggested that he mistakes the order of the gamut. Given the music theory attached to every early edition of the authorized psalter, Sternhold and Hopkins, *The Whole Book of Psalms* (1563 and repeatedly thereafter), however, this is perhaps even less likely than supposing that someone now would be ignorant of the words to "Doh, a deer, a female deer."

9. Abraham Fraunce, *The Arcadian Rhetoric* (1588; Menston: Scolar Press, 1969), H7.

10. Ros King, "Seeing the Rhythm: An Interpretation of Sixteenth-Century Punctuation and Metrical Practice," in *Ma(r)king the Text: The Presentation of Meaning on the Literary Page,* ed. Joe Bray, Miriam Handley, and Anne C. Henry (Aldershot: Ashgate, 2000), 235–52; Ros King, *The Works of Richard Edwards: Politics, Poetry, and Performance in Sixteenth-Century England* (Manchester: Manchester University Press, 2001). Cf. Charles Butler, *The Principles of Musik, in Singing and Setting* (1636).

11. King, *Edwards,* 52.

12. Plutarch, *Lives of the Noble Grecians and Romans,* trans. Sir Thomas North (1579), ed.W. E. Henley, The Tudor Translations, 6 vols. (London: David Nutt, 1895–96), 6:185.

13. Ibid., 6:184.

14. Ibid., 6:2.

15. Cicero, *Brutus,* trans. G. L. Hendrickson, Loeb Classical Library (London: Heinemann, 1952), 95.325, 13.51.

16. *Quintilian,* ed. H. E. Butler, Loeb Classical Library, 4 vols. (London: Heinemann, 1922), 12.10.1–17.

17. *Julius Caesar,* ed. David Daniell, Arden 3 (Walton-on-Thames: Thomas Nelson, 1998), 44.

18. *Quintilian,* 9.4.103.

19. Ibid., 4.9.112–14.

20. Thomas Wright, *The Passions of the Mind in General* (1601), ed. William-Webster Newbold (New York: Garland, 1986), 216–17.

21. Cf. Tirzah Lowen, *Peter Hall Directs "Antony and Cleopatra"* (London: Methuen, 1990).

22. Stanley Wells and Gary Taylor, et al. *William Shakespeare: A Textual Companion* (Oxford: Clarendon Press, 1987). Cf. *Macbeth*, ed. Nicholas Brooke (Oxford: Clarendon Press, 1990); and Thomas Middleton, *The Witch*, ed. Elizabeth Schafer, The New Mermaids (London: A & C Black, 1994). Holdsworth's published work on Middleton tends toward the identification of verbal similarities in pairs of texts. The report of his findings concerning Middleton and *Macbeth* recounted in Nicholas Brooke's single-volume Oxford edition seems to suggest largely the same approach. It is now more clearly recognized that this is a slippery way of establishing either precedent or common authorship.

23. Wright, *Shakespeare's Metrical Art*, 233.

24. The exception is Nigel Alexander, "The Necessity of Hecate," inaugural lecture, at Queen Mary College, University of London, 1977.

25. All quotations from Davenant's *Macbeth* are taken from *Five Restoration Adaptations of Shakespeare*, ed. Christopher Spencer (Urbana: University of Illinois Press, 1965).

26. Tiffany Stern identifies a difference between extensive revisions that would necessitate rewriting both promptbook and actors' parts and those designed to make no alteration to the actors' cues (106–10). On this principle, the kind of revision suggested by the Oxford edition would not have resulted in the partial rewriting (just Hecate's speeches, the cauldron scene, and the song titles) found in the Folio.

27. *Cymbeline*, dir. Danny Scheie, Shakespeare Santa Cruz, California, 2000.

# The Disappearing Wall: *A Midsummer Night's Dream* and *Timon of Athens*

### ALEXANDER LEGGATT

W HEN SHAKESPEARE IMAGINED WHAT LAY OUTSIDE LONDON, THE RESULT was usually more of England: Gloucestershire, Warwickshire, Windsor, St. Albans, York. Leaving London, we do not seem to be moving into another world, another mental and imaginative space: we are simply travelling across locations on a familiar map. Shakespeare's Mediterranean cities are another matter. He is more inclined to think of them as walled cities with gates, beyond which lies not just more of Italy or more of Greece but a space in which society has been replaced by something else. It is true that in the Italian plays we are aware that beyond one city—Verona or Padua—there are other cities: Milan, Pisa, Mantua. But in *The Two Gentlemen of Verona* there is also the wood of the outlaws, not just the green world that used to be a picturesque feature in the criticism of Shakespearean comedy, but a place of absurdity where normal codes and values break down, murder and kidnapping rank as petty crimes, and Valentine exercises his leadership of the robber band (which he acquired through his good looks and his command of languages) by trying to prevent them from robbing anybody.[1] In this context his attempt to turn Silvia over to Proteus as a token of forgiveness seems part of the general craziness. This is an early experiment, but it alerts Shakespeare to an idea he was to use over and over: that beyond the city lie not just more cities, or even a familiar countryside, but places of otherness and strangeness. Thus, beyond the Rome of *Coriolanus* there are the cities of the Volsces; but there is also the city of kites and crows, the fen of the lonely dragon. It is here, not just in a military encampment, that Cominius finds not Coriolanus but a man who refuses all names, who is a kind of nothing.

There are of course such places in *King Lear* and *Cymbeline*; and there are courts of a kind to set against them. But in those cases there is no clearly defined city. The contrast between city and wilderness seems to have been easiest for Shakespeare to imagine when he got out of England. The effect I want to explore is clearest in his two Athenian plays, *A Midsummer Night's Dream* and *Timon of Athens*, though I want to approach

194

the latter by a brief detour through *Titus Andronicus*. Shakespeare's imagination, like those of his contemporaries, was fuller of information and ideas about Rome than about Athens. It was therefore easier for Athens to be to him a generic city, reflecting not so much a particular history or culture as a general idea of city-ness. In *Dream* and *Timon* he imagines no other Greek cities beyond Athens. There is Athens, and there is the wood. Between them there is a wall.

The wall features more prominently in *Timon*, as we shall see, but Lysander's "Through Athens gates have we devis'd to steal" (1.1.213) implies a walled city.[2] To break out of Athens is to break out of an enclosure. And of course in *Pyramus and Thisbe* we encounter another wall, the best-spoken wall in English drama. One wall pens lovers in, in a city whose laws frustrate their desires; the other wall separates lovers from each other. This being a comedy, both walls disappear in the course of the action. The separation imposed by the city wall is not just geographical, and not just a division of city and wood. Athens is a male space dominated by the authority of Theseus on one level and Egeus on another. In the wood, authority is divided between Oberon and Titania, but at first it seems more her domain than his. The first acknowledgment of authority in the opening forest scene is "I serve the Fairy Queen" (2.1.8). In general the wood is a place for getting lost, as trackless and unmappable as its American equivalent in *The Blair Witch Project*. Its one significant location is Titania's bower, defined as a special place by Oberon's breaking into it. Oberon himself seems to have no headquarters; he ranges freely. The key location in the wood is Titania's bower, as the key location in the city is Theseus's palace.

Although Lysander recalls only one previous visit to the wood on a special occasion, "To do observance to a morn of May" (1.1.167), Hermia recalls regular visits with Helena for schoolgirl confidences "in the wood, where often you and I / Upon faint primrose beds were wont to lie, / Emptying our bosoms of their counsel [sweet]" (1.1.214–16). Once again the wood seems more a female space than a male one. The common factor is the otherness of the wood: whether it is a place of seasonal observance or a place of privacy, it is where you go to do things that cannot be done in the city.

The Athenians tend to compartmentalize and divide. Even in the wood Hermia insists on sleeping some distance from Lysander: "Such separation as may well be said / Becomes a virtuous bachelor and a maid" (2.2.58–59). She does not believe in bundling. Theseus's manager of mirth (Philostrate in the Quarto, Egeus in the Folio) insists on another kind of division, trying to keep the rude mechanicals out of the palace. Their play, he tells Theseus firmly, "is not for you" (5.1.77). He is in his own way a builder of walls. But something there is that doesn't love a wall, and whatever that something is, it is at work in this play. Hermia, in a way, is punished for keeping Lysander at a distance; it helps trigger Puck's mistake, and for a while she loses her lover altogether. In the end they lie side by side. And Theseus lets Quince's acting troop into his palace over the protests of his master of the revels, where they present, among other things, the play's most striking image of a barrier disappearing. Wall, his part ended, simply gets up and leaves: "Thus have I, Wall, my part discharged so; / And being done, thus Wall away doth go" (5.1.204–5). The departure of Wall is not just a practical move to clear the stage. It functions as a move within the story when Bottom assures the spectators, "the wall is down that parted their fathers" (5.1.351–52), suggesting an equivalent of the Capulet-Montague reconciliation at the end of *Romeo and Juliet*. As Bottom says this, at least two more divisions disappear: Pyramus, having died, returns from the dead in his original person as Bottom. Role dissolves into actor, and the barrier between the living and the dead is broken. So is the custom of politeness that normally keeps actors and audience from interrupting each other, the convention that in later ages of theater would be known as the fourth wall.

In Snout's impersonation of this crucial character, the division between animate and inanimate has also been challenged. This is a wall with human attributes, sweet and lovely when Pyramus expects to see Thisbe through the chink, wicked when no Thisbe appears: "Curs'd be thy stones for thus deceiving me!" (5.1.181). (This anticipates a scene in *Fawlty Towers* in which John Cleese whips a recalcitrant automobile with a tree branch, shouting, "You vicious bastard!") Wall is humanized, not just by the people who address it, but by its own gift of speech. As Theseus and Demetrius observe, "Would you desire lime and hair to speak better?" "It is the wittiest partition that ever I heard discourse" (5.1.165–68).

The wall that separates the families disappears, and even when it is in place it offers a comic challenge to the divisions and distinctions of normal life. How does it relate to that other wall, which we never see but whose significance we sense throughout the play, the wall that separates Athens from the wood? Does that wall also disappear? In a word, yes. Its separating function is challenged from the beginning—significantly, by the very players who invade the palace, and who were prepared to open a window and let in moonshine until they decided Starveling would do it better. Quince orders his fellows to meet him in "the palace wood" and identifies their rendezvous as "the Duke's oak" (1.2.101, 110). More than the lovers of the previous scene, he sees the wood as an extension of the city, a place where Theseus's authority runs as it does in Athens. Arriving for their rehearsal, the actors transform the wood, with no sense of effort, into an urban place, a theater: "This green plot shall be our stage, this hawthorn brake our tiring-house" (3.1.3–4). (The transformation does indeed require no effort, since the green plot *is* a stage and the hawthorn brake *is* a tiring-house.) Before their rehearsal is over, Quince and company will confront the strangeness of the woods at full force in the sight of the transformed Bottom. But theatrically their panic is set up by the easy familiarity with which they settle down in the wood and make themselves at home.

Their transformation of the green plot into a stage, their sense that there is no real difference between the wood and Athens, sets up another transformation, another crossing of barriers, at the end of the play. When the play is performed in realistic sets, the effect of its coda is that the fairies are doing just what they say they are doing, invading Theseus's palace. But in an unlocalized staging such as the original one, the first entry of Puck and the Fairy told us we were in the wood, and throughout the middle scenes the presence of the fairies kept that setting in place. Where the fairies are, there the wood is also. And so at the end when the fairies enter, the palace dissolves into the wood, bedchambers and all; it has been transported, or (like Bottom) translated. The wall has not just been breached; like its equivalent in *Pyramus and Thisbe* it has disappeared.

This dissolution of one thing into another reminds us of a book from the Mediterranean world that particularly fired Shakespeare's imagination, Ovid's *Metamorphoses*. But in the play, transformations seem arrested at a halfway point. Snug tries to become a lion as Snout tries to become a wall; but they are too talkatively themselves to be anything more than halfway there. Flute, with a beard coming, is in standing water between boy and man, man and woman. As when the green plot becomes a stage or the palace becomes the wood, there is the kind of vision Hermia reports, "When every thing seems double" (4.1.190).

The greatest of these incomplete transformations is of course that of Bottom. As he has the head of an ass, but only the head, he seems to have increasingly the appetites of an ass (hay, oats, and dried peas), but he expresses them in a voice that is recognizably his own. The hero of *The Golden Ass*, externally at least, went all the way. Bottom is more like Pooh bear, stuck halfway in the passage.[3] And the lovers, collectively, are stuck halfway when they come out of the forest. Lysander is disenchanted, but Demetrius is still enchanted and will remain so for the rest of his life. Or one could say that both men are enchanted, since Lysander now loves Hermia not because he is back to his old self but through the action of yet another drug. It is the women who remain themselves, the men who from now on will live in the wood when they think they are living in Athens. If we see the wood as a female space, this counterbalances the male authority implied by the women's silence throughout act 5, just as the blessing of the bride-beds recalls Titania's lyrical description of her pregnant votaress, and helps to restore some of the female authority she surrendered when she gave Oberon the Indian boy.

Throughout the play there have been echoes between the city and the wood. Demetrius, we learn, changed his affections in Athens without the help of drugs: there too he was a "spotted and inconstant man" (1.1.110). In both places there is a dispute over who has rights of property over a child: Hermia and the Indian boy. In both locations revelry is aborted: Theseus's call for general merriment is cut across by the cantankerous voice of Egeus calling on the dark side of city life, the working of an inhuman law; Oberon and Titania interrupt each other's revels. In the city and the wood there are problems, the same problems, and it is traffic across the border that allows for their solution.

Disappearing barriers may seem a characteristic function of comedy. But barriers protect, and their disappearance can be part of the terror of tragedy. This is certainly the case in *Titus Andronicus*, roughly contemporary with *A Midsummer Night's Dream*, where the walls of Rome are as porous as the walls of Athens. Titus brings Gothic prisoners to Rome, only to find that in short order they take over the city and he becomes an outcast. In the end his son Lucius is made emperor with the backing of an army of Goths. As Tamora calls herself "incorporate in Rome, / A Roman now adopted happily" (1.1.462–63), the distinction between Roman and Goth, a line Titus has spent his military career policing, dissolves.[4] This may account for one of the most disturbing parallels in the play: the silence of Lavinia as Bassianus and her family carry her off (in one kind of rape) anticipates the silence forced on her by Chiron and Demetrius (in another kind of rape). The actions of her husband and her family in the city foreshadow the actions of her Gothic assailants in the wood. The line between civil and savage, love and violence, is not so firm as we thought.

A literal wall figures in the action when Aaron recounts how, spying like Pyramus through the crevice of a wall, he wept with laughter at Titus's grief over the severed heads of his sons. Here the wall divides: tragedy on one side, comedy on the other. But again the division is insecure. Aaron does not seem to have noticed that later in the same scene Titus laughs too, and the laughter clears out his grief and starts him on his course of revenge. In that revenge he shows a cruel wit to match Aaron's own, and Aaron himself applauds the cleverness of Titus's insolent messages to the court. Aaron is a violator of thresholds, from his merry habit of digging up corpses and making them stand in doorways, to his telling reminder to Chiron and Demetrius that the black baby they want to kill is their brother. He is a spirit of misrule in a play in which barriers break and the wood comes into the city. As Titus puts it, "Rome is but a wilderness of tigers" (3.1.54). The animal transformations of Bottom and Snug took them only halfway there, so that they were fixed on the border just as Snout was embedded in the wall. Here the moral transformation of human to animal is complete, but the tigers still look like people.

In *Timon of Athens* we seem to have a radical contrast between the city and the wood; the city walls, of which we hear a good deal in this play, really do seem to divide. On the one side is the wealth and sophistication of a great city, with crowded scenes featuring a bewildering array of characters who keep dissolving into each other; on the other side, the solitude of the woods where life is at subsistence level and the drama takes on a Beckett-like austerity.[5] Apemantus mockingly draws the contrast between Timon's old life and his new one:

> What, think'st
> That the bleak air, thy boisterous chamberlain,
> Will put thy shirt on warm? Will these moist trees,
> That have outliv'd the eagle, page thy heels
> And skip when thou point'st out?
>
> (4.3.221–25)

But this city/wood division becomes as problematic as the others we have looked at. When Timon digs in the earth for roots, the first thing he finds is gold. Once again he has money. The difference is that while his fortune in Athens seemed to come from the earth only in a mediated way, through the rent of his land (a process in which Timon seems to have taken not the slightest interest), here it comes from the earth in the most immediate, literal way, through his own efforts. Living as we do in a society in which money comes from money, which comes from money (and in *Timon of Athens* the constant references to usury suggest a world like ours), it requires an effort of imagination to think of money coming from labor. But this is where Timon's second fortune comes from, the difference being that this time the labor is his own. He uses his new-found gold to spread corruption and destruction throughout Athens; arguably, that was what he always did, but this time he does it explicitly and intentionally. Timon's second life is his first life revisited, deepened, and clarified.[6] Life outside the wall is not that different from life inside it, just as the madness of love in the wood outside that earlier Athens is a farcically literal enactment of love as we hear of it in the town.

By the same token, life in Athens recalls the wilderness of tigers that is Rome. While the obliging Wall of *Pyramus and Thisbe* leaves the stage when its part is over, Timon has to curse the wall of Athens to make it disappear, though by addressing it as Pyramus does, for a moment he makes it seem as human as Snout:

> O thou wall
> That girdles in those wolves, dive in the earth,
> And fence not Athens! Matrons, turn incontinent!
> Obedience, fail in children! Slaves and fools,
> Pluck the grave wrinkled Senate from the bench,

And minister in their steads! To general filths
Convert o'th'instant, green virginity!
Do't in your parents' eyes!

(4.1.1–8)

Timon does not see the wall as protecting humanity from the wolves outside. It is the other way around: the wolves, like the tigers of Rome, are
inside the city, and the wall is to protect the wilderness. Then the wall
acquires a more disquieting symbolic function. It becomes a metaphor for
the internal barriers, moral and psychological, that restrain the Athenians
from expressing their true natures, protecting them from themselves and
each other, hiding what they truly are. That is the barrier Timon wants to
disappear. The beasts he wants to turn loose on the city are the beasts beneath the skin.

Apemantus has already seen Athens as a city, not of tigers, but of dogs
and monkeys. When the Painter tells him, "Y'are a dog," he replies, "Thy
mother's of my generation; what's she, if I be a dog?" (1.1.200–2). His
complaint, "The strain of man's bred out / Into baboon and monkey"
(1.1.250–51), implies a kind of reverse Darwinism. His own name, on the
page, irresistibly suggests "ape man." We might expect these satiric metamorphoses to intensify when Timon goes to the woods and lives more like
an animal, with only animals for neighbors. To some degree this happens:
when Apemantus, repeating one of his stock routines, declares, "The commonwealth of Athens is become a forest of beasts," Timon asks, "How
has the ass broke the wall, that thou art out of the city?" (4.3.347–50).
Once again the function of the city wall is to keep the animals in. When
Alcibiades asks him who he is, Timon replies, "A beast, as thou art"
(4.3.50). Yet in the same dialogue the distinction between beast and man
starts to reappear. Timon tells Alcibiades, "For thy part, I do wish thou
wert a dog, / That I might love thee something" (4.3.55–56). Behind the
obvious point that dogs are more lovable than people is the admission that
Alcibiades is not a dog. It would be better if he were, of course. Exchanging insults with Apemantus, Timon makes a similar point: when Apemantus complains that Timon is imitating his manners, Timon retorts, "'Tis
then, because thou dost not keep a dog; / Whom I would imitate"
(4.3.200–1). Apemantus is not a dog; better if he were. On the one hand
this deepens the satire: Timon prefers dogs as Gulliver comes to prefer
horses.[7] Yet the distinction these passages draw between beast and man
suggests a retreat from one of the play's key ideas, and an inclination to
re-erect the wall. It is in the wood that Bottom becomes an ass, and then
becomes Bottom again; it is in the wood that Timon, looking with detachment on the metaphorical dogs and monkeys of Athens, begins to realize
that real beasts and real men are not the same.

Apemantus has a similar moment. Taking his cue from Apemantus's idea that the world should be given to the beasts "to be rid of the men" while he himself would remain "a beast with the beasts" (4.3.323–25), Timon constructs a beast fable in which the animals act like people, rapacious and stupid (4.3.327–45). When Timon later returns to Apemantus's idea and demands that gold turn men against each other "that beasts / May have the world in empire!" Apemantus, who has had time to digest the full implications, is the first to blink: "Would 'twere so! / But not till I am dead" (4.3.392–93). He has glimpsed the exchange of human and animal, and he retreats. He wants the wall in place. He wants the city to do what cities should do—protect people and keep them human—and he wants to be inside with his fellow men.

Apemantus has always been a respecter of barriers. He offers what seems a perverse explanation of his presence in Timon's house: "I come to have thee thrust me out of doors" (1.2.25). He is self-dramatizing, wanting to highlight his own role as outsider; but he is also rebuking Timon for keeping open house, for not protecting his private space; he needs practice in throwing people out. A Senator who has lent Timon money and deplores his prodigal ways makes the point more directly: "No porter at his gate, / But rather one that smiles and still invites / All that pass by" (2.1.10–12). Even when he is ruined and locked into his house for his own protection, Timon bursts out of it like a wild animal breaking out of a cage. Society defines itself by the erecting of barriers; we glimpsed that in *Dream*, seeing Egeus, Philostrate, and even Hermia policing the borders. Timon is a breaker of barriers, and this makes him, even in his civic life, anti-social. His keeping open house for the unworthy is a sign of social breakdown.

When in the closing scenes of the play Alcibiades lays siege to Athens we become acutely aware of its walls, as we do with other besieged cities like Angiers in *King John* and Harfleur in *Henry V.* The wall that Timon cursed is still very much in place. The stage direction, "The SENATORS appear upon the walls" (5.4.2.1) invites us to visualize it. The Second Senator, by insisting "These walls of ours / Were not erected by their hands from whom / You have receiv'd your grief" (5.4.22–24), invites Alcibiades to look beyond the corrupt city of the present and see an older city, perhaps as old as Apemantus's trees that have outlived the eagle. It has a larger story and a more honorable tradition than the Athens the play has shown, and the wall stands for its past—as in some cities we can visit now, where the wall is the oldest thing still standing.

The wall enforces moral discriminations. The Senators invite Alcibiades to enter, on condition that he leave the savage part of himself outside: "Bring in thy ranks, but leave without thy rage" (5.4.39). On that condition, "So thou wilt send thy gentle heart before, / To say thou't enter

friendly" (5.4.48–49), the gates will open easily. The wall divides Alcibiades himself. It leaves outside the full violence of the soldier, a violence
like that of the follower he defended in the scene that provoked his banishment, and admits the civil citizen who will do measured justice, not destroying the town but killing only "the destin'd tenth" (5.4.33) who are to
be selected by a roll of the dice. Wholesale vengeance is transformed into
ritualized sacrifice. The gate is narrow, and Alcibiades' vengeance must
be trimmed to fit.

Yet we may find this an odd sort of civility. The Senators' invitation to
kill one tenth of the population, coupled with their insistence that Alcibiades' actual enemies are all dead, means logically that he will be killing
innocent people. Like the killing of Alarbus in *Titus*, this is ritually logical
but morally bizarre. And the claim that Alcibiades' enemies are all dead
is backed by an explanation so grotesque it compels disbelief: "Shame,
that they wanted cunning in excess, / Hath broke their hearts" (5.4.28–29).
The suggestion that this is a new Athens in which the bad old generation
has died off is usually countered in performance by the presence of the
same actors as we saw in the first half of the play—often still in their original characters.[8] Unless he was writing for the theater of the mind (a possibility that with this play cannot be ruled out). Shakespeare, knowing the
size of his company, must have expected this effect. The ambiguity of this
reformed, conciliatory Athens is matched by the ambiguity of the gesture
Alcibiades picks to show his mercy and forbearance: he throws down a
glove. When Alcibiades enters the city, behind the image of an accommodating town welcoming an invader who comes in peace is a shadow-action
in which an angry conqueror, having flung down his glove in a traditional
sign of challenge, breaks into a corrupt city to shed blood. The fact that
we have seen a couple of prostitutes in Alcibiades' entourage suggests that
even in the new Athens it will be business as usual.

The play's final scene seems to affirm the importance of walls: discrimi-
nating, dividing, protecting civil society by setting conditions for admission. It figures a return to civil life through a new sense of respect for its
divisions. But the sardonic overtones of the scene imply that the wall is
really a provocation to Alcibiades' belligerence, and a screen by which the
Athenians hide their continuing corruption. They let Alcibiades in when
he agrees to play the game as they have defined it. The wall does indeed
stand for society; that is what is wrong with it. (We flash forward a moment to the wall in Edward Bond's *Lear*.)

Timon meanwhile has crossed another border, the border between life
and death, symbolized by the border that separates the land from the sea.
Except that he does not really cross it. He is buried at a point where land
and sea keep changing places as the tide ebbs and flows. It is the equivalent of the twilight zone Oberon inhabits when he sports with the dawn; it

recalls the confusion of woods and palace at the end of *Dream*, the halfway transformations of Bottom, Snout, and Snug. In Timon's own words,

> Come not to me again, but say to Athens,
> Timon hath made his everlasting mansion
> Upon the beached verge of the salt flood,
> Who once a day with his embossed froth
> The turbulent surge shall cover.

(5.1.214–18)

Never a respecter of barriers, Timon is sporting with the border between life and death. His grave will be a house, a place to live. Having said he wants nothing to do with Athens, he keeps sending messages to it; this is one of many. "Say to Athens" is like the inscription at Thermopylae: "Go tell the Spartans." It is a message from the dead to the living.[9] He goes on sending such messages in the form of self-authored epitaphs. And what kind of dead man, we might ask, buries himself and sets up his own gravestone? In his last living speech he calls for the ending of language, and goes on talking for three more lines (5.1.220–23). In his exile he has spent much of his time receiving visitors in a demented intellectual *salon* in which he does most of the talking, and the ironically self-defeating manner of his rejection of society persists beyond death. His two epitaphs are inconsistent with each other, in that one withholds his name and the other proclaims it: "Here lies a wretched corse, of wretched soul bereft; / Seek not my name: a plague consume you, wicked caitiffs left!" and "Here lie I, Timon, who, alive, all living men did hate; / Pass by and curse thy fill, but pass and stay not here thy gait" (5.4.70–73). The sensible explanation is that the indecision is Shakespeare's; he intended to cancel one epitaph and never got around to it.[10] Yet the text as we have it has a value in reflecting Timon's own indecision. Is he dead or not? Has he a name or not? Is he alone or not? One factor common to both epitaphs is that while Timon has passed beyond society, he still expects visitors. Like Browning's bishop ordering his tomb, he is still very much in the world; he has not grasped what it means to be dead. And nothing, not even death, will shut him up.

Pyramus too went on talking after death: when he proclaimed "Now am I dead" (5.1.301) he was just getting warmed up. And he broke the final barrier by rising from the ground to assure Theseus, "the wall is down that parted their fathers" (5.1.351–52). Alcibiades' reading of Timon's last gesture sees it as working against his curses: "rich conceit / Taught thee to make vast Neptune weep for aye / On thy low grave, on faults forgiven" (5.4.77–79).

The inanimate world once again acquires human qualities. Does the sea's forgiveness of Timon imply a final restoration of the human bond? Could Timon and the world forgive each other beyond death? Has the last wall fallen? We can imagine Timon responding, "that is not what I meant at all, that is not it at all." But we have seen how hard it is for him to leave community behind; and Alcibiades has looked beyond his words to a more benevolent intention implied in the symbolism of his burial. Good fences make good neighbors, according to the neighbor in Robert Frost's "Mending Wall." But when the wood becomes indistinguishable from Theseus's palace, this allows the fairies to bless the bride-beds, and for Alcibiades Timon's burial in a spot which is neither land nor sea is a gesture of forgiveness. It may be that when Shakespeare contemplated the walled cities of the Mediterranean world one conclusion he came to was that for all society's dependence on the barriers that divide and distinguish, true communities are made not when walls are built but when they are taken down.

## Notes

1. In the old critical tradition of poking fun at *Two Gentlemen of Verona*, H. B. Charlton's comparison of them to the Pirates of Penzance stands as a high point. See *Shakespearian Comedy* (1938; reprint London: Methuen, 1966), 38–40.

2. The square brackets used in *The Riverside Shakespeare* to show textual emendations have been silently omitted in quotations from it.

3. As William C. Carroll puts it, "the boundary between the human and the animal seems, in his case at least, to be located precisely at the neck ."; *The Metamorphoses of Shakespearean Comedy* (Princeton: Princeton University Press, 1985), 149.

4. See Coppélia Kahn, *Roman Shakespeare: Warriors, Wounds and Women* (London: Routledge, 1997), 47; and Naomi Conn Liebler, *Shakespeare's Festive Tragedy: The Ritual Foundations of Genre* (London: Routledge, 1995), 142, 146.

5. Richard Fly sees a generic division. By getting outside the wall, Timon "appears to have moved from a structure whose radical of presentation is dramatic to one whose mode of address is essentially lyric and satiric." *Shakespeare's Mediated World* (Amherst: University of Massachusetts Press, 1976), 137. According to A. D. Nuttall, in the last two acts "We seem to have travelled back to the earliest period of Greek drama, in which the 'second actor' has not yet been invented and where . . . the same speaker came forward to address the audience in a succession of different masks." *Twayne's New Critical Introductions to Shakespeare: "Timon of Athens"* (Boston: Twayne, 1989), 89. He also calls the play "Shakespeare's *Endgame*" (135).

6. See Gail Kern Paster, *The Idea of the City in the Age of Shakespeare* (Athens: University of Georgia Press, 1985), 106.

7. Nuttall observes, "The favour shown to dogs in *Timon* is only a measure of the depth to which man has sunk. It is hardly a compliment to the dog to choose him for this particular purpose" (*Twayne Timon*, 132). He develops the comparison with Gulliver's last voyage (132–33).

8. This was the effect, for example, in productions by Michael Langham at

Stratford, Ontario, in 1963 (restaged at Chichester in 1964) and 1991; and by Robin Phillips at the Grand Theatre, London, Ontario, in 1983.

9. See Nuttall, *Twayne Timon*, 138.

10. According to Plutarch the first epitaph was Timon's own, the second the work of the poet Callimachus.

# Shakespeare's Outsiders

## Charles Marowitz

In HIS BOOK *THE SHIFTING POINT,* PETER BROOK WRITES THAT WHEREAS other writers merely "interpret reality," what we get from Shakespeare is not simply his "view of the world, it's something that actually resembles reality." Other artists may interpret reality, says Brook, but "what [Shakespeare] wrote is not interpretation, it is the thing itself."

This idea, enlarged and aggrandized, reappears in Harold Bloom's recent book *Shakespeare: The Invention of the Human,* in which Bloom argues that human character as we know it, was not simply observed by Shakespeare but actually invented by him, Shakespeare not so much an artist reflecting the world around him but an avatar creating the prototypes that eventually become sentient human beings. If we are to buy Professor Bloom's theory of Bardic Creationism, then we must believe that there were no brooding, young intellectuals before Hamlet; no obsessive, career-driven women before Lady Macbeth; no arrogant, foolhardy old rulers like Lear commanding love from his offspring; no wheedling, vengeful money-lenders before Shylock; no cynical, scoffing soldiers before Falstaff; no young men as besotted with juvenile love as Romeo or young girls as delirious with passion as Juliet. That all the variety of types depicted by all of Shakespeare's predecessors—Ovid, Homer, Spenser, Plutarch, Cinthio, Boccaccio—were simply laying small insignificant eggs that Mother Hen Shakespeare actually hatched.

I have a deep affection for Mr. Bloom and believe that as a critic and a scholar he brings an intelligence to the canon which is titillatingly insightful and often profound. Like a brilliant and eloquent docent, he shows us around the many wings of a fascinating old castle, dropping pearls-of-wisdom and rubies-of-perception wherever he goes. But academics have a strong tendency to overstate their case, sometimes to the point of absurdity, and although I am mightily impressed by Bloom's galaxies of insights, I find his central thesis preposterous.

Now why do I begin in this narky, sardonic way, bad-mouthing a highly esteemed Shakespearean scholar who has given me, and I'm sure you as well, innumerable hours of pleasure and stimulation? Mainly as a caution to myself, since what I am about to say about two of Shakespeare's plays, *The Merchant of Venice* and *Othello*, may strike those that hear it as just as fanciful and absurd as Bloom's thesis strikes me. I am openly acknowledging that curious sport in which we're all engaged here: a kind of theatrical balancing act which juggles theories, hunches, insights, propositions, analyses, paradoxes, paradigms, aberrations, and delusions. In short, the traditional claptrap of Shakespearean criticism. Only now, having made my disclaimer or, if you like, "Surgeon-General's Safety Warning," do I feel I can commence.

*The Merchant Of Venice* is not a play about money, venture capitalism, Judaism, Christianity, social justice, nuptial lotteries, or Shakespeare's hang-up with Marlowe's *Jew Of Malta*. It seems to me to be a play in which the author tries to balance three incompatible styles: Romance, Comedy, and Tragedy. The nuptial lottery, Bassanio's quest to win Portia, Antonio's deeply rooted affection for his wastrel friend (touchingly reciprocated by Bassanio), and Portia's partiality to this impecunious adventurer, is where the Romance is lodged. The Comedy grows out of Shakespeare's depiction of a stereotypical sixteenth-century Jewish usurer who sees people almost exclusively as property (a blind spot that extends even to his daughter), and the quiz show of the Three Sealed Boxes as performed by Portia, Nerissa, and the three male contestants who seek her hand, a kind of Renaissance version of "Who Wants To Marry a Millionairess"!

The Tragedy of course is rooted in the play's Trial Scene, in which Antonio's life is imperiled by a tenacious plaintiff who, demanding that the Court apply the letter of the law, is unaware that the law is not graven in stone but etched in tablets of clay, which can either bend or break depending on who handles them. Forbidding the spillage of a drop of blood in a forfeit that permits the cutting of a pound of flesh (Portia's brilliant trump card) is one of those legal anomalies so dear to professional attorneys which, to everyone else, seems only to make nonsense of the law, the equivalent of a dimpled chad that disqualifies an otherwise legitimate ballot. One might argue that Shylock's contract was illegal to start with, as its proper execution would necessarily violate a slew of other standing laws like those against Mayhem, Grievous Bodily Harm, or Conspiracy to Commit Murder. But theoretically the bond entered into between Antonio and Shylock was sanctioned and certified by the State or the case would never have come to trial in the first place. So, bloodthirsty as it may seem to us, it was obviously deemed legitimate within its own social context. If that is so, to contravene it by suddenly applying another statute that nullifies it could be construed as a cruel anomaly, entrapment, or simply playing fast and loose with the whole concept of the law. Striking down one law in favor of another that appears to contravene it is, at the very least, a case ripe for review by a court of appeal. But the Venetian Court, despite its lip service to impartiality, is clearly prejudiced against the plaintiff and will go to any lengths to foil his suit—even permitting a young, foreign whippersnapper of a justice to turn its statutes on their head. The tragedy then is that the law, as practiced in Venice, is not impartial but prejudiced against the Jew as later laws throughout Europe unquestionably were, and as American laws were against blacks from the birth of the Republic right up to the present day.

Without meaning to reopen old wounds, I must say that the preferences of the Florida legislature as expressed in the presidential election of 2000 were just as clearly prejudicial to the claims of Al Gore as the Duke's court was to Shylock. There too a plaintiff, but of the wrong political persuasion, was perceived as an "outsider" in regard to the prevailing political sympathies of the judges that presided over that court; so much so that they were prepared to find for his opponent whatever the official verdict might have been. A majority of the highest U.S. court, the Supreme Court, perpetuated that prejudice by refusing to permit a recount that might have produced a result inimical to their partisan preferences. Judges and attorneys have always manipulated the laws, and laws have been created in such a way that they lend themselves to being bent in whichever direction clever attorneys are able to bend them. Fortunately, there are so many laws that one can blithely be used against the other, as it was in Shylock's case, to achieve the desired end of a ruling faction. Some call this democracy at work; others see it as the smirking, unacceptable face of Democracy, which brings to mind H. L. Mencken's definition: "Democracy is the theory that the common people know what they want, and deserve to get it— good and hard!"

The law, as we see over and over again, is never absolute and almost never impartial. It has biases built into it because of the nature of the people who are wielding it. It is a weapon in the hands of those holding power to favor its friends and punish its enemies. Being man-made, it suffers from the moral flaws and egoistic prejudices of its creators. It is precisely because judges are mortal men and women that they wish to appear as emissaries of some divine power. That's why they disguise themselves in wigs and gowns, prop themselves up behind high benches, surround themselves with Roman columns, and preside beneath gold-embossed moralistic platitudes. They would have us believe that they are more prescient and more omnipotent than ordinary mortals who feel human surges such as spite, vindictiveness, rancor, and vengeance. Being Talmudic rather than worldly, intellectual rather than practical, Shylock fatally misreads the intentions of the Court. The fact is, Shylock, by being a Jew in a Christian community, is already guilty, and if he were half as bright as his clever badinage in the Trial Scene, he would have realized it and never brought a case that, no matter what its rights in law, he could not possibly win.

Ultimately, it's the Tragedy in *Merchant* that overwhelms both the Romance and the Comedy—so much so that in that last lyrical scene (act 5) we cannot possibly concentrate on the amusing squabbles of the four newlyweds because some part of us cannot shake the image of Shylock being stripped of his Jewish gabardine, his star of David roughly replaced by a crucifix and a copy of the New Testament.

The aftermath of Shylock's tragedy highlights the fact that Shakespeare has failed at blending his three selected elements of Romance, Comedy, and Tragedy into an organic whole. He commits the same mistake in *Measure for Measure*, where the sexual collisions between Angelo and Isabella subvert all of the Duke's ingenious acts of stage management. It doesn't matter how resolutely this so-called "comedy" resolves itself with the forced marriage of Mariana and Angelo, and the equally forced marriage of Isabella and the Duke. No arbitrary nuptial resolutions can obliterate the rancid taste of Angelo's corruption of power or the nun's realization that the world is not filled with beatific angels like Saint Clare but lustful sinners like Angelo and Lucio.

They are often referred to as "problem plays," but critics rarely identify what the problems are. Essentially, they represent a stylistic imbalance which the playwright, try as he may, cannot reconcile—which is why directors revive them over and over again, trying in their productions to resolve the contradictions the author was unable to resolve. That may well be the underlying raison d'être of all revisionist Shakespeare productions. Paradoxically, it is the plays' deeply embedded imperfections that are responsible for some of the most imaginative productions of them that we occasionally see:—directorial ingenuity and the acumen of talented actors compensating for a playwright's failings, one of the best kept secrets in the theater.

*　　*　　*

If Shylock is the black sheep of the Venetian community, what are we to call Othello, that other great misfit from the same city? One might argue that, as a hired mercenary and successful warrior, Othello provides an invaluable service to the State. But then, in a much less conspicuous way, so does a moneylender. The one fortifies the city's walls, the other its economy. Shylock and Othello are both outcasts in Venice, but so long as they can provide monetary or military services, they are tolerated and grudgingly accepted. Apart from their race and their both being war heroes, there are no striking parallels between Othello and General Colin Powell, the American Secretary of State, and yet they are both united by a painful contradiction. Othello provides his skills and military expertise in order to wage war against a brown-skinned enemy, the Turks, who threaten the security of the State.

Powell is a member of the ruling Washington elite in a democracy where he is well aware that blacks are often disenfranchised, economically disadvantaged, discriminated against, and racially profiled. He sees no contradiction in belonging to a party that many blacks view with suspicion and some with open contempt. Perhaps he justifies his role in the cabinet by arguing that he is in a position to enhance the lot of his people. Anything that shows able and effective black citizens rising to high office and being visible there helps to remove the inequality that is embedded in the nation's shameful history and must be counted as a virtue. Powell, by no stretch of the imagination "an outsider," becomes an exemplar for others of his race.

Othello is not so motivated. He is an outsider who pretends he isn't and indulges in no advocacy for Moors, Turks, or any other minority excluded from the seats of power. He eagerly enters into alliances against members of his own race. His services are bought and paid for and their value is openly acknowledged by his paymasters, who see it as a good bargain. He knows better than Montano, Brabantio, Ludovico, or the Duke how to fight battles and rout the enemy; and he knows his paymasters know it, and that gives him a certain grandiosity which is discernible in his manner, in his bearing, and in his language. Othello is like the obnoxious CEO that all the shareholders will regularly vote to maintain in office because he consistently increases the value of their stock, and, ultimately, that is what really counts in a corporation or in a government. But should he lose his usefulness, should he become volatile and unpredictable, so emotionally unstable as to create doubts about his efficiency, then his "outsiderness," invisible when efficacious, becomes a serious liability. If not a victorious warrior, then Othello is nothing. When his "occupation's gone," Othello is himself a goner. (How ironic that after his downfall it should be the crapulous and unstable Cassio who should rule in Othello's place in Cyprus. It seems to me to confirm the inherent corruptions of the Venetian government that Othello seems so proud to serve.)

The prejudice against Shylock the Jew is very thinly veiled, openly alluded to by both Gratiano and Antonio. But apart from Brabantio's indignation at losing a daughter and Iago's natural, barrack-room slurs against black-skinned men, Othello is respected. That is, his power-to-deliver-the-goods is not in question and so his "outsiderness" never becomes an issue. But it is always an issue in Othello's mind, and for that reason Iago easily kindles the fires by which his general is ultimately consumed. It is Othello's own deep-rooted fears that feed those flames.

The General is aware that he has intruded into alien territory by acquiring Desdemona. This is not simply another plume on his crest, another medal for bravery-in-action. This is an incursion into a world where, hitherto, he has been a tolerated outsider. A world into which no Moor, ever before, achieved such eminence. It is his knowledge of that fact, more than any suspicion planted by Iago, that prevents him from consummating his marriage. Some part of him readily believes that Cassio or another member of Desdemona's race could blithely cuckold him because, endemically, they belong to the charmed society in which he is only a hired mercenary. Iago has it easy; his work is done for him by Othello's deep-rooted suspicion that a white woman will never remain faithful to an outsider. His desire to strangle her is part-and-parcel of his perceived inability to possess her, and, because in the dark and rumbling boiler room of his soul he doesn't believe he ever truly can possess her, the hint that someone else has comes springingly to the fore.

After the murder of Desdemona and the discovery of Iago's treachery, Othello reverts to these deep-seated fears and suspicions: "I am black / And have not those soft parts of conversation / that chamberers have" (3.3.263–65). He knows that the thought that fathered his wife's murder was not spawned by his Ancient but by himself. His effusive love for Desdemona, as expressed in act 2, scene 1, when he reunites with her in Cyprus, exists to compensate for his doubts and fears about invading the Magic Circle to which he does not truly belong. "O my soul's joy," he exclaims, "If after every tempest come such calms, / May the winds blow till they have waken'd death!" And then, "If it were now to die, / 'Twere now to be most happy; for I fear / My soul hath her content so absolute / That not another comfort like to this / Succeeds in unknown fate." And then, "sweet powers! / I cannot speak enough of this content, / It stops me here; it is too much of joy" (2.1.184–97). And then, before the entire assembly, he kisses his bride. Othello's mode of expression with Desdemona brings to mind the effusive exhibitions of love and endearment often found between hastily married couples who, within months, are initiating divorce proceedings against one another. A histrionic display of excessive affection is always inspired by deeply-grounded fears of its dissolution, as if the "show of love" were a tonic that helped strengthen lovers' shaky sense of insecurity.

Iago's indignation at being passed over in favor of Cassio was a convenient hammer with which Othello could confront and ultimately bludgeon that sense of wrongful intrusion which haunted him from the outset for appropriating the forbidden Desdemona to himself. Forced to defend himself before the dignitaries of Venice, Othello says,

> Rude am I in my speech,
> And little bless'd with the soft phrase of peace;
> For since these arms of mine had seven years' pith,

Till now some nine moons wasted, they have us'd
Their dearest action in the tented field;
And little of this great world can I speak
More than pertains to feats of broils and battle,
And therefore little shall I grace my cause
In speaking for myself.

(1.3.81–89)

Royal lineage notwithstanding, he admits he is a man who doesn't speak the same language as those in his immediate social milieu: a prisoner-of-war then "sold to slavery," surviving in caves and empty deserts—now in the midst of Dukes, Senators, Officers, and Gentlemen. And not engrossed in military or political matters but defending himself for having stolen away a senator's daughter. How can he help but feel odd-man-out in such a situation and in such a society?

Shylock's loss of Jessica to Lorenzo is something akin to Othello's sense of betrayal in regard to Desdemona. In both instances, the characters' pain is commingled with a realization that an alien world has punished them for attempting to intrude upon it. Both have been punished for trespassing into a society to which they were not born. Shylock's response is vengefulness. He knows his enemies and tries to rout them using their very own weapons: the machinations of the law. Othello's is self-referential. In order to wreak his revenge, he must inflict punishment upon himself.

One of the hardest tasks for an actor playing Othello is making the transition from being head-over-heels in love with his new wife to rapidly suspecting her of base infidelity. After their loving reunion in Cyprus, there are only two short scenes before 3.3 in which Othello's loathing of Desdemona's betrayal begins to fester. One moment he is besotted with his "fair warrior" and the next he is asking bitterly, "Why did I marry?" It doesn't take a very astute psychoanalyst to note that the seeds of Othello's destructive impulses were there long before Iago conjured them into being. And if one deduces from this that the patient is criminally ambivalent, it would be a mistaken diagnosis, for Desdemona is simply a surrogate for the entire Venetian world into which Othello has allowed himself to be lured. Being a soldier, he has a sure instinct about his enemy, and being a soldier he lives in constant anticipation of his enemy. A soldier without an enemy is inconceivable, and Othello has a primordial need to seek out enemies and destroy them. Cassio is only a symbolic enemy. He is merely a representative of "the general camp, pioneers, and all" who may have "tasted" Desdemona's "sweet body" and Othello "nothing known."

His real animus was not so much against Cassio as against his own untenable position in a Venetian State in which he felt so much "the alien," that he construed marriage to Desdemona as some magical means of integration. This, ultimately, is what brands the play a tragedy. The whole of Othello's last speech is an attempt to exonerate his irrational murder of Desdemona by citing his valuable service to that state. "An honorable murderer" as he puts it, "for nought I did in hate, but all in honor." Having been manipulated into enmity against Cassio and then Desdemona and then Iago, he has finally found his true enemy, and it is himself; and being a good soldier, he destroys it.

*    *    *

If Othello's motives are repressed, unacknowledged by the General himself, Iago's are no less so. Since Coleridge, there has been much speculation about Iago's "motiveless malignity." But there is one underlying motive that seeps into the play from Cinthio's *Hecatommithi*, the known source material of Shakespeare's tragedy. In Cinthio, you will recall, Iago's hatred of the Moor comes out of his frustrated desire for Desdemona. But is this motivation entirely absent in Shakespeare's play simply because it is not directly incorporated into the action? At one point, he actually says he loves Desdemona not "out of absolute lust" but partly to feed his revenge. And when Desdemona arrives at Cyprus before Othello, his banter with her fairly crackles with double entendres in which, curiously, Desdemona merrily participates.

Iago, who is constantly living vicariously, turns Roderigo into a phallic surrogate, just as he will shortly try to turn Cassio into another. And what makes better psychological sense than that a man should elaborately destroy the obstacle that stands between him and the woman he lusts after? Not because by removing that obstacle he stands any better chance of winning her but, simply and maliciously, out of sexual spite. "If I can't have her—neither will you—nor will anyone else!" The age-old motive behind crimes-passionnels! And when he is finally confronted with his crime, why doesn't Iago tell Othello and the Venetian authorities what he has already told us? You passed over a more practiced and worthy soldier and gave the Lieutenantship to Cassio instead. Or why doesn't he blurt out, "I believe you seduced my wife, and so what I've done to you is simply tit for tat"? No, instead he says, "Demand me nothing; what you know, you know: / From this time forth I never will speak word." An obdurate, stonewalling silence, perhaps because he cannot come to grips with his own smoldering, unconscious compulsion, which was the lascivious desire to possess Desdemona the way Othello had, an admission he can barely confront in himself and finds impossible to declare to others. That is an overwhelming and understandable reason for pleading the Fifth Amendment to avoid the shame of self-incrimination. The whole of Iago's intrigue against the Moor, Roderigo, and Cassio is a kind of murderous, masturbatory fantasy stemming from a starved sexual lust that is never acknowledged, never confessed, but runs powerfully beneath the current of events.

\*          \*          \*

Many writers and critics have made the point that in terms of beliefs, and social and moral attitudes, Shakespeare is an Invisible Man. Was he a Royalist? A crypto-Catholic? A faithful Protestant? A Champion of the Establishment or a sly subversive? The fascination of the man is that he cannot be conclusively labeled according to his works, but in his treatment of Othello and Shylock, we have to recognize that he was the first writer of his time to humanize the villainous Jew and make us feel enormous sympathy for a tormented black man. It is his humanism that is so innovative and creates those tantalizing ambiguities that make it impossible for us to condemn either a flagrant usurer or a murderous general.

So in some sense, maybe Harold Bloom did get it right. If not the "inventor of the human," Shakespeare certainly held an active and prosperous franchise that remains in force to this day.

# "His master's ass": Slavery, Service, and Subordination in *Othello*

### Michael Neill

> Man's inability to moderate and restrain the emotions I call
> Bondage: for a man who is subject to the emotions is not his
> own master, but is ruled by fortune, and is so in her power that
> he is often forced, although he sees what is better for him, to
> follow that which is worse.
>
> —Spinoza, Preface to *Of Human Bondage*

*OTHELLO*, DECLARES THE WEST INDIAN PROTAGONIST OF MURRAY CAR-
lin's drama *Not Now, Sweet Desdemona* (1969), "is a play on the theme
of Race . . . a play about colour. It is the first play about colour that ever
was written. *Othello* is about colour, and nothing but colour."[1] With this
defiant assertion, Carlin's play, like the pioneering critical work of Eldred
Durosimi Jones and G. K. Hunter with which it was contemporaneous,[2]
sought to reinvigorate discussion of Shakespeare's tragedy by restoring it
to its original context in the foundational period of European "racial"
thought. What seemed an iconoclastic position in 1968, however, has now
become an orthodoxy; for the overwhelming preoccupation of *Othello*
criticism in the last two decades has been with the issue of race. The result
is that we now have a much more nuanced and historically grounded understanding of "racial" thinking in the culture that produced the play. Paradoxically, however, the more sophisticated critics have become in their
approach, the more they have been troubled by an uneasy sense that their
interrogation of the play's oxymoronic subtitle, "The Moor of Venice," is
being posed in inappropriate terms—even if they are the only terms we
have. For all the disconcerting familiarity of the hate language coined by
Iago, the play is fundamentally pre-racialist in its assumptions. In Early
Modern parlance, as Margo Hendricks and others have shown, the very
word *race* had yet to acquire anything like its modern meaning, referring
as it did to genealogy rather than ethnicity;[3] *Moor* was a description poised
uneasily between ethnological and religious distinctions; while even *color*
carried a different freight of associations from those we are accustomed

to, being (as Edward Pechter puts it) "not so much a thing in itself as the marker of a theological category"[4] yet from the opening scene of Shakespeare's tragedy there is no escaping the intensity of its preoccupation with the "quality" that constitutes Othello's otherness. Thus, as I wrote in another context, "to talk about 'race' in *Othello* is to fall into anachronism; yet not to talk about it is to ignore something fundamental to [the] play."[5] The problem is twofold, involving both the play's own discourse of alterity, and the interpretation to which it has been subjected. Shakespeare's contemporaries had no consistently evolved language for classifying and explaining the phenotypical differences on which European theorists would later erect the ideology of "race," with the result that the attitudes expressed in the play towards Othello's color are necessarily improvisational and incoherent; yet, precisely because the tragedy is so anxiously concerned with these differences, criticism of *Othello* has, from its very beginnings in the late seventeenth century, been profoundly entangled with the history of racial thinking—to the point where it is probably impossible to think our way back through this history to an undistorted reading of the protagonist's otherness and the social tensions that it appears to trigger.

Take, for example, the play's references to slaves and slavery: in the light of the subsequent record of European depredations in Africa, these are bound to seem loaded terms. Indeed Carlin's Othello-character insists that the play can be properly understood only if we remember that its writing coincided with the establishment of the great slave-trading forts along the sub-Saharan littoral; thus the play's references to slavery carry an historical charge that links them to its racial discourse. Shakespeare's Moor is now a general, but was once a slave: when Othello recalls how he was "taken by the insolent foe / And sold to slavery" (1.3.137–38),[6] he appears to sketch the first of those African slave-narratives whose history stretches through Aphra Behn's *Oronooko* to the journal of Olaudah Equiano and beyond; and when he denounces himself, after the murder of Desdemona, as "cursed, cursed slave" (5.2.276), it is as though he were willingly returning himself to the servile destiny marked by his skin: if he once learned to see himself in the mirror of Desdemona's rapt response to his exotic tales, he now recognizes himself again in a very different white gaze. But "slave" is also the epithet twice hurled at Iago in this same scene (5.2.243, 332), and it is unlikely that Othello's "history" of enslavement would have had the same resonances for the original audience. Of course, it is true that English involvement with the African slave trade can be traced back to the sixteenth century, with the voyages of John Hawkins in the 1560s; but these were relatively small-scale, experimental enterprises, insufficient to establish any automatic identification of blackness with servitude. The term *Moor*, moreover, was a notoriously unstable one: not only did it blur the distinction between North African and sub-Saharan peoples, it could also be used to embrace all Muslims regardless of their geographic location; and for this reason, as the work of Nabil Matar and Daniel Vitkus has demonstrated, "Moors" were, on balance, more likely to figure in the early seventeenth-century English imagination as enslavers than as slaves.[7] Othello's story of capture, enslavement, and "redemption thence" actually parallels the experience of many prisoners on both sides of a Muslim-Christian conflict that stretched back at least to the Crusades; and as such it belongs not to the industrialized human marketplace of the Atlantic triangle, but to the same Mediterranean theater of war as the Turkish invasion of Cyprus. In fact, slavery bore little or no relation to discourses of "racial" difference in early modern thought; rather, it was part of a much older construction of human difference in which the distinctions that mattered were not those between different "colors" or "races," but those between master and servant, or between bond and free.

It is, I think, in the context of contemporary debates over the nature and limits of service that the play's references to the slave condition are best understood. In the Latin *servus*, the conditions of "servant" and "slave" are indistinguishable; but the social and religious doctrine of Shakespeare's time, insisting as it did upon the sublime virtue of voluntary obedience, stressed the absolute distinction between "servile" and "liberal" (or free) servants—the former being those who were (in William Gouge's words) "born servants, or sold for servants, or taken in war, or ransomed," and the latter those who were "by voluntary contract made servants, whether at will, as some serving-men, journeymen, and laborers; or for a certain term of years, as prentices, clerks, and such like . . . whatsoever the birth, parentage, estate, or former condition of any have been."[8] This is the distinction on which Iago insists when he reminds Othello, "Though I am bound to every act of duty, / I am not bound to that all slaves are free to. / Utter my thoughts?" (3.3.134–36). For practical purposes, however, the two conditions must often have felt, especially for those in the lower ranks of the hierarchy of service, very little different. Thus the conservative social theorist William Gouge emphasizes the surrender of individual will and identity involved in the contract of service: "while the term of their service lasteth, [servants] are not their own, neither ought the things which they do, to be for themselves: both their persons and their actions are their master's: and the will of their master must be their rule and guide (in things which are not against God's will)."[9] In the eyes of Iago, whose rank of "Ancient" or Ensign explicitly reduces him to the mere sign of his master's presence, such self-effacement appears intolerably abject, no better than slavery or the condition of "his master's ass" (1.1.47). Characteristically, his animus against Othello and Desdemona expresses itself in a sardonic emphasis on their "free" condition (1.3.399; 2.3.320, 340), and in his vision of Othello "led by th'nose / As asses are" (1.3.401–2)—just as his discontent with his own position can be heard in his resentful nagging at the terms of subordination: *bound, serve, servant,* duty, and *office.*[10]

In an essay written some years ago, I argued that the key to Iago's murderous resentment was to be found in a complex of anxieties attaching to the idea of "place"; in this paper I want to concentrate on the significance of one aspect of place—that involving the rewards and humiliations of service. I will suggest that by paying more attention to such issues it may be possible to find a way around the anachronisms endemic to race-centered readings of the play. Matters of rank and status, authority and subordination, after all, were something that Shakespeare's contemporaries understood very well indeed, and for which (in sharp contrast to their confused articulations of "racial" difference) they had a highly sophisticated language. It is Iago's consuming bitterness about the proprieties of rank that informs the tirade with which he opens the play, where it emerges not just in his anger at Cassio's unwarranted promotion but in the sneering reference to his own commander as "his Moorship" (1.1.33). If this mock-honorific seems racially loaded, it is so only because of its sardonic perversion of a familiar vocabulary of deference. The genius of Iago's slur lies in the way that its lexical irregularity ("Moor" being substituted for "worth") contrives to suggest a social absurdity—as if there were something fundamentally ridiculous in the idea of superior rank's being vested in a Moor. Yet what follows consists not of any attempt to argue the inauthenticity of the Moor's claims to authority, but of a generalized tirade against the inequities and follies of all service. It is only when the topic shifts to Desdemona's elopement that Iago and Roderigo are able to make of Othello's conspicuous otherness the blemish that turns him from "the Moor" into "thick-lips," "an old black ram," and "a Barbary horse" (1.1.66, 88, 111–12). The scandal they pretend to discover is (as Hendricks's work would lead one to expect) primarily a function of those rules of descent, inheritance, and filial obedience that were so crucial to the patriarchal order of things. When Iago warns Brabantio, "you'll have your nephews [i.e. descendants] neigh to you" (1.1.112), or when Roderigo envisages Desdemona "Tying her *duty*, beauty, wit, and *fortunes* / In an extravagant and wheeling stranger" (1.1.135–36), what matters is less the issue of Othello's blackness in itself than the undoing of patriarchal authority and succession threatened by this unlicensed liaison.[11] The scandal of the Moor's difference, Iago implies, is that it will be passed on as the indelible sign of this affront to established hierarchy: hence Roderigo's sly emphasis on the degrading circumstances of Desdemona's transport "with a *knave of common hire*"—a detail with which he subtly reinforces the "gross" impropriety of the Moor's embrace (1.1.125–26); and hence too Brabantio's conviction that his is no "idle cause" but a matter of such importance that his fellow-patriarchs, the duke and his senatorial "brothers of the state, / Cannot but feel this wrong as 'twere their own" (1.2.96–97). His conclusion that if such actions are allowed to go unpunished "Bond-slaves and pagans shall our statesmen be" (99) is less a glance at Othello's former slave condition, or at his African origins, than a hyperbolic assertion of the general consequences of such an undermining of authority.

Before long, of course, color would indeed become an unmistakable marker of authority and subordination; and, once slavery had become a fully institutionalized part of the imperial economy, this reading of "race" would be thoroughly naturalized by enlightenment taxonomy and the Darwinian evolutionary hierarchy to which it gave birth. Even by the 1680s, Morgan Godwyn could claim that "[the] two words *Negro* and *Slave* [have] by custom grown Homogeneous and Convertible"[12]—articulating the assumption that would underlie Thomas Rymer's famously dismissive account of *Othello* a decade later: "With us a Blackamoor might rise to be a Trumpeter, but *Shakespeare* would not have him less than a Lieutenant-General. With us a *Moor* might marry some little drab, or Small-coal Wench: *Shakespeare* would provide him the Daughter and kin of some great Lord, or Privy-Councillor."[13] But for Shakespeare and his contemporaries, the relationship between ethnicity and subordination was by no means clear; and Iago's continuing hints that there is something recognizably unnatural about the vesting of authority in the Moor are seemingly annulled by the Duke's public show of respect, and by Montano's deference ("'tis a worthy governor," 2.1.30).

What is important, then, about Othello's Moorishness at the beginning of the play is not that it ranks, categorizes, or places him in any *agreed* way, but the opposite—that, in spite of his solemnly reiterated commitment to "office" and "place,"[14] it renders him to some degree anomalous, in need of placing, insecurely fitted to the received hierarchies by which Shakespeare's Venetians order their world. It is exactly this displacement that provides Iago with his opportunity; for, despite his furious efforts to stigmatize his general as "black Othello" (2.3.32), Iago's resentments have little to do with color (in and of itself), but everything to do with subordination. Color is simply the instrument he can use to destabilize the order he finds so oppressive, by exploiting a whole range of negative cultural associations that enable him to "discover" in Othello's skin the signs of animality, ungoverned passion, witchcraft, devilry, and so forth. But it is clear from the attitudes of most Venetians that, while the ready availability of these associations may account for Brabantio's suggestibility and the psychological vulnerability of Othello himself, they are by no means accepted as necessary and essential attributes of Moorishness.

The order against which Iago reneges is one held in place by the comprehensive ideology of "service" that I have explored elsewhere.[15] This was an ideological system that in Early Modern society embraced virtually all forms of human relationship, public as well as domestic, military as well as civilian; and it created a world in which authority and subordination of any kind could only be imagined (however anachronistically) in terms of the personal allegiance that had characterized the feudal regime[16]—one in which "desert" itself (as the etymology of the word clearly demonstrates) was simply a function of good service. But, however comprehensive it claimed to be, this was also an ideology under increasing strain—a strain that is nowhere more eloquently displayed than in the drama; and Iago joins a whole theatrical gallery of false servants (Ithamore, Mosca, De Flores, Bosola) who conspire to undo its irksome differences.

In *Othello*, not only the relationships between the major characters, but each character's reputation and self-image, are defined by the idea of service. Montano, the governor of Cyprus, a man whose high office and "free duty" identify him as the "trusty and most valiant servitor" of Venice (1.3.40), yields authority to Othello as one who "commands / Like a full soldier," a master whom he is proud to have "serv'd" (2.1.35–36). Cassio, similarly, invests his whole identity in the "place" secured by his "love and service" to Othello (3.3.17–18) and (more ambiguously) to Desdemona, whose "true servant" he gallantly professes himself to be (3.3.9). Drawing on the rhetoric of organic intimacy that was habitually deployed to define the relation of master and servant, the lieutenant declares his very existence contingent upon his continued capacity to perform "the *office* of [his] heart" by becoming once again "a *member* of [Othello's] love" (3.4.12–13);[17] and in his pleas for reinstatement he appeals to the merits of "service past" (3.4.116), as passionately as Othello himself. For Cassio, to "*attend . . . on the general*," as he insists to Bianca he must do (3.4.193, 200), is not simply to await his decision, but to *wait upon him* in the posture of the servant that he longs once again to be.

The same language of authority and subordination that characterizes relationships in what we might think of as the "public" world of state affairs and soldiership, governs the domestic world of husbands and wives, fathers and children. Just as *King Lear* conceives of the king's relationship with his daughters, his noble followers, and his household servants as being fundamentally of the same order, so *Othello* imagines the domestic "offices" of the family in a continuum with the "places" of military officers, and the ranks that order society at large. Thus it is more than mere wordplay or a loose analogy that links the erotic "office" that the Moor and Cassio have supposedly usurped in Iago's bedchamber (1.3.387–88, 2.1.307) with the military office (or "place") of which they have cheated him (1.1.11 ff.), just as it is more than mere hyperbole that allows Brabantio to denounce his daughter's elopement as a *"treason* of the blood" (1.1.169), or Cassio to describe Desdemona as "our great captain's captain" (2.1.74), or Iago to insist that "Our general's wife is now the general" (2.3.314–15). If Desdemona imagines her love as a form of glad subordination—"My heart's *subdu'd* / Even to the very quality of my lord," as the Folio has it (1.3.250–51)[18]—then in Iago's eyes Othello's love amounts to a kind of humiliating enslavement that strips him of both rank and identity:[19]

> His soul is so *enfettered* to her love
> That she may make, unmake, do what she list,
> Even as her appetite shall play the god
> With his weak function.
>
> (2.3.345–48; emphasis added)

Moreover, just as Desdemona's elopement is attacked by Brabantio and defended by Desdemona herself as an issue of proper "duty" and "obedience" (1.3.180–81), so the drunken Cassio is denounced by Iago as one who has "forgot all place of sense and duty" (2.3.167). The supposed adultery of Desdemona and Cassio, is thus construed as being as much a betrayal of the "place" and "duty" of each as a sexual betrayal—or rather, to put it more accurately, their sexual betrayal can only be thought of as the limit case of disobedience and displacement. In Desdemona's hand, Othello professes to read the signs of this perverse "liberty": "For here's a young and sweating devil, here, / That commonly *rebels*" (3.4.40, 42–43). "Obedient" is the word that Desdemona uses to affirm her love and constancy ("What e'er you be, I am obedient," 3.3.89), and the word that her "lord" throws in her face in act 4, scene 1, when she appeals to what she has "deserv'd" (l. 241): "And she's obedient: as you say, obedient, / Very obedient" (4.1.255–56). But obedience to her lord and master is also what the too loyal Emilia (anticipating the rebellion of Cornwall's servant in *Lear*) finally repudiates: "'Tis proper I obey him; but not now. / Perchance, Iago, I will ne'er go home" (5.2.196–97)—a repudiation of his domestic authority that invites Iago's denunciation of her as a "villainous whore" (l. 229), even as she ironically repeats the *non serviam* that is her husband's distinguishing utterance.

It is only within this larger scheme of authority and subordination, and the ideal of service by which it is governed, that the relationship between Othello and Iago can properly be understood. Othello's entire sense of self is measured not just by his ability to command service but by his capacity to give it: it is exactly his readiness to obey those whom he calls "My very noble and approv'd good *masters*" (1.3.77), subordinating the "life and being" he derives from "men of royal siege" to his chosen role as servant of the state, that gives the Moor his social and political "place," substantiating his paradoxical claim to be "of Venice": "My *services*, which I have done the signiory, / Shall out-tongue his complaints" (1.2.18–19). At the moment of crisis in act 4, when the lieutenant's supposed usurpation of Othello's husbandly authority seems mockingly duplicated by the Senate's command "deputing Cassio in his government" (4.1.237), the general reasserts his place precisely through his obedient willingness to surrender it: "I am commanded home. . . . Sir, I *obey* the mandate. . . . Cassio shall have my *place*" (4.1.258–61); for Othello is a man who speaks for himself, as every servant should, in the performance of his "free duty." No wonder, then, that in the closing moments of the play he has no other way to reclaim his Venetian identity than to reinvoke the language of proud subordination that he shares with Desdemona: "I have done the state some *service*, and they know't" (5.2.339).[20]

Iago, by contrast, defines himself from the start by his resentful loathing of what he revealingly calls "the curse of service" (1.1.35). In his eyes, the lot of any obedient servant, dutiful attendant, or loyal follower is to become a "duteous and knee-crooking knave," no better than "his master's ass" (1.1.45–47). Thus for Iago, the performance of any office is warrantable only as a *performance*—one of those "shows of service" whose "forms and visages of duty" contemporary domestic moralists (following St. Paul) dubbed "eye service":[21]

> I *follow* him to *serve* my turn upon him.
> We cannot all be *masters*, nor all *masters*
> Cannot be truly *followed*. . . .
>                    Others there are
> Who, trimm'd in *forms and visages of duty*,
> Keep yet their hearts *attending* on themselves,
> And throwing but *shows of service* on their lords,
> Do well thrive by them; and when they have lin'd their *coats* [i.e., livery],
> *Do themselves homage*. . . .
> In *following* him, I *follow* but myself;
> Heaven is my judge, not I for *love and duty*,
> But seeming so, for my peculiar end.

(1.1.42–60)

Conspicuously, it is not his general's race that fuels Iago's indignation here, but the mere fact of his mastership, and the sense that his bonds of "service" can only amount to "obsequious bondage," an abject servitude no different from slavery. Looked at from the point of view established by this litany of resentment, *Othello* may appear to be less about "race" than about rank—a tragedy that sits easily alongside such plays as *King Lear*,

*The Duchess of Malfi*, and *The Changeling*, as a dramatization of the felt crisis in the early modern institution of service.[22]

The depth of Iago's resentment, and the extent of the social threat it represents, can be fully appreciated only once we begin to reimagine the extraordinary pervasiveness of the ideology he rejects and the religious authority with which it was invested. Manuals of service such as William Gouge's *Of Domesticall Dvties* (1622) laid heavy stress on the performance of service as a fulfillment of Christian doctrine: "No inferiors [writes Gouge] are more bound to obedience then servants: it is their main, and most popular function, to *obey their masters. . . .* They who are contrary minded, who are rebellious, and disdain to be under the authority of another, and are ready to say of their Master, *We will not have this man to reign over us*, are fitter to live among Anabaptists, than orthodoxal Christians. For to what end is the lawfulness of authority acknowledged, if subjection be not yielded unto it?" (603–4). God, this doctrine asserted, was the supreme master from whose dispensation the authority of all heads of household and the subjugation of all subordinates derived; and underpinning it is the recollection of Lucifer's rebellion as the original act of disobedience. For this reason, any resistance to the master's command was to be understood as devilishly inspired. The "young and sweating devil" that Othello discovers on his wife's palm is explicitly a figure of rebellion as much as of lechery. But if it is Desdemona's disobedience that appears to mark her as a "fair devil," it is notoriously Iago, whose "I am not what I am" (1.1.65) constitutes a demonic parody of the divine *I am*, whom the play identifies with the false service that masks diabolic rebellion.[23]

Iago's "flag and sign of love" (1.1.156) is precisely the signature of hypocrisy that the handbooks of domestic government taught their readers to expect in false servants, who (according to Gouge) "have *a heart*, and a heart, making show of one heart outwardly, and have another, even a clean contrary heart within them" (617). Such servile hypocrites, according to Gouge and his fellow propagandist "I.M.," resemble "Judas, that false traitor, [who] . . . betray[ed] his own master, Christ," being "so possessed with a devil, as they will seek all the revenge they can, if they be corrected, [and] secretly endeavor to take away the life of their masters."[24] *Non serviam* (as Iago slyly reminds us when he sarcastically denounces Brabantio as "one of those that will not serve God if the devil bid you" (1.1.108–9), was notoriously the watchword of Lucifer; for if the faithful servant's office was to be understood as an expression of Christian duty and humility, Lucifer's sin of pride was imagined precisely as a refusal of service: "in heav'n they scorned to *serve*, so now in hell they reign," wrote Phineas Fletcher of the rebel angels,[25] anticipating the famous defiance of Milton's Satan, "Better to reign in hell, than *serve* in heaven," and the faithful Abdiel's wish only to "*serve* / In heaven God ever blest, and his divine / Behests *obey*" (*Paradise Lost* 1.263, 6.183–85). Just as Doctor Faustus's surrender to the devil is couched in the language of egotistical self-service ("The God thou *servest* is thine own appetite," A-Text, 2.1.11),[26] so Iago's rebellion is characterized as the self-homage of a man who acknowledges no "power and corrigible authority" save that of his own will (1.3.325–26). Thus it is no accident that Iago's defiant repudiation of "obsequious bondage" is immediately followed by the confrontation with Brabantio, in which the Ensign's hypocritical offer of "service" (1.1.110) masks an intention to "Plague him with flies" (1.1.71) that recalls the afflictions visited by Lucifer's companion, the demon Beelzebub, Lord of the Flies.

But, for all the weight of social and theological support for the institution of service, the very multiplication of texts like Gouge's massive treatise is a reminder of the felt fragility of the institution of service, confronted as it was by challenges from radical thinkers on the one hand and from disillusioned conservatives on the other. Gouge's own seventh treatise prefaces its account of the duties of servants, with an elaborate demonstration "*Of the lawfulness of a master's place and power.*" Gouge was responding to what he saw as the dangerously persuasive assault on the "*authority of masters, and subjection of servants*" mounted by Anabaptists and their sympathizers. According to these radicals, "we are expressly forbidden to be *servants of men*" (1 Cor. 7:23): "[i]t is against nature for one to be a servant, especially a bond-servant to another [for] it is the prerogative of Christians to be *all one*: [and] subjection of servants to masters is against that prerogative, [since it] is against the liberty that Christ hath purchased for us, and wherewith he hath made us free."[27] The power of Iago's rhetoric to compel a reluctant sympathy from the audience will have depended upon his eloquent mimicry of such dissidence.

If Iago's repudiation of "obsequious bondage" and his insistence on the independence of the individual will both chime with the radical positions denounced by Gouge, then his nostalgic appeal to "the old gradation" and denunciation of the habitual ingratitude of masters echoes the complaints of conservative social critics, who saw the institution of service as corrupted by the new commercial dispensation of wage-labor. Iago's bitter portrait of the servant who "Wears out his time much like his master's ass, / For naught but provender," only to be "cashiered," in his old age, looks forward to Richard Brathwaite's invective against "the unthankfulness or disrespect of *masters* towards their *servants*, when they have spent their strength and wasted them in their service."[28] The apparent menace of such ingratitude lay in its capacity to expose the empty fiction of "assured friendship" underpinning the ideology of service;[29] and the emotional force of Iago's complaint depends partly on the brutally material relationship that "cashiered" discovers beneath the chivalric rhetoric of military "service"[30]—one in which the possibility of cashierment is understood as a degrading condition of "soldiership."

Othello himself, though the play tactfully suppresses the fact, is a species of mercenary; and Iago makes clear to Roderigo that the consideration governing all human relations is cold cash ("Put money in thy purse," 1.3.339–71). In the Venetian world, he insists, where "the old gradation" founded upon natural ties of "love" and "duty" has been displaced by corrupt influence ("letter and affection"), service is best treated as a commercial contract—a system of pecuniary reward governed by legally enforceable "just term[s]" (1.1.35–39, 58). To imagine otherwise is to submit to a form of "obsequious bondage" in which the servant's livery is reduced (by a kind of etymological insult) to mere stable "provender"[31]—a slavery that mockingly disguises itself in the naturalized language of "bonds" and "following." Thus Iago presents his "forms and visages of duty" (1. 50) or "shows of service" (1. 52) as demonstrations of the paradoxically honest hypocrisy to which any serving-man will be driven if he is to resist the ideological cheat by which his profession is controlled.

From the perspective of conservatives like Gouge, true service involved a kind of self-surrender, subsuming one's individual identity in the larger social "countenance" of one's master, much as Desdemona "subdues" herself to "the very quality" of her lord. Iago's determination to "follow but myself" and "do [myself] homage" is a conscious renunciation of this doctrine that looks forward to the Leveller Richard Overton's claims for the "self-propriety" of the individual; and his loathing of "obsequious bondage" mirrors that of social dissidents like the musician Thomas Whythorne, who, determined to be "[his] own man," declared that "to be a serving-creature or servingman, it was so like the life of a water-spaniel, that must be at commandment to fetch or bring here, or carry there, with all kind of drudgery, that I could not like of that life."[32] Once we are alert to the social context of Iago's resentments, the smallest details of his relationship with Othello, like the moment when the General, with a patronizing "good Iago," orders his subordinate to "disembark my coffers" from the ship (2.1.207–8) will become charged with murderous feeling: for what else but the fetching of a water spaniel, or the labor of "his master's ass" is the Ensign being asked to perform? Even more importantly, the language of the temptation scene, with its elaborate parade of the loyalty, "duty," and "love" that servants (like wives) were supposed to owe their masters, will acquire a dangerous new edge—as, for example, when Iago responds to Othello's demand to know his thoughts:

> Good my lord, pardon me:
> Though I am *bound* to every act of *duty*,
> I am not *bound* to that all *slaves* are free [to].
>
> (3.3.133–35)

Equally loaded are the terms of his response to Othello's insistence upon proof:

> now I shall have reason
> To show the *love and duty* that I bear you
> With franker spirit; therefore (as I am *bound*)
> Receive it from me.
>
> (3.3.193–96)

The rhetoric of the speech is calculated to remind Othello of the maddening contrast between the frankness (freedom and honesty) of Iago's servantly "love and duty" and the deviousness of Desdemona's supposed betrayal of wifely fidelity.[33] But, for the audience, the heavy metrical stress on "bound" will act as a reminder of social bonds of a more abject kind, underlining the covert sarcasm in Iago's recollection of the "obsequious bondage" that he despises. With its elaborate profession of servile self-surrender, it prepares the way for the climax of the scene:

> Witness that here Iago doth give up
> The execution of his wit, hands, heart,
> To wrong'd Othello's *service*. Let him *command*,
> And to *obey* shall be in me remorse,
> What bloody business ever.
>
> (3.3.465–69)

If Iago's offer of hand and heart identifies the kneeling exchange of vows as a blasphemous troth-plighting, a parody of the wedding rite whose knot the tempter has patiently untied,[34] Iago means Othello to accept it as a formal reaffirmation of his "office," an exhibition of the "duty," "service," and "homage" that he privately reserves for himself (1.1.50–54), and an act of absolute self-surrender to the master's will ("I am your own for ever," 3.3.480). With proper magnanimity, Othello duly welcomes this seeming enactment of the reciprocal bonds between master and servant: "I greet thy love, / Not with vain thanks, but with acceptance bounteous" (3.3.469–70). But the bitter irony of this Judas-like ritual of submission is that Iago's eye-service has precisely reversed its ostensible meaning; for it is actually Othello who (like Faustus when he binds Mephostophilis to be "his servant") has indentured his soul to his own subordinate—as his unwitting confession earlier in the scene suggests: "I am *bound* to thee for ever" (3.3.213). Try as both the Venetians and Othello himself may, to reaffirm the proprieties of "service" and "place" (5.2.339, 369), it is difficult to avoid the leveling implications of a plot that leaves the master a "cursèd slave," rhetorically bound to his subordinate in the same abject condition of unfreedom—"Fall'n," as Lodovico puts it, "in the practice of a [damned] slave" (5.2.292).

# Notes

Baruch de Spinoza, "Of Human Bondage," in *The Philosophy of Spinoza*, trans. George Stuart Fullerton (New York: Henry Holt and Co., 1907), 153.

1. Murray Carlin, *Not Now, Sweet Desdemona* (Nairobi: Oxford University Press, 1969), 29, 32.

2. Eldred D. Jones, *Othello's Countrymen: The African in English Renaissance Drama* (London: Oxford University Press, 1965); G. K. Hunter, "Othello and Colour Prejudice," *Proceedings of the Bibliographical Association* 53 (1967): 139–63.

3. See Margo Hendricks, "Civility, Barbarism, and Aphra Behn's *The Widow Ranter*," and Linda Boose, "'The Getting of a Lawful Race': Racial Discourse in Early Modern England and the Unrepresentable Black Woman," both in *Women, "Race," and Writing in the Early Modern Period*, ed. Hendricks and Patricia Parker (London: Routledge, 1994), 35–54, 225–39; and Kim Hall, *Things of Darkness: Economies of Race and Gender in Early Modern England* (Ithaca: Cornell University Press, 1995).

4. Edward Pechter, *"Othello" and Interpretive Traditions* (Iowa City: University of Iowa Press, 1999), 34.

5. Michael Neill, "'Mulattos,' 'Blacks,' and 'Indian Moors': *Othello* and Early Modern Constructions of Human Difference," in *Putting History to the Question: Power, Politics, and Society in English Renaissance Drama* (New York: Columbia University Press, 2000), 269. For an essay that approaches the same issue through an analysis of visual representations of black subjects, see Peter Erickson, "Representations of Blacks and Blackness in the Renaissance," *Criticism* 35 (1993): 499–527.

6. The use of italics for emphasis in quotations from *Othello* is the author's. References are (with some minor changes of punctuation) to the Arden 3 edition, ed. E. A. J. Honigmann (London: Thomas Nelson, 1997).

7. See Nabil Matar, "Soldiers, Pirates, Traders, and Captives: Britons among the Muslims," chap. 2 of *Turks, Moors, and Englishmen in the Age of Discovery* (New York: Columbia University Press, 1999), esp. 71–82; Daniel J. Vitkus, "Turning Turk in *Othello*: The Conversion and Damnation of the Moor," *Shakespeare Quarterly* 48 (1997): 145–76; and Daniel J. Vitkus, ed., *Three Turk Plays from Early Modern England* (New York: Columbia University Press, 1999).

8. William Gouge, *Of Domesticall Dvties Eight Treatises* (1622), 160. In all quotations from primary texts, the spelling has been silently modernized.

9. Ibid., 604; the passage continues, "1. Servants may not go whither they will. . . . 2. They ought not to do their own business and affairs. . . . 3. They ought not to do what business they list themselves. . . . 4. They ought not to marry while the term of their covenant for service lasteth, unless their master give consent thereto. . . . 5. They ought not to dispose of their master's goods at their own pleasure. . . . 6. They may not before their covenanted time be expired go away from their master" (605–6).

10. The meaning of *office* was still essentially that of its Latin root, *officium*, 'duty,' 'service.'

11. In this regard it is significant that in *Titus Andronicus* the blackness of Aaron the Moor, insofar as it is anything more than a conventional sign of demonic villainy, matters only when he fathers a half-Moorish child on the Empress Tamora.

12. Morgan Godwyn, *The Negro's and Indian's Advocate* (1680), 3; cited in Bridget Orr, *Empire on the English Stage, 1660–1714* (Cambridge: Cambridge University Press, 2001), 21.

13. Thomas Rymer, *A Short View of Tragedie* (London, 1693), 91–92. Orr, however, cites the trenchant objections of Gildon (1694) and Theobald (1733) to Rymer's sneers, Gildon proclaiming that "there is no reason in the nature of things, why a *Negro* of equal Birth and Merit, should not be on an equal bottom, with a *German, Hollander, French-man, &c,*" urging Shakespeare's "contempt for the mere Accident of their Complexion" (*Miscellaneous Letters and Essays on Several Subjects*, 96; cited in Orr, *Empire* 23).

14. See Neill, "Changing Places in *Othello*," in *Putting History*, 207–36.

15. "Servant Obedience and Master Sins: Shakespeare and the Bonds of Service," in *Putting History*, 33–48.

16. Military "place" was not imagined as something *analagous* to domestic "office," but rather (as the use of the term "officer" in both domestic and military contexts suggests) as another aspect of the same system, something given (in the first instance, at least) to a particular individual—the commander of a company, who in turn served the "captain" or "general" above him (Neill, "Servant Obedience," 27–28).

17. Cf. John Dod and Robert Cleaver, *A Godly Forme of Household Government* (London, 1630), sig. Aa3: "[G]ood and faithful servants, liking and affecting their masters . . . obey them . . . not as a water-spaniel, but as the hand is stirred to obey the mind." On the subsumption of the servant's identity in that of his master, see Neill, "Servant Obedience," 20–28.

18. The idea of love as a kind of involuntary subordination is echoed in Othello's description of the handkerchief's occult power to "make [my mother] amiable, and *subdue* my father / Entirely to her love," and again in his description of his own "*subdued* eyes," melting at the consequences of his extreme love (3.4.59–60, 5.2.348).

19. The slur on the Moor's enfettered state is further emphasized by Iago's rhetorical stress on his own "free" advice and on Desdemona's "free" condition (2.3.337, 342).

20. Interestingly enough, in the parallel speech of self-justification that prefaces the suicide of Ward, at the end of Robert Daborne's *Christian Turned Turk*, the renegado appeals to "all the service I have done for you" (16.298), before renouncing his loyalty to the "slaves of Mahomet" and reclaiming his Christian allegiance. Daborne clearly models his protagonist's death on Othello's, even if Ward—who is denounced as "Inhuman dog!," "Unheard of monster!," "villain," and "wretch" (2.290, 314, 322, 323)—owes as much to Iago as to the noble Moor; and in each case it is "service" that has established the convert's claim to an alien identity. Cited from Vitkus, ed., *Three Turk Plays*.

21. See Gouge, *Of Domesticall Dvties* 165. Citing Eph. 6.6 ("Not with eye service, as men-pleasers, but as the servants of Christ, doing the will of God from the heart"), Gouge writes, "The vice here noted to be contrary to sincere service is termed *eye-service*. . . . And that is twofold, *Hypocritical, Parasitical*. Hypocritical service is that which is done merely in show: when that is pretended to be done which indeed is not done. . . . *Parasitical* service is that which is indeed done, but

in presence of the master: such servants are they who will be very diligent and faithful in doing such things as their masters see . . . but otherwise behind their master's back, and in things which they hope shall never come to his knowledge, they will be as negligent, and unfaithful as if they were no servants. Yet to satisfy their masters, and to sooth them, they will do any thing though never so unlawful" (165). See also Richard Brathwaite, *The English Gentleman* (London, 1630), 159.

22. See "Servant Obedience," 24–27, 31–33, 36–38, 45–46.

23. Compare the deceitful servant described in Fabio Glissenti's *Discorsi morali contra il dispiacer del morire* (1596) who reveals that "in the presence of the master I'm on guard and this rather pleases me, for he doesn't really come to know me, and in his presence I put on a show of being that which I am not"; cited in Dennis Romano, *Housecraft & Statecraft: Domestic Service in Renaissance Venice 1400–1600* (Baltimore: Johns Hopkins University Press, 1996), 193.

24. Gouge, *Of Domesticall Dvties*, 614, 617; and "I.M.," *A Health to the Gentlemanly Profession of Seruingmen* (London, 1598), 148.

25. Phineas Fletcher, *The Purple Island* (1633), 6.10.

26. Cited from Christopher Marlowe, *"Doctor Faustus" and Other Plays*, ed. David Bevington and David Rasmussen (Oxford: Oxford University Press, 1995).

27. Gouge, Of Domesticall Dvties, 591–94.

28. Brathwaite, *English Gentleman*, 158–59.

29. For a good account of the importance of "gratitude" in the Senecan doctrine of "benefits" that underpinned sixteenth-century ideas of generosity and housekeeping, see John M. Wallace, *"Timon of Athens* and the Three Graces: Shakespeare's Senecan Study," *Modern Philology* 83 (1986): 349–63; and Linda Levy Peck, *Court Patronage and Corruption in Early Stuart England* (Boston: Unwin Hyman, 1990), 12–14, 28–29.

30. It is symptomatic of the absence of real distinction between military and other forms of service that the verb *cashier* (a newly-coined term-of-art imported by soldiers returning from the Low Countries in 1585) was almost immediately extended to the domestic realm—so in *Histrio-mastix* (1599) the young lords are described as having "cashiered their traines" of servants (3.370). The sneering force of Iago's "cashiered" is enhanced by the quibble that links it to his denunciation of Cassio ("Cashio")—whose name itself appears to derive from the Italian, *casso* 'cashiered.'

31. As the term "livery stable" reminds us, "livery" originally denoted the master's obligation to supply his servants with food.

32. James M. Osborn, ed., *The Autobiography of Thomas Whythorne* (London: Oxford University Press, 1962), 10, 28; cf. also 46: "I do think that the teachers thereof [i.e., music] may esteem so much of themselves as to be free and not bound, much less to be made slave-like."

33. It is of course part of Iago's strategy to promote himself from the subordinate role of servant to the equality of "friend" (3.3.380). Plutarch's widely quoted and imitated essay in the *Moralia*, "How to Tell a Flatterer from a Friend," explores the problem of false friendship to which the great are especially vulnerable. Cf. Robert C. Evans, "Flattery in Shakespeare's *Othello*: The Relevance of Plutarch and Sir Thomas Elyot," *Comparative Drama* 35 (2001): 1–41.

34. See Neill, "Changing Places," 231–35.

# Shakespeare's *Odyssey*

## Yves Peyré

To unpath'd waters, undream'd shores
—*The Winter's Tale* 4.4.567

IN THE BEGINNING, HOMER CREATED THE MEDITERRANEAN. THE *ODYSSEY*, while undoubtedly an original, coherent creation, draws on a collection of traditional oral tales,[1] which it organizes into a system of myths. The Mediterranean sea is one of the unifying factors that bring together various legendary motifs around the theme of Ulysses' peregrinations.

The Homeric sea is multiple and uncertain, now favorable, now hostile; its "wine-dark" color suggests disquieting depths that harbor unknown monsters (3.158),[2] unless it is the "unresting sea" itself that is a huge monster, "dangerous and dismaying" (5.174), swallowing boats and men into its "frightening gulfs" (5.52). Though frequently described as "barren," the sea is also a broad bosom (εὐρέα κόλπον, 4.435), which allows for fecundity: "ἔπρησεν δ' ἄνεμος μέσον ἱστίον" (2.427), literally, "the wind puffed up the middle (or the center) of the sail"; A. T. Murray may have had Shakespeare's image in mind, of sails that "conceive / And grow big-bellied with the wanton wind" (*A Midsummer Night's Dream* 2.1.128–29), when he translated, "the wind filled the belly of the sail," thus stressing the fertile character of the otherwise barren sea. Reading Homer and Shakespeare in parallel, I shall be exploring the assumption that, despite widely different cultural backgrounds, purposes, and outlooks, the two authors can at times be mutually illuminating. If one could validate the hypothesis that Odyssean myths are still, at least subliminally, at work in Shakespeare's plays, then it might prove just as significant to rediscover Homer in the light of Shakespeare as to try to assess what Shakespeare owes to Homer, if only indirectly.

William M. Jones suggested in 1960 that Shakespeare was referring to the *Odyssey* when he gave Polonius's son the name of Ulysses' father Laertes and that he might have found the Orestes story in book 1 while working on *Hamlet*. Jones argues that Shakespeare may have read the *Odyssey* in Latin.[3] Several Latin translations were available throughout the sixteenth century,[4] as were translations into several vernacular languages,

German, Spanish, Italian, and French.[5] Chapman's translation was published only in 1614–15. Even if Shakespeare had read part of it in manuscript from 1611 onwards, it probably came too late to exert any influence on his plays.

At least two passages in Shakespeare have been thought to imply some knowledge of the Greek text. The third drawer's exclamation in *2 Henry IV,* "By the mass, here will be old utis" (2.4.19), has sometimes been taken, since Samuel Butler, as a possible reference to Ulysses' deception of Polyphemus under the false identity of "οὖτις" (nobody).[6] But "old utis" can easily be understood as a dialectal word meaning "confusion" or as "Utas," a period of festivity.[7] In *2 Henry VI,* (3.2.89), Aeolus looses the winds "forth their brazen caves," while in *Pericles* he is implored to "bind them in brass" (3.1.3). Noting that there is no mention of brass in Virgil's account of Aeolus (nor, for that matter, in any Ovidian allusion), Robert Kilburn Root assumed that Shakespeare must have remembered *Odyssey,* 10.3–4, where the island of Aeolus is said to have a "τεῖχος χάλκεον" a wall of brass, or bronze.[8] But one cannot infer a direct knowledge of Homer's text from such clues, since information of that kind was available in reference books: Lilio Gregorio Giraldi, for example, recalled in his *De Deis Gentium* that "Civitatis . . . suae moenia ex aere construxisse dictus" (The wall round his city is said to have been built of bronze).[9] So it is hardly surprising that even T. W. Baldwin, who was not given to underestimating Shakespeare's reading, should have concluded that "If Shakspere had any contact with Homer in grammar school or elsewhere, that contact was but of the slightest importance."[10] Unless evidence of some sort is produced that Shakespeare knew a Latin or a vernacular version, one can safely assume that he almost certainly never read the *Odyssey.*

Odyssean themes, though, undoubtedly reached him, through an indirect, diffuse, and multiple transmission that is particularly well suited to an exploration of the workings of mythical language, of the ways in which it survives despite distortions, misinterpretations, or reinterpretations.[11] More specifically, it lends itself to the study of how an essential, primitive, founding myth sometimes resurfaces in unexpected ways, reworks itself, and is revitalized in later occurrences.

Taking hints from Virgil's *Aeneid,*[12] medieval literature transformed Ulysses from noble hero into crafty liar.[13] At the end of the sixteenth century however, a new interest in the *Odyssey* emerged in England, that focused on the traveler and husband. In *The Scholemaster* (1570), Roger Ascham led the way when he understood Homer's adjective "polytropos" (of many turns) as meaning "skilfull in many mens manners and facions" and held Ulysses up as a model to be followed by young travelers wishing to avoid the dangers and pitfalls of Italy, which he saw as Circe's court.[14] In the same vein, Clerophontes advises his son Gwydonius, in Robert

Greene's *The Carde of Fancie* (1587), to beware the "subtill Syrens" and "sorcering Circes" he might meet in his travels: "he which will heare the Syrens sing, must with Ulisses tye himself to the mast of a ship, least happely he be drowned," and "who so meanes to be a sutor to Circes, must take a Preservative, unlesse he will be inchaunted."[15] Just as frequently, Odyssean themes were used in the context of a developing ideology in praise of married love. In 1570, John Balechouse painted *The Return of Ulysses to Penelope* for Bess of Hardwick.[16] Bess also bought a series of Brussels tapestries woven to a design by Michiel Coxie: they represent the story of Ulysses, as a symbol, one assumes, of Bess's own loyalty to her husband.[17] William Gager's *Ulysses Redux* (played at Christ Church College, Oxford, on 6 February 1591/92 and published in May 1592) dramatizes Ulysses' return, his revenge on the suitors, and his happy reunion with Penelope, whose constancy is praised in two choruses.[18] In 1587, Robert Greene published *Penelope's Web*, "a christall mirror of fæminine perfection" dedicated to the sister countesses of Cumberland and Warwick: in perfect reciprocity, while Penelope keeps "the Idea of Vlisses printed in her thoughts," Ulysses sails back to Ithaca, "to see the mistresse of his thoughts chast Penelope."[19]

We do not find any apparent trace of the Humanists' new moral Ulysses, wise traveler and faithful husband, in Shakespeare's plays. Instead, we have "sly Ulysses," who appears in Lucrece's tapestry (*The Rape of Lucrece*, 1399), and remains sly right up to *Troilus and Cressida*. Yet in The Winter's Tale, Autolycus, who inherits the name of Ulysses' crafty grandfather (probably through Ovid's *Metamorphoses*),[20] takes Ulysses' roguery into the subplot and margins of the play, which suggests perhaps that the essential lies elsewhere. In the *Rape of Lucrece*, wise Nestor speaks and the Greeks listen "As if some mermaid did their ears entice" (1411). The superposition and, it seems, adequation between Nestor's words of wisdom and the Sirens' lures contribute to blur usual distinctions. Nestor and the Sirens also blend in *3 Henry VI,* when Richard of Gloucester prepares himself both to "play the orator as well as Nestor" (3.2.188) and to "drown more sailors than the mermaids shall" (3.2.186). This program will also lead him to "Deceive more slily than Ulysses could" (3.2.189), and transform himself into a Ulysses who has become as dangerous as Circe and the Sirens. Consequently, *Richard III* seems to amalgamate all these threats, as a monstrous siren-like Richard sends his victims into a devouring sea: Clarence, who agonizingly experiences the descent to the bottom of the sea (1.4.22–23), and Hastings, who is also made "to tumble down / Into the fatal bowels of the deep" (3.4.100–101). In *The Merchant of Venice* Launcelot Gobbo declares Jessica to be "damn'd both by father and mother; thus when I shun Scylla, your father, I fall into Charybdis, your mother" (3.5.15–17); the joke is a grotesque caricature of a partial vision in which Scylla, as a cannibalistic, ogre-like Shylock, complements a Mediterranean sea that, Charybdis-like, devours the merchant's goods.[21] From Richard as siren to Shylock as Scylla, images of female monsters express fundamental fears. At the same time, unsounded human depths are as "savage-wild" as the most powerful and frightening natural forces, be they symbolized by bear or billow, "empty tigers or the roaring sea" (*Romeo and Juliet* 5.3.39).

In its cruelty, the sea does not so much devour as make "unjust divorce," as in *The Comedy of Errors* (1.1.104), which harks back to the archetypal separation story of the *Odyssey*. Onto his blend of *Amphitruo*, *Menaechmi*, and Gower's version of Apollonius, Shakespeare appropriately grafts Odyssean themes. All the characters seem to have "drunk of Circe's cup" (5.1.271) as they go through the destabilizing process of questioning their own identity in what looks like a darkly Ovidian metamorphic world. Antipholus of Syracuse finds in Luciana a fascinating siren, whose erotic charm would lure him to desirable death:

> O, train me not, sweet mermaid, with thy note,
> To drown me in thy sister's flood of tears.
> Sing, siren, for thyself, and I will dote;
> Spread o'er the silver waves thy golden hairs,
> And as a bed I'll take them, and there lie,
> And in that glorious supposition think
> He gains by death that hath such means to die:
>
> (3.2.45–51)

Beneath the colorful sensuality of a Renaissance picture lies the familiar assumption, expressed by Lydgate, that mermaids make a man

> Forgete hym silf & lese his remembraunce,
> Devoide hym clene from his owne thought,
> Til unwarly he be to meschef brought.[22]

Ulysses-like, therefore, Antipholus tries to tear himself from that "enchanting presence and discourse" (3.2.161) that he believes is leading him to destruction:

> But lest myself be guilty to self-wrong,
> I'll stop mine ears against the mermaid's song.
>
> (3.2.163–64)[23]

Yet, far from making him "traitor to [himself]" (3.2.162), as he fears, she enables him to find a new, stable identity, when the siren is finally transformed into a wife. In the scene where Antipholus of Syracuse starts courting Luciana, the boy actor's, or nowadays actress's, part, though brief, is particularly complex: it must express all at once, in a very delicate balance, Luciana's bafflement and incredulity, her indignation fighting off secret longings, when she hears his insistent praises and persuasions, "as if some mermaid did [her] eares entice." In this brief scene, Shakespeare creates the dramatic image of the suffering siren, an Ovidian metamorphosis of the Odyssean theme,[24] that he later developed and explored in *Antony and Cleopatra*, which dramatizes a tension between threatening woman and suffering woman.

Cleopatra is cast in the part of Dido, as George Wilson Knight noted in 1931.[25] Not only, as A. D. Nuttall suggests, because Dido unmanned Aeneas in her Carthaginian revels,[26] but also, as Jonathan Bate shows, because Dido expressed the pain of the forsaken lover in Ovid's *Heroides*.[27] Behind Dido stands Calypso, who shuddered (5.116–17) when she realized that she had to let her lover go. Antony tries to break free of those strong "Egyptian fetters" just as Ulysses dreams of escaping the nymph's island "though bonds of iron hold him," "οὐδ' εἴ πέρ τε σιδήρεα δέσματ' ἔχῃσιν" (1.204; Chapman speaks of "iron chaines," 1. 319). Surrounded by "seeming mermaids," Cleopatra is also Circe,[28] keeping her lover in the thraldom of sensuality.[29] Surrendering to "idleness itself" (1.3.94), Antony becomes as "*reses*" (inactive, stagnant") and "*tardus*" (slow, sluggish) as Ulysses' companions in Ovid's account (*Metamorphoses* 14.436); he is turned by "this enchanting queen" (1.2.128) into "a doting mallard" (3.10.19), soon to be "pluck'd" (3.12.3), and later changed into the bull of Basan (3.13.127–28), or the boar of Thessaly (4.13.2). But Cleopatra, a Circe who traps Antony in day-to-day unconsciousness, is also a Calypso whose myth making ensures immortality, the lovers' abandon to immediate pleasure and their desperate search for eternity being, for "the blown rose" and "the old ruffian," complementary ways of fighting the threats of old age; but the price to be paid is death to the reality of the world.

The question of mortality, connected with that of memory, is perhaps where Shakespeare's plays and the *Odyssey* come closest. The immortality offered by Calypso implies forgetfulness: "with soft and wheedling words she beguiles him that he may forget Ithaca" (1.56–57). Similarly, Circe drugs her victims so that "they might utterly forget their native land" (10.236). But while forgetfulness is lethal, memory can be a source of pain and confusion. Twenty years on, the husband or wife one recovers is no longer the remembered one. In the *Odyssey*, time separates more dangerously than even the sea can do. Penelope has cherished the memory of the young warrior who left for Troy. "So dear a face do I always remember with longing, my husband's" (1.343–44). Twenty years later she is courted by young pretenders, most of whom are no older than her own son.

Paradoxically, as she weaves and unweaves, she seems to freeze time, to be constantly setting the clock back; but, by refusing the pretenders, she also dissociates herself from the image of young Ulysses and prepares herself to welcome an unknown man, a Ulysses twenty years older, "for quickly do men grow old in evil fortune" (19.360). In William Gager's *Ulysses Redux* (971–72), Amphinomus warns Penelope that, were he to come back, Ulysses would be changed: "Inane praeter nomen, et larvam meram, / Rugasque, canitiemque, seniumque, et situm" (nothing but his name, a mere ghost, wrinkled, white-haired, decrepit, and filthy). The suitors, in Peter Colse's *Penelope's Complaint*, refer to themselves as "vs yongsters" (1. 1100) and contemptuously call Ulysses "Baldpate" (1. 1104). The French novelist Annie Leclerc recently rewrote Ulysses' return from the viewpoint of Penelope, who must await "not him who twenty years hence haunted my dreams, not the young man with handsome locks, the newly crowned king, glowing, generous, indestructible, but the real Ulysses, a man weighed down, worn out, changed Ulysses, returned from the distant shore, from the land of the dead, perhaps, having seen more marvels, fought more monsters and sorrows than you may conceive of, a brooding, irritable, fiery Ulysses."[30] Instead of "that beloved young man whom the waves bore away," "an old man whose face has been chiseled by the barren seas' countless storms . . . a stranger burnt by the sea-spray, crusted with blood and scars, bearing the memory of all those women."[31]

Ulysses, for his part, left behind a young Penelope, whom he dreams of returning to. In her study of the weaving motif in the *Odyssey*, Ioanna Papadopoulou-Belmehdi notes that "Homer's Ulysses is intent on returning to the wife who was but a 'young nymph' when he set out for Troy. Divine Calypso's invitation to immortality is countered not by a yearning for death but rather by the opposite, the barely suggested dream of recapturing those bygone days."[32] Instead, he must meet an aged woman, transformed by the natural metamorphosis of life, her "cheeks stained with tears" (18.173). While Homer's heroine complains that "All beauty that was mine the gods who hold Olympus have destroyed since the day *he* departed in the hollow ships" (18.180–81),[33] Ovid's Penelope insists, "Certe ego, quae fueram te discedente puella, / Protinus ut uenias, facta uidebor anus" (And I indeed, young though I was when you left, however soon you may return, aged will I appear to you, *Heroides* 1.115–16). William Gager's Penelope, remembering Ovid's, is equally aware of the changes brought on by the years: "Certe puella quae profecturo fui, / Anus videbor facta, redeunti statim" (Young indeed that I was when you left, aged will I appear to you when you come back, 876–77)." With her "wrinkling sorrowed face" (468), Peter Colse's Penelope adds her contribution to a well established theme:

> Ah when to Troy my true-loue wend,
> He left me shining maiden like,
> But when that he doth backward bend,
> He sure shal find me beldam-like
>
> (463–66)

An acute awareness of the passing of time, poised on the knife's edge between pathos and comedy, is expressed in the recognition scene of *The Comedy of Errors*, or rather the non-recognition scene, when Egeon tries to make himself known, but to the wrong son and the wrong servant; their blank memories cause him to deplore the havoc of time, which hampers recognition:

> O! grief hath chang'd me since you saw me last,
> And careful hours with time's deformed hand
> Have written strange defeatures in my face:
>
> (5.1.298–300)

The theme is further developed in Shakespeare's last plays, which, like *The Comedy of Errors*, partly derive from the Greek romances, and through them connect distantly with the Odyssean world.[34] Pericles appears "in sorrow all devour'd" (4.4.25), face unwashed and hair uncut, while Leontes has become old, crushed under the weight of guilt and grief. On seeing his wife's statue, he is surprised to find that she is not as he remembered her:

> But yet, Paulina,
> Hermione was not so much wrinkled, nothing
> So aged as this seems.
>
> (5.3.27–29)

Leontes' reaction expresses that moment of shock when the memory of sixteen years hence is suddenly forced to give way to present-day reality. Annie Leclerc has captured the dramatic impact of the reunion scene in the *Odyssey* in words that might apply to *The Winter's Tale*, when she imagines "the instant when your gazes meet, when you are driven to recognize each other, to put down your burden of suffering and resentment, to embrace at last, you poor humans."[35] The scene had already struck Spenser, who imaginatively recreated it in *The Faerie Queene*:

> Not so great wonder and astonishment,
> Did the most chast Penelope possesse,
> To see her Lord, that was reported drent,
> And dead long since in dolorous distresse,

Come home to her in piteous wretchednesse,
After long trauell of full twentie yeares,
That she knew not his fauours likelynesse,
For many scarres and many hoary heares,
But stood long staring on him, mongst vncertaine feares.

(6.7.39)

Thus does Leontes, with great wonder and astonishment, recover Hermione, who was reported dead long since in dolorous distress, and after a full sixteen years stands long-staring on her, 'mongst uncertain fears. Hermione's deep silence, like Emilia's and Egeon's in *The Comedy of Errors*, is the sign of intense dramatic emotion.

Yet beyond suggesting a moment that is all the more poignant since it was no longer hoped for, the *Odyssey* offers a complex imaginative system. Two worlds face each other in a mutual confrontation: comforting Penelope contrasts with the deadly monsters, Charybdis, Scylla, the Sirens; while the seductive, young Calypso offers immortality, challenging an ageing Penelope, who anchors one in mortality. The human and nonhuman, eternity and the injuries of time, the young nymphs and the ageing wife, are thus pitted against one another. Yet there is also a third term, a middle ground. Halfway between the nonhuman world of monsters and nymphs, and the civilized world of home and Penelope, lies the island of Phaeacia, a kind of threshold, or crossing over. Nausicaa lives there, and she helps Ulysses from one world to the other in much the same way as Perdita, Marina, and Miranda make it possible to pass from the world of evil and separation to the world of reintegration. Just as Pericles hails Marina as "Thou that beget'st him that did thee beget" (5.1.195), Ulysses gratefully acknowledges that "you, maiden, have given me life" (8.868). Like Marina, Nausicaa is a Diana figure (6.102–9, 151–52), while being, like Perdita, Marina, and Miranda, on the nubile threshold of womanhood.[36]

The confrontation between the older man and the younger girl might be read as a suggestion of incest, which the *Odyssey* fends off, not only because Nausicaa's parents are known, but because Ulysses is called, throughout this episode and nowhere else, "ξεῖνε πάτερ" (7.28, 48; 8.145, 408), or "father stranger," a phrase that states proximity while associating it with safe distance. The incest theme was developed by the Greek romances, from which the extant Latin *Apollonius of Tyre* that was taken over in Greene's *Pandosto* undoubtedly derives. Shakespeare tones the theme down and clarifies it: in Marina, Pericles finds the portrait of her mother Thaisa (5.1.102–13), and if Leontes is briefly taken by Perdita's beauty (5.1.222–23), it is because, at the very moment when Paulina has forbidden him to marry, "Unless another, / As like Hermione as is her picture, / Affront his eye" (5.1.73–75), he sees in his daughter the image of his wife as she was sixteen years earlier, and as she has lived on in his memory. That is why Nausicaa, the last helper on the homebound journey, is also the last temptation. If he accepted Alcinous's offer (8.314) and married her, Ulysses would be projected twenty years earlier. By tempting him out of time, Nausicaa is a second Calypso: at the door of Alcinous's palace stand two gold and silver dogs, "immortal they were and ageless all their days" (7.94), as a reminder that Calypso, herself "immortal and ageless" (5.218), wanted to make Ulysses in her image, "immortal and ageless all his days" ("ἤματα πάντα," 5.136).[37] When Ulysses tells Nausicaa, as he leaves her, "I will . . . pray to you as to a god all my days" ("ἤματα πάντα," 8.467–68), not only does he separate himself from her as a mortal stands removed from a goddess, but, as linguistic "polytropos," he gives a new turn or twist to Calypso's words. By changing the meaning of "ἤματα πάντα," he wards off the threat that Nausicaa embodies, the last temptation of immortality.[38] The unnaturalness of the Calypso and Nausicaa enticement is suggested by the reference to the love of the forever young Aurora and the endlessly senile Tithonus in the first line of book 5, when Ulysses leaves Calypso.[39] Furthermore, while Laertes' orchard, to which Ulysses finally comes back, is submitted to normal seasonal cycles (24.341–44), Nausicaa's garden produces fruit all year round because of an unnatural coexistence of all the stages of a plant's life; the same tree simultaneously produces blossom and fruit; while unripe grapes shed their blossom, others are turning purple (7.114–26).

There is a slight suggestion of Nausicaa's unnatural garden in *The Winter's Tale*. "Daffadils begin to peer" ( 4.3.1), and Perdita is "Flora / Peering in April's front" (4.4.2–3) at the time of the shearing season, "the year growing ancient, / Not yet on summer's death, nor on the birth / Of trembling winter" (4.4.79–81), while Polyxenes and Camillo clearly welcome the wintry rosemary and rue, "Grace and remembrance" (4.4.76): "well you fit our ages / With flow'rs of winter" (4.4.78–79). Perdita and Marina help Leontes and Pericles toward a reconciliation with life that includes an acceptance of mortality. Once the hero can dissociate the wife and the daughter figures, the latter helps him across a perilous sea, to reach what Homer calls "the threshold of old age" (15.246, 348; 24.212). At the same time, the great devouring gulf transforms itself into "this great sea of joys" (*Pericles* 5.1.192), and one is left with a vision of Perdita dancing like "A wave o' th' sea" (*The Winter's Tale* 4.4.141).

Collecting and reorganizing old tales that no doubt probe deep in the human psyche, Homer's *Odyssey* is a literary matrix of fundamental images and situations whose complexity and subtlety turn simple archetypes into flexible literary myths. In contrast with the *Iliad*, a man's world of battle where women play secondary, submissive roles,[40] the *Odyssey* presents prominent figures of women, to the extent that Samuel Butler considered that it could only have been written by a woman, whom he thought must have been Nausicaa.[41] Beyond that fanciful improbability lies a real intuition: more than a series of feminine types, the poem offers a vision of woman as akin to the sea, where opposites meet as one constantly crosses from one shore to another, between fear and desire, pleasure and suffering, a yearning for eternity and the acceptance of mortality. In Shakespeare's plays, similar mythical voices seem to be heard. They tell the story of woman as a frightful devouring monster and deceptive seductress, imagined as another form of death; they tell the story of her transformation from witch into comforter and victim. They also tell the story of the ambivalent daughter figure. If Shakespeare had no direct knowledge of Homer, then what Francis Bacon says of philosophy, that it "must be dismembred, so that a few fragments only, and in some places will bee found like the scattered boords of shipwracke,"[42] is also true of literary myths. Even after their dislocation, they retain enough power to reassemble and reactivate in an alien but welcoming land, where they create new configurations while keeping some distant but essential memory of their original country.

# Notes

1. See Gérard Lambin, *Homère le compagnon* (Paris: CNRS Éditions, 1995), 216–44.
2. All quotations are taken from *The Odyssey*, ed. A. T. Murray, rev. George E. Dimock, Loeb Classical Library, 2 vols. (Cambridge: Harvard University Press, 1995).
3. William M. Jones, "Shakespeare's Source for the Name 'Laertes,'" *Shakespeare Newsletter* 10 (1960): 9; John W. Velz, *Shakespeare and the Classical Tradition, A Critical Guide to Commentary, 1660–1960* (Minneapolis: University of Minnesota Press, 1968), 309.
4. Such as the version printed by Joannes Schottus in Strasburg in 1510; Raphael Volaterranum's version (Rome: Jacobum Mazochium, 1510; Lyons: S. Gryphium, 1541); or Simone Lemnio's (Paris: M. Juvenem, 1581).
5. For example, Simon Schaidenreisser's German version (Augsburg: A. Weissenhorn, 1537); Gonçalo Perez's Spanish version (Antwerp: J. Steelsio, 1556); Girolamo Baccelli's Italian version (Florence: Sermartelli, 1582). The first two books were translated into French by Jacques Peletier (Paris: C. Gautier, 1570), and the first three books by Amadis Jamyn (Paris: Breyer, 1584). A full translation into French was done by Salomon Certon (Paris: L'Angelier, 1604).
6. Nel Mezzo, "2 *Henry IV,* 2.4.21: Ulysses and Utis," *Notes and Queries* 4 (1911): 83–84; Velz, *Shakespeare and the Classical Tradition,* 174–75.
7. See A. R. Humphreys in his edition (London: Methuen, 1966), 63.
8. R. K. Root, *Classical Mythology in Shakespeare,* Yale Studies in English 19 (New York: Henry Holt, 1903), 34.

9. Lilio Gregorio Giraldi, *De Deis Gentium varia et multiplex Historia* (Basel: Johannes Oporinus, 1548), 253.

10. T. W. Baldwin, *William Shakspere's Small Latine & Lesse Greeke*, 2 vols. (Urbana: University of Illinois Press, 1944), 2:660–61.

11. Two main channels interacted. On the one hand, the literary reworkings of Virgil's *Aeneid*, and Ovid's *Metamorphoses* 13–14 and *Heroides* 1. The latter reverberates in Gower's *Confessio Amantis* 4.77–133. On the other hand, innumerable commentaries and interpretations: see Félix Buffière, *Les mythes d'Homère et la pensée grecque* (Paris: Les Belles Lettres, 1956, 1973); Robert Lamberton, *Homer the Theologian, Neoplatonist Allegorical Reading and the Growth of the Epic Tradition* (Berkeley and Los Angeles: University of California Press, 1986); Don Cameron Allen, "Undermeanings in Homer's *Iliad* and *Odyssey*," in *Mysteriously Meant: The Rediscovery of Pagan Symbolism and Allegorical Interpretation in the Renaissance* (Baltimore: Johns Hopkins University Press, 1970), 83–105; Jean Dorat, *Mythologicum ou interprétation allégorique de l'Odyssée X–XII et de l'Hymne à Aphrodite*, ed. Philip Ford (Geneva: Droz, 2000).

12. Elements for an overall history of the evolution of the character of Ulysses in literature are to be found in W. B. Stanford, *The Ulysses Theme* (Oxford: Basil Blackwell, 1968).

13. He is "fel Ulixes" (treacherous Ulysses) in the twelfth-century *Roman d'Eneas*, ed. Aimé Petit (Paris: Le Livre de Poche, 1997), 104. Lydgate's portrait was more balanced: although Ulysses is "Ful of wyles and sleighty at assayes / In menyng double and right deceyveable," he is also "In conseillynge discret & ful prudent," *Troy Book* 2.4600–4601, 4605, ed. Henry Bergen, 3 vols. (Millwood, N.Y.: Kraus Reprint Co., 1973), 1:276. Seneca's *Troades* reinforced that reputation. These portraits refer more to the politician of the *Iliad* than the husband and traveler of the *Odyssey*.

14. Roger Ascham, *English Works*, ed. W. A. Wright (Cambridge: Cambridge University Press, 1904), 225.

15. Robert Greene, *The Carde of Fancie*, in *Shorter Novels: Elizabethan*, ed. George Saintsbury (London: Dent, 1929), 184. So Lyly writes in *Euphues and his England*: "the Trauailer that stragleth from his own countrey, is in short tyme transformed into so monstrous a shape, that hee is faine to alter his mansion with his manners, and to liue where he canne, not where he would. What did Ulysses wish in the middest of his trauailing, but onely to see the smoake of his owne Chymnie?" *The Complete Works*, ed. R. Warwick Bond, 3 vols. (Oxford: Clarendon Press, 1902), 2:25. The last sentence is reminiscent of Du Bellay, *Les Regrets* (1558), Sonnet 31. Ascham's interpretation is echoed as late as 1619 in Fletcher and Massinger's *The Custom of the Country*, when Duarte declares: "If I traveld / Like wise Ulysses to see men and manners, / I would returne in act, more knowing, then / Homer could fancie him" (2.1.115–18).

16. See Anthony Wells-Cole, *Art and Decoration in Elizabethan and Jacobean England* (New Haven: Yale University Press, 1997), 250–51, 288–92.

17. Wells-Cole, *Art and Decoration*, 269.

18. *Ulysses Redux*, 1125–51, 1980–2009, in William Gager, *Meleager, Ulysses Redux, Panniculus Hippolyto Assutus*, ed. J. W. Binns (Hildesheim: Georg Olms, 1981).

19. Robert Greene, *Penelope's Web* (London: [Thomas Orwin?], 1587), sig. Br°. A second edition was printed by E. Allde for John Hodgets (London, 1601).

20. "Autolycus, his mother's noble father, who excelled all men in thievery and in oaths. It was a god himself who had given him this skill, to wit, Hermes" (*Odys-*

*sey* 19.394–97) becomes, in Golding's version of Ovid's *Metamorphoses*, "shee bare by Mercurye / A sonne that hyght Awtolychus, who provde a wyly pye, / And such a fellow as in theft and filching had no peere" (11.359–61).

21. Natale Conti had interpreted this Homeric episode as a warning against profligates' running into debt: *Mythologia*, 8, 12 (Frankfurt: Andreas Wechel, 1584), 881. Spenser seems to have used Conti in his account of Guyon's navigation between Charybdis and Scylla, or the Gulf of Greediness and the Rock of vile Reproach. *Faerie Queene*, 2.12.1–9.

22. Lydgate's *Troy Book*, 5.2068–70, ed. Henry Bergen, 2:831.

23. Ulysses did not stop his ears in Homer, but he did in Lydgate's *Troy Book*, 5.2079–81; and in Lodge's *Rosalind* (1590), ed. Donald Beecher (Ottawa: Dovehouse Editions, 1997), 139.

24. A landmark in the transformation of a threatening figure into a suffering figure was the traditional, post-Homeric story of the siren Parthenope, who drowned herself when Ulysses stopped his ears not to hear her song; it worked its way into Peter Colse's *Penelope's Complaint* (London: Valentine Simmes for H. Jackson, 1596), 929–30: "And when she saw I would not stay, / She drownd her selfe in surging sea."

25. George Wilson Knight, *The Imperial Theme* (London: Methuen, 1931), 297.

26. A. D. Nuttall, "Virgil and Shakespeare," in *Virgil and his Influence*, ed. Charles Martindale (Exeter: Bristol Classical Press, 1984), 71–93, 75.

27. Jonathan Bate, *Shakespeare and Ovid* (Oxford: Clarendon Press, 1993), 207–8.

28. Some of Cleopatra's Circean features were noted by Clifford Davidson in "*Antony and Cleopatra*: Circe, Venus, and the Whore of Babylon," *Bucknell Review* 25 (1980): 31–55.

29. Antony becomes like Circe's victims, who, according to Geoffrey Whitney, wished to remain in subjection: "when they might haue their former shape againe, / They did refuse, and rather wish'd, still brutishe to remaine"; *A Choice of Emblemes* (Leyden: Christopher Plantin, 1586), 82. The idea may take its origin in Giovanni Battista Gelli's *Circe*, a reflexion on the human condition, which was translated into English by Henry Iden (London: John Cawood, 1557).

30. "Non pas celui qui vingt ans durant a hanté mes rêves, le jeune homme aux belles boucles, le roi tout neuf, rutilant, généreux, indestructible, mais Ulysse pour de vrai, homme pesant, usé, changé, Ulysse revenu de l'autre côté des mers, et peut-être de la mort, ayant connu plus de merveilles, affronté plus de monstres et de chagrins que tu n'en peux concevoir, Ulysse assombri, irrité et brûlant. . . ." Annie Leclerc, *Toi, Pénélope* (Arles: Actes Sud, 2001), 88–89.

31. "le jeune homme bien aimé emporté par les flots," "le vieil homme au visage buriné par mille tempêtes de la mer inféconde, . . . l'étranger chargé d'embruns, croûté de sang et de blessures, chargé du souvenir de tant de femmes." Leclerc, *Toi, Pénélope*, 132.

32. "l'Ulysse d'Homère ne désire que retrouver l'épouse qu'il avait quittée 'jeune nymphe' en partant pour Troie. Face à l'immortalité offerte par la divine Calypso ne se dresse point le désir de la mort, mais le rêve inverse, à peine esquissé, d'atteindre un temps révolu," Ioanna Papadopoulou-Belmehdi, *Le chant de Pénélope* (Paris: Belin, 1994), 96.

33. And again 19.124–26: "all excellence of mine, both of beauty and of form, the immortals destroyed on the day when the Argives embarked for Ilium, and with them went my husband, Odysseus."

34. See Samuel Lee Wolff, *The Greek Romances in Elizabethan Prose Fiction*

(New York, 1912); Carol Gesner, *Shakespeare and the Greek Romance: A Study of Origins* (Lexington: University Press of Kentucky, 1970).

35. "le moment où vos yeux se toucheront, où vous serez bien forcés l'un et l'autre de vous reconnaître, de lâcher vos sacs de douleur et de ressentiment, de vous étreindre, oh pauvres humains." Leclerc, *Toi, Pénélope*, 177.

36. The older, weather-beaten captain and traveler, back from outlandish countries with his store of fantastic stories thus briefly meets the younger, inexperienced, girl, like an Othello who would not marry Desdemona. This parallel was suggested by George de F. Lord in "The *Odyssey* and the Western World," *Sewanee Review* 62 (1954): 406–27.

37. The phrase reverberates in 7.257 and 23.336.

38. Although Nausicaa describes him as "like the gods, who hold broad heaven" (6.243), Ulysses clearly rejects the suggestion: "I am not like the immortals, who hold broad heaven, either in stature or in form, but like mortal men" (7.209–10).

39. Annie Leclerc intuitively sees Nausicaa as Dawn: "Nausicaa is simply Aurora's other name, rosy-fingered Aurora, exquisite virginity" ("Nausicaa n'est que l'autre nom de l'aurore, d'Aurore aux doigts de rose, virginité exquise"); Leclerc, *Toi, Pénélope*, 200.

40. The heroic and political themes of the *Iliad* may have made it more popular than the *Odyssey*. It was published earlier and more frequently in England. The Greek text, *Homerou Ilias*, was printed by George Bishop (London, 1591); and, before Chapman Arthur Hall translated the first ten books (London: Ralph Newberie, 1581).

41. Samuel Butler, *The Authoress of the Odyssey* (London, 1897).

42. Francis Bacon, *The Wisedome of the Ancients* (London: John Bill, 1619), 60.

# Shakespeare's Mediterranean
## *Measure for Measure*

### GARY TAYLOR

### 1

MODERN AUDIENCES HAVE NO DIFFICULTY UNDERSTANDING WHY *Measure for Measure* is set in Vienna. In 1930, both Erich Ziegel in Hamburg and Iwan Schmith in Vienna updated the play to the modern Austrian capital, adorning it with lots of local color.[1] In 1956 American John Houseman directed the play as "a Strauss operetta," with the carefree atmosphere of an imperial capital at its cultural and political zenith. In 1974, in glaring contrast, Britain's Jonathan Miller located the play in the early 1930s, just before the Nazi coup, with a harsh score reminiscent of Schoenberg.[2] In 1975, Canada's Robin Philips set it in the city of Freud, in 1912, emphasizing the repressed sexuality of Isabella, a decadent upper class, and an empire on the eve of disintegration.[3]

But none of these associations was available to the play's original audiences. Nevertheless, spectators in the early seventeenth century, like their modern counterparts, could not have avoided reading the play's action in terms of its setting. Even without stage scenery, the play's setting is a signifier, part of what Keir Elam identifies as "the semiotics of theatre";[4] in particular, part of that moral, symbolic, ideological, and "poetic geography" that John Gillies has characterized as Shakespeare's "geography of difference."[5] Neither Elam nor Gillies has anything to say about the setting of *Measure for Measure*, but that setting would have been part of the visual and aural experience of any early audience. Shakespeare's contemporaries knew that inhabitants of different parts of Europe dressed differently than Englishmen;[6] acting companies indicated geographical and cultural identities synecdochically, by a few characteristic peculiarities of costume.[7] Moreover, the word "Vienna" is spoken twice in the very first scene and reiterated again in the next scene, and the next, occurring altogether nine times—as often as Messina in *Much Ado about Nothing*, Navarre in *Love's Labor's Lost*, or Dunsinane in *Macbeth*; more often than Verona in *The Two Gentlemen of Verona*, the Forest of Ardenne in *As You Like It*, Elsi-

243

nore in *Hamlet*, Belmont in *The Merchant of Venice*, or Ephesus in *The Comedy of Errors*.[8] References to Vienna in *Measure* are not randomly distributed, either, but bunched for emphasis in the first and last few minutes of the play in performance.[9]

So, what did the word "Vienna" mean to London audiences in 1603 or 1604, when the play was first performed?

It meant almost nothing. *Measure* is the only play written in England before 1660 to be set in Vienna or to feature Viennese characters.[10] Actually, it is the only play of the period set anywhere in Austria.

Although they were not associated specifically with Vienna, a few Austrian characters did appear on early modern stages. Three Elizabethan plays—the anonymous *Troublesome Reign of King John*, Shakespeare's *King John*, and Munday and Chettle's *Death of Robert Earl of Huntington*—all feature the same Austrian duke responsible for the murder of Richard the Lion-Hearted.[11] Chapman's *Conspiracy of Charles Duke of Byron*, in 1608, includes a walk-on part for the contemporary Archduke of Austria, on a diplomatic mission to Paris.[12] Obviously, none of these Austrians is of much help in deciphering *Measure*. Neither is Henry Chettle's *Tragedy of Hoffman*, written in 1602 and therefore closest in date to Shakespeare's comedy. In Chettle's tragedy, the Duke of Austria belongs to a family cast of characters entirely Germanic and northern European: the Duke of Prussia, the Duke of Saxony, and the Duchess of Luneberg; the play is also littered with references to the Baltic Sea, the Baltic island of Bornholm, Danzig, Elsinore, Germany, Heidelberg, Lubeck Haven, Norway, Pomerania, Wittenberg—and even the "Cimmerian mists" of the Arctic circle.[13] Chettle correctly identifies Austria as a Germanic state, linked most closely to the northern principalities of the Holy Roman Empire. But *Measure* does not associate Vienna with any of those places.

Indeed, *Measure* does not even associate Vienna with "Austria," a word that never appears in the play. "Austria is not an easy term for the historian to handle," admits one of the most distinguished modern historians of the House of Austria; in particular, in the sixteenth and seventeenth centuries there was "no effective imposition of an Austrian identity."[14] Although Shakespeare's contemporaries located Vienna in a vaguely defined region called "Austria," Austria itself was merely a province of Germany.[15] Vienna was just one city among several in what was then called "Upper Germany."[16] But "Germany" does not appear in *Measure*, either; nor does any reference to the Danube.[17]

Shakespeare only mentions Vienna once elsewhere, in Hamlet's explanation of *The Mousetrap*: "This play is the image of a murder done in Vienna" (3.2.226–27). Shakespeare's source for this material seems to have been the murder of a duke of Urbino, and Harold Jenkins suggests that "Vienna" in the Second Quarto may be a compositorial misreading or authorial mis-memory of "Vrbino";[18] the First Quarto reads "*guyana*" (sig. F4), a variant recently defended by Patricia Parker.[19] Vienna and Guiana would have been equally exotic places for the original audiences. Any of these names would convey the essential information that "This play, so relevant to recent events here in Denmark, is not set here in Denmark, but in some irrelevant other place, far away." Beyond that, it may be pointless to expect coherence or precision. Hamlet is at this point either acting mad, or actually mad; speaking "trapically"/"tropically," he absurdly entitles the play *The Mousetrap*, and uses "Duke" for the character elsewhere consistently described as "King" (even by himself). Vienna, Urbino, Guiana—what difference does the place-name make to the dramatic effect here? These are "wild and whirling words." They tell us nothing about the Vienna of *Measure*.

If Vienna meant anything particular in England in the period up to 1604, it was what George Abbot in 1599 called "now the principall Bulwarke of all Christendome against the Turke."[20] In 1529 the advance into Europe of the armies of Suleiman the Magnificent was halted at Vienna, and there are allusions to that famous siege in Marlowe's *Tamburlaine* (1588),[21] Jonson's *Every Man in his Humour* (1598),[22] and Barnabe Barnes's *The Devil's Charter* (1606);[23] in Thomas Goffe's *The Raging Turke* (1618), the title character threatens to "make *Vienna* all a Shambles."[24] Only two Elizabethan books headlined Vienna on the title page, and both advertised "newes, sent from Vienna" of "the Turke."[25] Hostilities between the Turks and the Holy Roman Empire recommenced in 1591; in 1601 Robert Johnson's popular translation, *The Travellers Breviat*, noted that "the princes of Austrich," sharing a larger border with the Turk than any other prince, were "constrained to spend the greatest part of their reuenues in the continuall maintenance of twentie thousand footemen and horsemen in garrison."[26] The Ottoman threat to Vienna persisted till the very end of the seventeenth century.

Islamic expansion was the subject of real anxiety in Elizabethan England, an anxiety expressed in books, plays, and ballads.[27] Like most of his contemporaries, Shakespeare took an interest in the Turks. He probably read Richard Knolles's *Generall Historie of the Turkes* soon after its publication (early October 1603);[28] there he would have found 150 folio pages devoted to the war then raging between the house of Austria and the Turks, culminating in "great harms" inflicted on the Christians in 1603, and warnings that the Sultan was "purposing . . . to make an inroad into Austria."[29] Whether or not he read Knolles, Shakespeare refers to Turks or Moors at least 119 times in eighteen different plays.[30] Indeed, in *Othello*—the play Shakespeare probably wrote just before or just after *Measure*—"Turk" or "Moor" or "Ottomites" occurs seventy-nine times.[31] Nevertheless, despite Shakespeare's general interest in such matters, and despite the specific reputation of Vienna, there is not a single reference to Turks or Moors or "the general enemy Ottoman" in *Measure*. And no one has ever interpreted *Measure* as a play set at the edge of the known Christian world.[32]

In early modern England, Vienna was not an important source of imports or an important market for exports; indeed, its economy was in decline.[33] Perhaps for that reason, or because it was not an independent city-state, Vienna had not developed a distinctive urban identity or reputation. Even sartorially, Vienna was anonymous: no Viennese fashions were illustrated among the five hundred woodcuts of the 1598 edition of Cesare Vecellio's classic *Habiti antichi, et moderni di tutto il Mondo*;[34] likewise, although the famous German *Tractenbuch* (1577) begins with ninety-three plates illustrating clothing in German-speaking Europe, neither Vienna nor Austria is identified, or credited, with a distinctive style.[35] Even if the King's Men had wanted to use costuming to signify "Vienna," they would have found it difficult to do so.

Sixteenth-century Vienna was, as one modern historian puts it, "a sleepy city." There was no resident English ambassador, and "contacts between Vienna and England were few."[36] Although troupes of English actors had begun touring in German-speaking Europe by the early 1580s, none visited Austria until 1607, or Vienna until 1617.[37] The English public had little access to news about central and eastern Europe until the beginning of the Thirty Years War, in 1618, led to the creation of the first printed news serials.[38] Moreover, Vienna had not yet become important intellectually or culturally; it was not the home of a single important poet, artist, musician, or architect familiar even to the most educated Englishmen.[39] In Stephen W. May's forthcoming comprehensive index of Elizabethan verse, Vienna gets mentioned only twice (in minor poems of the mid-1570s).[40] Many Englishmen visited France, Italy, and the Low Countries; a smaller number ventured into northern or western Germany; but Vienna did not become a canonical feature of the Grand Tour until after 1630, and even then represented its "farthest extension."[41] In 1593, Fynes Moryson did stay there "three daies"—not because he found the city interesting for any reason, but only "to ease my weary horse."[42]

To sum up: for London audiences in 1603–4, the reiterated place-name "Vienna" would have meant almost nothing, and absolutely nothing relevant to *Measure*. Why, then, does it appear in the play?

One explanation offered by some modern scholars is that the play's setting constitutes a "contemporary allusion."[43] In 1966, Josephine Waters Bennett, as part of her argument that *Measure* was specifically designed as a "royal entertainment," claimed that Shakespeare was influenced by the visit to the English court of Queen Anne's brother, Ulric, Duke of Holstein.[44] Bennett quoted John Chamberlain, who on 10 December 1604, wrote that "The Duke of Holst is here still procuring a levie of men to carie into Hungarie."[45] According to the Venetian ambassador, Ulric had arrived on 12 November.[46] He came "to raise ten thousand men for service in Hungary."[47] Bennett contended that a speech by Lucio "glances with polite ambiguity at the Duke of Holst in the audience and to the general political situation. The choice of Vienna as the locale of the play may also reflect current interest." Leah Marcus in 1988 endorsed and expanded Bennett's argument, arguing that Vienna was crucial to any "topical" or "local" reading of the play.[48] Brian Gibbons, in his 1991 Cambridge edition of the play, called Bennett's conjecture "almost certain";[49] he cited it as evidence that "in 1604 Vienna, the play's setting, would be associated with the efforts of the Holy Roman Emperor to suppress Protestantism in nearby Hungary."

This is all nonsense.[50] The King's Men did perform "*Mesur for Mesur*," by "Shaxberd," at court on 26 December 1604;[51] but that fact does not establish that Shakespeare wrote the play specifically for court performance, or that he wrote it in November and December.[52] Ulric's duchy, Holstein, was located in what is now northwest Germany, on the Jutland peninsula; neither he nor his sister Queen Anne had any personal connection with Vienna, or Austria. The court of the Holy Roman Emperor had been moved in 1583 from Vienna to Prague, and it stayed in Prague until 1611.[53] None of the extant documents recording Holstein's visit mentions either Vienna or Austria.

Holstein, moreover, did not make much of an impression at court. On 14 November the Earl of Shrewsbury wrote to a friend that "The Queen's Brother is come to Court, but not very rytche eny way."[54] The Venetian ambassador immediately appraised him as "a young Prince of twenty-four without much knowledge of the world," who "ignored all etiquette."[55] Chamberlain doubted that Holstein would raise many soldiers: "me thinckes they should have litle to do that wold adventure themselves so far with a man able to do them no more goode."[56]

The passage allegedly explained by Holstein's inauspicious visit to court is the beginning of the play's second scene:

> *Luc.* If the *Duke*, with the other Dukes, come not to composition with the King
>     of *Hungary*, why then all the dukes fall vpon the King.
> *1. Gent.* Heauen grant vs its peace, but not the King of *Hungaries*.
>                                                        (TLN 97–101; 1.2.1–5)[57]

There were no "other dukes" involved in Holstein's project, no "peace" in Hungary in 1603–4, and no peace negotiations under way to "come to composition" with the "King of Hungary."[58] Although it contains a

"Duke" and "Hungary," every substantive detail of this passage fails to fit the circumstances of Holstein or Hungary in 1603–4. Bennett admits that it is "difficult to discover what [Holstein] planned," but she conjectures that he was raising troops to support the Holy Roman Emperor against the Turks and their allies the Hungarian Protestants. This conjecture seems extremely unlikely. According to the Venetian ambassador, as soon as Holstein arrived in London, "he went straight to Court, and after a few words of compliment he said [to his brother-in-law, King James], *Sire, your Majesty has committed a great mistake in concluding peace with Spain, and you will soon find it out.*"[59] On 9 January he was again urging "renewal of the war with Spain."[60] Holstein thus, like many other Protestants, opposed peace with Spain; it is hard to imagine him, at the same moment, recruiting troops to support the Catholic Hapsburgs in their effort to suppress a Protestant rebellion in Hungary. But regardless of his intentions with respect to Hungary, during the period before and after the court performance of *Measure* Holstein was challenging the most important foreign policy initiative of King James, who was patron of Shakespeare's company; Holstein soon managed to alienate not only the resident Spanish and Venetian ambassadors, but his own sister the queen, and the king.[61] Why would Shakespeare go out of his way to endorse Holstein's jejune militarism?[62] Why would the King's Men side with Holstein against their new patron?[63]

The claim that this passage is an allusion to Holstein is implausible from every perspective, historical or theatrical. Why then have serious scholars taken it so seriously? Because the passage connects to nothing else in the text, it seems to make sense only as a reference to something outside the play's world. Scholars have suggested that this reference to the King of Hungary "looks much like an elusive half-memory of Corvinus King of Hungary" in one of Shakespeare's probable sources;[64] but the King of Hungary in that source is not engaged in negotiations with "the duke, and the other dukes," nor is there any threat of war or reason to disparage "the King of Hungary's" peace. Even if this "elusive half-memory" were less elusive than it is, it would make sense of the passage only by referring to something outside the text—something very few spectators could have known.

Perhaps centuries of scholars have failed to locate the referent of this passage because they have been looking in the wrong place. Lucio's first speech occurs in a passage of disputed date and authorship; almost all modern scholars and critics recognize that the first part of 1.2 must be a later addition to the text, and the only issue is how much later.[65] John Dover Wilson connected it to events in 1606, two years after the play was performed at court; Leah Marcus connected it to events in 1608.[66] Neither of these conjectures is convincing, but they attest to a consensus that the passage is later than the rest of the play. Days later? Years later? If the passage was written at some time after the rest of the play, then perhaps the referent for the allusion belongs to some period after 1604.

Our only text of *Measure* was published in 1623; it had been set into type and run through the press sometime in 1622. The manuscript from which it was printed was prepared by the scribe Ralph Crane, who began working for the King's Men in 1619.[67] That text has been systematically expurgated, in line with the 1606 Act to Restrain Abuses of Players; it contains act divisions, which reflect the theatrical practice of the King's Men after their acquisition of the Blackfriars in 1608. It also contains one stanza of a two-stanza song that appears in Fletcher's play *Rollo Duke of Normandy*, an extraordinarily popular play written between 1617 and 1620 for the King's Men; Fletcher's two-stanza version of the song, which translates a two-stanza Latin poem, was one of the most popular songs of the century.[68] Thus Lucio's remark about Hungary occurs in a text not printed until 1622, from a manuscript not in existence earlier than 1619, which contains multiple and interlocking evidence of use in the theater after 1606, after 1608, after 1617. And John Jowett has recently discovered an exact source for Lucio's remarks about the dukes and the King of Hungary in a printed English newsletter published on 6 October 1621.[69]

"Almost any play first printed more than ten years after composition and known to have been kept in active repertory by the company which owned it," G. E. Bentley concluded, "is most likely to contain later revisions by the author or, in many cases, by another playwright working for the same company."[70] Since the eighteenth century, editors and scholars have suspected that the Folio text of *Measure* shows signs of theatrical adaptation. Jowett's new evidence appears to clinch the case; in fact, the evidence for posthumous adaptation of *Measure* is now even stronger than the evidence for posthumous adaptation of *Macbeth*. In both *Macbeth* and *Measure* the evidence for adaptation is in part "external" evidence: parts of both plays (songs) also occur in other texts, attributed to other playwrights. In 1986 the Oxford Shakespeare identified Middleton as the probable author of the added material in 1.2;[71] the forthcoming Oxford edition of *The Collected Works of Thomas Middleton* will provide further evidence for Middleton's authorship of that passage, and of three other passages, amounting altogether to about 130 lines.[72]

If Middleton added that allusion to Hungary in 1621, then does the setting of *Measure* in Vienna belong to the text Shakespeare wrote in 1604, or does it belong to Middleton's adaptation of that text in 1621? Whereas Vienna would have meant nothing to London audiences in 1604, in 1621 Vienna was a subject of intense public interest in England. By 1621, Vienna was again the capital of the Holy Roman Emperor, now Ferdinand II: the focus of profound hostility in England, Ferdinand II was the leader of an aggressive Catholic campaign against the Protestants of Germany and central Europe, the person held responsible for deposing the Protestant daughter and son-in-law of King James himself. In 1619 King James sent Lord Hay on a diplomatic mission to Vienna;[73] in 1620, Sir Henry Wotton was dispatched to Vienna, to renew negotiations.[74] On 23 May 1621, King James dispatched a third special ambassador, Lord Digby, to Vienna; he arrived on 4 July. In August, the invading army of the King of Hungary was burning villages just outside Vienna; news of this had reached London by early September;[75] on 2 October 1621, a printed English news sheet reported that the King of Hungary was within one mile of Vienna.[76] Throughout 1621, English news sheets, Parliamentary debates, and private letters were full of references to Vienna.[77]

In 1621, for Middleton and Middleton's audiences, Vienna would have been an immediately recognizable and resonant geographical, political, and poetic signifier. In 1604, for Shakespeare and Shakespeare's audiences, Vienna would have meant nothing—or the wrong thing. Moreover, Shakespeare in 1604 would have had to deliberately and self-consciously intrude that meaningless setting into his play. *None* of the many known sources and analogues for *Measure* sets it in Vienna.[78] Not one.

We are therefore faced with a very simple choice. Either Shakespeare or Middleton changed the setting of the story to Vienna. Shakespeare in 1604 had no reason to do so. Middleton in 1621 had every reason to do so. Given this choice, it seems reasonable to conclude that Middleton, not Shakespeare, was responsible for setting *Measure* in Vienna.


## 2


Where then did Shakespeare set it? In one sense, the answer is as obvious to me as it has been to other interpreters of *Measure* since the Restoration. In 1662 Davenant's theatrical adaptation set the story in Italy; in 1833 Pushkin's narrative adaptation set it in Italy;[79] in 1834–36 Wagner's operatic adaptation set it in Italy;[80] in 1979 the BBC Shakespeare set it in Italy; in 1997, in his book *The English Renaissance*, Alistair Fox included it among "the Italianate plays of Shakespeare."[81]

This unanimity is not difficult to explain. The dramatis personae list calls the Duke "Vincentio," a common Italian name Shakespeare used for an Italian character in *The Taming of the Shrew*. "Lucio" is also an Italian name, used by Shakespeare in *Romeo and Juliet* (1.2.73); so, of course, is "Juliet." Italians are named "Claudio" in Shakespeare, Lyly, and Marston; "Isabella," "Angelo," "Mariana," "Francisca," and "Barnardine" are also names given elsewhere to specifically Italian characters. Shakespeare apparently acquired the odd name "Escalus" from his chief source for

*Romeo*, and used it for the Prince of Verona; it appears in Early Modern plays only there, in the Florentine scenes of *All's Well that Ends Well*, and in *Measure*.[82] The prisoner with the unique name Ragozine (4.3.71, 4.3.76, 5.1.533; TLN 2153, 2158) is a pirate, apparently from Ragusa (modern Dubrovnik) on the Adriatic coast;[83] it would be easiest to account for his presence if the prison were an Italian one. In *Measure*, as in the Padua of *Shrew* and nowhere else in Shakespeare, there is a church called "Saint Luke's" (3.1.264; TLN 1485); in the very same line, there is a "grange," as in the Venice of *Othello* and nowhere else in Shakespeare. Vineyards are mentioned three separate times (4.1.29, 30, 33; TLN 1800, 1801, 1804); like other Renaissance Englishmen, Shakespeare associated wine with Italy, not Austria.[84] Finally, when Pompey the bawd is arrested, he is incriminated by possession of "a strange Pick-lock" (3.2.17; TLN 1506); as scholars have recognized since the eighteenth century, the "lock" this is designed to "pick" was a chastity belt, an object almost always associated with Italy, and regularly cited by Englishmen as evidence of the obsessive jealousy of Italian men.[85] More generally, Italy was notorious for sexual licentiousness and in particular prostitution; "fornication in Italy is not a sinne wincked at, but rather may be called an allowed trade."[86] Prostitution and other forms of illicit sexuality are, of course, the chief vices associated with the city portrayed in *Measure*. By contrast, Vienna was a part of Germany, where Fynes Moryson reported that "no doubt the men are very chast, and the wemen not only exceeding modest . . . but in my opinion most chast in the worlde." Moryson reports, from personal experience, a traditional characterization of Germanic peoples, one that goes back to Tacitus. Indeed, the sexual coldness of northern Europeans had been contrasted to the sexual heat of Mediterranean peoples as early as the Greek medical treatises attributed to Hippocrates.[87]

Shakespeare, writing *Measure*, was thinking of Italy, not Germany. But the play is set in a specific town, which it never leaves; in the play Shakespeare wrote, that Italian town must have been given a name. As Mark Eccles noted in his Variorum edition, among the many possible sources and analogues for Shakespeare's story of sexual blackmail, "an important series" is set in northern Italy. François de Belleforest set it in Turin. But in 1559, Georg Lauterback associated it with "the Duke of Ferrara," and that association was perpetuated in a series of Latin, German, French, and English versions of the story, well into the seventeenth century.[88] Shakespeare could have read this "Duke of Ferrara" version in, for instance, Thomas Beard's *Theatre of God's Judgements*, published in London in 1597.[89] We don't know whether Shakespeare read that book, but we do know that he read Giambattista Cinzio Giraldi's enormously popular *Ecatommiti*. Since Shakespeare certainly used Tale 37 for *Othello* and Tale 85 for *Measure*, it is reasonable to assume that he read the whole book; Mary

Lascelles, Geoffrey Bullough, and Michele Marrapodi have all argued that, in writing *Measure*, Shakespeare also drew on Tale 56, and in particular was influenced by the role in that story of a "Duke of Ferrara."[90]

As is made clear in the front matter of all of its many sixteenth-century editions, *Ecatommiti* was written while Cinzio was living in Ferrara. In the sixteenth century, under the patronage of the Este family, the independent city-state of Ferrara rivaled and in many ways surpassed Florence as the center of Italian literary culture. Like Montaigne and many others, Fynes Moryson visited Ferrara; indeed, he mentions it on the first page of his table of contents and gives a full description of its geography, history, architecture, and accommodations.[91] The Duke of Ferrara was a patron of both Tasso and Guarini, who together created a model of tragicomedy that began to influence English drama—including, in particular, *Measure*—at the very beginning of the seventeenth century. Ferrara was also the home of Ariosto, whose play *I suppositi*, translated into English by Gascoigne, was a major source for *The Taming of the Shrew*.[92] In both Ariosto's play and Gascoigne's translation readers are told at the outset that "The Comedie [is] presented as it were in *Ferrara*" (111). Shakespeare, having read *The Supposes*, knew that "the Citie of *Ferrara*" (121) was, like the city in *Measure*, a walled town, with "gates" (122, 134), governed by a "Duke" (120, 123, 124), using "Ducates" as the local currency (117, 124, 151); one of the characters owns a "Grange" (132, 134). The entire play, of course, is driven by disguises, deceptions, and premarital sex. A character named "Litio" says "have you not often heard tell of the falsehood of *Ferara*" (142), and later insists again, twice, upon "the falsehood of *Ferrara*" (143, 152); another character claims that "these *Ferareses* be as craftie as the Devill of hell" (126). Nevertheless, another character insists that the city is governed by "a most juste prince" (145), and the libelous Litio is rebuked: "you do not well to slaunder the Citie" (142). All Litio's libels about "the falsehood of Ferrara"—like Lucio's libels about the Duke—are eventually disproved.

Ferrara, unlike Vienna, was familiar to Shakespeare and his contemporaries. Illustrations of typical Ferrarese clothing appear in influential sixteenth-century costume books by Cesare Vecellio,[93] Bartolomeo Grassi (see figure 9),[94] Hans Weigel, and Jost Amman.[95] Ferrara is the first Italian city mentioned in John Florio's *Second Fruits*.[96] Elizabethans could glimpse its role in the military and diplomatic chaos of sixteenth-century Italy in the famed histories of Machiavelli and Guicciardini, available in both Italian and English (and other languages);[97] they could read, in Florio's translation of Montaigne's *Essays*, of Montaigne's own visit to Ferrara, and his encounter there with the mad and imprisoned poet Tasso.[98] Shakespeare referred to a "league between his highness and Ferrara" (*All is True; or, Henry VIII* 3.2.323); Jonson in 1600 has a traveler in *Cynthia's*

Plebea *ferrarese*.    Nobile *vergine ferrarese*.    Contadina *ferrarese*.

Rustique de Ferrare.    Noble Vierge de Ferrare.    Paysane de Ferrare.

9. Bartolomeo Grassi, *Dei veri ritratti degl'habiti di tutte le parti del mondo* (Rome, 1585), p. 19, plate 12: three figures, "Plebea ferrarese. Nobile vergine ferrarese. Contadina Ferrarese," reproduced here by kind permission: Typ 525.85.435, Department of Printing and Graphic Arts, Houghton Library of the Harvard College Library.

*Revels* claim to have tasted wine "authentically from the Duke of *Ferrara's* bottles."[99] Ducal Ferrara is also mentioned in plays by Barnabe Barnes, John Fletcher, Thomas Heywood, and Sir Aston Cokain;[100] in nondramatic works by Chaucer, Stephen Gosson, Thomas Heywood, Thomas Nashe, William Painter, Barnabe Rich, Henry Roberts, John Taylor, William Warner, and Lady Mary Wroth;[101] in John Harington's translation of Ariosto, Fairfax's translation of Tasso, and Sylvester's translation of Du Bartas.[102] Ferrara, with its duke, is the setting of James Shirley's *Love's Cruelty* and *The Opportunity*, of Thomas Nabbes's *The Unfortunate Mother*, and William Lower's *The Amorous Phantasm*. Characters from Ferrara also show up in Heywood's *Fair Maid of the West, Part II*, Robert Davenport's *The City Nightcap*, Shirley's *The Imposture*, Brome's *The Cunning Lovers*.[103] More specifically, in John Mason's *The Turk* (1607) and in John Fletcher's *The Chances* (1617), a Duke of Ferrara is not only a major character; in both plays the Duke disguises himself.[104]

The disguised Duke of Ferrara in the plays by Mason and Fletcher probably draws upon an earlier dramatic tradition, one immediately relevant to

*Measure*. Other scholars have noted a cluster of "disguised duke" plays, written for different companies in 1603 and 1604. As Thomas Pendleton has demonstrated, there is no English play earlier than 1603 "which is structurally dominated by a disguised monarch who observes, exposes, thwarts, and judges the vices and follies of his realm."[105] One of the disguised duke plays written at the very beginning of James I's reign, and according to Pendleton a major source for Shakespeare's characterization of the Duke in *Measure*, was Middleton's *The Phoenix*, performed at court in February 1604. *The Phoenix* is set in Ferrara, and includes a Duke of Ferrara among its characters; in the very first scene, the Duke's son announces an intention to travel, but then disguises himself in order to observe the vices of his own city, which are primarily sexual; at the end of the play, he reunites the major malefactors, accuses them of various crimes, is himself accused of treason, dramatically removes his disguise, and comprehensively dispenses justice. Likewise, in Marston's *Parasitaster, or the Fawn*, a disguised Duke of Ferrara, observing and manipulating the sexual follies of other characters, dominates the entire action. The date of *Parasitaster* is disputed, but David Blostein, in the Revels edition, concludes that "the most likely date" is 1604; Blostein also calls attention to the similarities between the central character in *Parasitaster*, *The Phoenix* and *Measure*. A group of English actors touring in Germany in 1604 were performing another play, similar but not identical to Marston's, that featured a disguised duke of Ferrara.[106]

Why did Middleton and Marston choose Ferrara? In part, no doubt, simply because it was an Italian city familiar to their audiences; one out of four early modern English plays was set in Italy.[107] Both Marston and Middleton made a habit of using Italian locations to comment upon English vices. But there were also particular reasons to use the dukedom of Ferrara, in the first years of the seventeenth century, in a satirical play. As late as the 1590s, Ferrara was an important diplomatic player; King James himself, while still in Scotland, received and dispatched ambassadors to Ferrara as late as 1597.[108] But in 1598, the dukedom of Ferrara ceased to exist; the last duke of the Este line died without a legitimate heir, and Pope Clement VII, aggressively taking the military and diplomatic initiative, successfully reclaimed the city as a papal territory. This was a major triumph for an invigorated Counter-Reformation papacy, and it was celebrated in an extraordinary series of pageants and diplomatic meetings in Ferrara throughout 1598—including the marriage there of an Austrian Duke to a woman named "Isabella," a marriage that required one of the parties to abandon a religious vow of celibacy.[109] From the viewpoint of Protestants like Marston and Middleton (or Thomas Gainsford and Fynes Moryson), Ferrara was a warning of what could happen to England if it did not keep up its guard.[110] Moreover, for any English dramatist, in 1603 or 1604, the papal conquest meant that no actual powerful duke of Ferrara could take offence at the portrayal of a fictional duke of Ferrara.[111]

Andrew Gurr and Roslyn Knutson have called attention to the tendency of the rival acting companies in London to mirror each other's repertoires: *Two Angry Women of Abington* versus *The Merry Wives of Windsor*, *Henry IV, Part 1* versus *Sir John Oldcastle*, and so on.[112] The disguised-duke plays of 1604 clearly belong to that pattern. The pattern would have been even more obvious if Shakespeare, like some of his sources, had set *Measure* in Ferrara.

Of all the possible locations of the story told in *Measure for Measure*, in all the known sources, *Ferrara* is the only one with the same metrical structure as *Vienna*.[113] If Shakespeare had originally written "If any in Ferrara be of worth," or "Mortality and mercy in Ferrara," or "My absolute power and place here in Ferrara," or "Here in Ferrara, sir," or "Made me a looker-on here in Ferrara," it would have been easy enough for Middleton to substitute "Vienna," and thus change the setting of the play by changing a mere nine words of the text.

# 3

This essay has so far made two distinct claims. Part 1 argued that Shakespeare did not set *Measure for Measure* in Vienna. In Part 2 I argued that he did set it in Ferrara. Obviously, the two claims reinforce one another: the argument for Ferrara follows from the argument against Vienna, and the argument against Vienna is strengthened by the ready availability of a plausible Shakespearean alternative. But it is nonetheless important to keep the two arguments separate. The specific claim for Ferrara is intrinsically more conjectural than the case against Vienna. We can know that something is wrong without knowing how to correct it—or know that something new has been substituted, without being equally confident about what it displaced. Shakespeare could have used the name of some other Italian city; "Ferrara" is simply the most conservative solution to the problem.

The text that we possess, the object of all critical and theatrical interpretation, is *Measure* as adapted by Middleton. Any attempt to recover Shakespeare's original inevitably depends upon a speculative reconstruction of the lost process by which Middleton in 1621 transformed what Shakespeare had written in 1604. It is certainly possible to identify elements of the 1623 text as the work of Middleton, but it will always be harder to reconstruct the process of transformation. Nevertheless, there are anomalies in the 1623 text that could be the result of Middleton's alteration of the play's setting. The claim that "Vienna" is an un-Shakespearean locale does not depend upon these anomalies; the evidence for that claim has already been given. But once we have established, on other grounds, that the play's setting was changed, then we may also better understand certain other oddities of the text.

For instance, editors have long been puzzled by the fact that the dramatis personae list gives the duke a name ("Vincentio"), despite the fact that no name is preserved anywhere in the play itself, in dialogue, speech prefixes, or stage directions. The simplest explanation for this unique anomaly is that Crane knew the name because it was in the original promptbook, but had been crossed out. "Vincentio" is, of course, an appropriately Italian name for a duke of Ferrara; indeed, it was in 1604 the name of the reigning duke of Mantua.[114] Both playwrights would have wanted to establish the play's setting in the first moments of the first scene; insofar as the name of the Duke reinforces that setting, we would expect Shakespeare to have used it in the first scene. Indeed, he might have used it in the very first line. "Escalus," the Duke commands, and Escalus replies, "My lord." But perhaps Escalus originally replied "My lord Vincentio"—as in *The Tempest* the Duke of Milan is addressed as "my lord Antonio" (5.1.264). Shakespeare often followed "my lord" with a proper name.[115] If he did so here, the play would have begun with a full verse line, instead of the anomalously broken opening found in the First Folio.[116] Certainly, the name would be as inappropriate for Middleton's setting as it is appropriate for Shakespeare's. "Vincentio" does not sound like the name of an Austrian Hapsburg duke of Vienna. Middleton, wishing to establish a German setting, would not have wanted to begin the play with an Italian ducal name.

Middleton presumably left all the other Italian names because changing them would have required too many minuscule alterations of the actors' parts. The first rule of early modern theatrical adaptation was, as far as possible, not to fiddle with the texture of the dialogue, but instead to deal in large discrete chunks (like the passages added at the beginning of 1.2, 4.1, and 4.3).[117] It would be easy enough to remind Escalus to leave out the name in his first line, and to remind everybody that they should say "Vienna" instead of "Ferrara." In 1621, Vienna would be on their minds, anyway. Middleton did not need to change all the play's names, because the presence of a few un-Germanic names would hardly have disturbed his audiences. My argument against "Vienna," in part 1, does not depend upon the presence in the play of Italian names, because the Holy Roman Empire extended south as far as the Adriatic.[118] Englishmen in 1603–4 may not have been particularly aware of that (or of much else about Austria), but by 1621 Englishmen were certainly alert to the extent of papal influence upon the Emperor's court (by then relocated in Vienna). A reigning archduchess of Austria was named Isabella. Likewise, although Shakespeare himself clearly associated the name "Escalus" with Italy, the name itself is Latin—as are several other names in the 1623 Folio text (Valencius, Crassus, Flavius, Varrius). Such Latinity could characterize either Shakespeare's Italy or Middleton's Holy Roman Empire. Thus, although a specifically Italian name for a Duke in the play's first lines would be misleading, once the play's setting had been established in Vienna the other names could be left unchanged. With Middleton's characteristic economy, the alteration of nine words and the omission of one significantly alters our perspective on the play.[119]

Recognizing that Shakespeare's original was probably set in Ferrara allows us to resituate *Measure* critically. We do not have to call Shakespeare's original a "problem play" or a "City comedy"; many of the City-comedy elements are Middleton's additions, and some of the problems result from the clash between Middleton's vision and Shakespeare's. The original was one of Shakespeare's many Italian plays, linked specifically to the source for *Shrew*, and linked chronologically to *Othello*, the Italian tragedy Shakespeare wrote as a companion piece to his Italian tragicomedy (set in an adjacent Italian city-state). We can now relate *Measure* to Middleton's and Marston's Ferrara plays of the same year; we can relate it to *Macbeth*, the other Jacobean play by Shakespeare later adapted by Middleton; we can relate both to *Timon of Athens*, the one play Middleton and Shakespeare apparently wrote in collaboration. More generally, we can relate the adapted version to the history of Shakespearean adaptations, and to other plays by Middleton, and to events and plays of the early 1620s.

Relocating *Measure* geographically also relocates it critically, in many ways that remain to be explored. For example, I have argued elsewhere that Shakespeare was Catholic, or at the very least sympathetic to Catholicism;[120] an English Catholic in 1604 would be critical of Puritans like Angelo, but would see nothing necessarily sinister about Italy, nuns of the order of St. Clare, a friar who has just come with special instructions from the Holy See, auricular confession, or an absolutism that "like power divine" is absolutely benevolent and can therefore characterize any dissent as vicious slander.[121] But Middleton was a Calvinist, and English Calvinists in 1621 felt threatened by Vienna, by devious absolutism, by the suppression of dissent, by the fanaticism and sexual hypocrisy of the Counter-Reformation, and by the efforts of an English gentlewoman to create a new English order of St. Clare.[122] Our own clashing, diametrically opposed interpretations of the text published in 1623 derive, in part, from the clash between Shakespeare and Middleton. Whether we read Angelo as a Puritan or a Jesuit, whether we read the Duke as a saint or a tyrant, whether we see Lucio as a fop or a blunt soldier, whether we see the play from the perspective of Vincentio or of Lucio, depends upon whether we are reading Shakespeare or reading Middleton, reading like Shakespeare or reading like Middleton. In *Measure for Measure*, the two greatest dramatists of the English Renaissance met in hand-to-hand combat, somewhere between Vienna and Ferrara.

# Notes

1. Wilhelm Hortmann, with Maik Hamburger, *Shakespeare on the German Stage: The Twentieth Century* (Cambridge: Cambridge University Press, 1998), 78–79.

2. For the productions by Housman and Miller, see Brian Gibbons, ed., *Measure for Measure*, New Cambridge Shakespeare (Cambridge: Cambridge University Press, 1991), 65, 70. N. W. Bawcutt, in his edition (Oxford: Oxford University Press, 1991), notes more generally that "in the past forty or so years" the play in the theater has regularly "been brought forward into modern times, frequently to Vienna in the late nineteenth or earlier twentieth century" (38).

3. Ralph Berry, *On Directing Shakespeare: Interviews with Contemporary Directors* (London: Croom Helm, 1977), 92–99.

4. Keir Elam, *The Semiotics of Theatre and Drama* (London: Methuen, 1980).

5. John Gillies, *Shakespeare and the Geography of Difference* (Cambridge: Cambridge University Press, 1994).

6. Even without consulting the many sixteenth-century costume books, Londoners would have seen many of the differences for themselves in the clothing worn by tourists and traders in one of Europe's busiest port cities.

7. Ann Rosalind Jones and Peter Stallybrass, *Renaissance Clothing and the Materials of Memory* (Cambridge: Cambridge University Press, 2000), 175–206; Jean MacIntyre, *Costumes and Scripts in the Elizabethan Theatre* (Edmonton: University of Alberta Press, 1992).

8. Outside the title, Verona is named only two or four times (depending on whether 3.1.81 and 5.4.127 are emended), Ardenne (or Arden) four, Elsinore four, Belmont seven, Ephesus eight. These and all other verbal statistics are taken from Marvin Spevack, *The Harvard Concordance to Shakespeare* (Cambridge: Harvard University Press, 1973).

9. *Measure* 1.1.22, 1.1.44, 1.2.87, 1.3.13, 2.1.187, 2.1.219, 2.1.230, 5.1.266, 5.1.314. References to Shakespeare are keyed to *The Complete Works*, general editors. Stanley Wells and Gary Taylor (Oxford: Clarendon Press, 1986).

10. Thomas L. Berger, William C. Bradford, and Sidney L. Sondergard, *An Index of Characters in Early Modern English Drama: Printed Plays, 1500–1660*, rev. ed. (Cambridge: Cambridge University Press, 1998), 100. All my figures for the geographical origin of characters (Vienna, Austria, Ferrara) derive from this invaluable reference work. It does not index plays that survive only in manuscript, but for such plays I have checked W. W. Greg's *Dramatic Documents from the Elizabethan Playhouses: Commentary* (Oxford: Clarendon Press, 1931) and the available Malone Society editions of manuscript plays known or unknown to Greg. Berger's only other entry for *Viennese* is *Hamlet*, presumably in deference to Hamlet's description of "The Mousetrap" (discussed below). Even if we accept that locale, the characters appear only within the play-within-the-play; the audi-

ence is not asked to believe that they are *really* Viennese (or *really* from Urbino, or Guiana).

11. According to Leah S. Marcus, "In near-contemporary plays like Shakespeare's *King John* and Munday's *Downfall* and *Death of Robert, Earl of Huntington* 'Vienna' and 'Austria' are clearly enemy territory"; *Puzzling Shakespeare: Local Reading and its Discontents* (Berkeley and Los Angeles: University of California Press, 1988), 162. But the place-name "Vienna" appears in none of those plays. "Austria" is the site of Richard the Lion-Hearted's misfortune because it lay on the crusaders' route to the Holy Land; these plays thus belong to the more general Elizabethan association of Austria/Vienna with the war against Islam (on which see below).

12. *The Conspiracie of Charles Duke of Byron*, in *The Plays of George Chapman: The Tragedies*, general editor Allan Holaday (Cambridge: D. S. Brewer, 1987), 1.2.165–81, 214–24.

13. Henry Chettle, *The Tragedy of Hoffman*, ed. John Jowett (Nottingham: Nottingham Drama Texts, 1983): Baltic 24, 142; Wittenberg 258, 1484; Danzig 290, 501, 502, 908; Bornholm 336, 1780; Elsinore 419; Heidelberg 444; Pomerania 444, 1059; Norway 1067; Germany 1286, 2313; Lubeck 1641; Cimmerian mists 1580.

14. R. J. W. Evans, *The Making of the Hapsburg Monarchy, 1550–1700* (Oxford: Clarendon Press, 1979), 157, 164.

15. George Abbot, *A Briefe Description of the Whole Worlde* (1599), STC 24: "That corner of Germanie which lieth neerest to Hungarie, is called *Austria*, which is an Archdukedome. . . . In this countrie standeth *Vienna*" (sig. A7).

16. See Fynes Moryson, *An Itinerary* (1617), ed. Charles Hughes, 2d ed. (New York: Benjamin Blom, 1967), Kkk6, 3.2.3: "*Germany* is diuided into the vpper & the lower. The vpper lying vpon the Alpes, & neere the Riuer *Danow*, is subdiuided into 11 Prouinces, *Austria* [etc.]. . . . *Austria* . . . is vulgarly called *Oestreich*, that is, the Easterly Kingdome. . . . It hath many ancient & famous Cities whereof the chiefe is *Vienna*, (vulgarly *Wien*) built vpon the banke of *Danow*." Many other writers, less precisely than Moryson, locate Vienna in what was then called Germany. See, for instance, Lady Mary Wroth, *The First Part of the Countess of Mountgomery's "Urania,"* ed. Josephine A. Roberts (Binghamton: Medieval and Renaissance Texts and Studies, 1995), 463: "he came to the neerest part of Germany, and so passd . . . Buda, Prague, Vienna, all places he saw that were of worth, and traveld over the most part of Germany" (ll. 29–35).

17. The Shakespeare canon contains twenty-one references to "German[s]" or "Germany," including specifically "upper Germany" at *All Is True/Henry VIII* 5.2.64. Shakespeare does not elsewhere refer to the Danube (or "Danow"), but several Elizabethan plays do mention it: see Edward H. Sugden, *A Topographical Dictionary to the Works of Shakespeare and his Fellow Dramatists* (Manchester: Manchester University Press, 1925), 145–46. "The mightie riuer *Danubius*," running through "*Austria* and *Hungarie*," is also mentioned in Abbot's *Briefe Description*, sig. A7; Moryson's first sentence on Vienna is followed by a description of the river and the bridges over it (sig. F4).

18. *Hamlet*, ed. Harold Jenkins, New Arden Shakespeare (London: Methuen, 1982), 102, 507–8.

19. Patricia Parker, "Murder in Guyana," *Shakespeare Studies* 28 (2000): 169–74. As Parker notes, Guiana can be linked to published reports from the 1590s, to *Merry Wives.*, to the pun on "tropically," and to the play's interest in "blackness"; for the latter, see Gary Taylor, "*Hamlet* in Africa 1607," in *Travel*

*Knowledge*, ed. Ivo Kamps and Jyotsna Singh (New York: St. Martin's Press, 2000), 211–48. I argue there that *Hamlet* is Shakespeare's "most European play," deliberately referencing an extraordinary range of European places, histories, and practices that might reflect the influence of the lost Ur-*Hamlet*, especially if that lost play were by Thomas Kyd, who delighted in such cosmopolitan mixtures. Within that context, "Vienna" is just another European site, meaningful only as a further token of the text's inclusiveness.

20. Abbot, *Briefe Description*, sig. A7. Abbot continues, "from whence Solimon was repelled by Ferdinandus King of Hungarie, in the time of Emperour Charles the fift. It was in this countrie, that Richard the first King of *England*, in his returne from the holy land, was taken prisoner by the Archduke of *Austria*" (thus clearly linking the Richard/Austria story to the battle against Islam). Fynes Moryson likewise called Vienna "a famous Fort against the Turkes": *Itinerary*, sig. F3v (1.1.5). He later notes that it is "famous not so much for the Vniuersity, & the trafficke of the place, as for that it is most strongly fortified to keepe out the Turkes, & it is subject to the Emperour, as he is Arch-duke of *Austria*" (Kkk6, 3.2.5). Sugden characterized Early Modern perceptions of Vienna as "the outpost of European civilisation against the Turks and Slavs" (547).

21. Christopher Marlowe, *Tamburlaine the Great*, ed. J. S. Cunningham, Revels Plays (Manchester: Manchester University Press, 1981), *Part II*, 1.1.86–87 ("I am he That with the cannon shook Vienna walls"), 1.1.103 ("Vienna was besieged, and I was there"). Marlowe associates Vienna with Hungary, Boheme, the Palatine, "the Austric Duke" (1.1.94–95)—and with the Danube (1.1.7, 33–38, 79).

22. Ben Jonson, *Every Man in His Humour* (1598), ed. Robert S. Miola, Revels Plays (Manchester: Manchester University Press, 2000), 2.1.62 ("I was twice shot at the taking of Aleppo, once at the relief of Vienna")—this after a list of other exotic places associated with battles against Turks, "Bohemia, Hungaria, Dalmatia, Poland" (2.1.58).

23. Barnabe Barnes, *"The Devil's Charter": A Critical Edition*, ed. Jim C. Pogue (New York: Garland, 1980), 3.3: "I my selfe . . . Have serv'd against the *Turkes* and *Sarazines*, Where at *Vienna* . . . I did unhorse three *Turkie* Janizaries" (1407–14).

24. Thomas Goffe, *The Raging Turke* (London, 1631), Actus Quinti, Scena Decima, sig. O2. Dates cited in the text are those of probable first performance, as indicated in Alfred Harbage, *Annals of English Drama, 975–1700*, rev. S. Schoenbaum, rev. Sylvia Stoler Wagonheim (New York: Routledge, 1989).

25. *News from Vienna the .5. day of August. 1566. of Jula in Hungary, assaulted by the great Turke* (1566), STC 24716; and *True and most certaine newes, sent from Vienna in Austria, the 17. of June last, 1595. Howe Ferdinand earle of Hardeck, generall ouer Raab in Hungaria, trecherously yeelded to the Turke* (1595), STC 24716.5.

26. *The Travellers Breviat* (1601), STC 3398, p. 51 (sig. H2). This book (printed twice in 1601, and thereafter in 1603, 1608, 1611, 1616, etc.), is Robert Johnson's translation and epitome of Giovanni Botero's *Relationi Universali*. It also refers to the siege of Vienna (pp. 60, 64, sig. I2v, I4v), and concludes, "what prince bordering vpon so puissant an enemie, but either by building of fortresses, or by intertaining of garrisons, is not almost beggered, I will not say, in time of warre, but euen during the securest peace? . . . retaining in wages continually twenty thousand soldiers, keeping watch and warde vpon the borders of Hungarie[;] . . . let vs not shut both our eares, and say, he is farre from vs, when he stands at our doores, yea close by our sides" (p. 68, sig. K2v).

27. See Samuel C. Chew, *The Crescent and the Rose: Islam and England during the Renaissance* (New York: Oxford University Press, 1937), 100–49; Daniel J. Vitkus, ed., *Three Turk Plays from Early Modern England* (New York: Columbia University Press, 2000), 1–53.

28. See Stanley Wells, "Dating *Othello*," letter to the *Times Literary Supplement*, 20 July 1984.

29. Richard Knolles, *The Generall Historie of the Turkes* (1603), STC 15051, pp. 1007–1157 (war), 1157, sig. 5E6v (warning of invasion of Austria). Knolles describes the siege of Vienna (610–14), repeatedly mentions the importance of the Danube (611–12), and in an unpaginated final assessment of Turkish military power warns that the house of Austria will have "much ado to defend themselues against the Turke" (sig. 5G1).

30. I include in this total occurrences of "Moor" (and related compounds), "Ottoman," "Ottomites," "Saracen," "Sultan," and "Turk" (and related compounds). I have also—like all editors—taken as an allusion to the Sultan's court the Captain's speech at *Twelfth Night* 1.2.58–59 ("Be you his eunuch, and your mute I'll be. / When my tongue blabs, then let mine eyes not see"). The number of occurrences would rise to 128, and of plays to twenty, if I included "pagan(s)," which—like "paynim"—in Shakespeare as in other writers often clearly refers to Moslems. Between *The Merchant of Venice* (1597) and *Macbeth* (1606), references to the Turk occur in every play except the classical *Julius Caesar* and *Timon of Athens* (where they would be anachronistic), and *Measure*.

31. On the proximity of *Measure* and *Othello*, see Gary Taylor, "The Canon and Chronology of Shakespeare's Plays," in Stanley Wells, Gary Taylor, et al., *William Shakespeare: A Textual Companion* (Oxford: Clarendon Press, 1987), 125–26.

32. Austria often appears in early modern catalogues of exotic places. In *Summers Last Will and Testament*, Nashe had imagined going to Samos, Paphos, Austria, Phasis, Arabia, Meander, Orcades, Phrigia, Malta, and half a dozen other places: see *The Works of Thomas Nashe*, ed. R. B. McKerrow, 5 vols. (Oxford: Blackwell, 1966), 3:296. Similarly, in *The Phoenix in her Flames: A Tragedy* (1639), William Lower speaks in one breath "of Tartaria, of Austria, Of Egypt, Babylonia" (3.1).

33. John P. Spielman, *The City and The Crown: Vienna and the Imperial Court, 1600–1740* (West Lafayette: Purdue University Press, 1993), 17–22. The Ottoman expansion disrupted central European trade, and New World gold diminished the significance of eastern European mines. Peter Musgrave complains that there has been "very little recent work" on the economy of Germany (including Austria) in this period: see *The Early Modern European Economy* (Basingstoke: Macmillan, 1999), 120.

34. All the illustrations from the enlarged second edition of Cèsare Vecellio's *Habiti antichi, et moderni* (Venice, 1598) are reproduced in *Vecellio's Renaissance Costume Book* (New York: Dover, 1977).

35. Hans Wiegel and Jost Amman, *Habitus Praecipuorum Populorum . . . Tractenbuch* (Nuremberg, 1577).

36. James M. Osborn, *Young Philip Sidney, 1572–1577* (New Haven: Yale University Press, 1972), 96, 120. Sidney was one of the few important Englishmen to visit Vienna in Elizabeth's reign; but his private visit—in the context of a prolonged European tour—took place when Shakespeare was nine, thirty years before composition of *Measure*.

37. Jerzy Limon, *Gentlemen of a Company: English Players in Central and*

*Eastern Europe, 1590–1660* (Cambridge: Cambridge University Press, 1985), 3, 121, 199.

38. See Folke Dahl, *A Bibliography of English Corantos and Periodical Newsbooks, 1620–1642* (London: The Bibliographical Society, 1952); Joseph Frank, *The Beginnings of the English Newspaper, 1620–1660* (Cambridge: Harvard University Press, 1961); Richard Cust, "News and Politics in Early Seventeenth-Century England," *Past and Present* 111 (1986): 60–90.

39. It was famous, if at all, for its library: see Osborn, *Young Philip Sidney,* 99; and Sir Thomas Browne, *Pseudodoxia Epidemica*, ed. Robin Robbins, 2 vols. (Oxford: Clarendon, 1981), 1:422. *Measure* does not refer to any library, or even to the reading of books.

40. Stephen May, *Bibliography and First-Line Index of English Verse, 1559–1603* (London: Mansell Press, forthcoming). My thanks to Steven May and Paul J. Voss for supplying me with this information. The two poems occur in John Bale's *The Pageant of Popes*, trans. with additions by John Studley (1574), STC 1304, sig. D3v, and *The Familiar Epistles of Sir Anthony of Gueuara*, trans. Edward Hellows, "now corrected & enlarged" (1575?), STC 12433, sig. 2A3v.

41. John Stoye, *English Travellers Abroad, 1604–1667*, rev. ed. (New Haven: Yale University Press, 1989), 119. Long before it became a "canonical" part of the tour, Vienna was visited by the indefatigable traveller Henry Wotton (in 1590–91). See Antoni Macsak, *Travel in Early Modern Europe*, trans. Ursula Phillips (Cambridge: Polity Press, 1995), 189.

42. Moryson, *Itinerary*, F4.

43. Gibbons, ed., *Measure* 22–23.

44. Josephine Waters Bennett, *"Measure for Measure" as Royal Entertainment* (New York: Columbia University Press, 1966), 10–11.

45. *Letters of John Chamberlain*, ed. N. E. McClure, 2 vols. (Philadelphia: American Philosophical Society, 1939), 1:198.

46. Nicolo Molin, letter of 1 December 1604, in *Calendar of State Papers Venetian* (hereafter referred to as *SPV*), 10 (1900): 301. "The Duke of Holstein arrived in London last Monday week, the 22nd of November," Molin records, using New Style dates, ten days later than the English calendar. Bennett did not cite this letter, instead indicating only that Holstein arrived "before November 14" (10)— thus allowing for the possibility that he may have been in London quite a bit earlier, and easing the timetable for Shakespeare to have written *Measure* after Holstein arrived but before the court performance on 26 December.

47. Nicolo Molin, 17 November 1604, in *SPV* 10:295.

48. Leah Marcus, *Puzzling Shakespeare*, 160–64, 184–202. Marcus cites Bennett on p. 255 n. 47, saying that she "gives a good sense of the contemporary preoccupation with Hungary."

49. Gibbons, ed., *Measure*, 22 n. 3.

50. Bennett's case is so flimsy that it was not mentioned at all by Mark Eccles in his New Variorum Edition of *Measure* (New York: Modern Language Association, 1980), either in his notes on this passage (20–21) or in his appendix on "The Date of Composition" (299–301). Presumably for the same reason, Leeds Barroll ignores it in his account of the influence of Holstein's sister: *Anna of Denmark, Queen of England: A Cultural Biography* (Philadelphia: University of Pennsylvania Press, 2001). I pay so much attention to it here only because of its potential relevance to the choice of setting and because it was ignored in my own earlier discussions of the play's date.

51. For the Revels document, see Eccles, *Variorum*, 299–300, 467. It seems

unlikely that the King's Men, or the Lord Chamberlain, would have chosen a play performed in the previous Christmas season to begin the 1604–5 court Christmas season; the Revels document thus tends to confirm the consensus that Shakespeare wrote the play in 1604, not 1603.

52. For a devastating critique of "the King James Version" of *Measure*, see Richard Levin, *New Readings vs. Old Plays: Recent Trends in the Reinterpretation of English Renaissance Drama* (Chicago: University of Chicago Press, 1977), 171–93.

53. R. J. W. Evans, *Rudolf II and His World* (Oxford: Clarendon Press, 1973), 22. Although she cites Evans elsewhere in her chapter, Marcus claims that Vienna "was one of the capitals of the Holy Roman Empire, much in the news in the year 1604 as the traditional seat of the Hapsburg dynasty, the administrative hub of a vast and shifting Catholic alliance with which the English had been on hostile terms for decades" (*Puzzling Shakespeare*, 162). Her use of "traditional" here may be a tacit acknowledgment that Vienna had in fact not been the seat of the Hapsburg dynasty "for decades." See also Evans, *Hapsburg Monarchy*, who notes that in the fifteenth and sixteenth centuries "several other cities, notably Prague, rivalled Vienna as imperial residences," and that Vienna did not come into its own until after 1612 (191). Moreover, despite her assertion here, her chapter provides no evidence that Vienna itself (rather than Catholic Hapsburgs in Spain and the Netherlands) was "much in the news in the year 1604."

54. John Nichols, *The Progresses, Processions, and Magnificent Festivities of King James the First* (London, 1838), 1:466; cited by Bennett, not in the main text but in a note (167), perhaps because it was not in her interest to call attention to the unimpressive character of his arrival.

55. Nicolo Molin, 1 December 1604, in *SPV,* 10:301.

56. *Letters of Chamberlain*, 1:198.

57. Quotations from *Measure* cite the Eccles (Variorum) text, an unemended reproduction of the Folio, with its through line numbers; for convenience of reference I also cite the act-scene-line numbering of the Oxford *Complete Works*.

58. Marcus identifies the play's "dukes" as "the Hapsburg dukes" (*Puzzling Shakespeare*, 162); "the duke and the 'other Dukes' were all Hapsburg archdukes" (187); "The actual 'Duke of Vienna' in 1604 was Archduke Matthias" (189). But, as her own prose indicates, the Hapsburg "dukes" were never identified as mere "dukes" but insisted upon their more elevated status as "archdukes" (a word that never appears in *MM*). Moreover, as her coy quotation marks perhaps acknowledge, there was no actual "Duke of Vienna"; Matthias was Archduke of Austria.

59. Nicolo Molin, 1 December 1604, in *SPV,* 10:301.

60. Vincent to Benson, 9 January 1605, *Calendar of State Papers Domestic*, 12.186.

61. See *SPV,* 10:323, 333, 363, 374, 384.

62. Shakespeare's sympathy with James's ecumenical peacemaking has been convincingly demonstrated by Robin Headlam Wells, *Shakespeare on Masculinity* (Cambridge: Cambridge University Press, 2000).

63. On the increasing dependence of Shakespeare's company upon royal patronage, see J. Leeds Barroll, *Politics, Plague, and Shakespeare's Theater: The Stuart Years* (Ithaca: Cornell University Press, 1991); and Alvin Kernan, *Shakespeare, the King's Playwright: Theater in the Stuart Court, 1603–1613* (New Haven: Yale University Press, 1995). Since the eighteenth century scholars have recognized in the play particular allusions apparently intended to flatter James; Bennett's *Royal Entertainment* presupposes such a strategy (without acknowledging that the alleged Ulric allusion contradicts it).

64. Eccles, Variorum, 20, referring to George Whetstone's play *Promos and Cassandra* (reprinted by Eccles, 306–69).

65. For a summary of existing opinion on the duplication in 1.2, see John Jowett and Gary Taylor, "With New Additions: Theatrical Interpolation in *Measure for Measure*," in *Shakespeare Reshaped, 1606–1623,* by Taylor and Jowett (Oxford: Clarendon Press, 1993), 151–55. Gibbons, ed., *Measure* (1991), also accepts that the passage was written later than subsequent parts of the scene (199).

66. For Wilson's conjecture linking the play to the 1606 treaty with the Turks, see Eccles, Variorum, 21. For Marcus, see *Puzzling Shakespeare*: "The king of Hungary was then the emperor Rudolf II. The duke and the 'other Dukes' were all Hapsburg archdukes. . . . Discontented with the unstable Rudolf's administration of the areas under his direct control, the 'Duke and the other Dukes' banded together to deprive him of effective power, eventually expelling him (since he obstinately refused to 'come to composition') from the thrones of Hungary and Bohemia" (187). For this Hapsburg infighting, Marcus cites Roger Lockyer, *Hapsburg and Bourbon Europe, 1470–1720* (London: Longman, 1974), 317–29; and George W. Keeton, *Shakespeare's Legal and Political Background* (London: Pitman and Sons, 1967), 374–76; but neither text supports her claim that these divisions had become public by 1603–4; in fact, both make clear that this result happened "eventually" only in 1608. (See also Evans, *Hapsburg Monarchy*, 52, for the same chronology.) Nor does Marcus provide any evidence that anyone in England in 1604 was aware of the simmering divisions between the Hapsburg brothers. Instead, she generalizes about English interest in Hungary (186–87), citing Bennett. For fuller consideration of Marcus's interpretation, see "Canon and Chronology" in *Thomas Middleton and Early Modern Textual Culture*, ed. Gary Taylor (Oxford: Oxford University Press, forthcoming).

67. For a summary of relevant scholarship on the printing of *Measure*, and Crane's preparation of printer's copy, see Eccles, Variorum, 291–98; and Jowett and Taylor, "New Additions."

68. For expurgation, see Gary Taylor, "'Swounds Revisited," in Taylor and Jowett, *Shakespeare Reshaped*, 51–106; for act divisions, see Taylor, "The Structure of Performance," in Taylor and Jowett, *Shakespeare Reshaped,*, 3–50; for the song, see Jowett and Taylor, "New Additions," 123–40, 260–95.

69. John Jowett, "The Audacity of *Measure for Measure* in 1621," *Ben Jonson Journal* 8 (2001): 229–47.

70. G. E. Bentley, *The Profession of Dramatist in Shakespeare's Time, 1590–1642* (Princeton: Princeton University Press, 1971), 263.

71. For Middleton's authorship of the beginning of 1.2, see Taylor and Jowett, *Shakespeare Reshaped*, 186–226.

72. The passages most strongly linked to Middleton are 1.2.1–82 (TLN 96–175), 2.1.266–75 (TLN 718–30), 4.1.6–24 (1776–96), 4.3.1–18 (2078–95). In *The Collected Works*, Jowett also argues that the description of Barnardine as "A Bohemian borne" (4.2.130, TLN 1996) may belong to the Middleton adaptation, since Bohemia was so topical in 1621.

73. Bertuci Contarini, 16 November 1619, in *SPV 1619–21*, no. 86. This letter also notices the outbreak of plague in Vienna, as does no. 92 ("precautions with all those coming from Germany and Vienna in particular").

74. Girolamo Lando, 2 October 1620, in *SPV,* no. 565.

75. Girolamo Lando (from London), 10 September 1621, in *SPV,* p. 126.

76. Jowett and Taylor, "New Additions," 183; for a more detailed account of English public interest in the king of Hungary's attack on Vienna, see Jowett, "Audacity."

77. Robert Zaller, *The Parliament of 1621: A study in Constitutional Conflict* (Berkeley and Los Angeles: University of California Press, 1971), 11, 142–45, 149–52. See also the index entries for "Austria," "Digby," and "Ferdinand II" in Wallace Notestein, Frances Relf, Hartley Simpson, eds., *Commons Debates, 1621*, 7 vols. (New Haven: Yale University Press, 1935).

78. On sources and analogues, see Eccles, Variorum, 301–5, 387–92. Like many other scholars, Eccles cites a letter written in 1547 by "a Hungarian student in Vienna" (388–89), but this letter itself sets the story in Milan; nor does anyone claim Shakespeare knew this particular private letter, written in Latin from someone in Vienna to someone in Hungary more than half a century before. It is a measure of the meaninglessness of the play's setting in 1604 that scholars have so often seized upon the fact that this letter—whose account of sexual blackmail and retribution differs from Shakespeare's play in almost every particular—was written "in Vienna."

79. Zdeněk Stříbrný, *Shakespeare and Eastern Europe* (Oxford: Oxford University Press, 2000), 42.

80. Richard Wagner, *Das Liebesverbot oder Die Novize von Palermo*: see Bryan N. S. Gooch, David Thatcher, et al., *A Shakespeare Music Catalogue*, 5 vols. (Oxford: Clarendon Press, 1991), no. 7805.

81. Fox, *The English Renaissance: identity and representation in Elizabethan England* (Oxford: Blackwell, 1997), 205–11.

82. Eccles, Variorum, 4; Berger et al., *Index of Characters*, 43. All my statements in this paragraph about the national identity of names in the play are based upon Eccles and Berger. In *All's Well That Ends Well*, Escalus is coupled with Antonio, the eldest son of the Duke of Florence (3.5.78); a Florentine native, the Widow, identifies both Antonio and Escalus; in the next line, Helen asks about "the Frenchman," suggesting that the previous identities have all been Italian.

83. Eccles, Variorum, 216; see also *OED*, s.vv. "ragusan," "argosy."

84. See, for instance, Abbot, *Briefe Description*; although his chapter "De Italia" is only three octavo pages long, Abbot takes time to mention the country's "great varietie of wines" (sig. A4). He devotes a paragraph each to Venice, Florence, Milan, Rome, and Naples, and then ends, "There be moreouer in Italy, many other prince-domes & States, as the Dukedome of Ferrara," giving it pride of place over Mantua, Urbino, Parma, Placentia, Luca, and Genoa.

85. Eccles, Variorum, 159, citing parallels in *Volpone, Cymbeline, A Chaste Maid in Cheapside*, and Robert Tofte's *Ariosto's Satires*; see also *A Mad World My Masters* 1.2.21–23; and *Women Beware Women* 3.1.212. All these examples associate the practice with Italy.

86. Fynes Moryson, *Shakespeare's Europe: A Survey of the Condition of Europe at the end of the 16th century, being unpublished chapters of Fynes Moryson's Itinerary (1617)*, ed. Charles Hughes, 2d ed. (New York: Benjamin Blom, 1967), 411. Although most European cities had shut down the official medieval bordellos by the mid-sixteenth century, Italy did not: see *A History of Women in the West*, vol. 3: *Renaissance and Enlightenment Paradoxes*, ed. Natalie Zemon Davis and Arlette Farge (Cambridge: Harvard University Press, 1993), 460. There are of course innumerable late Elizabethan and Jacobean examples of this association of Italy with sexual vice, and particularly with female prostitutes: see for instance *All's Well*, 2.1.19 ("those girls of Italy"), and *Cymbeline* 1.3.29 ("the shes of Italy") and 3.4.49 ("some jay of Italy").

87. *Shakespeare's Europe: Unpublished Chapters*, 293; Hippocrates, *Airs, Waters, Places*, in *Hippocrates*, trans. W. H. S. Jones, 6 vols., Loeb Classical Li-

brary (London: William Heinemann, 1923), 1:125 (par. xxv); Richard F. Thomas, *Lands and Peoples in Roman Poetry: The Ethnographical Tradition*, Cambridge Philological Society (Cambridge: Cambridge University Library, 1982), 11–12.

88. Eccles, Variorum, 388–89.

89. Thomas Beard, *The Theatre of Gods Judgments . . . Translated out of French, and augmented by more than three hundred Examples* (London, 1597), 313–14 (where *"Gonzo* duke of Ferrara," twice specified, is the only character in the story named or identified). The story is immediately followed by another involving "Vincentia" (314). Eccles gives full details for the other "Duke of Ferrara" versions by Georg Lauterback, *Regentenbuch* (Leipzig, 1559), bk. 2, chap. 15, sigs. P2–3; Hans Wilhelm Kirchhof, ed. Oesterley (Frankfurt, 1603), 4:186–87; and Sigmund Feyerabend's *Theatrum Diabolorum* (Frankfurt, 1569, 1575), f. 305$^v$. See also Henning Grosse's Latin *Tragic seu tristium historiarum . . . librie ii* (Eisleben, 1597), 107–8; and Simon Goulart's *Histoires admirables* (Paris, 1601), 221r–v.

90. Mary Lascelles, *Shakespeare's "Measure for Measure"* (London: Athlone Press, 1953), 32–36; Geoffrey Bullough, vol. 2 of *Narrative and Dramatic Sources of Shakespeare: The Comedies, 1597–1603* (London: Routledge, 1958), 115; Michele Marrapodi, "English and Italian Intertexts of the Ransom Plot in *Measure for Measure*," in *Shakespeare and Intertextuality: The Transition of Cultures between Italy and England in the Early Modern Period*, ed. Michele Marrapodi (Rome: Bulzoni, 2000), 103–17.

91. Moryson, *Itinerary*, 1:90–92, 291; 3:104, etc.

92. Bullough, *Narrative and Dramatic Sources*, 1 (1957); I cite Bullough's edition of *Supposes* (111–60).

93. Cèsare Vecellio, *Habiti antichi, et moderni* (1598), plates 202 (unmarried woman of Ferrara) and 203 (street dress of matron of Ferrara).

94. Bartolomeo Grassi, *Dei veri ritratti degl'habiti. di tutte le parti del mondo* (Rome, 1585), plate 12 (19), with three figures, "Plebea ferrarese. Nobile vergine ferrarese. Contadina Ferrarese," reproduced here by kind permission: Typ 525.85.435, Department of Printing and Graphic Arts, Houghton Library of the Harvard College Library. Although Grassi has many illustrations of northern and eastern European clothing (plates 36–49), he gives no examples from Vienna or Austria.

95. Hans Wiegel and Jost Amman, "Nobilis Foemina Ferrariensis," *Habitus Praecipuorum Populorum . . . Tractenbuch* (Nuremberg, 1577), plate 124 (124).

96. John Florio, *Second Frutes* (1591), STC 11097, p. 8 (sig. B4v); also mentioned on 106–7 (sig. P1v–P2).

97. Nicolo Machiavelli, *Discourses on Livy*, trans. Henry C. Mansfield and Nathan Tarcov (Chicago: University of Chicago Press, 1996), 166 (2.17.4), 228–29 (3.6.14), 245 (3.11.2); *I Discorsi* was printed in London in 1584 by John Wolfe (STC 17159). See also Machiavelli, *The Florentine History*, trans. W. K. Marriott (London: Dent, 1909), 27, 342–43, 347; printed in London by Wolfe in 1587 (STC 17161) and also translated by T. Bedingfield in 1595 (STC 17162). Francesco Guicciardini is more thorough, and therefore refers more often to Ferrara: even in Sidney Alexander's abridged translation of *The History of Italy* (New York: Macmillan, 1969) there are eighteen references; Guicciardini was translated by George Fenton (1579, repr. 1599) and also epitomized (1591), STC 12461.

98. *The Essays of Montaigne*, trans. John Florio (1603), Modern Library (New York, n.d.), 2.12.438. See also E. Vittorini, "Montaigne, Ferrara and Tasso," in *The Renaissance in Ferrara and its European Horizons*, ed. J. Salmons and W. Moretti (Cardiff: University of Wales Press, 1984), 145–70.

99. Ben Jonson, *Cynthia's Revels* (1.4.27–28), in *Ben Jonson,* ed. C. H. Herford, Percy Simpson, and Evelyn Simpson, 11 vols. (Oxford: Clarendon Press, 1925–52), 4:54–55.

100. Sugden, *Topographical Dictionary,* 189, citing Barnes's *The Devil's Charter,* 4.3.2196–2200; Cokayne's *Trappolin Creduto Principe,* 2.3 ("Civil Ferrara, Ariosto's town"); Fletcher's *Custom of the Country,* 2.3 ("Ferrara's royal duke"); Heywood's *Fair Maid of the West, Part 2,* 3. Chorus (alluding to the seacoast of Ferrara); and the anonymous manuscript play *Laelia* (1590), ed. G. C. Moore Smith (Cambridge: Cambridge University Press, 1910), 1.4.91 ("Dux Ferrariae"). See also Heywood's *A Maidenhead Well Lost* (1634), act 3: "Ferrara hath a faire and hopefull Heire" (not noted by Sugden).

101. Chaucer, "The Clerk's Prologue," fragment 4 (Group E), 51 ("of Ferrare, and Venyse"); Stephen Gosson, *The Ephemerides of Phialo* (1579), at least seventeen passages; Thomas Heywood, *Troia Britanica* (1609), canto 17 ("Now Venice and Ferara peace discuss"); Thomas Nashe, *The Unfortunate Traveller* (1594), in *Works,* ed. R. B. McKerrow, 2d ed., 5 vols. (Oxford: Blackwell, 1966), 2:299 ("these courses of reuenge a Merchant of *Venice* tooke against a Merchant of *Ferrara*"); William Painter, *The Palace of Pleasure,* 1 (1566), Novell 33: 2 (1567), Novell 22, 28; Barnabe Rich, *Don Simonides,* tome 2 (1584), and *Riche his Farewell to Militarie profession* (1581); Henry Roberts, *Honours Conquest* (1598), chaps. 23, 28, 29; John Taylor, in *A Bawd,* in *All the Works* (1630), refers to "Lucretia Borgia's marriage to Alphonsus D'Est Duke of Ferara," and also refers to Ferrara in *A Conference holden in the Castle of St. Angello betwixt the Pope, the Emperour, & the King of Spaine*; William Warner, *Albions England* (1602), bk. 12, chap. 73, ll.135–36 ("Ferrara, Vrbine, Mantua, Placence, and Parma are / Braue Cities, great for State, and please those which to them repare"); Lady Mary Wroth, *Urania,* 304 ("the Princes of Florence, Milan, Ferrara, Naples").

102. Edward Fairfax, trans., *Godfrey of Bulloigne* (1600), 17:602; John Harrington, trans., *Orlando Furioso* (1591), 40:49; 43:52; Joshua Sylvester, trans., *The Divine Weeks and Works of Guillaume de Saluste Sieur Du Bartas,* ed. Susan Snyder, 2 vols. (Oxford: Clarendon Press, 1979), 2.1.1.544–46 (referring to the famous fountains of "rich Ferrara's stately Cardinall"). Ferrara is also mentioned repeatedly in Robert Toft's translation of Ariosto's satires, *Ariosto's Seven Planets* (1611).

103. For characters from Ferrara in plays, see Berger, *Index of Characters,* 45. (I have checked all these plays to confirm the presence of Ferrarese.)

104. In Shirley's *The Opportunity* someone else is disguised as the Duke of Ferrara.

105. Thomas A. Pendleton, "Shakespeare's Disguised Duke Play: Middleton, Marston, and the Sources of *Measure for Measure,*" in *Fanned and Winnowed Opinions: Shakespearean Essays Presented to Harold Jenkins,* ed. John W. Mason and Thomas A. Pendleton (New York: Methuen, 1987), 81.

106. John Marston, *Parasitaster, or The Fawn,* ed. David A. Blostein, Revels Plays (Manchester: Manchester University Press, 1978), 32–39.

107. Sugden, *Topographical Dictionary,* 275 ("About one-fourth of the plays of our period have their scene in Italy during the 16th and 17th cent[uries]").

108. George Leslie to Mr. Browne, 4 September 1597, Historical Manuscripts Commission, *Calendar of the Manuscripts of the Most. Hon. The Marquis of Salisbury,* 14 (London: H. M. Stationary Office, 1923), 20.

109. Bonner Mitchell, *1598: A Year of Pageantry in Late Renaissance Ferrara,* Medieval & Renaissance Texts & Studies, 71 (Binghamton: Medieval & Renais-

sance Texts & Studies, 1990). The Archduke left his monastic vows in order to marry—in Ferrara, by proxy—the Infanta of Spain, Isabella, thus uniting the Spanish and Austrian branches of the House of Austria; this was an important marriage dynastically and in terms of the European balance of power.

110. See Michael J. Redmond, "*Measure for Measure* and the Politics of the Italianate Disguised Duke Play," in *Shakespeare and Intertextuality,* ed. Marrapodi, 193–214.

111. As the duke of Florence took offense at the publication of Robert Dallington's *A Survey of the Great Dukes State of Tuscany* (1605), STC 6200, which was as a result suppressed. See *SPV*: "The Council has ordered all copies of that book on the Italian States to be burned, and this was publicly carried out at St. Paul's. The author has been confined to his house till the Grand Duke's pleasure be known" (Molin, 1 June 1605). See also Anna Maria Crino, *Fatti e figure del seicento Anglo-Toscano* (Florence: L. Olschki, 1957), 41–48.

112. Andrew Gurr, "Intertextuality at Windsor," *Shakespeare Quarterly* 38 (1987): 189–200; Gurr, "Intertextuality in Henslowe," *Shakespeare Quarterly* 39 (1988): 394–98; Roslyn Knutson, *The Repertory of Shakespeare's Company, 1594–1613* (Fayetteville: University of Arkansas Press, 1991).

113. The alternative settings for the "monstrus ransom" story were Julio, Innsbruck, Milan, Turin, Burgundy, Milan, Como, and Turin; Shakespeare—like other English writers—consistently used "Milan," not "Milano."

114. See Eccles, Variorum, 3. Vincenzio Gonzaga made strenuous efforts to be elected king of Poland; this might explain why Shakespeare's Duke spreads rumors that he has "travelled to Poland" (1.3.14).

115. See also "my lord Sebastian" (*Tempest* 2.1.137), "my lord Biron" (*Love's Labor's Lost* 1.1.305, 4.1.104, 5.2.841), "my lord Bassanio" (*Merchant of Venice* 1.1.69, 3.2.189, 4.1.449, 4.2.6, 5.1.179).

116. In *Shrew* the meter usually requires "Vincentio" to have four syllables; if it had four syllables here, the only irregularity of the line would be a missing initial unstressed syllable, a license common enough in Shakespeare's verse by 1604. Eccles, contesting Wilson's conjecture that something has been cut from the beginning of the first scene, claims that Shakespeare begins *Timon* with a broken line of verse (Variorum, 8); but the first line of *Timon* is simply a regular line divided between two speakers. This leaves only *Hamlet* as a parallel for the abrupt beginning of *Measure*; but "Who's there?" makes a much more naturally disjunctive opening.

117. On patterns of interpolation, see John Kerrigan, "Revision, Adaptation, and the Fool in *King Lear*," in *The Division of the Kingdoms: Shakespeare's Two Versions of "King Lear,"* ed. Gary Taylor and Michael Warren (Oxford: Clarendon,1983), 195–246.

118. Evans, *Making of the Hapsburg Monarchy*, 157–62: Italian was spoken "all around the southern periphery, from Bozen to Fiume" (162).

119. For a discussion of the critical significance of Middleton's other alterations to *Measure* see Taylor and Jowett, *Shakespeare Reshaped,* 233–36, and Jowett's introduction to the adaptation in *Collected Works*. It is possible that a few other words have been altered or omitted in the text to accommodate the change of locale; see Jowett's commentary.

120. See Gary Taylor, "The Fortunes of Oldcastle," *Shakespeare Survey* 38 (1985): 85–100; Taylor, "Forms of Opposition: Shakespeare and Middleton," *English Literary Renaissance* 24 (1994): 283–314; Taylor, "Divine [ ]sences," *Shakespeare Survey* 54 (2001): 13–30.

121. For an analysis of Shakespeare's attitude toward Lucio in the original play, see Gary Taylor, "Power, Pathos, Character," in *Harold Bloom's Shakespeare*, ed. Christy Desmet and Robert Sawyer (New York: Palsgrave, 2002), 43–64.

122. For Mary Ward and her efforts to set up an English convent of poor Clares, see "Relation of England of Girolamo Lando," 21 September 1622), *CSPD*, 17:449–50.

# Playtext Reporters and *Memoriones*: Suspect Texts in Shakespeare and Spanish Golden Age Drama

Jesús Tronch-Pérez

In her thorough study of memorial reconstruction, *Shakespearean Suspect Texts*,[1] Laurie Maguire devotes a two-page section to examining external evidence from Spanish Golden Age drama that may support the hypothesis that the so-called "bad" quartos were memorially reconstructed; and concludes with an expression of the need for further research on the subject in order to see how useful this evidence is.[2] Although I am not a competent Hispanist myself, as she suggests that anyone interrogating this evidence should be, I have taken up her request and tackled this investigation, not without the assistance of Hispanists such as Evangelina Rodríguez Cuadros, Joan Oleza, José María Ruano de la Haza, and José Luis Canet, to whom I wish here to express my gratitude.

This is ongoing research, and what I will present here today is an analysis of a well documented case of the memorial reconstruction of a Spanish Golden Age play, Lope de Vega's comedy *La dama boba* (*The Lady Nit-Wit* or *The Idiot Lady*). This play preserves two textual versions that stem from a memorial reconstruction, not by an actor or actors, as assumed in the Shakespeare "bad" quartos, but by a spectator—perhaps two spectators—someone with a very effective memory, for whom the Spanish language has a set of specific words: *memorión*, *memorilla*, or *memorioso;* that is, "memory man." One can confidently state that these two textual versions of *La dama boba* stem from a memorially reconstructed text on the basis of the following documentary evidence. First, in a book published in 1615, Cristóbal Suárez de Figueroa refers to the deeds of a *memorión*, Luis Remírez de Arellano, able to "take from memory an entire play on hearing it three times," and specifies the titles of three Lope de Vega plays this memory man memorized: *La dama boba*, *El príncipe perfecto*, and *La Arcadia*.[3] No memorial version survives of the last two; only *La dama boba* preserves these interesting texts: manuscript 14,596 at the Biblioteca Nacional in Madrid (ascribed copy) and the text printed in the *Novena Parte* of Lope's plays in 1617.[4]

Second, this non-holographic manuscript of *La dama boba* has an additional final leaf bearing the signature of Luis Remírez himself. There are other signatures in the form of the initials "D.l.R$^z$.A." at the end of acts 1 and 2, and "D.J.Rz.A" at the end of act 3, which are assumed to belong to an assistant of Remírez, perhaps his brother Juan, since further documentary evidence refers to Remírez's being aided by a *memorilla*, although not specifically on *La dama boba*.[5]

Third, for the text printed in the *Novena Parte*, in the publication of which Lope personally intervened,[6] a letter by Lope to his patron, the duke of Sessa (who supplied the playwright with original manuscripts Lope had given him), tells us that the duke never had *La dama boba*, because it belonged to the actress Jerónima de Burgos, and that Lope had to print it from a copy signed with his name.[7] Further internal analysis, detailed below, connects this "copy" with the scribal manuscript signed by the *memoriones*.

Taking into account that the standard or "good" text of this comedy has come to us directly from Lope's hands in his holograph, signed in Madrid on 28 April 1613, handed over to the theater company of Pedro de Valdés (husband of Jerónima de Burgos), and now in the Biblioteca Nacional,[8] we have the good fortune of having, as Victor Dixon states,[9] the best documented case (at least for the scribal manuscript) to examine how the *memoriones* worked. I have analyzed the three early texts of *La dama boba* and their verbal variations in order to observe the kind and frequency of memorial alterations presumably produced by a *memorión* or *memoriones*, and I have compared these alterations with those features that Shakespeareans endorsing memorial reconstruction have catalogued as characteristic of "bad" quartos and symptomatic of faulty playtext reporting—features that Maguire discusses thoroughly. But a brief description and assessment of the relationship between the early texts of *La dama boba* needs to be included. The nature and quantity of agreements and disagreements between the three texts[10] leads one to infer a common ancestor from which the surviving Remírez-signed manuscript and the printed version both derive. The following stemma helps visualize these relationships.

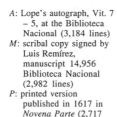

*A*: Lope's autograph, Vit. 7 – 5, at the Biblioteca Nacional (3,184 lines)

*M*: scribal copy signed by Luis Remírez, manuscript 14,956 Biblioteca Nacional (2,982 lines)

*P*: printed version published in 1617 in *Novena Parte* (2,717 lines)

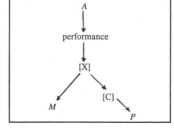

Although the highly reputed scholar Maria Grazia Profetti has hypothe-sized that the text of *La dama boba* printed in the *Novena Parte* corre-sponds to Lope's latest intentions, and that its features result from a coherent and carefully planned process of authorial revision,[11] from my own analysis I concur with García Soriano and Victor Dixon, who infer that the scribal manuscript and the copy C (now lost) behind the printed text must stem from a common ancestor X (also lost), which must have been the text reconstructed from memory by Luis Remírez and perhaps his assistant.[12] In order to analyze the memorial innovations produced by these *memoriones*, it is therefore necessary to limit our analysis to the assumed ancestor X as inferred from the extant documents; that is, to readings in which *M* and *P* agree against the holograph (also paying attention to read-ings in which both *M* and *P* deviate differently from the autograph), in addition to those *M*-only lines that must have been part of the performance version but were later taken out by other agents intervening between the ancestor X and the printed text *P*.

We may well begin our analysis of this memorial reconstruction with some statistics in order to have an overview. The number of lines deviating from the holograph amounts to 509, which means that, taking this memo-rial version to have 2,996,[13] 84 percent of Lope's lines are rendered intact by Luis Remírez or the two *memoriones*. If we take into account that 80 percent of the altered lines consists of deviations of only one word, and that a number of these must have been carried out by actors during per-formance and therefore may not be attributed to the *memoriones*, these figures certainly tell of a prodigious memory.[14]

As far as the kinds of verbal alteration in the dialogue are concerned, substitutions constitute an overwhelming majority, 85 percent, followed by 10 percent of transpositions. Within the type of substitutions, only sixty-three cases involve different meaning (thirty-three of them consisting of one-word substitution). The following passages provide good exam-ples:[15]

| line | A | M and P |
|------|---|---------|
| 2175 | *Nise*. El amor se ha de tener | *Nise*. **Poner freno a la mujer** |
| 2176 | adonde se puede hallar; | **es poner límite al mar.** |
| 2178 | que como no es elección, | **Extrañas quimeras son** |
| 2179 | sino sólo accidente, | que amor como es accidente |
| 2180 | tiénese donde se siente, | tiénense donde se siente, |
| 2181 | no donde fuera razón | no donde fuera razón |

| | A | M | P |
|---|---|---|---|
| 3019 | *Duardo.* ¿Cómo vos le | *Duar.* Vuestra desdicha | *Duar.* Vuestra desdicha |
| | habéis mandado | he sabido | he sabido |
| 3020 | que de los hombres se | y siento como es razón. | y siento como es razón. |
| | esconda? | | |
| 3021 | *Otavio.* No sé, por Dios, | *Oct.* Y yo que en esta | *Fenis.* Y yo que en esta |
| | qué os responda. | ocasión | ocasión |
| 3022 | Con ella estoy enojado, | haya perdido el sentido. | haya perdido el sentido. |
| 3023 | o con mi contraria | *Fenis.* ¡Qué lástima! | *Oct.* Que ya era cuerda |
| | estrella. | | entendí, |
| | | *Duard.*        Nise bella | y estaba loco de vella. |
| 3024 | *Miseno.* Ya viene Liseo | con Liseo viene aquí. | *Mis.* ¡Qué lástima! |
| | aquí. | | *Duard.*        Nise bella |
| 3025 | Determinaos. | *Fenis.* Determinaos. | con Liseo viene aquí. |
| 3025 | *Otavio.*        Yo, por mí, | *Oct.*        Yo, por mí, | |
| 3026 | ¿qué puedo decir sin | ¿qué puedo decir sin | |
| | ella? | ella? | |

Examples of one-word substitutions are:

| | A | M and P |
|---|---|---|
| 30 | *Liseo.* [...] ha de llegar cuando pueda | *Liseo.* [...] ha de llegar **cuanto** pueda |
| 31 | lucir. | **antes.** |
| 31 | *Turín.* Muy atrás se queda | *Turín.* Muy atrás se queda |

| | A | M (whole scene omitted in *P*) |
|---|---|---|
| 271 | *Otavio.*  Casémosla; que temo | *Octavio.*  Pues casémosla; que temo |
| 272 | alguna necedad de tanto estremo | alguna **novedad** de tanto estremo |

The variants "cuando"/"cuanto" and "novedad"/"necedad" are similar in sound.

The rest of the substitutions are those rendering the same or similar sense and those minor substitutions involving grammatical items. In the first case, I have counted 201 examples, consisting of

(1) paraphrased lines, 43 deviations (e.g., l. 288: "todo se viene a saber] todo se deja entender");

(2) partly paraphrased lines, 41 (l. 75: "Dicen que es también hermosa] Oigo decir que es hermosa");

(3) one-word synonymic substitutions, 58 (l. 209: "Pero ver tan discreta y arrogante] Pero ver tan entendida y arrogante"); or

(4) semantically related words, 59 (l. 226: "en amar y servir] en servir y agradar").

As for minor substitutions of grammatical items, there are 152 cases, such as demonstratives (19); pronouns (22); articles and determiners (13); adverbs (18); connectives, conjunctions, and prepositions (38); exclamations (3); and grammatical inflexions (39, involving singular/plural changes, verb tense, and personal endings).

As we can see by these numbers, synonymic or near-synonymic substitution—whether of lines, groups of lines, or single words—is the most common alteration made by our *memorión* or *memoriones*.

Interestingly, seven deviations involve the adjectives *boba*, *necia*, and *simple* (idiot, simple, and silly), which are characteristic of the play's title role. Five cases alter numerals, and five alterations correspond to what Maguire has termed "formulae," a feature that she judges to have little value as a symptom of faulty memory if taken individually, but "when they appear in abundance . . . they suggest an uninventiveness more likely to stem from a reporter in difficulty."[16] Only five cases of formulaic alterations appear in *La dama boba* (line number precedes the reading in *A*, the holograph):

991    Dios os guarde ] El cielo os guarde.
1950   No entre en mi casa / Laurencio más] Locura extraña. / No entre aquí Laurencio.
1796   ¿Hay cosa semejante?] ¿*Hay* ignorancia *tal*?
2542   Válgame el cielo ] ¿*Hay tal* locura?
2791   Así es verdad] ¿*Hay tal* cosa?

Note the last three repeating the pattern "¿Hay tal . . . ?" (Is there such . . . ?).

Paraphrase occurs mainly in one-line substitutions, two examples involving two lines, one of which follows:

|  | *A* | *M* (passage omitted in *P*) |
|---|---|---|
| 1614 | yo os doy sus esperanzas y favores; | yo os doy todas mis cartas y papeles; |
| 1615 | mis deseos os doy y mis amores, | mis regalos os doy y mis suspiros, |

But there is no paraphrase of larger groups of lines except for the three-line letter by the gallant Laurencio to Finea, which is significantly the only prose passage in the play:

|  | *A* | *M* and *P* |
|---|---|---|
| 1504 | "Agradezco mucho la merced que me has hecho, aunque toda esta noche la he pasado con poco sosiego, pensando en tu hermosura" | "Estoy muy agradecido de la merced que me haces aunque he pasado toda esta noche contemplando tu hermosura" |

Inter-play borrowings have been adduced to detect memorial reconstruction in a suspect playtext. In the reconstructed *La dama boba*, I have observed only one case—the three unique lines "poner freno a la mujer / es poner límite al mar. Extrañas quimeras son" (ll. 2175–77, appearing in the first example)—which may lead one to suspect an external echo, although it should be further confirmed as such. After consulting the CD-ROM database *Teatro del Siglo de Oro* published by Chadwyck[17] (which includes some nine hundred plays, although only printed ones and by sixteen major playwrights), I have observed that the phrase "extrañas quimeras" is unique to Lope's printed plays and appears in five plays written before *La dama boba*, two of them printed before 1615 and therefore susceptible of having been known by the *memoriones*[18]. The lines "poner freno a la mujer es poner límite al mar" have a close resemblance in thought and wording to Lope's *La ocasión perdida* (act 2, line 91), "apréstese la gente, que es en vano poner freno a la mar, ni a amor olvido," which was published in the *Segunda Parte* in 1609 and certainly written before 1604, when Lope mentions it in the list of his plays he included in the edition of his novel *El peregrino en su patria*. Maguire argues correctly that external echoes are unconvincing as memorial errors if they are of a proverbial or commonplace character,[19] and these two lines are precisely of a proverbial character.

Supporters of memorial-reconstruction theory have pointed out internal repetitions as errors committed by playtext reporters, whether anticipations or recollections. In the memorial version, I have found forty cases of internal repetition, thirty-two being repetitions of one word.[20] Seventeen cases (thirteen anticipations and four recollections) are repetitions of words within an immediate four-line context—which are common scribal or compositorial errors. And twenty-one cases repeat words standing at considerable distance: ten anticipations from words further away (some from 150 and one 190 lines; for instance, after line 1649 there is an added half-line, "Y habrán disimulado," anticipating a sentence thirteen lines after); and eleven recollections of precedent words standing at distances from six to forty-four lines before. In my opinion, these figures show a frequency of internal repetitions higher than that expected in scribal or compositorial transmission.[21] Maguire argues that for an internal repetition to be a reliable sign of faulty memory, it should be a run of lines showing distinctive vocabulary.[22] There is only one example of this in the reconstructed *La dama boba*, in act 2, scene 7, lines 1952–64 (see table on next page).

Repetitions of an interlocutor's immediately preceding line, which have been identified as a feature of memorial reconstruction, do not appear in this memorial version.

Substitution is also the most common alteration in speech headings.[23] Interestingly, most misattributions happen among related characters. The three gallants courting the intelligent sister are usually confused.[24] Both

| | A | M | P |
|---|---|---|---|
| 1952 | *Nise.* Es error, porque Laurencio la engaña: | *Nise.* Es yerro, **que él y Liseo la engañan,** | *Nise.* Es yerro, **que él y Liseo la engañan,** |
| 1953 | que él y Liseo lo dicen | **y aquesta traza han buscado** | **y aquesta traza han tomado** |
| 1954 | no más de para enseñarla. | no más de para enseñarla. | no más de para enseñarla. |
| 1955 | *Otavio.* De esa manera, yo callo. | *Octav.* ¡Oh! Pues ¿con eso yo callo? | *Octav.* ¡Oh! Pues ¿con eso yo callo? |
| 1956 | *Finea.* ¡Oh! Pues ¿con eso nos tapa | *Finea.* ¡Oh! Pues ¿con eso nos tapas | *Finea.* ¡Oh! Pues ¿con esa nos tapas |
| 1957 | la boca? *Otavio.* Vente conmigo. | la boca? *Octav.* Ven allá dentro. | la boca? *Octav.* Ven allá dentro. |
| 1958 | *Finea.* ¿A dónde? *Otavio.* Donde te aguarda | | |
| 1959 | un notario. *Finea* Vamos. *Otavio.* Ven. | | |
| 1960 | ¡Qué descanso de mis canas! *Vanse Nise sola* | ¡Qué descanso de mis canas! *Vanse Finea y Octavio, queda Nise* | ¡Qué descanso de mis canas! *Vanse Octavio y Finea* |
| 1961 | *Nise.* Hame contado Laurencio | *Nise.* Hame contado Laurencio | *Nise.* Hame contado Laurencio |
| 1962 | que han tomado aquesta traza | **que él y Liseo la engañan** | que han tomado aquesta traza |
| 1963 | Liseo y él, para ver | **y aquesta traza han tomada** | **él y Liseo por** ver |
| 1964 | si aquella rudeza labran, | **no más de para enseñarla** | si **aquesta** rudeza labran, |
| 1965 | y no me parece mal. | y no me parece mal. | y no me parece mal. |

servants, Turín and Pedro, are exchanged at line 2560. Instead of the lady Finea, her servant Clara announces the father's entrance at line 845. The intelligent sister Nise and not the father Otavio orders the idiot sister Finea to be quiet at line 959.

Transposition, which for Taylor "is among the easiest forms of memorial errors,"[25] is the second most numerous type of alteration, although far less copious than substitutions. Following Taylor's classification of transposition, the most frequent type of transposition in Remírez's reconstruction is that involving words immediately juxtaposed, such as subject-verb and subject-object order within a sentence, the type that Taylor discards in his reporter-identification method because they "may be made by compositors easily enough."[26] There are a few examples of transposition of words in doublets or catalogues (five cases); of words performing the same syntactical function in grammatically parallel phrases (four cases); of vocatives, interjections, and other floating elements (nine cases); of clauses within a speech (five cases); and, finally, of whole self-contained fragments or speeches (three cases). A thirty-two-line transposition occurs in act 2, scene 3, when the intelligent sister Nise reproaches Laurencio for leaving her in favor of her idiot but rich sister Finea. In Lope's autograph, Nise asks her servant to speak in order to give testimony of the betrayal (l. 1276); the servant does so, and Nise carries on her reproach (ll. 1277–308) until she expresses a lament (l. 1309) that ends in a final reproach. In the memorial version, after Nise asks her servant to speak, Nise begins her lament followed by the final reproach, and then the servant intervenes to give testimony followed by Nise's reproach. The alteration produces no dramatic awkwardness: Nise's contradiction in beginning a lament just after she has asked her servant to speak may be seen as a sign of Nise's state of agitation.

In act 3, scene 22, two quatrains (ll. 2963–66, 2983–86) beginning with the phrase "En el desván" (In the attic) are transposed to earlier moments in a dialogue between the protagonist Finea and her servant Clara discussing the kinds of people living in an attic, the place to which the former has been confined by her father. These transpositions are probably prompted by the fact that many of Clara's speeches begin with "En el desván."

If omitted lines that may probably be cuts in the performance version are not counted, omission is not a conspicuous memorial error in Remírez's reconstruction. Most omissions involve one word and do not affect meter.[27] The omission of one line (1513) in an enumeration of gallants courting the intelligent sister leaves a rhymeless line in a passage of rhymed pairs of hendecasyllables. Another omitted line (3143) occurs before a transposition of three lines (ll. 3144–46) before line 3170, which is then followed by an added line in order to keep the *romance* versification scheme.

| A | | M[28] | |
|---|---|---|---|
| 3142 | *Otavio*. ¡Rasgaréle aquella boca! | 3142 | *Otavio*. ¡Rasgaréle aquella boca! |
| 3143 | *Miseno*. Este es caso sin remedio. | 3147 | *Miseo* Octavio, vos sois discreto: |
|  |  |  | [...] |
|  |  | 3168 | *Laurencio*. [...] si ella me de la |
|  |  |  | memoria |
|  |  | 3169 | de cuarenta mil ducados. |
| 3144 | *Nise*. ¿Y la Clara socarrona | 3144 | *Turín*. ¿Y la Clara socarrona |
| 3145 | que llevaba los gazapos? | 3145 | que llevaba los gazapos? |
| 3146 | *Clara*. Mandómelo mi señora. | 3146 | *Clara*. Mandómelo mi señora. |
| 3147 | *Miseo* Otavio, vos sois discreto: | +1 | *Turín*. ¡Oh! Cuál se los meterían. |
| 3148 | ya sabéis que tanto monta | 3170 | *Pedro*. Y Pedro, ¿no es bien que |
|  |  |  | coma |

Other omissions consist of two-line to four-line groups for which it is difficult to discern whether they were cut or memorially omitted. One group contains a proverbial sentence (ll. 1311–12), another is part of an enumeration (ll. 1616–17), and another is repeating the idiot sister's command to hide herself in the attic (2874–75). No omission has produced nonsense.

Additions are neither numerous nor generally extra-metrical. Only one exclamation ("¡[Oh] Caballeros!" [l. 1650]) is added in a two-line passage of deficient meter; but, for instance, in the above-mentioned example at line 271 a connective is added to pad a pronoun omission:

| A | M |
|---|---|
| 270 *Miseno.*      Un casamiento | *Miseno.*      Un casamiento |
| 271 os traigo **yo.** | os traigo. |
| 271 *Otavio.*      Casémosla; que temo | *Octavio.*      **Pues** casémosla; que temo |
| 272 alguna necedad de tanto estremo | alguna novedad de tanto estremo |

Half-lines (at ll. 343, 358 + 1, and 1979 + 1) and a vocative (at l. 172) are inserted to compensate for a half-line omission. There are no additions consisting of topical or local references, or of expanded clowning— features regarded as indicative of memorial reconstruction.

Deficiencies in versification are also a textual feature attributed to playtext reporters. Lope's autograph of *La dama boba* shows the usual combination of different stanzas with various rhyme patterns and line lengths, 85 percent being octosyllables.[29] In such a rhyme-patterned dialogue, any verbal alteration, especially of the end word of a line, that affects versification is easily noticed by a trained audience. Remírez's reconstruction reveals effective attempts to preserve the versification, as shown before when discussing omissions and additions. At lines 2663–70,

| A | M |
|---|---|
| 2663 *Laurencio.* [...] ¿Querrás buscar ocasión | ¿Querraste casar **así** |
| 2664 para querer a Liseo, | |
| 2665 a quien ya tan cerca veo | |
| 2666 de tu boda y posesión? | |
| 2667 Bien haces, Nise; haces, bien. | |
| 2668 Levántame un testimonio, | Levantando un testimonio |
| 2669 porque de este matrimonio | y de aqueste matrimonio |
| 2670 a mí la culpa me den. | echarme la culpa **a mí?** |

Remírez was not able to remember the three lines 2664–66, so he summarized the whole quatrain in the first line "¿Querraste casar así" (Will you thus marry me?), which belongs to a single *redondilla* quatrain made up of the last three lines of the following quatrain, which contains the important words "testimonio" and "matrimonio," necessary for the plot. For the last line (2670) to rhyme with the first new line, Remírez transposed the indirect object "a mí" (to me) from the beginning to the end of the line.

Of the 2,996 lines in this memorial version, around a dozen are metrically defective or rhymeless. There are no fragments showing the kind of jerky style or wrecked verse found in Elizabethan suspect texts, neither the macaronic combination of verse and prose, nor the verse made up of unscannable lines found in *Pericles*.[30]

Aural errors, as Maguire states, "can arise in almost any kind of transmission" and cannot function "as diagnostic evidence of memory,"[31] but eleven instances of them appear in Remírez's version, fewer than in the First Quarto *King Lear*:[32] for instance, "apenas halla un] apenas hay un"(l. 248); "varia, culta] varia, oculta" (l. 299); "Lamícola, Arañizaldo] Lamícol, Aramizaldo" (l. 465); "enoja] en hoja" (l. 936); "alma, señora] almas, señora" (l. 1187); "de esos brazos] de esos abrazos" (l. 1528); "tan bien] también" (l. 2060).

The following features have been pointed out as errors of playtext reporters, but they are *not* observed in the memorial reconstruction of *La dama boba*: length of speeches not rising above fourteen or twenty lines, erroneous factual references and allusions, stylistic unevenness, verbal characterization and poor verbal comedy, banal and stereotyped exit lines, reduction in subject matter or in playing time in favor of a less sophisticated audience, reduction of the cast for a smaller company, and serious plot inconsistencies or contradictions. There is only one inconsistency (l. 2323), when the father Octavio tells the gallant that Duardo will marry the wrong sister, Finea, instead of the expected Nise. Yet this inconsistency is present also in Lope's autograph and is therefore an authorial oversight that was not corrected in the performance version.[33]

The "tired reporter" theory explaining the gradual diminution in verbal correlation found in the Shakespeare suspect texts is partly confirmed by my analysis: while on the one hand the number of altered lines is even throughout the text (190 lines in act 1, 195 in act 2, and 194 in act 3),[34] on the other hand, the most serious alterations occur near the end of the play, involving the largest groups of lines (2879–93, 3019–24, 3170–82) and compound errors involving misattributions and substitutions of different meaning.

Stage directions are in the indicative (in contrast to Lope's usual subjunctive or imperative) and are sometimes descriptive of action, as in the fifth scene when the idiot lady is having her reading lesson. There is the added direction "Ponense en medio Nise y Celia" at line 356 Nise and Celia get in between [Finea and the teacher]"); and just before, when the desperate teacher has resorted to physical punishment as a teaching method at line 351, Lope provides the curt direction "Saca una palmatoria" (he takes out a rod), which is replaced by "Dale una palmcta y ella echa a correr tras él" (he gives her a rod and she runs after him]: on stage it is Finea that wrenches the rod from the hand of the teacher who was about to beat her, but from a distance it appeared to the *memorión* that the teacher gave her the punishing instrument. The teacher's name is "Rufino" in Lope's initial stage direction, but his name is not mentioned in the dialogue, and therefore in Remírez's reconstruction he is "un maestro de leer" (a teacher of reading) with no personal name and with his precise task in the scene indicated in the stage direction (l. 307). The same happens with another minor character, the student Leandro, who is given a nameless "un estudiante" (student) in both the stage direction and speech headings by the *memorión* (ll. 81, 171). A stage direction incorporating a descriptive epithet occurs when the servant Turín enters in order to cry out that his master is going to duel with the rival gallant Laurencio: "Sale Turín muy alborotado" (Turin enters in great distress), l. 1529, which is analogous to the famous "Enter the ghost in his night gowne" in the First Quarto *Hamlet* (G2v.28), or "Enter Juliet somewhat fast, and embraceth Romeo" (Q1 *Romeo and Juliet,* E4r.31). Specifications of scene location at the beginning of each scene (for example, "Sala en casa de Otavio en Madrid" [A room in Otavio's house in Madrid], ll. 184, 1063, 1667, 2032) are consistently absent. All this clearly indicates that the *memorión* had no visual access to a playscript but reported what he saw on stage, thus confirming the assumptions held by supporters of memorial reconstruction with respect to stage directions. On other occasions, the autograph's stage directions provide some properties that are omitted by the *memorión*: for instance, at line 272 the idiot lady Finea does not enter with "dos cartillas" (two notebooks) as specified in the holograph.

This study leads me to several conclusions.

As far as I have been able to determine, it is not clear whether the *memoriones* were a common or a marginal phenomenon. The memorial capacity of this *memorión*, Luis Remírez, was so exceptional as to lead one to suspect that there would not be many men of such prodigious memory as to be able to put together an entire play from memory.[35]

The fact that there is not in English a term as specific as *memorión* may indicate either that there were no *memoriones* stalking the London or provincial playhouses, or that this phenomenon was not very widespread in Elizabethan and Jacobean England.

Of the twenty-eight features discussed by Laurie Maguire that were "identified by the New Bibliographers as characteristic of suspect texts and symptomatic of memorial reconstruction,"[36] only eight (perhaps nine, if one takes into account the still-to-be-confirmed external echo "poner freno a la mujer . . . Extrañas quimeras son" (to curb a woman . . . Wild chimeras are) receive some support from the memorial reconstruction of *La dama boba*. The clearest support comes from the nature of stage directions. Prominent memorial alterations, though not conspicuously excessive, are synonymic or quasi-synonymic substitutions of words and lines and paraphrases, anticipations and recollections, transpositions, and misattributions. Less support is given by the presence of aural errors, and partial support is accorded to the "tired reporter" theory.

The fact that internal repetition is a significant error gives support to Maguire's assertion that internal repetitions are the most reliable indicators of faulty long-term memory.[37] Interestingly, on the other hand a number of the textual features in this memorial reconstruction, such as aural errors, transpositions, and descriptive stage directions, were judged by Maguire to have little or no value in her diagnostic analysis of memorial reconstruction. The Remírezes also committed the kind of errors that are equally explained as by scribal or compositorial agents. And I am inclined to think that if we applied Maguire's diagnostic method to their memorial version, and assume her cautious and skeptical attitude, we would probably *not* come out with a verdict of memorial reconstruction, since one case of internal repetition clearly produced by faulty long-term memory and five cases of formulas, together with a positive stylistic assessment, would incline us to absolve this playtext from the guilty verdict of "memorially reconstructed." This should not lead one to think that the soundness of her method has been undermined by this analysis; rather, it causes one to acknowledge the exceptionality of this spectator's memory.[38]

And if the present analysis reveals a confirmation of many of the verbal features that previous supporters of memorial reconstruction attributed to actors-reporters, this should not lead one to think that their analyses were right. If this memorial version of *La dama boba* did not have the documentary evidence described above to confirm this play text as the work of *memoriones*, I am inclined to think that many supporters of memorial reconstruction would not have judged it as such. The nearly six hundred alterations made by the *memorión* are fewer in number than the 1,141 variants between the suspect First Quarto *King Lear* and its First Folio collateral text, or the 1,934 variants between the suspect First Quarto *Richard III* and its Folio counterpart,[39] alterations variously explained by the agency of compositors, bookkeepers, scribes, adapters, and author. The quality of the text and its dramaturgy is not "bad," and one may find arguments, as Profetti does, to support authorial revision in many variants. Only the fact that the reconstructed *La dama boba* presents more synonymic substitutions, one-word internal repetitions, or misattributions than expected in scribal or compositorial transmission, would give one reason for second thoughts on the final verdict. What this last remark induces me to endorse is the observation made by both New Bibliographers and Maguire that the combination of several alleged memorial errors and their high frequency provides a firm basis for hypothesizing reconstruction from memory in a text.

# Notes

1. Laurie Maguire, *Shakespearean Suspect Texts: The "Bad" Quartos and Their Contexts* (Cambridge: Cambridge University Press, 1996).

2. Ten years ago I attended the Tokyo World Shakespeare Congress as a postgraduate student, and I wondered if one day I would be taking the floor and talking to a Shakespearean audience about my findings on a given subject. That dream has come true today and I am sincerely thankful to the World Shakespeare Congress Committee for the opportunity to give a short paper here.

3. Cristóbal Suárez de Figueroa, *Plaza Universal de todas las ciencias y artes* (Madrid: Luis Sánchez, 1615), fol. 237. The Spanish original reads, "Hállase en Madrid al presente un mancebo grandemente memorioso. Llámase Luis Remírez de Arellano, hijo de nobles padres y natural de Villaescusa de Haro. Este toma de memoria una comedia entera de tres veces que la oye, sin discrepar un punto en traza y versos. Aplica el primer dia a la disposición; el segundo a la variedad de la composición y el tercero a la puntualidad de las coplas. Deste modo encomienda a la memoria las comedias que quiere. En particular tomó así *La dama boba*, *El príncipe perfecto* y *La Arcadia*, sin otras" (There is in Madrid at present a young man of very capacious memory. His name is Luis Remírez de Arellano, son of noble parents and born in Villaescusa de Haro. He takes from memory an entire play by only hearing it three times, without differing the least in either plot or lines. He devotes the first day to the plot disposition, the second to the variety of writing, and the third to the precision of the verses. In this way he entrusts any play he wishes to his memory. In particular he took *The Nit-Wit Lady*, *The Perfect Prince*, and *Arcadia*, and no others). This is quoted in part by Gary Taylor in the general introduction to *William Shakespeare: A Textual Companion*, ed. by Stanley Wells and Gary Taylor (Oxford: Oxford University Press, 1986), 23. Another contemporary reference to Luis Remírez comes from Vicente Espinel in his *Vida del escudero Marcos de Obregón* published in 1617 (see edition by M. S. Carrasco Urgotti [Madrid: Castalia, 1972], 2:211–12).

4. Lope de Vega Carpio, *Doze comedias de Lope de Vega, sacadas de sus originales por el mismo. Novena Parte* (Madrid: Viuda de Alonso Martin, 1617).

5. See J. de Entrambasaguas, *Estudios sobre Lope de Vega* (Madrid: Consejo Superior de Investigaciones Científicas, 1946), 245–47; Justo García Soriano, "Prólogo," *Obras de Lope de Vega* (Madrid: Real Academia Española, 1929), 9:xxxiii. In his prologue to *La Arcadia*, published in *Trezena Parte de las comedias de Lope de Vega Carpio* (Madrid: Viuda de A. Martín, 1620), Lope de Vega complains about "the stealing of comedias by those whom the vulgar call, the one *Memorilla*, and the other *Gran Memoria*, who, with the few verses they learn, mingle an infinity of their own barbarous lines" (English translation quoted from Gary Taylor, "General Introduction," 23).

6. Maria Grazia Profetti, "Editar el teatro del Fénix de los Ingenios," *Anuario de Lope de Vega* 2 (1996): 141–43; Victor Dixon, "La intervención de Lope de Vega en la publicación de sus comedias," *Anuario de Lope de Vega* 2 (1996): 45–64.

7. "En razon de las comedias nunca Vex.ª tubo *La dama boba*, porque esta es de Geronima de Burgos, y yo la ymprimi por una copia, firmándola de mi nombre" (With respect to the plays, your lordship never had *La dama boba* [The Nit-Wit Lady] for it belongs to Geronima de Brugos, and I printed it from a copy, signed with my name). A. González de Amezúa, *Epistolario de Lope de Vega* (Madrid: Real Academia Española, 1942), 3:308.

8. Shelfmark Vit. 7–5.

9. Victor Dixon, "Tres textos tempranos de *La dama boba* de Lope," *Anuario de Lope de Vega* 3 (1997): 64.

10. The holograph contains 3,184 lines, the scribal manuscript omits 202 lines,

and the printed text retains fourteen of these omitted lines and omits another 279 lines. The Remírez-signed manuscript and the printed text differ in 186 lines.

11. Maria Grazia Profetti, "Editar el teatro," 129–51.

12. García Soriano, "Prólogo," xxxv; Dixon, "Tres textos," 53, 57. The readings peculiar to the printed text may be transmission errors, and deliberate alterations by an editor or by Lope on supervising his publication. The readings peculiar to the scribal manuscript may be common errors of transmission, or further deliberate modification by the *memoriones*.

13. The 188 omitted lines that this inferred memorial version must have had are of a nature equally explained by abridgement before performance and by faulty memory, although most of them consist of self-contained passages or lines, leaving versification unaffected, and therefore are likely to have been already cut in the performance version.

14. This is clearer if we measure the degree of textual variation according to the system of five categories of verbal correlation used by Kathleen Irace in *Reforming the "Bad" Quartos: Performance and Provenance of Six Shakespearean First Editions* (Newark: University of Delaware Press, 1994), 116, and compare them with the results of her analysis of six Shakespeare "bad" quartos. Remírez's *La dama boba* shows a proportion of 85 percent in the *all* category and of 14 percent in the *most* category (in which more than half of the words match). That is a total of 94 percent of *all* and *most* lines, conspicuously higher than the 83 % of Q1 *Henry V,* 79 percent of Q1 *Romeo and Juliet,* 59 percent of Q1 *Hamlet,* and 44 percent of Q1 *Merry Wives of Windsor* (Irace, 186).

15. Line numbers are keyed to Diego Marín's edition (Madrid: Cátedra, 1986). The Spanish text is regularized to modern spelling and punctuation.

16. Maguire, *Shakespearean Suspect Texts,* 177.

17. *Teatro del Siglo de Oro,* CD-ROM (Chadwyck-Healy España, 1998).

18. Lope de Vega, *La fuerza lastimosa,* in *Segunda Parte de las Comedias de Lope de Vega Carpio* (Madrid: Alonso Martín, 1609), act 1, 1. 388; de Vega, *La noche toledana,* in *Tercera Parte de las comedias de Lope de Vega* (Barcelona: Sebastián de Cormellas, 1612), act 3, 1. 755; de Vega, *El exemplo de casadas,* in *Flor de las comedias de España de diferetes autores. Quinta Parte* (Barcelona: Sebastián de Cormellas, 1616), act 2, 1. 266, probably written between 1599 and 1608; de Vega, *Los porceles de Murcia,* in *El Fénix de España . . . Séptima Parte de sus comedias* (Madrid: Viuda de Alsonso Martín, 1617), act 3, 1. 1125, probably written between 1599 and 1608; de Vega, *El animal de Hungría,* in *Novena Parte,* (1617), act 3, 1. 1097, probably written between 1608 and 12. Conjectural dates of composition are from S. G. Morley and C. Bruerton, *Cronología de las comedias de Lope de Vega* (Madrid: Gredos, 1968), originally published as *The Chronology of Lope de Vega's Comedias* (New York: MLA, 1940). "Extrañas quimeras" appears also in *Los bandos de Sena,* (1635), act 3, 1. 248. Morley and Bruerton date it between 1597 and 1603 (288), whereas E. Cotarelo y Mori judges it a mature piece, since it is not included in Lope's list of his plays in the 1618 edition of *El peregrino en su patria* ("Prólogo," *Obras de Lope de Vega* [Madrid: Real Academia Española, 1917], 3:xxiv).

19. Maguire, *Shakespearean Suspect Texts,* 166–67.

20. The exceptions are: two two-word repetitions, e.g. at 1. 2638 "a lo que mi amor desea] a lo que mi alma desea" ("el alma" appears in 1. 2636); two one-line repetitions after 1. 1943. where the addition "que tanta pena me daban" in *M* and *P* repeats 1. 1902; and one two-line repetition at ll. 1952 and 1962, which is shown below.

21. For instance, Q2 *Hamlet* shows two cases of anticipation, according to J. Dover Wilson (*The Manuscript of Shakespeare's "Hamlet"* [Cambridge: Cambridge University Press, 1934], 55). Interestingly, he points out twenty-three anticipations in F1 *Hamlet* (ibid., 59–64), a figure comparable to the twenty-three anticipations found in Remírez's reconstruction (thirteen in the immediate four-line context and ten in a remote place). While J. Dover Wilson attributed all F1 *Hamlet* anticipations to the active memory of a playhouse copyist familiar with the text, Harold Jenkins observed that the sixteen anticipations of words in the immediate context may well be the work of a scribe or compositor, and that the other anticipations, those of words standing further away, may be due to the memory of actors (*Hamlet,* Arden Shakespeare [London: Methuen, 1982], 63). Anticipations in F1 *Hamlet* appear in the stints of both compositors B and I.

22. Maguire, *Suspect Texts*, 170.

23. Deviations in speech headings are twenty-six substitutions, six omissions, and one transposition.

24. Feniso and Duardo, sometimes including the accompanying Miseno (at ll. 503–4, 551–52, 627–69, 1067–68, 1135, 1147, 1860, 1906–7, 2734, 2789–91, 2990, 3110, 3123).

25. Gary Taylor, "Corruption and Authority in the Bad Quarto," in *Modernizing Shakespeare's Spelling with Three Studies in the Text of "Henry V,"* by Stanley Wells and Gary Taylor (Oxford: Clarendon Press, 1979), 161.

26. Ibid., 161. There are twenty-four instances of this kind of error in Remírez's reconstruction: e.g., "Estas son letras también] Letras son estas también" (ll. 325), and "has dicho a Finea / requiebros] has dicho requiebros / a Finea" (ll. 1281–82).

27. Connectives (ten) and pronouns (seven), plus one adverb and one imperative verb.

28. The printed version (*P*) also transposes ll. 3144–46 (also attributed to the servant Turín) before l. 3170, but the added line reads "¡Oh! Cuál los engullirían."

29. In stanzas such as *redondilla* (8a 8b 8b 8a) and *romance* (8x 8a 8x 8a), which are stylistically close to conversational prose (Marín, *La dama boba*, 39–40).

30. Variously explained. (1) As reported text by E. K. Chambers, *William Shakespeare: A Study of Facts and Problems* (Oxford: Oxford University Press, 1930), 1:521; W. W. Greg, *The Editorial Problem in Shakespeare*, 3d ed. (Oxford: Clarendon Press, 1962), 74; F. D. Hoeniger, ed., *Pericles*, New Arden Shakespeare (London: Methuen, 1963), xxxi–ix; J. M. Maxwell, ed., *Pericles*, New Shakespeare (Cambridge: Cambridge University Press, 1969), 88; Gary Taylor, "The Transmission of *Pericles,*" *PBSA* 80 (1986): 193–217; Wells and Taylor, *Textual Companion*, 556–60; and *The Riverside Shakespeare*, 2d ed., 1559. (2) As memorial reconstruction by two reporters with different reporting methods. Philip Edwards, "An Approach to the Problem of *Pericles,*" *Shakespeare Survey* 5 (1952): 25–49. (3) As part foul papers, part memorial reconstruction by S. Musgrove, "The First Quarto of *Pericles* Reconsidered," *Shakespeare Quarterly* 29 (1978): 389–406. (4) As revised authorial copy: H. Craig, "*Pericles* and *The Painfull Aduentures,*" *Studies in Philology* 45 (1949): 100–5.

31. Maguire, *Shakespearean Suspect Texts*, 197.

32. Variously explained. (1) As authorial draft: M. Doran, *The Text of "King Lear"* (Stanford: Stanford University Press, 1931); M. Warren, "Quarto and Folio *King Lear* and the Interpretation of Albany and Edgar," in *Shakespeare: Pattern of Excelling Nature*, ed. D. Bevington and J. L. Halio (Newark: University of Delaware Press, 1976), 95–107; S. Urkowitz, *Shakespeare's Revision of "King Lear"* (Princeton: Princeton University Press, 1980); P. W. M. Blayney, *The Texts of "King Lear"* (Cambridge: Cambridge University Press, 1982); Wells and Taylor,

*Textual Companion*, 510; and Jay L. Halio, ed. *The Tragedy of "King Lear,"* New Cambridge Shakespeare (Cambridge: Cambridge University Press, 1992), 69–70. (2) As shorthand report: E. K. Chambers, *William Shakespeare*, 465; and W. W. Greg, *Editorial Problem*, 95–100. (3) As reported text by an actor reading from "foul papers" and relying on his memory and another actor hearing the text: A. Walker, *Textual Problems of the First Folio* (Cambridge: Cambridge University Press, 1953); and G. I. Duthie, ed., *King Lear*, New Shakespeare (Cambridge: Cambridge University Press, 1960). (4) As memorial reconstruction by one or more actors: L. Kirschbaum, *The True Text of "King Lear"* (Baltimore: Johns Hopkins University Press, 1945), 6–7; J. K. Walton, *The Quarto Copy for the First Folio of Shakespeare* (Dublin: Dublin University Press, 1971); and G. I. Duthie, ed., *Shakespeare's "King Lear": A Critical Edition* (Oxford: Blackwell, 1949), 6, 21–116. And (5) as longhand report by audience member: P. W. K. Stone, *The Textual History of "King Lear"* (London: Scolar Press, 1980).

33. Another authorial inconsistency occurs at l. 521 when Lope substitutes the form of the name "Eduardo" for the usual "Duardo."

34. This counting includes misattributions and variants in which the three early texts differ.

35. Ruano de la Haza points out an interesting piece of external evidence ("La relación textual entre *El Burlador de Sevilla* y *Tan largo me lo fiáis*," in *Tirso de Molina: Del Siglo de Oro al Siglo XX*, ed. Igancio Arellano et al. [Madrid: Revista "Estudios," 1995], 292) from a study on Lope published in 1935 that deals with an actor's involvement in memorial reconstruction and that I think deserves to be repeated here: a contract, signed in 1606 between the *autor de comedias* or theater manager Alonso Riquelme and the actor Juan de Ribera, binds the latter, in case he would leave the company, not to give away the plays and plots he knows or has been given by the manager, or to compose (*compondrá*) the stories and plots of these plays or other plays he has seen or would see playing in the company. Ruano de la Haza remarks that if a theater manager took pains to prevent an actor of his company from giving plays, stories, or plots to anyone not connected with the company, it was due to the fact that this was general practice. This piece of evidence does not clarify to what extent memory is used in the surreptitious composition of texts, however. The kind of textual transmission inferrable from this contract is the reconstruction from the actor's knowledge of plays as participant and spectator, and from manuscript material the actor possesses. Moreover, it is the stories or plots that are reconstructed, not the lines of the whole play. In that sense, this evidence is analogous to the passage in Robert Taylor's play *The Hog Hath Lost His Pearl*, dated 1614, which recognizes the involvement of an actor in reporting a text from memory in a surreptitious activity (Taylor, "General Introduction," 26). Further investigation into documentary evidence dealing with actors has so far proved to be fruitless.

36. Maguire, *Shakespearean Suspect Texts*, 223.

37. Ibid., 325.

38. Maguire is interested in the most reliable features that, either individually or accompanied by other features, indicate reconstruction from memory; that is, the most likely features to be caused by long-term faulty memory, and therefore relevent in diagnosing a play text in its own terms. Hers is a defect-spotting method (on the sensible assumption that memorial reconstruction leaves defects in the text), so when it is applied to a suspect text that, seen in its own terms, has few deficiencies, as Remírez's reconstruction of *La dama boba* shows, it seems not to work properly.

39. Figures taken from M. Spevack, *A Complete and Systematic Concordance to the Works of Shakespeare*, vol. 9, *Substantive Variants* (Hildesheim: Georg Olms Verlag, 1980).

# Part Three
## Contextualities

# Shakespeare's Islands

## JONATHAN BATE

FERNAND BRAUDEL WRITES IN *THE MEDITERRANEAN AND THE MEDITERRA-nean World in the Age of Philip II,*

> Every sea tends to live off itself, to organize the shipping circuits of its sailing vessels and small boats into an autonomous system. This was also true of the two great basins of the Mediterranean, east and west. They communicated and had links with each other but tended to organize themselves into closed circuits, notwithstanding a certain number of contacts, alliances, and relations of interdependence.
>
> This is underlined only too clearly by sixteenth-century politics. What a marvellous geopolitical map one could draw of the western half of the Mediterranean between the middle of the fifteenth and the middle of the sixteenth century, with arrows showing the old and new directions of Spanish imperialism, the positions it seized and exploited in order to gain control of the western sea. . . . The Ionian Sea, the "Sea of Crete," was by contrast the Ottoman sea. . . . These two different Mediterraneans were vehicles, one almost might say they were responsible for the twin empires. . . . Politics merely followed the outline of an underlying reality. These two Mediterraneans, commanded by warring rulers, were physically, economically and culturally different from each other. Each was a separate historical zone.[1]

William Shakespeare lived on a small island of minor international influence far to the north of the great geopolitical theater where the Cold—and sometimes Hot—War of his age was played out between two rival super powers, sometimes on land but mostly at sea.

Hold an image of the Mediterranean in your head and divide it at its narrow midpoint between Sicily and Tunis: the western half is the Spanish sea, the eastern half the Ottoman. Then divide the western sea north and south. The northern shore, from Cadiz to Naples to Messina, is under the influence of Spain. The southern shore, from Alcazar to Algiers to Tunis, is a place of uncertainty, ruled by a wild mix of client regimes and wayward corsairs. A successful privateer could make his fortune there; a captured one could lose not just his life but his immortal soul. A Spanish dispatch in the year of Shakespeare's birth announced that it was raining Christians in Algiers.

Sixteenth-century navigational technique was a matter of hugging the shorelines. "More precisely, according to the galley accounts of a Ragusan vessel, it was a matter of buying one's butter at Villefranche, vinegar at Nice, oil and bacon at Toulon. Or, as a Portuguese chronicler puts it, traveling from one seaside inn to another, dining in one and supping in the next." On the rare occasions when ships ventured beyond the sight of land, it was to follow one of a handful of time-honored routes: from Spain to Italy by the Balearics and the south of Sardinia, which was often called "sailing by the islands"; from Sicily to Tunis; from Rhodes to Alexandria; or from the straits of Messina or Malta to Aleppo in Syria via the coasts of Crete and Cyprus.[2] The islands were the essential pressure points. As Cuba and the Philippines were of inestimable strategic importance in a later era of super-power rivalry, so in this one much depended on control of Sicily, of Cyprus, of Rhodes.

I want to suggest that Shakespeare was more aware of this fact than we have sometimes given him credit for, and that he was interested in islands because they constitute a special enclosed space within the larger environment of geopolitics, perhaps a little like the enclosed space of the theater within the larger environment of the city. An island is an experimental place where opposing forces are brought together in dramatic confrontation.

As in so many areas, Christopher Marlowe established the paradigm. High Elizabethan tragedy was born with Tamburlaine's great westward sweep from Scythia through Persia to the Ottoman empire and beyond. Part 1 turns the old "fall of princes" motif on its head, offering a fantasy of a nobody from the distant East overthrowing the mighty Turkish Bajazeth. Part 2 begins with a bewildering ethnic mix as King Sigismund brings from Christendom "his camp of stout Hungarians, / Slavonians, Almains, Rutters, Muffs, and Danes," while the opposing Ottomans muster "revolted Grecians, Albanese, / Sicilians, Jews, Arabians, Turks, and Moors, / Natolians, Sorians, black Egyptians, / Illyrians, Thracians, and Bithynians."[3] The Ottoman army defeats first the Christians and then Tamburlaine's third force drawn from "Afric's frontier towns," the Barbary lands of Morocco, Fez and Argier. The two-part drama charts the rise and fall of the atheistic Tamburlaine, the fall and re-rise of the Ottoman empire. It is Mohammed, not the Christian God, who finally strikes down Tamburlaine. Marlowe recognizes that in the eastern Mediterranean and all along the Afric shore, the Christians constitute a weak, embattled, and marginal minority.

*Tamburlaine* is a land play. It name-checks the whole of known Asia and Africa, but ignores the islands of the Mediterranean. Marlowe fills that gap in *The Jew of Malta*. Recognizing that *Tamburlaine*'s dramatic weakness was its episodic structure, the inevitable consequence of the Scythian shepherd's long-distance marches, he invents a story that focuses the contest between Christianity and Islam on a single pressure point, the island of Malta. As befits a writer who had a second career as a spy, he turns his gaze from invasion to subversion. The third force in the gap between Christianity and Islam is no longer the Scythian outsider but rather the alien within—the combination of Jew (Barabas) and hybrid Moor (Ithamore).

To the Elizabethans, the name Malta would instantly have suggested the Knights of St. John, defenders of Christian pilgrims against the Muslim. Jew and Malta would therefore have been perceived as an oxymoronic pairing.[4] The play may reveal the Christian Friars as avaricious, lustful hypocrites, but it is hardly a surprise that the Jew is represented as a double-crosser who betrays the island. *The Jew of Malta* fulfills the expectation set up by its title. It was an enormously popular and influential play—witness the influence of Barabas and Ithamore on Shakespeare's Aaron in *Titus Andronicus*. An audience member going along to a new play called *The Moor of Venice* would therefore have had a similar expectation: that this Moor too will be a Barabas or Aaron, a barbarian who puts Venice in peril.[5]

\*     \*     \*

*Othello* is a play rich in allusion to the southern shoreline of the Mediterranean: a maid called Barbary, the Arabian tree, an encounter in Aleppo once. And yet Giovanni Battista Giraldi Cinthio's story in *Gli Hecatommithi* concerning a Venetian lady, a Moorish captain, and his ensign is very unspecific in its atmosphere. The narrative is confined entirely to plotting and dialogue; there is no realization of historical setting beyond the broad context that all the stories in the collection are narrated by a group of aristocrats who have escaped to Marseilles from the war, famine, and plague attendant upon the sack of Rome in 1527. It was Shakespeare who gave the story local texture—Venetian, Cypriot, and Moorish—courtesy of such recently published books as Lewis Lewkenor's 1599 translation of Contarini's *The Commonwealth and Government of Venice*, John Pory's 1600 translation of *A Geographical History of Africa* by "Leo Africanus," and Richard Knolles's 1603 *Generall Historie of the Turkes*.

In Cinthio the Venetian lords merely decide to change the guard in Cyprus, choosing the Moor as commandant of the new group of soldiers sent there. Desdemona insists on going with him and they arrive safely in Cyprus. There is no storm and there are no Turks. Whereas Cinthio's story was set, and indeed written, before the Turkish assault on Cyprus, Shakespeare updates the narrative and offers an invented variation on more recent history. The Turkish context is his most far-reaching addition to

Cinthio. The representation of Cyprus as an island embattled in the Ottoman sea was surely inspired by Marlowe's treatment of Malta.

"Valiant Othello, we must straight employ you / Against the general
enemy Ottoman," says the Duke of Venice.[6] The audience hears a conso-
nance, heightened by the rhetorical epanalepsis, between the names of the
captain-general "Othello" and the general enemy "Ottoman." This would
have been especially apparent if, as is likely, the original pronunciation of
the hero's name was Otello. Othman was the founder of the Turkish empire; Ottoman-ness is thus suggested by Othello's name, but he is turned
against the origin implied by that name.[7]

To Shakespeare and his contemporaries, Turk, Arab, and Moor all represented the Islamic "other," but they were not necessarily homogenized
into a single image of generic "barbarianism." Arabian culture was frequently associated with learning and civilization, in contrast to the prevailing images of Turk and Saracen. A Barbar could be "brave" rather than
"barbarous": George Peele's *Battle of Alcazar in Barbary*, a play based
on recent historical events, has both "a barbarous Moor, / The negro Muly
Hamet," and a "brave Barbarian Lord Muly Molocco."[8] A Moor could
help you out in your war against the Turk—or, for that matter, the Spaniard. How one judges the Islamic "other" depends not only on ideological
stereotype but also on the particularities of diplomatic liaison and changing allegiance in a world of super-power rivalry. At the end of *Alcazar*, the
evil Moor Muly Mahamet is defeated (just before the end we see him on
the battlefield crying "A horse, a horse, villain a horse" [1414]—this in a
play written well before *Richard III*). The throne of Barbary goes to Abdelmelec's virtuous brother, who is also called Muly Mahamet and who was
the real historical figure whose ambassador Abd-el-Oahed ben Massaood
visited the Elizabethan court in 1600 in order to explore the possibility of
forming an alliance to conquer Spain with a mixture of the English navy
and African troops.[9] Shakespeare's company played at court that Christmas, so he may have seen the Barbarian delegation in the flesh.

Peele's play mingles historical matter with a more general sense of the
barbarian, the other, the devilish—bad Muly Mahamet surrounds himself
with devilish and underworld associations. Audiences would have come to
*Moor of Venice* with the expectation of something similar, but witnessed a
remarkable inversion in that here it is a sophisticated Venetian who is associated with the devil and damnable actions.

The primary usage of the term "Moor" in Early Modern English was as
a religious, not a racial, identification: Moor meant "Mohammedan," that
is, Muslim. The word was frequently used as a general term for "not one
of us," non-Christian. To the play's original audience, one of the most
striking things about the figure of Othello would have been that he is a
committed Christian. The "ground" of the play is laid out in the first

scene, when Iago trumpets his own military virtues, in contrast to Cassio's "theoretical" knowledge of the art of war (Cassio comes from Florence, home of such *theorists* of war as Machiavelli):

> And I, of whom his eyes have seen the proof
> At Rhodes, at Cyprus, and on [other] grounds
> Christen'd and heathen.
>
> (1.1.28–30)

These lines give an immediate sense of confrontation between Christian and heathen dominions, with Rhodes and Cyprus as pressure points. Startlingly, though, the Moor is fighting for the Christians, not the heathen.

Again, consider Othello's response to the drunken brawl in Cyprus:

> Are we turn'd Turks, and to ourselves do that
> Which heaven hath forbid the Ottomites?
> For Christian shame, put by this barbarous brawl.
>
> (2.3.170–72)

Such Christian language in the mouth of a Moor, a Muslim, is inherently a paradox. It suggests that Othello would have been assumed to be a convert. The "baptism" that Iago says he will cause Othello to renounce would have taken place not at birth but at conversion. The action of the play re-converts Othello from Christianity, through the machinations of Iago. In this sense, it is fitting that Iago appeals to a "Divinity of hell" and that Othello acknowledges at the end of the play that he himself is bound for damnation.

The notion of conversion was crucial in the Elizabethan perception of the relationship between European Christianity and the Ottoman Empire. The phrase "to turn Turk" entered the common lexicon.[10] And the "renegade" became a dramatic type. In *The Tragedy of Solyman and Perseda* (1588, possibly by Kyd), a character called Basilisco turns Turk because the Turks, unlike the Christians, recognize his value and excellence as a soldier. There is a hit here at the poor pay of English soldiers, but Basilisco is also mocked as a braggart knight. Fun is had at his expense over the lopping of a collop of his flesh when he turns Turk, that is to say, when he is circumcised.

Islam was as powerful an alien force to Europeans in the sixteenth century as Communism was to Americans in the twentieth. "To turn Turk," was to go over to the other side. It could happen in a number of different ways: some travelers converted by a process of cultural assimilation, others who had been captured and enslaved did so in the belief that they would then be released. It is easy to forget how many English privateers became Ottoman slaves—on one occasion, two thousand wives petitioned

King James and Parliament for help in ransoming their husbands from Muslim captivity.[11]

If Shakespeare read all the way through Knolles's *Generall Historie of the Turkes*, he would have learned that once every three years the Turks levied a tax on the Christians living in the Balkans: it took the form of ten to twelve thousand children. They were deported and converted (circumcised), then trained to become soldiers. They formed a highly feared cadre in the Turkish army known as the Janizzaries—there is an elite guard of them in *The Battle of Alcazar*, while Bajazeth's army in *Tamburlaine* combines "circumcised Turks / And warlike bands of Christians renegade."[12] Othello is a Janizzary in reverse, not a Christian turned Muslim fighting against Christians, but a Muslim turned Christian fighting against Muslims. Although Lewkenor reports that the captain-general of the Venetian army was always a "stranger," historically speaking, conversion in Othello's direction, from Muslim to Christian, was much rarer than the opposite turn.

The second Elizabethan sense of the word "Moor" was specifically racial and geographical: it referred to a native or inhabitant of Mauretania, a region of north Africa corresponding to parts of present-day Morocco and Algeria. This association is invoked when Iago falsely tells Roderigo toward the end of the play that Othello "goes into Mauretania, and takes away with him the fair Desdemona" (4.2.224–25). Ethnic Moors were members of a Muslim people of mixed Berber and Arab descent. In the eighth century they had conquered Spain. Is it possibly in memory of this that Othello's second weapon is a sword of Spain?

Given that the Spanish Empire was England's great enemy, there would have been a certain ambivalence about the Moors—they may have overthrown Christianity, but at least it was Spanish Catholic Christianity. Philip II's worst fear was an uprising of the remaining Moors in Granada synchronized with a Turkish invasion,[13] just as Elizabeth I's worst fear was an uprising of the Irish synchronized with a Spanish invasion. As it was, the Turks took a different turn: in 1570, shortly after the end of the Morisco uprising and Philip's ethnic cleansing of Granada, they attacked Cyprus.

The alliance of European Christians against the Ottomans was uneasy because of post-Reformation divisions in Europe itself. Independent lesser powers such as Venice and England found themselves negotiating for footholds in the Mediterranean theater. Hence the diplomatic maneuvering that brought the Barbary ambassadors to London—and hence also the blow to Venice caused by the loss of Cyprus in 1571.

Martin Amis, in his wonderful book *Experience*, quotes Christopher Hitchens on the moment when the twentieth-century Cold War threatened to turn hot—that island drama known as the Cuban Missile Crisis: "I remember exactly where I was standing and who I was with at the moment that President Kennedy nearly killed me."[14]

Think of the wave of relief at the end of that week in October 1962. Map it back onto Shakespeare, and you might think of the wave of relief in act 2 of *Othello* with the news of the dispersal of the Turkish fleet by the Christian God's stormy hand. But you might also think of the wave of relief in 1588 after the dispersal of the Spanish fleet by the Protestant God's stormy hand. And with that conjunction you see the greater complexity of sixteenth-century geopolitics compared with twentieth: there were two Cold (sometimes Hot) Wars, not one—between the Christian western Mediterranean and the Islamic east, and between the Protestant north of Europe and the Catholic south.

In *Purchas his Pilgrimage* Algiers is referred to as "the whip of the Christian World, the wall of the Barbarian, terror of Europe, the bridle of both Hesperias (Italy and Spain), scourge of the Islands." North Africa— where Othello and Caliban are conceived—is a demonic "alien" territory. But at the same time, the Turks and their satellite states were vital trading partners for the English. Algiers had a golden age of commercial prosperity around the turn of the century, while at the other end of the sea Aleppo was a key trading -post on the silk route to China.

In *Othello*, it is not the Turk but Iago who "turns" Othello back to barbarity. If we want to read the play for a contemporary political "message," the newly-anointed King's Men might be saying to the new king, "It's not the stranger, the alien power, the Turk, who is now the threat—they have been defeated, as you reminded us in your poem on the battle of Lepanto;[15] no, the danger is the cunning, self-serving politicker, the enemy within." One might even go so far as to identify that enemy with Catholicism and Spanish sympathy. Why does the Venetian Iago have a Spanish name, reminiscent of St. Iago of Compostella, who was known as Matamoros, the Moor killer?[16]

Should we consider it part of the hinterland of the play that in the late sixteenth century there was a fair bit of snuggling up between the English and the Turks because their common enemy was Catholic Spain? In the 1580s we find Elizabeth's diplomats in Istanbul pointing out that English Protestantism shared with Islam a rejection of that veneration of idolatrous images which characterized Spanish and Papal power. The queen actually sent some fragments of broken images to the sultan as a token of her good intent.

There is deep irony in Iago's "Nay, it is true, or else I am a Turk" (2.1.114), for it *is* Iago who does the Turkish work of destroying the Christian community. All three major characters invert audience expectation: Othello is a counter-Janizzary, Desdemona is—contrary to ethnic stereotyping—a Venetian lady who is not lascivious, and Christian Iago is a functional Turk.

This said, I don't actually see the play as a direct "intervention" into contemporary diplomatic maneuvering in the way that Pory's translation of Leo Africanus was in 1600 and Knolles's *Historie of the Turkes*, with its dedication to King James, was in 1603. Shakespeare's plays use history, but they subsume geopolitics into interpersonal encounters; they are not overtly polemical; they present questions and debates, not propaganda and positions. That is why they are so amenable to re-inflection in new cultural circumstances.

There is, however, good evidence that Shakespeare read Knolles shortly before writing the play.[17] One link seems to me decisive: where did Shakespeare get the business in act 1, scene 3, about the uncertainty whether the Turks are heading for Rhodes or for Cyprus? It must be from the passage in Knolles that describes the events of April 1571. The previous year Selimus, emperor of the Turks, had made plans to invade Cyprus. He gave a commission to one Piall Bassa, a base-born Hungarian who had "turn[ed] Turk and giv[en] himself to arms." Piall fought against the Christians and was raised to the rank of Basso. He was sent by Selimus to keep the Venetians from sending reinforcements for their garrison in Cyprus. He departed from Constantinople and, says Knolles, cut through Propontis and Hellespont (a juxtaposition of names that might have stuck in Shakespeare's mind—remember the Pontic sea that keeps due on to the Propontic and the Hellespont). But Piall then heard that there was plague at Venice, so it was unlikely that the Venetians would be taking any action in the short term. He therefore diverted and attacked the island of Tenedos in the Cyclades, which had been in Venetian possession but desisted because his superior general, Mustapha, summoned him to Rhodes with the intention of joining their two armies together and sailing against Cyprus. This must be the source of the Messenger's announcement that the Turks

> Steering with due course toward the isle of Rhodes,
> Have there injointed them with an after fleet . . .
> Of thirty sail; and now they do restem
> Their backward course, bearing with frank appearance
> Their purposes toward Cyprus.

(1.3.34–39)

Even more specifically, Knolles tells of how one Angelus Sorianus was sent with his galley to meet the Venetian ambassador who bore the Turkish ultimatum demanding possession of Cyprus: this is surely the source of the messenger from the galleys saying, "So was I bid report here to the state / By Signior Angelo" (1.3.15–16).[18]

Knolles has been accepted as a source by most scholars for some time, but I don't think anyone has paused on the significance of Piall Bassa, the renegade Christian Hungarian who turned Turk and led the attack on Venetian-controlled Cyprus. I suspect that it was the story of Piall that furnished Shakespeare with the idea of giving depth and historical specificity to Cinthio's tale of the Venetian Moor sent to defend Cyprus: like Piall, Othello has risen from an obscure background to become a great general and in so doing changed his religion. But he is a reverse renegade.

There is another suggestive passage in Knolles. How were the Venetians in control of Cyprus in the first place? In the early fifteenth century it had been an independent kingdom, but in 1523 the throne passed to one King John, who lacked courage and gave himself to pleasure, Knolles writes that "according to the manner of his effeminate education, [he] showed himself in all things more like a woman than a man." His wife took over the running of Cyprus while he devoted himself to vain pleasures. The wife was in turn ruled by the counsel of her nurse. And the nurse was ruled by her daughter. "So that the people commonly said the daughter ruled the nurse, the nurse the queen and the queen the king." The result of this was a disordered kingdom, usurpation, civil war, and an eventual league that brought in the Venetians to restore order. They paid off the Egyptians, who had a longstanding claim for the island, and ruled it peaceably for over a century. But Selimus I conquered Egypt, and in 1570 Selimus II, reviving the Egyptian claim but now on behalf of the Ottomon empire, attacked Cyprus, taking the capital Nicosia and—the following year, through the fleet of Mustapha and Piall Bassa—the fortified port of Famagusta.

Shakespeare changes history. He sees off the Turk and implies instead that the real danger to the isle comes from the internal collapse of civil society. The story of how the Cypriots originally lost control of their own island due to emasculation serves as a model for this: think of Othello's harsh reaction to Cassio's drunkenness, the idea that having been saved from the Turks the Venetians are now destroying themselves and "fright[-ing] the isle / From her propriety" (2.3.175–76); and think of how central it is to Iago's scheme that he should persuade Cassio that Othello is ruled by his wife—that Desdemona has become our captain's captain in the manner of the wife of old King John of Cyprus (though, fortunately, she is not ruled by her nurse). Venice regarded Cyprus as a key Christian outpost against the Turk, but what happens in the play is that it is "heathenized" from within rather than without.

Montano, the governor of Cyprus, is an interesting figure in this respect. Despite his name, he seems to be a Cypriot, not a Venetian regent. He is addressed as one of the "men of Cyprus" and later as a "gallant of Cyprus." His welcome of Othello and the Venetians is thus like the old history of Venice helping to restore order after the reign of the effeminate King John. But the falling out between Cassio and Montano becomes symbolic of Venice's losing Cyprus. The divine intervention of the storm means that the island is not lost to the Turk, but destabilized through internal division. "For even out of that will I cause these of Cyprus to mutiny" (2.1.274–75), says Iago: Cyprus being an occupied state, the danger of mutiny within and of civil war is greater than the threat from without.

A lesson for early Jacobean Ireland perhaps? Like the imaginary Turkish fleet in the play, the real Spanish armadas that had made for Ireland in 1596 and 1597 were dispersed by storms—but this did not make life any easier for the occupying English military garrison. Shakespeare was a typical post-Armada Englishman: as he had showed in his history plays, the true threat to the polity was rebellion rather than invasion.

Othello dies on a kiss, an embrace of black and white, perhaps a symbolic reconciliation of the virtues of West and East, Europe and orient; but the public image he wants to be remembered by in the letter back to Venice is of confrontation between Christian and Turk, with himself as the defender of Christianity in Aleppo, that point of eastern extremity in Syria. In smiting himself, he recognizes that he has now become the Turk. By killing Desdemona he has renounced his Christian civility and damned himself. He symbolically takes back upon himself the insignia of Islam— turban, circumcision—that he had renounced when he turned Christian. He has beaten a Venetian wife and traduced the state. He has been turned Turk—not, however, by the general Ottoman but by the super-subtle Venetian, the "honest" Iago.

\*     \*     \*

I now want to turn to late Shakespeare, beginning from an enduring puzzle. Robert Greene's popular romance *Pandosto* told the story of a king of Bohemia who mistakenly believed that his wife was pregnant by his old friend the king of Sicilia. Shakespeare's most celebrated alteration of this story when he dramatized it into *The Winter's Tale* was the resurrection of the wronged queen, but his most puzzling was the inversion of the kingdoms. The jealous fit falls upon Sicilia instead of Bohemia.

The winter weather in Prague is somewhat colder than that in Palermo. Would it not therefore have been better to follow the original by locating the chilly court of Leontes in snowy middle Europe and the summer shepherding in sunny Sicily, which was, besides, the reputed birthplace of Theocritus, father of the pastoral genre? If Hermione is to be made the daughter of the emperor of Russia, would it not—from both a geographical and a dynastic point of view—have been more plausible to marry her to the king of nearby Bohemia rather than that of a distant Mediterranean island?

Various explanations have been proffered. Perhaps Shakespeare made the reversal so that Perdita would become a daughter of Sicily, thus furthering her resemblance to Proserpine, her mythic prototype and fellow transformer of winter to spring.[19] Or perhaps it was because "Sicily was well known for crimes of jealousy and revenge, while Bohemia with its fabled sea-coast was currently a frequent center for romantic adventure."[20] Stephen Orgel argues that the location of the shipwreck and Antigonus's death on the coast of Bohemia, which was in reality landlocked, as opposed to Sicilia, which is in reality an island, should be regarded, like the title of the play, as something that purposefully "removes the action from the world of literal geographical space as it is removed from historical time."[21]

These explanations are genre-dependent. They grow from a perception of the play as romance, myth, pastoral, tale. They ask us to detach Bohemia and Sicilia from their counterparts in the real world of early modern European geopolitics. Similar explanations would not have been forthcoming if Shakespeare had swapped England and Scotland in a history play. But are we to suppose that Shakespearean romance is wholly divorced from history and geopolitics? *The Tempest* is very interested in statecraft and dynastic liaison, while *Cymbeline* is one of Shakespeare's two extended meditations on what political historians call the "British Question." *The Winter's Tale* opens, in the exchange between Camillo and Archidamus, with the language of courtiership, not that of fairy. (And even to invoke that latter word is to be given an instant Spenserian reminder that for the Elizabethans the poesy of romance and pastoral was a powerful medium for the exploration of courtiership and the expression of royal compliment.)

Shakespeare wrote all his later plays in the knowledge that the King's Men were required to give more command performances at court than any other theater company. Would he not have paused for a moment to consider the diplomatic resonances of such names as Bohemia and Sicilia in *The Winter's Tale*, Milan and Naples in *The Tempest*? After all, he knew from his run-in with the descendants of Sir John Oldcastle a decade earlier that to attach the wrong associations to a particular name could easily offend.

However removed from historical reality the action may be, to invoke the kingdoms of Bohemia and Sicilia, especially in front of court audiences that might include visiting diplomats, would inevitably create a penumbra of geopolitical associations.

In the time of Shakespeare's father, the difference between the two realms in terms of political association would have been nugatory. As Holy Roman Emperor, Charles V ruled the greater part of Europe, including both Sicily and Bohemia. But Shakespeare himself lived after the division of the House of Habsburg into distinct Spanish and Austrian branches. In his time, the two kingdoms fell under separate spheres of influence. Sicilia—or more exactly, the kingdom of the two Sicilies, one consisting of the island and the other of southern Italy (otherwise known as the kingdom of Naples)—was at the heart of the Mediterranean empire of Philip II of Spain, while Bohemia became the core of the Holy Roman Empire. When Rudolf II became emperor in 1576, he moved the seat of his government from Vienna to Prague. In Shakespeare's time, the title of King of Sicilia belonged to Spain, while the King of Bohemia was the senior secular elector of the Habsburg Empery.

The other crucial difference was religious: Sicily was Catholic, whereas for two hundred years the Bohemians had been divided from Rome; the Hussite rising of 1419–20 was in effect the first Reformation in Europe. In the words of Rudolf II's modern biographer, "If to be Protestant is to be anti-papal, anti-clerical, and fiercely fundamentalist on matters of morality, then the majority of Czechs became Protestants *avant la lettre*."[22]

Fictional and fanciful as *The Winter's Tale* may be, the fact is that when the play was written the king of Sicilia was Philip III of Spain, and the king of Bohemia was the emperor Rudolf II. There were strong links between the courts of James in London and Rudolf in Prague. Rudolf's court was famously hospitable to English intellectuals, ranging from John Dee, the magician, to the young woman who became one of the most famous poets in all Europe, Elizabeth Jane Weston. There were also striking resemblances between the two monarchs, especially in the areas of their interest in magic and their desire for European peacemaking through interdenominational matchmaking.[23] These two preoccupations were closely related: Rudolf's obsession with alchemy, natural magic and Rosicrucianism was not some eccentric aberration of his melancholy personality, but rather a way to a deeper religious vision and unity beyond the confessional divisions that racked his empire. Magic and royal matchmaking were also, of course, distinctly late Shakespearean subjects.

Conversely, despite the Catholicism of James's queen and the king's various attempts to match his children to clients of Spain, the residual English hostility to all things Spanish, dating back to the Armada and beyond, had not gone away. In these circumstances, it seems eminently plausible that on deciding to dramatize a story about the kings of Sicilia and Bohemia, and knowing that the play would at some point go into the court repertoire, Shakespeare thought it would be politic to make the monarch with Spanish, as opposed to Rudolfine, associations the one who is irrational, cruel, and blasphemous. I am not proposing that Leontes is in any sense a representation of Philip or Polixenes of Rudolf, but rather that tact was required in the invocation of the names of European kingdoms.

Shakespeare's tact towards Bohemia, a synecdoche for the Austro-Germanic Habsburg territories, was indeed such that *The Winter's Tale* could be played at court without embarrassment during the 1612–13 festivities in celebration of the wedding of King James's daughter Elizabeth to the Habsburg princeling, Frederick the Elector Palatine—who, as it happens, would later become king of Bohemia.

Stephen Orgel's admirable Oxford edition of *The Winter's Tale* touches on the Bohemian connection, but says nothing about the status of Sicily in Shakespeare's time. There is, however, firm evidence that Shakespeare knew it was controlled by Spain. The principal source of his other Sicilian play, *Much Ado about Nothing*, is a story in Bandello set at the precise moment when Spain assumed power over Sicily.[24] Shakespeare substitutes an army for Bandello's navy, but the Messina of Don Pedro is manifestly in Spanish hands.

Whether or not I am right in supposing that geopolitical sensitivity lay behind Shakespeare's transposition of Sicilia and Bohemia, *The Winter's Tale* can still be thought of as a play that works on a north-south axis, as opposed to the east-west one of *Othello*. The weird temporal syncretism of *The Winter's Tale* enacts the early modern rebirth of classical civilization: Apollo thunders and Ovid's Pygmalion is reborn as Giulio Romano; the setting moves between the temple of the Delphic oracle on a balmy Greek island, a very English-seeming sheep-shearing feast, and a private chapel reached via a picture gallery and housing a Madonna-like statue. The essential geographical structure, meanwhile, is an opposition between a hot-blooded, court-dominated—hence Catholic?—south and a more relaxed, temperate north in which ordinary people (shepherd and clown) have a voice, as they do in the Protestant world where the Bible is available in the vernacular.

*     *     *

About 150 years after the house of Aragon seized Sicily, Alfonso V took the kingdom of Naples. Both Sicily and the southern half of Italy were under Spanish control throughout the sixteenth and seventeenth centuries. The Spanish crown also held considerable territories in the northern half of Italy, including the garrison city of Milan. Which brings me to *The Tempest*. We tend to think of Milan in that play as an autonomous dukedom and Naples as a sovereign kingdom. Insofar as we think about it all, we assume that the dynastic liaison established by the marriage of Miranda and Ferdinand represents some kind of north-south unification of Italian statelets intended to counterbalance the papal power of Rome. In the imaginary afterlife of the play's plot, Ferdinand, son of Alonso, will one day be both king of Naples and duke of Milan. In the historical reality of early modern Italy, both Milan and Naples were under the dominion of the Spanish crown.[25]

I am not sure that editors of *The Tempest* have noted how profoundly the name Ferdinand—perhaps also Alonso, if we hear in it an echo of Alfonso—was associated with Spanish dominion over Naples.[26] Alfonso V, the first Iberian king of Naples, was succeeded by his illegitimate son Ferdinand, who struggled to maintain his kingdom against Turkish inroads, baronial revolts, and Venetian hostilities. He was succeeded by his son, another Alfonso, who after a brief and unpopular reign made a Prospero-like retreat: he "renounced his state unto his son Ferdinand . . . and sailed into Sicily, where he gave himself to study, solitariness, and religion."[27] This Ferdinand lost Naples to the French, withdrew to Sicily, recovered Naples with the assistance of the Spaniards and the Venetians, then died suddenly, bringing the line of the illegitimate Ferdinand to an end, after which the kingdom of Naples was ruled by the Spanish crown through a viceroy. It has been suggested that Shakespeare knew William Thomas's *History of Italy*, where this sequence of four generations of Alfonsos and Ferdinands is outlined, but regardless of the question of specific sources, the names carry the aura of Spanish power.

William Warner in *Albion's England* refers casually to "The free-*Italian* States, of which the *Spaniards* part have won: / As *Naples*, Milan, royal That, and Duchy This."[28] Our thinking of the play in relation to imperialism receives a jolt from the idea that Milan was a colonized city-state and the kingdom of Naples a dominion of Spain. To a Jacobean audience— especially a court audience in the historical and diplomatic know— Prospero is more likely to have been regarded as the victim of intrigue that had Spanish villainy somewhere behind it than as any sort of imperial adventurer. Perhaps we should think of him as a displaced General Vichy rather than a prototypical Cecil Rhodes. But then again perhaps we should think of him as either neither or both, for what is striking about *The Tempest* is its pointed absence of allusion to Spanish matter, its lack of referential anchorage. This is not the Spanish Italy of *Much Ado about Nothing*.

*The Tempest* begins on a ship bound from Tunis to Naples. The exchange in act 2 about Carthage and "widow Dido" has led critics to read this voyage in relation to Virgil's *Aeneid* and the legendary foundations of Rome. Reflection on the legacy of Rome has a similar effect on us to that of the imaginary alliance between Milan and Naples: it makes us think about nation and *imperium* in Italian terms. But the reality of sixteenth- and early seventeenth-century Tunis was that it was a flashpoint between Spain and the Ottomans. Just as he is quiet about Spanish Naples and Milan, so Shakespeare is intriguingly silent about the allegiance of Claribel's "African" husband. We are not told where in historical time the marriage should be imagined: when Tunis was a Spanish puppet state, when it was under the autonomous control of Euldj Ali, the corsair king of Algiers, or after Ali had enlisted the support of the Turks.[29]

Similarly with Algiers. The supposed coupling of Sycorax and the devil suggests that Caliban is the product of some form of miscegenation, of hybrid union. Around the time *The Tempest* was written, Algiers had what Braudel calls "a fabric of many colors." It housed some twenty thousand prisoners, about half of them Christian (Portuguese, Flemish, English, Scottish, Hungarian, Danish, Irish, Slav, French, Spanish, and Italian), the other half "heretics and idolaters" (Syrians, Egyptians, Japanese, Chinese, Ethiopians, inhabitants of New Spain)—"and every nation of course provided its crop of renegades."[30] Samuel Purchas reckoned that there were two hundred thousand Christians resident in Algiers, most of them renegades.[31] But instead of making Caliban the product of some specific union between a Christian and a Muslim, Shakespeare suggests various more abstract kinds of hybrid encounters, between the human and the devilish, the human and the animal, the land and the sea ("A strange fish!"). This process of abstraction from the particularities of Mediterranean setting that had characterized *Othello* has been crucial to the afterlife of the play.

In *The Tempest* Shakespeare is careful to remove precise references to historical time and geographic place. Most obviously, he does not name or locate the island. The dialogue about Tunis and Carthage draws pointed attention to the dangers of making historical equations, of arguing by the sort of parallelisms beloved of Plutarch and Fluellen:

—This Tunis, sir, was Carthage.
—Carthage?
—I assure you, Carthage.
—His word is more than the miraculous harp.
—He hath rais'd the wall, and houses too.
—What impossible matter will he make easy next?
—I think he will carry this island home in his pocket, and give it his son for an apple.
—And sowing the kernels of it in the sea, bring forth more islands.

(2.1.84–94)

Gonzalo is wrong. Tunis is not on the exact site of Carthage. Neither physically nor politically is the modern city a replication of the ancient one. To suppose that ancient history can be brought back to life is to outdo the music of Amphion's harp, which magically rebuilt the walls of Thebes.

Similarly, the realities of the island do not conform to the "Golden Age" image conjured up by Gonzalo. It follows that we must be wary of parallelisms that propose *The Tempest* as a modern *Aeneid* and the island as an allegory of either Mediterranean or new world empires. At the same time, the very placelessness of the island—its U-topian quality— encourages the spectator to pick it up like Gonzalo's apple and scatter the seeds so that other islands—Caribbean, Irish, and so forth—grow magically from it.

The art of *The Tempest* makes impossible matter easy. By veiling the real history of the sixteenth-century Mediterranean, Shakespeare takes his play out of contemporaneous geopolitics and gives it the potential to live in later history. As critics such as Jeffrey Knapp and historians such as David Armitage have shown, there was really no such thing as an English empire (beyond Ireland) during Shakespeare's lifetime.[32] The great continental shift of geopolitics from the Mediterranean to the Atlantic was in its earliest infancy. The evacuation of historical specificity from *The Tempest* is a conjuring trick that creates the illusion that Shakespeare prophesied the subsequent history of British imperialism. This made possible the manner in which the play was most frequently read in the post-Vietnam, postcolonial portion of the twentieth-century Cold War.

*Othello* is located on the east-west frontier between Christianity and Islam, with Othello himself functioning as the *tertium quid* that veers between the world's two dominant religions. *The Winter's Tale* plays off the Catholic south and the Protestant north. *The Tempest* returns to Marlowe's strategy in *The Jew of Malta* of compressing all the world onto the stage of a single island. But with a difference. Shakespeare *could* have grounded his play in the Balearics and made Caliban a renegade, Prospero an exile from Spanish power, and Stephano and Trinculo English privateers. He did not. He replaced Malta with Utopia, rendering the island a pure conceptual space—or rather a purely theatrical space, for it is here that our sense of the resemblance between an island and a theater is strongest.

The play thus becomes readable as a drama of north, south, east, and west. That is why it is (along with *Hamlet*) Shakespeare's most Shakespearean work, and why it is (beyond even *Hamlet*) the play most amenable to richly productive reappropriation. "Politics merely followed the outline of an underlying reality," wrote Braudel of the environmental influence on Mediterranean history. Not so in *The Tempest*: by displacing the underlying reality of the early modern Mediterranean, Shakespeare mirrors the gigantic shadows cast by future history. We have learned to acknowledge this play as the legislator of a whole new world. It offers, in John Pitcher's fine phrase, "a theatre of the future."[33]

Shakespeare lives when he is read and performed in ways that are simultaneously tuned to the present and true to the text. The "new world" reading of *The Tempest* has been achieved at some cost in the latter respect. I sometimes worry that we have brought up a whole generation of students to make the tacit assumption that the play is located somewhere near Bermuda, and that Prospero's "rotten carcass of a butt, not rigged, / Nor tackle, sail, nor mast" (1.2.146–47)—not to mention Sycorax's boat to exile—has somehow made the long Atlantic crossing.

Predictions are odious, but there is a strong likelihood that twenty-first-century *Tempest*s won't have this problem. Assuming that the United States and China will find ways of accommodating each other, the focus of geopolitical tension will return to the Mediterranean. Shakespearean interpretation in the second half of the twentieth century was shaped by post-colonial anxiety and a Cold War-induced preoccupation with the rights of the individual and the limits of the state. In our not-so-brave new millennium, the battle lines will be closer to those of the sixteenth-century Mediterranean: between the forces of global capitalism and the imperatives of Islam. *The Tempest* will, I suspect, be drawn back toward Tunis and Algiers. Shakespeare's Venice, meanwhile, will serve as a paradigm of global capitalism, and a new spin will be given to the thorny problem we have been grappling with for so long now: how shall we best represent the "alien"? Aaron and Shylock and Othello and Caliban will remain center-stage.

## Notes

1. Fernand Braudel, *Le Méditerranée et le Monde Méditerranéen à l'Époque de Philippe II*, trans. Siân Reynolds, abr. Richard Ollard (London: HarperCollins, 1992), 100–1.

2. Braudel, *Le Méditerrainée*, 65–67.

3. *2 Tamburlaine* 1.1.21–22, 61–64, quoted from *Tamburlaine*, ed. J. W. Harper (London: Black, 1971).

4. For the complex interplay of Christian, Muslim, and Jew in the early modern Mediterranean, see Bernard Lewis, *Cultures in Conflict: Christians, Muslims and Jews in the Age of Discovery* (Oxford: Oxford University Press, 1995). For the process of linked demonization, A. H. and H. E. Cutler, *The Jew as Ally of the Muslim: Medieval Roots of Anti-Semitism* (Notre Dame: University of Notre Dame Press, 1986).

5. Does an oxymoronic conjunction unite opposites or highlight contradictions? See the discussions relating Othello to Leo Africanus in Emily Bartels, "Making More of the Moor: Aaron, Othello, and Renaissance Refashionings of Race," *Shakespeare Quarterly* 41 (1990): 433–54; and Michael Neill, "'Mulattos,' 'Blacks,' and 'Indian Moors': *Othello* and Early Modern Constructions of Human Difference," *Shakespeare Quarterly* 49 (1998): 361–74. For Bartels, a positive reading of Leo leads to a perception of Othello as an assimilated Christian: the Moor *of Venice*. But for Neill, Leo's "amphibian" identity as both Muslim and Christian suggests a hybridity that would have been regarded as inherently monstrous: the *Moor* of Venice.

6. *Othello* 1.3.48–49.

7. There may also be a more distant resonance: "Othman" was also an alternative spelling of Uthman, third caliph of the Islamic Empire back in the seventh century. A son-in-law of the prophet Muhammad, it was under his rule that the Arabs became a naval power and extended their rule to North Africa and Cyprus. Before being assassinated, he oversaw the compilation of the authoritative version of the Qur'an.

8. George Peele, *The Battle of Alcazar 1594* (London: Malone Society Reprints, 1907), ll. 9–10, 15.

9. See Bernard Harris, "A Portrait of a Moor," in *Shakespeare and Race*, ed. Catherine M. S. Alexander and Stanley Wells (Cambridge: Cambridge University Press, 2000), 23–36 (first published in *Shakespeare Survey* 11, 1958).

10. On this, see Daniel J. Vitkus's excellent article, "Turning Turk in *Othello*: The Conversion and Damnation of the Moor," *Shakespeare Quarterly* 48 (1997): 145–76.

11. See Nabil Matar, *Islam in Britain, 1558–1685* (Cambridge: Cambridge University Press, 1998), 27. I am deeply indebted to this admirable study.

12. *1 Tamburlaine* 3.1.8–9.

13. See J. H. Elliott, *Europe Divided, 1559–1598*, 2d ed. (Oxford: Blackwell, 2000), 122–25.

14. Martin Amis, *Experience* (London: Jonathan Cape, 2000), 137 n.

15. On Lepanto and *Othello*, see Emrys Jones, "*Othello, Lepanto*, and the Cyprus Wars," *Shakespeare Survey* 21 (1970): 47–52. For the historical context, see Andrew Hess, "The Battle of Lepanto and its place in Mediterranean History," *Past and Present* 57 (1972): 53–73. For suggestive remarks on Shakespeare's creation of "a seemingly historical background by transforming international violence into dreamland peace," see Philip Edwards, "Shakespeare, Ireland, Dreamland," *Irish University Review* 28 (1998): 227–39 (232).

16. See Barbara Everett, "'Spanish' Othello: The Making of Shakespeare's Moor," *Shakespeare and Race*, 64–81 (first published in *Shakespeare Survey* 35, 1982).

17. Since *The Historie of the Turkes* was published in 1603, this to my mind disproves Ernst Honigmann's argument in his recent Arden edition for a 1601–2 rather than the traditional 1603–4 date for *Othello*.

18. Because Honigmann wants to argue for an early date, his Arden edition says nothing of any of this.

19. Ernst Honigmann, "Secondary Sources of *The Winter's Tale*," *Philological Quarterly* 34 (1955): 27–38. Cf. Jonathan Bate, *Shakespeare and Ovid* (Oxford: Clarendon Press, 1993), 232.

20. Geoffrey Bullough, *Narrative and Dramatic Sources of Shakespeare*, 8 vols. (London: Routledge and Kegan Paul, 1957–75), 8:125.

21. Stephen Orgel, introduction to his edition of *The Winter's Tale* (Oxford: Oxford University Press, 1996), 37.

22. R. J. W. Evans, *Rudolf II and his World: A Study in Intellectual History, 1576–1612* (Oxford: Clarendon Press, 1973), 29.

23. On this, see Evans, *Rudolf II*, 80–83. For speculations as to Rudolf's possible influence on the figures of the Duke in *Measure for Measure* and Prospero in *The Tempest*, see Robert Grudin, "Rudolf II of Prague and Cornelius Drebbel: Shakespearean Archetypes?" *Huntington Library Quartery* 54 (1991): 181–205. David Scott Kastan speculates interestingly on the Rudolfine context of *The Tempest* in his *Shakespeare after Theory* (New York and London: Routledge), 191–94.

24. Known to Shakespeare possibly in the French version of Belleforest.

25. The large body of scholarship on Shakespeare's representations of Italy is highly variable in the extent to which it does or does not attach weight to the Spanish influence. For starting points, see *Shakespeare's Italy: Functions of Italian Locations in Renaissance Drama*, ed. Michele Marrapodi et al. (Manchester: Manchester University Press, 1993).

26. Although Orgel again comes closest, when he makes passing mention of the

Aragonese connection in a note on how "The search for historical figures behind the play in fact offers some possibilities that resonate tantalizingly"; *The Tempest*, ed. Stephen Orgel (Oxford: Oxford University Press, 1987), 43 n.

27. Thus W. Thomas, *History of Italy* (1549), cited by Bullough, *Sources of Shakespeare*, 8.249–50, as a book that Shakespeare probably knew.

28. *Albion's England*, 12.75, quoted in Jeffrey Knapp, *An Empire Nowhere: England, America and Literature from "Utopia" to "The Tempest"* (Berkeley and Los Angeles: University of California Press, 1992), 334n.

29. For further speculation on the significance of Tunis, see Richard Wilson, "Voyage to Tunis: New History and Old World in *The Tempest*," *ELH* 64 (1997): 333–57. Also several valuable essays in *"The Tempest" and its Travels*, ed. Peter Hulme and William Sherman (London: Reaktion, 2000).

30. Braudel, *Le Méditerranée*, 645.

31. See Matar, *Islam in Britain*, 16.

32. Knapp, *An Empire Nowhere*; David Armitage, "Literature and Empire," in *The Oxford History of the British Empire, vol. 1, The Origins of Empire* (Oxford: Oxford University Press, 1998), 99–123.

33. John Pitcher, "'A Theatre of the Future': *The Aeneid* and *The Tempest*," *Essays in Criticism* 34 (1984): 193–215.

# Painted Devils and Aery Nothings: Metamorphoses and Magic Art

MARINA WARNER

ON THE HELLENO-ROMAN WORLD MAP, THE MEDITERRANEAN WAS CALLED "Our Sea," but not because it was familiar or tame—or homely. Besides its natural perils of pirates and storms, it was a supernatural sea, of cyclopes and sirens, whirlpools and typhoons, ordeals and prodigies, monsters and miracles; and it was charted according to imaginary journeys, fabulous quests, and heroic epic. It is not the earliest ocean of story, but from the pillars of Hercules to the west, the Atlas Mountains to the south, the cauldron of Charybdis and the cave of Scylla near Sicily in the middle, to the gulf where Io, maddened by a sting, plunged to her death, and the peninsula—or island—where Circe cast her spells and where Delos, birthplace of the sun and the moon, lies floating, to the eastern end where Leto turned her persecutors into frogs and the slave girl Fotis gave Lucius the wrong ointment and he turned into a donkey, the Mediterranean was mapped by faerie. It could be unfolded, like the roll of a harbor-front storyteller, to follow the voyages of Ulysses, Jason, Roland, Guy of Warwick, Sinbad, or Aladdin. Those who have swum in the Mediterranean also include Europa, the nymph whose rape by Zeus in the form of a bull founded this continent, and Persephone and Dante, who descended into hell from these shores.

In the Thyssen collection in Madrid, there is a small, exquisite painting by the Ferrarese artist Ercole de' Roberti (himself named after Hercules, that Mediterranean hero), which shows Jason and his companions on the Argo sailing out of Colchis: Jason is standing protectively by Medea, who has just eloped with him, betraying her father and making off with his treasure. De' Roberti, interestingly, shows Medea's hand resting on her tummy, expressing that slowed time of pregnancy: the artist has inhabited the famous story so intimately that, proleptically, he imagines the birth of the child who will eventually be killed, when it is Jason's turn to turn traitor to his bonds.

In *The Voyage of Argo*, written in the third century B.C. by Apollonius of Rhodes (another fabulous island of Our Sea), the flight of Jason and

Medea takes them to Aeaea, to see Medea's aunt, Circe, daughter of the sun god Helios, and one of the most skillful of all magicians. The lovers beg her to purify them, but, the night before their coming, Circe has dreamed of walls streaming with blood, of fire and cacophony and terror, and so she sees that what they have done lies beyond her powers of blessing; she can offer sacrifice on their behalf, but not forgive them or save them from their fate, and she sends them uneasily on their way again.[1] Circe appears earlier of course in the *Odyssey*, with Calypso the nymph, her counterpart in charm, in music, and in seduction. She has many daughters in the tragic-comic romances that the Mediterranean carried from one port to another over the centuries before Shakespeare threw his fine-meshed nets into the same waters: the enchantress Alcina in the Roland cycles; and, in the Arthurian material carried by the Normans when they voyaged south, the fairy called Morgan le Fay—King Arthur's immortal sister, who lived in Sicily under the sea and, to divert the lovers she made captive, raised fairy spectacles, aery nothings, insubstantial pageants, and "cloud-capp'd towers" for their amusements. This meteorological phenomenon, which occurs in Sicily, is still known by her name, Fata Morgana, or in English, quoting Carlyle's comment on Coleridge's preference for fantasy, fatamorganes.

The Mediterranean was not only the seabed of legends, and the zone of metamorphosis, but more particularly of female magic, and that magic was characterized not by the sex of its makers alone, but by the kind of magic they made: spectacular and ravishing to the senses. "If this be magic," says Leontes, at Paulina's performance, "Let it be lawful as eating . . .": a prime gratification, the simple lineaments of a child's desire.

*　　*　　*

Many years ago, I sent a short story to a famous magazine; it was inspired by Ariadne's love of Theseus and her subsequent switch to Dionysus, on another island, Naxos. The editor wrote back saying that it was the policy of the magazine not to run reworkings of old tales, but to concentrate exclusively on original material.

That was in the 1970s. I am positioning my writing struggles, not claiming kinship (!) when I say that it was Shakespeare's practice to graft, splice, prune, and, of course, profoundly transform his sources, and that this approach has returned in the writing of many of the most compelling contemporary writers—for example, Margaret Atwood, Toni Morrison, Derek Walcott, Carol Ann Duffy, Anne Carson, Peter Carey—Shakespeare becoming metamorphic himself, in poetry, plays, and novels. One aspect of this form of textual horticulture, of the sort spurned by Perdita in her pastoral aspect (Perdita the stern opponent of the postmodern), intrigues me at present more than others: the return of the uses of female magic and the supernatural in storytelling, which has grown in concert, it seems, with the rise of the mythical and dream plays and the once-disparaged romances, and coexists almost unexamined with our "secular agnosticism." When I first began reading re-visioned fairy tales by Angela Carter, published in the late 1960s in the magazine *Bananas*, neither *Pericles* nor *Cymbeline* was the subject of many productions, let alone *Titus Andronicus*, with its ogreish revenges of a markedly fairytale character. Deborah Warner, who read *The Bloody Chamber* and absorbed its late Gothic admixture of cruelty and horror and delicacy and desire, was the first director to reveal to me the neglected *Titus*'s stunning dramatic power. Angela Carter herself went on to write *Wise Children*, which is saturated with plot devices, images, and characters from *A Midsummer Night's Dream* above all, but deliberately includes elements from every single one of Shakespeare's plays.

I am going to explore Shakespeare's fairy-tale uses of magic, on a map of the Mediterranean drawn according to *mentalité* rather than geography or history. In three sections, I will take metamorphosis through some of the protean wrestling holds with which Shakespeare struggles to hold the supernatural in his plays: as phantom or diabolical delusion; as a spectacle performed through stagecraft of word and magic; as Pythagorean metempsychosis, or non-Christian shape-shifting; and finally, as the conflict within poetic language itself over the heathen grotesque as ornament, as artifice, as error.

Since listening to other writers, especially Jonathan Bate, picturing the conflicting religious interests of Shakespeare's time, and Richard Wilson, arguing for Shakespeare's Catholic connections, this quartet of themes seems to me to correspond suggestively to principles of Catholic thought, as they have impinged in my imagination and writing since my childhood. For, even though I have long been an apostate to the Catholicism of my upbringing, I have found that its patterns have proved inescapable and I have given up the attempt to reconfigure them ("Once a Catholic . . ."). These principles, axiomatic to the faith, include: first, a belief in the power of images; second, a ritual practice of sacramental or performative speech; and, third and above all, a view of time as folded, like an ironed handkerchief, so that its edges meet, and extremes touch, not able to unfurl, progressively, to stream in the wind. This is providential time, which allows for change and reversal, for conversion and repentance, for all things to be recapitulated in a new form.

*     *     *

I am going to begin with some general remarks about magic, and then, as I have already written about *A Midsummer Night's Dream* and *The Tempest* elsewhere,[2] I will examine the magical themes in *The Winter's Tale*.

When Macbeth quails from the visions brought to him by his inner demons, Lady Macbeth taunts him, "'tis the eye of childhood / That fears a painted devil" (*Macbeth* 2.2.51–52). So does she dismiss made-up fantasies—both the immaterial, inward stuff that dreams are made on, and the material embodiment, made by art. Both are figments, and, as will be proven mistaken in this tragedy, she scorns their power to issue warnings and consequently prevent Macbeth from taking action. But, in her skepticism, and her chiding, is Lady Macbeth adopting the view of a proto-rationalist, anti-clerical, and enlightened philosopher when she deems the devil's illusions and such credulity childish? She is declaring herself against images in the mind's eye; as they appear to resemble pictures, implicitly she is here rejecting the theory of the icon, that an image partakes of the nature of its original. In so doing, she occupies, interestingly enough, the more accepted cultural attitude toward devils among a London audience today, but not, it is likely, that of Jacobean England. And she is shown to be rash and proud in this disbelief. Her hubris forms part of her transgressive unsexed desires, which makes her place herself outside the limits of womanly as well as creaturely humility.

Devils are invoked in many tones and registers throughout Shakespeare's plays and those of his contemporaries: they are summoned by magic; they are conjured by Joan La Pucelle in *Henry VI, Part 1*; they are seen ominously in dreams, as in *Julius Caesar*'s portents; they were raised by Sycorax, who is "a devil's dam" as well as a devil-worshipper, as Prospero reports in *The Tempest*; they are connected with Puck's merry feats and the light, mischievous sprites and fairies of *A Midsummer Night's Dream*. The three witches work their spells under the devil's auspices, or so it is strongly implied, though never explicitly stated. The hell broth that they stir in their cauldron contains ingredients that witch-hunters identified in the flying ointment used to enable participants to gather at the Witches' Sabbath; they do not tryst on the heath on foot, but sail in a sieve or "hover through the fog and filthy air." The human characters in the plays in general believe in the supernatural, which they conjure, even when it is done in jest: in *The Winter's Tale*, Paulina, who is play-acting a prodigy of metamorphosis, invests the spectacle of Hermione's resurrection with liturgical solemnity—which in turn gives it power over Leontes and the other witnesses, as well as over us in the audience. Prospero does not doubt his art; it is so manifestly present, active and reliable to him that he has to renounce its instruments—his staff, his magic cloak, his grimoire or handbook of spells—by strong measures of shattering and drowning. Nobody else doubts his powers, either, or Sycorax's for that matter before him.

So imagine a visitor from the New World to Shakespeare's England, with a twenty-first-century ethnographer's curiosity about other people's religions and beliefs: would such a tourist have been able to deduce from

Shakespeare's plays much about Christianity as a faith or a moral system? The plays would have provided plenty of research material on magic as an expression of supernatural powers—but on the Christian scheme of redemption? A sequence of unearthly phenomena—"rough magic"—moves the action; it stirs the characters to their next move: think of the opening of *Macbeth* and the creepy oracle of the three weird sisters, of the opening of *Hamlet* and his father's eerie call for remembrance and revenge. Fiendish motives, devilish plots, the narrative heartbeat of pagan and Renaissance magic—supernatural spirit forces, not the incarnate savior or the Holy Ghost, let alone the saints, work at a great depth in these stories; they nourish the very bone marrow of the plays. The vehicles of devilry are magic, and metamorphosis counts among its chief effects and prime manifestations; transformation is the dynamic and dramatic consequence of supernatural agency. Not transformation as in the natural processes of generation but aberrational disruptions in the expected course of developments govern these stories. They give a turn of the screw to the horror (*Macbeth*), or heighten the atmosphere of grotesque comedy (Bottom's translation), or add color and character to fairy enchantments. But such metamorphoses are not always staged as taking place for real: like the devils themselves, they may or may not be illusory. In *Hamlet*, the watch on the battlements sees his father's ghost before he does: these are shared, unchallenged sightings of spirits. But in *Macbeth*, the uncanny becomes internal, a private, agonizing haunting of the criminal and his accomplice: this tragedy plumbs inner depths more deeply than even *Hamlet*, for it blurs the boundaries between inner and outer manifestations of the supernatural, depicts individual fantasy itself as possessed by devils, so that nobody else, besides guilty Macbeth, sees Banquo's ghost. Vision here becomes subjective dreaming, only the private conscience fabricating phantoms, not verifiable by shared experience.

# 1

Specters inhabit Shakespeare's strongly projected interior landscapes of the mind, the dream zones into which his characters are thrust, often by some momentous crisis. Even a commonsensical secondary character, such as Antigonus in *The Winter's Tale*, becomes haunted as he prepares to carry out the order to expose the baby girl whom Hermione has borne: in a long speech, he describes how the wronged queen appeared to him the night before "in his cabin where he lay." She told him to name the child Perdita, and she predicted that, on account of his part in this crime, he would never see his wife Paulina. Antigonus imagines he's seeing a ghost:

I have heard, but not believ'd, the spirits o' th' dead
May walk again: if such thing be, thy mother
Appear'd to me last night; for ne'er was dream
So like a waking. To me comes a creature
                    . . . in pure white robes,
Like very sanctity. . . .

(3.3.16–19, 22–23)

And at this stage, the first audiences of the play would not have known that the report of Hermione's death was not true and that Antigonus was not being vouchsafed a classical monitory dream, in which the soul of the departed, in a characteristic shroud of white, appears to one still living— usually in order to save him from committing a terrible crime.[3] Shakespeare's dramatic duplicity here intensifies the effect by evoking a wild and emotional Hermione, very different from the dignified, composed, and silent bearing of the queen in front of Leontes' fury, and far more like a conventional shade, gibbering and squeaking. For, after describing the spouting torrents of her tears, Antigonus adds, "And so, with shrieks, / She melted into air" (3.3.36–37)—like the witches who appear to Macbeth and Banquo. His thought grows contradictory, and he seems unable to make up his mind about the status of the visitation. This might count as a characteristic passage of inward puzzlement and soliloquizing indirection, but it also moves to the jumpy indecisiveness about portents, visions, and imaginings that Stuart Clark has emphasized as the central dilemma in contemporaneous attitudes to the supernatural. As it is for the Macbeths at the beginning of their hauntings, "the question [is], is vision veridical?" He writes,

The intellectual history of the period (from the Protestant Reformation to the Scientific Revolution) is marked by a pervasive sense of vision's precariousness and fallibility—a feeling that it was not only the noblest of the five senses and the key to all forms of wisdom and enlightenment, but also the most vulnerable, the most unreliable, and the most problematic, and a realization, too, that this was a major obstacle that had to be confronted and perhaps overcome before anything else could be achieved.[4]

Of his uncertain dream, Antigonus first says, "Affrighted much, / I did in time collect myself, and thought / This was so, and no slumber." Then he adds, turning it over in his mind in short, broken phrases, "Dreams are toys; / Yet for this once, yea, superstitiously, / I will be squar'd by this" (3.3.37–42). So, dreams are toys: childish things. Like belief in painted devils. But they are also prophetic.

The theme of childish make-believe and adults' corresponding fancy threads its colors through *The Winter's Tale* with more revealing significance; it links up to Lady Macbeth's mistaken scorn for "the eye of child-hood" and to the great question about dream reality and magic's power not only to give the illusion of life but also to animate and change phenomena.

At the start of act 2, when Mamillius is encouraged by his mother, Hermione, to tell a tale, merry or sad, for her and her ladies of the court, the boy responds with an intertextual allusion to the play's title, "A sad tale's best for winter: I have one / Of sprites and goblins" (2.1.25).[5] His mother teases him, that he should do his best to "fright" her; "you're pow'rful at it" she adds, encouragingly (2.1.27).

In *Shakespeare's Language*, Frank Kermode takes the tale as sad, and comments that Mamillius's story is "perhaps a precognition of his own death and the fate of his mother, to whom alone he is willing to tell it."[6] But this sense of melancholy intimacy misses Mamillius describing his sad tale as "one with sprites and goblins"; Mamillius's telling it "softly" in his mother's ear, unheard by the audience, might be spooky whispering, in order to fright her more with the climax. From the opening: "There was a man . . . Dwelt by a churchyard. . . ," the story promises specters. M. R. James, the great antiquarian and classicist writer of ghost stories, identified it as a perennial piece of folklore: a man violates a grave for the treasure buried there, and the corpse rises from the tomb and comes after him, coming closer and closer. The story involves a game, climaxing in a variety of Boo! for the teller also draws closer and closer until he suddenly pounces on his hapless listener. M. R. James writes, "With a hoarse scream of 'You've got it!,' the ghost seizes back his gold from the grave-robber." James imagined Mamillius suddenly raising his voice and even jumping up on "the youngest of the court ladies present."[7] Such games played among children, are even depicted on Greek vases and Roman sarcophagi, often with one of the players masked, in adult disguise, as ogre or satyr.[8]

Shakespeare did not need to write out the whole tale, but, as it were, fades it behind the eruption of Leontes with his rage upon him, an apparition that is all too real. The crucial point is that such a bogeyman game replicates, in its foolery, the horror of the delusion that grips Leontes when Hermione's infidelity becomes the overwhelming reality for him, and affects him so powerfully that he loses all sense of anything else, overthrowing his judgment.

The speech that has been reckoned the obscurest and most confused in Shakespeare then returns to the paradoxical condition of dream experience; it becomes the prime analogy of Leontes' terror that he has been betrayed. This distracted soliloquy is overheard rather than addressed to any listener, even though Leontes is actually looking in Mamillius's eyes. Here, as with "painted devils," the illusion exists between word and act, a magic conjuration.

> may't be?—
> Affection! . . .
> Thou dost make possible things not so held,
> Communicat'st with dreams (how can this be?),
> With what's unreal thou co-active art

(1.2.137–41)

That the bugbears of child's play—joke phantoms conjured by false vision and not dispelled by reason—have an analogy in the disturbed mental terrors provoked by superstition or by madness, such as Leontes' jealousy, furnishes one of the major metaphors at work in this romance. It echoes in the exchanges about dreams between Leontes and Hermione in act 3. Hermione declares, "My life stands in the level of your dreams, / Which I'll lay down." Leontes replies, "Your actions are my dreams" (i.e., his worst nightmares). Hermione then accepts her banishment, falling back on the language of her son Mamillius's game: "The bug which you would fright me with, I seek" (3.2.80 ff.), where bug means spook, or devil. The Coverdale translation of the Bible, for example, which was made for Henry VIII and published in 1535, is known as the "Bug Bible" on account of its translation of Psalm 91:5: "Thou shalt not nede to be afrayed of eny bugges by night"—and the line does not mean mosquitoes. It is Beelzebub, one of the devil's most vivid names, who is termed "Lord of the Flies"—that is to say bugs—in the Second Book of Kings (1:2).

The ambiguity of dream evidence achieves its climactic spectacle in the daring *coup de théâtre* of Hermione's waking; for this resurrection fulfills dream longings for Leontes; her return to life shares the character of a ghostly visitation; like Macbeth's victims, the innocent Hermione, dead from Leontes' wrongdoing, comes back to life before his eyes. Paulina makes great play with her role as magician: she explicitly evokes conjuring, only in order to dismiss it; her spell is lawful, she says, as she acts the magician to full effect. Leontes is struck with wonder as he sees his long-lost wife breathe again: "There is an air comes from her. What fine chisel / Could ever yet cut breath?" (5.3.78–79).

This truly marvelous act is staged—both by Hermione and Paulina for Leontes, and by Shakespeare for us—in the form of a masque, foreshadowing the summoning of the three goddesses of fertility by Prospero's magic art. When Hermione is restored—in a scene that when staged has power to move the spectator to tears again and again—Paulina comments that such a twist "should be hooted at / Like an old tale" (5.3.116–17).

Playing with the wilder reaches of conventional storytelling brightens the wonderful, Monty-Pythonesque banter about ballads between Autolycus and the Shepherdesses and Clown—and the songs' far-fetched plots and outrageous, irreducible claims to absolute truth. The stories stand to the statue of Hermione as Mamillius's game of Boo!—his own illusion, his own scary, sad winter's tale—stands to dream evidence, to the monsters produced in Leontes' disordered brain. In the hall of mirrors that is representation, artifacts, such as a painted statue, can make as convincing a pretense of reality as a shameless ballad or winter's tale, full of improbabilities, that succeeds in frightening one out of one's wits. Kermode has noted how frequently (eight times) the word "mock" and variations occur in this play: mockery and foolery have a way of turning out to be real.[9] Analogously, in *The Merry Wives of Windsor*, Shakespeare invents a mock metamorphosis, when Falstaff plays Herne the Hunter, and imagines himself to be Jupiter in various guises; here, on a different register of buffoonery and revenge, his pretense brings down real consequences on his head.

But in this business of scaring and tricking and deluding, authority has passed to children and to women: only an unsexed female like Lady Macbeth could angrily condemn this order of experience. (I think here that the argument of Ted Hughes in *Shakespeare and the Goddess of Supreme Being* deserves a more careful appraisal than it received. Hughes proposed that Shakespeare's enforced disavowal of the Roman church involved him in a larger rejection of the female principle, embodied by Venus and the Virgin Mary, and that this profound conflict can be seen in his poetry [*Venus and Adonis*] and in his plays.[10]) One passage in *The Winter's Tale* has proved a riddle: the New Arden editor comments, "it sounds a likely folklore theme that might be found in ballad or play, but it has not been traced."[11] But it might have been inspired by a medieval miracle story, and this would represent a deepening of Shakespeare's concern with the connectedness of art and vision, of the perceptual affinity between the imaginary life of an image in stone and the illusion of a figure in a dream. Paulina is talking to Leontes about the second marriage his courtiers are urging on him; he does not need much encouragement from Paulina to renounce any such possibility:

> One worse,
> And better us'd, would make her sainted spirit
> Again possess her corpse, and on this stage
> (Were we offenders now) appear soul-vex'd,
> And begin, "Why to me?"
>
> (5.1.56–59)

He then imagines how a first wife, hearing the news of a new marriage, might appear to her husband and upbraid him—and then, even, "incense me / To murther her I married" (5.1.61–62).

There are two immediately striking aspects of this conversation: proleptically, Leontes and Paulina elaborate together, voluptuously, a scene of ghosts walking, of nuptial nostalgia and female haunting that Paulina later stage-manages with Hermione; secondly, Leontes uses a metaphor borrowed from theatrical spectacle that recalls *Macbeth*, a connection Paulina catches in an open echo of *Hamlet*. But over and above this promise of supernatural, performance trickery, the possible source of Shakespeare's allusion here tightens the strict association with the alarming enigma of statues. For one of the most improbable and perverse of medieval miracle stories features the Virgin Mary as a jilted first bride, who returns, in a vision, to fetch back her errant spouse on his wedding night. In fury at his betrayal of her, she demands that he forsake his new wife, and then carries him off to heaven with her. As far as I have discovered, however, the Virgin does not go so far as to urge her betrothed to kill her rival; his death suffices.

In a fourteenth-century collection of miracle plays, *Miracles de la Notre Dame par Personnages*, the young protagonist, also on his wedding night, receives a visit from the Virgin Mary, who is indeed incensed and berates him for abandoning her for a mere "terrienne femme": "You must be drunk to give your whole heart and all your love to a woman of this earth? And to leave me, the lady of heaven?" She threatens the young man with hellfire; eventually, he runs from his wife's nakedness and leaves a letter saying that the Virgin Mary is

> Si jalouse
> De lui qu'en paradis son lit
> Lui avoir fait pour grant delit
> Qui lui sera du tout defait.

[So jealous of him that she'd made him a bed in paradise, but by his great wickedness, he had undone it all.]

In some variations, the story begins with the young man unwittingly marrying the virgin when, playing ball in a cathedral precinct, he takes off his fiancée's ring and places it for safe keeping on the finger of a statue of the Virgin carved on the fabric of the building; her hand closes on it *"si fermement que nus ne l'en peust retraire"* (so firmly that nobody could draw it off), and she insists on his troth; he agrees, only to forget later that he has done so, with fatal consequences. The statue slides into bed with him on his wedding night, and he wakes up in terror. The Virgin then swears at him very roundly—in Gautier de Coincy's verse—and, again, ends the marriage. William of Malmesbury tells this old tale, but the statue in this case is of Venus and stands in the forum, in Rome.[12]

The animation of statues recurs as a motif, both in the practice of magicians and in stories about the magic arts: it is the fundamental metamorphosis of lifelessness into vitality, the governing metaphor of generation in myths of human origin, in the Genesis account of Adam fashioned from earth and breathed into being by God, or the Hesiodic passages about Prometheus, making the first human being like a potter working with clay; and in the story of Pandora, the first woman. Paulina's marvel, so circumstantially described by her as the most up-to-date, expensive, commissioned portrait from Italy, the supposed polychrome living likeness of Hermione by Julio Romano, draws some mythological vitality from the Pygmalion story in the *Metamorphoses* of Ovid, and Jonathan Bate has discussed how profoundly Shakespeare was himself colored by Ovid.[13] But it also taps into the confusion between spectacle, dream illusion, and supernatural visions that so preoccupied Shakespeare and his contemporaries, especially after the Reformation ended the Catholic cult of icons. Paulina is even called, early on in the play, "a [mankind] witch" (2.3.68).

However, the awakening of Hermione does not change her (unless one accepts the far-fetched theory that she was a statue all these sixteen years): it is a mock metamorphosis, stage-managed by Paulina to mimic—to ape—the conventions of the mythological and poetic genre. The fictive Hermione's lip is not stained with oily paint—though the actor's well might be. Inside the frame of the plot, she belongs to the order of nature, not of representation; she is a natural woman, not using artifice (indeed, she is famously "wrinkled"). She is distinguished from the "painted and streak'd gillyvors" produced by grafting and culture that Perdita rejects. Pastoral botany's pristine blooms include the virtuous and unstained Hermione, as well as her "blossom," as the infant Perdita is called by Antigonus. By contrast, "counterfeit stones" have earlier appeared among the trumpery and trinkets of the thieving peddler Autolycus, and prepared us for this contrast between the true woman (in more senses than one) and her false, dead double.

Although the scene includes much repetition of the stoniness of Hermione's effigy, her painted condition points in the direction of two rituals known to Shakespeare's contemporaries. First, there is the carrying of a funeral effigy after the death of a king. These predecessors of royal waxworks, wearing their own robes and regalia, can still be seen in London in Westminster Abbey, in the Undercroft; they include Edward III and Charles II, most resplendent in his Garter robes, and his mistress, the duchess of Richmond. These living likenesses of the dead, bewigged and arrayed, survived the change in state religion. They will develop, in the late eighteenth century, into the spectacle of a Mrs. Salmon or a Madame Tussaud's waxworks.[14] But Hermione's full-color, fully costumed state, placed in Paulina's chapel, did already belong to an existing, known category of spectral apparition, raised, in the manner of the game of Boo! in respect and simultaneous defiance of death's dominion. Kenneth Gross, in

*The Dream of the Moving Statue*, has discussed perceptively the resistance to the hyperbolic lifelikeness of the invoked statue, calling attention to the "anxiety that is here attached to the artifices of animation,"[15] pointing out that Shakespeare only once explicitly evokes the Pygmalion story from Ovid by name, and then with chilly lewdness, in *Measure for Measure*.

But the waxwork, as secular reliquary of the hero's body, has another, even more eloquently Mediterranean progenitor: the ex voto effigy. In S. Maria dei Miracoli, a still popular pilgrimage church near Mantua, the walls are covered in wax life casts of limbs, breasts, and organs cured by the intercession of the Madonna venerated there; above these there are lines of fully clothed, life-size polychrome figures, wearing the suits of armor in which they providentially escaped death on the battlefield, or the rags they were wearing when they went to the gallows and the rope broke in answer to their prayers and saved them. These three-dimensional images were made to resemble their grateful donors as closely as possible—taken from life—and offered in thanksgiving for the miracle, together with their possessions at the time of their unexpected reprieve.

Such sculptures freeze time. Hermione's "stone," her "picture" relates to the brisk, even blithe handling of time in *The Winter's Tale*: at the opening of act 3, Shakespeare daringly sweeps through the intervening sixteen years in order to catch us up into the magical denouement. Hermione's apparent effigy halts that flow of time: her fixity, invoked twice ("but newly-fix'd" and "the fixure of her eye") is the stasis of art's condition and it counters nature's metamorphic process of melting and fusion, generation and blossoming; its unchanging condition (which of course has its virtue elsewhere in Shakespeare's work) here tragically embodies obduracy, stoniness, the contraries of Leontes' new state of repentance. As Gross writes in *The Dream of the Moving Statue*, "She stands, indeed, as a figure for the nothing he [Leontes] has made of himself, of their shared love, or their children, of the erotic decorums of the social world, of all criteria of value, through his terror and fixation.[16]

Several other celebrated metamorphoses sound echoes in this scene with classical and Christian literature, tales of petrification from Ovid's poem. Above all, Hermione recalls the distraught Niobe turned to weeping stone after the deaths of all her children. The miracle stirs memories of magical organicism, too: the sowing of stones after the flood by Pyrrha and her husband Deucalion who is mentioned in the play (4.4.442), and, from the Bible, the terrible temptation of Christ, to turn stones into bread (Matt. 4:3), which is itself a hideous mockery of transubstantiation, the central, imperceptible, and most problematic metamorphosis in Catholic doctrine. Yet another story from the Bible reverberates more strongly, I think, and it can offer a way of thinking in particular about the temporal shape and texture of Shakespeare's drama: the story of Lot's wife, the most notorious and mysterious fate suffered by a wife and mother and one of the few metamorphoses in the Old Testament. Her crystallization, into a kind of monument to grief, a pillar of salt, is the penalty for her looking back at the blasted cities of Sodom and Gomorrah after Lot and his family have been ordered to leave them without a backward glance. Retrospection costs her her life, according to the typological interpretation of the highly compressed, indeed hermetically singular Biblical sentence (Gen. 19:26: "But his wife looked back from behind him, and she became a pillar of salt"). In a stained glass window of Canterbury Cathedral, made around 1175–80, one of the places in England where the story of this nonclassical metamorphosis is told, the episode is paired with another difficult passage, in this case from the First Book of Kings, in which a prophet successfully puts an end to the idolatry of King Jeroboam. In this extremely recondite piece of medieval iconography, Jeroboam is shown sacrificing to a golden calf; the prophet's message, "Nor turn again by the same way that thou camest" (1 Kings 13:9) is inscribed on a scroll above the altar. Between these two episodes from the Old Testament, a scene from the New Testament completes the pattern of recapitulation and prefigurement in this "elaborate display of twelfth century theology";[17] the three kings are warned by the angel not to return to Herod and tell him where Jesus has been born.

This stained glass window is a survivor; it is one of the few lancets from the chancel of Canterbury Cathedral to have escaped the Protestant iconoclasm of the civil war (and the ravages of World War II); its iconography exemplifies the way that, according to the pre-Reformation model of providence, time folds to meet itself across eons.[18]

Exegetical picture books, such as the *Biblia Pauperum* and the *Speculum Humanae Salvationis*, which were widely disseminated in numerous manuscripts and printed versions, place the escape of Lot and his daughters from the rain of fire on Sodom alongside three types of "liberation": the delivery from Hell's Mouth of the just who died before Christ, the escape of the children of Israel from Pharoah's destruction, and Abraham's deliverance from Ur of the Chaldees. In one illustrated volume, Lot's wife appears in the woodcut changing into a portrait bust on a column: the pillar of salt unequivocally understood to be a statue, with the full active force of the pun on com*bust*um, consumed by fire, embodied by the image.[19] Thus she fails to be delivered, unlike a romance heroine, whose fate liberates her from past suffering and who can undergo the positive metamorphosis of conversion, and escape both combustion and crystallization. Paradoxically, the salting of Lot's wife, one of the very scant instances of the phenomenon of metamorphosis in Christian folklore, exemplifies the dangers of refusing another kind of transformation: repentance, conversion.

The lesson goes that fidelity to the true god entails leaving evil ways behind: the sacrificial passage of the virtuous from the past into the future demands an end to old attachments, with their stained practices, a close to human nostalgia, to hankering. Recollection here becomes dyed with impure longings and a turning away from righteousness: Lot's wife is punished for failing to keep her eyes on the road ahead, the way forward out of iniquity. It is not altogether wild to find an echo of this morality in Shakespeare's *tableau vivant* of a woman who escapes a stony fate when a king shows he too has put the past behind him. *The Winter's Tale* diverges from the tragedies precisely in this attitude to time and memory: in the romances the past does not weigh on the present and can be set aside; the mysterious reconciliations that conclude the late plays demand an effort of forgetting, of not looking back. It is the essence of fairy tales that their protagonists don't have long memories, even though they may live for a thousand years. It is the promise of the New Covenant, a New Testament reprieve, a possibly Catholic-inflected dynamic of forgiveness, renewal, and rebirth that the unlikely happy ending of *The Winter's Tale* works out in its triumphant close.

It is worth noting, too, that after their mother's very particular kind of petrification, Lot's daughters decide to seduce their father—in order, the Bible says, to continue the family line. This story is told, advisedly, in the book of Genesis, of origin, of generation. Without their mother, future generations—in the male line—would not come into being.

Reading the story of Hermione's make-believe petrification through this strange episode in the Bible clarifies the play's struggle with futurity—the theme of issue that so constantly preoccupies Shakespeare, in *Titus Andronicus*, in *Macbeth*, and in *The Tempest*. Leontes's rage has killed his family: Mamillius has died, the infant daughter has been exposed to die. Hermione's mineral apparition thus embodies the issue of the future as it would have been if Leontes had indeed suffered the appropriate retribution of his murderous and barren jealousy. Lot's anonymous wife becomes a body of frozen tears, imprisoned forever in a highly unusual, if not unique, form of mortal spoil. Hermione as statue is likewise stone: the word is repeated six times in the scene, four times by Leontes. The miracle of metamorphosis that then takes place tilts the balance of three metaphorical pairs conveying the play's dramatic reversal of death into life: it turns painted artifice into unadorned nature, sterile stone into flesh, and the timeless eternity of marble into the "wrinkled," hence timebound, fruitfulness of the mother. The first *speech* of Hermione rediviva leaves off embracing Leontes to address her daughter, Perdita, and it closes with a pun on the word "issue":

> thou shalt hear that I
> Knowing by Paulina that the Oracle

Gave hope thou wast in being, have preserv'd
Myself to see the issue.

(5.3.125–28)

Issue here could mean both the outcome of the oracle and her offspring, Perdita. Hermione is saying that she survived because of her child's promised survival: she did not look back at Leontes' crime, but held fast to the deliverance of the future, through his lineage and restored authority—established through the giving of a daughter in marriage, as in *The Tempest*.

This tremendous scene also develops the relationship between painted devils and aery nothings in Shakespeare's use of magic. For in order to bring Hermione back into the unfolding story, Paulina turns to stagecraft, that is, pretence; she performs equivalent arts of intervention, of painting, of performance, and in so doing, she appears to summon Hermione's eerie "double." The capacity of theater to produce the illusion of real presence vexes Shakespeare, because of its connections to diabolical illusion, to sorcery, and, within sorcery, to Catholic magic of transubstantiation, and iconodulia, the forbidden worship of graven images. In the second century, Celsus, a scourge of Christians, vituperated belief in magicians "who make things move as though they were alive although they are not really so, but only appear as such in the imagination."[20]

The trope of the living statue is related to ekphrasis, the classical topos, most famously represented by Homer's evocation of the shield of Achilles. Julio Romano's rare skills in rendering the supposed dead queen to the life displays the prized esthetic quality of *enargeia*, vividness, also known as hypotyposis. The resulting ambiguity about the status of the image's "picture-flesh" (Maurice Merleau-Ponty's brilliant term[21]) enhances the hallucinatory atmosphere of the play's closing scene. Both Leontes and Hermione are poised between sleep and waking states; as the statue awakes, to Paulina's command, Leontes still thinks it might be an illusion, as in a dream: "O, she's warm!" he exclaims in surprise when he embraces her, for dreams rarely offer evidence to the sense of touch. And diabolical illusions never do (though they can—and do—stink!).

The paradoxes of ekphrasis—its material immateriality—relate to the illusions of presence in spectral conjuring. The sorcerer becomes a paradoxically material agent, and his entertainment counterpart, the conjuror, becomes a maker of tricks and illusions: dreams in this sense are indeed toys. The historian of theater Iain Wright has uncovered evidence, shortly to be published, that the first performances of *Dr. Faustus* and of *Macbeth* may have used early magic lantern effects, projections onto smoke and through glass, to summon painted devils.[22] When Prospero talks of his "insubstantial pageant," it is hard not to imagine stagecraft of an optical variety. Indeed, in his famous speech, he says, "We are such stuff as dreams are made *on*," and "on" suggests that dreams appear on something, perhaps on the screen of fantasy (*Tempest* 4.1.14 ff.)[23] Theatrical illusion offers an analogy to the spectral conjurings of enchanters as well as to the phantasms of haunted minds, and the faery entertainments of Fata Morgana. In *Dream* Theseus talks of "shaping fantasies" (5.1.5), and Hippolita of "fancy's images" (5.1.25). Reversing Prospero's metaphor, Theseus also says that actors themselves are "shadows"; Puck repeats this in the play's envoi ("If we shadows have offended" (5.1.423 ff.).

However, so far, the first reports of such experiments come from the second half of the seventeenth century and the activities of that truly Faustian figure, Athanasius Kircher, the Jesuit, who, in the Jesuit college in Rome, practiced his catoptrical arts with smoking lamps, compound crystals, and various camera obscuras with lenses and slides. The earliest illustrations reveal an intrinsic, unexamined equivalence between the technology of illusion and supernatural phenomena: Kircher projected souls in hell, leering devils, and other products of imagination, not observation. He was consequently called a magician by his peers, and only half in jest.

Thomas Aquinas, following Augustine, had determined that the devil could not be capable of actually performing metamorphoses, or of being in two or more places at once (the divine gift of ubiquity); or of knowing the future, since these were the unique prerogatives of God. But the devil was an ape, a mimic, a deceiver, who could create the illusion of such feats.[24] In some sense, devils are always "painted," that is counterfeit, since they assume the forms they do in order to manifest themselves to humans. *Macbeth*, interestingly, contains examples of both inner and outer vision: both the male protagonist and Lady Macbeth are privately haunted by their own, personal demons—the dagger, Banquo's ghost, the kings stretching to the crack of doom—but in the play the oracular witches, who, it is implied, have magicked themselves to their gathering, and will do so again, are visible to everyone accompanying Macbeth.

The condition of Shakespeare's apparitions is strictly uncanny: in Scottish demonology, the devil could conjure a spirit double, or fetch, sometimes called "a joint-eater," a phantasm such as Helen of Troy, when she appears at the summoning of Mephistopheles in Christopher Marlowe's *Dr. Faustus*. Likewise, Banquo's ghost is both there and not there, visible but not palpable.

Keeping with the theme of metamorphosis as an illusion created by magic craft, I want to turn now from statues to projections—to *The Tempest*'s insubstantial pageants and *A Midsummer Night's Dream's* "aery nothings," to which "the lunatic, the lover, and the poet / Give . . . a local habitation and a name" (5.1.7, 16–17).

**2**

Frank Kermode, in his edition of *The Tempest*, influentially distinguishes between theurgy (good or natural magic) and goety (or sorcery)—the dark arts, and their foul deeds, called *maleficium* by the witch hunters.[25] But in *The Tempest* and *Dream*, the two modes of supernatural manipulation are in practice confused, because the same persons perform both: Prospero and Oberon. Nor are ghosts and specters raised only by adepts, sorcerers, or witches: Horatio recalls the portents that warned of Julius Caesar's death, after Hamlet's father has appeared to the watch, and that potent ghost of memory is seen—and debated—by several witnesses. As we have heard, in *The Winter's Tale* Antigonus sets aside his skepticism when visited by what he takes to be Hermione's ghost. Oberon who as king of the fairies, is in a position to know, is careful to discriminate between the many different orders of supernatural beings: referring to ghosts, he says, "We are spirits of another sort."

Even in the enchanted forest of *Dream*, the supernatural packs a certain menace. The fairies used to be cast as tiny tots and costumed in confections of gauze and tulle. But recent productions have paid more attention to their odd, eldritch, dusty, and even piquant names: Cobweb and Moth, Peaseblossom and Mustardseed. Still, these dingy sprites range themselves against even darker forces of nighttime disturbance: Titania asks them to sing her "a roundel and a fairy song" before she goes to sleep and before they go off on their "war" against cankers in the musk rose, against bats and owls—a combat of good and evil in the sphere of botany. In the "sweet lullaby" that follows, these elvish guardians of freshness, ripeness, and light, list the creatures that endanger even the queen of the fairies. Titania's guardian fairies sing,

> You spotted snakes with double tongue,
> Thorny hedgehogs, be not seen,
> Newts and blind'worms, do no wrong
> Come not near our fairy queen.

(2.2.9 to 12)

These bugs and bogeys are familiar characters, for they are also tossed into the pot by the three weird sisters, to the accompaniment of another, more famous cantrip, the famous "Double, double, toil and trouble" (*Macbeth* 4.1).

Elsewhere in Shakespeare's plays, a diverse, uncanny population flourishes that resembles the curious, alarming *Secret Commonwealth* of the Rev. Robert Kirk's book, written at the end of the seventeenth century:[26] lobs and pucks and sprites and phantoms and elves and ouphes (pronounced *owfs*), a kind of elf, who are conjured up under this name among the troop of fairies by Mistress Quickly at the comic finale of *The Merry Wives of Windsor*.

But above all, both malignant and beneficent magic phenomena inhabit analogous zones of metaphor they speak or sing through similar patterns of imagery and of prosody, of verse forms. Any clear difference between witchcraft and fairy lore, and between good and evil origin, true or false messages totters and fails, though the plays tend—and this is true not only of the comedies—toward resisting bane and releasing, fostering, allowing boons and blessings to flourish, toward, as Puck puts it in the closing line of *Dream*, "restoring amends." This work of repair sees ghosts laid to rest, fairies' mischief quietening, Ariel set free, and order in Scotland, in Denmark, and in Milan, reestablished. But the conflict between good and evil never takes the Manichaean form of a simple combat myth, such as animates the movie *Star Wars* or even Harry Potter's duel with Lord Voldemort; the power of Shakespeare's uncanny rises from this ambiguity, which can be shivery, thrilling, and sometimes terrifying. The guardian fairies of Titania's rest, for example, do not themselves altogether escape the cauldron's realm of reptiles, night creatures, and other creepy-crawlies. They are bug-like in scale, and she gives them sinister-sounding tasks: Titania's close instructions to make candles for Bottom's siesta are both practical, in the manner of a cunning woman, but also rather more surgical than one might want:

> The honey bags steal from the humble-bees,
> And for night-tapers crop their waxen thighs,
> And light them at the fiery glow-worm's eyes
> To have my love to bed and to arise;
> And pluck the wings from painted butterflies,
> To fan the moonbeams from his sleeping eyes.
>
> (3.1.168–73)

A friend told me that when her daughter was taking part in a primary school production of *Dream*, this speech was cut as being too upsetting for young children.

The imagery of insects dominates the visual lexicon of horrors and frighteners today; similar elements—scales, proboscoes, pincers, gleaming carapaces, elaborate mouthparts and bristling antennae from the hidden, subterranean territory of "creepy-crawlies"—characterize the scary cast of current fantasy. Dislocations of size belong with the unsettling capacity to change shape, and they do not belittle the fairies' power, but increase their eeriness: Titania can stroke Bottom's large soft ears in a woman's way, even though her attendants flit about, hanging dewdrops on cowslips.

It is not anachronistic to respond to Titania's imagery of bees' legs and plucked insect wings with a shudder. Entertainment imagery today is again closing the gap between "bug" meaning "insect" and "bug" meaning "devil"; this is the intermediate space where Shakespeare's busy elves are poised.

Like devils, Shakespearean fairies and aerial creatures are shape shifters; they can also change others' shapes. Bottom the weaver is "translated" into an ass. Puck boasts that he can change himself into "a filly foal" or "a roasted crab"; Ariel, under orders from Prospero, turns into a harpy, a water-nymph, and the lightning of St. Elmo's fire. Both Puck and Ariel know how to disappear from human sight—indeed the impossible stage direction occurs, "enter Ariel, invisible." Invisibility is a frequent and most coveted power of the magician: as Richard Kieckhefer comments, in his spirited commentary on a fifteenth-century German manual of necromancy, "it is in the nature of these experiments that in one way or other most of them are *shared*: in some cases the result of the magical is a spectacle that may be put on for the wonderment of others, and even when the point is for the magician to become invisible, his very state of non-visibility is a way of relating to others."[27] Christopher Marlowe stages a lengthy comic scene that depends on Mephistopheles' invisibility, and indeed the shadow of his magic play projects over these images of witchcraft, like lantern slides themselves, for Dr. Faustus's devil reveals to him powers of metamorphosis as well as other spells. The fairy banquet that vanishes into thin air in *The Tempest* recalls the invisibly served delicacies in Cupid and Psyche from *The Golden Ass*, itself burlesqued in the Induction of Sly at the beginning of *The Taming of the Shrew*.[28] Celsus scorned Christian belief in miracles by comparing them with the feats of street magicians "who, for a few obols make known their sacred lore in the middle of the market-place . . . displaying expensive banquets and dining-tables and cakes and dishes which are non-existent."[29] A grimoire such as the Munich manuscript that Kieckhefer translated contains detailed instructions on how to conjure an illusory feast: "You have often seen me exercise at your court the art of summoning banquet-bearers . . . ," he begins. "First one must invoke fifteen spirits, in this manner . . ." Elaborate measures are then described, involving much brandishing of a hoopoe, a bird ascribed strong necromantic powers. "You must know that no matter how much they [the banqueters] eat, they will be all the more hungry, because they will seem like dishes but they will not exist."

The writer of this long, sly handbook was enjoying himself, Kieckhefer argues. At this date, "His tricks are meant fundamentally as entertainment, chiefly for himself, perhaps, but potentially for others as well—and certainly for the reader who, in the privacy of his chamber, fantasizes about these wonders much as one might share in the fantasies of romance and related literature." In the fifteenth century, the beliefs of the witch hunters had not yet turned such make-believe dangerous.[30] However, as Shakespeare's characterization of Joan of Arc as a fully fledged witch reveals, his audience as highly sensitive to the powers of sorcery, fascinated and enthralled, and Prospero's avowal, at the opening of the play, that he left off his duties as duke of Milan to pursue his studies of the secret arts, would have invoked a recognizable, fascinating—and dangerous—area of knowledge.

The argument about art and nature in *The Winter's Tale*, explored in the intense exchange between Perdita and Polixenes, about piedness and streaked gillyvors, about hybridity and grafting versus pristine purity, informs the tension about the uncanny as well. As Stuart Clark discusses in *Thinking with Demons*, the need to distinguish natural magic, the preternatural or even monstrous and occurring in nature, from magic that is diabolical in origin, excited profound anxiety throughout the seventeenth century.[31] The opposition between nature and artifice, as in the dispute about horticulture, can be resolved by absorbing one category into the embrace of the other, as Polixenes' attempt does when he ingeniously summarizes, saying,

> Yet nature is made better by no mean
> But nature makes that mean: so, over that art,
> Which you say adds to nature, is an art
> That nature makes.
>
> (*Winter's Tale* 4.4.88–92)

Cabinets of Curiosities, exhibiting *artificialia* alongside *naturalia,* adopted a classificatory system that assimilated artifacts as elaborations of nature's own wonders. Interestingly, the language of magic in Shakespeare often turns to the grotesque: For example, Ariel's eerie, beguiling song, "Come unto these yellow sands," ends inexplicably "Bow wow bow wow"—a nod to the canine metamorphoses of spirits in the play, but also a jarring note after the lyrical picture of the preceding lines. And Bottom's turning into a donkey is the fullest metamorphosis Shakespeare tackles— and the funniest. But it is not for comic effect alone that Shakespeare puts near-doggerel to work: the witches' uncouth rigmaroles from *Macbeth*, grotesque as they are, do not inspire laughter, not even horrid laughter.

In the domain of enchantments, of painted devils and aery nothings, the supernatural and the preternatural have to be kept apart precisely because the devil could ape divine handicraft. He is the master of the grotesque—an esthetic mode that deliberately focuses on transmogrifications, even disfigurements of pristine natural forms—and the leader of the monkeys' comic dance.

A further difficulty arises, however, that if the origin of a phenomenon, such as Prospero's "cloud capp'd tow'rs" can be demonstrated to be natural, not demonic, the magic used to bring it into being becomes human; if human, are these materializations part of the natural world? In what sense can such ephemeral materializations be in nature? Unless materialism embraces a spiritual dimension, and a human conjuror, such as Prospero, breaks through the borders of the physical into the metaphysical. Here's the rub, which Shakespeare often puzzles over, in his explorations of the meaning of dream experience; for the immaterial materiality of dreams, their eidetic condition of being both real and not real, actual and not actual, there and not there, lived and not lived, offers a homologous zone to the natural magic that Prospero must command if he is not to be a diabolical sorcerer, like Medea. So, as Stuart Clark has deduced, the difference between natural and demonic magic ultimately resides in the character of the magician: hence the church's—and the witch hunters'—obsession with diagnosing the origin of the visionary's powers.[32]

## 3

Theater realizes illusions, setting up a perceptual paradox about the play-world that cannot be resolved. The dramas that seem to resolve the problem of the supernatural, by breaking the spell, ending the enchantment, relegating or at least limiting the powers of ghosts and fairies, are the selfsame plays where Shakespeare meditates most obsessively about the nature of the state of illusion itself, of the power of fantasy. "These are all actors," Prospero tells his new son-in-law, Ferdinand, "all spirits, and / Are melted into air, into thin air" (5.1.149–50). The vision Ferdinand has experienced since the shipwreck stands on a "baseless fabric." The puzzle this produces relates to the condition of language itself, oscillating between event with consequences, and an utterance or description as airy and ephemeral as the breath taken to speak. Shakespeare explores language as event: he makes his poetry work to change experience: "So long lives this, and this gives life to thee," he concludes, sacramentally, at the end of the eighteenth sonnet.

In the plays, curses, blessings, spells, and incantations perform crucial dramatic acts to push forward the story, transform the characters. These kinds of speech thus become the very tools of metamorphosis and of stagecraft. But can this supernatural agency spill over the edges of the stage, diffuse its mists with dry ice, and fork its lightning into the audience's interior spaces of fear and terror? Can it reach into our dreams? Or, to put it the other way round, is Life Itself a dream? And what does this imply for the status of dreamed realities? The answers to these questions interestingly do not depend on the audience's belief at any one time: you could say, "oh, but people *then* believed in ghosts and oracles and omens, in magic and even, perhaps, metamorphosis, that a man could become a donkey." But *we* do not entertain such childish fancies *now*; it is different for *us*. Our language of the supernatural continues, but our faith does not. The magic or supernatural machinery of the stories does not present a problem of faith because its effects are created in the virtual realm of theater, which we enter and inhabit, and this realm, I propose, embodies a current model of the mind, in which fantasy and dream produce impossible phenomena. The supernatural has become co-extensive, even consubstantial, with imagination itself, enacted through theatrical representation or at work in fiction.

Shakespeare was puzzling over this, all those years ago before the unconscious was discovered or cognitive psychologists pondered the structure of the visual cortex and attempted to analyze consciousness itself. Theseus in *Dream* meditates on the interrelationship in one of the crucial speeches in Shakespeare's thinking about his writing. First, when Theseus is discussing the lovers' madness, he comments, "such tricks hath strong imagination. How easy is a bush suppos'd a bear" (*Dream* 5.1.18, 22). His mind is still running on metamorphosis and illusion while watching the performance of "Pyramus and Thisbe," when he says of the actors, "The best in this kind are but shadows, and the worst are no worse, if imagination amend them" (*Dream* 5.1.211–12).

Fantasy supplies something more, when engaged with theater, as it also does for dreamers and lovers—"imagination bodies forth / The forms of things unknown" (*Dream* 5.1.14–15). This movement of the mind makes amends, which art's reparatory power imitates through invention. For the poet's pen "Turns them to shapes"—that is to say wields the magic power of metamorphosis and, as quoted earlier, "gives to aery nothing / A local habitation and a name" (*Dream* 5.1.16–17).

However, this activity does not contain its power—or its threat. The convergence between the dream space of magic and metamorphosis and the theater space of performance, acting and illusion makes one leak into the other both inside the plays and outside them. Inside the plays, Hamlet stages "The Mouse Trap" to spring Claudius from his equanimity—and succeeds. For Claudius, the events enacted on the stage prove too real to endure and he calls for lights and storms out. The play Hamlet has composed for the Players crosses the divide between insubstantial pageant and actual existence. So does Paulina's *coup de théâtre*. Life and art become mixed up: this is the dangerous magic of acted words; this is the basis of casting spells, as the weird sisters demonstrate, as the fairies' lullaby attempts. As we have seen, Autolycus's trumpery wares include ballads alongside "counterfeit stones."

Magic is made by performative speech: its commands bring their contents into being, as in the priest officiating at a sacrament. "With this ring I thee wed" accomplishes a marriage; Oberon's love spell on Titania makes her fall in love with Bottom. The words "chant," "incantation," "cantrip" reveal the relationship of verbal music and song to spells and charm; such formulas do not record or describe, they produce events, they inaugurate change, they effect conversion and transformation.

More and more deeply entangled in the difficulties that the painted devils and aery nothings of his own stagecraft raised for him, what does Shakespeare do, to elude the charge of conjuring? I think, if we fold back the theme to the beginning, to the old tales and the tall stories of the ballads and that preoccupation, in *The Winter's Tale*, with the limits of nature, we can find one response to the problem. Shakespeare sought to escape pied artistry, "streak'd gillyvors" and "painted devils" and sea-changed works and wonders into a supposed natural magic, whose equivalent in representation became for him a vernacular poetic diction, a spoken, as it were natural, language. "Juggling fiends . . . / That palter with us in a double sense" (*Macbeth* 5.8.19–20) could be dispelled, outfaced, and undone by the verbal equivalent of Perdita's artless flowers, or the human equivalent of Hermione's restored organic, living flesh (the miracle that Deucalion and Pyrrha achieve), blossom against counterfeit stones. The meshes of this paradox set another, deeper snare, but one that cannot be unsnarled here: for the question continues to hang, spectrally, in thin air; how can language utter truth within the mendacious illusion of representation itself?

# Notes

1. Apollonius of Rhodes, *The Voyage of Argo: The "Argonautica,"* trans. E. V. Rieu (Harmondsworth: Penguin, 1971), 165–67.

2. Marina Warner, "'Rough Magic and Sweet Lullaby': Shakespeare's Supernatural," BBC Radio, 31 October 2001, 3, Warner,, "'The foul witch' and her 'freckled whelp': Circean Mutations in the New World," in *"The Tempest" and Its Travels*, ed. Peter Hulme and William Sherman (London: Reaktion Books, 2000), 97–113.

3. See Jean Claude Schmitt, *Ghosts in the Middle Ages: The Living and the Dead in Medieval Society*, trans. Teresa Lavender Fagan (Chicago: University of Chicago Press, 1998).

4. Stuart Clark, "Demons, Natural Magic and the Virtually Real: Visual Paradox in Early Modern Europe," paper from October 2000, kindly lent by the author, to whom I am most grateful for help with this and other materials.

5. See Stanley Cavell, "Recounting Gains, Showing Losses," in *Disowning Knowledge in Six Plays of Shakespeare* (Cambridge: Cambridge University Press, 1987), 193–221.

6. Frank Kermode, *Shakespeare's Language* (London: Allen Lane, 2000), 273.

7. Jacqueline Simpson, "'The Rules of Folklore' in the Ghost Stories of M. R. James," *Folklore* 108 (1997): 9–18.

8. See Marina Warner, *No Go the Bogeyman* (London: Chatto & Windus, 1998), 167–72.

9. Kermode, *Shakespeare's Language*, p. 268

10. Ted Hughes, *Shakespeare and the Goddess of Supreme Being* (London: Faber & Faber, 1992), 49–93.

11. *The Winter's Tale*, ed. J. H. P. Pafford, New Arden Shakespeare (London: Methuen, 1963), 138.

12. See Marina Warner, *Alone of All Her Sex* (1976; reprint, London: Vintage, 1990), 156 ff.

13. Jonathan Bate, *Shakespeare and Ovid* (Oxford: Oxford University Press, 1999). Giulio Romano in fact painted several classical metamorphoses at the Palazzo Te, Mantua, including a fresco cycle of Cupid and Psyche, inspired by Apuleius.

14. See Marina Warner, "Waxworks and Wonderlands," in *Visual Display Culture Beyond Appearances*, ed. Lynne Cooke and Peter Wollen (New York: DIA Center for the Arts, 1995).

15. Kenneth Gross, *The Dream of the Moving Statue* (Ithaca: Cornell University Press, 1992), 101.

16. Ibid., 100.

17. Madeline Harrison Cavines, *The Early Stained Glass of Canterbury Cathedral, 1175–1220* (Princeton: Princeton University Press, 1977), 55.

18. Ibid., 50 ff.

19. Adrian Wilson and Joyce Lancaster Wilson, *A Medieval Mirror 1324–1500* (Berkeley and Los Angeles: University of California Press, 1984), 195.

20. Richard Kieckhefer, *Forbidden Rites: A Necromancer's Manual of the Fifteenth Century* (London: Sutton, 1997), 44, quoting Origen, *Contra Celsum* (1.68), ed. Henry Chadwick (Cambridge: Cambridge University Press, 1953), 62–63.

21. Maurice Merleau-Ponty, *Le Visible et l'Invisible*, ed. Claude Lefort (Paris: Gallimard, 1964), 189–204, 302–15.

22. Iain Wright, "All Done With Mirrors: Politics, Magic and Theatrical Illusion in *Macbeth*," paper given at the Shakespeare Symposium, Humanities Research Centre, Australian National University, Canberra, 26–28 June 2001; to be published in a forthcoming study of *Macbeth*.

23. Cf. Steven Connor, "Fascination, Skin and Screen," *Critical Quarterly* 40, no.1 (1998): 9–24.

24. Stuart Clark, *Thinking with Demons: The Idea of Witchcraft in Early Modern Europe* (Oxford: Oxford University Press, 1999), 80 ff.

25. *The Tempest*, ed. Frank Kermode, New Arden Shakespeare (1958; reprint London: Methuen, 1987), xl.

26. Rev. Robert Kirk, *The Secret Common-wealth*, ed. Stewart Sanderson (Cambridge: D. S. Brewer, 1976).

27. Kieckhefer, *Forbidden Rites*, 45.

28. See J. J. M. Tobin, *Shakespeare's Favorite Novel: A Study of "The Golden Asse" as Prime Source* (Lanham, Md.: University Press of America, 1984).

29. Ibid., 44.

30. Kieckhefer, *Forbidden Rites*, 64.

31. Clark, *Thinking with Demons*, 233–50.

32. Ibid., 459–71.

# From Shakespeare's Italy to Italy's Shakespeare: Biographical Fantasies of Love and Power

## Paul Franssen

OVER THE LAST FEW DECADES, THERE HAS BEEN A MARKED SHIFT IN
Shakespeare studies. Not so long ago, it went without saying that Shakespeare's works should be studied for their intrinsic meaning, as if they
were a kind of supplement to the Holy Scriptures. Nowadays, many scholars have turned their attention to the way Shakespeare has been appropriated, *made* to mean something. We have seen studies of productions,
editions, and critical analyses of Shakespeare's works, whose meaning has
come to be seen as a cultural construct. It is not just the works that lend
themselves to such an approach: his biography, his portraits, and the entire
Shakespeare industry, down to the use of the bardic image on beer mats
and bank notes, have been analyzed from a cultural-materialist perspective.[1]

There is, however, one aspect of the Shakespeare industry that is only
beginning to attract the notice of most critics: the deployment of Shakespeare as a literary character in novels, stories, plays, films, and other
kinds of fiction.[2] Because we know so little of Shakespeare the man, his
life is, as it were, a text full of gaps. With reference to A. C. Bradley's
analysis of *Hamlet*, Terence Hawkes has argued that any text is opaque
and will inevitably be read in the reader's own image; but it is not just the
words that lend themselves to an infinity of readings, but also the silences,
the gaps and indeterminacies, between these words.[3] If we transfer this notion of silences to Shakespeare's life, it becomes clear that this text particularly lends itself to appropriation, since there is so much silence, so little
text. As a consequence, it is precisely in fictional lives that the forces that
made Shakespeare into a national and even an international myth, and the
uses to which that myth has been put in any particular era, can be seen
in their most undiluted form. In particular, where the Shakespeare myth
intersects with another great western myth, that of the Mediterranean as
the cradle of European civilization, fictions of Shakespeare's life inevita-

bly reflect and help to shape political constructions such as the notion of the *translatio imperii*, the periodical transfer of world leadership.

Before turning to fictions of Shakespeare, however, it seems worth considering briefly an authentic Shakespearean passage. In *The Merchant of Venice*, Bassanio finds a miniature portrait of his beloved Portia inside the casket:

> *Bassanio*. What find I here? [*Opening the leaden casket.*]
> Fair Portia's counterfeit! What demigod
> Hath come so near creation? Move these eyes?
> Or whether, riding on the balls of mine,
> Seem they in motion?

(3.2.114–18)

Some fifteen years later, the English traveler Thomas Coryate recorded seeing a very similar portrait with moving eyes in a painters' workshop in Venice: "the picture of a Gentlewoman, whose eies were contriued with that singularitie of cunning, that they moued vp and down of themselues, not in a seeming manner, but truly and indeed. For I did very exactly view it. But I believe it was done by a vice [*sic*] which the Greeks call *automaton*."[4] What the resemblance shows is that Shakespeare had some detailed knowledge of Venetian expertise in *trompe l'oeil* painting; but how did he come by it?

This apparently authentic detail of Shakespeare's Mediterranean world is, of course, only one among many similar instances that have been noted over the centuries. Shakespeare's use of local color, especially in his depictions of Venice, has been widely praised, despite occasional lapses. This has led also to speculation about whether he ever visited the country, for instance during the plague year, 1593, when all the theaters were closed. It has been objected that he could have learned all he knew from written sources, from oral reports of travelers, or from Italian immigrants such as John Florio or the Bassano family.[5]

In some cases, such speculation about Shakespeare's travel to Italy seems to be motivated by factors other than mere scholarly curiosity. A case in point is the late Professor Ernesto Grillo, an Italian scholar who worked at Glasgow University until his death in 1946. In his study *Shakespeare in Italy*, Grillo again asks the familiar question, "Did Shakespeare visit Italy?" and answers in the affirmative. The evidence he produces is not in itself remarkable: for a century or so, scholars had been making similar points. What *is* remarkable is the lyrical note on which Grillo ends his essay, which allows us to catch a glimpse of extraneous reasons for his need to show that Shakespeare had visited Italy:

> In conclusion we may affirm that of all the English poets who visited Italy . . . no one has depicted our scenes, our life, our character and our nature better than

Shakespeare. The portrayer of the spirit of humanity, the genius of the English Renaissance, in whose works we find not only true life and passion, but all European institutions with their chivalry, courtesy and ambitions, could not have sung the praises of the classical yet ever romantic land of Italy without having paid her at least a fleeting visit. It need occasion no surprise therefore if we imagine the great lover of our country travelling through many Lombardian and Venetian cities "waving friendly together the British and the Italian flag, and talking of the Alps, the Apennines, and the River Po." These words of the dramatist proved truly prophetic, for the Anglo-Italian flags waved victoriously together in the Crimea, in Sicily on Garibaldi's disembarkation in 1859 and on the sacred battlefields of more recent wars for the defence of that civilization which is the glory of the Latin peoples.[6]

Grillo's military metaphors of battlefields and waving flags suggest cooperation between equal partners: the Mediterranean world, the cradle of Western civilization, and the Anglo-Saxon world, which has inherited that cultural capital, personified in Shakespeare. In actual fact, of course, by the end of the war there was hardly any equality between the West and the South in terms of power. Besides, by evoking "Anglo-Italian flags wav-[ing] victoriously together in the Crimea," Grillo consciously constructs a counterweight to that more recent war in which Italy had been pitched against Britain. During the war, the survival of what Grillo sees as Italian civilization depended largely on military intervention by the Anglo-Saxon world, Britain, and the United States; and after the war, economic assistance was to come from the same corner. This is where the symbolic function of Shakespeare's putative visit to Italy comes in: it makes tangible the idea of a cultural exchange between the South and the West. The West has inherited its culture from the South, and flourished because of it; for that reason, it should now feel a moral obligation to come to the aid of the South, to preserve and protect the roots of its own cultural heritage.

Not all Shakespearean scholarship conducted by Italians has this political agenda, and most scholars, Mario Praz in particular, have actually been very careful not to confuse wishful thinking with painstaking scholarship. Fiction writers, however, are not bound by such restraints, and have been free to imagine Shakespeare traveling through Italy. In the following, I will address two-and-a-half examples of this fantasy, for each of them asking myself what cultural meanings Shakespeare is made to represent here, and what is the contribution of the Mediterranean setting. None of my examples is actually by Italians; yet all of them are variations on Grillo's sense of a power shift within Europe, from the Mediterranean to the North Sea basin, and ultimately away from Europe to the United States; an economic, political, and cultural change that was initiated in the Early Modern period and completed after World War II.

My first example is a little-known work that came out in 1916, the tercentenary of Shakespeare's death: the *Shakespeariad* by the American Denton J. Snider.[7] As I shall argue, Snider's Shakespeare fantasy serves to illustrate the notion of the transfer of empire, which in Snider's prophetic vision takes place in two stages: from Italy to England in the Early Modern period, and from England to the United States in the early twentieth century.

The form of the *Shakespeariad* is most unusual. In the "Argument," the author explains that he has sought to "unite the epic and dramatic forms into a higher kind." As in a Spenserian epic, the eponymous hero appears only intermittently in his own person, and interacts with allegorical characters such as "Pandora from Hellas and the East, and young Prospero from Atlantis and the West." Most of the over-four hundred pages are populated by Shakespearean characters from diverse plays, interacting with each other and occasionally with Shakespeare in dramatic blank-verse dialogue.

Shakespeare does not make his first appearance until the middle section, entitled "The Venetian Trilogy." As a tourist in Venice, he meets a young English nobleman by the name of Lord Falconbridge, who asks him to act as his interpreter in the wooing of Portia. Thus Snider's Shakespeare actually witnesses some of the events that he is to write about in *The Merchant of Venice* later. While Falconbridge woos Portia, only to be revealed as the English fop that is the butt of Portia's ridicule in *Merchant*, Shakespeare wants to win her in a different way, as a subject for literature. Her haughtiness fascinates him as something to be conquered; and he will conquer by adapting her story for the English stage.

Equating writing about a woman with possessing her may seem whimsical, but Snider infuses this literary domination with allegorical significance: Shakespeare's capture of Portia is a sign of the *translatio imperii* from Venice to England. Snider's Shakespeare sees Venice as a symbol of mutability and decadence.[8] Because his art will outlast life, however, he may be able to salvage something from that decay by eternalizing Portia, who in her splendor and arrogance symbolizes Venice to him:

> Ah me! this Portia here must vanish soon,
> All beautiful Venice seems now drooping down,
> I feel their transitory gayety;
> Can I not fix them in their primal bloom,
> And this Venetian palace and its folk
> Wrest from the vicious blows of assassin Time?

(238)

The apparent aestheticism veils a political theme. Speaking of Portia, the "grand prize" of the age, Shakespeare says, "She means to my thought

this question: who is to be the successor of Venice in the world's inheritance? . . . Is the Venetian heirship to fall to our England?" (224).

As Othello's case may show, Venice has become so decadent that its
security depends on "foreign mercenaries even of a different race" (226).
What is obviously needed to preserve the glory of Venice—that is, western
culture—from complete decay is an infusion of creative energy from some
other part of Europe, and Shakespeare feels he has been chosen to take
this "task God-sent" upon his shoulders. Saving Venice can only be ac-
complished by transforming it, however: most of all, Portia will have to
speak English on the stage, a language that now she scorns to speak to
Falconbridge. This again has a deeper significance, as Shakespeare fore-
sees the day when English will be the "universal tongue," he himself "of
poesy's world-empire the next heir" (239). This English hegemony in the
fields of culture and language is then explicitly linked to the English colo-
nizing exploits in America. Snider's Shakespeare thus becomes the figurehead of a triple British Imperialism: political, linguistic, and poetic.

Yet, as I have suggested, to Snider this is not the end of the matter. The
episode is full of topical allusions to the international situation in 1916, in
particular the Great War in Europe, with the United States as then still
neutral. When Falconbridge and Shakespeare are traveling to Belmont in
their "English gondola," the rival German suitor makes his boat collide
with theirs on purpose. It is not necessarily a coincidence that in 1916 the
English and German fleets clashed off Jutland in one of the century's main
naval encounters. Besides, the German is described in terms that are more
reminiscent of wartime propaganda than of Portia's description of his
counterpart in *Merchant*: "In the morning he is pious or perhaps philo-
sophic; but at midday he is full of fight, will whip the whole world and
make it more German; in the evening his beer gets the better of him and
he droops. Still he knows more than all the rest of these suitors, and as he
is evermore the soldier he may try to storm Portia and all Belmont by
straight assault" (232). Later, during the wooing at Belmont, the German
quarrels with the French suitor "over precedence of positions" (257). All
this suggests, of course, that Snider has an eye on the war raging in Europe. Moreover, he is prophetically aware of the threat to British hegemony: the description of Venice as a decaying empire that needs the help
of "foreign mercenaries even of a different race" (226) is at least as appli-
cable to Britain in 1916 as it is to Venice in Shakespeare's time. The wheel
has come full circle, and the time has come for another transfer of empire.

The identity of the new world power is revealed more clearly later in the
poem. In a Venetian library, Shakespeare overhears a number of characters
discussing the shortcomings in his work, when one of them suggests that
the answer to these lies in the country of Atlantis, clearly meaning
America. Shakespeare himself takes up this suggestion, and muses that his

works may be foreshadowings of greater things to be realized across the
ocean:

> My very last shapes of peopled creation
> Are only buds of a higher efflorescence
> Perchance to be seen in Atlantis.
> Once I stood on the sea-shore at Bristol
> And gazed at the prophetic sails of the ships
> As they pushed out westward bound for Virginia,
> Breaking over our insular limits
> To dare the limitless future.
> So I felt mine own spirit beating within
> To wing itself over all boundaries,
> And now I know my Genius aspiring
> Even beyond the walls of my Shakespearopolis.

(351–52)

The issues left unresolved in Shakespeare's works include racial inequality
and the position of women. These, we are told, will one day be solved, and
Shakespeare's works will be superseded as the culmination of humanity,
in the "coming Seculum" of New Atlantis. Shakespearopolis, exemplary
for its period yet flawed by its class system and bigotry, will be superseded
by "new folk-ordered Prosperopolis"—the city of Young Prospero from
the West, the first American.

Thus, somewhat surprisingly, Snider fulfills the expectations aroused by
the epic genre. Like many classical epics, the *Shakespeariad* is nationalistic, and in a moment of crisis it looks back to the great figures of the national past. True, Shakespeare was not really an American, but his use of
the English language makes him a sort of honorary U.S. citizen. Besides,
who ever asked Aeneas for his green card? The migration of a culture to
new shores, leading to a renewal of empire, is an age-honored convention
of the epic genre.

My second example, the half example, most resembles Grillo's appropriation of Shakespeare for Italy. In the second volume of his autobiography, *You've Had Your Time*, Anthony Burgess recounts how his 1964
novel on Shakespeare, *Nothing Like the Sun*, had an abortive offspring in
the seventies, when he himself was living in Italy. Burgess was asked to
write a script for a television project, to be entitled *Shakespeare da Noi*,
Shakespeare among us, "us" being the Italians.[9] The program was to center on two stages of Shakespeare's contact with Italy: first through his acquaintance with Giordano Bruno, in exile in England, and later through
his actual visit to northern Italy, accompanying the earl of Southampton
on a diplomatic mission to the Veneto. Burgess realized that there was no
evidence whatsoever that Shakespeare ever left England, but he was not

deterred: "All this was fanciful, but it might make good television" (309). This exercise in appropriating the Bard for Italy was to be partly financed by the Italian television network, RAI.

Burgess leaves little doubt about his own incentive to collaborate on this project: money. But what was on the minds of the backers from RAI? Why make a film about Shakespeare's completely fictitious visit to Italy, rather than a historically accurate portrait of any of the dozens of great artists and thinkers of the Italian Renaissance? Obviously, what was on the minds of the financiers of a scheme that was never realized is not an easy question to answer. Still, the project described by Burgess looks like a diluted version of Grillo's theory, and might have served to reinforce the national glory of the Italian Renaissance with the icon of Anglo-Saxon supremacy, William Shakespeare, as a symbolic acknowledgment of where the real power lay now, in the twentieth century.

It was not to be, however. As Burgess reports, RAI was unwilling to put up the necessary funds for their part of the deal. What was made instead was, in Burgess's words, "a shoestring abomination made with British money alone, with my script rejected and [not surprisingly] the Italian element wholly expunged."[10]

Whereas Burgess never got beyond the "first draft scripts" of his project, some years later we find a similar plot in *Serenissima* (1986) by Erica Jong, a personal friend of Burgess's. Although Jong has identified Virginia Woolf's *Orlando* as her source of inspiration, there are also uncanny resemblances to Burgess's project: for instance, in a framing device, Jong speaks of a film version of Shakespeare's life, which like her own novel is called *Serenissima* and features a visit by Shakespeare and Southampton to Venice.[11] Besides, Jong makes Burgess himself a character in her novel: Björn, the director of the film, goes "in hiding . . . in Lugano, staying with Anthony and Liana Burgess."[12] His project is in danger after a scandal has caused RAI to pull out from their financial commitments (94). The resemblance to the real Burgess's experience of having his Shakespeare project canceled because RAI pulled out is too close to be a mere coincidence.[13]

Despite these resemblances, Jong obviously gives her own twist to the plot of Shakespeare in Venice, especially by seeing it from a female perspective. More accurately, one might speak of a double female-perspective, which allows Jong to juxtapose past and present. The narrator, Jessica Pruitt, is a modern-day American film star who visits Venice in 1984 to sit on the jury of the Venice film festival. During her stay there, Jessica is miraculously transported to the year 1592, where she merges with Shylock's daughter Jessica, the role she was to have played in the film version of *Serenissima*; and she meets Shakespeare and Southampton, who have fled the plague by making the Grand Tour to Italy.

Shakespeare, in this fairy tale for modern women, is cast as Prince Charming, albeit one meant for adult consumption. The book confirms the same cliché that has more recently been used in *Shakespeare in Love*, that of Shakespeare as the greatest lover the world has ever known. It goes without saying that, in an Erica Jong novel, the greatest lover is also expected to perform in bed. With uncharacteristic coyness, the narrator asks, "Was Will Shakespeare good in bed? Let the reader judge!" (172). Then she proceeds to give that reader the evidence on which s/he may base his/her judgment: "we were caught up in a sort of natural disaster, an act of God, a shipwreck, a typhoon, a tempest over which we had absolutely no control" (172). In spite of the mention of disasters, the answer seems to be an unequivocal "yes."

Jong's Shakespeare, then, is not a model of chastity, nor is he expected to be. Here, of course, looms an obstacle from the documented facts of Shakespeare's life that Jong has to circumvent: can the perfect lover simultaneously be a heartless philanderer, enjoying himself with an exotic beauty in Venice while his wife Anne is minding the kids in Stratford? Jong's Shakespeare does not feel any pangs of conscience over Anne, since they have become estranged by her scolding him and mocking his profession. Still, the narrator is aware of Anne's perspective, too: she has become materialistic out of the need to feed her children (130). Biological and social pressures have caused them to drift apart.

Paradoxically, this greatest of all lovers is expected to be monogamous in relation to Jessica, whereas Jessica herself is not completely averse to the advances of Southampton, and she is free from guilt because he forces himself upon her (183). What begins as rape ends as passionate lovemaking (208). Here Jong characteristically turns the patriarchal double standard on its head, albeit at the considerable risk of suggesting that women can be forced into the enjoyment of sex.[14]

All in all, Jong's Shakespeare portrait seems to be a sketch of what she sees as the ideal man for the 80s: an experienced lover, yet monogamous, a good and caring father, sensitive and tender-hearted, and with just a bit of old-fashioned derring-do: "poets think they can do everything—deliver babies, sail Venetian barks, defeat death itself—and Will is no exception" (143). But this Early-Modern Alan Alda has a few weaknesses, too: he gambles (121), he becomes seasick (154), and he is envious of his more successful rival Marlowe to the point of (prophetically) wishing him dead (173). In spite of his love for Jessica, he is indecisive when it comes to protecting her from being raped (183). On the road with her and a foundling baby, fleeing from his creditors, he is "frightened for his life" (155), and she even thinks of him as another baby she has to care for (206). It is his very lack of machismo, however, that gives Jessica her chance to grow: "His fear made me brave. If it is true, as has sometimes been said, that the human species is distinguished by its ability to be best when things are worst, then I am a charter member of the human species. For the worse things get, the better I am. . . . Give me a boy's doublet, two assassins and a lover in pursuit, noble lines to speak, a baby to protect—in short, a heroine's role—and all is well with my world. But leave me alone in a cozy room with a clock ticking away the minutes and I may just go mad!" (155).

If Shakespeare represents the perfect lover, from another perspective he also symbolizes a strangely idealized past. Jessica's journey to the past is a liberating experience in spite of the horrors and repression she witnesses. At worst, the past is seen as just another version of the present: Jessica in 1984 is as tied down by legal restrictions imposed by her grandfather's will as Portia is by her father's (86 ff.). Jessica muses that men, even Shakespeare and Southampton, have always fought over women, then as now, the main thing being the relations between these men rather than the women themselves. As a Jew's daughter, her freedom of movement in 1592 is circumscribed as it would not be in her life as a film actress, but she has ways of evading the control. In fact, the repressiveness has its bright side, too: "Exciting it surely was, for sex was dangerous then—and therefore more piquant. Sex most dangerous is most rare. If nothing can come of it (neither plagues nor babies), then perhaps there is no existential risk and the mystery is less" (172). At best, the past as the narrator imagines it is superior to the present: she sees Queen Elizabeth as the greatest of all feminists, whereas "all the last four hundred years had been a falling away from the feminism that Elizabeth herself embodied" (39). Even so, Jessica realizes that Jews in 1592 Venice are subject to persecution. She actually witnesses a pogrom. But lest the reader see such barbarities as typical only of the past, in present-day Venice the narrator comes across a "plaque commemorating the Venetian Jews deported in 1943–44," which is "a somber reminder that the persecutions of the Jews have accelerated, not diminished, throughout history" (109–10).

The opposition between past and present also has a geographical correlative. The novel opens with the heroine traveling on a jet plane from L.A. to Venice across six time zones, and this in itself is compared to time travel. Like Shakespeare, Venice stands for the Old World, which has retained some of the magic of the past. Jessica's home country, America, was an unspoiled world in Shakespeare's age, but it is now "a whole continent consecrated to greed, and given over to the rape of nature and the death of art" (196). Thus it appears that Jong's view is that America stands in need of an infusion of some old-world *joie de vivre* rather than the reverse. In the transfer of political, military, and economic power, the cultural domain has somehow been forgotten, and left behind in Europe.

There is a further dimension to the book's Venetian setting, in its being vaguely reminiscent of the "green world" of Shakespeare's comedies.

Venice, in both 1984 and 1592, is described as a "city of illusions where reality becomes fantasy and fantasy becomes reality" (8). It is a city of mirrors and reflections, down to the reflection on the ceiling of the shimmering water outside, for which the Venetians have a special idiom (1). Jessica spells out the thematic implications of all this mirror imagery: "Each time one comes to Venice, it reflects back another self, another dream, as if it were partly your own mirror" (8). The particular dream Venice gives her this time is one of Shakespeare, the man that fulfills all her desires, in the setting of an idealized Renaissance. This is not intended to be a true picture of the essential Shakespeare. Jessica's conception of both the Renaissance and Shakespeare is presented as a self-projection and wishful thinking. Yet it is an enabling fantasy, which frees the woman that immerses herself in it. Jessica's return to the present is described as a rebirth, resembling Botticelli's Venus rising from the waves (220).

In this respect, we may perhaps see Jong's fabulation as a fictional analogue to the work of many feminist critics, who have come to regard Shakespeare as not necessarily feminist in himself, but as lending himself to appropriation in the cause of emancipation. In particular, it is the comedies featuring strong and independent-minded young women such as Helena, Viola, Rosalind, Portia, and Jessica that have been seen to support this view.[15] In her novel, Jong appropriates both one of these plays and its author. In her time-travel fantasy, Jessica elopes with Shakespeare dressed as a boy, thus reenacting the liberating experience of many Shakespearean heroines, including the original Jessica; and on Shakespeare she projects the complementary fantasy of the man that such an emancipated woman needs.

Jong's structural principle, then, is not a three-way split between Renaissance Italy, Shakespeare's England, and twentieth-century United States, as it was in Snider; nor is there an antithesis between South and West, Italy and Shakespeare, culture and power, as in Grillo and, embryonically, in Burgess's RAI project. For Jong, Shakespeare and Italy together seem to stand for art, the imagination, the past, and liberation, the antithesis of modern-day philistine and materialistic America from which her protagonist flees to Europe. Snider's theme is thus stood on its head: here it is the New World that requires an infusion of cultural energy from the Old, rather than the reverse, nor has the New Atlantis resolved the issue of the position of women quite so satisfactorily as Snider had predicted some seventy years earlier.

Thus the facts of Shakespeare's life, or rather the authors' fantasies about his life, are made to reflect various concerns, including American imperial ambitions, Italians' pride in their cultural heritage, and feminism, respectively. In all these fantasies of Shakespearean travel, the notion of the shift of power and cultural prestige from the south of Europe to the west is projected back onto Shakespeare's life, yet the interpretations differ widely in their applications.

As far as Shakespeare's plays are concerned, the existence of appropriations in the name of a wide variety of political and social causes has long been recognized. When it is the life that is appropriated, however, the effect can be even more extreme, yet such uses of the Shakespeare-myth are still too often disregarded. For that reason alone, fictions of Shakespeare's life should be an interesting and challenging new field of study.

# Notes

1. See, for instance, Terence Hawkes, *Meaning by Shakespeare* (London: Routledge, 1992); and Graham Holderness and Bryan Loughrey, "Shakespearean Features," in *The Appropriation of Shakespeare: Post-Renaissance Reconstructions of the Works and the Myth*, ed. Jean I. Marsden (London: Harvester-Wheatsheaf, 1991), 183–201. I am indebted throughout this paper to the support and advice of my colleague Ton Hoenselaars.

2. A few notable exceptions are Samuel Schoenbaum's monumental *Shakespeare's Lives*, rev. ed. (Oxford: Oxford University Press, 1991); and Michael Dobson, *The Making of the National Poet: Shakespeare, Adaptation and Authorship, 1660–1769* (Oxford: Clarendon Press, 1992); but in neither of these is the deployment of Shakespeare as a character more than a sideline. Maurice J. O'Sullivan has anthologized a number of Shakespearean fictions in his *Shakespeare's Other Lives* (Jefferson, N.C.: McFarland, 1997). For the phenomenon of historical authors as fictional characters in general, see *Biofictions: The Rewriting of Romantic Lives in Contemporary Fiction and Drama*, ed. Martin Middeke and Werner Huber (Rochester, N.Y.: Camden House, 1999); and *The Author as Character: Representing Historical Writers in Western Literature*, ed. Paul Franssen and Ton Hoenselaars (Madison, N.J.: Fairleigh Dickinson University Press, 1999).

3. Terence Hawkes, *That Shakespeherian Rag: Essays on a Critical Process* (London: Methuen, 1986), in particular chap. 2.

4. *Coryats Crudities* (1611; London: Scolar Press, 1978), 254.

5. According to Samuel Schoenbaum, the suggestion that Shakespeare had visited Italy goes back at least to Charles Armitage Brown, in his *Shakespeare's Autobiographical Poems* (1838), followed by the German scholar Karl Elze in 1874. See Schoenbaum's *William Shakespeare: A Compact Documentary Life*, rev ed. (Oxford: Oxford University Press, 1987), 169 n.; and his *Shakespeare's Lives*, New Ed. (Oxford: Oxford University Press, 1993), 187. For a considered view of the likelihood of an Italian journey, see Mario Praz, "Shakespeare's Italy," *Shakespeare Survey* 7 (1954): 95–106. The theory has been practically discounted by Harry Levin, "Shakespeare's Italians," in *Shakespeare's Italy: Functions of Italian Locations in Renaissance Drama*, ed. Michele Marrapodi, A. J. Hoenselaars, et al. (Manchester: Manchester University Press, 1993), 28; and by Agostino Lombardo, "The Veneto, Metatheatre, and Shakespeare," in the same volume, 144. Angela Locatelli speaks of the evidence for Shakespeare in Mantua as "still inconclusive" (*Shakespeare's Italy* 79), and then proceeds to enumerate obvious gaps in Shakespeare's geographical knowledge. David C. McPherson, *Shakespeare, Jonson, and the Myth of Venice* (Newark: University of Delaware Press,

1990), gives an extensive survey of the various kinds of sources from which Shakespeare and Jonson could have learned about Venice without ever going there in person (17–26).

6. Ernesto Grillo, *Shakespeare and Italy* (Glasgow: Glasgow University Press, 1949), 148–49. Grillo's quote conflates *Cymbeline* 5.5.480–81 with *King John* 1.1.202–3, disregarding the latter passage's ironic attitude towards foreign travel.

7. Denton J. Snider, *Shakespeariad: A Dramatic Epos* (St. Louis: Sigma Publishing, 1916). On Snider's later preoccupation with *Hamlet*, see also Ann Thompson, *"The New Wing at Elsinor, The Redemption of the Hamlets* and Other Sequels, Prequels and Offshoots of *Hamlet,"* in *Renaissance Refractions: Essays in Honour of Alexander Shurbanov* (Sofia: Sofia University Press, 2001), 217–31.

8. Although Snider's aesthetic phrasing may seem anachronistic, Venice really was in decline by the late sixteenth century and perceived as such in England: see J. R. Mulryne, "History and Myth in *The Merchant of Venice,"* in *Shakespeare's Italy,* 87–99; and McPherson, *Shakespeare and the Myth,* 30–32.

9. Anthony Burgess, *You've Had Your Time* (London: Heinemann, 1990), 308–9.

10. Burgess does not name the scriptwriter responsible for this "shoestring abomination," but judging from the date in the early seventies, the reference must have been to John Mortimer's TV series, *William Shakespeare: The Untold Story.* A novelized version of that script was published afterwards as John Mortimer's *Shakespeare: The Untold Story* (1977; n.p.: Dell, 1978). For Mortimer's own view of the series, see his "Shakespeare and a Playwright of Today," in *Shakespeare, Man of the Theatre,* ed. Kenneth Muir et al. (Newark: University of Delaware Press, 1983), 18–33.

11. See Cynthia Thompkins, "Erica Jong," *Dictionary of Literary Biography* 152 (1995): 105.

12. Erica Jong, *Serenissima: A Novel of Venice* (London: Bantam, 1987), 94. Another edition of the novel is entitled *Shylock's Daughter: A Novel of Love in Venice* (New York: HarperCollins Publishers, 1995).

13. Burgess himself speaks of Jong as "my friend" in *You've Had Your Time,* 128, and mentions his own appearance in her book on page 382.

14. According to Carol Johnston, Jong's typical "method is the redefinition of stereotypes through the inversion of time-honored myths of human sexuality" ("Erica Jong," *Dictionary of Literary Biography* 2 [1978]: 253).

15. Cf. Gary Waller, introduction to *Shakespeare's Comedies,* ed. Gary Waller (London: Longman, 1991), 12–14. For a critical view, see Deborah E. Barker and Ivo Kamps, in "Shakespeare and Gender: An Introduction," *Shakespeare and Gender: A History* (London: Verso, 1995), 7.

# Gender on the Periphery

## JEAN E. HOWARD

IN THE 1590S AND THE FIRST DECADES OF THE SEVENTEENTH CENTURY, pirates, adventurers, and privateers became popular figures on the English stage. For example, *The Famous History of Sir Thomas Stukeley* (1596) dramatizes the life of an English man of fortune who served many of the monarchs of Europe before dying at the Battle of Alcazar in North Africa; *Fortune by Land and Sea* (1607–9) contains scenes depicting the capture of the infamous pirates, Clinton and Purser; *The Fair Maid of the West, Part 1* (1598?) follows the adventures of an imaginary English tavern girl who eventually becomes a privateer against the Spanish before conquering the Moorish king of Morocco with her dazzling beauty; and *A Christian Turned Turk* (1612) makes the notorious English pirate, John Ward, the protagonist of a lurid drama featuring the encounter of Jewish, Christian, and Muslim cultures in the North African port city of Tunis. In exploring plays such as these I will argue that collectively they helped to articulate both the ambitions and the anxieties of a nation poised to refigure its position on the world stage. In historical terms, these plays can best be understood through the intertwined categories of genre, gender, and nation. By creating the genre of the adventure play featuring a distinctive kind of swashbuckling masculine hero, the Early Modern theater forged an important cultural vehicle for exploring the contradictions of a particular moment in England's ongoing engagement in the international arena.[1]

Significantly, the adventure drama that I will examine is almost always set in the Mediterranean: in the cities of Italy, Spain, and Greece, but also in the towns and ports of North Africa and the Levant such as Tunis, Fez, and Antioch. Since classical times, the Mediterranean world, including by 1600 much of the powerful Ottoman Empire, had been the center both of culture and of commerce for the West. England, which produced the adventure plays about which I am writing, was decidedly peripheral to this great concentration of power in the Mediterranean world.[2] Consequently, the title for this essay, "Gender on the Periphery," is meant at least in part as a provocation. In the sixteenth century the English often described themselves, on their northern and foggy island, as a dull and cold-blooded

344

race with an immature culture, a crude diet, and an underdeveloped commercial life. They were anxious about whether their language could support a national literature and anxious about whether their island fortress might fall before the might of Spain.[3] One might logically assume, therefore, and with some historical justification, that in this essay I will be dealing with gender issues in plays set in England, the nation on the periphery of Northern Europe on the edge of a world system centered on the Mediterranean.

Instead, I am deliberately reversing the actualities of history in order to explore another strand in England's cultural life at this time; namely, its nascent national self-assertiveness, including its attempts to imagine itself as a central player on the world stage. The two phenomena, national self-assertiveness and national insecurity, were flip sides of one coin. Fearing itself belated in regard to the cultural and economic powers of the Mediterranean, England nonetheless harbored clear territorial, cultural, and economic ambitions. For example, in the late sixteenth century, England began newly to assert itself as a trading presence in the Mediterranean world even as the public theater was presenting "Eastern" dramas featuring Mediterranean people and places, especially those of North Africa and the Levant. Increasingly, the English theater cast its gaze both east and south, imagining, with hubris and anxiety co-mingled, the Mediterranean world that was—to the English—on the periphery of their actual and imaginative experience. In exploring the adventure play and the problematics of its cross-cultural representations, I frame my central question this way: how, in this particular genre, did a theater situated on the rim of Northern Europe dramatize the cultures of the less immediately familiar corners of the Mediterranean basin, and why did gender figure as it did in these representations? As I hope to show, by elaborating a particular kind of stage narrative and creating a particular kind of masculine hero, the adventure play could embody both the ambitions and the anxieties of a peripheral nation attempting to be something more.

## Theater and Genre

Contemporary work on the Early Modern theater has for several decades been influenced by New Historicism that made effective use of Foucault's idea of discourse to investigate links between texts we call literary and other kinds of texts and social practices. Discourse analysis typically works on a horizontal axis; that is, it investigates the appearance, across a range of sites, of the languages and practices that together constitute a specific strand of discourse, whether one involving sexuality, the law, religion, housewifery, or divine-right monarchy. Such work has successfully shown links between texts, subjects, and the sites of power through which discourses circulate and gain authority. It has been less successful in offering accounts of historical change.

By contrast, literary historians often link texts on a vertical axis, with emphasis on the ways the dominant forms and languages of literary works alter over time. Because they often construct literature as an autonomous entity, however, traditional literary historians frequently are oblivious to what most interests New Historicists, namely, the ways in which texts designated as literary are linked to other texts and practices in the culture at large.[4] In this essay I am turning to the concept of genre, or textual kinds, to effect a bridge between these two forms of inquiry and to reanimate investigations of the historicity of literary texts, a project involving attention to literary forms as well as to discursive context. Examining genre allows one to investigate not only how the special properties of the literary system work on or transform the discourses by which texts are traversed but, equally, how the literary system itself is altered by its implication in a broader social formation. The emergence of new generic forms, alterations in existing genres, generic hybrids—these are all symptoms of the dialectical process by which the textual system plays a mediating role in cultural change.[5]

Paying renewed attention to the historical function of genre is especially productive when thinking about the Early Modern stage, where generic experimentation and hybridization were common. Critics agree that this stage was unusually central and sensitive to cultural change, registering and producing the new through innovative dramatic forms and conventions.[6] The adventure play is one such innovation, and fully to understand its significance would involve situating it in relation to other stage genres such as the national history play, set in England; or tragedies of state, set primarily in Europe outside England; or domestic tragedy, set in rural gentry households. It is part of my larger argument that these textual kinds can be distinguished not only by particular features of style and construction, but also by their use of geographical setting, the class investments negotiated through each, and their representations of gender. Since, however, I cannot here examine the entire field of Early Modern dramatic kinds, I will focus on the particular features of the adventure play and begin to outline the particular cultural work it performed in Early Modern England.

Typically, adventure plays feature non-aristocratic English heroes who engage in notable actions in lands far distant from England itself. In terms of dramatic lineage, adventure plays owe something to heroic dramas such as Marlowe's *Tamburlaine, Parts 1 and 2*, that established the popularity of a certain hyperbolic rhetoric as the signature of martial heroism and also popularized "the East" as the exotic locale where martial exploits might occur.[7] Adventure plays also draw on popular chivalric romance dramas such as *Sir Clyomon and Clamydes* or *The Four Apprentices of London*, both of which imitate medieval aristocratic romance but do so to satisfy the tastes of the middling sort. This is the kind of play hilariously satirized in Beaumont and Fletcher's *Knight of the Burning Pestle*, in which a grocer's apprentice becomes a wandering knight.[8]

Most adventure plays, however, are more solidly rooted in contemporary time and place than the chivalric romance drama is. Often, their heroes are stage versions of actual historical figures such as Thomas Stukeley and John Ward, to whom I referred in the opening lines of this essay; or the notorious Shirley brothers—Anthony, Thomas, and Robert—who featured in the 1607 adventure play, *The Three English Brothers*. A few works in this genre, such as Heywood's *Fair Maid of the West*, notable for a female adventurer, do not foreground an historical protagonist, but *through* Bess a very important historical figure, Queen Elizabeth, is repeatedly referenced; and like all adventure plays, *The Fair Maid* is set in actual and locatable geographical places: Plymouth, Cadiz, Fez. Likewise, *A Christian Turned Turk* takes place primarily in the cosmopolitan and disreputable city of Tunis, as does Massinger's *The Renegado*.

Moreover, although the adventure play resembles the chivalric romance in its emphasis on the martial prowess of an adventuring hero, the protagonists of the adventure play are typically of a lower social class and move through "real" geographies, not the unlocatable spaces of romance. The spatial mobility of adventure heroes, moreover, often mirrors their social mobility. To use Robert Nerlich's terms, adventure drama refunctions narratives of aristocratic chivalry in the interests of a different social group.[9] Poor commoners such as Bess Bridges or penniless gentlemen such as Thomas Stukeley, through bravery and skill, achieve prominence as military leaders, privateers, or, more disreputably, as pirate captains. This suggests what we would now call the class aspirations coded within this genre, the aspirations of social and economic interlopers who rise above their stations and in so doing signify both national self-assertion and vulnerability.

Although the geographical arena for adventure plays is most often the Mediterranean world, especially North Africa and the Levant, adventuring heroes frequently first move along the west coast of Europe, stopping at ports in Ireland, the Azores, or Spain. There are good reasons for the Mediterranean's being the destination of the adventurer. As historians such as Robert Brenner have shown, the late sixteenth century saw the English involved in a vastly expanded network of commercial activities, including the founding of the Elizabethan joint-stock companies. As Italian and Spanish dominance of the Mediterranean declined, the English, through the activities of the Turkey Company (1581), the Barbary Company (1585), the Levant Company (1592), and the East India Company (1599), began to increase their trade in the busy Mediterranean ports stretching from Tangier to Aleppo.[10] Both legitimate merchants and privateers/pirates saw this region as a place where fortunes could quickly be made and also, of course, lost. Imagined as a site of possibility and of danger, the Mediterranean was home to the much-feared Barbary pirates and partially ringed by the empire of the Ottoman Turks.[11]

As part of the cultural work it performed, the adventure play "mapped" this Mediterranean world for the average Elizabethan playgoer, to whom Tunis, Turks, and Barbary pirates were places and beings with whom they very seldom had had first-hand acquaintance. And while at first blush the adventure play may appear a naive genre, the imaginative mapping it performed was a complex and often contradictory exercise. It did not, of course, involve mimetic realism, providing "accurate" accounts of foreign peoples and places. Rather, plays in this genre usually dealt in stereotypes and melodramatic oppositions between Englishmen and various categories of imagined others, most notably Spaniards, Moors, Turks, and Jews. Adventure drama was thus a prime site for producing Early Modern religious, cultural, and racial categories of difference. Through its technologies of costumes, wigs, and dyed skin, the stage rendered such differences spectacularly visible.

And yet, the complexities of the historical moment within which these adventure plays were produced made this process of category construction fraught and unstable. As G. K. Hunter reminds us, in the sixteenth century "the European nations were inexorably emerging from the matrix of Christendom; but they did not yet stand distinct enough from one another to allow simple dramatic opposition";[12] that is, the breakdown of Catholic hegemony coincided with the first emergence of modern nation-states. Hence, while a common Christian culture still to some extent bound Europeans together, nationalism and the effects of the Reformation drove them apart, with the result that Europe was often divided against itself rather than seamlessly united against an Islamic enemy in the Mediterranean. In the 1590s, as Richard Helgerson and others have shown, England defined its Protestant nationhood in sharp opposition to Spain's Catholic dominion,[13] and Spain was another European power. At the same time, England was undertaking more extensive trade with parts of the Ottoman Empire, with which it was also supposedly in religious conflict. Since the medieval Crusades, Christians had in theory aligned themselves against the Islamic infidel. In this confusing historical context, categorization itself became newly difficult. It was impossible for the adventure play simply to circulate stable images of England and its racial or religious others, since these categories were constantly being redefined, realigned, and triangulated.

In what follows, I examine several adventure plays, focusing in particular on how gender functions in this genre to express and sometimes allay anxieties about England's place in this fraught international arena. I will argue that adventure drama is premised on a certain kind of male subject at its center, what I will simply call the "renegade male."[14] Typically constructed as a locus of English patriotic sentiment, the swashbuckling heroes of adventure drama are both attractive and dangerously unstable, antiheroes as often as heroes. Their masculinity is of a bellicose, insubordinate, and extravagant character. Through such figures the theater captured both the energy of English popular ambitions and the fear that such ambitions might lead to the confounding of English identity. Women are almost never the protagonists of adventure drama and comprise only a small fraction of the cast of any play. While the few women who do appear in this genre certainly perform crucial narrative and ideological functions, the adventure genre does not make marriage its animating telos, as does Early Modern romantic comedy. Rather, at the heart of adventure drama lies a conversion paradigm, the actual or threatened transformation of the English hero into something alien: into a Turk, a Muslim, a traitor, a renegado.[15] Frequently, it is sexual congress with an alien woman that triggers or emblematizes this transformation, but I will argue that the pervasive fantasy that the heroes of this genre will turn into their opposites underwrites adventure narratives even when the trope of conversion through sexual union is missing.

## Thomas Stukeley and Renegade Masculinity

To define the masculine hero of adventure drama more precisely, I turn to an "actual" historical figure, Sir Thomas Stukeley, one of the most colorful of the Elizabethan adventurers. Although he was eventually denounced as a traitor and a "Romanist" by Queen Elizabeth, Stukeley nonetheless was presented as a hero, and a specifically English hero, in a number of cultural productions from the late sixteenth century, including several ballads celebrating his exploits, a play, *The Famous History of Sir Thomas Stukeley* (1596), and another play, George Peele's *The Battle of Alcazar*, probably written in the late 1580s but published in 1594, in which Stukeley's name appears rather incongruously on the title page, a sure sign that its presence was assumed to enhance the play's popularity.[16] In fact, the full title reads: *The Battle of Alcazar, fought in Barbarie, betweene Sebastian king of Portugall, and Abdelmelec King of Marocco, With the Death of Captaine Stukeley.* Evident here is Peele's aspiration to link his homebred adventurer to the most significant events, and people, on the world stage.

So who was this Captain Stukeley? Historically speaking, he was the son of a Devon sheriff without much money who tried to make his way in the world by putting himself in the service of prominent noblemen: at a young age he served in the household of the duke of Suffolk, later fought in France with the forces of Henry VIII, still later served the duke of Somerset, and at mid-century moved back and forth between France and England seeking various employments under Mary, Edward, and then Elizabeth.[17] In the 1550s he married Anne Curtis, daughter of a rich London alderman, and he was said to have married for money. The money, however, did not last long in the face of Stukeley's prodigality, and throughout the 1560s Stukeley petitioned Elizabeth for funds and men to undertake a number of projects to improve his fortunes and, supposedly, hers, including a plan to settle Florida.

Under both Mary and Elizabeth, Stukeley sometimes acted as a privateer, an adventurer who with covert monarchical support raided the ships of France and Spain carrying goods and bullion across the Atlantic or along Europe's western shores. The problem with privateering was that the very monarchs who encouraged the practice and benefited monetarily from it often felt forced to repudiate the activities of privateers who were captured.[18] On the other hand, monarchs also often had difficulty controlling the men who undertook privateering missions. The line between state-sanctioned raids on the shipping of England's enemies and entrepreneurial piracy was often a slim one, and Stukeley seems to have fallen into that class of Elizabethan adventurers whose activities were always a cause of concern for those in authority. For example, in the 1560s Stukeley went to Ireland where he became an intermediary in negotiations with the Irish leader, Shane O'Neill. When he asked to be named marshall in Ireland, however, Elizabeth and Cecil said no, probably judging Stukeley too unreliable to entrust with serious state office. In 1569 he was accused of inciting the Irish hostilities against Elizabeth and imprisoned in Dublin for seventeen weeks. He then promised Elizabeth that he was ready to come to court to answer the charges, but once on-board ship, he headed not for England but for Spain, where he put himself in Phillip's service, supporting his bid to invade Ireland. Phillip knighted Stukeley in 1571; he fought for the Pope in the Battle of Lepanto, all the while attempting to raise money for a long-planned invasion of Ireland. In 1577 the Pope finally granted him the resources for a small-scale incursion. Traveling from Rome with a number of Italian soldiers, Stukeley stopped in Lisbon, where he was persuaded by Don John of Portugal to join his expedition going to North Africa to give aid to Muly Mohamet, the usurper whose uncle, Abdelmelic, was attempting to recapture the Moroccan throne. Spain promised to help Portugal in "this holy Christian war" (*Alcazar* 2.4.635), but instead secretly sided with Abdelmelic and detained the promised aid. The Portuguese forces were resoundingly and disastrously defeated in 1578 at Alcazar, where Stukeley died.

In many ways Stukeley was a perfect protagonist for the adventure-play genre. An impoverished gentleman with enormous personal ambition, he was acknowledged to be a strong military leader, and those skills took him to Ireland, Lepanto, and Alcazar. At the same time, many of his actions were unreadable. Was he an English hero in Ireland or a traitor? Was he dangerously self-serving, or was he upholding English honor in distant lands? Hero or anti-hero? Privateer or pirate? It was possible for Elizabeth and Cecil to think one thing and for Stukeley to be presented in quite another light in the popular drama or the ballad literature.

To underscore precisely what kind of masculinity Stukeley came to represent on the stage and its suitability for what I am calling the characteristic narratives of conversion that define the adventure genre, I want to turn to an anonymous play of 1596, *The Famous History of Sir Thomas Stukeley*. Throughout, Stukeley's Englishness is stressed. He is referred to variously as "the English Captain" (ll. 1782, 1834), "a gallant Englishman" (l. 1707), "a fond Englishman" (l. 2190), and "this Englishman" (ll. 1917, 2297); and he lays claim to "a noble English hart" (l. 1484) and "a faithful English hart" (l. 1503). The play featuring this Englishman is structured episodically. Each act is set in a particular place: England, Ireland, Spain and Portugal, Rome, and finally North Africa. (Most of act 4, the one set in Rome, is now lost, and its action is summarized by a Chorus.) This episodic structure and the geographical progress it maps construct the protagonist in a certain way. He is a wanderer, someone who moves further and further from "home," in the process crossing not only national boundaries but religious and racial ones, as well. For a London audience, it is hard to imagine what would have been more "foreign," the wild Irish, the Spanish Catholics, the Pope, or the "Negro Moor" Muly Mohamet. Stukeley interacts with them all and is allied with several, demonstrating at once his daring and courage and also his dangerous capacity to resemble what is supposedly most alien to him.

For example, in the second act, set in Ireland, the hotheaded Stukeley arrives at the English garrison there that is being besieged by the forces of Shane O'Neill. Almost immediately, Stukeley draws his sword against Captain Herbert, the English commander of the garrison, because the two of them had had a private quarrel back in England. Here Stukeley puts his own personal honor before his official mission to reinforce the English garrison. Moreover, in the first skirmish outside the walls of the garrison, Stukeley refuses to obey the signal for retreat and is shut out of the garrison for the night. This is as much a symbolic as a literal excursion, marking the Englishman as unfit for the civil and civilized enclosure represented by the garrison. Although it is *against* the Irish that Stukeley here fights, it is *in close proximity* to the Irish that he spends the night in the fields. Stukeley's brand of English masculinity is colored with a dangerous wildness that becomes the defining mark of the adventure hero.

In this regard, the definitive moment of Stukeley's life in *The Famous History* may well be his decision to abandon the London career for which his father had destined him. In act 2 he attends the Inns of Court and makes a City marriage with Anne Curtis to improve his financial standing. He is thus tied to a variety of specifically London places and institutions, yet he rebels against them all, turning his back both on a career as a lawyer and on the role of husband. Three days after he marries Anne Curtis, he uses her dowry to outfit himself for the Irish expedition then afoot. Leaving behind both the bounded domestic space and the bounded national space of England, Stukeley never returns to either. Implicitly renouncing the citizen values of thrift, civic duty, domesticity, and fidelity to the monarch, he increasingly embodies a hyperbolic attachment to chivalric honor and self-assertion, here severed from their origins as part of aristocratic life and appropriated by an impecunious gentleman with ambitions to be a king. These ambitions potentially convert Stukeley into the mirror image of the "foreign" and dangerous inhabitants of the world beyond England's borders: the wild Irish, the treacherous Spaniards, and finally, the Moors of North Africa.

To see how this is so, consider the last two acts of the "other" Stukeley play, George Peele's *Alcazar*, in which Stukeley joins forces with Don Sebastian of Portugal to bring aid to Muly Mohamet, the Moroccan king whose occupation of the Moroccan throne is being challenged by his uncle, Abdelmelic. Peele's play records the difficulties facing an English playwright trying to make sense of this historic event even as it reveals the paradoxical status of the adventure hero. On the one hand, the battle of Alcazar could be understood as a Christian crusade against a fearsome Islamic enemy. This is how both the Pope and Don Sebastian describe their participation in the battle against Abdelmelic. On the other hand, this way of understanding the battle is obviously inadequate, since Christendom is decidedly *not* unified in *Alcazar*, and neither is the Muslim world. The Protestant states are not allies of the Pope, and Catholic Spain betrays Catholic Portugal by deliberately withholding its promised aid. In Peele's play, Don Sebastian is called a "Christian king" (3.3.870, 5.1.1448) or a "Christian Prince" (3.2.842), while Phillip is repeatedly labeled the "Catholic king" (for example, 3.1.762, 3.1.776, 3.2.841, 5.1.1337), perhaps suggesting that Portugal is less Catholic than Spain and so a worthier English ally. On the other side, in what is essentially a civil war, the Moorish king, Abdelmelic, fights his own nephew, Muly Mohamet, and both are Muslims. Against the older paradigm of Christian-Muslim enmity is set the reality of the fragmentation of Europe into rival states whose alliances are determined not by an imagined Christian unity but by intra-

Christian struggles for commercial and political preeminence. In this context, Stukeley holds a complicated position. From an English perspective, he entered the battle on the "right side," in that he followed Don Sebastian of Portugal, who was betrayed by the treacherous Phillip of Spain, England's dearest enemy. On the other hand, he also entered the battle on the "wrong side," in that both he and Don Sebastian back Muly Mohamet, who is depicted in racialized and racist terms as a black barbarian and kin murderer, who does not deserve the throne to which he aspires.

The relationship between Stukeley and Muly is crucial to understanding both the mode of English masculinity foregrounded in the adventure play and also the implicit anxiety about the transformation or conversion of the male hero that haunts the genre. In *Alcazar* Stukeley is explicitly rebuked by the governor of Lisbon for being a traitor to his country in undertaking an expedition against Ireland. The governor says,

> Under correction, are ye not all Englishmen,
> And longs not Ireland to that kingdome Lords?
> Then may I speake my conscience in the cause,
> Sance scandall to the holy see of Rome,
> Unhonorable is this expedition,
> And misbeseeming yo to meddle in.

(2.2.403–8)

Yet Stukeley is also lionized as the Englishman who died with kings, the Englishman whose overweening ambition and overblown rhetoric make him a native Tamburlaine. As he says at one point, "Huffe it brave minde, and never cease t'aspire, / Before thou raigne sole king of thy desire" (2.2.466–67). Importantly, in Peele's play, Muly Mohamet emerges as the figure who most closely mirrors Stukeley and who is also used to manage the anxiety aroused by Stukeley's treachery to his country and his overweening, somewhat lawless ambition. The Moorish king thus reveals what is dangerous about Stukeley and yet also allows that danger to be displaced onto a racialized dark body.

In *Alcazar*, like Stukeley, Muly employs a huffing, over-reaching rhetoric; and like Stukeley, though in more lurid form, he transgresses his country's deepest taboos. The opening dumb show of Peele's plays shows Muly presiding over the murders of his brothers and his uncle. Not only is this kin murder, but it also violates Moroccan laws governing monarchical succession. By Moroccan law, the crown passed from brother to brother, not from father to son.[19] Muly's father transgressively gave his throne to his son Muly rather than to his brother Abdelmelic; and Muly compounded the crime by killing all those family members who might block his own son's succession. Peele thus constructs Muly as a cruel despot whose evil is underscored by repeated references to his black skin ("Blacke in his looke, and bloudie in his deeds," prologue, act 1, l. 16) and by the epithet, "the Negro" Moor (prologue, act 1, l. 7; 3.2.851). By contrast, in regard to Muly's uncle, Abdelmelic, there is no mention of the color of his skin. Rather, he is subtly classicized: the Turks who guard his tent are compared to the Mermidons who guarded Achilles (1.1.68–69)—and consistently depicted as a rule-governed, law-abiding leader. At the end of the play, when Muly is defeated, the victorious brother of Abdelmelic orders Abdelmelic to receive a royal burial, but of Muly he says,

> That all the world may learne by him to avoide,
> To hall on princes to injurious warre,
> His skin we will be parted from his flesh,
> And being stifned out and stuft with strawe,
> So to deterre and feare the lookers on,
> From anie such foule fact or bad attempt,
> Awaie with him.

> (5.1.1442–47)

Thus perish traitors.

The *other* traitor in the text, of course, is Stukeley, but the spectacular foregrounding of the bestial black body and the bloody deeds of Muly displace the onus of treachery away from the Englishman, allowing Peele to construct a recuperative ending for the play, in which Stukeley dies remembering his native country and praying to be remembered there (5.1.1328–72). Yet by acting as the Englishman's dark double, Muly Mohamet reveals the implicit transformation-motif at the heart of the adventure play. Stukeley is an exemplar of English heroism, but one whose ambition and whose adventures in the alien courts of Spain and Rome, and in the sands of North Africa, render him vulnerable, with a vulnerability imagined as the transformation into something alien, here given riveting stage embodiment in the person of Muly Mohamet, the Negro Moor.

## Sexual Contact and the Conversion Paradigm

I now want to move forward in time to 1612 when a play called *A Christian Turned Turk* was first published, and further east in space to the great port city of Tunis where most of the action occurs. *Turk* provides perhaps the most outlandish embodiment of the motifs and tendencies I have been examining in earlier parts of this essay. In Daborne's play the term "renegade masculinity" takes on a new piquancy, in that the English protagonist of this play literally becomes a *renegade*; that is, one who leaves his Christian faith to embrace Islam, rather than simply a man who in a more general way is something of an outlaw. The potential in the Stukeley narrative for the hero to be transformed or converted into his antithesis is here actualized in a drama that at its center stages an elaborate ritual of religious conversion.

Like Stukeley, Daborne's protagonist, John Ward, was an actual person, an Englishman from common origins. Early in his life he was a fisherman. Eventually, however, he put his seafaring skills to a different use and became a pirate working out of Tunis, which was at that time controlled by the Turks.[20] Ward raided shipping moving through the Mediterranean, much of it from Christian countries, and took his booty back to Tunis where he sold it to the Ottoman governor, who in turn resold it for a much higher price. It was Ward's life as a pirate that won him notoriety in England. Several pamphlets about him were published in 1609, and he was singled out in King James's 1609 *Proclamation Against Pirates*, though he was never successfully punished for his piracy.[21] The historical Ward did, at some point in his life, convert to Islam, and he eventually died of old age in Tunis.

Daborne shaped his play to emphasize, certainly, Ward's depradations, but also, less predictably, his grandeur. Like Stukeley, Ward's vaulting language propels him to larger-than-life status. The following salvo is typical of Daborne's hero:

> The sway of things
> Belongs to him dares most. Such should be kings,
> And such am I. What Nature in my birth
> Denied me, Fortune supplies. This maxim I hold:
> He lives a slave that lives to be controlled.
>
> (sc. 4, ll. 83–87)

Like Stukeley, Ward has Faustian ambition. In actuality, he had even further to rise than Stukeley, who was at least a gentleman by birth, though a poor one. The Chorus that opens the play melodramatically stresses both Ward's low birth and his spectacular rise to public prominence as a criminal:

> Our subject's low, yet to your eyes presents
> Deeds high in blood, in blood of innocents:
>
> . . . . . . . . . . . . . . .
>
> What heretofore set others' pens awork,
> Was Ward turned pirate; ours is Ward turned Turk.
> Their trivial scenes might best afford to show
> The baseness of his birth, how from below
> Ambition oft takes root, makes men forsake
> The good thy enjoy, yet know not.
>
> (prologue, ll. 3–4, 7–12)

What is interesting here—aside from the relish with which the Chorus talks of the great crime of apostasy—is that the dramatist imps his wing on Ward's. The greater the transgression, the higher the pitch the muse must fly, reaching toward tragedy. If one recalls that the Early Modern stage was a hardscrabble place where men of low estate made a living by thrusting their vaulting rhetoric into the mouths of lowborn actors, one can see the identification, as well as the dis-identification, involved in retailing the life of a Kentish fisherman who became notorious, if only for villainy.

The adventure play, of which *A Christian Turned Turk* is simply a nicely vulgar instance, walks the knife's edge between adulation and disavowal in chronicling the exploits of its heroes. Social and economic interlopers, men of ambition and no cash, privateers and soldiers of fortune—that is the social group whose spectacular energies were given dramatic embodiment and powerful vocalization through the adventure play. At times useful to the state in harassing and plundering Spanish and French shipping, or in opening trading outposts in hazardous sites, these figures could also be a problem for someone like Elizabeth to control, as we saw with Stukeley. *A Christian Turned Turk* is a more decidedly tragic drama than *The Famous History*, and its hero more decisively criminalized, in part because by 1612 the great age of Elizabethan privateering had passed. James, at the urging of the members of the Levant Company, had taken a hard line against both interlopers attempting illegally to enter the Mediterranean trade and pirates who pestered "legitimate" English shipping all through the Mediterranean region.[22] To James, Ward was neither amusing nor useful, though on the stage he retained an aura of glamor.

Typically, in fact, on the stage adventure heroes were constructed through narratives that wove together powerful discourses of patriotic pride (this is the hotheaded Englishman, the English Captain, the English pirate king) and anxiety (this is the Englishman who might deal with Catholics, turn Turk, go native, undergo circumcision, infuse Englishness with the imagined wildness of distant places). The geographical journeys that took adventure heroes away from "home" and never allowed of return put them on the front line of contact with an array of stigmatized, exoticized, and slenderly understood peoples: the Irish, the Spanish, the Moors, the Turks, and the Jews. In a moral register, one can say that the social transgressions enacted by the adventure hero courted anxiety as they evoked narratives of overreaching, monstrous pride, and social subversion. That these transgressions were so often enacted in what were to the English peripheral spaces, spaces on the edge of their known and experienced world, produced fictions in which the excesses of a renegade masculinity ended in overt or sublimated fantasies of conversion *into* the peoples of the periphery. Thus Stukeley is doubled and mirrored by Muly Mohamet, and, more straightforwardly, John Ward turns Turk.

In *A Christian Turned Turk*, conversion is effected through sexual contact with a woman from the periphery. In Daborne's play, Ward's main activity in the first two acts is to capture and loot a French ship and take prisoner her crew. Ward eventually makes his way to Tunis to dispose of his booty, and there, in a city constructed as a cosmopolitan mixture of Muslims, Jews, and Christians, the Turkish governors of the port first invite Ward to convert. He resists until introduced to Voada, the Muslim sister of the Captain of the Janissaries in Tunis. Love of Voada finally leads Ward to embrace Islam. The spectacular centerpiece of Daborne's play is a lengthy dumb show in which Ward undergoes a ritual enacting his conversion. It is described as follows:

> Enter two bearing half-moons, one with a Mahomet's head following. After them, the Mufti, or chief priest, two meaner priests bearing his train. The Mufti seated, a confused noise of music, with a show. Enter two Turks, one bearing a turban with a half-moon in it, the other a robe, a sword: a third with a globe in one hand, an arrow in the other. Two knights follow. After them, Ward on an ass, in his Christian habit, bare-headed. The two knights, with low reverence, ascend, whisper the Mufti in the ear, draw their swords and pull him off the ass. He [is] laid on his belly, the tables (by two inferior priests) offered him, he lifts his hand up, subscribes, is brought to his seat by the Mufti, who puts on his turban and robe, girds his sword, then swears him on the Mahomet's head, ungirts his sword, offers him a cup of wine by the hands of a Christian. He spurns at him and throws away the cup, is mounted on the ass, who is richly glad, and with a shout, they exit. (S.D. following sc. 8, l. 10)

Later we learn that Ward at this ceremony has undergone circumcision, presumably when laid on the table by the two knights who pull him from his ass. Just how this was effected is unclear, though the English were good at the technologies of stage blood and presumably could have produced a blood-stained cloth at a strategic moment. This would have enhanced an already spectacular stage moment with the Mufti, or high priest, in full Turkish stage costume surrounded by the banners of Islam, a head of Mohamet, a full complement of attendants, and an ass.

This moment of his conversion into an anti-Christian, anti-English self marks the end of Ward's rise. Afterwards his love affair with Voada is thwarted and his ships are burned in the harbor by a fellow pirate attempting to find a way to return to European society by destroying Ward's pirate fleet and murdering the Jewish middleman, Benwash. Tunis itself is set afire, and in this dismal landscape of wrecked hopes and thwarted love, Ward stabs himself. Having renounced his conversion and turning fiercely against the Turks and Voada, he says,

Who will soar high
First lesson that he learns must be to die.
Here's precedent for him.
You're slaves of Mahomet,
Ungrateful curs, that have repaid me thus
For all the service that I have done for you.
He that hath brought more treasure to your shore
Than all Arabia yields! He that hath shown you
The way to conquer Europe—and did first impart
What your forefathers knew not, the seaman's art;
Which had they attained, this universe had been
One monarchy. May all your seed be damned!

. . . . . . . . . . . . . .

O may, O may, the force of Christendom
Be reunited and all at once requite
The lives of all that you have murdered,
Beating a path out to Jerusalem
Over the bleeding breasts of you and yours.

. . . . . . . . . . . . . .

Lastly, O may I be the last of my country
That trust unto your treacheries, seducing treacheries.
                    (sc. 16, ll. 293–304, 309–313, 315–16)

This speech is a fitting ending for an essay about the generic properties and the historical function of the adventure play. Such plays almost always end with a recuperative gesture through which renegade masculinity looks homeward, renounces the seductions of the periphery, and is reconciled to a larger English or Christian community, here imagined as gathering its forces to reclaim Jerusalem and as the source of the seafaring technology that the Muslims supposedly could not invent for themselves. Yet even in the act of renunciation, the signature of the adventure hero remains his overreaching rhetoric and his bravura gestures. Ward makes this speech *after* stabbing himself. Unlike the historical Ward, he has, in most un-Christian fashion, taken his own life. Ward's renegade masculinity remains intact even at his death.

## Coda

Let me close by suggesting that the plays I have been examining were part of a large number of similar dramas that collectively form the Early Modern adventure genre, though each play is somewhat differently nuanced. In *The Fair Maid*, the feminine gender of the protagonist results in the muting of the heroine's rhetoric. Bess is a fiercely patriotic, lowborn lass who rises to mistress of a privateering vessel, but gender decorum prevents her being given a version of the male adventure hero's mighty line. Moreover, in her case, the threat of sexual contact with men of North Africa presents a particularly salacious danger. When the Moorish King of Fez kisses Bess, a comic character voices fear of miscegenation by remarking repeatedly on the incongruity of a black face touching Bess's white skin. In Massinger's play, *The Renegado*, the European hero converts to Islam for love of Turkish women, but then renounces the conversion and converts the women to Christianity. They flee Tunis, and in this case a conversion narrative ends in a wedding and a return to Europe. Typically, however, plays in this genre feature male overreachers, wavering between heroism and criminality, whose renegade masculinity bodies forth the ambitions and anxieties of a nation on the periphery, aspiring to centrality, but fearing incorporation, conversion, and death.

To conclude, I turn from the periphery of the English dramatic canon— from the "bad" plays we so seldom read and teach—to Shakespeare, the imagined center. Doubtless the adventure play was part of the stage inheritance that informed Shakespeare's creation of *Othello*, *Antony and Cleopatra*, and *Pericles*. In a major innovation, *Othello* reverses the dynamics of most adventure dramas but is thoroughly conversant with them. In most such plays an English hero goes to the Mediterranean, interacts with the alien peoples he encounters there, and is threatened by that encounter, often through contact with a foreign woman. In *Othello*, a non-English Moorish hero comes to the other side of the Mediterranean, to Venice, and is eventually undone by this experience, in part through his encounter with the white daughter of a Venetian senator. As Dan Vitkus has shown, Othello is first and foremost constructed as a barbarian, though a noble one, who has ventured into the heart of Christian Europe and adopted its ways, but whose Christian civility hideously gives way to something akin to Oriental despotism.[23] The question of Othello's "true" identity is as unstable as that of Stukeley, Ward, and other adventure heroes whose soaring rhetoric and tales of martial prowess initially define their heroism but who eventually align themselves with their country's enemies, though without ever quite shedding their identities as Englishmen and Christians. Under the combined pressure of his passion for Desdemona and the manipulations of Iago, Othello's self fissures. About to die, he describes himself as *both* a "malignant and a turban'd Turk" *and* the Venetian officer who kills "the circumcised dog" (5.2.353, 355). Othello is both what he was and also what his new subject position has made him. Like Ward, he dies by his own hand, denouncing his follies, yet trying to reclaim another self. Through the fissured heroes of the adventure play and its cognates, the theater let audiences imagine the dangers—and the excitement—of Mediterranean encounters in which English heroism could be displayed and tested, and England's place in the international arena reimagined. The insecurities that dogged these fictions are evident, not least in the regularity with which its heroes pass over to the enemy, become traitors, turn Turk, commit suicide, and end their days on foreign soil. It is not surprising that at the inaugural moments of their expanded traffic with the world beyond their borders, the English should have been drawn to plays that so powerfully and rawly embody the ambitions and the insecurities of a small Northern nation imagining a place in the sun.

# Notes

1. I use the term "adventure play" to describe a type of drama the distinguishing features of which typically include a hero often drawn from real life; an emphasis on the maritime exploits of the hero, often as he or she functions as a privateer or pirate; a Mediterranean setting for some or all of the action; attention to realistic details of geographical locale and the everyday environment in which events occur; and patriotic or nationalistic overtones. In *Middle-Class Culture in Elizabethan England* (Chapel Hill: University of North Carolina Press, 1935), 603–54, Louis B. Wright discusses this type of drama as one which seems to have appealed particularly to an emerging middling-sort audience. At first, he asserts, plays of knightly or chivalric adventure were popular, but these were quickly supplemented by plays drawing on the period's expanding travel and pamphlet literature dealing with the pirates, seafaring merchants, and adventurers of all kinds. See, in particular, 614–20.

2. For a concise introduction to the process whereby northern Europe replaced the Mediterranean as the dominant economic and cultural region in the West see Samir Amin, *Eurocentrism* (New York: Monthly Review Press, 1989). See also Immanuel Wallerstein's *The Modern World System*, vol. 1., *Capitalist Agriculture and the Origins of the European World-Economy, in the Sixteenth Century* (New York: Academy Press, 1974); and vol. 2, *Mercantilism and the Consolidation of the European World-Economy 1600–1750* (New York: Academy Press, 1980).

3. For a powerful analysis of the fear that at its origins England was a savage nation unable to match the sophistication of other European nation states, see Jodi Mikalachki, *The Legacy of Boadicea: Gender and Nation in Early Modern England* (London: Routledge, 1998).

4. Certain new historicists, such as Leonard Tennenhouse, made genre a central variable in their historical work, as did Louis Montrose in his investigations, in particular, of Renaissance pastoral. I think the generalization holds that genre has not been as crucial to new historical criticism, however, as, for example, to Marxist work. See also my "Shakespeare and Genre," in *A Companion to Shakespeare*, ed. David Scott Kastan (Oxford: Blackwell, 1999), 297–310.

5. See Fredric Jameson, *The Political Unconscious: Narrative as a Socially Symbolic Act* (Ithaca: Cornell University Press, 1981), esp. 17–102.

6. The literature on this topic is voluminous. For key texts see Walter Cohen, *Drama of a Nation: Public Theater in Renaissance England and Spain* (Ithaca: Cornell University Press, 1985); Stephen Greenblatt, *Shakespearean Negotiations: The Circulation of Social Energy in Renaissance England* (Berkeley and Los Angeles: University of California Press, 1988); Jean E. Howard, *The Stage and Social Struggle in Early Modern England* (London: Routledge, 1994); Louis Mon-

trose, *The Purpose of Playing: Shakespeare and the Cultural Politics of the Eliza-bethan Theatre* (Chicago: University of Chicago Press, 1996); Steven Mullaney, *The Place of the Stage: License, Play and Power in Renaissance England* (Chicago: University of Chicago Press, 1987); Karen Newman, *Fashioning Femininity and the Renaissance Stage* (Chicago: University of Chicago Press, 1991); Robert Weimann, *Shakespeare and the Popular Tradition in the Theater: Studies in the Social Dimension of Dramatic Form and Function*, ed. Robert Schwartz (Baltimore: Johns Hopkins University Press, 1978).

7. For an excellent study of the Marlovian hero's overweening rhetoric and its impact on subsequent drama, see Eugene Waith, *The Herculean Hero in Marlowe, Chapman, Shakespeare, and Dryden* (New York: Columbia University Press, 1962). See also Stephen Greenblatt, "Marlowe and the Will to Absolute Play" in *Renaissance Self-Fashioning: From More to Shakespeare* (Chicago: University of Chicago Press, 1980), 193–221; and Emily Bartels, *Spectacles of Strangeness: Imperialism, Alienation, and Marlowe* (Philadelphia: University of Pennsylvania Press, 1993).

8. *The Knight of the Burning Pestle* (1607) refers to both a number of chivalric-romance dramas and to the more realistic adventure plays such as those I will discuss in this essay. The existence of Beaumont and Fletcher's parody suggests that the conventions of both kinds of plays were so entrenched by 1607 that audiences could recognize and take pleasure in seeing them sent up.

9. For "refunctioning" see Robert Nerlich, *The Ideology of Adventure: Studies in Modern Consciousness, 1100–1750*, vol. 1 (Minneapolis: University of Minnesota Press, 1987), esp. 61–62.

10. See Robert Brenner, *Merchants and Revolution: Commercial Change, Political Conflict, and London's Overseas Traders, 1550–1653* (Princeton: Princeton University Press, 1993).

11. For studies of privateering/piracy in the Mediterranean, see Kenneth Andrews, *Trade, Plunder and Settlement: Maritime Enterprise and the Genesis of the British Empire, 1480–1630* (Cambridge: Cambridge University Press, 1984); Godfrey Fisher, *Barbary Legend: War, Trade, and Piracy in North Africa, 1415–1830* (Oxford: Clarendon Press, 1957); David Debison Hebb, *Piracy and the English Government, 1616–1642* (Aldershot, U.K.: Scolar Press, 1994).

12. G. K. Hunter, "Elizabethans and Foreigners," in *Dramatic Identities and Cultural Tradition: Studies in Shakespeare and His Contemporaries* (New York: Barnes and Noble, 1978), 24.

13. Richard Helgerson, *Forms of Nationhood: The Elizabethan Writing of England* (Chicago: University of Chicago Press, 1992), esp. 181–87.

14. *OED2*, s.v. "renegade": (1) "an apostate from any form of religious faith, esp. a Christian who becomes a Muslim," first citation 1583. By 1665 it also had come to mean (2) "one who deserts a party, person, or principle, in favour of another; a turn-coat." I am using the term to encompass both its more general and also its particular religious meanings.

15. For a trenchant discussion of the Early Modern English fear of "Turning Turk," see Dan Vitkus, "Turning Turk in *Othello*: The Conversion and Damnation of the Moor," *Shakespeare Quarterly* 48 (1997): 145–76. For the reverse phenomenon, the conversion of an Eastern woman to Christianity, see Ania Loomba's "Shakespeare and Cultural Difference," in *Alternative Shakespeares 2*, ed. Terence Hawkes (London: Routledge, 1996), 164–91, esp. 182–85.

16. For the dating of *The Battle of Alcazar* see John Yoklavich's discussion in his introduction to *The Battle of Alcazar* in *The Dramatic Works of George Peele*,

gen. ed. Charles Prouty (New Haven: Yale University Press, 1966), 2:221–25. All references will be to this edition. For *The Famous History of the Life and Death of Thomas Stukeley*, references will be to the Malone Society edition, ed. Judith C. Levinson (Oxford: Oxford University Press, 1975).

17. For information on Stukeley's life I am indebted to "The Biography of Sir Thomas Stucley" prepared by Richard Simpson in *The School of Shakspere* (London: Chatto and Windus, 1878), 1–156. For an account of the life much embellished by literary flourishes, see John Izon's *Sir Thomas Stucley c. 1525–1578: Traitor Extraordinary* (London: Andrew Melrose, 1956).

18. Under Elizabeth, privateers, often barely distinguishable from pirates, became tools of national policy and received letters of marque from the sovereign to carry on their work. They were important in plundering French and Spanish vessels plying the Atlantic coast. Nonetheless, Elizabeth frequently was forced to recall, reprimand, and punish privateers when other nations complained too vociferously about their acts. See Hugh Rankin, *The Golden Age of Piracy* (New York: Holt, Rinehart and Winston, 1969); and Kenneth Anderson, *Trade, Plunder and Settlement* (Cambridge: Cambridge University Press, 1984).

19. Muly Mahmet Xeque, ruler from 1518 to 1557, established the tanistry-like rule of brothers that Muly Hamet and his father both violate. See John Yoklavich's introduction to *The Battle of Alcazar*, 227, and, for the play's account of the establishment of this practice, 1.1.122–27.

20. For an account of Ward's life and of the prose pamphlets about this notorious figure, see the introduction by Dan Vitkus to his edition of *Three Turk Plays From Early Modern England* (New York: Columbia University Press, 2000), 23–39. All references will be to this edition.

21. In *Piracy and the English Government, 1616–42*, David Hebb gives a full account of James's prolonged attempt to combat the Barbary pirates and also those Englishmen who turned pirate to prey on Mediterranean trading ships. For "A Proclamation Against Pirates," issued 8 January 1609, see James F. Larkin and Paul L. Hughes, *Royal Proclamaion of King James I, 1603–25* (Oxford: Clarendon, 1973), 203–6. The proclamation mentions Ward by name.

22. Hebb, *Piracy*, 7–20.

23. Dan Vitkus, "Turning Turk in *Othello*." As he writes, "A baptized Moor turned Turk, Othello is 'doubly damned' for backsliding" (176).

# Rediscovering Artemis in
## *The Comedy of Errors*

### RANDALL MARTIN

SHAKESPEARE LOCATES THE ENDINGS OF *THE COMEDY OF ERRORS* AND *Pericles* in the temple of Artemis, or Diana, at Ephesus. The setting is implied in the comedy and explicit in the romance, but in both cases its interest lies in the contrasting mythologies suggested by the dual identities of the goddess: Diana represents the familiar Greco-Roman patron of chastity, the woods, and hunting; whereas Artemis is the Hellenistic deity of fertility, animal husbandry, and childbirth who descends from the Anatolian earth-mother Cybele. The Asian origins and distinctive attributes of Artemis—above all her association with maternal power, sexual divinity, and child rearing—often go unnoticed because in most of his other plays Shakespeare refers exclusively to the solitary, celibate, lunar huntress.[1] And when the presence of her Eastern ancestor does become visible, he tends to mingle the virtues of both under one name, Diana. Yet Shakespeare, like other Early Modern readers, was aware of the differences between these two figures, and investigating them is a crucial starting point for reconstructing the eastern Mediterranean counter-histories of these plays, and considering their Early Modern production of non-European spatial and cultural identities.

Shakespeare's knowledge of Ephesian Diana is evident in several plays besides *The Comedy of Errors* (which I will return to as the focus of this essay). In *Pericles*, when Thaisa is recovered and revived by Cerimon after seeming to die while giving birth to Marina on board ship and being buried at sea, she exclaims, "O dear Diana, / Where am I?" (3.2.104–5). Awakening in Ephesus from the threshold experience of what she calls her "eaning [i.e., birth] time" (3.4.6), when her womb is open and regenerative, Thaisa calls on Diana in her ancient roles as goddess of fertility, protector of women in labor, and guardian of children. Only later when she decides to enter the temple of Diana in a "vestal livery" as Pericles' widow do the associations merge with those of the goddess of chastity, whose body is symbolically closed.[2] These divergent roles remain partly connected by the fact that both Artemis and Diana were known as "virgins." The classi-

363

10. **Statue of Artemis flanked by sacred hinds from Ephesus, second century A.D., now in the Ephesus Museum. © Casa Editrice Bonechi.**

cal understanding of the term did not exclude sexual activity, but signified the unmarried state and female independence of Artemis and her disciples, the most famous of whom were the Amazons. The Asian and Hellenistic worship of Artemis as supernally fructifying earth mother, and the European tradition of Diana as sexually and morally pure, were both assimilated by the new Christian religion when Mary, their avatar, was officially declared "mother of god" at the purposefully situated Council of Ephesus in A.D. 431.[3]

Another revealing example occurs in *2 Henry IV,* when the Page refers to Falstaff and his Eastcheap drinking companions as "Ephesians . . . of the old church" (2.2.150). This alludes to the Ephesians' biblical reputation as "boon companions" (*OED* s.v. "Ephesian"), revellers, and sensualists, according to Paul's epistles.[4] But behind these fleshly traits lies the wider historical conflict—also biblical—between local pagan spirituality and Paul's new monotheistic and patriarchal religion. The Geneva version of Acts 19 refers four times to "the great goddesse Diana" (vv. 27, 28, 34, 35), clearly distinguishing the Eastern *magna mater* from her celibate European namesake.[5] For Elizabethan readers and spectators, the Page's phrase carries additional topical allusions to the period's officially displaced Catholicism, and, more obliquely, to the religion of the play-wright's family. Moreover, marginal glosses in the Geneva Bible explain that first-century Ephesians protested against the new Christians "because they left the olde religion [of Artemis], & broght in another trade of doc-trine" (19.24; NT QQiiiiv). One note in particular equates the worshippers of this "church" with those of its modern Roman counterpart. Such inter-textual associations, as well as Shakespeare's abundant allusions to Ephe-sians and Acts in *The Comedy of Errors*, demonstrate his knowledge of Ephesian Diana's historical and allegorical significance.[6]

*The Comedy of Errors* describes her temple as a "priory"or "abbey" presided over by Emilia, who is reunited with her husband Egeon and their two sons at a "gossips' feast" after a thirty-three year "travail." The Christian coloring of Emilia's language is related to Shakespeare's under-lying decision to set the play in Ephesus, rather than the Epidamnum of his main source, Plautus's *Menaechmi*. Ephesus was known to Elizabe-thans for its temple, the Artemision, which was one of the seven wonders of the classical world.[7] And as editors have long noted, the city was famil-iar to Elizabethan playgoers as a major commercial seaport from St. Paul's epistles as well as from the history of his missions there and across the Mediterranean recorded in Acts.

It is usually assumed that Shakespeare chose Ephesus to lend a hint of supernatural agency to Plautus's non-numinous world. *The Comedy of Er-rors* alludes at various points to the city's reputation for witchcraft and "curious artes" (Acts 19.19). For instance, when Antipholus of Syracuse is treated strangely and mistaken for other people, he plausibly—though erroneously—ascribes the cause to magic and sorcery:

> They say this town is full of cozenage:
> As nimble jugglers that deceive the eye,
> Dark-working sorcerers that change the mind,
> Soul-killing witches that deform the body,
> Disguised cheaters, prating mountebanks,
> And many such-like liberties of sin:
> If it prove so, I will be gone the sooner.
>
> (1.2.97–103)

Overall, such references create a potential atmosphere of exotic mystery and suspense. They likewise deepen the moral seriousness of lost and mis-taken identities, and they adumbrate a sense of divine wonder when the day's confusions are clarified.[8] To the extent that the play presents a dra-matic fiction in a historical setting, Antipholus's viewpoint derives reflex-ively from Paul and later Christian Europe, which Elizabethans heard in church and presumably accepted. Its validation concurrently affirms the cultural differentiation of earlier pre-Christian practices and local beliefs focused on the worship of Diana. By having Christianized characters express a discourse that is anachronistically hegemonic but, historically, was contested and marginal, Shakespeare represents Ephesus as a place intersected by several temporal horizons as Christian values and Western narratives mingle with Hellenistic and Eastern ones. The city's identity, to borrow Doreen Massey's terms, is progressive, since its social relations are defined by "extra-verted" encounters of subjects across time and space: illegal arrivals from European Mediterranean cities and states, domesticated foreigners (assimilated to apparently varying degrees), and native urban dwellers in Asia Minor.[9] Ephesus is therefore a palimpsest of perspectives owned by more than one culture.[10] Its proliferation of religious signs and social histories generates plural cultural subjects and meanings. And dramatically the play authorizes these signs and histories as productively dynamic, since its ending stages personal and symbolic reconciliations that remain provisional, ambiguous, and unfinished.

# 1

In traditional readings and performances of the play, the displaced temple of Diana and its "Lady Abbess" become the authoritative seat of differentiation where the play's personal separations, errors, and misfortunes are reunited and redeemed within an idealized context of communal Christian values. Stage productions typically costume Emilia in a nun's habit, and affix Christian emblems such as a cross to the "house" into which Antipholus and Dromio flee for refuge (5.1.36–37). Yet there is little in the authoritative Folio text to prevent Emilia's "priory" or "abbey" from being alternatively understood and represented as the older pre-Christian site. The names "priory" or "abbey" are not strictly definitive, since they only represent the conventional medieval and Early Modern practice of using familiar Christian terms to describe classical and non-European religious sites and entities. This is evident from the way in which Shakespeare's known and probable sources describe the temple of Diana. In the tale of Apollonius of Tyre related by John Gower's *Confessio Amantis*, which Shakespeare used (as he did later in *Pericles*) for the framing story of Egeon and Emilia's shipwreck and family reunion, Gower describes the Emilia figure, Lucina, dedicating herself to "religion" in the temple after being separated at sea from her husband and children:

> The feste and the profession
> After the reule of that degre
> Was mad with gret solempnete

Where as Diane is seintefied.
Thus stant this lady justefied
In ordre wher sche thenkth to dwelle.

(Bullough, 53)

Eventually she becomes "Abbesse there."[11] We cannot be certain whether Shakespeare knew *The excellent and pleasant worke of Iulius Solinus Polyhistor* (1587), which describes "the Temple of *Diana*, buylded by the Amozons" in "the most famous Cittie *Ephesus*" (Aaiiiv; see the illustration of an Amazon from the altar of the Artemision, dating from the fourth century B.C.). But the fact that he calls the Duke "Solinus" in the opening line of the play suggests that he did. If that is the case, it is telling that Arthur Golding, the English translator of Solinus, calls the temple "thys holy church."

The diction of Emilia's speeches is likewise transhistorical, inflected by both Christian and pre-Christian associations. When she rebukes Adriana at 5.1.68–86 for her husband's "madness," her arguments are based on

11. **Amazon from the altar of the Artemision in Ephesus. © Kunsthistorisches Museum, Vienna.**

traditional ideas deriving from Hippocrates, Galen, and other classical authorities about the relationship between unbalanced physiological and
mental states, and on humoral disorders such as melancholy. She refers to
using "wholesome syrups, drugs, and holy prayers, / To make of [Antipho-
lus] a formal man again" (5.1.104–5), and to her aid as being "A charitable duty of my order" (108). What is remarkable about her vocation is
its ecumenism, since her remedies are entirely compatible with services
dispensed at the Hellenistic temple of Artemis/Diana cited in well-known
accounts by Plutarch, Pliny, and Paul.[12] The Artemision's fame as a "sanctuary" (5.1.94) was especially well known, since it was reported that the
Amazons' request for asylum there led to their rebuilding of the Hellenistic temple in monumental marble, adorned with statues of themselves in
the pediment. When Cleopatra's sister Arsinoe took sanctuary in the temple, Marc Antony forced the chief priestess to bring her out, whereupon
he murdered her to assure himself and Cleopatra of the Egyptian throne.[13]

When in the end Emilia welcomes everyone inside to a "gossips' feast,"
traditional assumptions about her as a Christian figure have led editors to
define "gossip" along similar lines: the anticipated celebration becomes
a symbolic christening in which the fortuitous recovery of long-lost and
mistaken identities manifests a redemptive Providence.[14] She also says her
"travail" has lasted thirty-three years. This period is inconsistent with the
timelines of her family's earlier separation and journeys, but it does correspond with the lifetime of Jesus, and so reinforces the sense of Christian
agency at work. Shakespeare may have chosen the figure to impart a sense
of divine *commedia* to the play's closure, thereby creating a seasonal connection with the occasions of its first recorded performances, for the
Christmas revels at Gray's Inn on 28 December 1594, and again at court
on Innocents' Day, 27 December 1604.[15]

Yet this implied spiritual triumph becomes problematized in an ending
whose personal reconciliations are not in all cases self-evident or acknowledged in the text.[16] Emilia's pregnancy-and-childbirth metaphor suggests
that "gossips" can be equally understood in a nonsectarian sense as referring to friends of the mother (in traditional social practice, all women) who
are present at her delivery (*OED* s.v. "gossip"). Given the final scene's
gathering of rediscovered relations of both sexes (ibid.), "gossip" becomes gender-neutral in this context. The Duke further widens the word's
meaning when he vows to "gossip at this feast," a line the *OED* cites to
define the verb: "To act as a . . . familiar acquaintance; to . . . be a boon-
companion." This suggests the "gossips' feast" will be as much a home
gathering of "Ephesians . . . of the old church" as of a new one.[17]

During his two-year stay in Ephesus, Paul encountered fierce resistance
to his evangelizing missions at two public sites: the temple of Artemis,
and the theater. Classical and biblical accounts confirm the city's strong

loyalty to the Eastern "great goddess" for her regenerative powers materialized through ritual sex and magic. With this temporal perspective in mind, it is worth noting the main biblical story that unfolded in Ephesus, which has been overlooked in discussions of Shakespeare's sources, yet is more prominent than the sporadic references to witches and magic. In Acts 19.23–41, a local silversmith named Demetrius galvanizes his fellow craftsmen against Paul because the new religion was hurting their business in shrines of Artemis. Demetrius also objects that the state being "reproued" and that "the temple of the great goddesse Diana shulde be nothing estemed, and that it wolde come to passe that her magnificence, which all Asia and the worlde worshippeth, shulde be destroyed" (27). The protesters stormed the theater and drove away two of Paul's companions who were preaching there; Paul himself was persuaded not to inflame the protesters by appearing. A local Jewish leader, Alexander, tried to calm the situation, but again there "arose such a shoute almoste for the space of two houres, of all men crying, Great is Diana of the Ephesians" (34). The silversmiths and their supporters were finally pacified by the "towne clarke," who assured them that the city's devotion to its ancient patron was undiminished, and he encouraged them to express their complaints in established legal forums. Paul left the city shortly afterwards and later spoke bitterly about his experience (1 Cor. 15.32, quoted below). While Christianity continued slowly to grow in Ephesus, local worship of Artemis persisted until the fourth century, when St. John Chrysostom destroyed the temple.[18] The clash between city silversmiths and missionary Christians defines Ephesus as a place of competing loyalties to a long-established female-centered religion versus a transplanted patriarchal one, and of conflict between thriving commercial interests and a repressive anti-material and messianic ideology.

The contested status of Christian authority in Shakespeare's Ephesus is also related to the fact that, while the play alludes to the city's reputation for magic and makes comic capital out of characters' misperceptions based on it, there are in fact "no sorcerers or devils in Ephesus, no witches save those projected by male sexual anxiety. . . . The comedy's decorum rests upon the strict absence of supernatural agency."[19] Stephen Greenblatt makes these observations in the course of arguing that Shakespeare shares the skepticism of many contemporaries about the demonic. If that is the case, then the implied doubt about witches also works the opposite way, to "empty out" any authentic sense of Christian agency (which explains why certain contemporary authorities such as James I vigorously opposed absolute skepticism about witches). The play's exposure of demonic possession as a falsification of explicable but superficially mistaken natural phenomena foregrounds the city's openness to ideological competition and improvisation, the comic effects of which are "madness."[20] In historical terms it is likewise a place where subjects previously separated by geography, and their disjunctive beliefs, encounter and transform one another. In this regard Ephesus resembles better-known Mediterranean port-cities and states such as Venice and Cyprus. All are "contact zones" of contested social relations represented by local inhabitants and alien travelers from cultures dispersed around the Mediterranean.[21]

A microcosm of these conflicting agencies is represented by Nell, the "kitchen-vestal" who horrifies Dromio of Syracuse by laying claim to his body as his wife (3.2.71 ff.). She is sometimes assumed to be the servant named Luce who bars Antipholus of Ephesus from his house (3.1.48 ff.), in which case she punningly embodies "light" and "loose." On the other hand Nell may be a separate person, if one simply imagines Adriana and her husband as having more than one servant. Dromio caricatures her as a "very reverent body: ay, such a one as a man may not speak of without he say, 'Sir-reverence'" (3.2.90–91), "the formulaic apology for a harlot or 'light' woman" (Parker, 67). Much of the scene's humor lies in the fact that we never see Nell, so that Dromio's comic portrait remains a fantasy reaction to his own estranging experiences of the unfamiliar city. Echoing his master's fears of sorcery and satanic possession, Dromio labels Nell a "witch" and a "diviner." The second of these is usually glossed "magician," but the *OED* supplies other definitions—prophet, seer—which suggest the folk knowledge of a local wise-woman. This alternative identity also invites readers and spectators to divine beyond Dromio's mock-horror hyperbole to the non-European reality of the absent domestic servant. For Dromio's description of a gross, rampantly lusty kitchen-wench represents his first private encounter with a Near Eastern woman, and, allegedly, with her uncontained and unsubmissive physicality. His comic exaggeration of her hips, focusing on the reproductive center of her body, hints at Western associations of sexual orgasm with death, and thus his own fears of masculine annihilation. Dromio's succeeding tactics—to demonize, eroticize, and subjugate—make these underlying insecurities explicit:

> S. *Ant.* What claim lays she to thee?
> S. *Dro.* Marry, sir, such claim as you would lay to your horse; and she would have me as a beast; not that, I being a beast, she would have me, but that she, being a very beastly creature, lays claim to me.
>
> (3.2.84–89)

Dromio's words recall Paul's description of his encounter with the citizens of Ephesus after they had angrily driven him from the city: "I haue foght with beastes at Ephesus after the maner of men" (1 Cor. 15.32; Artemis was the goddess of beasts, and is often portrayed, like her ancestor Cybele, attended by a pair of lions, dogs, or other animals, as seen vestigially in

12. **Statuette of a seated goddess. Çatalhöyük, Anatolia (Turkey), ca. early 6000s B.C. © The Anatolian Civilizations Museum, Ankara, Turkey.**

illustration 10 as well as in illustration 11. This image depicts the earliest statue of a mother goddess, pregnant and giving birth, dating from the early 6000 B.C. It was found, like the statue reproduced on the previous page, at Çatalhöyük, in southwestern Anatolia, near present-day Konya). At the end of his comic routine, as Patricia Parker observes, Dromio alludes explicitly to Paul's letter: "I, amaz'd, ran from her as a witch. / And I think, if my breast had not been made of faith, and my heart of steel, / She had transform'd me to a curtal dog" (3.2.144–46).[22] And if we continue to "divine" Dromio's description of Nell, it also recalls images of Ephesian Diana and her Anatolian ancestor Cybele in their roles as global earth-mother. Nell's fertile and undulating body threatens the European Dromio with its sexual power and resistance to patriarchal mastery. Varying his humor, Dromio continues by responding to Antipholus's questions about Nell's complexion:

S. *Ant.* What complexion is she of?
S. *Dro.* Swart, like my shoe, but her face nothing like so clean kept: for why? she sweats, a man may go over shoes in the grime of it.

(3.2.101–4)

**13. Statuette of a mother goddess flanked by two cats and depicted giving birth, Çatalhöyük, Anatolia (Turkey), ca. early 6000s B.C. © The Anatolian Civilizations Museum, Ankara, Turkey.**

Nell's "swartness" invokes stereotyped racial associations with darker non-European skin colors and lower-class criminality, as Dromio implicitly contrasts her appearance with fashionable Early Modern European preferences for fair complexions. Insofar as she resembles traditional physical traits of the Eastern "great mother," her darkness also recalls negative Christian descriptions and images of Artemis as the "black Diana," distinguishing her from the light skinned, sexually regulated, and notionally closed body of her Roman namesake (see illustration 11).[23] There are likewise hints of a primitive aesthetic in Dromio's association of Nell's greasiness and dirt with pre-deluge human history. In his final move to contain and reproduce her, Dromio redraws Nell's body as a Eurocentric *mappa mundi*. His mock-blazon burlesques the Petrarchan poet who fragments the physical features of his resistant beloved into discrete parts, thereby disciplining and reordering them according to his desires. Nell is simultaneously figured as a "naturally" primitive, unregenerate, and dangerous subject prior to the arrival of the Western cultural gaze, and then "domesticated" in terms of English zones of commercial expansion and competition. The initially threatening and dominant Near Eastern women is reduced to the "rest of the world" by the inverting perspective of Western hegemony (Pratt, 4–5).

## 2

I mentioned earlier that the cultural openness of Emilia's "house"—which Antipholus and Dromio of Syracuse literalize by slipping into easily, in striking contrast to Adriana's gated home—is related to Emilia's transcultural status and function. When I teach the play, students often wonder why she treats Adriana as harshly and unfairly as she does. The conventional answer is that Adriana's jealousy and near-hysteria need to be corrected by an older, wiser, "female patriarch"—her future mother-in-law.[24] But Emilia's mistaking of Adriana as the cause of Antipholus's madness undermines her authority as a Christian peacemaker. And it seems clear that she deliberately goads Adriana into rhetorical extremes in order to entrap her:

> *Abbess.*   Which of these sorrows is he subject to?
> *Adriana.*       To none of these, except it be the last,
>            Namely, some love that drew him oft from home.
> *Abbess.*   You should for that have reprehended him.
> *Adriana.*   Why, so I did.
> *Abbess.*        Ay, but not rough enough.
> *Adriana.*   As roughly as my modesty would let me.

14. **Thirteenth-century French manuscript illustration (Trinity College, Cambridge, MS R.16.2, f. 29v) depicting St. John Chrysostom destroying the temple of Artemis at Ephesus in 401 A.D. © Trinity College Library, Cambridge.**

**15. Detail from Figure 14.**

| | |
|---|---|
| *Abbess.* | Haply, in private. |
| *Adriana.* | And in assemblies too. |
| *Abbess.* | Ay, but not enough. |
| *Adriana.* | It was the copy of our conference: |
| | In bed he slept not for my urging it; |
| | At board he fed not for my urging it; |
| | Alone, it was the subject of my theme; |
| | In company I often glanced it; |
| | Still did I tell him it was vild and bad. |
| *Abbess.* | And thereof came it that the man was mad. |

(5.1.54–68)

Emilia marginalizes Adriana's rights to minister to her husband in favor of the social privileges and authority of her own position. Her opposition creates two rival "homes," Adriana's and her own, within which different concepts of female power, deriving from Eastern and Western heritages, are valued and asserted. Shakespeare gives Adriana powerful theological and cultural arguments: by sundering husband and wife, Emilia directly contradicts Christian scripture and custom. Ironically, it is the hitherto submissive and deferential Luciana who speaks up to defy Emilia's accusations of jealousy and domestic disorder, urging her sister not to remain silent: "Why bear you these rebukes, and answer not?" (5.1.89). For a moment, Adriana feels vulnerable: "She did betray me to my own reproof" (5.1.90). This somewhat ambiguous response could be glossed: "She revealed the negative role I have secretly reproached myself for (in the past)." Presumably this refers to the stereotype of the shrewish wife that Adriana fears becoming, and finds difficulty in separating from her justified complaints about her husband's mistreatment. Luciana had earlier accused her sister of jealousy, but forcefully denies it here, and on the whole the play validates her changed opinion, since Adriana's suspicions of her husband's adultery are shown increasingly to be plausible.[25] When, for example, Antipholus of Ephesus mentions that his previous meetings with the Courtesan have been innocent (3.1.109–14), his offhand disclaimer seems designed to safeguard his reputation in the eyes of his male friend Balthazar, and is later discredited by the knowing familiarity with which the Courtesan talks about him (4.3.81–96).

As noted earlier, Emilia's associations with Christian hierarchical authority and iconic female chastity are also problematized by her culminating metaphor suggesting that the time spent apart from her family has felt like a thirty-three year labor. The implications of social regeneration through female sexual agency are consistent with her acculturation as an Artemisian "virgin" and "abbess." Emilia says nothing about when and how she came to the city, only that the separation from one son and Dromio took place in Epidamnum, following their initial separation from her husband, other son, and his servant at sea, and that sometime later "fortune" brought her to Ephesus (5.1.350–56). As Robert S. Miola observes, Shakespeare reveals Emilia's identity, a crucial and surprising plot element, only at the very end.[26] The play says nothing about celibacy, even though critics—taking for granted a Christian context and her "widowed" status—assume this axiomatically.[27] Her Amazonian defiance of Adriana and associations with maternal healing and rebirth—activities functionally and socially related to "a gossips' feast"—suggest the co-presence of older and newer values based upon changing experiences in Europe and Asia minor, and which now personally interact in her plural roles and identity. Like the city that she to some degree epitomizes, Emilia is a subject-in-process, continuing to undergo personal growth and cultural redefinition.

3

Shakespeare's representation of Ephesus as a frontier space of gendered ideological encounters also becomes visible in the conflicts between the play's three main women, Luciana, Adriana, and Emilia. Early in the play, Luciana articulates an impeccably orthodox view of female subjection to patriarchal hierarchy and natural order based upon scriptural authority and traditional cosmography: "There's nothing situate under heaven's eye / But hath his bound in earth, in sea, in sky" (2.1.16 ff.). Adriana, "warrior against double standards,"[28] forcefully and movingly challenges this view in several speeches by pointing to her husband's self-interested disregard for ethical and material boundaries: "But, too unruly deer, he breaks the pale / And feeds from home; poor I am but his stale" (2.1.100–101). In the next scene Adriana extends her thoughts to the proper relationship of wives and husbands, echoing Paul's well-known image (deriving from Ephesians 5) of marriage as a union of "one flesh." But in her model based on companionable mutuality rather than Luciana's model of rigid gender hierarchies, Adriana also reinterprets Paul's letter in strikingly untraditional ways. The epistle's most frequently quoted verse asserts a paradigm of female subordination: "Wiues, submit your selues unto your husbands, as vnto the Lord" (22). Paul then focuses on the husband's duty: "Housbands, loue your wiues, euen as Christ loued the Church, & gaue him self for it" (25). This revises the social paradigm with a competing one of unconditional love, based ultimately on the spiritual imperative to love others as oneself.[29] Paul repeats this injunction twice more: "So oght men to loue their wiues, as their owne bodies: he that loueth his wife, loueth him self" (28); "Therefore . . . let euerie one loue his wife, as him self, & let the wife see that she feare her housband" (33). The patriarchal domination Paul initially endorses is radically constrained, and arguably canceled out, by the moral imperative of self-giving love and mutuality.[30] In the play's context of Hellenistic Ephesus, it is as if Luciana is the "youngling,"[31] reading Paul's message vehemently but narrowly as a new convert. Her preference for remaining unwed on the grounds of avoiding "troubles of the marriage-bed" (2.1.27) is more cryptic. It may hint at her personal sexuality, or it may be connected to Paul's counsel of celibacy in the early Christian context of preparation for the Second Coming—the imminently anticipated event that is a fundamental assumption underlying much of Paul's spiritual and social advice, but alien to local Eastern Mediterranean culture.

Adriana's position, on the other hand, derives from a reinterpretation of Ephesians 5 that mirrors the conflicting discoveries of many Early Modern women writers when they began to read the Bible for themselves. In terms of the several temporal horizons that intersect in Ephesus, Adriana's robust assertion of mutuality, and denunciation of her husband's failure to love her as himself, can be traced directly to the paradoxes of Paul's scriptural teaching. Yet in the context of her historical position as an Ephesian woman, her demands for personal respect also reflect the traditional gynosocial values of Artemis. Adriana, like Emilia, is a woman living in a city undergoing cultural transition and conflict. She encounters "primitive" Christianity—famously derided by Roman patricians as a religion of slaves and women—before it was reconstructed in ways that reversed its founder's concepts of spiritual and gender equality. Adriana "reads" Ephesians 5 differently because her religious and social heritage as a Greek Artemisian leads her to expect to find a place in her daily life for female virtues and social integrity, and thus for personal mutuality in her marriage. She is a subject divided between her indigenous culture and the new, partially adopted one, which historically was in the process of suppressing matriarchal divinity and essentializing female sexuality to make its ideology more acceptable to European patriarchal values and customs.

These multiple perspectives all unfold from Shakespeare's initial decision to set the play in Hellenistic, Asian, and Pauline Ephesus rather than in Roman Epidamnum.[32] Traces of Artemis/Diana and her Eastern attributes and practices are visible in the play's dialogue and action amidst Western discursive displacements. The presence of both worlds in one space creates a layered representation of settled urban values—non-European daily life "already there"[33]—and of new cultures—historically tentative but reflexively hegemonic—being constructed by emergent Christian and European ideology.

# Notes

1. E.g., *Coriolanus* 5.3.64–67: "The noble sister of Publicola, / The moon of Rome, chaste as the icicle / That's curdied by the frost from purest snow / And hangs on Dian's temple."

2. In the BBC video production, however, the final scene of *Pericles* is introduced by a frame of Ephesian Diana (known as "Beautiful Artemis," a Roman-replica statue of the second century A.D. now in the Ephesus Museum and reproduced here (see illustration 10). A very similar statue is in the Museo Archeologico Nazionale, Naples; a third statue, the Amazon depicted in the second illustration, and sections of the Hellenistic temple, are displayed in the Ephesosmuseum, part of Vienna's Kunsthistorisches Museum). Another example of Diana's opposed attributes occurs in *All's Well That Ends Well*, when the independent-minded Helena, having had her practical and assertive discussion with Parolles about keeping and losing her virginity, defends her desires for Bertram to the Countess by appealing to her understanding of Diana's dual aspects of sexually reproductive and chastely virtuous love: "but if yourself . . . / Did ever in so true a flame of liking / Wish chastely, and love dearly, that your Dian / Was both herself and Love" (1.3.209–13).

3. "Ephesus," *New Catholic Encyclopedia* (New York: McGraw Hill, 1967).

4. Eph. 2.1, 3; 4.19; 5.3, 5, 18. The *OED* cites no other examples besides *Errors* and *Merry Wives* 4.5.17–18, where the usage and context are identical: "[To Falstaff] It is thine host, thine Ephesian, calls."

5. A distinction familiar from the different designations applied to Christian saints bearing the same name; e.g., St. James the Great (or "Jacques le Grand"— see *All's Well*) and St. James the Less.

6. Ephesians seems to have been one of Shakespeare's favorite books of the Bible. For its prominence beyond these two plays, see D. J. Palmer, "Casting off the Old Man: History and St. Paul in *Henry IV*," *Critical Quarterly* 12 (1970): 267–83; and Harry Morris, "Prince Hal: Apostle to the Gentiles," *Clio* 7, no. 2 (1978): 227–46. Patricia Parker discusses *Errors*'s "concentrated allusiveness" to scriptural passages in "The Bible and the Marketplace: *The Comedy of Errors*,"

*Shakespeare from the Margins: Language, Culture, Context* (Chicago: University of Chicago Press, 1996), 56–82.

7. See Thomas Cooper's entry for Ephesus in his *Thesaurus Linguae Romanae* (London, 1565). "Artemis," he says simply, "Is a name of Diana"; but Cybele has many names, such as the now more familiar Cretan "Rhea," attesting to her associations with numerous mother-goddesses cults around the Mediterranean. Cooper also says that Cybele is "named of Paynims the mother of the goddes," alluding to her Anatolian and later title, "great mother."

8. *Narrative and Dramatic Sources of Shakespeare*, ed. Geoffrey Bullough, vol. 1 (New York: Routledge and Kegan Paul, 1957), 9; Robert S. Miola, "The Play and the Critics," in *"The Comedy of Errors": Critical Essays*, ed. R. S. Miola (New York: Garland Press, 1997), 11.

9. Doreen Massey, "Power-Geometry and a Progressive Sense of Place," in *Mapping the Future: Local Cultures, Global Change*, ed. Jon Bird et al. (London: Routledge, 1993), 59–69. A somewhat different form of this article appears under the title "A Place Called Home" in *Space, Place, and Gender* (Minneapolis: University of Minnesota Press, 1994), 158–84.

10. Parker, "The Bible and Marketplace," 56.

11. In his Arden edition (London: Methuen, 1962), R. A. Foakes records H. F. Brooks's observation that "such 'naturalization' of literature goes back at least to Alfred; at first not deliberate, it becomes a principle after being a habit," xxxii, n. 1.

12. The Artemision was renowned as both a religious and commercial site in Asia Minor, visited by merchants who shared their profits with, and pilgrims who brought their offerings to, the city's patron. It was linked to Alexander the Great, who was born on the night an arsonist burnt it to the ground (31 July 356 B.C.). Alexander later helped substantially to rebuild it (see Plutarch's "Life of Alexander" [paired with the life of Julius Caesar], chap. 3, of *Plutarch's Lives*, ed. B. Perrin, 11 vols. (London: William Heineman), 7:229–30. Marginal notes in the Geneva Bible cross-reference Pliny and supply brief historical and legendary details about the temple and its cult.

13. Bluma L. Trell, "The Temple of Artemis at Ephesos," in *The Seven Wonders of the Ancient World*, ed. Peter A. Clayton and Martin J. Price (London: Routledge, 1988), 83–84.

14. For a recent reading of the play along these lines, see Glyn Austen, "Ephesus Restored: Sacramentalism and Redemption in *The Comedy of Errors*," *Literature and Theology* 1 (1987): 54–69.

15. As the traditional emendations of editors such as Theobald and Capell demonstrate, "thirty-three" is easily interchangeable with other figures, and may originally have been one number among others. The first-performance dates may also explain Emilia's double emphasis on "nativity" (5.1.404, 406, which some editors have assumed is erroneous). See Arthur F. Kinney, "Shakespeare's *Comedy of Errors* and the Nature of Kinds," in *Critital Essays,* ed. R. S. Miola.

16. Parker, "The Bible and Marketplace," 74–75; Barbara Freedman, "Reading Errantly: Misrecognition and the Uncanny in *The Comedy of Errors,*" in *Critical Essays,* ed. R. S. Miola, (1997).

17. A point slyly conveyed by the BBC production when the Duke escorts the Courtesan into the abbey during the final exit.

18. It had, in any case, been only partially restored after being destroyed by the Ostrogoths in A.D. 262.

19. Stephen Greenblatt, "Shakespeare Bewitched," *New Historical Literary*

*Study*, ed. Jeffrey N. Cox and Larry J. Reynolds (Princeton: Princeton University Press, 1993), 119–20.

20. Duncan Salkeld, *Madness and Drama in the Age of Shakespeare* (Manchester: Manchester University Press, 1993), 68–71.

21. Mary Louise Pratt, *Imperial Eyes: Travel Writing and Transculturation* (London: Routledge, 1992), 4–7. Pratt defines contact zones as "social spaces where disparate cultures meet, clash, and grapple with each other, often in highly asymmetrical relations of domination and subordination" (4). Although her main subject is the relationship between travel narratives and imperial conquest from the eighteenth century onwards, her concepts usefully illuminate Shakespeare's encoding of spatially defined ideological conflict and cultural hybridity that were historical features of Hellenistic and early Christian Ephesus, and of the Early Modern Ottoman and European Mediterranean.

22. Compare Eph. 6: "Put on the whole armour of God, that ye may be able to stand against the assauts [*sic*] of the deuil. For we wrestle not against flesh and blood, but against . . . powers, and against the worldlie gouenours, the princes of the darkenes of this worlde. . . . Stand therefore, and your loines girde about with veritie; & hauing on the brest plate of righteousnes. . . . Aboue all, take the shield of faith, wherewith ye may quench all the fyrie dartes of the wicked" (11–12, 14, 16).

23. Leslie A. Fielder, *The Stranger in Shakespeare* (New York: Stein and Day, 1972), 68–69; Robert Turcan, *The Cults of the Roman Empire* (Oxford: Blackwell, 1996), 37.

24. W. Thomas McCory, in "Friends and Lovers," *Shakespeare's Comedies*, ed. Gary Waller (London: Longman, 1991), 36.

25. Ralph Berry observes that while Adriana may overdo her complaints—a matter of social and perhaps dramatic decorum—"this is not the same thing as saying she has no grounds for complaint"; *Shakespeare's Comedies: Explorations in Form* (Princeton: Princeton University Press, 1972), 72.

26. Miola, "The Play and the Critics," 16.

27. "Emilia renounces sexual power over men and chooses thirty-three years in holy orders; so doing, she assumes the authority of the patriarchal institution that shelters her and takes center stage as restorer of family and community" (Miola, "The Play and the Critics," 17).

28. Laurie Maguire, "The Girls from Ephesus," in *"The Comedy of Errors": Critical Essays*, ed. R. S. Miola (New York: Garland Press, 1997), 356–91.

29. Elisabeth Schüssler Fiorenza, *In Memory of Her: A Feminist Theological Reconstruction of Christian Origins* (New York: Crossroad Publishing, 1992), 266–70.

30. Which has remained the suppressed reading; compare the concept of marriage defined by one standard legal reference work, *The Guide to American Law: Everyone's Legal Encyclopedia*, 12 vols. (St. Paul: West Publishing Company, 1983–85): "The traditional legal principle upon which the institution of marriage is founded is that a husband has the obligation to support a wife and a wife has the duty to serve" (7:275).

31. Katherine Parr, *The Lamentation of a Sinner* (London, 1547): "the younglinges and vnperfect . . . so muche the more as they shew themselues feruent in their [grudging and murmuring against their neighbor], they are iudged of the blynde worlde, and of them selues, great zealebearers to god" (E5v).

32. Alexander Leggatt, *Shakespeare's Comedy of Love* (London: Methuen, 1974), 4–14.

33. C. L. Barber and Richard P. Wheeler, *The Whole Journey: Shakespeare's Power of Development* (Berkeley and Los Angeles: University of California Press, 1986), 68.

# The Religious Dimension
# of Shakespeare's Illyria

PETER MILWARD

IN HIS MASTERPIECE OF LITERARY DETECTION, *THE FIRST NIGHT OF "Twelfth Night,"*[1] Leslie Hotson comes to deal with what he calls in his heading for chapter 7, "Illyria for Whitehall." Here he asks the natural question, "Were the connotations of *Illyria* for (Shakespeare) and his audience the lyric, the idyll, or the illusion that the romantic sound of the name so often suggests in a modern ear?" The shocking answer he gives is, "Far from it!" Instead, he provides what he calls "something more robustious," in view of the contemporary reputation of Illyria for riot and drunkenness, as exemplified by that "rudesby" (as Olivia calls her uncle) Sir Toby Belch, and for piracy, as exemplified by Antonio as seen through the eyes of Olivia, that "notable pirate" and "salt-water thief." In Hotson's eyes, such characters are more typical of the real Illyria than the romantic figures of the Duke Orsino and the Countess Olivia.

Far be it from me to dispute the presence of such boisterous elements in Illyria. They are, after all, what the dramatist has put into his play for the Feast of Fools, celebrated on the feast of the Epiphany, 6 January, the "twelfth night" after Christmas—no less than on the feast of the Holy Innocents, 28 December. Only I would point out that to maintain the realism of Illyria it is not necessary to reject or minimize its romance. The dramatic genius of Shakespeare is not restricted to the low comedy of the subplot, in which Sir Toby's presence serves to emphasize the "boisterous" connotation of Illyria. Rather, like the clown who is appropriately named Feste (as Master of the Revels at the Feast of Fools), Shakespeare can "sing both high and low" (2.3.41). He can imply both connotations of Illyria, both the realistic or "boisterous" one and the romantic one, even though in this play the main plot is subordinated in emphasis and impressiveness to the subplot. So the main character of the play, aimed at in the ambition of every leading player, is not Orsino, nor Sir Toby, nor Feste, but Malvolio.

True, the name of Illyria comes up far more frequently in the subplot of *Twelfth Night* than in the main plot: eight times in the former, as against only twice in the latter. So it may be said that its "boisterous" sense receives more emphasis than its idyllic sense. But this at least shows that the idyllic sense is by no means absent, as Hotson would have it. Twice may be even more significant than eight times, considering the way the place-name is twice mentioned with no small emphasis at the beginning of the play. On the occasion of her safe arrival on land after her shipwreck, Viola questions the captain who has rescued her concerning the name of the country. When the captain simply answers, "This is Illyria," she comments—with a typical Shakespearean pun, glancing at the romantic connotation of the name—"And what should I do in Illyria? / My brother he is in Elysium" (1.2.2–4). She is afraid her twin brother Sebastian has been drowned and so preceded her to Elysium, the land of the blessed. Yet in this very contrast between the real land of Illyria, on the Dalmatian coast of what is now Croatia, and the ideal land of "Elysium" Viola brings the two names together in a very Shakespearean association. Hotson is much too one-sided. At the end of the play, too, we come upon a similar association, as it were, between earth and heaven, drawn by the romantic Duke Orsino, when he first sets eyes (within the play) on the Countess Olivia. "Here comes the Countess," he exclaims; "now heaven walks on earth" (5.1.97).

In the ensuing scenes, as we follow Viola to the ducal palaces, Hotson skillfully introduces us to the setting of the stage in the royal banqueting hall of Whitehall, in the course of chapter 3, "Shakespeare's Arena Stage." He points out two "houses" at either side of the stage, one for Orsino and the other for Olivia. It is between them that the play is for the most part to be acted, once we have put the coast of Illyria behind us. On the one hand, it is to the former house, that of Orsino, that the idyllic aspect of Illyria chiefly belongs, the aspect Hotson sadly tends to overlook. It is an aspect emphasized in the opening words of the duke, when he calls at the outset of his dreamy soliloquy for music as "the food of love." It is also emphasized in the songs of Feste, both the romantic love song he sings for Sir Toby and Sir Andrew, "O mistress mine, where are you roaming?" (2.3.39), and the "old and antique song" he sings in compliance with the melancholy mood of the duke, "Come away, come away, death" (2.4.51). This latter song the duke significantly contrasts with the "light airs and recollected terms / Of these most brisk and giddy-paced times" (2.4.5–6). Nor is he alone among Shakespeare's characters in his distaste for such current fashions. Portia in *The Merchant of Venice* is also, we may observe, out of liking for "these naughty times" (3.2.18). Orlando, too, in *As You Like It* commends his old servant Adam on not being "for the fashion of these times" (2.3.59). The French king in *All's Well That Ends Well* likewise complains of "younger spirits, whose apprehensive senses / All

but new things disdain" (1.2.60–61). Romance after all feeds on such idyllic memories of the past, as on the dreamy ideal (already for Shakespeare
a memory of the medieval past) of "merry England."

From this point of view one may relate the idyllic land of Illyria (on the
side of Orsino) both to the country home of Portia at Belmont and to the
country setting of the Forest of Arden, however much Hotson may prefer,
with his emphasis on the subplot in Olivia's house and on the implied
presence of the Virgin Queen, to relate Illyria to Whitehall. Thus one may
think of Illyria in terms not only of its precise Croatian setting but also of
Venice or Italy in general, of the French Ardennes, even of England, and
again in terms both of the Hampshire Belmont, the home of Southampton's good cousin Thomas Pounde, and of the Warwickshire Arden close
to the dramatist's country home. As for Whitehall, it was then, as Hotson
ably demonstrates, the setting for a stately encounter between Queen Elizabeth and her noble Italian visitor, Don Virginio Orsino, duke of Bracciano.

Turning now to the religious dimension of the play, this was, in plainer
words, an encounter between the Catholic "house" of the Italian, even
Papal, Duke Orsino, and the Protestant "house" of the English-Welsh
Tudor Queen Elizabeth. In thus accepting the queen's hospitable invitation, it might seem, as Hotson well emphasizes in chapter 2, "Orsino," as
if the Catholic duke was venturing to put his head into a Protestant lion's
den. After all, his duchy was within the papal states, and he himself had
been appointed by Pope Sixtus V "prince attendant to the Papal throne."
At this particular moment, however, he was out of favor with Sixtus V's
successor, Pope Clement VIII, a fact that may have the more endeared him
to the Protestant queen. Anyhow, considering that the play was to be presented at court for the entertainment of the queen and the duke, it is understandable that the Catholic and papal connotations of the visitor's position
receive no special emphasis; whereas when we turn to the opposite
"house" of the Countess Olivia, standing for Queen Elizabeth, we may
well be surprised at the frequency of Protestant allusions.

First and foremost, it is the figure of the surly steward Malvolio who
most stands out in this connection. He might hardly seem fit for the main
role in this comedy but for the fact that at this point in Shakespeare's dramatic career, thanks in no small measure to the influence of Falstaff, the
subplot has come to prevail over the main plot. It is as if aristocracy has
been overwhelmed by democracy, and patricians by plebeians. In particular, he is described by Maria as "a kind of Puritan," which means—for all
the learned reservations of commentators—still a Puritan, if not quite so
extreme as the Brownists, in Sir Andrew's estimation (2.3.139; 3.2.31–
32). Ironically, he is baited in prison by the clown, who mimics the clerical
Puritan as "Sir Topas the curate." His Puritanism appears in his assump-

tion of a gown for the purpose, and his accompanying remark, "I would I were the first that ever dissembled in such a gown" (4.2.2, 5–6)—with a dig at those Puritan ministers who insisted on wearing no more than a gown at liturgical ceremonies. (Cf. the other clown's remark in *All's Well* 1.3.93–95: "Though honesty be no puritan, yet it will do no hurt; it will wear the surplice of humility over the black gown of a big [i.e., proud] heart.") Even the form of speech affected by the clown glances at the sanctimonious manner of Puritans: "Malvolio, Malvolio, thy wits the heavens restore! Endeavor thyself to sleep, and leave thy vain bibble babble!" (4.2.95–97)—where the very use of "bibble babble" may be derived from the words of the Puritan exorcist John Darrell in his contemporary apologia, *A True Narration* (1600).

On the other hand, it may seem strange to associate Sir Toby with Puritanism, in view of his rejection of Puritan sobriety and prohibition of "cakes and ale" (2.3.116). Yet he, more than Malvolio, stands for the basic Protestant doctrine, going all the way back to Martin Luther, of faith without works—a doctrine in which the Puritans naturally concurred, though by their time it had come to receive a more nuanced interpretation. This is the point of Sir Toby's exclamation on the arrival of the handsome young Cesario at the house of Olivia: "Let him be the devil and he will, I care not; give me faith say I" (1.5.128–29). In his drunken condition he mistakes Viola as Cesario for the devil Lechery come to tempt him to sexual sin. But he is convinced that, so long as he has a saving faith, he is immune from sin and its consequences, according to the notorious saying of Luther in his *Letter to Melanchthon* (1556), "Be a sinner, and sin strongly." In this respect he may well be seen as a "cousin" to Sir John Falstaff, who shows a similar faith without works in his remark concerning Poins, "O, if men were to be sav'd by merit, what hole in hell were hot enough for him?" (*1 Henry IV* 1.2.107–9). Also in this respect we may see in Maria a fit spouse to Sir Toby, considering her acceptance of the Christian hope "to be sav'd by believing rightly," in contrast to the ridiculous behavior of Malvolio (3.2.62–63).

In such ways, the "house" of the Countess Olivia, representing Queen Elizabeth, may be seen as a place where various forms of Protestantism—Lutheranism, moderate Puritanism, and even the more extreme Brownism—come together. Yet neither Olivia nor her prototype Elizabeth are entirely Protestant. Elizabeth herself was no less opposed to the Puritans than to the Catholics, and she persecuted either side with a cruel impartiality. So she no doubt enjoyed the anti-Puritan satire in *Twelfth Night* as the dramatist no doubt intended her to. She even liked to retain certain elements of Catholic ceremony, such as the crucifix, in her royal chapel; and she objected to a married clergy, not least in her bishops, though her disapproval was not so effective. On Olivia's side, we find her arranging for herself and Sebastian (imagining him to be Viola-Cesario) to be married by a Catholic priest in a Catholic wedding. This is to be performed, she says, by a "holy man" under the "consecrated roof" of a nearby "chantry" (4.3.23–25); whereas in England all chantry chapels that had survived the pillage under Henry VIII had been destroyed by order of Elizabeth's Protestant brother Edward VI early on in his reign. All rites of consecration were, moreover, regarded by Protestants as Catholic and superstitious. Olivia also addresses the priest as "father," a title not to be used of a Protestant minister. She goes on to ask him to explain the marriage rite he has just performed (5.1.156–63). This he does in such a way as to recall Jaques's ideal of a "good priest" in *As You Like It*, one who "can tell you what marriage is" (3.3.85–86).

As for the illusion in Illyria, which Hotson rejects out of hand, it is surely all-pervasive in the play, affecting almost everyone, not least the two central figures, the Italian duke and the English queen, as represented by Orsino and Olivia. This illusion takes the form of imaginings of romantic love, as Orsino, Malvolio, and Sir Andrew all imagine themselves in various ways either as loving or as being loved by Olivia; while Olivia in turn imagines herself in love with Viola-Cesario, only to find herself married to her twin brother Sebastian. The whole play is thus another "comedy of errors," consisting of shipwreck, identical twins, and mistaken identity. At the same time, there are two other figures no less central to the play than Orsino and Olivia: the heroine Viola-Cesario and the fool Feste. Whereas Orsino and Olivia belong to their respective houses and are rarely seen outside them until the last scene, Viola and Feste move equally between both houses, though Viola belongs to the one and Feste to the other. They alone know the truth about themselves beneath their respective disguises (for the fool's motley is also a kind of disguise), as well as the truth about others beneath their illusions. They somehow stand apart from the scenario in which they have their parts to play. They are endowed with a precious wisdom, which the heroine recognizes in the fool, though he not so clearly in her (3.1.60). They may thus be seen as standing for the main theme of *Twelfth Night*, considering that the feast being celebrated that 6 January is not only a Feast of Fools but also the Feast of the Epiphany, commemorating the coming of the wise men to Bethlehem.

Thus in spite of all Hotson says to the contrary, Illyria may be seen as standing in the dramatist's mind for two countries in addition to the real Illyria on the Eastern coast of the Adriatic as identified in the play. There is, on the one hand, the Catholic country of Italy, the home of Duke Orsino, regarded not just as a fiction of the dramatist's imagination but as the queen's noble visitor at Whitehall. It represents the ideal and idyllic land across the seas, akin to Belmont and the Forest of Arden, whether in Hampshire or Venetia, whether in Warwickshire or the Low Countries.

There is, on the other hand, the Protestant country of England, centered on the court of Queen Elizabeth in Westminster, where the play is enacted for the royal and ducal entertainment. In this connection it may well be remembered that the queen was also patroness (in Spanish eyes) to such notable pirates as Sir Francis Drake, whom she even knighted in 1581 after his notorious expedition of piracy around the coast of South America and across the Pacific Ocean, and to Protestant rebels abroad in Scotland, France, and the Low Countries. Considering all this, it is indeed a marvel how daringly and skillfully the dramatist contrived to present it all under the very nose and eyes of the queen, and to put her in a good humor withal! Thus he may be hailed as the quintessential subverter of the English Protestant establishment, once we approach the play from a religious and Catholic point of view.

At the same time, and on a deeper level, we may interpret the play as "the thing" by which the dramatist hopes to "catch the conscience" of the queen (*Hamlet* 2.2.604–5). It may be seen as his way of appealing to her inner mind and heart on the occasion of this visit of an Italian duke close to the Pope at Rome. This duke, as Hotson points out, in visiting this Protestant queen was in serious danger of incurring the wrath both of Pope Clement VIII and of King Philip III of Spain—which may have been the reason (as noted above) why he received such a warm welcome from the queen. Yet in this meeting Shakespeare may have seen an opportunity of "dialogue" between the two opposing sides in the religious conflict, Catholic and Protestant. And as an outcome of the dialogue, he may have envisaged an easing by the queen of her long continued persecution of the English Catholics.

Unfortunately, this hope of Shakespeare's (if such it was) remained unfulfilled, partly owing to the failure of the Essex rebellion barely three weeks after "the first night of *Twelfth Night*." For then Essex derived support from some desperate Catholic gentlemen, including Shakespeare's distant cousin (on his mother's side) Robert Catesby, who also went on— with the probable connivance and blackmail of Sir Robert Cecil—to concoct the extraordinary Gunpowder Plot of 1605. Partly also, we may add, owing to the outbreak about this time of a scandalous controversy between a disaffected group of seminary priests and some of the leading Jesuits, notably Robert Persons, back in Rome. The former group, in their opposition to the "Hispaniolated" Jesuits, appealed to the queen for toleration in consideration of their professed loyalty to her; but her only answer was to issue the last proclamation of her long reign, banishing them. So the poor Catholics still had to wait, with hopes now pinned on the coming of a new, Scottish reign on the heels of the old, Welsh reign—hopes whose disappointment was admitted by the prosecutor at the plotters' trial as the immediate cause of their hare-brained resort to the Gunpowder Plot.

## Postscript

What, it may now be asked, has this account of "the religious dimension in Shakespeare's Illyria" got to do with the seminar subtitled of "heterotopies, identities, (counter) histories?"

First, it may be answered, by "heterotopies" one may, according to the literal meaning of the word, understand other places, unexpected places, places of paradox or seeming self-contradiction. Obviously, the place intended as the setting of *Twelfth Night* is the land of Illyria, otherwise known as Dalmatia or Croatia, on the eastern coast of the Adriatic Sea, whether regarded as an ideal, idyllic land of illusion or as a real place of drunken riot and piracy. Yet it also points, according to the ingenious theory of Leslie Hotson, to the real court of Queen Elizabeth at Whitehall and to the banquet she gave there in honor of the visiting duke of Bracciano, Don Virginio Orsino. And so we are subtly led back from Illyria to England, and at the same time from England to Italy and the papal states. This implies a further contrast between the Protestant country of Elizabethan England and the Catholic country of Italy, even where the latter is most Catholic, at Rome. This background may explain why there are so many Protestant, even Puritan, references in the subplot centered on the house of Olivia (standing as she does for Elizabeth), but fewer Catholic references in the main plot centered on the house of Orsino.

Secondly, the "identities" of the characters in this play are all confused in a plot of endless love-delusion and class or gender confusion, culminating in Viola's identification of Olivia, "That you do think you are not what you are," followed by her own admission, "Then think you right: I am not what I am" (3.1.139, 141). Only the heroine Viola and the fool Feste (as noted above) know themselves rightly, and only they are truly wise according to both the Socratic ideal of self-knowledge and the celebration of this feast of the wise men, the Epiphany. The others are all fools in their various ways, not knowing who they are or what they are doing. At the same time, the use of disguise in the play may point to the situation of Elizabethan Catholics, who were obliged to dissemble their true identity in order to escape the cruel laws passed by Puritan-dominated Parliaments against them. It was above all their priests who had to resort most of the time to real disguise, even while recognizing, with Viola, that it was "a wickedness" (2.2.27). Moreover, behind the characters who appear in the play as *dramatis personae*, Hotson points to the real persons of Queen Elizabeth as the Countess Olivia and Don Virginio Orsino as Duke Orsino, as well as the comptroller of the queen's household Sir William Knollys as Malvolio and possibly Mary Fitton as Maria. For Shakespeare is never averse, as we may see in not a few of his plays, to the use of what has been called (by Alice Lyle Scoufos) "topological satire."

Thirdly, by "counter histories" one may understand not only the story of the play, whether as derived from one or more "sources" such as Barnabe Riche's *Farewell to Military Profession* (1581), or from the immediate occasion of the play for the royal entertainment at Whitehall, but also the history behind the play, in which the dramatist looks at once to the romantic lands of the Mediterranean symbolized by "Illyria" (with its connotation of Elysium) and to the harsh reality (especially for Catholics) in Elizabethan England. This harsh reality pervades the action not only of *Twelfth Night*, imparting to the play its characteristic tone of melancholy (as in the madrigals of the time, many of whose composers were recusants or at least sympathizers), but also of almost all the comedies, not least the earlier *Comedy of Errors* to which it is commonly compared, and of those tragedies that are envisaged in the oddly sad ending of *Twelfth Night*, namely *Hamlet*, seen as a sequel to Malvolio's vow of revenge, and *King Lear*, seen as a sequel to Feste's concluding ditty on the sadness of human life.

*Note.* It may be worthwhile to say a few words about the religious divisions mentioned in this article. The basic division is, of course, that between Catholic and Protestant, which originated in the revolt of Martin Luther from Rome but became fully explicit at the Diet of Spires in 1529 when the reformers came to be known as "Protestant" from the formal *Protestatio* they drew up on that occasion. This term, therefore, covers all countries, including Edwardian and Elizabethan England, which generally accepted the reforms inaugurated by Luther. The Puritans, however, were the more radical Protestants in England, who opposed the bishops on the ground of the rites and ceremonies ordered in the Book of Common Prayer, and for this the Puritan ministers were ejected from their livings first by Archbishop Parker in the 1560s and later by Archbishop Whitgift in the 1580s. Most of them still remained members of the Church of England, recognizing the queen as its lawful governor; but the more extreme of them, first known as Brownists (from Robert Browne) and more generally as Separatists, refused to accept the Church of England as a valid church of Christ. Hence Robert Persons, writing in 1592, was able to distinguish "three religions" in the England of those days: Catholic, Protestant, and Puritan—where by "Protestant" he evidently refers to the Church of England. The Catholics were, however, commonly called "Papists" by their opponents, for their allegiance to the Pope; and so one may speak of these three religions for convenience as "the three Ps." Needless to say, within these main divisions there were innumerable subdivisions, which fail to come to the surface only on account of the prevailing persecution in the name of religious conformity.

## Note

1. Leslie Hotson, *The First Night of "Twelfth Night"* (London: Hart-Davis, 1954).

# The True History of Romeo and Juliet: A Veronese Plot of the 1830s

PAOLA PUGLIATTI

THE ARCHIGINNASIO PALACE IN BOLOGNA IS PROBABLY THE MOST IMPORtant historic building in town. It was built in 1562–63 by Antonio Morandi, called the Terribilia, to accommodate the various schools of the *Studium*, until then scattered about the city, mostly in the private houses of the doctors. Its construction was promoted by Pope Pius VI, who charged Cardinal Carlo Borromeo, at the time his legate in Bologna, to further the enterprise. Until 1803, the imposing building was the seat of the University; the seven thousand coats of arms, either sculpted or painted in the court, on the staircase, in the passages, and in the halls, belonged to students' corporations, chancellors, deans, and others associated with the *Studium* during the sixteenth and seventeenth centuries. Since 1803, when the *Studium* was removed, the building has become the seat of the civic library. Proud of its unmanageable "historical catalogue," of its uncomfortable benches, of the dim light that falls from the high ceiling and from the tall, narrow windows, the place carries readers back in time: the time of its building and the time—two-and-a-half-centuries later—when the library was established. It was in that library that months ago I came by chance across the book of which I am going to speak.

At first sight, this bulky volume does not stimulate much critical reflection; rather, it invites one to tell a story, a tiny piece of provincial cultural history—or better two stories two-and-a-half-centuries removed from each other, two tales of a city, Verona. The book enacts the two moments in time that are evoked by the library where it is kept, and it is with those two moments in time that my paper is concerned: the sixteenth century, when the story of Romeo Montecchi and Giulia Cappelletti was first narrated and when it spread itself in a number of writings of different genres; and the early nineteenth century, when—in an entirely different mood and atmosphere—it was passionately revived, again in a number of forms and genres. The aim, this time, was to show the story's indisputable truth, in a debate that, as we shall see, involved the whole of a micro-society of eminent citizens.

The book was printed in Pisa in 1831 by Nistri, a printing house still in existence. Its editor, Alessandro Torri, was from Verona; but he was a voluntary exile from his native town because he had been persecuted by the Austrian regime.[1]

The collection presents four units, which have been marked in arabic numbers by the librarian. Unit 1 is a new imprint, while units 2 to 4 are reprints. The first unit contains what the editor calls "the historical *novella*" by Luigi Da Porto with a preface (written by Signor Bertolotti), a biography of Da Porto by the same Torri and numerous annotations, both historical (excerpts from sixteenth- and seventeenth-century chronicles about the families of Monticoli and Cappelletti) and textual (comments on the variants of the two first editions of Da Porto's *novella*); then follow various cases of prolonged sleep or apparent death induced by potions; the *novella*s by Masuccio Salernitano and by Matteo Bandello; the poem by "Clizia Veronese" and lines by Ardeo on Clizia's death. The second unit contains three letters by Filippo Scolari—a Veronese historian, a friend of Torri's, and a staunch defender of the truth of the story—two of which had been published previously, followed by various poems. Unit three is a short pamphlet published the previous year (1830) in Padua: the pamphlet illustrates the fine old custom of presenting writings on the occasion of weddings. In this case, it is a letter by Giuseppe Todeschini (the champion of the skeptic party) to Giacomo Milan, written on the occasion of "the most happy Porto wedding." Giacomo Milan, the dedicatee of the letter, was uncle to the bridegroom; both the bride and the bridegroom, in turn, were descendants of Luigi Da Porto. Finally, the fourth unit contains Michele Leoni's translation of Shakespeare's play.[2]

Torri dedicated "queste pietose pagine onde il tuo core era scosso" (those compassionate pages by which your heart was moved) to a woman, Anna, Countess Schio, lately deceased.[3] In the letter that follows, addressed by the editor to Count Pietro degli Emilj from Verona, Anna's husband, Torri quotes a passage from a letter that the countess had sent to him "not many days before she was taken by her mortal illness," encouraging him to publish the present miscellany. "La prefazione, che voi porrete avanti la Novella del Da-Porto sul tristo avvenimento di Giulietta," Anna wrote, "sarà assai calda, spero, e ne dimostrerà la verità incontrastabile"[4] (The preface that you will write as an introduction to the *novella* by Luigi Da Porto on the sad story of Juliet will be very warm, I hope, and will show beyond all doubt the truth of the story).

Torri then declares that he was persuaded to publish the book by the fact that some people had lately expressed doubts and others had altogether denied the truth of the story; he therefore decided to gather all the documents, both pro and con, that concerned the "trial" (this is the word he uses) celebrated at the time in Verona, whether the story of Romeo and

Juliet, as narrated by Da Porto in his *novella* and related by Girolamo Dalla Corte in his *Istorie di Verona*,[5] is true or not.

Although he shows and declares equanimity in presenting some of the writings of the adverse party, it is clear that Torri belonged to those who, in the present "trial," intended to bear witness to the truth of the story. He then adds his own evidence *pro veritate* to those produced by his friend Filippo Scolari. Among these are various cases of "apparent death" or "lethargic sleep," including that of a lady still living in Verona, who had been taken by a deep sleep lasting forty-eight hours owing to an overdose of opium.[6] The framework of the gestation and publication of the book can be inferred by reading its last pages, where the editor presents the volume "A' suoi concittadini veronesi / Associati alla novella di Luigi Da Porto / sopra la storia di Giulietta e Romeo / con altri scritti relativi" (To his Veronese fellow citizens / Associated with the *novella* by Luigi Da Porto / about the story of Romeo and Juliet / together with other related writings).[7] Torri then speaks of an engagement taken with a group of worthy Veronese citizens to publish Da Porto's *novella* with a comment on the variants that appear in its two sixteenth-century editions (the first probably published in 1531 and the second in 1535), and to offer part of the income from the book's sale to an otherwise unspecified "casa di ricovero" (probably a children's home). On the last page of the book, a list of 110 names of notable Veronese citizens is printed. These seem to have been the promoters (it is not clear whether material or simply moral) of the book. The enterprise, then, seems to have involved a considerable number of people—historians, literati, noblemen, noblewomen, professional people, simple citizens—in a passionate debate that seems to have developed in the then-appropriate mood of love for one's homeland and its traditions.

For months I questioned that book, paying repeated visits to the library, simply leafing through its pages and reading here and there, trying to absorb the context that had produced it and to understand what it was that made it such a peculiar reading experience in my eyes and also what it was that connected it so closely to the place where I was reading it. In the end I realized that I was not interested in the fact that the book gathered together the Italian sources of Shakespeare's tragedy (or the sources of its sources); nor was I interested in collating the variants appearing in the story's different versions; least of all was I attracted by the idea of comparing and evaluating the evidence, either pro or con, for the authenticity of the fact. In short, what appeared to me stimulating was not the story itself but the various circumstances in which it had been narrated and discussed. In this way, I became aware that attention had to be shifted from the texts to the contexts of their production, from the contents of the story in its different versions to the circumstances of its many utterances, from the body of those texts to their thresholds: the half-hinted or unwritten dialogue surrounding them.

So I decided to look at the dedicatory letters and the introductory lines of those texts, and these started to unveil a deeply intriguing network of relations.

Da Porto's *novella* has precedents in the homologous stories of tragic love by Boccaccio[8] and by Masuccio Salernitano;[9] Luigi Da Porto, however, was the first who named the lovers Romeo Montecchi and Giulia Cappelletti, and the first who set the story in Verona (he was from Vicenza, near Verona), "at the time of Signor Bartolomeo della Scala."[10] The date 1531 is attributed by general consent to the first impression of the *novella*, which had a second edition in 1535.[11] Da Porto dedicated the *novella* "To the most beautiful and graceful Lady Lucina Savorgnana,"[12] his friend and kinswoman. In the first lines of the dedicatory letter, Porto writes,

> Poscia che io, già assai giorni con voi parlando, dissi di voler una compassionevole *novella* da me già più volte udita, ed in Verona intervenuta, iscrivere, m'è paruto essere il debito in queste poche carte distenderla, sì perché le mie parole appo voi non paressero vane, sì anco perché a me, che misero sono, de' casi de'miseri amanti, di ch'ella è piena, si appartiene.[13]

> [Since many days ago, conversing with you, I told you that I wanted to write down a pitiful story that took place in Verona and that I have heard many times, I thought it was my obligation to you to unfold it in these few leaves, both in order to show that my words to you were not idle and because the story suits my miserable self, being full of miserable cases of miserable lovers.]

Let me remark two things: in the first place, the writing down of the *novella* was preceded by a conversation with the Lady, in which Porto promised that he would write down the story; secondly, Porto (in the case of the dedicatory letter the author, not the narrator, of the story) declares that he has *heard* the story told many times; he therefore claims that his task was simply that of translating an orally transmitted tale into a written text.

The first long paragraph of the story introduces Porto's narrational mask (Porto himself, only temporally at some remove from Porto the redactor of the *novella*), the character of the person who had orally transmitted the story to him and the circumstances of its enunciation. Let us retrieve just a few pieces of information from the *incipit* of the *novella*: the oral narrator is an archer; he is from Verona, and his name is Peregrino. Porto's *novella* is not part of a corpus of stories; since it stands on its own, these are the only paratextual hints we may glean from it.

The case of Bandello is completely different. His *novella*s constitute a huge corpus that was originally published in four volumes (the first three appeared in Lucca in 1554, the fourth posthumously in Lyon in 1573).[14]

Bandello's 214 *novella*s do not have a fictional framework like Boccaccio's, and Bandello himself declares, in the foreword to the third volume
of his work, that his *novella*s have not been written according to any principle of continuity or order.[15] This statement has too often been taken at
face value, and indeed few critics have tackled the corpus in a systematic
way. In recent discussions, however, the stress has been put on the complex and extremely rich and varied system of social relations that the dedicatory letters highlight. As G. Mazzacurati has said, these constitute "a
whirl of fictitious presences and of evoked absences which goes through
almost the whole of Italy and makes of the entire courtly world (surveyed
in that huge simulation of epistolary which the dedicatory letters constitute), the new 'brigade,' the disseminated framework, the physically ex-
ploded circle which is socially recomposed in the author's memory."[16] In
other words, as Daria Perocco argues, "the thematic aggregation suggested
by Boccaccio's model has been substituted by a polymorphous tension
whose nucleus is not inside the *novella*s but outside, in the world of
courtly discussion, in the performance of each story and in the sometimes
explicit debate which frames them."[17]

The framework to which both Mazzacurati and Perocco allude is extremely rich and complex. Each of Bandello's *novella*s has its own dedicatory letter, and each has an introductory passage in which a certain number
of things are almost invariably specified: the circumstance and place of
its enunciation, the participants in the conversational circle, the topic of
discussion from which the argument of each *novella* is suggested, the identity of the oral narrator of the story, and so on.

Let us see briefly what the framework of the *novella* concerning Romeo
and Juliet is.

Bandello dedicated the *novella* to an eminent Veronese, Girolamo Fracastoro, a literary man, a physician, and a scientist. In the letter, Bandello
relates a visit to the thermal baths of Caldero, a spa fifteen kilometers from
Verona, where he had followed his protector Cesare Fregoso, who had
been staying there for a while to drink the salubrious waters. While staying
in Caldero, Fregoso was a guest of a Veronese gentleman, Matteo Boldiero. Bandello praises the virtues of the waters that, he reminds the dedicatee of the letter, he had experienced some time before on the advice of
the same Fracastoro and that had rid him of a terrible backache. He then
tells about the way in which his patron had spent the time in Caldero,
"usando de l'onesta libertà la quale a chi beve quell'acque si concede,
ricreandosi di brigata con quelli che ai bagni si ritrovavano" (using the
honest liberty that is convenient to those who drink the waters, enjoying
the company of a brigade that was wont to gather at the baths). "Venivano
anco," he adds, "dalle cittati circonvicine gentiluomini assai a visitarlo, i
quali tutti esso signore lietamente riceveva e con ricca e sontuosa mensa

onorava"[18] (Many gentlemen came to visit [Fregoso] from nearby cities, and he received them cheerfully and honored them with rich and sumptuous meals). One day, when the brigade was conversing about the mischances that sometimes befall lovers, one of them told "una piertosa istoria che a Verona al tempo del Signor Bartolomeo della Scala avvenne" (a pitiful story of events that had occurred in Verona at the time of Signor Bartolomeo della Scala).[19] The teller of the story, Bandello says, was "Captain Alessandro Peregrino." This said, he closes the letter to Fracastoro by hinting at a literary relationship with the dedicatee, who had written an epigram in praise of Bandello's poem "Le tre parche."

Let me add a few pieces of extratextual information. Matteo Boldiero, Fregoso's host, was probably the uncle of Gherardo Boldiero (or Boldieri) to whom Bandello dedicated the twelfth *novella* of the second volume and who is the narrator of the forty-first *novella* in the same volume; in addition, Matteo was uncle to Dalla Corte, the first who gave a historical imprint to the story.[20] More importantly, Gherardo Boldiero has been identified as the author of the poem on the story of Romeo and Juliet published in 1553 (that is, one year before the first three volumes of Bandello's *novella*s appeared) under the pseudonym "Clizia Veronese."[21]

I wish to pick out and examine a few elements from Bandello's letter to Fracastoro. Again, as we have seen in Porto, the author hides himself behind an oral report, of which he is merely a receiver and which he transcribes simply because the case seems to him to be worthy to be kept in a permanent memory that the oral report does not allow; in the second place, Bandello never mentions the story in Porto's version; obviously we do not know whether he read it or even knew about it; it is a fact, however, that the oral teller of Bandello's story is the same Peregrino from Verona from whom Porto said he had heard it. The third—and most important—thing to be remarked is the framework in which the story is heard; that is, the conversational courtly context in which the primacy of the spoken word is supreme. It appears, therefore, that—not unlike Porto's—Bandello's *auctoritas* is an oral source, connected to the circumstance of the gathering of the "brigade" of Cesare Fregoso's friends and fully in keeping with that model of interpersonal relationships that was the custom of the "civil conversation," that custom which, in 1574, was to produce one of the great institutional books of the Italian Renaissance, *La civil conversazione* by Stefano Guazzo.

According to Guazzo, the civil conversation is the one that takes place in a "virtuosa raunanza" (virtuous gathering), and *civil* is defined as "onesta," "lodevole," "virtuosa" (honest, praiseworthy, and virtuous).[22] The ideal circumstances in which the *civil conversazione* develops are therefore not different from those we witness at the thermal baths of Caldero described by Bandello.

Let me open a brief parenthesis in order to quote a few passages from Guazzo's work in which the primacy of oral social interaction in conversational exchange is established: " 'l principio e 'l fine delle scienze dipende dalla conversazione" ("conuersation is the beginning and end of knowledge");[23] " 'l sapere comincia dal conversare e finisce nel conversare" ("knowledge starts in conversation and ends in conversation");[24] "giova più al letterato un'ora ch'egli dispensi nel discorrere ch'un giorno di studio in solitudine" ("it more auayleth a student to discourse one hour with his like, then to studie a whole day by himselfe in his studie");[25] until we encounter the paradoxical allusion to the fact that the very book we are reading is an almost powerless didactic tool:

> . . . sarebbe errore il credere che la dottrina s'acquisti più nella solitudine fra i libri che nella conversazione fra gli uomini dotti, percioché la prova ci dimostra che meglio s'apprende la dottrina per l'orecchie che per gli occhi, e che non accaderebbe consumarsi la vista né assottigliarsi le dita nel rivolgere i fogli degli scrittori, se si potesse aver del continuo la presenza loro e ricever per le orecchie quella viva voce, la quale con mirabil forza s'imprime nella mente. (Guazzo, fols. 15v–16)

> [it were a great errour to beleeue, that learning is more gotten in solitariness amongest Bookes, then in the companie of learned men. For this is a maxime in Philosophy, and experience showeth it, That learning is easier gotten by the eares then by the eyes: neither should a man neede to dimme his sight, and weare his fingers in turning over the books of wryters, if hee might alwayes see them present, and receiue by hearing that natural voyce, which by wonderfull force imprinteth it selfe in the minde.] (Pettie, trans. trans., fol. 14v)]

But the network of conversational relationships becomes even more intriguing if we remember that the person who affirms the primacy of conversation in Castiglione's *Cortegiano* is Federico Fregoso, uncle to Bandello's patron. The relevant passage in *The Courtier* is the following:

> Onde, consentendo con le opinioni sue (del Conte Ludovico di Canossa), ed oltre al resto circa la nobiltà del cortegiano e lo ingegno e la disposizion del corpo e grazia dell'aspetto, dico che per acquistar laude meritamente e bona estimazione appresso ognuno, e grazia da quei signori ai quali serve, parmi necesario che e' sappia componere tutta la vita sua e valersi delle sue bone qualità universalmente nella *conversazion* di tutti gli omini senza acquistarne invidia.[26]

> [Therefore, agreeing with his [Count Ludovico of Canossa's ] opinions . . . about the nobility of the courtier, his brilliance, the posture of his body, and the gracefulness of his appearance, I say that in order to deserve the praise, the good estimation, and the favor of everybody and the benevolence of those whom he

serves, it seems to me necessary that he should be able to order all his life and avail himself of his good qualities universally in the conversation of all men.]

We may now go back to the early nineteenth century. In those years, Verona, and the whole of Lombardo-Veneto, were oppressed by the Austrian regime. The year 1831, when Alessandro Torri edited the book from which I started my study, is a significant date in the history of Italy's striving for independence. For the third time in ten years, an uprising, which this time had started in Modena, had failed, and its leaders had been executed. Probably, then, the revival of the story of Romeo and Juliet in that climate meant also the vindication of local identity and the pride of one's own traditions and history. The social tone, however, has changed. As Giacomo Leopardi remarked on 28 September 1823, in one of the thoughts of his *Zibaldone*, the art and institution of conversation is now extinguished, and therefore, "in Italy, there is but very little society. . . . no social tone which can be said to be Italian."[27] But the outlook on the written sources of that tradition also has changed. In the fully romantic mood and atmosphere in which the story is revived, what was originally presented as *oral* and as the outcome of a workshop of *civil conversazione* has made way for the romantic idea of originality, authority, and authorship; indeed, in the present trial, the written sources have even become *evidence* of the truth of the fact, with no apparent distinction between chroniclers and historians and writers of *novella*s. No longer assembled in the "virtuous gathering" of a brigade, the participants in the "trial" are engaged in exchanging individual letters, in formulating written answers to written challenges, each time enacting a duologue of arguments.

In a peculiar passage, the historian Scolari produces a singular narratological argument, holding that the *novella*s are more truthful than the historical novels:

> Il romanzo istorico dei moderni poi è cosa affatto diversa dalle Novelle, in quanto che se le Novelle hanno per iscopo la rappresentazione di un fatto singolare avvenuto, il Romanzo storico ha bensì per base la narrazione di un fatto che per lo più è supposto, ma questo per aver occasione a poter far conoscere lo stato, e rappresentare per esso la condizione del tempo e dei costumi ai quali lo si vuol riferire.[28]

> [The modern historical novel is completely different from the *novella*s; indeed, while the *novella*s aim at the representation of a real notable event, the historical novel, on the contrary, has at its base the narration of something that is in most cases fictional, which it uses as an opportunity . . . to represent the circumstances of the time and costumes to which the story refers.]

Thus the debate concentrated on the reliability of single authors and on the basic truthfulness of the novelistic genre; in harmony with a new historiographic mood and with the taste for ruins and for graveyard poetry, it also concentrated on *monuments*, with an exceptional stress laid on the stone that was visited as Juliet's tomb.

Although Shakespeare has not been the main focus of my talk, I cannot end these notes without asking myself what the function of his tragedy may have been in the mind of the editor. The tragedy by Guglielmo Shakespeare is introduced by a brief note in which it is defined as "one of the masterpieces of English theatre"; Shakespeare is the only non-Italian author who appears in the collection; neither Boaistuau nor Brooke is even mentioned in the book. But Shakespeare means both *authorship* and *auctoritas* to the Romantics; besides, with an understandable paradoxical inversion, his tragedy seems to represent a further vindication of nationhood because rendered in Italian in the native hendecasyllabic line, the line of Dante and of Petrarch. What seems curious, however, is that his work, not unlike Da Porto's, Bandello's, or the chronicler Dalla Corte's, is subsumed as further *evidence*, as another authoritative *monument* to the truth, of the two lovers' unhappy story. In short, in a rather confused and paradoxical way, Shakespeare's tragedy, from rewriting and representation of the story, becomes one of the relevant sources of the event.

On 7 November 1816, Shakespeare's countryman Lord Byron wrote a skeptical note to his friend Thomas More: "I have been over Verona. The amphitheatre is wonderful—beats even Greece. Of the truth of Juliet's story, they seem tenacious to a degree, insisting on the fact—giving a date (1303), and showing a tomb." Byron, however, seems to have been infected by the Veronese idolatry, for he goes on, "I have brought away a few pieces of the granite, to give to my daughter and my nieces."[29]

Byron's gesture was precisely what the Veronese attributed to the insensitivity of certain tourists: "Incresce purtroppo alle anime di dolce tempera," Giovan Battista Persico wrote in 1820, "il veder quell'arca esposta al suo disfacimento, sminuendosi tutto il dì dal levargliene pezzetti per farne gioielli" (Sweet-tempered minds are sorry to see that tomb exposed to decay, daily diminished by those people who remove small pieces from it in order to make jewels . . . ).[30]

But was Byron's gesture really one of insensitivity?

One of the founders of the *Annales*, Lucien Febvre, wrote that "a remarkable part, and maybe the most fascinating, of a historian's work lies in the continuous effort of making dumb objects speak, of making them say things which by themselves they would not say."[31] In spite of his apparent skepticism, Byron must have felt a similar need before Juliet's tomb, if in the same letter he shows that he tried to make that stone speak to his imagination: "It is a plain, open, and partly decayed sarcophagus," he wrote, "with withered leaves in it, in a wild and desolate conventual garden, once a cemetery, now ruined to the very graves." And, in some peculiar way, that stone must have shaken his skepticism, for in the closing of the passage a few presuppositions of truth slipped from of his pen: "The situation struck me as very appropriate, being blighted as their love."[32]

# Notes

1. From the last words of the letter to Count Pietro degli Emilj, which prefaces the collection, it appears that Torri no longer lives "in our dear Verona, my beloved homeland" (xii). The fact that the book was published in Pisa suggests that it is from there that he writes; the reasons of his Pisan exile are not clear from what he writes, but if one is persistent enough in consulting the "historical catalogue" of the library, one will find an obituary of Torri, dated 27 June 1861 and signed by the same Count degli Emilj to whom Torri had addressed his book (Pietro degli Emilj, "Necrologia di Alessandro Torri," *L'indicatore bresciano*, 30 June 1861). Degli Emilj depicts Torri as a sincere patriot in love with liberty; he speaks of the fierce persecution he had suffered under the Austrian regime, which had determined his decision to go an exile far from his beloved Verona and take shelter in the more hospitable Pisa, where he had established a printing house and where he lived until his death. We also learn that Torri had become a distinguished Dante scholar and that Gray's "Elegy" was one of the many things his Pisan printing house had published. Degli Emilj closes his obituary by writing, in an old-fashioned style of trite patriotic rhetoric, "Io credo che a quella pace suprema gran parte si avesse il saper egli che moriva libero figlio di una libera e forte Nazione e col ciglio umido ancora di quelle lacrime soavissime che la festività nazionale del 2 Giugno gli faceva spargere" (I believe that to that supreme peace greatly contributed the fact that he knew he died the free son of a free and strong Nation, his eye still wet with those most sweet tears which the national celebration of 2 June made him shed). Degli Emilj was obviously alluding to the fact that in 1860, after long strife, Italy achieved unity and independence.

2. Leoni translated Shakespeare's tragedies starting with *Julius Caesar* in 1811; in the following years he published the complete translations in one single work, *Le tragedie di Shakspeare* 14 vols.(Verona: Società Tipografica, 1819–22).

3. Torri, ed., unit 1, p. iii.

4. Ibid., p. vi.

5. G. Dalla Corte, *Istorie di Verona*, 2 vols. (Verona, 1596).

6. Torri, ed., unit 1, p. viii.

7. Ibid., unit 4, last page but one of the volume, unnumbered.

8. G. Boccaccio, *Decameron*, IV day, *novella* 1, which tells how Tancredi, prince of Salerno, killed the lover of his daughter Gismonda and sent her the young man's heart in a gold cup, and how Gismonda killed herself by drinking the poison she had poured into the cup. Masuccio Salernitano, *Il Novellino* (1476), *novella* 33. The *novella* tells of the unfortunate love of Gianozza and Mariotto and the death of Gianozza on the lifeless body of her lover.

9. Masuccio Salernitano, *Il Novellino* (1476), *novella* 32.

10. The title of Da Porto's *novella* is "Istoria novellamente ritrovata di due nobili amanti con la pietosa loro morte intervenuta già nella città di Verona nel tempo del Sig. Bartolommeo della Scala" (The newly found story of two noble lovers with their pitiful death occurred in the city of Verona at the time of Signor Bartolomeo della Scala).

11. Quotations in this article are from the first edition, the one reproduced in Torri's collection. The editor also lists the variants that occur between the first and the second edition.

12. Alla bellissima e leggiadra madama Lucina Savorgnana (17).

13. Torri, ed., unit 1, p. 17.

14. M. Bandello, *La prima, seconda, terza parte de le novelle del Bandello*, 3 vols. (Lucca: V. Busdrago, 1554); *La quarta parte de le novelle del Bandello, nuovamente composte né per l'addietro date in luce* (Lyon: A. Marsilii, 1573).

15. Bandello explains the random sequence as follows: "non essendo le mie novelle soggetto d'istoria continovata, ma una mistura d'accidenti diversi, diversamente e in diversi luoghi e tempi a diverse persone avvenuti e senza ordine veruno recitati" (since my *novellas* do not represent a continuous story but rather a mixture of different accidents happening at different times and in different places, and told in no particular order). Quotations are from Matteo Bandello, *Giulietta e Romeo*, ed. D. Perocco (Venezia: Marsilio, 1993), 11.

16. G. Mazzacurati, "La narrazione policentrica di Matteo Bandello," in *Gli uomini, le città e i tempi di Matteo Bandello* (Tortona: Litocoop, 1985), 85.

17. D. Perocco, ed., introduction to *Giulietta*, by Bandello, 12.

18. Ibid., 43–44.

19. Ibid., 44.

20. In his letter to Giacomo Milan quoted above, Giuseppe Todeschini argues against the historicity of Dalla Corte's account in his *Istorie di Verona* by showing that whole passages of his report reproduce *verbatim* Bandello's text (Torri, ed., unit 3, pp. 1–43, 21–23).

21. The poem was reprinted in Torri's miscellany (unit 1, pp. 143–94).

22. Quotations are from the first edition: S. Guazzo, *La civil conversazione* (Brescia, 1574); first English translation from the French by G. Pettie, *The ciuile conuersation of M. Steuen Guazzo* (London, 1581).

23. Guazzo, fol. 15; Pettie, trans., fol. 14.

24. Guazzo, fol., 29.

25. Guazzo, fol. 17r–v; Pettie, trans., 16.

26. B. Castiglione, *Il cortegiano*, book 2:7.

27. The whole passage reads, "In una città piccola, massime dove sia poca conversazione, non essendo determinato il tuono della società, . . . ciascun fa tuono da se, e la maniera di ciascuno, qual ch'ella sia, è tollerata e giudicata per buona e conveniente. Così a proporzione in una nazione, dove non v'abbia se non pochissima società, come in Italia. . . . Infatti non v'è tuono di società che possa dirsi italiano. Ciascuno italiano ha la sua maniera di conversare, o naturale, o imparata dagli stranieri, o comunque acquistata" (In a small city, especially where there is little conversation, not being determined the tone of the society, . . . each one has a distinct tone and each one's manner, whatever it is, is tolerated and deemed good and convenient. Thus happens in a nation where, as in Italy, there is but very little society. . . . Indeed there is no social tone that can be said to be Italian. Every Italian has his own style of conversation, either natural or learned from foreigners or however acquired). G. Leopardi, *Zibaldone di pensieri*, ed. G. Pacella (Milano: Garzanti, 1991), 1:852–53. According to Leopardi, the art and the institution of conversation has now migrated to France, a sociable nation where the peculiar conversational hue and style, its special *tournure*, is a component of the national identity (107).

28. Torri, ed., unit 1, p. 46. The example that Scolari probably had in mind was Manzoni's *I promessi sposi*, the first edition of which was published in 1827.

29. L. A. Marchand, ed., *Byron's Letters and Journals*, 6 vols. (London: William Clawes and Sons, 1973–76), 5:126. The passage quoted is in a postscript dated "November 7th 1816."

30. G. B. Persico, *Descrizione di Verona* (Verona, 1820), pt. 1, p. 140. The passage is reported in Torri's miscellany, unit 1, 140.

31. L. Febvre, "Vers une autre histoire," *Revue de métaphysique et de morale* 58 (1949): 419–38, 428; my translation.

32. Marchand, ed., *Byron's Letters*, 5:126.

# Illyria Revisited: Shakespeare and the Eastern Adriatic

GORAN STANIVUKOVIC

To JUDGE BY THE ACCOUNTS OF ENGLISH TRAVELERS AND MERCHANTS who in the sixteenth and seventeenth centuries sailed along the eastern coast of the Adriatic Sea on their way to Jerusalem and Turkey, the eastern Adriatic was an inhospitable sea known for its strong winds and big storms. In 1610, writing about the Adriatic, which was known in the Renaissance as the Gulf of Venice (Golfo di Venezia), George Sandys, traveler and translator of Ovid's *Metamorphoses*, recorded in his journal that "The Gulf deuided *Italy* from *Illyria*, ioyning Eastward with the *Mediterraneum*, about the cape of *Otranto*. . . . [It is] a sea tempestuous and vnfaithfull: at an instant incensed with sudden gusts; but chiefly with the Southerne winds. . . . But more dreadful are the Northerne, beating vpon the harbourless shore."[1] Sandys's ship might have sailed along the same sea route as Egeon's in *The Comedy of Errors*, since the warning about storms in the Adriatic had already been echoed in Egeon's story of a shipwreck:

> A league from Epidamnum had we sail'd
> Before the always-wind-obeying deep
> Gave any tragic instance of our harm:
> But longer did we not retain much hope.
>
> (1.1.62–65)[2]

As Egeon's "sailors sought for safety by our boat" (1.1.76), his ship was "sinking-ripe" (1.1.77) somewhere just off the coast of what was once the prosperous commercial port city of Epidamnum, but Durrez or Durazzo under the Turks (Durrës in modern Albania). Epidamnum provides a partly homonymic pair with the legendary Epidaurus, believed to have been a place near Ragusa (Dubrovnik in modern Croatia), not the one in Greece "famed for its temple of Aesculapius."[3] The reference to Epidaurus not only creates an auditory image, but also evokes the world of the legendary past before it was eclipsed by the Turks, whose possession of Epidamnum brought, in this comedy, the eastern Mediterranean and its threats close to Venice.[4]

400

Sandys's "harborless shore" of the eastern Adriatic, the shore of Illyria, however, may be his invention, for Abraham Ortelius, a famous Renaissance cartographer, quotes an earlier geographer, Strabo, as saying "that this country [Illyria] hath good hauens."[5] Both Richard Hakluyt and Nicholas Nicolay, two travelers in the eastern Mediterranean, mention Illyrian harbors. The eastern Adriatic was never a final destination of western travelers; it was a coastline one sailed along. The wind, the storms, and the Turks, which caused much anxiety to the travelers, were probably the reason that the knowledge of the eastern Adriatic was always partial, based more on imagination than on experience. Leafing through the pages of the Renaissance travel accounts of the Adriatic's eastern coast—for example, in George Sandys, Nicholas Nicolay, Richard Torkington, Joannes Boemus, Robert Stafforde, Richard Hakluyt, and William Lithgow—one feature of these accounts becomes immediately apparent: the amount of text and information and the abundance of description about the eastern Adriatic are much sparser—it seems that the narrators merely glanced at the region—compared to any other part of the Mediterranean including north Africa; as if between Venice and Corfu, where the richness, length, and descriptive detail in those narratives pick up again, there was not much worth attention but a mere few port cities worth a passing reference, and a coast that did not warrant descriptive detail. In the Renaissance, both the geographical Adriatic and the Adriatic of the English drama embody what Alexander Leggatt says of the sea in the last plays and in *Twelfth Night* (I would also add *The Comedy of Errors*.): "[T]he sea is invoked throughout, and carries suggestions of a power beyond human will—frightening, destructive, yet finally benevolent—the devouring sea of Orsino's love fantasies."[6]

George Sandys's occlusion may simply be a rhetorical gesture to emphasize the inhospitableness of the sea, but it provides a fitting starting point for his long account of the degradation and desolation of Christian culture in the eastern Mediterranean. He says that "large territories [of the Eastern Mediterranean are] thinly inhabited: goodly Cities made desolate, sumptuous buildings become ruines" (sig. A2v). Similarly, the earliest classical references to Illyria, references that might have influenced the idea of Illyria in the English Renaissance, suggest the indifference with which Illyria's apparent inferiority was approached. That history probably begins with Pliny's view that only a few of the names of the Illyrian nations "are . . . worthie or easie to bee spoken," which I am here quoting from Philemon Holland's 1601 translation of *Natural History*, published less than a year before Shakespeare probably wrote *Twelfth Night*.[7]

In the emerging discipline of geography, Illyria was described as a region whose boundaries and location were subjects of dispute, as Robert Stafforde observes: "No certaine limits can be giuen of this Countrie [Illyria]: For all Geographers that write, doe disagree about it" (sig. D1v).[8] Some of the confusion about the boundaries and naming of Illyria, however, goes back to classical geography. Ortelius's description of Illyria reminds us of those earliest debates about that country. According to Ortelius, Illyria's "confines are not distinguished by euery one with sealfe same, but with different boundes, for Pliny encloseth her betweene the riuers Arsia and Titia: but Ptolome doeth stretche the same from Histria, vntill the borders of Macedonia, acordinge to the sea coasts."[9] Ortelius's Illyria also comprises "Sclauonia, Croatia, Carnia or Carinthia, Istria, Bosnia, & c" (N1v). This flurry of names of the lands in the Adriatic hinterland, partially extending into the Balkans, suggests that Illyria was not always thought of as a maritime country. In fact, looking at various geographical maps of the sixteenth and seventeenth centuries, one notices that "Illyria" was a relatively flexible term used to designate a large area of land stretching from the eastern coast of the Adriatic sea to modern Croatia in the west and sometimes even as far east as the Pannonian plain in the east.[10] The question then asked by many a Renaissance geographer has its dramatic equivalent, one might say, in *Twelfth Night*, in Viola's question, "What country, friends, is this?" (1.2.1). Viola may not know the name of the country she has found herself in, but then the period did not have a clear sense either of what actually constituted that country. While the name of the country is missing, the implication of what that country might be like is signaled in Viola's next line, suggesting that Illyria is not like the "after-death island"[11] of Elysium ("My brother he is in Elysium," 1.2.4) with which Illyria is paradoxically contrasted through the homonymic link.[12] Just as the geographical (and historical) Illyria was a composite of numerous and often varied places and provinces, so is Shakespeare's Illyria several places in one. It is Renaissance London, a fictive country (a sort of *no*place), and a region on the margin of the Mediterranean.

Renaissance constructions of Illyria as an ambivalent and, to judge by the plot of *Twelfth Night*, unpleasant location were coupled with the myths about it that had negative connotations, and with fantasies that, in both classical-period and Renaissance England traditions, associated Illyria with violence. Cicero makes Illyria a place of origin of "Bardulis, the Illyrian bandit" (*De officiis*, 2.11.40).[13] In his anti-Puritan pamphlet, *An Almond for a Parrat* (1590), Thomas Nashe refers to the Illyrians as "riotous," making them precursors to the drinking pranksters, Sir Toby Belch and Sir Andrew Aguecheek.[14] Yet, for Ovid, Illyria is a destination of last refuge, where parents look for their children from whom they have been separated. This is where, in book 4 of the *Metamorphoses*, looking for their lost son, Illirio, Cadmus and his wife Hermione, as Golding translates, "fleeting long like pilgrims, at the last / Upon the coast of Illirie . . .

were cast" (H4r).[15] Illyria is also a region where Egeon has one day to look for his lost "youngest boy" (1.1.124). A place of violence and grief, never a desired destination but an unexpected last resort, the eastern Adriatic of *The Comedy of Errors* and *Twelfth Night* is a space where shipwreck and sorrow are the conditions of existence, where towns are dangerous and identities are unstable; it is a land in which courtship and fear mix, and in which comedy stems out of the confusion of space and time—as befits romance, a genre that depends on quest and geography.[16]

Romance, geography, travel, and history were in the Renaissance intricately connected. As some of the passages from the geographical records and travel accounts I have quoted suggest, even what was meant to be an experiential account based on observation and history was very often affected by imagination and fantasy. This is why I think that the Adriatic and Illyria—the two tend to be juxtaposed in the English Renaissance travel accounts—of Shakespeare's comedies cannot be separated from romances, whose currents intersect with the comedic plots of his Adriatic plays. Nor can the eastern Adriatic of Shakespeare's plays be looked at separately from contemporary attitudes toward and fantasies about Illyria. As Northrop Frye reminds us, "[t]he frequent association of romance with the historical . . . is based . . . on the principle that there is a peculiar emotional intensity in contemplating something . . . that we know has survived."[17]

Myth and romance underlie the Illyrian plot of *Twelfth Night*, but even before Shakespeare some of this romance nature of Illyria could already have been traced in the Early Modern descriptions of it; for example, in Thomas Cooper's 1565 reference to Illyria as "Sclauony, or Wendenlande."[18] The word Wendenlande, which Cooper, a famous lexicographer-encyclopedist, offers as a vernacular name for the Latin Illyria, associates Illyria with mutability, travel, and unpredictability. The *Oxford English Dictionary* defines *wend*, and its variant *went*, as words of Teutonic origin, meaning "to turn from one condition or form to another; to change to or into" (7. obs.), "to pass away; disappear, perish, decay" (12 obs.), and "to go forward, proceed; to travel, journey" (13 obs.). The land of wandering, Wendenland, the eastern Adriatic, Illyria, becomes in Cooper's imagination not only a decaying land but also a land of forward journeying, and not an entirely hopeless one, either. As a land of wandering and loss, Illyria is where "Hopeless and helpless doth Egeon wend, / But to procrastinate his liveless end" (*Comedy of Errors* 1.1.157–58).

The resemblance between travel and romance in the Renaissance rests on the "viewing experience" in approaching geographical and travel accounts, and romance.[19] This mode of perception comes out of the transforming power of imagination to change nature. In *An Apology for Poetry*, Sidney says of this transforming power of imagination that "[o]nly the poet, disdaining to be tied to any such subjection, lifted up with the vigour of his own invention, doth grow in effect into another nature, in making things either better than Nature bringeth forth, or, quite anew, forms such as never were in Nature."[20] Looked at from the perspective of this innovative critical thought, imagination enables the romance mode of viewing in both geography and literature. The rhetoric of voyaging and discovery in geographical and travel accounts underlies the poetics of discovery (of self-discovery) in Shakespeare's dramatic topography. When Maria's mockery of Malvolio metaphorically turns the Puritan's face into a richly ornamented geographical map—"He does smile his face into more lines than is in the new map, with the augmentation of the Indies" (3.2.78–80)—Shakespeare turns the new geography of Dutch cartographers into the subject of his drama.[21]

Yet is Illyria, as Kenneth Muir suggests, only "a geographical compromise, and a conveniently obscure location," only because it is neither Modena of Gl'Ingannati, nor Constantinople in Barnaby Riche's novella, "Apolonius and Silla," which Muir identifies as the two main sources of Twelfth Night?[22] Shifting the setting of Twelfth Night from Italy and Turkey to Illyria, to what Geoffrey Bullough calls "that little-known coast," brings Twelfth Night closer to romances that are typically set in the maritime but marginal locations in the eastern Mediterranean, a region for sea wanderings of the Apostolic Fathers in the Apocrypha.[23] Common to all the speculations about Illyria, from the earliest myths to contemporary criticism, is the impulse to push the boundaries of the description and definition of Illyria further east, and to represent it, though close to, in fact remote from, the civilizations of classical Rome and Renaissance Italy.

In 3.3 of Twelfth Night, Sebastian suggests to Antonio that they go sightseeing. "What's to do?" in Illyria, asks Sebastian, "Shall we go see the reliques of this town?" (3.3.18–19). He suggests to Antonio that they should "satisfy [their] eyes / With the memorials and the things of fame / That do renown this city" (3.3.22–24). Where are those "memorials and things of fame"? They might be in Ragusa, the most, and often the only, admired city in Illyria, according to some contemporary travel accounts. Its urban topography was described as early as 1511, in Pylgrimage of Sir Richarde Guyilforde, as "ryche & fayre in su[m]ptuous buyldynge with maruexlous strengthe and beautye togyther with many fayre Churches and glorious houses of Relygyon[;] . . . there be also many other grete Relyques."[24] Sebastian's Illyria might also be Zara (modern Croatian Zadar), the Illyrian city second in importance to Ragusa. Robert Stafforde records that in Zara there "is a church called Saint Iohn de Maluatia, which was built by a company of Mariners, that were in a dangerous tempest, and made a vow, that if they escaped, they would build a Church vnto the honour of S. Iohn de Maluatia."[25] Stafforde proceeds to tell us that many a stranded traveler would pay a visit to this church, this relic and memorial of fame, in gratitude for making it to the shore—much like Sebastian. Have Sebastian and Antonio found themselves in Ragusa or Zara? Or, is Shakespeare using picturesque but dangerous Illyria, an Adriatic location conveniently remote from the moral restrictions of England, to disguise the sudden, potentially homoerotic encounter between Sebastian and Antonio, between a shipwrecked youth and an eager sea captain? It might be, then, that this ambivalent location became a space for the inscription of transgressive desire that complicates the gendered plot of *Twelfth Night*. Seen either from the angle of Sebastian's eagerness to see the relics, or from Antonio's desire to see Sebastian in the room at "The Elephant," Illyria becomes a place of expectations and hopes, of mysteries and anxieties, a space in which desire and fear uncomfortably mix.[26]

In contrast to some earlier constructions of the Illyria of shifting boundaries and ambivalent naming, there have been attempts in modern criticism to place the geographical Illyria of Shakespeare's *Twelfth Night* in a specific geographical and topographic location on the coastline of the eastern Adriatic. This Illyria has been identified as the modern Croatian cities of Zadar, Split, and Ragusa.[27] But this modern appropriation of Illyria has more to do with cultural and, perhaps national, yearning to claim a part of Shakespeare's canon for another culture than with an impulse to generate new meaning. Critical assessments of this modern cultural appropriation of Shakespeare, however, should not mistake the historical and cultural reality of a place and the period's fantasies of it, constructions—cultural prejudices and artistic imaginings—motivated by complex, political, ideological, strategic, religious, and ethnographic currents that prompt one culture to define and construct itself against another culture. In that sense, the idea of Illyria in Renaissance England is similar to that of Italy. For Renaissance Englishmen, Italy was ambivalently known as a place both of civility and legality and as a country of unruliness and debauchery. Renaissance England admired Italy's institutions and culture (as Francis Bacon does in his essay "Of Travel"), and at the same time decried its propensity for violence and sodomy (as Thomas Nashe does in *The Unfortunate Traveller*).[28] If one were to construct a picture of Renaissance Italy by looking at the Elizabethan and Jacobean drama, especially comedies, one would easily notice that it was the other, Epicurean side of Italy that often appeared more attractive to English dramatists. Something remotely similar might have happened with Illyria in the English Renaissance consciousness of the eastern Adriatic.

The historical and geographical Illyria of the eastern Adriatic, though first a Roman province and later a Venetian colony, was a region with a relatively rich culture, which can be attested by numerous archaeological findings and surviving "reliques," to use Shakespeare's word, dating back to both classical and Renaissance periods.[29] Yet Renaissance England was not necessarily aware of this heritage. In fact, given the relative unimportance of the eastern Adriatic—it was unimportant because Renaissance England, indeed the Renaissance West, associated that coast with Venetian domination and the imminent threat of Turks, and hence tended to stay away from it—to English political, cultural, and even commercial interests, it is likely that Renaissance England had little knowledge of its relative cultural richness. Or, if England had that knowledge, it was fragmented and superficial, and the eastern Adriatic featured in it, naturally, as an extension of Italy. If indeed Renaissance England had been either familiar with or had any interest in Illyria, it would be reasonable to assume that there would have been more specific references to Illyrian heritage (as there are to Italy, Greece, Troy, and Mediterranean Africa) in the pages of the English travelers' accounts of the Mediterranean. As it turns out, there are but a few scarce references to details of the major ports in the eastern Adriatic. Thus it is the surviving written and printed records from the Early Modern period, not our present knowledge of what actually existed in Illyria but was not recorded during the Early Modern period, that give us an idea about how the period saw a specific geographical, historical, and cultural space, Illyria in this case. Those textualized discourses, fantasies, and constructions are, consequently, of more help to literary criticism. Despite its actual presence on the cultural map of Mediterranean Renaissance, the eastern coast of Adriatic remained, for the English, a land of mystery and imagination. The lack of an extended knowledge of Illyria in Renaissance England was probably the reason that the earlier textual criticism was reluctant to place Shakespeare's Illyria in any specific location in the eastern Adriatic.

One hundred years ago, in 1901, glossing Viola's famous line, "What country, friends, is this?" Horace Howard Furness, paraphrasing Edward W. Godwin, dismissed the play's Dalmatian connection as arbitrary. Furness says, "Although the action of this play is directed or described as taking place in a city of Illyria, there are but few words in the text which give anything like a Dalmatian complexion. If we accept Illyria, we have a city or seaport of the Venetian Republic under the local government of a duke, or, more correctly, a count, this last being the title given him by the law officer who arrests Antonio."[30] Bearing in mind that any cultural archaeology that modern critics are engaged in when uncovering the meaning of early texts always rests on proximity, Furness, *pace* Godwin, suggests something important about how we might want to think about the Adriatic in Shakespeare; that is, to understand what really happens on the Adriatic's eastern shore, we ought to look at it from its western coast, from Italy. I would like to suggest, then, that given Shakespeare's predilection for the Mediterranean, and for Italy in particular, we approach his Illyria "as a moment of art and as a sign of time,"[31] as a location whose historical connection with Italy *and* romance—rather than only with comedy and an ambivalent location somewhere in Dalmatia—generates meaning in a play set in a borderline region between West and East, one that was constantly under foreign—Venetian and Hungarian—administration. Looking at Illyria from a specific historical position of the eastern Adriatic helps us see that dramatic location not only as a fantasy land but also as a historically determined land of the Mediterranean romance.

At the time when Shakespeare wrote *Twelfth Night*, the eastern Mediterranean, and the eastern Adriatic, Fernand Braudel suggests, the world was compartmentalized into small lands isolated from one another, yet trying to make contact and survive with one another.[32] Venetian counts and governors, who lived and traveled in Illyria, left numerous accounts of poverty, backwardness, and civic discord between the nobles and plebeians of the eastern Adriatic. In 1553, in his lively and very detailed account of Illyria, *Itinerario*, Giovanni Battista Giustiniani says, "It seems pretty clear that in most coastal cities [north of Ragusa] there were social conflicts and that these conflicts lasted for centuries with varying degrees of intensity. However, they rarely menaced either the privileged position of the patricians or the overall Venetian domination."[33] Something of this sense of Illyria as a disorderly place is what Antonio might have in mind when he explains to Sebastian why he does "not without danger walk" (3.3.25) the streets of Illyria. "[T]he danger of this adverse town" (5.1.84), as Antonio puts it, makes Illyria an uncomfortable place. "Once in a sea-fight 'gainst the Count his galleys," says Antonio, "I did some service, of such note indeed / That there were I ta'en here it would scarce be answer'd" (3.3.27–28). And when Sebastian asks him, "Belike you slew great number of his people?" (3.3.29), we hear a dramatic echo of the historical situation in which internal and petty feuds in Illyria were typically fuelled by or resulted in "the many murders of nobles and plebeians."[34] And so Antonio, a plebeian, proceeds to tell Sebastian,

> Th' offense is not of such a bloody nature,
> Albeit the quality of the time and quarrel
> Might well have given us bloody argument.
> It might have since been answer'd in repaying
> What we took from them, which for traffic's sake
> Most of our city did. Only myself stood out,
> For which if I be lapsed in this place
> I shall pay dear.
>
> (3.3.30–37)

Unlike in the historical Illyria from the pages of Giustiniani's travel diary, the feud in Antonio's Illyria is "not of such a bloody nature," though given that the grudge is ancient, it might have been ("Albeit the quality of the time and quarrel / Might well have given us bloody argument"). It is this crumbling authority of local nobility and citizens that, among other reasons, opened up a space for foreign domination of Illyria. What helps resolve the feud in Shakespeare's Illyria is the pragmatic need "for traffic's sake," trade and (possibly) navigation, which is precisely what another Italian in Illyria, Vittore Barbarigo, formerly Venetian count in Zadar, recorded in his travel diary, telling us that through navigation and travel some citizens of Illyria managed to survive in an environment always destabilized by either internal strife or fear of the Turks.[35] After swinging back and forth between foreign and self rule, with the reestablishment in 1409 of Venetian dominion in the parts of the eastern Adriatic north of the independent Ragusa and its autonomies, Venice solidified the eastern Adriatic as its dominion, and the turbulent situation in the urban societies of Illyria remained unchanged for centuries to come.[36] That was still the case at the time when Shakespeare wrote his two Adriatic plays.

The discursive context, if not the actual subtext, of the Illyrians' feud in Antonio's speech, and for the Giustiniani connection, could be traced even further, in Renaissance London. Giustiniani, Palavicino's official in London, was one of the four arbitrators appointed by the English authorities to help resolve a major dispute between two Illyrians, Marin Mencetic and his young relative Nikola from Ragusa. The dispute, which deteriorated into violence, was over the will of Nikola Gucetic, an old and illustrious Ragusan merchant living in London who after his death in late 1595 left behind over £26,000—a huge amount by Elizabethan standards—and some property in Ragusa. But before his death, after dismissing the executor of his will, Nikola Gucetic named a new Nikola Mencetic as executor of the will. The old merchant's money was to have been distributed to various churches and monasteries in Italy and the Republic of Ragusa, but Queen Elizabeth's court, whose coffers were empty after the defeat of the Invincible Armanda, tried to prevent such a large amount of money from leaving the country. At the same time, two things complicated the execution of the will: first, the young and inexperienced Nikola did not follow the correct procedure for the execution of a will, but, without witnesses present, wrote letters to the Ragusan inheritors to inform them of their share. The Ragusan relatives were represented by Marin Mencetic, already in London. He was meant to help Nikola Mencetic sort out the old merchant's papers and assist him with the execution of the will. Second, when the news of death of the old and famous Ragusan merchant spread among the circles of bankers and merchants of Europe, they all rushed to settle their business affairs with his house. Caught in the triangle between the powerful and cunning of Queen Elizabeth's court, relatives from Ragusa headed by Marin, and the financial power-mongers of Europe, young Ni-

kola could barely handle his task. But, not only was Marin's task in helping him becoming more and more difficult with all the parties involved,
but he also suspected that young Nikola embezzled for himself a portion
of the money that belonged to him; and this is where the real trouble
started. So, in addition to having to deal with a long and complex legal
case over the will, which started to unravel and involved not only foreign
officials as arbiters but lawyers in several countries, and Elizabeth's court
itself, Marin and young Nikola started to fight bitterly; and it was at this
point that the English authorities appointed an arbiter in their case: none
other than Giovanni Battista Guistiniani. The case, which gradually turned
into a scandal of international proportions and was in part made public,
lasted until 1598, when Nikola Menčetić ended up in a London prison,
after he had been caught in Flanders fleeing England with a hefty sum
money.[37] Why this historical digression? We can, of course, only speculate
whether Shakespeare, living in London at the same time as this event involving the foreigners from Illyria was occurring, had this story at the back
of his mind while writing Antonio's speech. The point of juxtaposing a
play and a contemporary event, however, is not to suggest its influence on
Shakespeare but to speculate about what kind of knowledge of the Illyrians, their behavior, and their public presence in London might have given
rise to the ideas about their national traits and actions in the English poetic
imagination. In a play in which the foreigners and the English mingle and
clash, and in which the plot gets complicated when the two foreigners,
Viola and Sebastian, both from an imagined though Italian-sounding
place, Messaline, are shipwrecked in Illyria, the ideas, or rather fantasies,
about national traits become some of the central defining features of characters that live in and wander about Shakespeare's Illyria and London. For
even though this is a play about the encounter of the Illyrians with strangers and foreigners, some Illyrians—Sir Toby Belch and Sir Andrew
Aguecheek—have English-sounding names.[38]

Idleness and an archaic sense of status make the Illyrian nobility, according to Vittore Barbarigo, examples of a crumbling order within a dominion in which their power does not extend much beyond the walls of
their decadent dukedoms and households. Both Orsino's and Olivia's
households are examples of those few prosperous noble houses that, like
islands of cultural melancholy in midst of the poverty and decay of Illyria,
were recorded by both the Italian governors and the English travelers in
the eastern Adriatic. Twelfth Night abounds with comical examples of how
unruliness and decadence become tropes of knowing, of seeing the colony
of the eastern Adriatic as backward and provincial, and as a romance land
to which England displaces its own unruliness and vices, its own provincialism vis-à-vis the civilized Renaissance Europe, and perhaps even its

own restlessness over the failed and fantasized colonization of the eastern Mediterranean.[39]

Sir Toby's comment on drinking—"I'll drink to her [his niece] as long as there is a passage in my throat, and drink in Illyria" (1.3.38–40)—or Sir Andrew's pronouncement about trivialities, answering Sir Toby's question whether he is good at "kickshawses" (1.3.115), suggests that the main preoccupation of Illyria's decadent nobility and idle plebeians is centered on the unpolished low life. A version of the Illyrians' disorderly life and a lack of urban civility is echoed in Sir Andrew's comment on the lawlessness of Illyria. Sir Andrew, thinking Sebastian to be Viola, tells Sir Toby, "I'll have an action of battery against him, if there be any law in Illyria" (4.1.34–35). The Illyrians seem to be governed not by laws but by ferocious passions, which shocks both Viola responding to Sir Toby's impulse to stir up a feud—"This is as uncivil as strange" (3.4.253)—and Olivia, who calls the duel between Viola/Cesario and Sir Andrew an "uncivil and unjust extent" (4.1.53); that is, a barbarous event.[40] The spoofing of the chivalric in this duel is an effect of the confusion of gender and the deprecation of status. By extension, Viola dressed as a man is in this context a parody of heroic masculinity, just as Sir Andrew here and elsewhere in the drama is a parody of humanist nobility. These kinds of personal and public instability are the fabric of romances, popular in the early seventeenth century when the idea of chivalric masculinity became increasingly often replaced by that of romantic masculinity.

At the extreme end of the parodic representation of a provincial nation stands Malvolio's irrationality, which borders on lunacy that is made to sound almost like a national trait, as when he says to Feste, "I tell thee I am as well in my wits as any man in Illyria" (4.2.107). In the conversation that follows, Feste pushes Malvolio on the issue of madness, wanting to know whether or not he feigns it ("counterfeit" is Feste's word). Malvolio denies his madness, but the skeptical Feste does not believe him, saying "I'll ne'er believe a madman till I see his brains" (4.2.116). The proof that supports Feste's suspicion, however, is in Malvolio's silly love poetry, whose form, content, and purpose reveal the real quality of his brains. At this moment the scene ends, as if suggesting that Feste's suspicion of Malvolio's witlessness needs no further proof, except that it will be proved again, visually and hilariously, later in the play when, cross gartered, he appears to Olivia.

Displacements of Illyria beyond the boundaries of the familiar, beyond the here and *now*, are what defines it in *Twelfth Night*. When Feste wittily tells Viola that, in playing a go-between ("pander") in the match between Orsino and Olivia, he "would play Lord Pandarus of Phrygia . . . to bring a Cressida to this Troilus" (3.1.51–52), his comical deflation is both aesthetic and cultural, simultaneously extending to the country and to the characters. Pandarus and Phrygia may just reflect Feste's inventiveness with language and Shakespeare's predilection to adapt figures of sound to the arts of theater. But Phrygia also brings other echoes in the play. The Pandarus of *Troilus and Cressida*, a play "probably written soon after *Twelfth Night*,"[41] and Troilus and Cressida of that play, belong to the heroic world of classical Troy. In *Twelfth Night*, however, Feste imagines Pandarus as originating not in the heroic world of the ancients, but in the Phrygia of Asia Minor, once associated with Troy. A country in the legendary Natolia, or Turkey, Phrygia was most commonly evoked in the Renaissance as a decayed land of early Christianity, a country that in romances became a space for courtship, sexual liberties, and chivalric adventures. It was also a country most frequently described in Renaissance atlases and geographical writings as poor and desolate, and populated by hostile non-Christians. Thus in *Twelfth Night*, the shift from heroic Troy to unheroic Illyria, in which Olivia plays Cressida to Orsino's Troilus, turns the amorous conquest into parody. The imaginative space within which this deflation of heroic masculinity and heroic love are subjects of comedy brings into the world of Illyria the Turkey of romance literature and of Shakespeare's sources for *Twelfth Night*: Emanuel Ford's prose romance, *Parismus*, and perhaps even Barnaby Riche's romance *Brusanus*, both of which are set in Phrygia and Constantinople.[42] This comic deflation of heroic to romantic love, of heroic to a liminal and romantic place, is an aspect of Illyria's emasculating effect, which we have already witnessed in the parody of the heroic duel between Viola/Cesario and Sir Andrew, in Antonio's desire for Sebastian, in Orsino's ambivalent detachment from courtship into the lonely world of romantic melancholy, in Viola's playfulness with masculinity, and in Sir Toby's drunken boisterousness as a parody of the heroic action.

*Twelfth Night* is not only a romantic comedy that elicits laughter by playing with love melancholy, complicating desire, and confusing identities. It is also a comedy whose humor targets both the English and the foreigners, both *us* and *them*. As such, *Twelfth Night* is probably one of the first major, if implicit, artistic mockeries of the provincialism of the eastern Adriatic in English Renaissance drama. Illyrian provincialism will later become a convenient vehicle for any other kind of ethnic, even racial, deprecation, as in an early-nineteenth-century Italian adaptation of *Othello*. In Carlo Federici's *Otello, ossia lo Slavo. Azione tragica di spettacolo inedito* ("Othello, or the Slav. Tragic action of an unpublished performance"), Shakespeare's black Moor became a white Slav, probably from the neighboring Illyrian provinces.[43] In this Italian adaptation of Shakespeare, race is a matter not only of skin color but of ethnicity based on nationality, as well. Thus in Federici's *Othello*, the replacement of one denigrated race, Moorish, by another, Slavic, is based not only on the

Western prejudice against Slavs but on the Slavs' lack of national independence, which dispossessed them of their national freedom. In this case, racial deprecation arises from the political subordination, or imperial enslavement, of Illyria to the imperial powers of Italy and Hungary that ruled the eastern Adriatic.

Ambivalently located in the eastern Adriatic, lawless, violent, unpleasant, and emasculating, Shakespeare's Illyria of decadent nobility and inebriated plebeians has become part of what Andrew Hess calls the Mediterranean's "forgotten frontier,"[44] a zone between the coastline of northern Africa and the eastern Mediterranean, that is Turkey. Seen as part of that zone, the eastern Adriatic closes off a region that marks precisely the historical realm of the imperial fantasies, diplomatic frustrations, and commercial ambitions of West and East, England and the Levant, Venice and Turkey. The threshold of that "forgotten frontier" is Illyria, the eastern Adriatic, and the marginal colony of the civilized and powerful Venice. Contrary to our wishes to place, by location and name, Illyria firmly on the Renaissance geographical map somewhere in the eastern Adriatic, the play has always "pulled both away from and towards our dashed expectations."[45] The geographical and historical Illyria is just like the imagined Illyria of Shakespeare's romance and comedy: a liminal place, partially known, mysterious, and always already provincial.

# Notes

1. George Sandys, *A Relation of a Journey begun An.Dom: 1610* (1621), sig. B1v; STC 21726. Early printed books were printed in London except as otherwise noted.

2. Horace in Ode 1.3 also refers to the strong winds of the Adriatic, saying, "quo non arbiter Hadriae / maior, tollere seu ponere volt freta" (whether it [the south wind] the greater lord of the Adriatic wishes to raise or calm the waves). I thank Geraldine Thomas for help with the Latin, which is quoted from *Horace: The Odes and Epodes*, ed. C. E. Bennett, Loeb Classical Library (Cambridge: Harvard University Press, 1960).

3. *The Comedy of Errors*, ed. T. S. Dorsch, New Cambridge Shakespeare (Cambridge: Cambridge University Press, 1988), 45.

4. Turkish context, especially costumes, set, and music, were used in the 2000 RSC production of *The Comedy of Errors*, dir. Lynne Parker, RST, Stratford-upon-Avon.

5. Abraham Ortelius, *An Epitome of Ortelivs, His Theatre of the World, Wherein the Principal Regions of the Earth are Described in Smalle Mappes* (1602), sig. N1r.

6. Alexander Leggatt, *Shakespeare's Comedy of Love* (London: Methuen, 1974), 249.

7. *The Historie of the World. Commonly called, The Naturall Historie of C. Plinius Secundus*, trans. Philemon Holland (1601), 68; STC 20029.

8. Robert Stafforde, *A Geographicall and Authologicall Description of all the Empires and Kingdomes, both of Continent and Ilands in this Terrestriall Globe* (1618), sig. D1v.

9. Abraham Ortelius, *His epitome of the Theater of the Worlde* (1603), sig. M1v; STC 18856.

10. The Novacco Collection of—mostly Italian—Renaissance maps of the Mediterranean at the Newberry Library (Chicago) contains several maps of the Adriatic only, which illustrate a further ambiguity of the representation of Illyria. Iacoppo da Gastali's 1560 *Carta dell' Adriatico* (shelfmark 4F 118) shows the region that might have been known as Illyria as stretching deep into the Balkan Peninsula and in parts of Croatia. Even the first separately printed map of the Adriatic Sea (1565; shelfmark 2F 150), which shows the coast of the eastern Adriatic clearly, does not mention Illyria. A 1571 German map of the Adriatic sea, printed by "B. X." (shelfmark 2F 59), shows only two coastal cities in Illyria, Zara and Sebenico (i.e., Zadar and Šibenik), and depicts the region that might have been known as Illyria as a large territory that covers the entire hinterland beyond the coastline of the eastern Adriatic. The absence of the name Illyria in any of these Italian maps suggests that its designation was ambiguous, even relative, in Renaissance consciousness and contemporary cartography.

11. Philip Brockbank, "The Politics of Paradise: 'Bermudas,'" in *The Creativity of Perception: Essays in the Genesis of Literature and Art* (Oxford: Basil Blackwell, 1991), 29.

12. This is how this line is glossed in *Twelfth Night*, ed. Roger Warren and Stanley Wells, Oxford Shakespeare (Oxford: Oxford University Press, 1995).

13. Cicero, *De Officiis*, trans. Walter Miller, Loeb Classical Library (Cambridge: Harvard University Press, 1961).

14. J. J. M. Tobin, "Gabriel Harvey in Illyria," *English Studies* 61 (1980): 318–28. Tobin (318) also suggests that Shakespeare's reference to Illyria was derived from Plautus's comedy, *Menaechmi*, l. 265.

15. *The.xv.Bookes of P. Ouidius Naso, entytuled Metamorphosis, translated oute of Latin into English meeter, by Arthur Golding Gentleman* (1567), facsimile ed., The English Experience, no. 881 (Norwood, N.J.: Walter J. Johnson, Inc., 1977).

16. Bruce R. Smith refers to *Twelfth Night* as a romance in his book *"Twelfth Night": Texts and Contexts* (New York: Bedford/St. Martin's Press, 2001), 115–17. Stanley Wells briefly discusses *Twelfth Night* and *The Comedy of Errors* as romances, especially in terms of romantic love, in his essay "Shakespeare and Romance," in *Later Shakespeare*, ed. John Russell Brown and Bernard Harris, Stratford-upon-Avon Studies 8 (London: Edward Arnold Ltd., 1966), 49–79.

17. Northrop Frye, *The Secular Scripture: A Study of the Structure of Romance* (Cambridge: Harvard University Press, 1976), 176.

18. Thomas Cooper, *Thesaurus Linguae Romanae et Britannicae* (1565), sig. K3v.

19. W. T. Jewkes, "The Literature of Travel and the Mode of Romance in the Renaissance," *Bulletin of the New York Public Library* 67 (1963): 233.

20. Sir Philip Sidney, *An Apology for Poetry*, ed. Geoffrey Shepherd (New York: Barnes and Noble, 1973), 100.

21. For explanation of the topical allusion in Maria's lines, see John Gillies, *Shakespeare and the Geography of Difference* (Cambridge: Cambridge University Press, 1994), 49–50. Gillies also points out that Fabian's reproach to Sir Andrew (3.2.24–28) is related to the discovery of *Novaya Zemlya* by the Dutch.

22. See Kenneth Muir, *The Sources of Shakespeare's Plays* (London: Methuen, 1977), 138–39. Constantinople is used as a location for the similar kind of romance plot in Barnaby Riche's romance, *Brusanus* (1592).

23. Geoffrey Bullough says, "it may be that [in *TN*] Shakespeare shifted the setting from Italy and Turkey (Riche) to Illyria . . . because on that little-known coast the mixture of Mediterranean romance and northern realism would be more plausible"; see *Narrative and Dramatic Sources of Shakespeare*, ed. Bullough, vol. 2: *The Comedies, 1597–1603* (New York: Columbia University Press, 1968), 284.

24. Quoted from Rudolf Filipovic̀, "Shakespeareove Ilirija," *Filologija* 1 (1957): 131–32.

25. Robert Stafforde, *A Geographical and Anthological Description*, sig. D2r.

26. The anxiety over the potentially homoerotic encounter between Sebastian and Antonio in Illyria might be juxtaposed with the homophobic panic in Renaissance Dubrovnik, a place that was, more than any other in Renaissance Italy, notorious for its Draconian laws against homosexuals, which included the death penalty. See Bariša Krekić, "*Abominandum crimen*: Punishment of Homosexuals in Renaissance Dubrovnik," *Viator* 18 (1987): 337–45.

27. See Vinko Krišković, "Shakespeare i mi: Češka morska obala u *Zimskoj priči*," *Hrvatska revija* 14 (1941): 1–5; Filipović, "Shakespeareova Ilirija," 123–39; Mira Jankovic, "Grad u Shakespeareovoj Iliriji," *Filoloki pregled* 1–2 (1964): 141–45; Josip Torbarina, "The Settings of Shakespeare's Plays," *Studia Romanica et Anglica Zagrabiensia* 17–18 (1964): 21–60; Veselin Kostić, *Kulturne veze izmedju jugoslovenskih zemalja i Engleske do 1700. godine* (Beograd: Srpska akademija nauka i umetnosti, 1971), 182–84; Murray J. Levith, "Illyria, Italia, Englandia," in *Shakespeare's Italian Settings and Plays* (Houndsmill, U.K.: Macmillan, 1989), 1–11.

28. Much has been written on this ambivalent representation of Italy in the English literature of the Early Modern period. For a very good, concise view of the problem, see Jonathan Bate, "The Elizabethans in Italy," in *Travel and Drama in Shakespeare's Time*, ed. Jean-Pierre Maquerlot and Michèle Willems (Cambridge: Cambridge University Press, 1996), 55–74.

29. On the historical Illyria in Croatian Renaissance literature, see Bruna Kuntic-Makvić, "Tradicija o našim krajevima u antičkom razdoblju kod dalmatinskih pisaca XVI i XVII stolječa," *Živa antika* 34 (1984): 155–64. I am grateful to Robert Matijašić for making this article available to me.

30. In the New Variorum edition of *Twelfth Night* (London: J. B. Lippincott, 1901), 22, the editor Horace Howard Furness refers to Edward W. Godwin's note in the London newspaper, *The Architect*, 24 April 1875.

31. Brockbank, *Creativity*, 26.

32. For a more detailed account, see Fernand Braudel, *The Mediterranean and the Mediterranean World in the Age of Philip II*, 2 vols. (London: Collins, 1972–73), esp. vol. 1.

33. Quoted from Bariša Krekić, "Developed Autonomy: The Patricians in Dubrovnik and Dalmatian Cities," in *Urban Society of Eastern Europe in Premodern Times* (Berkeley and Los Angeles: University of California Press, 1987), 205.

34. Ibid., 203.

35. Quoted from *Commissiones et relationes venetiae*, ed. Šime Ljubic, *JAZU* [*Jugoslavenska akademija znanosti i umjetnosti*] 2 (1877): 45.

36. For a detailed account of the political and civic situation in Dalmatia, especially Zadar and Dubrovnik, see Krekić, "Developed Autonomy," 185–215.

37. The full critical account of this event, and the archival documents support-

ing it, appear in Veselin Kostic, *Dubrovnik i Engleska, 1300–1650* (Beograd: Srpska akademija nauka i umetnosti, 1975), 284–96, 521–23.

38. Smith, *Texts and Contexts,* 116.

39. I owe these ideas about the possible political implications of the relationship between England and Illyria to Michael Redmond and Martin Prochazka.

40. See gloss for this line in Warren and Wells's Oxford edition.

41. See Warren and Wells's gloss to Feste's line (155).

42. There have been attempts in the theater to stage Illyria in the oriental setting of the eastern Mediterranean; e.g., the production of *Twelfth Night* directed by Tim Supple at the Young Vic in July 1998 was set somewhere in the oriental Mediterranean, and the atmosphere created by the oriental instruments and music, as Zara Bruzzi suggests, "gave to the discourse of the play an esoteric exoticism part eastern Mediterranean, part African, part Asian." See Zara Bruzzi, "'A Most Extracting Frenzy': *Twelfth Night*, Performance and the Traditions of English Petrarchism," in *Shakespeare and Italy*, ed. Holger Klein and Michele Marrapodi (Lewiston, N.Y.: Edwin Mellen Press, 1999), 190–210.

43. N.p., n.d. The dates of the minor playwright Carlo Federici (1778–1848) suggest that his book might have been published sometime in the early nineteenth century. I am grateful to Shaul Bassi for drawing my attention to this source and translating the Italian.

44. Andrew C. Hess, *The Forgotten Frontier: The History of the Sixteenth-Century Ibero-African Frontier* (Chicago: University of Chicago Press, 1978).

45. Brockbank, *Creativity*, 40.

# "Every third thought": Shakespeare's Milan

## RICHARD WILSON

JUST BEFORE DAWN ON 25 JUNE 1580, EDMOND CAMPION LANDED BENEATH Dover Cliff, and "climbing a great rock, fell upon his knees to commend to God his cause and his coming" to restore the faith to England. The night before, he wrote from Calais that the wind was set fair for his mission by "the incredible comfort" it had received in Milan from Carlo Borromeo, so "I think we are now safe, unless we are betrayed in these sea-side places." The grand narrative of Catholic return seemed about to be fulfilled. In fact, we know Campion's movements had been relayed to Lord Burghley, from the day he set foot in Italy from Prague in the Emperor's coach, by a ring of spies, who included the double agent Anthony Munday. But disguised as a "merchant," who had for sale "a pearl of great price," like the one in Matthew (by which he meant his martyrdom), the Jesuit was waved on by the mayor of Dover, to join his partner Robert Parsons, before setting out on the first stage of their missionary crusade, which took them from the London home of Sir William Catesby to his house at Lapworth Park, near Stratford.[1] There, during September, the young priests distributed copies of the Testament of Catholic faith they had been given by Borromeo; and because one of the very first to sign, we think, was John Shakespeare, it seems important to consider what this mission from Milan might have meant to his son, whose career would start, in *The Two Gentlemen of Verona*, with a broken journey to the city, and end, in *The Tempest*, with hope of finally arriving there, where "Every third thought" shall be a grave (5.1.312). Certainly, news from Milan was challenging, because the Testament, composed by Borromeo to stiffen opposition to Protestantism, compounded the reputation of his diocese as doctrinally more ultra than even its nominal duke, Philip II of Spain. The charismatic cardinal was perceived in Madrid, indeed, as a fundamentalist rival to the occupying Hapsburgs, who might "provoke a revolt in Milan to chase the Spaniards out."[2] His subsidy of the missionaries, and promise to "receive with all charity" any recruits they sent to him,[3] might support Campion's claim to be innocent of Spanish politics, therefore, but suggests that one reason why Milan stayed in Shakespeare's imagination as a final goal and destina-

416

tion was of its association with martyrdom: the first and last of all those places in his plays that lie beyond the horizon of the text: invisible worlds elsewhere, so utopian and extreme that they retain the indeterminacy of "a pearl of great price."

"He had learned and most godly speeches with us," Parsons reported, after the fanatic cardinal had asked the English priests to debate for eight nights, "tending to contempt of this world and perfect zeal for Christ, whereof we saw so rare an example in himself, being nothing in effect but skin and bone, through continual fasting, penance, and pains."[4] Carlo Borromeo's canonization in the year of *The Tempest* would glorify such asceticism, along with his orders to "be careful with your eyes, guard your heart," and "remember how we are continually tempted," that seem to be echoed by Prospero.[5] For, as John Bossy has written, this Borromean taboo on physical contact was part of a "Copernican revolution" that rigidly separated public from private space by suggesting that sin was "all in the mind." So John Shakespeare's Catholic Testament was just one of a "proliferation of forms, files, receipts, and regulations" invented by the archbishop of Milan to make "self-examination available to the average man," accessories of his most coercive device to divide the seen from the unseen, the confession box.[6] Designed about 1550, this miniature baroque theater was made mandatory in Milan in 1576, when Borromeo's specifications for a double-seated closet partitioned by a grille no finger could penetrate terminated the medieval practice of communal confession and instituted a modern confessional economy in which sin was internalized. Recent studies have explored Foucault's suspicion of the affinity between this new binary space and the torture chamber, since the impossibility of touching, confidentiality, and invisibility all combined to separate the confessor from a drama of which he was truly a *deus ex machina*.[7] So when they began confessing in Warwickshire according to the cardinal's *Instructions*, the Jesuits might have planted an image of ultramontane Milan as, in the words of a historian, so "rationalized, bureaucratized, hierarchized, officered, and submissive," as to be "the most developed cultural space in Europe,"[8] but they must also have terrorized the Midlanders with an impression of this perfect utopian place as the final invisible repository of all their secrets, like that copy of Borromeo's Testament that John Shakespeare was wise—or frightened—enough to hide in his roof tiles. In Valencia, followers of the Milanese saint took to the streets during Holy Week in ecstatic flagellant processions; but in Stratford-upon-Avon they took to their attics.

One of the 1580 mission who did not arrive from Milan was a brother of the Stratford schoolmaster, Thomas Cottam, who had been described by Munday in such detail that he was arrested at Dover. He had in his pocket a letter from Shakespeare's cousin, Robert Debdale, a seminarian

in Rome, in which he "commended Cottam to his parents in Shottery" and
sent to them and his brother-in-law John Pace, a neighbor of the Hatha-
ways, "certain tokens": coins, a medal, a crucifix, and two rosaries.[9] Later,
it would be the grisly relics of the Jesuit himself that Debdale would use
in the exorcisms that made him notorious, before he followed him to the
gallows; but it was Munday's crowing over Cottam's execution, as he died
"trembling and fearful,"[10] that makes it so telling that when Shakespeare
wrote his play about the journey to Milan, which opens with Proteus com-
mending Valentine to his "holy prayers" and pledging to be his "beads-
man" (*Two Gentlemen* 1.1.18), he should model it, as Giorgio Melchiori
has pointed out, on Munday's comedy of *The Two Italian Gentlemen: Fedele and Fortunio*.[11] For Munday had returned from the Jesuits in Rome to
stage-manage the executions of his fellow students with a baroque sense
of theater as a space of revelation, and if his play has a key it is the surveil-
lance service operated by his persona, Crackstone, who insinuates himself
"in every company, knows where every gallant loves, and sees the remedy." So its plot initiated what William Slights terms the "multi-perspec-
tivism" of Elizabethan drama, where in a universe of intelligencers and
searchers no one finds it possible "to locate any private space or sanctuary" from exposure.[12] Francis Meres would praise Munday as "our best
for plotting," and Charles Nicoll agrees that the "facility would serve him
well," in espionage as entertainment.[13] So *The Two Italian Gentlemen* is
in the grip of the informer's law that the last laugh belongs to those who,
"Unseen by any, yet viewing all . . . take a knave in a pitfall," and its
action relies on the watch committee's motto, that spies "look down" on
all our lives.[14] Shakespeare would turn its story—of a groom tricked into
denouncing his bride—against all such paranoid "noting" in *Much Ado
about Nothing*; but in *Two Gentlemen* he at first answers Munday with a
play that seems destined to find "happiness . . . in Milan" (1.1.61), and
then avoids any such incriminating disclosure.

    "To Milan let me hear from thee by letters," Proteus urges his friend,
"And I likewise will visit thee with mine" (1.1.57); but their mail must
have a delayed delivery, because, after being reported to have "parted to
embark for Milan" (71), the next we learn of him is that the "youthful
Valentine / Attends the Emperor in his royal court" (1.3.26); and soon Proteus has heard how he is "daily graced by the Emperor" (58), and is himself joining one Don Alphonso with "other gentlemen . . . journeying to
salute the Emperor," and "commend their service to his will" (39–42),
while even the servant Launce is "going with Sir Proteus to the Imperial's
court" (2.3.4). Editors offer numerous explanations for this detour "to the
Emperor's court" (1.3.38), proposing that Milan and the empire are one
place, that references to a spectral emperor come from a source, or that
scenes have been cut. Tantalizingly, though, when he rejoins Valentine,

Proteus has earned "commendation from great potentates" that testify how fit he is "to be an emperor's counselor" (2.4.70–79); and it is these credentials that suggest why the royal road to the emperor might offer an alternative path, not taken in this text, toward a different end. For there were, Bossy explains, two roads to Rome that Elizabethan Catholics could choose. Both met in Milan, but unless the Netherlands were blocked by war, the French way was less used than the "imperial route," via a quick crossing to Antwerp, along the postal road to Augsberg, with spurs to Vienna and Prague, and into Italy by the Brenner Pass. As if suddenly alarmed by the implications, *Two Gentlemen* seems to recoil from this trans-Alpine choice, which would lead, Bossy proposes, to a split among English Catholics between supporters of Hapsburg and Stuart claimants to the throne.[15] For it is, of course, the Hispanic company of "Don Alfonso" that points to the court of the Hapsburg Rudolf II in Prague as a lost location in this play, and the English College in Rome, under its rector, Alphonso Agazzari, as the final destination for those émigrés who attend the emperor. In 1577 Campion had written from Prague to Robert Arden, a Warwickshire Jesuit, later a canon of Toledo, thought to be related to Shakespeare's mother, that his "abundant harvest" of Midland recruits should be told of the welcome awaiting them if storms of persecution drove them to be "cast gently on the pleasant and blessed shore" of Bohemia.[16] But if the dramatist did not come so perilously close as Philip Sidney to joining English Catholics in one of the emperor's "studious universities," his false starts and textual prevarications in this play suggest that the chance to "Hear sweet discourse" and "converse with noblemen" (1.3.10, 31) in some Bohemian college had triggered his wariness about such an absolutist world elsewhere.

"Some say he is with the Emperor of Russia; and other some, he is in Rome": Rudolf II's "mad, fantastical trick to steal from the state" and abandon Vienna in 1583 for a scholarly "beggary he was never born to" (*Measure for Measure* 3.2.88–94) may have prompted the dramatist in the Rudolfine strategy—aborted in *Two Gentlemen* but perfected with *Measure*—of having some "ghostly father" (4.3.48) shadow his plot. Recently, David Scott Kastan has argued that the reclusive Rudolf ghosts *The Tempest*, too, as a double of the Duke of Milan;[17] so, if even the Bohemian scenes of *The Winter's Tale* can be glimpsed in the Czech diversion of the early comedy, that is because Shakespeare seems there, as editors complain, to want to visit so many places at once. This play may originally have had just two settings, but from the moment Valentine enters to exit, and "see the wonders of the world abroad," rather than stay "dully sluggardised at home" (1.1.6–8), Shakespeare's technical need to keep his dangerous liaisons moving, so the travelers can write to one another, seems to complement his quest for a similar "enfranchisement" (*Two*

*Gentlemen* 2.4.90, 3.1.151). Thus, although almost the entire plot consists of scenes of farewell, no one is ever certain where they are going, or whether they have arrived at Milan, Verona, or even Padua. This hesitation may express the writer's own deep misgivings about an ultramontane future, for there is something sinister in the Duke of Milan's patronage of "heaven-bred poesy"—after Proteus assures him that "Orpheus' lute was strung with poets' sinews" (3.2.71–77)—seeing how "the Thracian singer" had been ripped to pieces by enraged "Bacchanals" (*A Midsummer Night's Dream* 5.1.48). Tridentine Milan may have seemed a papist Parnassus for the "exquisite detail" with which its artists were supervised,[18] but from the day his teacher, Simon Hunt, left in 1576, Shakespeare had witnessed a generation of scholars depart Stratford for Italy, only to die there or at Tyburn. He was probably among the "school-fellows and common people," for instance, who saw off the saintly Edward Throckmorton in 1580, bound for an early death in Rome, amid "tears of relations and lamentations of servants . . . as if in a funeral procession";[19] but if so, he distanced himself from such hysteria with Crab's dogged refusal to "shed one tear," when, according to Launce, "A Jew would have wept to see our parting" (*Two Gentlemen* 2.3.1–32). Instead, a text by the most famous of all murdered poets, Christopher Marlowe, prefaces *Two Gentlemen* with an epigraph suggesting that religious exile is more profound in fiction than in fact:

> *Proteus.*  Upon some book of love I'll pray for thee.
> *Valentine.* That's on some shallow story of deep love,
>           How young Leander crossed the Hellespont.
> *Proteus.*  That's a deep story, of a deeper love,
>           For he was more than over shoes in love.
> *Valentine.* 'Tis true; for you are over boots in love,
>           And yet you never swum the Hellespont.
>
> (1.1.20–26)

With its splitting of boats and boots, or ships and sheep, and anxiety that "My father at the road / Expects my coming, there to see me shipped" (53–56), Shakespeare's earliest comedy condenses all the uneasiness of an enforced Elizabethan journey to Milan, but, notoriously, *by sea*. This is a play, in other words, that seems so evasive in its geography because it encodes the reluctance of one who (we can assume) "never swum the Hellespont" to take that passage to the capital of the Counter-Reformation that carried so many English martyrs to their deaths, "blasting . . . in the prime," as Valentine grieves, "all the fair effects of future hopes" (1.1.47–50). Luckily, the only victim in this particular mad Italian escapade is not even the dog Crab, but another little dog "stol'n . . . by the hangman's boys in the market place" (4.4.56); and if the young voyagers never do quite arrive in Milan, that is because the Duke's daughter discovers a secret exit that provides an alternative to this violent public space, when Silvia foils her father's "spies" by escaping "Out at the postern by the abbey wall," promising to confess "at Friar Patrick's cell" (5.1.3–9). "Friar Patrick" was, in fact, the alias of Campion, adopted at Lough Derg in Ireland, where St. Patrick had supposedly discovered the mouth of Purgatory. As Stephen Greenblatt has now reminded us, the "vast unreal space" of Purgatory, invoked in Borromeo's Testament and by Hamlet, as a dungeon where ghosts are bound to walk, was one of the most terrifying inventions of the Catholic baroque, so the mere mention of "confession / At Patrick's cell" (5.3.40) opens a gaping chasm beneath Shakespeare's text.[20] But tellingly, the lovers of *The Two Gentlemen* never do meet at his cell, preferring to return home with outlaws, who look reassuringly like actors. Evidently, that ancient tunnel through the Abbey provided a bolt-hole not only from the Duke's spies, but from sectarian extremes. So what the writer rivals called an "upstart crow"[21] seems to admit in the forest scenes of this play is how he changed a clerical black for player's plumes, as he groped in this prototype of all his works for a way out of his liaison with those real Jesuit outlaws who followed "Friar Patrick" from Milan. And by evading the piazza with the cruel hangman's boys, and rerouting its lovers around the derelict Abbey and "St. Gregory's well" (4.2.84), *Two Gentlemen* also reveals how his proximity to Campion's mission may have shaped Shakespeare's entire dramatic strategy, which in an age of totalitarian extremes seems traumatized into resisting the petrifying spaces of the baroque, and into endlessly deferring the arrival in absolutist Milan, by taking refuge in some secluded retreat—halfway between England and Rome—such as a ruined convent, moated grange, holy well, or wayside shrine. Like the attendant lords expecting simply to "swell a progress, start a scene or two" in Tom Stoppard's comedy, when confronted by the Europe of the Counter-Reformation it seems that Shakespeare's two young gentlemen just "want to go home."[22]

"I Pandulf, of fair Milan Cardinal . . . Do . . . religiously demand / Why thou against the Church, our Holy Mother, / So willfully dost spurn": if, as editors note, Shakespeare altered the very title of the papal legate in *King John*, to make him a delegate as much of "fair Milan" as of Rome (3.1.138–42), that may have been because—in this play that expresses, as Donna Hamilton shows, a sly resistance to the Tudor state,[23]—the forbidden city of Borromeo had come, through Campion's disaster, to signify the illusoriness of any such militant alternative to the Anglican Church. So, while it is no surprise that the failure of the "holy lord of Milan" (5.2.120) to broker English subjection was censored from the text in the 1640s by the Holy Office,[24] this does not mean, Gary Taylor notes, that

"Shakespeare was not a Catholic; only that like most English Catholics in the late sixteenth century [he] did not agree with papal policies."[25] Shakespeare—who may well have signaled in the very title of his play, *The Moor of Venice*, sympathy with the persecuted co-religionists of Thomas More—was quite capable, that is to say, of distinguishing what he seems to have called "our fashion" of quietist English Catholicism from the "thralled discontent" (*Sonnets* 124) that his audiences may have identified with a Spanish-sounding Iago and the conquistadores of Compostella: the shrine of St. James, at which (again significantly) the Helena of *All's Well That Ends Well* never arrives. Thus the cardinal archbishop of Milan becomes the figurehead, in *King John*, for a papist reconquest forever retreating from the play; and such may also be the connotation of Shakespeare's most enigmatic allusion to the Borromean city, which is the comparison, in *Much Ado*, of Hero's wedding dress to "the Duchess of Milan's gown that they praise so" for being fashioned in a truly baroque style: from "cloth o' gold, and cuts, and lac'd with silver, set with pearls, down-sleeves, side-sleeves, and skirts, round underborne with a bluish tinsel" (3.4.18–23). To an English audience, there had only ever been one duchess of Milan, and her wedding dress was indeed enskyed with the "bluish tinsel" of Marian symbolism, when she had been married in spectacular and popish pomp at Winchester Cathedral, in a ceremony during which her father-in-law had solemnly bestowed the Milanese duchy on the groom and bride. But when this one and only duchess of Milan had afterwards been buried in that same garish and ill-fated Italian gown, the dynastic hopes of England's recusant community had been interred with it, as well; for she was, of course, the daughter-in-law of the Emperor Charles V and wife of Philip II, whom her Protestant subjects would resent for ever as "Bloody" Mary Tudor.[26]

"She died . . . but whiles her slander liv'd" (5.4.66): and so, although Hero is restored to life—like the English faith reborn—we see that her bridal dress, "worth ten" of the duchess's, "for a fine, quaint, graceful, and excellent fashion" (3.4.24), has been elaborately designed to outshine that blood-stained signifier, and to purify "the chapel" (5.4.71) of the legend of the "absolutist" duchess of Milan. For "Absolute Milan" (*Tempest* 1.2.109), which had come so menacingly close to Shakespeare's England, is indeed what his plays seem deliberately constructed to defer as, poised between the rival confessional extremes of London and Rome, they dedicate "Every third thought" to arriving at last, sometime tomorrow, in what Prospero so prudently denominates instead as "my Milan" (5.1.311). In 1610 "poor Milan" had, indeed, been on the eve of just such an ending, since the champion of the ecumenical middle way, Henry IV of France, had been about to liberate "The dukedom yet unbowed" (1.2.115) when he was assassinated.[27] This failure to free the dukedom ensured, however, that up to the final moment in *The Tempest* Milan would remain what Prospero envisions: a final destination and place of last resort, the shining city over the mountains, forever receding, as the characters troop into the shelter of his cell, beyond the horizon of the stage.

# Notes

1. Richard Simpson, *Edmund Campion: A Biography* (London: John Hodges, 1896), 171, 176, 224, 251–52.
2. Agostino Borromeo, "Archbishop Carlo Borromeo and the Ecclesiastical Policy of Philip II in the State of Milan," in *San Carlo Borromeo: Catholic Reform and Ecclesiastical Politics in the Second Half of the Sixteenth Century*, ed. John M. Headley and John B. Tomaro (Washington: Folger Books, 1988), 95.
3. Letter to Alphonsus Agazzari, 30 June 1580; quoted in Simpson, *Edmund Campion*, 157.
4. Ibid.
5. Quoted in Adriano Prosperi, "Clerics and Laymen in the Work of Carlo Borromeo," in Headley and Tomaro, eds., 135.
6. John Bossy, "The Social History of Confession in the Age of the Reformation," *Transactions of the Royal Historical Society* 25 (1975): 28–31.
7. Michel Foucault, *The History of Sexuality: Introduction* (Harmondsworth: Penguin, 1978), 59; Elizabeth Hanson, *Discovering the Subject in Renaissance England* (Cambridge: Cambridge University Press, 1998), 49–50; Jeremy Tambling, *Confession: Sexuality, Sin, the Subject* (Manchester: Manchester University Press, 1990), 67–69, 84–85.
8. Marc Venard, "The Influence of Carlo Borromeo on the Church of France," in Headley and Tomaro, eds., 221.
9. Simpson, *Edmund Campion*, 190–91. For evidence that Debdale's great-aunt was Shakespeare's maternal grandmother, Mrs. Robert Arden, née Palmer (Debdale's alias), see Edgar Fripp, *Shakespeare's Haunts near Stratford* (Oxford: Oxford University Press, 1929), 33, 53.
10. Anthony Munday, *The English Roman Life*, ed. G. B. Harrison (Edinburgh: Edinburgh University Press, 1966), 66.
11. Giorgio Melchiori, "In Fair Verona: *Commedia Erudita* into Romantic Comedy," in *Shakespeare's Italy: Functions of Italian Locations in Renaissance Drama*, ed. Michele Marrapodi et al. (Manchester: Manchester University Press, 1997), 100–111.
12. Anthony Munday, *Fedele and Fortunio*, ed. Richard Hosley (New York: Garland, 1981), 2.1.21; William Slights, *Ben Jonson and the Art of Secrecy* (Toronto: University of Toronto Press, 1994), 21, 26, 98.
13. Francis Meres, *Palladis Tamia* (London, 1598), quoted in Charles Nicoll, *The Reckoning: The Murder of Christopher Marlowe* (London: Picador, 1992), 174.
14. Munday, *Fedele*, 2.1.86, 3.1.54.
15. John Bossy, "Rome and the Elizabethan Catholics: A Question of Geography," *Historical Journal* 7, no. 1 (1964): 135–42; and see also Peter Guilday, *The English Catholic Refugees on the Continent, 1558–1795* (London: Longmans & Green, 1914), 95–96.

16. 6 August 1577; quoted in Simpson, *Edmund Campion*, 120–21 and no. 92, 521.

17. David Scott Kastan, *Shakespeare after Theory* (London: Routledge, 2001), 210.

18. A. D. Wright, "The Borromean Ideal and the Spanish Church," in Headley and Tomaro, eds., 190.

19. Robert Southwell, "Life of Edward Throckmorton," quoted in Christopher Devlin, *The Life of Robert Southwell: Poet and Martyr* (London: Longmans & Green, 1956), 21.

20. Simpson, *Edmund Campion*, 58–59,153: "They wanted to call Campion Petre; but he, remembering how well he had escaped from Ireland under St. Patrick's patronage, would take no name but his old one of Patrick"; Stephen Greenblatt, *Hamlet in Purgatory* (Princeton: Princeton University Press, 2001), 50.

21. Robert Greene, quoted in Samuel Shoenbaum, *Shakespeare's Lives* (Oxford: Clarendon Press, 1970), 50: "There is an upstart crow beautified with our feathers." In *The Phoenix and Turtle*, the "treble-dated crow," who creates "sable gender . . . With the breath thou giv'st and tak'st" (17–19), looks very like a Jesuit who sends his seminarians to the deaths with which he then inspires their successors.

22. T. S. Eliot, "The Love Song of J. Alfred Prufrock," in *The Complete Poems and Plays of T. S. Eliot* (London: Faber and Faber, 1969), 16; Tom Stoppard, *Rosencrantz and Guildenstern Are Dead* (London: Faber and Faber, 1967), 27.

23. Donna Hamilton, *Shakespeare and the Politics of Protestant England* (Lexington: University Press of Kentucky, 1992), 30–63.

24. See Roland Mushat Frye, "The Roman Catholic Censorship of Shakespeare, 1641–1651," in *Shakespeare and Christian Doctrine* (Princeton: Princeton University Press, 1963), 275–93.

25. Gary Taylor, "Forms of Opposition: Shakespeare and Middleton," *English Literary Renaissance* 24, no. 2 (1994): 303–4.

26. John Lynch, *Spain under the Habsburgs*, 2 vols. (Oxford: Basil Blackwell, 1964), 1:100. The duchy was excluded from the terms of Philip's later marriages.

27. Roland Mousnier, *The Assassination of Henry IV*, trans. Joan Spencer (London: Faber and Faber, 1973), 135–37.

# Ben Jonson and Cervantes: The Influence of Huarte de San Juan on Their Comic Theory

### Yumiko Yamada

## Poetics and Medicine

THE AIM OF THIS PAPER IS TO DISCUSS THE INFLUENCE OF HUARTE DE SAN Juan's (1530?–88?) *Examen de ingenios para las ciencias* (1575) on the comic theory of Jonson and Cervantes,[1] continuing the project begun with my book, *Ben Jonson and Cervantes*, "a reassessment of Cervantine and Jonsonian—and, by extension, early modern Spanish and English—Aristotelianism."[2] Huarte's treatise is a guide to vocational aptitude based on humoral theory, asserting that every young man should choose his occupation according to specific dispositions (or humors). Not only did it affect many Golden Age writers in Spain,[3] it also became a bestseller throughout Europe and was translated into French (1580), Italian (1582), English (1594), Latin (1622), and Dutch (1659).[4] Ten editions were published in Spain prior to part 1 of *Don Quixote*,[5] and Huarte's influence on Cervantes has been generally acknowledged.[6] In England it was first translated by Richard Carew in 1594. Jonson had close contact with Carew through the Cotton Circle,[7] and Harry Levin says that it was undoubtedly read by Jonson.[8] In *Don Quixote*, the clinical studies in madness are made in relation to humoral theory,[9] and in Jonsonian comedy of humors the behavior of eccentric characters is often anatomized along humoral lines.

But this does not fully confirm Huarte's influence. The theory of humors itself was a pan-European vogue. Cervantes cites other medical treatises in his books, and Huarte is considered to be of only marginal influence on his literary theory.[10] Still less can Huarte's influence be traced in Jonson, who had plenty of domestic sources, from Linacre to Elyot, without having to depend on an unfamiliar Spanish scholar.[11] What especially attracts our attention is that Jonson's enthusiasm for humors coincides with that for Aristotelian dramatic canons. In *Every Man in His Humor* and *The Magnetic Lady*, the alpha and omega of his comedy of humors,[12] Jonson appropriates Aristotelian dramaturgy.[13] Still more interesting is it that key passages in both are taken from the defense of classical dramaturgy by the Canon of Toledo and the Curate (1:48) from Thomas Shelton's translation of part 1 of *Don Quixote* (1612).[14]

Both Cervantes and Jonson were frustrated classical playwrights who tried to reform the theater of their nations according to the newly advocated Aristotelian-Horatian principle, but were overwhelmed by the popular drama and dramatic formulas of Lope de Vega and Shakespeare, respectively.[15] Apart from the term "humor," Jonson's comedy belongs basically to a classical Plautus-and-Terence mold, with a variety of moral characters. Likewise, Cervantes's yearning for the theater derived from observing Lope de Rueda's troupe with its classical comedy in the Italian Renaissance style.[16] The relationship between classical dramaturgy and humoral theory—involving a strong connotation of physiology—has eluded convincing explanation, however. These seemingly disparate elements begin to converge when we trace the Hippocratic-Aristotelian connection in the history of medicine, for which Huarte's *Examen* offers us a very helpful hint: Huarte declares that the ground plot of his treatise is Galen, who claimed that the writings of Peripatetic philosophers fortified the physiology of Hippocrates.[17] Aristotle's father was a court physician of the Hippocratic school, and his philosophy is said to be deeply imbued with the influence of Hippocratic medicine.[18]

Jonson was the most learned English poet of his age—worthy of the M.A., according to Silvette.[19] And Cervantes, a surgeon's son, is regarded as no less an authority: He dedicated a sonnet to a medical treatise of Dr. Francisco Díaz, and there is an anecdote that Richard Blackmore, William III's court physician, recommended to Thomas Sydenham that he read *Don Quixote* to increase his knowledge of medicine.[20] It is important to remember that their interest in the *Poetics* was based on an understanding of the corpus of Aristotelian philosophy as a whole, rather than involving pedantic controversies over the so-called rules.[21] In the same way, their concern with humors is based not so much on the minute classification of the four cardinal humors as on understanding the core principle of Hippocratic (or Galenic) medicine. If we add the Galenic notion of physiology provided by Huarte to their common Aristotelianism, it will shed new light on their classical literary principles.

## Therapeutic Methods

The two writers' interest in medical science is most clearly reflected in their therapeutic attitude. Jonson, who offered to anatomize "the times diformitie," thought that the poet's duty was to cure the minds of people by using "sharpe medicine" as the physician does in the cure of the body (*Discoveries* 2312–17). The plot of *Don Quixote* is a case history of a *hidalgo* who loses his wits through infatuation with books of chivalry. The effects of this theatrical therapy on Don Quixote, however, are dubious. Symptoms are treated as they appear, individually and imperfectly, utterly unrelated to the whole design of the work.[22] Not only does it lack a systematic and overall perspective, but the hero's cure seems to inhibit his own scheme of salving the ills of society by the "righting of wrongs and undoing of injuries" (1:19).[23] As if to justify his cause, the world of the novel is inhabited by people who may be sane but are mostly engaged in indecent, immoral—or at best worthless—business.[24] The hero's good moral discipline shimmers in contrast: in his madness he is "valiant, courteous, liberall, well mannered, generous, gentle, bold, mild, patient, an indurer of labours, imprisonments" (1:50). But his therapeutic efforts are consistently mentioned as abnormal, nevertheless, and the conciliatory restoration of his sanity is celebrated as a manifestation[1] of "the meere mercy of my [his] God" (2:74). What is the point of curing the hero, if it results in his being mixed again with the vulgar dregs of humanity?

The same may be said of Jonson. While he promises "to informe yongmen to all good disciplines, inflame growne men to all great vertues, keepe old-men in their best and supreme state" (*Volpone* Dedication 26–28), his comedy notoriously lacks moral consistency. Characters of higher moral principles are often ridiculed or disgraced, while immoral acts are sometimes overlooked and go unpunished.[25] Instead of showing the positive effects of therapy, he shows us "a collection of pathological specimens, labelled and classified," beyond any hope of remedy.[26] In the end we learn that the world is populated by incurably knavish or native fools.[27]

Interestingly, Shakespeare, Jonson's rival and target of criticism, has a vision of remedy very similar to that of Don Quixote. And as the author of *Don Quixote* tried to frustrate the hero's therapeutic efforts, Jonson appears to contradict Shakespeare's therapeutic plan, which is more systematic and thoroughgoing. In Shakespeare's plays, and in the mind of Don Quixote, humanity is linked in a great chain of being, extending from God to the lowest inanimate: "the paragon of animals," "infinite in faculties," "noble in reason," "like an angel in action, like a god in apprehension" (*Hamlet* 2.2.303–7).[28] In Shakespeare's plays and in the fancy of Don Quixote, the world has a cosmic order, with an organic correspondence between the microcosm and macrocosm. Regicide or other grievous crimes or sins cause thunder, lightning, tempests, gaping sepulchers, and other prodigious phenomena. Frequently the time is out of joint, the leading characters are challenged to set it right, and the hopeful remedy is implied in the end. But in the works of Jonson and Cervantes, whatever injustices may prevail on earth, heaven keeps silence to the last. Here man is but "the quintessence of dust" living in a world without special providence. Their pessimistic outlook has been ascribed to their cynicism, or to their spirit of mirth, which allows a saturnalian vision of the world upside-down. Yet there is room to think otherwise.

As I have shown elsewhere, Shakespeare's plays belong to the tradition of chivalric romances that preoccupy Don Quixote's mind.[29] To Cervantes and Jonson, the term "chivalric romance" was a metaphor for all literature that noticeably deviated from the classical norm and "for any medium which could plunge an individual or body politic into insanity, by asserting what is false to be true."[30] If Cervantes earnestly decried chivalric romances, and Jonson seriously attacked Shakespeare's plays, then it is probable that they were satisfied with their seemingly imperfect therapeutic method in their world of squalid reality.

## Every Man in His Humor

The two writers' mysterious attitudes toward therapy become clear when we read Huarte's *Examen*. Huarte demonstrates that if we apply Galen's theory to our bodies, every one of us cannot but be either a fool or a knave or both, as Jonson and Cervantes artfully demonstrated. Huarte's idea of vocational aptitude derives from the premise that no person can be perfect in two arts without failing in one of them. In Galen's physiology, the Hippocratic theory of four humors—that in the human body there are four humors: choler, melancholy, blood, and phlegm, whose right proportion leads to health, and disproportion causes illness—is combined with Aristotle's four first qualities: hot, cold, moist, and dry (21). Thus choler is hot and dry, melancholy cold and dry, blood hot and moist, and phlegm cold and moist (58–60).

Moreover, there are three kinds of intellectual faculty: the understanding, the memory, and the imagination; and different kinds of vocation require different kinds of faculty:

The Arts and Sciences which are gotten by the memorie, are these following, *Latine, Grammer*, or of whatsoeuer other language, the *Theoricke* of the lawes, Diuinitie positiue, *Cosmography*, and *Arithmeticke*.

Those which appertaine to the vnderstanding, are Schoole diuinitie, the *Theoricke of Physicke, logicke, natural and morall Philosophy*, and the practicke of the lawes, which we tearme pleading. From a good imagination, spring all the Arts and Sciences, which consist in figure, correspondence, harmonie, and proportion: such are Poetrie, Eloquence, Musicke, and the skill of preaching: the practise of Phisicke, the Mathematicals, Astrologie, and the gouerning of a Common-wealth, the art of Warfare, Paynting, drawing, writing, reading, to be a man of gratious, pleasant, neat, wittie in managing, & &c all the engins & deuises which artificers make. (103)

The faculty of understanding requires the brain to be dry, the memory moist, and the imagination hot. Yet it is impossible to be dry and moist at once, or hot and cold at the same time; so the brain can be dry and hot, dry and cold, moist and hot, or moist and cold. Accordingly, "a man may haue a great vndertanding and a great imagination, & much memorie with much imagination: and verely, it is a miracle to find a man of great imagination, who hath a good vnderstanding, and a sound memorie" (64).

After thus proving that the human race is not so wise as it believes, Huarte goes on to deny its inherent virtue. The temperate mind requires the brain, the seat of the reason, to be kept cold, while the healthy body requires heat in the digestive and generative organs for nutrition and procreation (247-48).[31] Because it is impossible for a human body to be cold and hot at once, the temperate mind and the healthy body are not compatible with each other. Thus, "By this reckoning it appeareth, that nature cannot fashion such a man as may be perfect in all his powers, nor produce him inclined to vertue. How repugnant it is vnto the nature of man, that he become inclind to vertue, is easily prooued, considering the composition of the first man . . . shaped by the hands of so great an artificer" (248)

In modern paraphrase, when we replace four humors and qualities with what we call the constituent elements of the body and their individual temperatures, mental faculties are determined by physical elements and factors. According to Huarte, people tend to attribute to God or the universal cause what ought to be ascribed to the particular causes of nature. He attempts to correct this "fallacy" from the viewpoint of "natural philosophy" based on Galen's notion of physiology. The term holds broad meaning: the study of nature (physiology), biology, and a large part of physics.[32] He asserts that God allowed nature to take its own course when He created the world: "for when *Aristotle* sayd, that God and nature did nothing in vaine, he meant not, that nature was an vniuersall cause, endowed with a iurisdiction seuered from God, but that she was a name of order and concent, which God hath bestowed in the frame of the world, to the end that the necessarie effects might follow, for the preseruation thereof. . . . God left miraculous effects reserued for himself, neither gaue allowance vnto naturall causes, that they might produce them" (18). Cervantes and Jonson likewise steer clear of the universal cause—under the pretext that it is too profound for our understanding: "*nor ought it* [i.e., the novel] *to Preach unto any the mixture of holy matters with profane, (a motley wherewith no Christian well should be attyred)*" (*Don Quixote* part 1, preface). And Jonson says, "For to utter Truth of God (but as hee thinkes only) may be dangerous; who is best knowne, by our not knowing" (*Discoveries*, 525–27).

The separation of science from religion goes back to Hippocratic tradition. Inheriting the rationalism of the Milesian natural philosophers, who explained the world in terms of visible constituents without recourse to supernatural intervention, the sixty-odd works of the Hippocratic corpus are virtually free from supernatural elements.[33] Aristotle, whose philosophy is said to form commentaries on the physiology of Hippocrates, preferred as the object of his study perishable things on earth—plants and animals among which we live—to heavenly knowledge, because we have better information about the former (*Parts of Animals* 1.5).[34] Huarte says that the supreme goal of the Hippocratic or Galenic natural philosophy is to attain the understanding of Aristotle (242).

Aristotle's central point would have been his assertion that studies of the soul belong to the field of natural science: "Consequently their [i.e., affections'] definitions ought to correspond, e.g. anger should be defined as a certain mode of movement of such and such a body (or part or faculty of a body) by this or that cause and for this or that end. That is precisely why the study of the soul—either every soul or souls of this sort—must fall within the science of nature. Hence a physicist would define an affection of soul differently from a dialectician; the latter would define e.g. anger as the appetite for returning pain for pain, or something like that, while the former would define it as a boiling of the blood or warm substance surrounding the heart. The one assigns the material conditions, the other the form or account" (*On the Soul* 1.1).

Citing Genesis, Huarte points out that God instrumentalized the body of Adam before he created his soul (39): Adam, who was created in the age of youth, with perfect faculties for nutrition and procreation, was definitely inclined to evil; only for a while he had been protected from sins by "originall Iustice," or the supernatural quality, which might keep down his "inferiour part"; when he offended, he lost this special quality (250). When the composition of the first man, shaped by the hands of God, was thus inclined to vice, still more so with us, his distant descendant. It is impossible for a healthy man, Huarte declares, to follow his own natural inclination without committing sinful deeds; he can be "virtuous" only when struck by "an impotencies of operation" or with "the speciall aid of God" (250). Jonson echoes Huarte's remarks when he admonishes Justice Adam Overdo, "Remember you are but *Adam*, Flesh, and blood! you haue your frailty, forget your other name of Ouerdoo," who is punished with the other two stern moralizers in *Bartholomew Fair* (5.6.96–98). His charge is over-pursuing "justice" by his inflexible and rigid standard. Every man is destined to be in his humor—or to have faults and defects inherent in flesh and blood. From this point of view, any attempt to rectify human beings according to moral discipline would be in vain; still more illusive would be a project of universal remedy.

In *Don Quixote*, the Curate and the Barber, allegorically in charge of mind and body, try to cure the mad hero; but their chief concern is always for his physical health. We are made to realize how hard the hero fights against the laws of nature. Cervantes clinically depicts the hero's physical condition changing in various circumstances with detailed descriptions of his sleep, diet, and excretions; and the causes and treatments of wounds, bruises, bone fractures, loss of teeth, and the like, until his death, which is the inevitable consequence of his overtaxing his body. He is presented as a guinea pig that the author tests to see what may happen if his "virtuous mind" tries to keep down the "inferiour part" not only of his own body but also of many others, according to the strict code of chivalry.

## The Castle of Health

Hippocratic (or Galenic) medicine spread mainly from the University of Padua, the center of Aristotelian studies in Europe. There they adopted double standards of truth: the Church's dogmas on one hand and independent philosophical thinking on the other.[35] Far from outdated, Galenism at this period was considered synonymous with progress.[36] Aristotle and Galen remained alive not only in the seventeenth century but even into the early eighteenth century, to bring forth the full bloom of anatomy.[37] Galenism did not remain within the narrow compass of medicine, however, and Thomas Linacre played a great role in advocating medical humanism in the Renaissance, returning to England from Padua as a humanist scholar specializing in Greek medicine. He thus cemented the connection between the universities and the College of Physicians,[38] and his Latin translation of Galen's *De sanitate tuenda* (1517) deeply influenced the leading humanists including More, Erasmus, Budé, Elyot, Vives, Vesalius, and even Rabelais (see *Gargantua and Pantagruel* 4:67).[39] Jonson and Cervantes, who admired these humanists including Vives and Erasmus, had been completely ready to accept Huarte. Their common slogan was, "a wise man should care for his body as carefully as of his mind," as Elyot wrote in his *Castel of Helthe* (1541).

In his dedication to Philip II, Huarte emphasizes that a good guide to proper vocational placement is necessary especially in the fields of divinity and medicine, which concern the mind and body: "For that at this day such a diligence is not vsed, those who had not a wit for Diuinitie, haue destroied the Christian religion. So doe those who are vntoward for Physicke, shorten many a mans daies." Conversely, a great number of souls and bodies would be saved by preventing wrongdoers from occupying these important professions, and this is the true aim of his treatise. What they were striving to do, after all, was to separate natural science from religion—a division by which we are authorized to choose health before virtue, without losing our conscience. And it was not only to be applied to Elyot's "wise man" but to all, without exception.

Gifford ascribed Jonson's relative "unpopularity" (when compared with Shakespeare) to his lack of what he calls "just discrimination": "He seems to have been deficient in that true tact of feeling of propriety which Shakespeare possessed in full excellence. He appears to have had *an equal value for all his characters*, and he *labors upon the most unimportant, and even disagreeable of them with the same fond and paternal assiduity* which accompanies his happiest efforts."[40] In the Shakespearean universal therapeutic scheme, the deaths of lesser characters, Polonius, Rosencrantz, and Guildenstern, for example, are treated lightly as an inevitable consequence of intruding themselves "between the mighty opposites," when they belong to "the baser nature" (*Hamlet* 5.2.58–62).

Yet following Huarte's argument, it is impossible to decide who is "the most unimportant, and even disagreeable," when every one of us is equally vicious and foolish, without much difference. Huarte asserts that every man ought to be cured in a method conformable to his particular constitution. When we have a hundred thousand patients, we have to apply a hundred thousand ways of therapy, one most suitable to each of them who has a bodily constitution particular to himself (175). Jonson agrees with him when he quotes Quintilian (2:8) in the *Discoveries*: "There are no fewer formes of minds, then of bodies amongst us. The variety is incredible; and therefore wee must search. Some are fit to make *Divines*, some *Poets*, some *Lawyers*, some *Physicians*; some to be sent to the plough, and trades" (672–76). Respect for the individual also derives from Hippocrates, who used proper pronouns for his patients in his records concerning the epidemic disease (*Epidemics I and III*).[41] This attitude is reflected in Aristotle's belief that the state of individuation, rather than being an integrated state as a species, is the "true" form of living, on the ground that the individual is more operative than the class in generation or procreation (*Generation of Animals* 4. 3).

In addition to showing the Hippocratic-Aristotelian connection, Huarte's treatise provides still another hint for understanding the relationship between the two writers' interest in the application of humoral theory to their comic theory. Huarte points out that Galenic physiology is a science that requires deeper consideration and wisdom than any other. Since its principles are far less certain than mathematics's, it is less suitable for young men (74). This reminds us that Aristotle prohibited youths' being spectators of *iambi* or of comedy until they are of a suitable age (*Politics* 7.17), not only because they are sometimes licentious but because comedy showed "virtue and vice" not in a dualist simplicity but in countless ways according to each particular situation (see *Politics* 1.13).

Galen strongly suggests that the *Characters* of Theophrastus, Aristotle's best disciple, also inherit the Hippocratic tradition of physiology. Theophrastus is said to have influenced Menander, writer of New Comedy, who in turn influenced Plautus, Terence, and numerous other Roman writers. And this implies that their aim was not just to exhibit a variety of stock characters.

In *Every Man in His Humor,* Jonson reconstructed the size and heterogeneity of London with the pathology-spotted speeches and dialects of his multitudinous characters: gallant, soldier, bourgeois, countryman, street seller, and so forth.[42] Similarly, Cervantes is said to have included the whole of Spain in his novel. In *Don Quixote* he dealt with 708 characters from the higher to the lowest of the social classes—merchants, lawyers, divines, soldiers, shepherds, peasants, and outlaws—portraying them according to their features, temperaments, clothes, food, religions, and other customs and habits.[43] To them every character was "nature's dearest son,"[6] irreplaceable by anyone else; he should quietly enjoy his own liberty and pursue his own happiness without unjustly invading others'.[44]

This must have been the very essence that Huarte's *Examen* tried to convey under the guise of "a dull treatise of little value, on the corporeal and mental qualities of men and women."[45] The treatise endorses John Donne's enigmatic comment that Jonson's comedy wisely showed the necessary way to save our souls in a revolutionary way, negotiating the laws of men and God.[46] It is tempting to suppose that Donne's "revolutionary way" implied "showing every one of us a particular way to save his/her own body, according to his/her humor or temperature." The remark is true also of the work of Cervantes, who shared the same comic theory with Ben Jonson.

# Notes

1. Quotations from *The Examination* (*Examen,* for short) are taken from *The Examination of Mens Wits,* trans. Richard Carew (1594; reprint, New York: Da Capo Press, 1969).

2. Yumiko Yamada, *Ben Jonson and Cervantes: Tilting Against Chivalric Romances* (Tokyo: Maruzen, 2000), revised by Edward H. Friedman, in *Revista de Estudios Hispánicos* 34, no. 3 (2000): 663–64.

3. Adrienne Laskier Martín cites Alonso López Pinciano, Luis Carvallo, Baltasar Gracián, and Jerónimo de Mondragón in *Cervantes and the Burlesque Sonnet* (Berkeley and Los Angeles: University of California Press, 1991), 69.

4. Norio Shimizu, *The Century of Don Quixote: Reading the Golden Age Spain* (Tokyo: Iwanami, 1990), 298 (Japanese).

5. Mauricio de Iriarte, S.J., *El doctor Huarte de San Juan y su Examen de Ingenios* (Santander: Aldus, 1939), 314; quoted in Martín, *Cervantes and the Burlesque Sonnet,* 69, 246 n.

6. Raphael Salillas, in *Un gran inspirador de Cervantes, el doctor Juan Hu-*

*arte y su "Examen de Ingenios"* (Madrid: Eduardo Arias, 1905), was the first to point it out. See also E. C. Riley, *Cervantes's Theory of the Novel* (Oxford: Clarendon Press, 1962), 9–10, 68, 76, 153; and Martín, *Cervantes*, 68.

7. In his "Execration upon Vulcan" (*The Underwood* 43), he refers to the books "Which noble Carew, Cotton, Selden lent" (100). See also *Conversations with Drummond*, 261–62; *Ben Jonson*, ed. C. H. Herford, Percy Simpson, and Evelyn Simpson, 11 vols. (Oxford: Clarendon Press, 1925–52) 1:35, 70. All quotations from Jonson are from this edition, hereafter "H&S."

8. Harry Levin, ed., *Veins of Humor* (Cambridge: Harvard University Press, 1972), 8.

9. Martín, *Cervantes*, 69.

10. Riley, *Cervantes's Theory of the Novel*, 9.

11. For details see C. R. Baskerville, *English Elements in Jonson's Early Comedy* (1911; reprint, New York: Johnson Reprint Corporation, 1972).

12. See *The Magnetic Lady* Induction, 99–111: "The *Author*, beginning his studies of this kind, with *every man in his Humour*; and after, *every man out of his Humour*: and since, continuing in all his *Playes*, especially those of the *Comick* thred, whereof the *New-Inne* was the last, some recent humors still, or manners of men, that went along with the times, finding himselfe now neare the close, or shutting up of his Circle, hath phant'sied to himselfe, in *Idæa*, this *Magnetick Mistris*."

13. *Every Man in His Humor* (1616 Folio), Prologue, 1–16:

> Though neede make many *Poets*, and some such
> As art, and nature haue not bettered much;
> Yet ours, for want, hath not so lou'd the stage,
> As he dare serue th'ill customes of the age:
> Or purchase your delight at such a rate,
> As, for it, he himself must iustly hate.
> To make a child, now swadled, to proceede
> Man, and then shoot vp, in one beard, and weede,
> Past three score yeeres. . . .
> He rather prayes, you will be pleas'd to see
> One such, to day, as other playes should be.
> Where neither *Chorus* wafts you ore the seas;
> Nor creaking throne comes downe, the boyes to please.

*The Magnetic Lady*, 1 Chorus, 15–27: "So, if a Child could be borne, in a *Play*, and grow up to a man, i' the first Scene, before hee went off the Stage: and then after to come forth a Squire, and bee made a Knight: and that Knight to travell betweene the Acts, and doe wonders i' the holy land, or else where; kill Paynims, wild Boores, dun Cowes, and other Monsters; beget him a reputation, and marry an Emperours Daughter for his Mistris; convert her Fathers Countrey; and at last come home, lame, and all to be laden with miracles."

14. For a detailed analysis, see Yamada, *Ben Jonson and Cervantes*, chap. 1.

15. For details, see ibid., chap. 3.

16. Jean Canavaggio, *Cervantes*, trans. J. R. Jones (New York: W. W. Norton & Company, 1990), 159.

17. Galen, *On the Natural Faculties*, trans. and ed. A. J. Brock, Loeb Classical Library (1916; reprint, Cambridge: Harvard University Press, 1991), 2:4.

18. James Longrigg, *Greek Rational Medicine: Philosophy and Medicine from Alcmaeon to the Alexandrians* (London: Routledge, 1993), 149.

19. Henry Silvette, *The Doctor on the Stage: Medicine and Medical Men in*

*Seventeenth-Century England*, ed. Francelia Butler (Knoxville: University of Tennessee Press, 1967), 121.

20. Shimizu, *The Century of Don Quixote*, 166.

21. See Yamada, *Ben Jonson and Cervantes*, chap. 6 and conclusion.

22. See, for example, H&S, 1:378–79.

23. The quotations from *Don Quixote* are from Thomas Shelton's translation (1612, 1620), ed. James Fitzmaurice-Kelly, 4 vols. (1896; reprint, New York: AMS Press, 1967).

24. Daniel Eisemberg, *Romances of Chivalry in the Spanish Golden Age* (Newark, Del.: Juan de la Cuesta, 1982), 156 n.

25. The biggest controversy over Jonson's "immorality" would be between Dryden, preface to *The Mock Astrologer*, and Jeremy Collier, *The Short View of the Immorality and Profaneness of the English Stage*, 151–56. For details see Yamada, "Jeremy Collier and Ben Jonson," *Studies in Humanities* 45, no. 4 (1993): 1–20 (Japanese).

26. H&S, 1:378.

27. James Hirsh, "Cynicism and the Futility of Art in *Volpone*," in *New Perspectives on Ben Jonson*, ed. James Hirsh (Madison, N.J.: Fairleigh Dickinson University Press, 1997): 106–27; cited in Robert S. Miola, ed., *Every Man in His Humour* (Manchester: Manchester University Press, 2000), 77 n.

28. Shakespeare also spoke of his therapeutic method in terms of humors, yet compared with Jonson he speaks with more feeling than as a mere observer of the ravages of the disease (Silvette, *Doctors on the Stage*, 219). See also Yamada, "Shakespeare's Humour Plays," *Shakespeare Studies* 21, The Shakespeare Society of Japan (1985): 35–64. Shakespeare's therapeutic attitude will be discussed in detail on a later occasion, owing to lack of space here.

29. Yamada, *Ben Jonson and Cervantes*, chap. 5.

30. Ibid., 145.

31. Huarte says that healthy digestion and procreation require heat in the heart (wrathful and concupiscent power), the liver (digestive power), and the "cod" (procreative power).

32. Brock, ed., *On the Natural Faculties*, xxvi–xxvii.

33. Longrigg, *Greek Rational Medicine*, 26.

34. Citations of Aristotle are from *The Complete Works of Aristotle*, ed. Jonathan Barnes, 2 vols. (Princeton: Princeton University Press, 1984).

35. Sem Dresden, *Humanism in the Renaissance*, trans. Margaret King (New York: McGraw-Hill, 1968), 27–28.

36. Richard J. Durling, "Linacre and Medical Humanism," in *Essays on the Life and Work of Thomas Linacre, c. 1460–1524*, ed. Francis Romeil et al. (Oxford: Clarendon Press, 1977), 76–106.

37. Walter Pagel, "Medical Humanism: A Historical Necessity in the Era of the Renaissance," in *Essays on Linacre*, 375–86.

38. Charles Webster, "Thomas Linacre and the Foundation of the College of Physicians," in *Essays on Linacre*, 198–222.

39. Durling, "Linacre and Medical Humanism," 103; Stanford E. Lehmberg, *Sir Thomas Elyot: Tudor Humanist* (Austin: University of Texas Press, 1960), 17–20.

40. William Gifford (1816), 1:ccxvii–ccxix, quoted in Frances Teague, *The Curious History of "Bartholomew Fair"* (Lewisburg, Pa.: Bucknell University Press, 1985), 101; emphasis mine.

41. *Hippocrates and the Fragments of Heracleitus*, trans. and ed. W. H. S. Jones

and E. T. Withington, 4 vols., Loeb Classical Library (1923; reprint, Cambridge: Harvard University Press, 1984), 1:139–288.

42. Peter Womack, *Ben Jonson* (Oxford: Blackwell, 1989), 80; cited in Miola, ed., *Every Man in*, 53.

43. Alberto Sánchez, "Don Quijote y los españoles": Estudios Conmemorativos del XXV *Aniversario de la Fundacion del Departamento de Estudios Hispánicos* (Universidad de Estudios Extranjeros de Kioto, 1989), 55–80.

44. See Richard Tuck, *Natural Rights Theories: Their Origin and Development* (Cambridge: Cambridge University Press, 1979), 60–75.

45. *DNB*, s.v. "Richard Carew."

46. John Donne, "Amicissimo, & meritissimo BEN: IONSON" (1607), 1–4; quoted in J. F. Bradley and J. Q. Adams, *The Jonson Allusion-Book: A Collection of Allusions to Ben Jonson from 1597 to 1700* (1922; reprint, New York: Russell & Russell, 1971), 56.

# Appendix A
## Complete List of Papers
## from the Program of the Conference

## Shakespeare and The Mediterranean
18 to 23 April 2001, Valencia
The International Shakespeare Association

### Plenary Sessions

"Shakespeare's Islands," Jonathan Bate
"Self-Consistency in Montaigne and Shakespeare," Robert Ellrodt
"Painted Devils and Aery Nothings: Metamorphoses and Magic Art," Marina Warner
"Shylock's Tribe," Stephen Orgel
"John Gielgud: Tradition, Magic, and Continuity in the Modern Shakespearean Theater," Michael Coveney

### Short-Paper Sessions

Chair: Andrew Gurr

"The First Permanent Playhouse in Madrid: *El Corral de la Cruz* (1579)," Charles Davis
"Staging Shakespeare and Calderón: Comparison and Contrast," John J. Allen
"Actors and Theatrical Documentation in Sixteenth- and Seventeenth-Century Spain: Development of a Database," M. Teresa Ferrer Valls

### Confusing Venice

Chair: J. R. Mulryne

"The Strange Mediterraneans of Marlowe and Shakespeare," J. Leeds Barroll

"Hybridizing Sheep with Ships: Commercial and Cultural Trading in *The Merchant of Venice*," Philippa Berry
"The Prince of Morocco's Choice of the Golden Casket: An Allegory of the Political and Cultural Rapprochement between Elizabethan England and Morocco," Gustav Ungerer

Chair: Niels B. Hansen

"Shakespeare's Mediterranean *Measure for Measure*," Gary Taylor
Playtext Reporters and *Memoriones*: Suspect Texts in Shakespeare and Spanish Golden Age Drama," Jesús Tronch-Pérez
"'Every third thought': Shakespeare's Milan," Richard Wilson

## Shakespeare and Mediterranean Bodies: Three Approaches

Chair: Gail Kern Paster

"Mediterranean Bodies in Shakespeare and Medical Discourse," Carol Thomas Neely
"'Vail your stomachs': Self-Restraint in Fruitful Lombardy," Keir Elam
"Organizing the Body/Organizing Knowledge: Shakespeare and Others," Jonathan Sawday

## Globalizing Shakespeare

Chair: Peter Donaldson

"Dot Shakespeare: 'This [Electronic] 0,'" Michael Best
"Performing Shakespeare in China, 1980–1990: A Multimedia Project," John Gillies and Ruru Li
"Globe Links: Prattle and Practice," Gabriel Egan and Patrick Spottis-woode

## Elizabethan Theaters and *Corrales de Comedias*: Origins and Evolution

Chair: John J. Allen

"The 1629 Corral de Comedias at Almagro and the Reconstructed Globe Theater, London," Franklin J. Hildy

"The Antiguo Teatro Cervantes in Alcalá de Henares: From *Corral de Comedias* to Cinema," Miguel Angel Coso Marin

Chair: Shen Lin

"Metaferocities: Jealousy in Verdi and Shakespeare," Graham Bradshaw
"The True History of Romeo and Juliet: A Veronese Plot of the 1830s," Paola Pugliatti
"Spanish Reception of Sampson's Linguistic and Sexual Ambiguity," Purificación Ribes

Chair: Poonam Trivedi

"Shakespeare and the Holocaust: Julie Taymor's *Titus* Is Beautiful; or, Shakesploi Meets (the) Camp," Richard Burt
"The Mediterranean Triangle: Sex and Conquest in *Antony and Cleopatra*," Ellen Caldwell
"Gender on the Periphery," Jean E. Howard

Chair: Yuji Kaneko

"The Disappearing Wall: *A Midsummer Night's Dream* and *Timon of Athens*," Alexander Leggatt
"Shakespeare's *Odyssey*," Yves Peyré
"Illyria Revisited: Shakespeare and the Eastern Adriatic," Goran Stanivukovic

Chair: Hanna Scolnicov

"Elizabethanism in Verona," John H. Astington
"Maids for All Markets?" Helmut Bonheim
"'We open in Venice . . .': On Location in Shakespeare's Italy," Russell Jackson

Chair: Aimara da Cunha Resende

"Shakespeare's Outsiders," Charles Marowitz
"The Pronouns of Propriety and Passion: *you* and *thou* in Shakespeare's Italian Comedies," Penelope Freedman
"Shakespeare and the Early Modern Mediterranean: Theater, Commerce, and English Identity," Daniel Vitkus

Chair: Suheyla Artemel

"A 'man right fair' and a 'woman coloured ill': Race and the Pseudo-Portraits of Shakespeare's Sonnets," David Schalkwyk
"Ben Jonson and Cervantes: The Influence of Huarte de San Juan on Their Comic Theory," Yumiko Yamada
"*Titus Andronicus*: Some Editorial Problems in Digital Editions," Vicente Forés Lopez

Chair: Lali Kereselidze

"Translating Arden: Shakespeare's Rhetorical Place in *As You Like It*," Swapan Chakravorty
"From Shakespeare's Italy to Italy's Shakespeare: Biographical Fantasies of Love and Power," Paul Franssen
"The Trouble with Old Virgins: Elizabeth and La Serenissima," Nancy Hodge

# Appendix B
## Seminars, with Their Leaders and Registered Participants

### 1. Shakespeare's Mediterranean Plays and Renaissance Travel Writing

*Leaders*: Philip Edwards and Mary Fuller
*Participants*:
  Edmund Campos
  Herschel Johnson
  Vassiliki Markidou
  Beate Neumeier
  Camille Wells Slights

### 2. Shakespeare and the Graeco-Roman World

*Leaders*: Supriya Chaudhuri and Coppélia Kahn
*Participants*:
  Rita Banerjee
  Silvana Carotenuto
  Sarbani Chaudury
  Alice Clark
  Naomi Conn Liebler
  Christy Desmet
  Roberto Ferreira da Rocha
  Robin Headlam Wells
  Christine Hutchins
  Ann Kaegi
  Paulina Kewes
  Arthur Little
  Katharine Maus
  Hoshang Merchant
  Robert S. Miola

### 3. Staging the Stranger

*Leaders*: Carol Chillington Rutter and Boika Sokolova
*Participants*
  Alexey Bartoshevitch
  Clara Calvo
  Nicoleta Cinpoes
  Anthony B. Dawson
  Stuart Hampton-Reeves
  Niels Bugge Hansen
  Helen Ostovitch
  Sue Tweg
  Tony Voss

### 4. Shakespeare and the Romantic Ideal of Italy

*Leaders*: Murray Levith and Michele Marrapodi
*Participants*:
  Frances Barasch
  Necla Cikigil
  Michael J. Redmond
  Nina da Vinci Nichols
  Susanne Wofford

### 5. "... I other accents borrow / That can my speech diffuse": Accents, Pronunciation, and Dialects on the Shakespearean Stage

*Leaders*: Charles Edelman and Andrew Gurr
*Respondent*: Peter Holland

*Participants*:
  Alison Findlay
  Richard Fotheringham
  Brian Gibbons
  Ros King
  Leanore Lieblein
  Jeremy Lopez
  Patricia Parker
  James R. Siemon
  Lingui Yang

**6. Shakespeare from the Twenty-First-Century Left; or, Material Shakespeare for the New Millennium**

*Leaders*: John Drakakis and Hugh Grady
*Participants*:
  Denise Albanese
  Barbara Correll
  Mustapha Fahmi
  Evelyn Gajowski
  Edward Gieskes
  Kim Hall
  Terence Hawkes
  Don Hedrick
  Robert Weimann

**7. Shakespeare and Sonnets: The English Form and the European Tradition**

*Leaders*: Mario Domenichelli and Katherine Duncan-Jones
*Participants*:
  Jane Carducci
  Angelo Deidda
  Werner Habicht
  Rafael Velez Nunez
  Donatella Pallotti
  Susan Payne
  Kay Stanton
  Paul R. Thomas

**8. A Boundless Sea: Shakespeare's Mediterranean on Film**

*Leaders*: José Ramón Díaz Fernández and Peter Donaldson

*Participants*:
  Iska Alter
  Ann Jennalie Cook
  Herbert R. Coursen
  Samuel Crowl
  Anthony Davies
  Kathy Howlett
  Hyon-U Lee
  Patricia Lennox
  Alfredo Michel Modenessi
  Yukiko Mori
  Martha P. Nochimson
  Sharon O'Dair
  Daryl Palmer
  Kenneth S. Rothwell
  Hanna Scolnicov
  Kay H. Smith
  Gulsen Teker
  Bob White
  Robert F. Willson, Jr.

**9. Shakespeare and Opera in the Mediterranean Milieu: Rewriting Texts, Staging Polyphonies, and Acting the Music**

*Leaders*: Marga Munkelt and Giovanna Silvani
*Participants*:
  Marco Capra
  Sheila Cavanagh
  Elena Sala Di Felice
  David Lindley
  Giorgio Melchiori
  Romana Zacchi

**10. Moving around the Mediterranean in the Plays of Shakespeare and His Contemporaries**

*Leaders*: Anthony Parr and Chong Zhang
*Participants*:
  Joan Fitzpatrick
  Jeanie Grant Moore
  Joan Larsen Klein
  Genevieve Love
  Jim Lusardi

Richard Nochimson
Kevin Pask
June Schlueter
Anne M. Tanaka
Marilyn Williamson
Eric Wilson

## 11. Messengers and Communication in Shakespearean and Renaissance Drama

*Leaders*: Lloyd Davis and Michael Dobson
*Respondent*: Philippa Kelly
*Participants*:
  Derek Cohen
  Manfred Draudt
  Gabriel Egan
  Corinna Evett
  Maria Amelia Fraga
  Linda Gregerson
  Elina Huhtikangas
  Mark Lawhorn
  David Linton
  Richard Madelaine
  Ninian Mellamphy
  Barbara Traister

## 12. Shakespeare in Non-Anglophone Countries

*Leaders*: Sukanta Chaudhuri and Chee Seng Lim
*Participants*:
  Etsuko Fukahori
  Margarida Gandara Rauen
  Keith Gregor
  Lawrence Guntner
  Younglim Han
  Kumiko Hilberdink-Sakamoto
  Alexander Huang
  Dennis Kennedy
  Shen Lin
  Shormishtha Panja
  Emil Sirbulescu
  Harish Trivedi
  Li Lan Yong

## 13. "Here I am . . . yet cannot hold this visible shape": Early Modern Man

*Leaders*: Martin Orkin and Bruce Smith
*Respondent*: Avraham Oz
*Participants*:
  Douglas A. Brooks
  Maurizio Calbi
  Casey Charles
  Charles R. Forker
  Barbara Fuchs
  Judith Haber
  Ursula Hehl
  Andreas Hoefele
  Richard Levin
  Simon Palfrey
  Jennifer Panek
  Phyllis Rackin
  Craig Rustici
  Alan Sinfield
  Ian Smith
  James Stone
  Suzanne Trill
  Jacqueline Vanhoutte
  Jennifer Vaught

## 4. Shakespeare's Nineteenth-Century Performers

*Leaders*: Gail Marshall and Mariangela Tempera
*Participants*:
  Nicholas Clary
  Patricia Kennan
  Krystyna Kujawinska-Courtney
  Lisa Merrill
  Adrian Poole
  Robert Sawyer
  Isabelle Schwartz-Gastine

## 15. Theory and Methodology in Authorship/Attribution Studies

*Leaders*: Jonathan Hope and David Kathman
*Participants*:
  Jayson Brown
  Charles Cathcart
  Marcus Dahl
  Kate McLuskie
  Gordon McMullan

Lucy Munro
Lene Petersen
Richard Proudfoot
Rebecca Rogers

## 16. Creative and Critical Appropriations of Shakespeare

*Leaders*: Sonia Massai and Barbara
Sebek
*Participants*:
Linda Burnett
Walter W. Cannon
Aimara da Cunha Resende
Patty Derrick
Suzanne Gossett
Michael Anthony Ingham
Maria Jones
Elizabeth Klein
Kaori Kobayashi
Ruru Li
Zoltan Markus
Clare McManus
Michael Shapiro
Frances A. Shirley
Brandie R. Siegfried
Christel Stalpaert
Poonam Trivedi
Ramona Wray

## 17. Staging the Boundaries of Law in Early Modern Drama: English Dramatic Presentations of Continental European Justice

*Leaders*: B. J. Sokol and Barbara I.
Kreps
*Participants*:
Stephanie Chamberlain
Imtiaz Habib
Rolf Müller
Mary Polito
Terry Reilly

## 18. Shakespeare's Illyrias: Heterotopies, Identities, (Counter) Histories

*Leaders*: Mladen Engelsfeld and Martin
Procházka
*Participants*:
Ann Blake
Marcus Cheng Chye Tan
Sara Hanna
John J. Joughin
Yoshiko Kawachi
Robert Matijasic for Bruna Kuntic-
Makvić
Peter Milward
Zdeněk Stříbrný

## 19. Re-framing *Othello:* Contexts, Para-texts, and Critical New Directions

*Leaders*: Michael Neill and Edward
Pechter
*Participants*:
Linda Anderson
Malvina Aparicio
Crystal L. Bartolovich
Shaul Bassi
Joanna Byles
Lawrence Danson
William Flesch
Dave Golz
Rafat Karim
Natasha Korda
Thomas Moisan
Joseph A. Porter
Michael W. Shurgot
Steve Sohmer
Mark Sokolyansky

## 20. Revenge as a Mediterranean Phenomenon Before and After "Hamlet"

*Leaders*: Carla Dente and Ann
Thompson
*Participants*:
Hardin L. Aasand
Monica Chesnoiu
Susan L. Fischer
Charles A. Hallett
Frederick Kiefer
Akiko Kusunoki

Markus Marti
Alessandra Marzola
Steven Mullaney
Giuseppina Restivo
Ildiko Elizabeth Solti
Neil Taylor
Linda Woodbridge

## 21. Shakespeare and Montaigne Revisited

*Leaders*: Tom Bishop and Peter
   Holbrook
*Respondent*: Lars Engle
*Participants*:
   Robert Bennett
   William Hamlin
   John Lee
   Kathleen Lynch
   Michael Mack
   Gail Price
   Chris Roark
   Herb Weil
   Judith Weil
   Paul Yachnin

## 22. Mediating the Mediterranean in the Drama of Shakespeare and His Contemporaries

*Leaders*: Ton Hoenselaars and Virginia
   Mason Vaughan
*Participants*:
   Rui Carvalho Homem
   Raymond Gardette
   R. Chris Hassel
   Diana E. Henderson
   Bindu Malieckal
   Linda McJannet
   John McKellor Reid
   Rachana Sachdev
   John D. Sanderson
   Peter Womack

## 23. Shakespeare's Biography

*Leaders*: E. A. J. Honigmann and Lois
   Potter

*Participants*:
   Edward S. Brubaker
   Agnes Fleck
   Reg Foakes
   Park Honan
   Jean-Marie Maguin
   Penny McCarthy
   Charles Pastoor
   Enno Ruge
   John Joseph Tobin
   Bruce Young

## 24. Editing Shakespeare's Mediterranean Plays

*Leaders*: Jay Halio and Charles
   Whitworth
*Participants*:
   Peter Alscher
   Tom Clayton
   Yuji Kaneko
   William Long
   Barbara Mowat
   Michael Skovmand
   Tiffany Stern
   Richard Weisberg

## 25. Machiavelli in Shakespeare and Early Modern English Playwrights up to 1642

*Leaders*: Sergio Mazzarelli and Martin
   Wiggins
*Participants*:
   N. W. Bawcutt
   Cyndia Susan Clegg
   John D. Cox
   Neslihan Ekmekçioglu
   Scott Fraser
   Reiko Fujita
   Cristina Malcolmson
   Tom McAlindon
   Hisao Oshima
   Jürgen Pieters
   Jill Phillips
   Mihoko Suzuki
   Soko Tomita

**26. Venice and English Identity in Shakespeare and His Contemporaries**

*Leaders*: David C. McPherson and J. R. Mulryne
*Participants*:
    Juliette Cunico
    Celia Daileader
    Jason Gleckman
    Paul Harvey
    Maurice Hunt
    Fritz Levy
    Joseph Woolwich

**27. Shakespeare and the Mediterranean: The "Non-European" Edge**

*Leaders*: Emily C. Bartels and Bulent Bozkurt
*Participants*:
    Randall Martin
    Shankar Raman
    Alan Rosen
    Jyotsna G. Singh

**28. Shakespeare's Narrative Poems**

*Leaders*: Christa Jansohn and Georgianna Ziegler
*Participants*:
    Judith Anderson
    Clara Calvo
    Hugh Craig
    Kate Green
    Dieter Mehl
    Madalina Nicolaescu
    John Roe
    John Velz

**29. Spain and Early Modern Drama**

*Leaders*: Janet Clare and Hiroshi Ozawa
*Participants*:
    Ivan Canadas
    Ed Esche
    José Manuel González
    Anita Howard
    Susana Marchetti
    Constance Rose

**30. www.shakespeare.com**

*Leaders*: Susan Bennett and Christie Carson
*Participants*:
    Susan Brock
    Elizabeth Hageman
    James L. Harner
    Barbara Mathieson
    Jim Shaw
    Alan Somerset
    Mary Steible
    Fran Teague
    Alan Young

**31. Commedia dell' arte and the Performance of Shakespeare**

*Leaders*: Andrew Grewar and Stephen Hazell
*Participants*:
    Melissa Aaron
    Gian Giacomo Colli
    Rob Conkie
    Luke Dixon
    Ronald Hall
    Clarissa Hurley
    Hilde Slinger

# Notes on Contibutors

JOHN J. ALLEN, Professor Emeritus of Spanish at the University of Kentucky, is author of *Don Quixote: Hero or Fool?* and *The Reconstruction of a Spanish Golden Age Playhouse*; co-author of *Los teatros comerciales del siglo XVII y la escenificación de la comedia* (The Commercial Playhouses of the 17th Century and the Staging of the Comedia); editor of a Spanish edition of *Don Quijote*; and co-editor of Calderón's *El gran teatro del mundo*.

JOHN H. ASTINGTON is Professor of English and Drama at the University of Toronto, and Director of the Graduate Centre for Study of Drama. He is the author of *English Court Theatre, 1558–1642* and of numerous articles on drama and on theatrical and cultural history. He is also a former editor of the journal *Modern Drama*.

JONATHAN BATE is Professor of Shakespeare and Renaissance Literature at The University of Warwick. His many works on Shakespeare include *Shakespeare and Ovid* (1993) and *The Genius of Shakespeare* (1997). His book on *The Elizabethans* for the New Oxford English Literary History will be published in 2004.

SWAPAN CHAKRAVORTY is Professor of English at Jadavpur University, Calcutta. He is the author of *Society and Politics in the Plays of Thomas Middleton* (1996), and a contributing editor of the forthcoming Oxford *Collected Works of Thomas Middleton*.

ANN JENNALIE COOK, Professor Emerita at Vanderbilt University, has published *The Privileged Playgoers of Shakespeare's London*, *Making a Match: Courtship in Shakespeare and His Society*, and many articles. She has received Guggenheim, Rockefeller, and Folger Fellowships. After serving as Executive Director of the Shakespeare Association of America for twelve years, then as Chair of the International Shakespeare Association for eight years, she is currently Vice President of the ISA and a Life Trustee of the Shakespeare Birthplace Trust.

MICHAEL COVENEY is theater critic of the *Daily Mail* in London. He took a degree in English at Oxford University in 1970 and has since worked as editor of *Plays and Players* (1973–78) and as chief theater critic for both the *Financial Times* (1981–89) and *The Observer* (1990–97). His books include critical biographies of Maggie Smith, Mike Leigh, and Andrew Lloyd Webber, and a history of the Glasgow Citizens Theatre.

ROBERT ELLRODT is Professor emeritus of English at the Sorbonne Nouvelle and the author of (besides other works) *Neoplatonism in the Poetry of Spenser, Poètes métaphysiques anglais* (1960), *Seven Metaphysical Poets: A Structural Study of the Unchanging Self* (2000), a commentary on *King Lear* in the new *Pléiade Shakespeare* (2002), a bilingual edition of the *Poems* of Shakespeare (2002), and translations of *Doctor Faustus* and *'Tis Pity She's a Whore* (forthcoming).

PAUL FRANSSEN teaches British Literature at the University of Utrecht, the Netherlands. He has co-edited *The Author as Character: Representing Historical Writers in Western Literature* (1999), and published a wide range of articles on Shakespeare, Marvell, Sterne, and others. In addition, he edits *Folio*, the journal of the Shakespeare Society of the Low Countries.

PENELOPE FREEDMAN studied Classics and Philosophy at St. Hilda's College, Oxford, and worked as a teacher before moving into Applied Linguistics. For the next nine years, at the University of Kent, she taught Discourse Stylistics and directed at the University theater. She is now based at the Shakespeare Institute, University of Birmingham, where she wrote her Ph.D. thesis. She has also worked as a theater critic, and her publications include short stories as well as book and theater reviews.

FRANKLIN J. HILDY is Head of the Ph.D. program in Theatre and Performance Studies at the University of Maryland, and Director of The Shakespeare Globe Center (U.S.A.) Research Archive. He is a specialist in theater architecture, theater archaeology, and historic stage; and author of *Shakespeare at the Maddermarket* (1986), editor of *New Issues in the Reconstruction of Shakespeare's Theatre* (1990), and co-author with Oscar Brockett of two editions of *History of the Theatre* (1999 and 2003).

JEAN E. HOWARD is Professor of English at Columbia University, where she teaches Renaissance literature and feminist studies. Her most recent books include *Engendering a Nation: A Feminist Account of Shakespeare's English Histories* (with Phyllis Rackin, 1997), *The Norton Shakespeare* (ed. with Stephen Greenblatt, Katharine Maus, and Walter Cohen, 1997), and *Marxist Shakespeares* (ed. with Scott Shershow, 2001). She is finishing

*Theater of a City: Generic Innovation and Social Change on the Early Modern Stage.*

Ros King, who lectures in English at Queen Mary College, University of London, is a musician, theater director, and dramaturg. She is the author of *The Works of Richard Edwards: Politics, Poetry and Performance in Sixteenth-Century England*, (2001) and is completing a book on *Cymbeline*.

Alexander Leggatt is a graduate of the University of Toronto and the Shakespeare Institute. He is currently Professor of English at University College, University of Toronto. He has published extensively on English drama, particularly Shakespeare and his contemporaries. Recent publications include *English Stage Comedy 1490–1990: Five Centuries of a Genre* (1998) and *Introduction to English Renaissance Comedy* (1999). He is editor of *The Cambridge Companion to Shakespearean Comedy* (2002). He has held the Guggenheim and Killam Fellowships.

David Lindley is Professor of Renaissance Literature at the University of Leeds. His published work includes editions of and essays on the Court Masque, a study of Thomas Campion, an investigation of the notorious career of Frances Howard, and, most recently, an edition of *The Tempest* for the New Cambridge Shakespeare.

Charles Marowitz is a critic-playwright-director whose specialty has been Shakespeare since his earliest work in England as co-director with Peter Brook of the Royal Shakespeare Company Experimental Group. He has published over two dozen books, the most recent *The Roar of the Canon: Kott & Marowitz on Shakespeare* (2002). His free adaptations of Shakespeare's plays have been performed worldwide and collected in *The Marowitz Shakespeare*. He is currently Artistic Director of the Malibu Stage Company in California.

Randall Martin is Professor of English at the University of New Brunswick. He has recently edited *Henry VI, Part 3* for the Oxford Shakespeare and Oxford World's Classics, and is currently writing a study of Early Modern women's-crime pamphlets.

Peter Milward was formerly Professor of English at Sophia University, Tokyo. His books on Shakespeare include *Shakespeare's Religious Background* (1973), *Bibilical Influences in Shakespeare's Great Tragedies* (1987), and *The Catholicism of Shakespeare's Plays* (1997); and, on the period, surveys of printed sources on *Religious Controversies of the Eliza-*

*bethan Age* (1977) and *Religious Controversies of the Jacobean Age* (1978).

MICHAEL NEILL is Professor of English at the University of Auckland. He is the author of *Issues of Death* (1997) and *Putting History to the Question* (2000). He has edited *Antony and Cleopatra* for the Oxford Shakespeare and is currently preparing *Othello* for the same series.

STEPHEN ORGEL is the Jackson Eli Reynolds Professor in Humanities at Stanford. His most recent books are *The Authentic Shakespeare* (2002) and *Impersonations: The Performance of Gender in Shakespeare's England* (1996). He has edited *The Tempest* and *The Winter's Tale* in The Oxford Shakespeare, and *Macbeth*, *King Lear*, *Pericles*, *The Taming of the Shrew*, and *The Sonnets* in the New Pelican Shakespeare, of which he is a general editor.

YVES PEYRÉ is Professor of English at the University of Montpellier (France). He has published several essays on the influence of the classics on Elizabethan literature, and is author of *Les voix des mythes dans la tragédie élizabethaine* (1996).

ADRIAN POOLE is Reader in English and Comparative Literature at the University of Cambridge and a Fellow of Trinity College. He has written on Greek and Shakespearean tragedy, on translation from the Classics, and on nineteenth-century authors including Dickens, Eliot, Hardy, Gissing, James, Stevenson, and Kipling. He delivered the 1999 British Academy Shakespeare lecture ("*Macbeth* and the Third Person"), and is currently completing *Shakespeare and the Victorians* for the Arden Shakespeare.

PAOLA PUGLIATTI is Professor of English at the University of Florence. She has written extensively on the theory of literary genres and on the genetic study of modern manuscripts, especially of Joyce's *Ulysses*. On Shakespeare, she has written essays on *Titus Andronicus*, *King Lear*, *Henry V*, *Henry VI, Part 2*, and *Henry VIII*; and two books, on *King Lear* and the history plays, respectively. Her forthcoming book is entitled *Beggary and Theatre in Early Modern England* (2003).

GORAN STANIVUKOVIC is Associate Professor of English at Saint Mary's University, Halifax, Canada. He is the editor of *Ovid and the Renaissance Body*. His essay, "Recent Studies of English Renaissance Literature of the Mediterranean," appeared in *English Literary Renaissance*, and his forthcoming publications include *A Critical Edition of Emanuel Ford's "Orna-*

*tus and Artesia"* and *Prose Fiction and Early Modern Sexualities in England, 1580–1640*, co-edited with Constance Relihan.

GARY TAYLOR is Professor of English and Director of the Hudson Strode Program in Renaissance Studies at the University of Alabama. He general-edited *William Shakespeare: The Complete Works* (1986) with Stanley Wells and is general editor of *The Collected Works of Thomas Middleton* (forthcoming). His most recent books are *Castration: An Abbreviated History of Western Manhood* (2000) and *Buying Whiteness: Race, Sex, and Slavery, from the English Renaissance to the African American Renaissance* (2003).

JESÚS TRONCH-PÉREZ is tenured Lecturer at the University of Valencia and member of the Instituto Shakespeare (a group of scholars who study and translate Shakespeare's plays). His research interests are textual criticism in general, and in particular the textual and editorial problems of Early Modern drama. He has published a monograph on the *First Quarto "Hamlet"* (1994) and *A Synoptic "Hamlet": A Critical-Synoptic Edition of the Second Quarto and First Folio Texts of "Hamlet"* (2002).

MARINA WARNER is a novelist, historian, and critic. She has written award-winning studies of mythology and fairy tales, and has contributed essays to art journals and catalogues, curating *The Inner Eye: Art Beyond The Visible*, a touring exhibition (1996); and selected a show on the theme of transformation for the Wellcome Institute, London (2002). In autumn 2001 she was a Visiting Fellow at All Souls College, Oxford, where she gave the Clarendon Lectures on *Fantastic Metamorphoses: Other Worlds* (2002). Her fifth novel, *The Leto Bundle*, was published in 2002.

RICHARD WILSON is Professor of Renaissance Literature at the University of Lancaster. His books include a critical study of *Julius Caesar* (1992) and *Will Power: Essays in Shakespearean Authority* (1993). He has edited *Christopher Marlowe: A Critical Reader and New Historicism* (1999) and, with Richard Dutton, *New Historicism and Renaissance Drama* (1992). He is currently completing *Secret Shakespeare*, a book exploring Shakespeare's Catholic connections; and is editor, with Richard Dutton and Alison Findlay, of two volumes of essays, *Lancastrian Shakespeare: Religion and Europe* and *Lancastrian Shakespeare: Region, Religion and Patronage* (2003).

YUMIKO YAMADA is Professor of English, Kobe College, Japan, and the author of *Ben Jonson and Cervantes: Tilting against Chivalric Romances*

(2000). Her recent studies include "Are Jonson and Rabelais Elegant or Grotesque?" (*Connotations* [1998]), "*The Masque of Queens*: Between Sight and Sound" in *Hot Questrists after the English Renaissance* (2000), and "Henderu to Arashi [Handel and *The Tempest*]" in *Sheikusupia wo Yominaosu* (rereading Shakespeare, 2001).

# Index

453